A POLITICAL HISTORY OF THE GAMBIA, 1816–1994

ROCHESTER STUDIES In
AFRICAN HISTORY and the DIASPORA

Toyin Falola, Senior Editor
The Frances Higginbotham Nalle Centennial Professor in History
University of Texas at Austin

(ISSN: 1092–5228)

A complete list of titles in the Rochester Studies in African History and the Diaspora, in order of publication, may be found at the end of this book.

A POLITICAL HISTORY OF THE GAMBIA, 1816–1994

Arnold Hughes and David Perfect

University of Rochester Press

First published 2006

University of Rochester Press
668 Mt. Hope Avenue, Rochester, NY 14620, USA
www.urpress.com
and Boydell & Brewer Limited
PO Box 9, Woodbridge, Suffolk IP12 3DF, UK
www.boydellandbrewer.com

ISBN: 1–58046–230–8
ISSN: 1092–5228

Library of Congress Cataloging-in-Publication Data
Hughes, Arnold.
  A political history of The Gambia, 1816-1994 / Arnold Hughes and David Perfect.
       p. cm. — (Rochester studies in African history and the diaspora, ISSN 1092-5228 ; v. 26)
  Includes bibliographical references and index.
  ISBN 1-58046-230-8 (hardcover : alk. paper)   1. Gambia–Politics and government.   I. Perfect, David, 1960-   II. Title.   III. Series.
  DT509.5.H84 2006
  966.51′02–dc22
                                        2006016874

A catalogue record for this title is available from the British Library.

This publication is printed on acid-free paper.
Printed in the United States of America.

This book is dedicated to the memory of Deyda Hydara

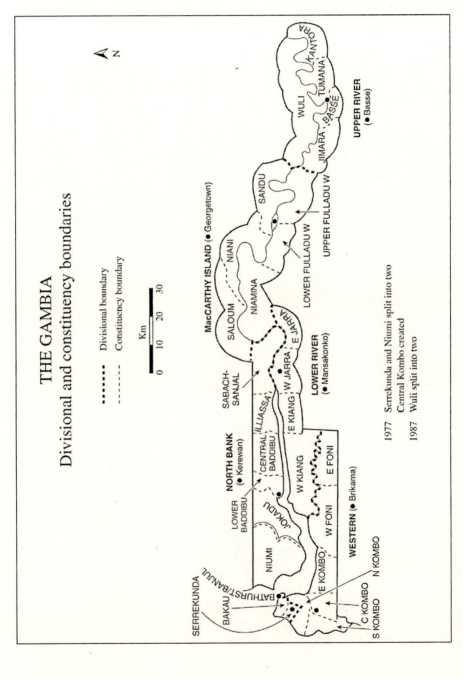

Map. The Gambia: Divisional and Constituency Boundaries

CONTENTS

TABLES

INTERVIEWEES

(all in Bathurst/Banjul unless stated)

Arnold Hughes

Sanjally Bojang:	February 1972; April 1992 (*both Kembuje, The Gambia*)
Assan M. Camara:	March 1987; January 1997; November 1997; December 1997; December 1999
Bakary B. Dabo:	July 1995; May 1996; June 1996 (*all Birmingham, England*)
Sheriff M. Dibba:	April 1977; March 1984; May 1992
Rev. John C. Faye:	April 1975
Kebba W. Foon:	September 1973; April 1977
John R. Forster:	February 1972
Ibrahima M. Garba-Jahumpa:	April 1977
Sam Goddard:	February 1977; April 1977
Paul Gore:	February 1992 (*Woodbridge, England*)
Ibrahima Jallow:	August 1997; November 1997 (*both Birmingham, England*)
Antouman ("Antoine") Jatta:	April 1977
Sir Dawda K. Jawara:	August 1998 (*Haywards Heath, England*)
Melvin B. Jones:	April 1975; March 1984
M. B. ("Tex") Khan:	October 1981
Lamin M'Boge:	September 1973
Pierre S. N'Jie:	March 1972; August 1973; September 1973; March 1977; April 1982
Henry Oliver:	September 1973 (*Bakau, The Gambia*)
Femi Peters:	November 1997; December 1997
Halifa Sallah:	April 1992 (*Bakotu, The Gambia*)
Braimah Sanyang:	May 1992
Bakary K. Sidibeh:	September 1973
Sheriff S. Sisay:	September 1973
Kenneth G. S. Smith:	August 1985 (*Sherborne, England*)
Ba M. Tarawale:	March 1972; April 1972; May 1992 (*Bathurst/Banjul*); December 1999 (*Latrikunda*)
Andrew Winter:	August 1994

Sir Percy Wyn-Harris: April 1974 (*Woodbridge, England*)

David Perfect

Alieu E. Cham-Joof:	May 1984
Rev. Roderick N. Coote:	November 1997 (*by post*)
Rev. John C. Faye:	June 1984; September 1984
Ibrahima M. Garba-Jahumpa:	June 1984
Sam Goddard:	April 1992
Femi Peters:	August 1984

Fatma Denton

Sir Dawda K. Jawara:	March 1996 (*Haywards Heath, England*)
Mbai M'Bengue:	August 1996 (*Dakar, Senegal*)

ACKNOWLEDGMENTS

In the course of the researching of this book, the authors have reason to be grateful to a great many individuals, non-Gambian as well as Gambian. The list is too long to mention every person by name, but our gratitude to all those who assisted us through personal recollections, analytical observations, and access to documentation in their possession, remains.

Two non-Gambians deserve particular mention: Professor David Gamble, formerly of California State University, San Francisco, and the doyen of Gambian studies, whose monumental multivolume bibliography of The Gambia has to be the starting point of any serious research on The Gambia, also made available a number of difficult-to-obtain newspaper cuttings and other documents relating to Gambian politics from the early post-World War II period in his possession. Henry Oliver, whose long career in the Gambian colonial administration culminated in the post of senior commissioner, offered invaluable insights into official thinking and the means of contacting other former British administrators, as well as being a generous and entertaining host.

Among the many Gambians, again two names stand out: the late Joseph ("Uncle Joe") Cates and Baboucar ("Ba") Tarawale. Indeed, it can be truthfully said that without the help of these two gentlemen, the research could never have started, let alone progress. Joe Cates provided affordable and hospitable accommodation to one of the authors in 1972, when he first visited The Gambia, and provided him with a range of invaluable contacts for extending his research. Both authors stayed with him on numerous subsequent occasions. Among these contacts was Ba Tarawale, a leading political journalist and former activist in the People's Progressive Party. Ba, more than any other individual, provided a wealth of information and understanding of the intricacies of Gambian politics from the late 1950s to the closing period of our research.

Our indebtedness to numerous other Gambians is partly revealed from our noted acknowledgments, but has to include a far greater number of individuals who in various ways furthered our investigations and offered us hospitality and friendship. Political activists of all political coloring, journalists, lawyers, civil servants, trade union leaders, and archivists, are among the many Gambians who advanced our understanding of Gambian politics and made our research visits to The Gambia pleasurable as well as instructive. We would also like to acknowledge our indebtedness to the pioneering scholarship of Dr. Florence Mahoney, herself descended from the Liberated African community in Banjul, for our analysis of nineteenth-century political history in Chapters 3 and 4. It is a matter of regret to us that her doctoral thesis, "Government and Opinion in the Gambia 1816–1901," remains unpublished.

We would particularly like to acknowledge the assistance of two of our former colleagues and friends. The late Professor Douglas Rimmer, formerly Director of the Centre of West African Studies, University of Birmingham, generously provided very useful comments on Chapter 1 despite increasing ill health at the time. Our fellow analyst of Gambian politics, Dr. John Wiseman, formerly of the University of Newcastle-upon-Tyne, engaged in many debates with both authors. Tragically, John died in 2002 before he could comment on the final drafts of the book; but his widow, Gill, greatly assisted our research by offering us John's substantial collection of modern Gambian newspapers and other West African magazines. We would also like to thank the two (Gambian) academic readers of the book, who provided very helpful comments on the penultimate draft. The University of Rochester Press deserves our particular gratitude for agreeing to publish such a lengthy work, as do the three members of its editorial staff, Suzanne Guiod, Sue Smith, and Katie Hurley, for dealing so patiently and efficiently with our many queries. Our thanks go as well to Harry Buglass of the University of Birmingham for drawing the map of The Gambia. Furthermore, the research for the book could not have been undertaken without the continued and generous financial support of the University of Birmingham and its Centre of West African Studies. Despite our indebtedness to all these individuals, any errors or shortcomings are solely the responsibility of the authors.

Finally, on a more personal note, we would like to thank our respective wives, Diana (Hughes) and Jill (Perfect), who have had to live with all things Gambian for more years than they would care to remember.

ABBREVIATIONS

AA	Administrative Areas
ACR	*Africa Contemporary Record*
AFPRC	Armed Forces Provisional Ruling Council
AMRC	Assets Management and Recovery Commission
APRC	Alliance for Patriotic Re-orientation and Construction
ARPS	Aborigines' Rights Protection Society
AT	*The African Times*
BanCC	Banjul City Council
BATC	Bathurst Advisory Town Council
BBM	Black Brotherhood Movement
BCC	Bathurst City Council
BO	*The Bathurst Observer and West African Gazette*
BTC	Bathurst Town Council
BTU	Bathurst Trade Union
BUDC	Bathurst Urban District Council
BYMS	Bathurst Young Muslims Society
CCYC	Central Council of Youth Clubs
CFAO	Compagnie Française de l'Afrique Occidentale
CILSS	Comité permanent intre-états de la lutte contre la sécheresse dans le Sahel
CO	Colonial Office
CRD	Central River Division
DCA	Democratic Congress Alliance
DO	Dominion Office
EEC	European Economic Community
ECOMOG	ECOWAS Cease-Fire Monitoring Group
ECOWAS	Economic Community of West African States
ERP	Economic Recovery Programme
Ex. Co.	Executive Council
FAO	Food and Agricultural Organization
FCO	Foreign and Commonwealth Office
FO	Foreign Office
GA	Gambian National Archives
GATU	Gambia Amalgamated Trade Union

GBA	Gambia Bar Association
GCDB	Gambia Commercial and Development Bank
GCP	Gambia Congress Party
GCU	Gambia Cooperatives Union
GD	*The Gambia Daily*
GDP	Gambia Democratic Party
GE	*The Gambia Echo*
GFCMA	Gambia Farmers' Co-operative Marketing Association
GG	*The Gambia Gazette*
GLU	Gambia Labour Union
GMC	Gambia Muslim Congress
GMDA	Gambia Medical and Dental Association
GNA	Gambian National Army
GNAssocn	Gambia Native Association
GNB	*The Gambia News Bulletin*
GNDU	Gambia Native Defensive Union
GNG	Gambian National Gendarmerie
GNL	Gambia National League
GNP	Gambia National Party
GNU	Gambia National Union
GNYC	Gambia National Youth Council
GO	*The Gambia Outlook and Senegambian Reporter*
GPP	Gambia People's Party
GRC	Gambia Representative Committee
GSRP	Gambia Socialist Revolutionary Party
GTU	Gambia Teachers' Union
GUSRWP	Gambia Underground Socialist Revolutionary Workers Party
GW	*The Gambia Weekly*
GWC	Gambia Workers' Confederation
GWU	Gambia Workers' Union
HDI	Human Development Index
HIID	Harvard Institute of International Development
ICFTU	International Confederation of Free Trade Unions
ICS	Institute of Commonwealth Studies
ILO	International Labour Office
IMF	International Monetary Fund
ITUC-NW	International Trade Union Committee of Negro Workers
IUP	Irish University Press
KNMF	Kwame Nkrumah Memorial Foundation
KSV	Kent Street Vous
LAI	League Against Imperialism
Leg. Co.	Legislative Council
LGA	Local Government Area
LRD	Lower River Division

LRDept	Labour Research Department
MBE	Member of the British Empire
MBHS	Methodist Boys' High School
MCC	Manchester Chamber of Commerce
MDMU	Motor Drivers' and Mechanics' Union
MEA	Ministry of External Affairs
MFDC	Mouvement des Forces Démocratiques de la Casamance
MID	MacCarthy Island Division
MOJA-G	Movement for Justice in Africa–The Gambia
MOJA-L	Movement for Justice in Africa–Liberia
MPLA	Movimento Popular de Libertação de Angola
NBD	North Bank Division
NCBWA	National Congress of British West Africa
NCP	National Convention Party
NCSL	National Council of Sierra Leone
NISER	Nigerian Institute of Social and Economic Research
NLP	National Liberation Party
NSS	National Security Service
OAU	Organisation of African Unity
OBE	Order of the British Empire
OIC	Organisation of Islamic Conference
OMVG	L'organisation pour la mise en valeur de la fleuve gambienne
OUP	Oxford University Press
PAIGC	Partido Africano da Independência da Guiné e Cabo Verde
PDOIS	People's Democratic Organisation for Independence and Socialism
PDP	People's Democratic Party
PDS	Parti Démocratique du Sénégal
PLP	Parliamentary Labour Party
PPA	People's Progressive Alliance
PPCA	Parliamentary Papers Colonies Africa
PPP	People's Progressive Party
PPS	Protectorate People's Society
PRO	Public Record Office
ProtPP	Protectorate People's Party
PSD	Programme for Sustained Development
PWD	Public Works Department
RDP	Rural Development Project
RILU	Red International of Labour Unions
RPA	Bathurst Ratepayers' Association
SA	Senegalese National Archives
SAC	Structural Adjustment Credit
SADR	Sahrawi Arab Democratic Republic
SAS	Special Air Service

SDR	Special Drawing Rights
SLPP	Sierra Leone People's Party
SLWN	*Sierra Leone Weekly News*
SP	Sessional Paper
TSG	Tactical Support Group
UAC	United Africa Company
UDI	Unilateral Declaration of Independence
UDP	United Democratic Party
UGCC	United Gold Coast Convention
UNDP	United Nations Development Programme
UNIA	Universal Negro Improvement Association
UP	United Party
URD	Upper River Division
WA	*West Africa*
WASU	West African Students Union
WAYL	West African Youth League
WBHS	Wesleyan Boys' High School
WD	Western Division
WFTU	World Federation of Trade Unions
WMMS	Wesleyan Methodist Missionary Society
WO	*Weekend Observer*

INTRODUCTION

This is the first full-length account of the modern political history of The Gambia, covering the period from the establishment of the British settlement of Bathurst on St. Mary's Island (site of the modern capital, Banjul) on the estuary of the River Gambia in 1816, to the overthrow of the elected government of President Sir Dawda Jawara in an army coup in July 1994. During this long period, British colonial rule gradually spread up river to form the British Protectorate of Gambia. Initially disputed over with the French, this territory subsequently was contested by African political movements seeking a transfer of power to an elected Gambian parliament. This was achieved with Gambian independence in February 1965.

Following independence, Gambians refuted the claims of skeptics, British as well as African, that such a small state could not long survive the economic challenges of statehood without being absorbed by its larger neighbor, Senegal; or only surviving as a client-state of its former rulers. Adroit political leadership kept the Senegalese at bay, even during the crisis years of the early 1980s, and established an uncommonly harmonious and unexpectedly equal relationship with Britain.

Doubts were also expressed about the political skills of the country's newly elected and inexperienced political leaders. Yet here too, The Gambia came to acquire a reputation both for political stability and an unusually democratic system of government. Credit for this enviable state of affairs goes as much to Gambians themselves as to their leaders. Gambian politics has been characterized by a lack of extremism: relations with the British were seldom rancorous and those between rival political parties conducted within a shared system of political beliefs that repudiated the systematic use of violence in pursuit of political objectives; or authoritarianism to maintain those objectives when once in power.

Likewise, no doubt reflecting their country's smallness, Gambians have escaped the pretensions and extravagant posturings of larger African countries in their external relations. Instead, a low-key realism and pragmatism has informed foreign policy decision making.

For some three decades, this smallest of mainland African states overcame the all-too-familiar fate of ethnic conflict and authoritarian regimes, civilian or military, of most other African countries. Ironically, it was as late as 1994, when the rest of Africa was successfully moving away from single-party or military rule, that

1

The Gambia itself succumbed to an army coup. Even when this happened, the country avoided bloodshed and maintained its territorial unity.

Modern forms of political activity among Gambians go back over a century and a half. Initially this was confined both geographically and socially to Western-educated elements among the African populace of the small Crown Colony on St Mary's Island, on the estuary of the River Gambia. The first of these, strictly speaking, were not Gambians (not that there were any "Gambians" at this time), but "Liberated Africans" or "Recaptives" from Sierra Leone and other locations in West Africa, who themselves, or their immediate forebears, were rescued from slavery by the Royal Navy and settled in Freetown or Bathurst.

Gradually acquiring prominence in commerce and the educational and religious institutions established by the British, as well as entering government employment, these individuals came to form a distinct political community. Their relations among themselves or with the European mercantile community and British colonial administration defined the structure and objectives of the wider African political community for some fifty years.

Political positions were often fluid rather than determined by race. The "Liberated African" leaders often worked together with the British and the European merchants in pursuit of shared commercial and political objectives: usually with respect to meeting the challenges from the French. At other times, of significance for later political developments, they clashed with merchants and administrators on the one hand, and among themselves on the other.

Episodic political organization around issues of the period gradually evolved into more permanent organizations. Such embryonic political associations were fluid and headed by socially and economically prominent individuals. An essentially elitist and personalist system of African representation emerged by the late nineteenth century, the forerunner of the more formal political system of the twentieth century. Such political brokers sought to speak for the growing African political community, while at the same time promoting their own interests. The personalization of power would remain a feature of postcolonial Gambian politics, particularly following the adoption of a republic in 1970.

Over time, the British conceded a right of representation on the territory's Legislative Council to representatives of the educated African community. For some sixty years, the conservative Forster family, father and son, monopolized this representation, although not always as compliant allies of the administration. Nevertheless, personal and political rivalries led to challenges to this familial domination, as well as to the limited and non-elective system of representation.

During the interwar years, wider political currents were felt—the pan-African claims of the National Congress of British West Africa and the remoter Garvey Movement, even Marxist socialism—but there was little support for such radical ideas among the essentially parochial Gambian political class. Even the leading radical voice of these years, the journalist-nationalist, Edward Small, spent most of his time in local factional fighting or seeking to ameliorate rather than overthrow British rule.

The Gambia's constitutional advance followed that of the other British West African dependencies and direct elected representation for the territory was only obtained after World War II. Only then could the various political pressure groups take the form of political parties. Initially, these were confined practically, as well as constitutionally, to the Colony proper, and the larger hinterland, or Protectorate, did not emerge politically until the end of the 1950s, when the British conceded direct territorial elections. For this reason, this book does not attempt any detailed reconstruction of politics within the Protectorate area before this period.

Three small and highly personalized political parties, the United Party, the Gambia Democratic Party, and the Gambia Muslim Congress, came into being in Bathurst in the 1950s, but proved unable to retain their political domination once the provincial masses were enfranchised and set up their own political party. The Protectorate People's Party (subsequently People's Progressive Party [PPP]), under the leadership of Dawda Jawara, emerged as the largest political organization during the general elections of 1960 and 1962 and was accepted by the British as their successors.

The post-independence era witnessed a steady consolidation of the PPP's power, as it repositioned itself politically as a national rather than as a Protectorate party and effectively used newly-available state patronage to undermine rival parties. Although The Gambia became a republic, following a second referendum in 1970, Jawara resisted the pressure to use this position and overwhelming electoral victories in subsequent decades to create either a dictatorship or a one-party state. Even so, as executive president, he came to wield considerable power in determining government policy and political appointments; while the PPP's permanent parliamentary majority led to a de facto if not de jure one party form of government, depicted as "one-party dominant" rule elsewhere in Africa.

From 1966 to 1994, the PPP effectively destroyed its old rivals—most notably the United Party—and resisted challenges from break-away parties set up by former vice presidents: the National Convention Party led by Sheriff Dibba in the mid-1970s and the Gambia People's Party, formed by Assan Musa Camara in the 1980s. Political divisions in Gambian politics have always been based predominantly on personal and factional interests, with very little ideological differences between rival leaders and parties. Regional-ethnic divisions tended to fade after independence as the PPP strove to replace its former Mandinka-Protectorate position with a more national outlook, embracing the former Colony and Protectorate areas and all ethnic groups. This and a middle-of-the-road position on major political and economic issues enabled the ruling party to marginalize rival parties, which found it difficult to offer a credible or original alternative political agenda.

The only distinct alternative ideological position came from a few small and marginal urban political groups espousing versions of Marxist or radical Pan-Africanist critiques of PPP policy and its conduct of government; but it was only in July–August 1981, when elements of these teamed-up with disaffected paramilitary policemen to stage a coup, that Jawara and the PPP were seriously threatened.

Even so, rapid Senegalese military intervention put down the insurrection and restored the Government to power.

Yet the political longevity of the Jawara government, in itself, continued to cause dissatisfaction, leading critics to claim that it clung to office by electoral malpractices, even if it avoided authoritarian rule. More seriously, it was accused of tolerating, if not promoting, persistent corruption on the part of senior politicians and public officials. The failure to deal firmly with frequent exposures of corruption both undermined the legitimacy of the administration and impeded its efforts at economic and social development. As elsewhere in Africa during these years, government and leadership survival rested less on broader ideological appeals than on the self-interest of an array of powerbrokers, who delivered electoral victory in return for political and economic patronage. Some of this patronage was redistributed at local level, but too much ended up with politicians and their cronies in the business community.

These criticisms eroded popular support for Jawara and the PPP during their second insurrectionary crisis in July 1994, and provided the dissident soldiers who seized power with the justification for their actions. In consequence, the overthrow of president and government was a rapid and bloodless event, neither opposed within The Gambia itself, nor by its previous protector, Senegal. The international community's response to the illegal removal of the Jawara government was also limited; public condemnation and a period of economic sanctions, rather than military intervention, were all that the exiled Jawara was granted. Three decades of multiparty democracy—however flawed—was replaced by an authoritarian military regime and elected parliamentary government gave way to a self-appointed army junta.

The research on which this book is based spans three decades of visits to The Gambia by the authors, providing an unusual depth of time to their investigations. Political events were observed at first hand and numerous interviews were held with representatives of all political interests. Additionally, extensive research was carried out at the Gambian National Archives. These archives hold a considerable collection of original official correspondence and reports from the colonial period; together with more limited material from the independence period. The irregular runs of local newspapers held by the archives were also consulted, as were documents at the Gambia National Library and various government ministries. Limited material was also consulted in the Senegalese National Archives in Dakar.

The authors have also consulted British colonial and postcolonial records at the National Archives (Public Record Office) in Kew, London. This holds the surviving correspondence between the Gambian government and the Colonial Office and its successor bodies (currently the Foreign and Commonwealth Office), as well as a host of other official reports. Documents up to the start of the closed period, 1976, were examined. Gambian and other newspaper holdings of the British Newspaper Library at Colindale, North London, yielded valuable additional information.

Research was also undertaken in a number of academic libraries in Britain. The Institute of Commonwealth Studies, London, the primary repository for Gambian documents in Britain, holds many published and unpublished documents on The Gambia. The School of African and Oriental Studies at the University of London has a smaller Gambian collection, but also holds the archives of the Wesleyan Methodist Missionary Society. The latter contains the correspondence between European missionaries in Gambia in the nineteenth and early twentieth centuries and the society's headquarters in London, and other useful material. The John Rylands Library at the University of Manchester and the University of Birmingham Library, including the holdings of its Centre of West African Studies, have been further important sources of information. Rhodes House Library, University of Oxford, holds a number of personal records of former colonial officials in the Gambian government. These were supplemented by interviews and correspondence with several retired British colonial officials in Britain and The Gambia. Finally, the archives of the Labour Research Department in London contain files that are relevant to Gambian political developments between World Wars I and II.

1

SOCIAL AND ECONOMIC SETTING

Chapter 1 provides the socioeconomic context to the political events analyzed in subsequent chapters. A physical description of The Gambia is provided first, followed by a review of the available demographic data and a description of the major ethnic groups of the country. Religious beliefs, educational development, and the labor force are then examined from a historical perspective. Finally, the structure of the economy is outlined and its prosperity (or otherwise) assessed chronologically.

Physical Description

The Gambia is one of the smallest countries in Africa, having a total area of approximately 11,000 square kilometers (4,361 square miles). It consists of strips of land about 10 kilometers wide (about 6 miles) either side of the River Gambia (one of the most navigable rivers in West Africa) and extends 470 kilometers (292 miles) into the interior of Africa from the Atlantic Ocean.[1] A former British colony, it was known as either "Gambia" or "the Gambia" until independence in 1965; to avoid confusion, we have used the former term when referring *exclusively* to the colonial period. The Gambia's northern, eastern, and southern borders, which are all shared with Senegal, were defined by a wide-ranging Anglo-French Convention of 1889 and demarcated between 1891 and 1905 (its eastern border was slightly modified in 1976).[2]

The 1889 treaty with France considerably expanded the size of Gambia. The British Crown Colony consisted of a few scattered settlements along the River Gambia with an estimated total area of only 110 square kilometers (69 square miles). St. Mary's Island at the mouth of the river, on which the capital, Bathurst (now Banjul) was located, was purchased in 1816; MacCarthy Island, 241 kilometers (150 miles) up river, was acquired in 1823; the "Ceded Mile," a tract of land on the north bank of the river 1.6 kilometers (1 mile) in breadth and 58 kilometers (36 miles) in length, was ceded in 1826 (and extended in 1832); British Kombo

6

(which was later called Kombo St. Mary), an area of 40 square kilometers (25 square miles) to the west of Bathurst was ceded in 1840 (and extended in 1853); Albreda, a trading post on the north bank of the river, was exchanged by France in 1857; and a few other districts were annexed in the 1880s.[3] These settlements were later termed "the Colony" to distinguish them from "the Protectorate," the land acquired under the 1889 Convention that, until independence, was administered quite differently. The first Protectorate Ordinance was passed in 1894 and between 1895 and 1902, all the settlements other than St. Mary's Island were placed under the Protectorate system of administration (although technically remaining part of the Colony). Kombo St. Mary was transferred back to the Colony for administrative purposes in 1946.[4]

Dense mangrove swamps line the banks of the River Gambia for the first 150 kilometers upstream, although in some places the mangrove has been cleared for rice cultivation. Behind the swamps are areas of savannah called "banto faros," which are slightly higher areas above river level. These remain arid in the dry season and swampy during the rainy season. The dry season lasts between November and June; the rains usually begin in late June and end in mid-October. On average, 85 percent of the annual rainfall (in Banjul) falls between July and September. The soil further up river is light and sandy and is suitable for groundnuts.[5]

Administrative Areas

The newly established Protectorate was subdivided into two administrative areas (covering the North Bank and the South Bank of the River Gambia) in 1893, with a third (Kombo) added in 1895. The incorporation of new territory within the Colony in 1902 led to a reorganization of the administrative boundaries, so that by 1906, there were five Provinces: North Bank, MacCarthy Island, South Bank, Upper River, and Kombo-Foni (or Fogni). Each was administered by a provincial commissioner (who was initially known as a "travelling commissioner").[6] These were renamed Divisions after World War II. Even though the formal distinction between the Colony and the Protectorate was abolished at independence, divisional commissioners continued to administer the former protectorate areas. There were four Divisions at independence—Lower River Division (LRD), MacCarthy Island Division (MID), Upper River Division (URD), and Western Division (WD). A fifth Division, North Bank Division (NBD), was created out of that part of LRD located on the North Bank of the River Gambia in 1968, and MID was renamed Central River Division in the 1990s. In the early 1960s, seven Local Government Areas (LGAs) were established: Bathurst; Brikama (which covered WD and Kombo St. Mary); Georgetown (which covered Georgetown itself and the parts of MID on the south bank of the River Gambia); Kuntaur (the north bank of MID); Kerewan (the north bank of LRD); Mansakonko (the south bank of LRD); and Basse (the whole of URD). By the early 1970s, an eighth LGA had been created through the creation of Kombo St. Mary LGA (later renamed Kanifing Urban District Council); Georgetown was renamed Janjangbureh in 1995.[7]

Demographic Context

During the nineteenth century, the population of the Crown Colony probably never exceeded 15,000 (table 1.1). In most years, the majority of its population lived in Bathurst. After 1871, the population of MacCarthy Island and British Kombo was in decline and Bathurst accounted for two-fifths of the Colony's population in both 1881 and 1891; in 1901, in part because of the temporary presence of troops from Sierra Leone, it comprised as much as two-thirds of it.[8] Table 1.2 shows the population of Gambia at successive census dates between 1901 and 1963 (the last census to be carried out before independence).

The population of the Protectorate was undoubtedly underestimated in 1901 and probably also in 1911, but overestimated in 1921, and the population of Bathurst in 1944 was temporarily increased by a large number of migrant workers from the Protectorate.[9] As table 1.2 also shows, the Protectorate always had a far larger population than the Colony and accounted for four-fifths of the national population in 1963.

Table 1.3 shows the population nationally and by LGA at each census date since 1963. Population growth since the 1970s has been particularly striking and, with an estimated population density of 111 people per square kilometer in 1995, The Gambia is now one of the more densely populated countries in Africa.[10] Table 1.3 also demonstrates that the distribution of the population between the eight LGAs

Table 1.1. Population of the Crown Colony, 1819–1901

	1819	1833	1839	1851	1871	1881	1891	1901
Bathurst	704	2,825	3,514	4,262	4,591	6,138	6,239	8,807[2]
MacCarthy Island	n/a	841	1,162[1]	1,171	1,263	908	906	797
Ceded Mile	n/a	n/a	n/a	206	3,917	4,047	4,207	2,211
British Kombo	n/a	n/a	n/a	1,246	4,419	3,057	1,705	1,641
Other	–	–	–	54[2]	–	–	1,209[3]	–
Total	**704**	**3,666**	**n/a**	**6,939**	**14,190**	**14,150**	**14,266**	**13,456**

[1]1836 "census"; Kuczynski's estimate of the population at this time was 1,600.
[2]Population of Cape St. Mary.
[3]Combined population of Tendabah, Bai, Kansala, and Bajana, which were added to the Colony in the 1880s.

Sources: R. R. Kuczynski, *Demographic Survey of the British Colonial Empire* (London: Oxford University Press, 1948) vol. 1, 318–28; and [Colonial Office], *Census of the British Empire 1901* (London: HMSO, 1906), 139.

Table 1.2. Population of Gambia, 1911–63

	1901	1911	1921	1931	1944	1951	1963
Colony	13,456	7,700[1]	9,227	14,370	21,152	27,297	40,017
Bathurst	8,807	7,700	9,227	14,370	21,152	19,602	27,809
Kombo St. Mary	1,641	1,963[2]	n/a	n/a	7,597[2]	7,695	12,208
Protectorate	76,948	138,401[2]	201,303	185,150	199,357[3]	n/a	275,469
Total	**90,404**	**146,101**	**210,530**	**199,520**	**220,509**	**n/a**	**315,486**

[1]Kuczynski (328) gives a figure of 13,157 for the population of the Colony; this included the areas which had been placed under the Protectorate administration.
[2]Included within Protectorate total.
[3]Annual estimate of the Protectorate.

Sources: Kuczynski, *Demographic Survey*, vol. 1, 318–31; 776; David P. Gamble, *Contributions to a Socio-Economic Survey of the Gambia* (London: Colonial Office Research Department, 1949), 25–27; K. C. Zachariah and Julien Condé, *Migration in West Africa: Demographic Aspects* (Oxford: Oxford University Press, 1981), Table 17.

Table 1.3. Population by Local Government Area, 1963–93

LGA	1963	%	1973	%	1983	%	1993	%
Bathurst/Banjul	27,809	9	39,179	8	44,188	6	42,326	4
Basse	58,049	18	86,167	17	111,388	16	155,059	15
Brikama	55,393	18	91,013	18	137,245	20	234,917	23
Georgetown[1]	35,752	11	54,232	11	68,410	10	88,247	9
Kerewan	63,045	20	93,388	19	112,225	16	156,462	15
Kombo St. Mary/ Kanifing	12,208	4	39,404	8	101,504	15	228,214	22
Kuntaur	29,003	9	47,669	10	57,594	8	67,774	7
Mansakonko	34,227	11	42,447	9	55,263	8	65,146	6
Total	**315,486**	**100**	**493,499**	**100**	**687,817**	**100**	**1,038,145**	**100**

[1]Renamed Janjangbureh in 1995.

Sources: [Gambia Government], *Population Databank 1995* (Banjul: National Population Commission Secretariat, 1996), Table 1.2.

has changed since 1963, with the growth of Kanifing (the former Kombo St. Mary) being particularly striking. A major reason for this was large-scale immigration from neighboring African countries; in 1993, non-Gambians accounted for 20 percent of its population. Mainly as a result of the growth of Kanifing, 37 percent of the population was urbanized by 1993, compared with only 23 percent in 1973.[11]

Ethnic Groups[12]

As later chapters will show, the politicization of ethnicity has been an important factor in Gambian politics, and in African politics more generally. It is therefore important to examine the major ethnic groups of The Gambia in some detail and, in this section, the available qualitative and quantitative census data are used to examine the characteristics of the ten Gambian ethnic groups separately identified in the 1993 census. We seek to assess each group's share of the national population, its geographical location, its typical occupations, and its typical religious beliefs.[13]

Although each ethnic group is shown separately, it is important to note that intermarriage between ethnic groups has been common in The Gambia over the past couple of centuries and many Gambians perhaps more properly should be described as being of mixed ethnic origin. Additionally, further interethnic blurring has occurred as a result of cultural assimilation among various peoples, with minority groups adopting the language and customs of dominant groups. For example, there has been Jola acculturation to Mandinka in LRD, and Wolof has been adopted as a *lingua franca* in the urban areas around Banjul (as it has in urban areas in Senegal). As noted in later chapters, several prominent politicians were among those who were "Wolofized" through long residence in or near the capital.[14] Finally, most Gambian ethnic groups have historically had a similar social structure—the caste system—which has also moderated differences between them.[15]

Nineteenth Century

Because the first attempt to record the ethnic composition of the Colony's population was not made until 1881, it is not possible to provide firm evidence of the ethnic breakdown in the early years of the settlement. As table 1.4 shows, the most numerous ethnic groups in the late nineteenth century were the Wolof and the Mandinka and, whereas the former predominated in Bathurst, the latter comprised the bulk of the population in the rest of the Colony. It is also evident that former slaves, who were known to contemporaries as "Liberated Africans," and their descendants, formed the second largest group of Bathurst's population in the 1880s and 1890s. However, there were fewer Liberated Africans in other parts of the Colony.

Colonial Period

Tables 1.5 and 1.6 show the population of the constituent parts of the Colony and the Protectorate at various dates between 1911 and 1963. Table 1.5 reveals that the Wolof remained the largest numerical group within Bathurst until independence and that the Aku were the second largest group until 1963 when they were overtaken by the Mandinka. In contrast, the Mandinka and the Jola between them comprised over half of the total population of Kombo St. Mary in 1951; at independence, the Mandinka alone accounted for more than one-quarter of its total

Table 1.4. Population of the Crown Colony by Ethnic Group, 1881–1901

	1881		1891		1901	
	Bathurst	Other Colony	Bathurst	Other Colony	Bathurst	Other Colony
Natives of British Gambia	2,875[1]	2,158[1]	4,072[2]	1,517[2]	n/a	n/a
Natives of Sierra Leone/Liberated Africans	824[3]	133[3]	n/a	n/a	n/a	n/a
Wolof	829[4]	277[4]	n/a	n/a	3,666	818
Mandinka	189	3,333	412	2,347	350	2,066
Jola	757[5]	1,430[5]	650	1,502	493	638
Serere	n/a[5]	n/a	593	1,072	715	301
Fula	35	258	210	496	176	202
Aku	n/a	n/a	n/a	n/a	819	99
Ibo	n/a	n/a	n/a	n/a	294	58
Manjago	n/a	n/a	n/a	n/a	83	30
Bambara	n/a	n/a	n/a	n/a	33	48
Other Africans	470	406[6]	240	1,092	1,847	375
West Indians	59	12	n/a	n/a	3	3
Europeans	100	5	62	1	217	4
Other Non-Africans	n/a	n/a	n/a	n/a	111	7
Total	**6,138**	**8,012**	**6,239**	**8,027**	**8,807**	**4,649**

[1]This probably mainly consists of Wolof born in the Crown Colony and the descendants of Liberated Africans.
[2]This probably mainly consists of Colony-born Wolof, Liberated Africans, and "Natives of Sierra Leone" and their descendants.
[3]Presumably excludes the descendants of Liberated Africans.
[4]Probably consists of Wolof born outside of the colony only.
[5]Includes Serere, who were not separately identified in 1881.
[6]Includes 106 "Bathurst people" in British Kombo.

Sources: [Gambia Government], Detailed Account of the Census of the Population of the British Settlement on the River Gambia, taken on the 4th April 1881 (Bathurst: Government Printer, 1881). This can be found in CO 87/117, Gouldsbury to Rowe, September 9,1881. [Gambia Government], A Report of 1891 Census by WC Cates Acting Registrar. This can be found in CO 87/139, Llewelyn to Secretary of State, July 21, 1891. [Colonial Office], Colony of the Gambia, Census 1901, Report of the Superintendent. (London: HMSO, 1902). This can be found in CO 87/163, Denton to Chamberlain, June 24, 1901.

population. Kombo St. Mary also had a sizeable Wolof population, but very few Aku lived there.

Despite the obvious inconsistencies of the data, table 1.6 shows clearly that the Mandinka remained the most numerous ethnic group in the Protectorate throughout the colonial period and that the other major groups were the Fula and the Wolof.[16]

Table 1.5. Population of Bathurst and Kombo St. Mary by Ethnic Group, 1911–63

	1911 B	1921 B	1944 B	1951 B	1951 KSM	1963 B	1963 KSM
Wolof	3,705	3,069	10,130	9,544	1,237	11,311	1,723
Mandinka	269	425	2,412	1,801	2,314	3,338	3,319
Jola	423	571	1,710	1,351	1,620	1,422	1,431
Aku	749	592	2,564	2,552	131	2,515	202
Fula	228	262	1,063	1,018	893	1,021	1,006
Serere	579	563	1,075	951	405	732	493
Manjago	128	158	n/a	n/a	n/a	502	203
Serahuli	84	162	n/a	n/a	n/a	344	248
Bambara	61	189	n/a	n/a	n/a	181	218
Tukulor	n/a	97	n/a	n/a	n/a	110	28
Ibo	357	275	n/a	n/a	n/a	n/a	n/a
Other African	797	2,335[1]	1,924	1,993	943	6,014	3,191
European and other non-African	320[2]	529[3]	274[4]	392[5]	152[6]	319[7]	146[8]
Total	**7,700**	**9,227**	**21,152**	**19,602**	**7,695**	**27,809**	**12,208**

[1]Includes 1,215 "mixed tribe" population.
[2]Consists of 107 British and 213 other Europeans. Original census return gives a figure of 230 Europeans, but this is a misprint.
[3]Consists of 362 Europeans, 91 Arabs, 54 Syrians, and 22 West Indians.
[4]Consists of 101 Europeans and 173 Syrians and Lebanese.
[5]Consists of 230 Europeans and 162 Syrians and Lebanese.
[6]Consists of 113 Europeans and 39 Syrians and Lebanese.
[7]Consists of 197 British, 52 Asians, and 70 other non-Africans.
[8]Consists of 130 British and 16 other non-Africans.

Sources: [Colonial Office], *Report and Summary of the Census of the Gambia 1911.* London: HMSO, 1911. This can be found in CO 87/186, Denton to Secretary of State, June 27, 1911. [Gambia Government], *Report and Summary of the Census of the Gambia* (Bathurst: Government Printer, 1921), Table 3; *Report of the Census Commissioner for Bathurst, 1944* (Sessional Paper no. 2 of 1945) (Bathurst: Government Printer, 1945); *Report of the Census Commissioner for the Colony — 1951* (Sessional Paper no. 4 of 1952) (Bathurst: Government Printer, 1952), Table 5; *Report on the Census of Population of the Gambia Taken on 17th/18th April 1963 by H. A. Oliver* (Sessional Paper no. 13 of 1965) (Bathurst: Government Printer, 1965), Tables 34 and 105.

Post-Independence

Table 1.7 shows the ethnic composition of The Gambia at each census date between 1963 and 1993. It is evident that the rank order of the first six ethnic groups has remained unchanged since independence; however, the Mandinka share of the national population has fallen significantly. This is partly due to the faster population growth of other Gambian ethnic groups and partly due to the

Table 1.6. Population of the Protectorate by Ethnic Group, 1911–63

	1911		1931		1946[1]		1963	
	N	%	N	%	N	%	N	%
Mandinka	71,070	51	85,640	46	99,206	43	122,150	44
Fula	27,118	20	22,273	12	51,542	23	40,696	15
Wolof	22,367	16	25,864	14	31,714	14	27,771	10
Serahuli	4,535	3	12,316	7	13,093	6	20,726	8
Jola	9,540	7	19,410	10	20,636	9	19,193	7
Tukulor	n/a	n/a	11,653	6	n/a	n/a	4,493	2
Serere	1,036	1	n/a	n/a	2,084	1	3,033	1
Bambara	943	1	3,261	2	5,047	2	1,177	...[2]
Manjago	n/a	n/a	n/a	n/a	1,059	...[2]	1,030	...[2]
Aku	559	...[2]	786	...[2]	680	...[2]	257	...[2]
Other African	1,233	1	3,947	2	3,053	1	34,791	13
Non–African	n/a	n/a	n/a	n/a	n/a	n/a	152	...[2]
Total	**138,401**	**100**	**185,150**	**100**	**228,114**	**100**	**275,469**	**100**

[1]Annual estimate of the Protectorate.
[2]Fewer than 0.5 percent.

Sources: [Colonial Office], *Census Report, 1911*; [Colonial Office], *Annual Report on the Social and Economic Progress of the People of the Gambia, 1931* (Colonial Reports no. 1572) (London: HMSO, 1932); Gamble, *Socio-Economic Survey*, 27, Table II (for 1946); [Gambia Government], *Census Report, 1963*, Table 12.

growth of the non-Gambian African population since 1983. The ethnic groups which are separately identified in table 1.7 are described below.[17]

Mandinka

The Mandinka first moved into Gambia in the late thirteenth or early fourteenth centuries as the Mali Empire expanded. They were certainly fully established on both banks of the River Gambia when the first European explorers (from Portugal) arrived in the fifteenth century and by 1800, they provided the ruling class (and most of the inhabitants) of all bar one of the fifteen kingdoms below the Barrakunda Falls.[18] As discussed in Chapter 3, the region was subject to considerable unrest in the second half of the nineteenth century; nevertheless, despite these upheavals, the Mandinka still accounted for 49 percent of the total population of Gambia in 1911. They then comprised the bulk of the population in the North Bank and South Bank Provinces of the Protectorate and were the most numerous group in all bar one of the other three Protectorate Provinces.[19] However, even though Mandinka from the Kombo had been among the earliest African inhabitants of Bathurst, they made up only 3 percent of its population in 1911 (see table 1.5).[20] During the first half of the twentieth century, their share of

Table 1.7. Population of The Gambia by Ethnic Group, 1963–93

	1963		1973		1983		1993	
	N	%	N	%	N	%	N	%
Gambians:								
Mandinka	128,807	41	186,241	38	251,997	37	353,840	34
Fula/Tukulor	47,354[1]	15	79,994	16	117,092	17	168,284	16
Wolof	40,805	13	69,291	14	84,404	12	130,546	13
Jola	22,046	7	41,988	9	64,494	9	95,262	9
Serahuli	21,318	7	38,478	8	51,137	7	79,690	8
Serere	4,258	1	9,229	2	15,551	2	24,710	2
Manjago	1,735	1	5,596	1	10,741	2	16,550[2]	2
Bambara	1,576	. . .[3]	1,722	. . .[3]	3,035	. . .[3]	7,458[2]	1
Aku	2,974	1	4,386	1	5,032	1	6,194	1
Other Gambian	9,058	3	3,791	1	20,376	3	13,601	1
Total Gambian	*279,931*	*89*	*440,716*	*89*	*623,859*	*91*	*896,135*	*86*
Non-Gambians:								
African	34,938	11	50,843	10	58,273	8	130,634	13
Non-African	617	. . .[3]	1,159	. . .[3]	2,523	. . .[3]	3,484	. . .[3]
Not stated	n/a	n/a	781	. . .[3]	3,162	. . .[3]	7,892	1
Total	**315,486**	**100**	**493,499**	**100**	**687,817**	**100**	**1,038,145**	**100**

[1]The Tukulor were reclassified as Fula in 1973. In 1963, the Fula population was 42,723 and the Tukulor population was 4,631.
[2]Additional data supplied by Central Statistics Department from census tables.
[3]Fewer than 0.5 percent.

Sources: [Gambia Government], *Census Report, 1963*, Table 10; [Gambia Government], *Population Databank*, Tables 1.4 and 4.16.

the population declined slightly, although, as shown in table 1.7, they still comprised 41 percent of the total population in 1963 (46 percent of the Gambian population). By 1993, these figures had fallen to 34 and 39 percent, respectively.

In 1963, 48 percent of the Mandinka population lived in LRD. This was clearly the Mandinka heartland; Mandinka accounted for 76 percent of the total population of Mansakonko LGA (which consisted of the Kiang and Jarra districts) and 58 percent of that of Kerewan LGA (which consisted of the Baddibu, Niumi, and Jokadu districts). The Mandinka were also the most numerous ethnic group in all the other LGAs except Bathurst. However, after independence, the center of the Mandinka population began to shift westward. By 1983, there were more Mandinka living in Brikama LGA than in any other LGA and by 1993, the WD had become the main centre of the Mandinka population; 26 percent of the

Mandinka lived in Brikama and a further 16 percent in Kanifing. This compared with only 14 and 3 percent, respectively, in 1963. Although the Mandinka were still the predominant group in four LGAs (Brikama, Kanifing, Kerewan, and Mansakonko), they had been overtaken by the Fula in Georgetown and Kuntaur (in the latter, they were also now outnumbered by the Wolof) and by the Serahuli in Basse. Moreover, only in Mansakonko did they now form an absolute majority of the population. Nevertheless, because they comprised at least one-quarter of the *Gambian* population of all LGAs, they could justifiably claim to be the most "national" of the various ethnic groups.

Precolonial Mandinka society was organized on the basis of a caste system and, even since independence, caste has remained an important arbiter of social status. The highest caste ("foro") contained freeborn members of a lineage; the middle caste ("nyamalo") consisted of people carrying out specialist functions, for example as smiths, leatherworkers, potters, or praise singers; and the lowest caste consisted of slaves ("jongo").[21]

Until independence, almost all Mandinka lived in the rural areas; as late as 1963, 95 percent lived in the Protectorate. More recently, they have moved into the urbanized areas of Banjul and Kanifing where 21 percent lived in 1993. Since the late nineteenth century, male Mandinka in the rural areas have mainly grown groundnuts (it is thought that, by the late nineteenth century, they were responsible for three-quarters of the total groundnut production) and female Mandinka have generally cultivated rice. The few Mandinka who lived in Bathurst before the 1960s tended to be poorly educated and employed in semiskilled and unskilled jobs. More recently, the Mandinka have moved up the occupational hierarchy and those in employment in the Banjul area are particularly likely to be employed in the public sector.[22]

Most Mandinka were animist until at least the 1860s, but, following the Soninke-Marabout Wars, many had converted to Islam by the 1890s and virtually all had done so by the 1920s. There have never been many Mandinka Christians, although their number have included The Gambia's first prime minister and president, Sir Dawda Jawara (who later reverted to Islam) and Edward Singhateh, one of the leaders of the 1994 military coup.[23]

Fula and Tukulor[24]

There has apparently been a Fula presence in The Gambia since at least the seventeenth century and by the nineteenth century, the various Fula subgroups, together with the closely related Tukulor, accounted for a substantial proportion of the population of the Mandinka kingdoms.[25] In the 1870s and 1880s, a famous Fula leader, Musa Molloh, established a Fula kingdom north of the river centered on Fuladu and in 1911, when they made up one-fifth of the population of the Protectorate (see table 1.6), they resided mainly in the North Bank and Upper River Provinces.[26] During the next fifty years, the estimated Fula population fluctuated, but by 1963, the Fula and the Tukulor between them comprised 15 percent of the total population. Their share of the national population remained broadly the same over the next three decades, so that in 1993, they comprised 16 percent of the total, and 19 percent of the Gambian, population (see table 1.7).

In 1963, well over half the Fula population lived either in Basse or in Georgetown LGAs, whereas 86 percent of the Tukulor lived in Kuntaur; 96 percent of their combined population lived in the Protectorate. Since independence, the Fula/Tukulor have become more evenly distributed across the country, although, in 1993, they were still more likely to live in Basse and Georgetown than elsewhere; they now accounted for at least one-tenth of the Gambian population in all LGAs except Banjul. Moreover, they are now the most numerous ethnic group in both Georgetown and Kuntaur.

Until the nineteenth century, most Fula were pastoralists who tended the cattle of their Mandinka overlords in return for pasturage. Some Fula subgroups did take up farming in the nineteenth century and, in the view of Swindell, by the 1970s, the Fula were as heavily involved in groundnut cultivation as other Gambian ethnic groups. Nevertheless, the Fula are still associated with cattle breeding and even in the 1980s, the wealth of a Fula was measured by the number of cattle he or she owned. Urban Fula, at least until the 1950s, appear to have been mainly employed as petty traders or as unskilled workers.[27]

Some Fula subgroups, as well as the Tukulor, were strongly Islamized by the 1860s, but others remained animist well into the twentieth century.[28] There have never been many Fula Christians, in part because a concerted effort by Wesleyan Methodists in the 1830s to convert them to Christianity proved a complete failure. An Anglican attempt to proselytize among the Fula by the building of a mission station and a school at Kristikunda in URD in 1940 was probably only a little more successful.[29]

Wolof

Like the Mandinka, the Wolof were firmly established in Gambia by the fifteenth century. They entered the Gambia Valley from Senegal, where they continue to be the most numerous ethnic group, and established a kingdom in Saloum (or Salum), which, by 1800, was the only non-Mandinka kingdom below the Barrakunda Falls; however, there were relatively few Wolof in any of the Mandinka kingdoms until the mid-nineteenth century.[30] Some Wolof from the interior may have later migrated to Bathurst. Meanwhile, in the 1820s, a substantial number of Wolof moved directly to Bathurst from Gorée and St. Louis in the French colony of Senegal. They were sent there by their European employers and Mulatto slave owners to work as artisans on the construction of the town, or as domestic servants, and tended originally to live in an area of North Bathurst, known as Joloff Town until the 1960s. It is probable that in the early days of the settlement on St. Mary's Island, they formed the majority of its African population.[31] There appears to have been little contact between the Gorée Wolof of Bathurst and the Wolof of the interior, who formed distinct communities at least until the 1960s.[32] In the early twentieth century, the Wolof comprised nearly half of Bathurst's population; they also made up 16 percent of the Protectorate's population in 1911 (see table 1.6).

The number of Wolof living in the Protectorate increased relatively slowly up to independence, so that by 1963 they accounted for only 10 percent of its population. Most of these lived in the Sabach Sanjal district of Kerewan LGA, in the Saloum districts of Kuntaur LGA, and in Georgetown LGA. In contrast, the Wolof formed easily the most numerous ethnic group in Bathurst, comprising 41 percent of its total population and an absolute majority of Gambians. By 1993, this picture had changed in several respects. Only 7 percent of the Wolof lived in Banjul, compared with 28 percent in Bathurst in 1963, and the Wolof now barely outnumbered the Mandinka in the capital. Almost one-third of the Wolof lived in Kerewan LGA—as they had in 1963.

Male Wolof in the rural areas have tended to be groundnut farmers since the end of the nineteenth century, and female Wolof have tended to grow food crops. Wolof farmers in the 1990s were more likely to be defined as "large export oriented" farmers, than as "small export oriented" or "subsistence" farmers (although it should be emphasized that all Gambian farmers are fairly small scale in comparison with commercial farmers elsewhere in West Africa).[33] Bathurst Wolof were often employed as skilled manual workers (artisans) or traders in the nineteenth and first half of the twentieth centuries and, even in the mid-1950s, they were often artisans, drivers, mechanics, and clerks. However, thanks to improved education, they began to move into higher level civil service posts and the professions in greater numbers after World War II, a process that has continued.[34]

Since the end of the nineteenth century, most rural Wolof have been Muslims.[35] Moreover, it is probable that most Wolof in modern Banjul are Muslims; however, there has also been a significant Christian Wolof community in the capital since the earliest years of the settlement on St. Mary's Island. Some of the Wolof immigrants from Gorée were converted to Christianity by Wesleyan missionaries and formed the nucleus (and the lay leadership) of the Methodist Church in the 1830s and 1840s; for example, the first two African assistant missionaries of the Wesleyan church, John Cupidon and Pierre Sallah, were both Wolof ex-slaves from Gorée.[36] However, after the establishment of a permanent Roman Catholic mission in Bathurst in 1849 (see below), many Wolof converted to Catholicism, particularly after 1860, and Wolof Catholics came to outnumber their Protestant counterparts. Certainly by the mid-twentieth century, most Wolof Christians were Catholic.[37]

Jola

The Jola, who are generally considered to have been resident in The Gambia for longer than any other major ethnic group, have been the most numerous ethnic group south of the River Gambia and in the Casamance area of Senegal for several centuries.[38] In 1911, when they comprised 7 percent of the national population (see table 1.5), they lived mainly in small and isolated communal groups in the forests and swamps of the southern districts of Kombo-Foni Province;

a minority also settled in Bathurst. Indeed, a key feature of Jola society at least until independence was its fragmentary nature.[39] The Jola remained concentrated in the Kombos and Fonis up to independence; as late as 1963, 55 percent of all Jola lived in either Eastern or Western Foni, and a further 27 percent lived in Eastern or Western Kombo. This meant that 83 percent of the Jola lived in the Brikama LGA. There were smaller Jola communities in Bathurst and Kanifing, but few Jola lived elsewhere in Gambia. The number of Jola living in Kanifing LGA increased from 1,400 in 1963, to more than 35,000 in 1993; this meant that by 1993, more than one-third of all Jola lived in the area. However, the majority (58 percent) of Jola still lived in Brikama LGA.

Jola living in the rural areas in the nineteenth and early twentieth centuries tended to grow rice and millet, rather than groundnuts, and also collected palm kernels for export; while urban Jola were mainly employed as unskilled laborers as late as the 1950s.[40] Unlike most other riverine peoples, the Jola were very slow to convert to Islam in the nineteenth century and many remained animist as late as the 1960s. Most Jola are now Muslims, with a minority being Roman Catholic.[41]

Serahuli

The Serahuli, who may be of mixed Mandinka, Tuareg, and Fula origin, are popularly believed to have been the main inhabitants of the ancient empire of Ghana (which flourished between the eighth and eleventh centuries AD). After the decline of the Ghana empire, some Serahuli moved to Gambia. A further migration of Serahuli into Gambia occurred in the mid-nineteenth century. As early as the 1840s, Serahuli were growing groundnuts as "strange farmers" for Mandinka landlords in the upper river and they also served as mercenaries during the Soninke–Marabout wars; they were also successful long-distance traders in the pre-colonial period.[42] By 1911, they made up 3 percent of the total population of Gambia, being resident mainly in Upper River Province.

Over the next fifty years, the recorded Serahuli population increased more rapidly than that of most other ethnic groups, so that, like the Jola, they accounted for 7 percent of the total population in 1963. Again like the Jola, they were also heavily concentrated within one LGA; 82 percent lived in Basse LGA. Indeed, the Serahuli were the most numerous group in three districts within this LGA: Kantora, Basse, and Jimara. Most other Serahuli lived in Georgetown LGA. Few lived in Bathurst or Kombo St. Mary before independence. In the first three decades after independence, the pattern of Serahuli settlement changed in some respects; nevertheless, even in 1993, nearly three-quarters of all Serahuli lived in Basse. Most others lived in Kanifing.

It is probable that most Serahuli in the nineteenth and twentieth centuries were farmers, although some urbanized Serahuli were prominent in commerce, including more recently in international trade in diamonds and clothing.[43] Since the late nineteenth century, almost all have been Muslims. The Serahuli also have been the least willing of the major Gambian ethnic groups to adopt Christian or Western education.[44]

Serere

The Serere (or Serer) have been present in The Gambia for many centuries, although they comprise a higher share of the population of Senegal, where they constituted 15 percent of the population in 1988.[45] In the early nineteenth century, most Serere lived north of the river in the kingdom of Saloum, but in 1863, an estimated 2,000 fled to the Crown Colony to escape from the fighting in the interior and eventually settled in Bathurst and British Kombo.[46] In 1901, they formed the third largest ethnic group in Bathurst after the Wolof and the Aku, and in 1911, one third of all Serere in the Colony lived in the capital. However, in 1963, only 17 percent of Serere lived in Bathurst and the majority resided in Kerewan LGA. Since 1963, the center of the Serere population has shifted again; just over one-third lived in Kerewan and just under a third in Kanifing in 1993.

Traditionally either engaged in farming or fishing, male Serere in the rural areas of The Gambia and Senegal tend now to grow groundnuts, and female Serere produce millet and vegetables. Certainly in the nineteenth century (and probably for much of the twentieth), male Serere in Bathurst tended to be employed as unskilled laborers.[47]

During the nineteenth and first half of the twentieth century, the majority of Gambian Serere remained animist, but in recent decades, most have become Muslim. Christianity has never made much headway amongst Gambian Serere, unlike in Senegal, where a significant minority became Roman Catholic during the colonial period. Indeed, a concerted effort by the Methodist Church to convert the Serere in Bathurst in the 1870s proved abortive.[48]

Manjago

The Manjago, who account for about one-tenth of the population of modern Guinea-Bissau (where they are called Mandjack, Mandyako, or Manjaco) apparently arrived in Gambia from Portuguese territory to the south in the late nineteenth century; in 1911, 128 of them lived in Bathurst (see table 1.5).[49] In 1963, there were 1,700 Manjago in Gambia, one-third of whom lived in Bathurst and over the next two decades, the Manjago population grew rapidly to reach nearly 11,000 by 1983 and more than 16,000 by 1993. Since independence, the Manjago population has mainly resided in Brikama LGA.

Relatively little is known about the history of the Manjago in The Gambia. It would appear that in the nineteenth and early twentieth centuries, they were often employed as sailors around Bathurst. There is little available information on their main occupations in more recent periods (although some are palm-wine tappers in the Kombos). However, it is known that most are Christian and their educational levels are higher than average.[50]

Bambara

The Bambara, who are the most numerous ethnic group in Mali, comprising about 30 percent of its population, have been present in The Gambia since the early nineteenth century.[51] In 1911, nearly a thousand Bambara lived in the Protectorate and there was also a small Bambara community in Bathurst (see tables 1.5 and 1.6). The number of Bambara living in the Protectorate increased rapidly until after World War II, before apparently declining sharply by 1963; this decline was probably largely due to a reclassification of many Bambara as Malians. After independence, the Bambara population increased slowly until 1983 and then more than doubled up to 1993, probably in part due to a reclassification of some Malians as Gambian Bambara. In both 1963 and 1973, the majority of Bambara lived in Basse LGA. However, in 1983 and 1993, they were most likely to live in Kerewan LGA. It is likely that most Bambara in the Protectorate are farmers, whereas those living in the capital have traditionally been employed in low-status laboring jobs.[52] Probably almost all are Muslims.

Aku, Ibo, and Liberated Africans

The Aku form a quite distinctive group within Gambian society. Like the Creoles of Sierra Leone, they are mainly descended from African slaves who were liberated by the British naval squadron after the abolition of slavery throughout the British Empire in 1807. These former slaves, who were known to contemporaries as Liberated Africans (and to later commentators as "Recaptives"), were usually first taken to Freetown, the capital of Sierra Leone.[53] A handful was transferred from Freetown to Bathurst as early as 1818 and a few more were sent there in the 1820s at the request of the mercantile community in Bathurst. However, most immigration occurred between 1832 (after Lieutenant Governor Rendall had urged the secretary of state for the colonies to allow the transfer of a large body of Liberated Africans) and 1838 (when Lieutenant Governor Mackie prohibited it). Despite this prohibition, the transfer of Liberated Africans continued until 1843, when the Liberated African Department in Bathurst was closed down, by which time between three and five thousand Liberated Africans had been transferred to Gambia.[54] By the 1840s, these formed a significant proportion of Bathurst's population; for example, in 1841, the estimated 1,400 Liberated Africans in Bathurst comprised two-fifths of its total population.[55]

The Liberated Africans in Gambia were of diverse ethnic origin. Although it is not possible to provide precise figures, it is probable that most were Yoruba from modern Western Nigeria who, as in Sierra Leone, were called Aku. Ibo from Eastern Nigeria may have formed the second largest group; there were also people from Grand/Little Popo in what is now Togo, Moco from Cameroon, "Congos," and Hausa from Northern Nigeria.[56] When the first detailed assessment of the ethnic origin of the Colony's population was made in 1901, the Aku, followed by the Ibo, comprised the largest proportion of the descendants of the Liberated

Africans (see table 1.4). Indeed, by 1911, the term Aku was apparently being used in the census to cover all the descendants of the Liberated Africans except the Ibo, as well as freeborn immigrants from Sierra Leone and possibly the children of Wolof Protestants and of mixed Aku/Wolof parents.[57]

Both the 1911 and 1921 census returns showed that the Aku and the Ibo remained the most important groups within Creole society in Bathurst. The data presented in table 1.5 suggest that the Aku community in Bathurst grew substantially in the 1920s and 1930s, but it is possible that those of Ibo descent were classified as Aku in 1944, thereby accounting for at least part of the increase; there may also have been a change in the classification of immigrants from Sierra Leone.[58] After World War II, the Aku population increased slowly so that by 1983, they comprised only 0.7 percent of the national population, a proportion that fell further to 0.6 percent in 1993.

During the 1830s, official policy was to place as many Liberated African immigrants as possible on MacCarthy Island, although a settlement was also established in the Ceded Mile at this time and in British Kombo in the 1850s and 1860s. The settlement in the Ceded Mile did not survive for long (its inhabitants soon moved to Bathurst), but the Liberated African community on MacCarthy Island survived until a few years after the withdrawal of its military garrison in 1866. However, by the 1870s, all Liberated African communities outside Bathurst were in decline and, as shown in table 1.4, more than four out of five Liberated Africans and Sierra Leonean immigrants lived in the capital in 1881.[59] Even after the establishment of the Protectorate, the Aku and Ibo largely continued to reside in Bathurst; in 1911, for example, most Aku, and all Ibo, lived in the capital.

Over the next fifty years, the number of Aku who resided in the Protectorate remained very low; in 1963, 85 percent of the Aku population lived in Bathurst and a further 7 percent in Kombo St. Mary. Only 8 percent of the Aku were found in the Protectorate and these made up a mere 0.1 percent of its total population. Over the next two decades, the Aku population increasingly shifted from Banjul to Kanifing, although even in 1983, 48 percent of the Aku still lived in the capital. In 1993, 57 percent of the Aku population lived in Kanifing and only 30 percent in Banjul.

The first Liberated African settlers in Gambia tended to succumb to the hostile climate, and the survivors often remained illiterate, unemployed, and destitute.[60] Gradually, however, Liberated Africans and their descendants became better educated. By the 1860s, they were "amongst the foremost traders in the river Gambia" and were well represented in government service; by the 1870s, a few had become merchants and by 1911, they were said to comprise the majority of the educated class.[61] During the next fifty years, the Aku strengthened their position in the civil service and also supplied most African merchants and professionals. At independence, many senior civil servants were Aku and they have continued to be well represented in the senior ranks of the civil service.[62] Even in 1993, the Aku population had much higher educational levels than other ethnic groups; only 9 percent had had no formal education.[63]

A contemporary account suggested that in the 1860s, the majority of Aku (narrowly defined, i.e., those of Yoruba origin) and almost all Ibo living in The Gambia were Christian. Most of these would have been Protestant (mainly Methodist, but also Anglican); there appear never to have been many Aku Catholics. A minority of Aku were Muslim (popularly known as "Aku Marabouts").[64] The religious complexion of the Aku community (more broadly defined) remained broadly similar for more than a century. Most Aku were Methodist and accounted for almost all the leading lay members of the Wesleyan Church in the nineteenth and early twentieth century—but a minority continued to be Muslims.[65]

Non-Gambian Africans

There has been a sizeable foreign African population in the Gambia Valley since the 1840s, when "strange farmers" from Senegal and other French territory moved into the area to grow groundnuts on a sharecropping basis.[66] The presence of strange farmers remained an important feature of Gambian rural society thereafter, although their numbers fluctuated considerably. For example, there were 16,000 strange farmers from French and Portuguese territory in Gambia in 1945, but only 7,000 in 1948. A Farmers' Survey carried out in the mid-1970s, estimated that there were about 25,000 Guinean, Senegalese, and Malian strange farmers in The Gambia, but a 1990 survey found that there were less than 2,000 non-Gambian strange farmers in the country.[67]

Non-Gambian Africans have also moved to Bathurst in considerable numbers since the late nineteenth century. The first to arrive were probably Creoles from Sierra Leone who came to Bathurst initially to trade and then, from the 1870s onward, to seek clerical employment with the Gambian government.[68] As noted, many were eventually absorbed into the Aku community. The number of Sierra Leoneans in The Gambia declined after World War II and by the 1970s, Gambians were more likely to live in Sierra Leone than vice versa.[69] In the first half of the twentieth century, and perhaps particularly between World Wars I and II, Senegalese and other immigrants from French and Portuguese territory traveled to Bathurst during the trade season to load groundnuts.[70]

Table 1.8 shows that the total of non-Gambian Africans rose gradually until 1983, before more than doubling to 131,000 in 1993, when, as shown in table 1.7, they comprised 13 percent of the population. This was a particularly high proportion, which reflected the economic and political problems of its neighbors. Not surprisingly, the majority of foreign nationals in The Gambia are from neighboring Senegal. In the mid-1970s, there were nearly twice as many Gambians living in Senegal as Senegalese living in Gambia, but by the 1990s, the situation was very different.[71] By 1993, over half of all non-Gambians lived in either Kanifing or Brikama. Non-Gambian Africans were also much more likely to be employed in the "informal sector" of the economy than in the "formal" private sector or the public sector.[72]

Table 1.8. Non-Gambian African Population of The Gambia, 1963–93

	Senegal	Guinea [Conakry]	Guinea-Bissau[a]	Mali	Sierra Leone	Mauritania	Other	Total
1963	21,498	5,257	4,689	1,911	730	585	268	34,938
1973	25,309	10,137	6,817	5,467	436	1,883	794	50,843
1983	32,385	12,599	5,626	4,295	517	1,828	1,023	58,273
1993	81,567	27,797	8,488	6,370	1,605	2,243	2,564	130,634

Sources: [Gambia Government], *Census Report, 1963*, Table 10; [Gambia Government], *Population Databank*, Table 4.16.
Note: Data are for country of nationality.
[a]Portuguese Guinea in 1963 and 1973.

Europeans

Ever since the foundation of Bathurst, there has been a small, but influential, European population. The first civilian settlers were a group of British merchants who moved to Gambia from Gorée soon after the French had reoccupied their trading post in 1817.[73] By 1823, there were forty-five Europeans (including military officers) on St. Mary's Island and there were usually thirty to fifty resident Europeans in Bathurst during the nineteenth century (few lived outside the town). Most Europeans in the Colony at any one time were British, although following the abandonment of Albreda, there was also a small, but significant, French commercial community in Bathurst from 1860 when the first French firm (Maurel Frères) was set up in the town. In the first half of the twentieth century, the number of Europeans on St. Mary's Island increased, reaching 261 in 1939; in 1963, the British population of Gambia was 412. By 1983, the non-African population exceeded 2,500. Many of these would have been Asians or Americans; the European share is unknown, although they perhaps still comprised the majority of non-African expatriates.[74]

Most European residents in the nineteenth century were either officials or merchants (a handful were missionaries). No clear-cut distinction was made between the two groups; owing to a shortage of manpower, merchants were often required to take on official positions.[75] In the first half of the twentieth century, about one-third of all Europeans were officials and by the 1990s, most were probably employed either by the central government or by aid agencies on contract work.[76]

Mulattos

For most of the nineteenth century, there was also a distinctive Mulatto community in Bathurst. A total of 135 Mulattos was recorded as living on St. Mary's Island in 1824 and 116 in the 1901 census. Mulattos were the product of relationships between European men and African (mainly Wolof) women (known as "senoras" or "signaras") and, as in Senegal, there were important social distinctions between

them. At one end of the social scale were the offspring of British officials and merchants who were often educated in Europe, became merchants themselves, and
lived alongside Europeans (often in Portuguese Town in North Bathurst). At the
other end were the descendants of early Portuguese traders who were generally
employed as artisans, sailors, and domestic servants. The Mulatto community "disappeared" after 1901; some Mulattos were absorbed into the European community; others were no doubt reclassified as Wolof.[77]

West Indians

In the later nineteenth century, there was also a small, but politically important,
West Indian community in Bathurst; for example, there were fifty-nine West
Indians living in Bathurst in 1881 (see table 1.4). Some were officials, but most
were probably engaged in commerce or the professions; many West Indian settlers
may originally have served in one of the West Indian regiments stationed at different times in Gambia.[78] By 1901, most had died or left Gambia.

Lebanese

Finally, the first Lebanese (or, strictly speaking, Syrian) immigrants arrived in
Gambia (and Senegal) around 1900; there were fourteen Syrians in Bathurst in
1901 and fifty-four in 1921.[79] Like other Lebanese in West Africa, they found work
initially as small-scale retailers in the Colony and Protectorate. Again as elsewhere
in West Africa, later generations also concentrated on commerce with some families (notably the Madis) being extremely successful. The Lebanese community
(which is now fully integrated into Gambian society) remains heavily involved in
commerce and in tourism.[80] With the exception of the Madi family, Lebanese in
The Gambia have avoided public engagement in politics.

Religion

The Gambia is now an overwhelmingly Islamic country; 95 percent of the population was Muslim in both 1983 and 1993.[81] However, at the beginning of the nineteenth century, the religious composition of the population was very different.
Moreover, for much of the period under review, there were marked differences
between the religious composition of Bathurst and of the Protectorate. These distinctions were of considerable political significance and so are examined in some
detail.

In 1800, the great majority of people living along the River Gambia were animist. Islam had been introduced into the riverine region in the fourteenth century and, in the early 1800s, there were small Muslim communities in almost all the
kingdoms. However, they suffered discrimination from the majority animist population, being prohibited from owning land or holding the highest offices of state.

In the late 1840s, the underlying tensions between stricter Muslims (who were collectively known as Marabouts) and animists or laxer Muslims (known as Soninkes) led to conflict in the south bank kingdom of Kombo. More significantly, in 1861, Maba (or Ma Bah) Diakhou (or Jaakhu), a Fula Torodo who had been initiated into the Tijaniyya brotherhood around 1850, launched a successful Muslim jihad (holy war) against the Soninke ruling class in the kingdom of Baddibu. The conflict spread rapidly to other parts of the river and by the mid-1870s, the Soninkes had been defeated.[82]

Muslims were thereafter in the ascendancy in most of the area, which was to become the Protectorate in 1894 and by the early 1900s, accounted for four out of five persons in the Protectorate. Almost all the rest were animists (or "pagans" as they were described in the census returns); there were very few Christians in the Protectorate. This situation remained largely unchanged by the early 1930s. By the 1950s, Muslims accounted for nine-tenths of the population of the Protectorate, but sizeable animist communities remained, notably in the Foni region.[83] However, by 1993, only 800 people admitted to being followers of "traditional" religions. The decline of traditional religions was thus more complete in The Gambia than in some other countries in West Africa; for example, around 40 percent of the population in Cameroon and Liberia still adhered to traditional religions in the 1990s.[84]

Christianity was never well established in the Protectorate, but in Bathurst, the situation was very different. Its origins in The Gambia may be traced to the arrival of the first Wesleyan Methodist missionary, John Morgan, in February 1821.[85] It was initially intended that the Wesleyan mission should be based at Mandinari in the Kombo, but this station was abandoned in 1822 and thereafter Bathurst remained the focus of Wesleyan attention.[86] The earliest Wesleyan missionaries (and their families) suffered a very high mortality rate, but recorded church membership rose from approximately forty in 1830 to 250 by the end of 1834 and 559 by 1837. In 1837, 70 percent of Wesleyans lived in Bathurst and the remainder on MacCarthy Island, where a mission station had been successfully established in 1832. By 1841, a total of 634 "natives" in the colony were said to profess the Christian religion.[87] Almost all of these would have been Methodist. Although an Anglican chaplain had first been appointed in 1820, Anglicanism had made little headway thereafter; a Catholic mission established on St. Mary's Island in 1823 was quickly abandoned and a permanent mission was not established in Bathurst until 1849.[88]

During the 1860s, however, the composition of the Christian population began to change as Roman Catholic missionary endeavors became more effective. When the first religious census was taken in 1871, Methodists accounted for 67 percent of the Crown Colony's Christians, Catholics for 24 percent, and Anglicans for 9 percent. According to Administrator Anton, who conducted the census, almost all Anglicans and Catholics then lived in Bathurst, whereas Methodists were scattered throughout the settlement; in fact, the majority of full members of the Methodist Church were resident in Bathurst. By the 1890s, there were an estimated 1,500

Table 1.9. Population of Bathurst/Banjul by Religious Belief, 1881–1993

	1881	1901	1911	1921	1931	1944	1951	1983	1993
Christian[1]	3,078	3,229	3,288	3,948	4,681	4,995	5,172	4,590	3,026
Anglican	751	n/a	n/a	n/a	1,119	1,030	1,074	n/a	n/a
Methodist	n/a	n/a	n/a	n/a	1,477	1,479	1,695	n/a	n/a
Roman Catholic	n/a	n/a	n/a	n/a	2,064	2,486	2,383	n/a	n/a
Muslim	1,894	4,192[2]	3,957	4,928	9,291	15,866	14,219	38,932	38,662
Traditional	1,166	1,386[2]	455	351	398	291	211	22	9
Total	**6,138**	**8,807**	**7,700**	**9,227**	**14,370**	**21,152**	**19,602**	**44,188**[3]	**42,326**[3]

[1] Includes other Christians, who were not separately identified.
[2] Probably artificially high figures because of the presence of the Expeditionary force in Bathurst (which would not have affected the Christian community to the same extent).
[3] Includes other religions and not stated.

Sources: As for tables 1.4 and 1.5; see also [Gambia Government], *Report and Summary of the Census of the Gambia* (Bathurst: Government Printer, 1932). Data for 1983 and 1993 were supplied to the authors by the Central Statistics Department, Banjul. These supplement data in [Gambia Government], *Population Databank*, Table 1.6.

Catholics in Gambia and, as table 1.9 shows, by 1931, Catholics easily outnumbered Methodists in Bathurst.[89]

The number of Muslims in Bathurst began to increase during the 1860s and 1870s as refugees from the conflict in the riverine kingdoms fled to the town; by 1881, they comprised 31 percent of its population.[90] There were more Muslims than Christians living in Bathurst in 1901 and by 1911, they formed an absolute majority of its population. Christianity was now largely confined to the capital; whereas one in five Christians resident in the Colony had lived outside Bathurst in 1881, less than one in ten did so in 1901.[91]

As table 1.9 shows, during the twentieth century, the capital increasingly became a "Muslim" town. Muslims accounted for three-quarters of the population in 1944 and for more than nine-tenths in 1993. Christians still accounted for 43 percent of the population of Bathurst in 1911, but by 1944, their share had fallen to one-quarter and by 1993 to less than one-tenth. Catholics accounted for almost half of the town's Christian population, Methodists for one-third, and Anglicans for the remainder, a quite different pattern from the nineteenth century. Catholics also made up three-quarters of the Christian population of Kombo St. Mary at this time.[92] Religious belief was not recorded in either the 1963 or 1973 censuses (although one author estimated the Christian population to be 10,000, of whom 8,000 were Catholic, in 1970), but the recorded Christian population was 25,000 in 1983 and 42,000 in 1993. Most Gambian Christians were Catholic; at the end of 1996, the estimated Catholic population was just under 30,000. There were also an estimated 1,500 Anglicans, and most of the remainder were presumably Methodist. Whereas in the colonial period, most Christians lived in Bathurst, fewer than one in ten lived in Banjul in 1993; nearly half lived in Kanifing and one-third in Brikama LGA.[93]

Education, Health, and Poverty

Education

As noted, the first permanent missionaries in The Gambia were Wesleyan Methodists who were therefore also the first to set up schools; by 1841, there were 268 pupils in their three elementary schools in Bathurst, the Ceded Mile, and MacCarthy Island.[94] Catholic and Anglican elementary schools were founded in Bathurst by 1870, but at least until the 1920s, the Wesleyan school rolls were usually the highest and the Anglican rolls the lowest. In 1918, for example, there were 592 pupils on the rolls of the three Wesleyan schools in Bathurst and Georgetown (MacCarthy Island); 538 pupils on the rolls of the three Catholic schools, and 235 on the Anglican roll.[95] Until 1903, when the "Mohammedan School" opened in Bathurst, no schools provided a Koranic education; a handful of Muslims did, however, attend one or other of the Protestant mission schools. The Mohammedan School, which was managed by a Board of Management of Muslim notables, possessed 108 pupils in 1918.[96] There was only one secondary school in Bathurst before the 1920s, the Wesleyan (Methodist) Boys' High School (WBHS). The WBHS was founded in 1879 to train native missionary agents and to educate the sons of Liberated African entrepreneurs. It originally had 15 pupils, which had increased to 39 by 1918 and to 140 by 1955. By 1930, there were four secondary schools in Bathurst: two were Methodist and two were Roman Catholic.[97]

Bathurst's elementary schools were administered by the missions until 1945 when they were taken over by the Gambian government and converted into primary schools under the Director of Education. The Baldwin Report of 1951 recommended that the four small mission secondary schools be merged into one nondenominational government school. But it was not until 1959 that the two Wesleyan secondary schools in Bathurst finally formed the nucleus of the government-run Gambia High School; the two Catholic secondary schools retained a separate existence. By 1960, enrolment in Bathurst's twelve government primary schools and three private elementary schools exceeded 3,700 (compared with 1,698 for the six mission elementary schools in 1938), and combined enrolment in the four secondary schools in Bathurst was 622 (compared with 197 in these schools in 1938).[98]

As discussed, the Christian missions concentrated their resources on Bathurst. This meant that Protectorate education was almost entirely neglected and even as late as 1918, the only elementary schools outside Bathurst were one Wesleyan and one Catholic school in Georgetown on MacCarthy Island. The situation had improved slightly by 1938, when there were six elementary mission schools outside Bathurst and, as noted, an Anglican mission school was also established at Kristikunda in 1940. Meanwhile, a government school, Armitage School, had been established at Georgetown in 1927 (following the closure of the Catholic school). It originally provided Koranic teaching and an elementary education in agriculture and (like the Bo School in Sierra Leone) was deliberately designed to cater for the sons and near relatives of Protectorate chiefs. It later became a secondary school and adopted an academic curriculum.[99] Nevertheless, educational provision in the rural areas remained very limited. After World War II, the situation improved and by 1960, the thirty-seven village primary schools in the Protectorate were attended by 2,200 pupils. Even so, only 5 percent of the school-age population of the Protectorate attended school, compared with 85 percent of the school-age population of Bathurst and 47 percent of that of Kombo St. Mary. Moreover, at independence in 1965, 86 percent of the secondary school places were in Bathurst and Kombo St. Mary.[100]

Because educational provision remained so poor before World War II, it is not surprising that the proportion of the population that could claim to be educated remained very low, even in Bathurst. Sixteen percent of the population of Bathurst was recorded as having a "good" education in 1921, and even in 1951, only 27 percent of Bathurst's population was literate in English. Although a higher proportion of the Christian than Muslim population was literate in English, the number of educated Muslims was certainly increasing by the 1950s; for example, 87 out of 140 pupils at the WBHS in 1955 were Muslim. The extent of literacy in Bathurst also compared very favorably with the Protectorate, where only 345 people—a mere 0.2 percent of the Protectorate's population—claimed literacy in English in 1945.[101] Although it is likely that literacy levels had improved by independence, the overall picture of a relatively poorly educated population (particularly in the Protectorate) remained valid by comparison with other West African countries.[102]

After independence, the Gambian government devoted considerable resources to improving educational provision with the ultimate goal of achieving universal primary education. The number of pupils attending primary schools rose from 11,500 in 1964–65 to 26,000 in 1976–77, and 113,000 in 1994–95. There were also 32,000 secondary school pupils in 1994–95, compared with only 3,000 at the end of 1964. In the same period, the number of schools increased from 99 to 257 and the number of teachers from 956 to 3,370. The gross primary enrolment rate (the percentage of the relevant age group enrolled in primary school) also increased from approximately 21 percent in 1964–65 to 53 percent in 1980 and 73 percent in 1993, and the secondary enrolment rate rose from 11–19 percent between 1980 and 1993. However, the adult literacy rate remained as low as 36 percent in 1992.[103] Significant progress has been made since independence in improving the position of groups in society which had fared poorly before independence; for example, the female gross primary enrolment increased from 15 percent in 1970 to 61 percent in 1993. Nevertheless, some of the historic imbalances of the educational system, notably the advantages enjoyed by Banjul over the rest of the country and by men over women, have still to be rectified. The adult male literacy rate in 1995 (53 percent) was more than twice as high as the female rate (25 percent), whereas both primary and secondary enrolment rates were higher for boys than girls. Moreover, a number of studies have revealed that literacy rates and enrolment rates remain higher in urban areas than in rural areas.[104]

Health

As noted, the dry season in The Gambia lasts between November and June and the rainy season between the end of June and late October. Until World War II, the dry and wet seasons could equally have been termed the "healthy" and "sickly" seasons; St. Mary's Island was subject to seasonal flooding, which provided ideal conditions for the spread of malaria. There were also periodic epidemics of yellow fever (the last one as recently as 1934) and cholera, which gave the colony its unflattering reputation for high mortality.[105] As late as 1944, the American president, Franklin Roosevelt, could comment about Gambia at a press conference that "Disease is rampant, absolutely. It's a terrible place for disease."[106]

After World War II, government expenditure on health began to increase, but the overall health of the population remained poor. For example, as late as 1960, the estimated life expectancy at birth was still only thirty-two years.[107] After independence, the government made a determined effort to improve the health of the population; for example, between 1963–64 and 1976–77, actual recurrent expenditure on health more than doubled in real terms. Although no new general hospitals were built to complement the Royal Victoria Hospital in Banjul and Bansang Hospital in MID, the number of health centers increased from eight in 1964 to twenty-three in 1991. As a result of greater emphasis being placed on providing health services in the rural areas, 406 village health services had also been established by 1991.[108]

By 1996, life expectancy at birth had increased to fifty-three years, a substantial improvement on the situation in 1960, and the infant mortality rate fell from 185 to 79 per 1,000 live births between 1970 and 1996. The 1996 rates compared with sub-Saharan averages of 52 and 91, respectively.[109] An estimated 76 percent of the population had access to safe water in 1995, but only 34 percent had access to sanitation. Compared with sub-Saharan Africa averages, a higher proportion had access to safe water, but a lower proportion to sanitation. Moreover, as in the case of education provision, significant differences remained between the urban and rural areas, for example, in terms of access to safe water.[110]

Poverty

It was not until the early 1990s that attempts were made systematically to measure the extent of poverty in The Gambia. The first comprehensive assessment, the 1992–93 Household Economic Survey, found that 15 percent of Gambians could be classified as "extremely poor"; their annual mean income was below the food poverty line. An additional 18 percent were "poor"; their annual income was between the food poverty line and the overall poverty line. More than one in five (23 percent) of those living in rural areas were extremely poor, compared with only 9 percent of those in "other urban" areas and 5 percent of those in Greater Banjul. A more recent survey, the 1998 National Household Poverty Survey, reported that poverty had increased in the 1990s, with 51 percent of persons being classified as "extremely poor." Again, those living in rural areas were much more likely to be in poverty than their urban counterparts.[111]

In 1990, the United Nations Development Programme (UNDP) introduced the Human Development Index (HDI). This seeks to compare the record of countries according to three components: life expectancy at birth; educational attainment, which comprises adult literacy and a combined primary, secondary, and tertiary enrolment ratio; and income (as measured by real gross domestic product per capita). The Gambia ranked second from last out of 164 countries in 1990; in 1995, by which time the measurement of the HDI had been refined, The Gambia ranked 161st out of 174 countries.[112]

Labor Force

Bathurst's permanent labor force in the nineteenth century consisted mainly of skilled and unskilled manual workers, traders, shopkeepers, and domestic servants. Virtually no native Gambians were employed in professional occupations and relatively few in clerical work.[113] There was also a seasonal labor force of unskilled laborers, who migrated to Bathurst from up river each year to load groundnuts onto ocean-going vessels.[114] In the first half of the twentieth century, skilled manual workers accounted for one-third of the urban labor force; unskilled laborers for between one-fifth and one-sixth of the labor force (except in the unusual circumstances of 1944, when the proportion rose to one-third); and about one person in seven was in commerce. Clerical work gradually assumed a more important role, so that, by 1951, it accounted for 9 percent of the urban labor force, but even in the 1950s, there were still very few Gambian professionals.[115] There was also a seasonal labor force that, as noted, included many temporary migrants from neighboring French and Portuguese colonies, as well as Gambians from up river, during the 1930s.[116] Meanwhile, outside Bathurst, most economically active people were farmers.

More recent data on the industrial and occupational structure of employment are available from the 1983 and 1993 censuses, and from a series of household and labor force surveys. Agriculture remained the single most important source of employment even in 1993 accounting for 51 percent of the economically active population; two-thirds of economically active women, but only two-fifths of economically active men, worked in this industry. The other main sources of employment were wholesale and retail trade and community, social, and personal services. Not surprisingly, Gambians were most likely to work as crop producers or as skilled agricultural workers in 1993; this occupational category accounted for half the total, and nearly three-quarters of the rural, economically active population. The urban population was most likely to be employed as service and market sales workers. Only 2 percent of the population was employed as legislators, managers, or professionals; three-quarters of those in these high-level occupations were men.[117]

It is probable that before World War II, the majority of employed Gambians in the urban areas worked in the private rather than the public sector.[118] However, during and after the war, the government assumed an enlarged role as an employer and by the 1960s, at least two-thirds of employment in "larger" establishments was either in central or local government or in public corporations (parastatals). This proportion had risen to three-quarters by 1973. Between 1975–76 and 1985–86, the number of civil servant posts nearly doubled and by 1983, four out of five employed persons worked in the public sector.[119] However, following the retrenchment of approximately 3,000 permanent and temporary civil servants in 1986, the public sector share of employment had fallen to 64 percent by December 1986.[120] During the late 1980s and early 1990s, total civil service employment increased again to reach 10,700 in 1993–94, which was similar to the pre-1986 retrenchment level. The public sector was now similar in size to the formal private sector, although much smaller than the informal private sector. The development of The Gambia as a holiday destination, which is described below, meant that by the late 1980s, an estimated 7,000 Gambians were employed in services directly or indirectly linked to tourism.[121]

Structure of the Economy

Throughout the colonial period, Gambia, like other West African colonies, depended on the proceeds of international trade.[122] Until World War II, the greater part of government revenue was provided by customs receipts. These were generated by duties imposed on manufactured goods, clothing, and foodstuffs imported from Europe by trading companies and, to a lesser extent, by a duty (which was first imposed in 1863) on the principal export crop, the groundnut. Other sources of revenue, such as fines and licenses, were usually of much lesser importance and there was no income tax in the colony until 1940.[123] After World War II, development expenditure was largely financed by grants or loans from the British government. However, at independence, nearly two-thirds of domestic revenue (total revenue excluding foreign grants) was derived from taxes on international trade. Indeed, until 1988–89, international trade almost always accounted for at least 60 percent, and often more than 70 percent, of domestic revenue.[124] This pattern apparently changed after the introduction of a national sales tax in 1988; the share of domestic revenue provided by international trade declined to only 43 percent by 1989–90, a similar proportion to that in other West African states. However, as Basu and Gemmell have pointed out, the sales tax on imports is in effect a tax on international trade; taking that into account, international trade continued to account for the major proportion of total revenue in the 1990s.[125]

Main Trading Partners

Gambia's main trading partners before World War I were France, which took three-quarters of its exports, and Great Britain, which supplied three-fifths of its imports. Britain replaced France as the main recipient of Gambian exports during World War I.[126] It retained this position as The Gambia's main trading partner up to independence, when the United Kingdom took three fifths of Gambian exports and supplied more than a third of its imports. Trade links with Sierra Leone had been important between the 1880s and World War II, but by independence, *recorded* trade with other African states was negligible (although, as discussed below, there was also a thriving contraband trade).[127] Britain remained The Gambia's most important trading partner until 1979, when the Netherlands took the lead as the main recipient of Gambian exports for the first time.[128]

Imports and Exports before Independence

Between the mid-1840s and independence, the groundnut generally was the principal export item; indeed, its dominance was so great that the country was described as a "classic monoculture" as late as the 1960s.[129] However, in the early years of the settlement on St. Mary's Island, gum, beeswax, and hides and skins were the leading exports, and the most important imports included rum and spirits, guns, and gunpowder. Gum exports declined rapidly after the 1830s, and beeswax and hides and skins were superseded by the groundnut in the 1840s and never regained their former importance.[130] Meanwhile, although groundnuts had been grown for food in Gambia for centuries, they were not exported at all until 1830 and only in small quantities before 1837. The United States, which imported groundnuts for food, provided the initial market for groundnuts, before its market for Senegambian groundnuts was closed by the imposition of a substantial tariff in 1842. More significantly, France began to import groundnuts in increasing quantities in the early 1840s, particularly to make soap. There was no equivalent demand from Britain, which preferred to import palm oil from the Niger Delta to manufacture soap. Nevertheless, the demand from France was sufficient to ensure that the export value of groundnuts rose rapidly. By 1844, they accounted for 64 percent of export value and, by 1857, for 83 percent. Thereafter, in most years before 1900, groundnuts accounted for between 70 and 90 percent of export value. Since 1848, France had been the recipient of the greater part of the Gambian groundnut crop, a status it was to retain until World War I, when it was replaced by Britain.[131]

Until the establishment of the Protectorate in the 1890s, the greater part of the Gambian crop came from areas that were neither under British rule nor British protection. Moreover, a substantial proportion of the crop was produced not by Gambian farmers, but rather by "strange farmers" from the interior of Africa.[132] Groundnuts were exchanged by barter for goods imported from Europe, which indirectly increased the government's tax revenue. But the increasing emphasis on groundnuts was not wholly beneficial, because foodstuffs were often neglected. Imports of "foreign" rice rose steadily after 1857 and there were periodic food crises.[133] Other imports in the second half of the nineteenth century included cotton manufactured goods, which made up one-quarter of import value by the

1850s; tobacco; guns and gunpowder (particularly during the religious wars of the 1860s); and kola nuts. The kola nut was an acceptable substitute for alcohol for Muslims and so the trade increased markedly after the Muslim jihad of the 1860s. Kola nuts were imported from Sierra Leone, not from Europe, and the trade was dominated by Liberated African entrepreneurs rather than by European mercantile firms.[134]

In the first half of the twentieth century, the dominance of the groundnut (which was grown mainly on the north bank of the river and in upper river areas) became even more pronounced. In 1909, the hydrogenation process was perfected, which meant that cheaper liquid oil could be substituted for oleo in the production of margarine. This led to a huge increase in demand for Gambian nuts. Consequently, whereas the record export volume before 1910 had been 35,805 tons in 1900, export volume averaged over 60,000 tons between 1910 and 1938. The world market price fluctuated sharply, but in most years before World War II, groundnuts made up over 90 percent (and frequently as much as 98 percent) of export value (if re-exports and exports of specie and bullion are excluded). The export of hides and skins was significant during World War I, but less so after 1920, and apart from groundnuts, only palm kernel exports were worth more than £10,000 a year between the wars (and not again after 1929).[135]

After World War II, the British government (through the Colonial Development Corporation) attempted to provide an additional source of export income for Gambia, but the Wallikunda rice project and especially the infamous Yundum egg scheme were disastrous failures. Attempts to exploit ilmenite and oil resources in the mid-1950s were equally unsuccessful. The export value of palm kernels did rise significantly after the war, reaching a record total of £124,000 in 1958, but even then it made up only 3 percent of exports. Groundnuts continued to dominate external trade and in most years before independence made up at least 90 percent of exports and were therefore virtually the only source of foreign exchange earnings.[136]

Imports and Exports after Independence

After independence, the composition of imports and exports remained similar for nearly two decades, with groundnut products accounting for 90 percent or more of the value of domestic exports virtually each year until the late 1970s and again in 1983–84.[137] Thereafter, however, the groundnut's share of domestic exports declined sharply to only 63 percent in 1991–92 and an estimated 51 percent in 1994–95. In part, this was due to a gradual diversification into exports other than groundnuts; other exports—principally fish and fish products, cotton products, and horticultural products—were worth Special Drawing Rights (SDR) 7.0 million in 1991–92, compared with only SDR 3.6 million in 1983–84, and after declining in the next two years, were valued at an estimated SDR 7.3 million in 1994–95. More importantly, however, the value of groundnut exports fell sharply from a peak of SDR 31.7 million in 1983–84 (when output reached 151,000 tons) to a low point of SDR 8.5 million in 1985–86 (when output was only 75,000 tons), recovered somewhat over the next few years to reach SDR 12.9 million in 1989–90, before falling again to an estimated SDR 7.6 million in 1994–95.[138] The collapse of the groundnut sector in the mid-1980s was caused by a combination of factors. These included prolonged drought; parasite infestation; lower soil fertility (which to some extent was in turn due to the poor performance of the government parastatal, the Gambia Cooperatives Union (GCU), which had a monopoly on the supply of seed and fertilizer to farmers); and overtaxation, which discouraged farmers from growing export crops. World prices were also falling in the early 1980s. The partial recovery of the second half of the 1980s has been attributed to the subsidizing of the producer price at the behest of the International Monetary Fund (IMF); once this was removed in 1989–90, groundnut production fell sharply from 133,000 tons in 1989–90 to 76,000 tons a year later. Production continued to decline during the 1990s, falling to a new low of only 46,000 tons in 1996.[139]

As late as 1974–75, groundnuts accounted for 78 percent of the value of total exports. Recorded and estimated re-exports (and adjustments) accounted for a further 19 percent. Since World War II, there had been a substantial (but officially not quantified) contraband re-export trade with Senegal and other Francophone colonies, which involved the trans-shipment of rice, flour, and other consumer goods that had been imported into Banjul. By the mid-1960s, the contraband trade between The Gambia and Senegal was estimated to be worth about $2 million, or 15 percent of Gambian imports. During the 1970s and 1980s, the re-export trade grew in importance; by 1982–83, re-exports accounted for 62 percent of total exports.[140]

Reforms undertaken as part of the Economic Recovery Programme (which is analyzed in the next section), such as the introduction of a flexible exchange rate system in 1986, the removal of trade and exchange restrictions and major cuts in import tariffs, provided a further impetus to the re-export trade, because costs of importing goods into the West African region were now much lower via Banjul than through other locations. Economic and political problems in other countries (e.g., Sierra Leone and Liberia) also improved Banjul's relative position. Thus re-exports accounted for 88 percent of exports in 1992–93, before falling to an estimated 82 percent in 1994–95. The downturn in re-exports occurred mainly for political reasons; in August 1993, Senegal tightened border controls (as it had after the collapse of the Senegambia Confederation in 1989) and suspended repurchases of the CFA franc and in January 1994, the CFA franc was devalued by 50 percent, which contributed to a weakening of demand for imports, including via The Gambia. Political uncertainty in The Gambia, following the July 1994 coup, caused further difficulties for the re-export sector.[141]

The decline of the groundnut sector meant that by 1990–91, it contributed only 14 percent of foreign exchange earnings. Re-exports contributed a further 30 percent. But the main source of foreign exchange was now tourism; travel income contributed 49 percent of foreign exchange earnings in that year.[142] The total number of foreign tourists rose from fewer than 1,000 in 1967–68 to nearly 50,000 by 1982–83 and then increased rapidly to reach almost 102,000 in 1988–89. The total again exceeded 100,000 in 1990–91, but then fell back to the levels of the mid-1980s. Following the overthrow of the civilian government in July 1994, nine out of ten tour operators withdrew from the country and the number of tourists fell from 78,000 in 1993–94 to only 45,000 in 1994–95. Consequently, travel income fell by nearly two-thirds. However, the downturn proved short-lived; in 1995–96, the number of tourists increased to 77,000.[143]

Economic Trends

Before Independence

In the early years of the settlement on St. Mary's Island, the colony's revenue and expenditure were very low and revenue might not have exceeded £5,000 before 1835.[144] As noted, import duties comprised the greater part of government revenue, but the Colonial Office did not allow the Gambian government to impose duties on goods imported by French traders (who had been based at Albreda since 1817). These traders were not allowed to trade further up river than James Island, but they ignored the prohibition and goods imported legally into Gambia from Gorée were subsequently smuggled up river. The effect of this contraband trade was to reduce legitimate trade and therefore both customs duties and government revenue.[145]

The establishment of the groundnut trade in the 1840s meant that merchants could now import a greater volume of goods into the colony for onward sale by their agents to farmers up river. Consequently, government revenue increased and exceeded £10,000 for the first time in 1851. However, in the 1850s, French traders began to buy groundnuts with cash (the five franc piece remained legal tender until the 1920s) and because imports of specie and bullion were not subject to duty, customs revenue was reduced and total revenue fell from more than £17,000 in 1856 to £14,000 in 1860. In response, and after much debate in official circles, an export tax of three farthings per bushel (about five shillings per ton) was imposed on groundnuts in 1863.[146] Revenue subsequently rose to an average of £22,000 in the 1870s, but as the colony's expenditure, which was consumed largely by the salaries and pensions of officials, increased faster, budget deficits became the norm. There were budget deficits in all bar three years between 1849 and 1865 (including every year between 1859 and 1865) and in five out of eight years between 1869 and 1876 and a Parliamentary Grant was required between 1860 and 1871 to defray expenses.[147] Surpluses were achieved between 1877 and 1883, but there were five more consecutive deficits after 1884. In 1887, total revenue was the lowest since 1852, due to a combination of a poor groundnut crop and a very low market price.[148]

After its separation from Sierra Leone in 1888, Gambia enjoyed a period of fiscal prosperity that lasted until World War I. The buoyant groundnut export market meant that total revenue increased significantly after 1900 and averaged £95,000 between 1910 and 1914 (compared with a then record £49,000 in 1900). Expenditure also rose, although salaries and pensions still consumed a substantial proportion of the expenditure.[149] During World War I, the high value of the groundnut crop boosted export earnings and, although imports were restricted by a lack of available shipping in 1914–15 (which reduced customs revenue), there were surpluses each year between 1915 and 1920. Consequently, reserves reached nearly £329,000 by 1920 (or double the colony's expenditure in that year). But the restriction of imports also helped to double the cost of living in Bathurst between 1914 and 1920.[150]

Groundnut exports were worth a record £2,322,000 in 1920, a boom year in the colony, and export value remained high throughout the 1920s.[151] Consequently, except in 1921 and 1925, gross revenue always exceeded £200,000 during the decade. But the colony did not benefit fully from the favorable export market. In January 1922, the Gambian government was forced to demonetize the five franc piece, which had dropped considerably in value by the end of World War I, and to bear the full cost of doing so. Expenditure in 1922 was no less than £430,000 (a figure not to be exceeded until 1944) and the budget deficit in that year was £226,000 (which was not surpassed until 1956). Reserves fell to just under £100,000 in 1922 and proposed development projects, such as the drainage of part of the swamp at Half Die (situated at the southern end of Bathurst), were therefore either postponed or cancelled.[152] World groundnut prices fell to an average of only £8 per ton between 1930 and 1934, thereby reducing the value of groundnut exports and thus government revenue. The Gambian government responded by making retrenchments to balance the budget, but this was only achieved at a cost of increased urban unemployment.[153]

A surplus was achieved on the recurrent budget each year between 1940 and 1947 (except in 1944, when there was a very small deficit). The volume of groundnut exports, which were affected by a lack of shipping and a shortage of strange farmers, was low throughout the war and their value did not reach prewar levels until 1945. Import restrictions also reduced revenue from indirect taxation, although part of the shortfall was met by the introduction of income tax in 1940.[154] As in World War I, inflation was fuelled by import restrictions (and not checked by ineffective price controls) and the consumer price index of Bathurst more than doubled between 1940 and June 1942, before falling slightly in the second half of the war.[155] Unlike during World War I, wartime conditions also increased employment. Whereas there were perhaps only 2,000 waged workers in Bathurst in 1940, the War Department and allied concerns employed close to 20,000 in the capital and surrounding areas in 1942 (although wage employment did fall after the threat of an invasion from Vichy-controlled Senegal was lifted in late 1942).[156]

Groundnut exports were worth more than £2 million for the first time in 1948. They were valued at £3.56 million in 1952 and at more than £3 million in five out of eight years between 1955 and 1962, despite a falling world price. Despite the high value of exports, there were budget deficits in most years between 1948 and 1965 as expenditures increased.[157] Much of this expenditure was directed toward medical and social services. Thus the Medical and Health Department's budget rose from £56,000 in 1945 to £154,000 in 1958, and the Education Department's budget increased from less than £30,000 in 1948 to over £124,000 in 1958.[158] By 1961, the budgetary situation was so unfavorable that the Gambian government had to apply for "grant-in-aid" from the British government, and between 1962 and 1964, the recurrent budget was subsidized by a total of £1.5 million. As part of the deal, the British government reserved the right to scrutinize the draft estimates and to insist on economies; for example, 700 employees of the Marine and Public Works Departments were laid off in 1964.[159]

After Independence

Despite its vulnerable state in 1965, the Gambian economy performed reasonably well in the first decade after independence, particularly in the early 1970s. A combination of high output and high world prices resulted in record groundnut export receipts, which in turn produced large foreign exchange reserves (equivalent to ten months of imports in 1974–75) and meant that foreign debt remained low. Moreover, the recurrent budget was usually in surplus. During this period, aggregate real income increased substantially and average per capita income rose. Inflation (as measured by the consumer price index for the low income group in Bathurst and Kombo St. Mary) remained low until 1971, before increasing between 1972 and 1974; urban unemployment may also have started to rise around 1972.[160]

After 1974–75, the overall economic situation began to deteriorate. This was in part caused by external developments. The world oil crisis of 1973 sharply raised the foreign exchange cost of fuel (the increase in world oil prices in 1979 had a similar effect) and thus increased the cost of imports, which in turn fueled inflation in the urban areas.[161] Moreover, the onset of the prolonged Sahelian drought in the early 1970s affected production both of food and export crops and resulted in increasing imports of staple foodstuffs. As discussed, world groundnut prices also declined in the late 1970s and the early 1980s, thereby further reducing the value of exports. Inappropriate government policies were also to blame. Following the introduction of the first Five Year Plan in 1975, government expenditure on development projects, many of which made little net contribution to national income, increased dramatically. Civil service employment also expanded significantly in the 1970s, with most of the parastatals established in the 1970s making substantial losses between 1979 and 1982.[162] In addition, the exchange rate became overvalued, which boosted the demand for imports and damaged exports. Finally, large-scale public sector corruption, including the Rural Development Project I scandal and large-scale theft in the GCU, also undoubtedly contributed to economic decline.[163]

Radelet has shown that until the early 1980s, The Gambia was protected from many of the adverse economic trends noted. This was due in part to the foreign exchange reserves it had built up by the mid-1970s, but mainly resulted from substantial foreign grants and loans after 1975; between 1975 and 1985, The Gambia received one of the highest levels of per capita foreign aid in Africa.[164] However, by 1983, international donors began to withdraw their support as The Gambia fell into arrears on its debt service obligations, which in turn further reduced foreign exchange reserves. The government was forced to negotiate a stand-by agreement with the IMF in 1984; the dalasi was devalued by 25 percent to boost exports, but the economy continued to deteriorate. By mid-1985, foreign exchange reserves had fallen to the equivalent of two weeks of imports as foreign debts and external arrears mounted rapidly; inflation had risen sharply since 1984, shortages of basic commodities, such as fuel and rice, were commonplace, agricultural production was falling, and real per capita income was declining. Arrears to the IMF and other international creditors were also rising rapidly. When it became apparent that the government could not meet its obligations, the IMF cancelled its stand-by agreement. Because foreign donors made it clear that they would not bail the country out in the absence of IMF support, the government was forced to act. Consequently, in June 1985, the minister of finance, Sheriff Sisay, assembled a task force consisting of senior Gambian officials and two expatriate advisers to develop a reform program to halt the deterioration of the economy and lay the foundations for sustained economic growth. He then successfully persuaded President Jawara and the cabinet to endorse the program.[165]

Although there was no IMF input into its design, the four-year Economic Recovery Programme (ERP), was in many ways a typical example of the IMF's structural adjustment program in Africa.[166] Its key objectives were to reform the exchange rate by devaluing the dalasi; revitalize the agricultural sector through changes in pricing policies and other means; promote other productive sectors, such as tourism and fisheries; reduce the size of the civil service; improve the performance of the parastatal sector; cut the budget deficit through monetary and fiscal policies; reorientate the public investment program from new capital projects to rehabilitation and reconstruction; and reschedule and refinance the country's external debt.[167]

To achieve these objectives, a series of measures were enacted between 1985 and 1989. These measures have been analyzed in detail by McPherson and Radelet and other members of the Harvard Institute of International Development (HIID) team, which acted as consultants to Ministry of Finance staff between 1985 and 1992. Consequently, only the key reforms are outlined here. These included the floating of the dalasi in January 1986; the signing of performance contracts in 1987 with major parastatals; job cuts in the civil service in 1986 and a wage freeze until 1989; increased taxes on petroleum and rice; the raising of public transport and electricity prices; and a range of measures to improve agricultural production, including a sharp (but temporary) increase in the producer price for groundnuts in 1986, reforms to the groundnut marketing system, and the ending of the Groundnut Produce Marketing Board's monopoly on the export of groundnut products in 1990.[168]

The Gambia proved more willing than most African countries to fulfill the requirements of the IMF's structural adjustment program.[169] As the HIID study shows, some reforms were more successful than others. Nevertheless, by 1989, The Gambia had experienced an impressive economic recovery; the government budget deficit had been reduced, the annual inflation rate, which had risen sharply in the first stages of ERP to 56.6 percent in 1986, had fallen to 8.3 percent by 1989 (the lowest figure since 1981), agricultural production and exports had increased, and foreign exchange reserves had been built up. The confidence of foreign donors had also been restored and the external debt service arrears had been eliminated. One estimate is that real wages in the rural sector increased by 7 percent owing to the introduction of the subsidy on groundnuts. However, the economic recovery was achieved at a price. The real wages of civil servants and others on fixed incomes had fallen; many of the 3,000 civil servants who had been laid off remained unemployed or at least underemployed, and a quarter of all men aged 20–24 were unemployed in 1993.[170] Expenditures on social services, agriculture, and public works were cut significantly and were about half of their pre-ERP levels in real terms in 1988–89.[171]

These side effects notwithstanding, the ERP was generally judged a success by most external commentators, although with some reservations.[172] However, it was recognized by the Gambian government that the program had not even begun to remove the underlying constraints on sustained growth. The aim of the Programme for Sustained Development (PSD), which was adopted in December 1990, with the blessing of the IMF, was therefore to accelerate improvements in the living standards of the population by achieving a faster and sustained rate of economic growth. In many respects, the PSD sought to reinforce reforms begun under the ERP. For example, further fiscal reforms designed to increase tax revenue were introduced, and performance contracts were drawn up or extended with four parastatals, whereas others were leased or sold off to the private sector. But in addition, the PSD sought to address the social dimensions of adjustment and to alleviate institutional and human resource constraints.[173]

These were ambitious aims and, in the view of Hughes and Cooke, the record of the PSD up to the 1994 coup was mixed. On the positive side, the overall balance of payments remained in surplus because of the continued growth of the re-export trade until 1993–94; inflation remained low and foreign exchange generated by tourism was at higher levels than in the 1980s. Revenue and profits also increased in the parastatals where performance contracts had been drawn up. On the other hand, groundnut exports declined after 1989–90 and the overall value of domestic exports was also lower than in the late 1980s. The fall in the value of re-exports in 1993–94, owing to the tightening of the Senegalese border restrictions and the devaluation of the CFA franc, also reduced foreign exchange earnings.[174]

Notwithstanding the real achievements of the Gambian government's economic recovery policies, its failure to root out mismanagement in the public sector, together with continuing hardship arising from the implementation of its policies, bred discontent and undermined its authority, providing a motive for disaffected elements within the Gambian armed forces to stage a successful coup in July 1994.

Summary

The key characteristics of Gambian society, in respect of ethnic and religious diversity and disparity of social development, and the principal features of the economy in the nineteenth and twentieth centuries—with its uneven development as between Colony and Protectorate, general impoverishment and a heavy reliance on a vulnerable monocrop export trade in groundnuts—are set out in some detail, because, as later chapters reveal, these factors affected the course and nature of Gambian politics.

2

CONSTITUTIONAL CHANGE IN THE GAMBIA, 1816–1994

This chapter briefly describes the constitutional evolution of The Gambia between 1816 (the date of the foundation of Bathurst) and 1994; key events are analyzed in detail in subsequent chapters. The constitutional status of The Gambia is discussed first. The Gambia was a British colony between 1821 and its achievement of independence in 1965. It became a republic in 1970, but remains within the Commonwealth. The machinery of government is then considered. After 1843, this consisted of the typical colonial instruments of an Executive and a Legislative Council. The former functioned until 1963 and the latter until 1960.

During the colonial period, the Legislative Council enacted laws that affected both the Colony and the Protectorate; however, the two parts of Gambia were administered locally in very different ways. Because developments in the Protectorate had very little impact on politics at a national level, this is not a major focus of the book, but we nevertheless briefly discuss the process by which the Protectorate was governed.

In July 1994, the civilian government was overthrown by a military coup and the House of Representatives was abolished; it was eventually replaced by a National Assembly under a new constitution in 1997. For ease of reference, the constitutional changes described here are summarized in Appendix A.

The Constitutional Status of The Gambia, 1816–1994

The origins of modern Gambia can be traced to April 1816 when an expeditionary force from Gorée under Captain Alexander Grant took possession of Banjul Island, renamed it St. Mary's, and established a settlement.[1] Named Bathurst after the secretary of state for the colonies, Earl Bathurst, this was not the first settlement on the River Gambia. A British garrison had been established as early as 1661 at James Island, some 25 miles from the river mouth, but was abandoned (not for the first time) in 1779.[2] The "Company of Merchants trading to Africa," which had administered James Island between 1750 and 1766, had regained nominal control over the area in 1783, but had made no attempt to reoccupy the fort after 1788 and was not involved in the new venture.[3] The initiative had in fact been taken by Earl Bathurst, who had been persuaded that the suppression of the slave trade and the development of "legitimate" trade, could only be achieved if a British force were to control the river. Grant had therefore been sent by Sir Charles MacCarthy (the Governor of Sierra Leone) to build a new fort and, having concluded that the restoration of Fort James was impractical, obtained the right to occupy Banjul Island for an annual payment to the owner, the King of Kombo, of 103 bars of iron.[4]

The new settlement was in theory the dual responsibility of Parliament and the Company of Merchants until 1821, when an Act of Parliament divested the company of all its powers, both in Gambia and the Gold Coast. This followed criticism of its administration in the House of Commons.[5] Colonial rule thus resumed in Gambia after 38 years, James Island, together with St. Louis and other coastal trading bases in Senegal, having formed the grandiosely termed Province of Senegambia between 1765 and 1783.[6] Nevertheless, Gambia was not yet a full Crown Colony; along with the British forts on the Gold Coast, it was placed under the overall jurisdiction of the governor-general of Sierra Leone.[7] Local authority was wielded at first by the commandant of the garrison and then from 1829 by a lieutenant governor. This arrangement was very unpopular in Bathurst, but it was not until June 1843 that the administrative connection between Gambia and Sierra Leone was broken. Gambia thus became an independent Crown Colony with its own governor (who was answerable to the secretary of state for the colonies), Executive Council, and Legislative Council.

However, in February 1866, the administration of the British Settlements in West Africa (Gambia, Gold Coast, Lagos, and Sierra Leone) was centralized. The governor of Sierra Leone became governor-in-chief of the settlements and, in the other colonies, administrators (answerable to the governor-in-chief) were appointed and Executive Councils were abolished.[8] As noted in Chapter 1, the colony consisted solely of Bathurst, the area immediately around it and a few scattered settlements up river. British policy sought to avoid costly entanglements in the war-torn politics of the Gambian hinterland, save when the interests of the colony were directly threatened. Occasional military expeditions were launched, but these were intended to mitigate the effects of the wars between non-Islamic "Soninke" states and expansionist, jihadist Muslim or "Marabout" invaders up river, rather than to acquire additional territory. Indeed, when various local rulers offered to cede their territory to the colony in exchange for military protection, they were refused. Subsidies to interior rulers and mediation between the warring factions were the preferred options.[9]

In July 1874, the West African Settlements were divided into two; Gambia remained under Sierra Leone jurisdiction, and Lagos was placed under the Gold Coast.[10] Lagos was finally established as an independent crown colony in 1886 and, in November 1888, Gambia was separated from Sierra Leone for the final time, although it was not until 1900 that the head of government was upgraded from an administrator to a governor.[11] One reason for the reestablishment of Gambian "independence" was to make it easier for the Gambian government to resist French pressure in the region. This had increased since the 1870s, when Britain and France failed to achieve the exchange of Gambia for French territory.[12]

During the 1880s, the French adopted a forward policy in West Africa and began to confront militarily the jihadist states. Local pressure in the Gambian colony and a revision of imperial policy in Britain in response to French encroachment in the interior led to Britain also adopting a policy of direct intervention and territorial acquisition. The governor of the West African Settlements, Sir Samuel Rowe, was compelled to travel up river during a visit to Gambia to establish treaties with the rulers of the south bank states of Foni and Kiang in 1887.[13] However, it was not until August 1889 that a formal agreement was entered into with the French to partition the Senegambian region, as part of a wider colonial settlement which also affected the three other British colonies of Sierra Leone, the Gold Coast, and Lagos.

At the outset of the negotiations, the British government remained willing to cede Gambia to France in exchange for concessions elsewhere, but it soon became clear that the French were not interested in acquiring the territory. Eventually Gambia's boundaries were fixed at ten kilometers (six miles) north and south of the River Gambia as far up river as Yarbutenda.[14] This Anglo-French Convention fixed the colony's borders in principle, although it took another decade of careful boundary demarcation and the military defeat of remaining jihadist leaders, such as Fodi Sillah and Fodi Kabba, before the boundaries were finalized (although ownership of some border villages was not resolved until the 1970s). As noted in Chapter 1, a Protectorate was subsequently declared over the newly acquired territory, with the first Protectorate Ordinance being promulgated in 1894.[15]

In the early 1900s, negotiations over exchange were revived, but again to no avail.[16] Thereafter, the Colonial Office did not pay much attention to the constitutional position of Gambia in the first half of the twentieth century, although, in 1939, the Dufferin Committee did recommend consideration of the establishment of a federation between Gambia and Sierra Leone.[17] More importantly, the Committee on Smaller Territories established by the Attlee government proposed in 1951 that certain "Island" and "City" states should not be permitted to progress toward self-government like larger territories. They should instead maintain a permanent link with the United Kingdom and be administered locally by a state council. The report was welcomed by Governor Percy Wyn-Harris of Gambia (who remained a firm advocate of what he termed the "Channel Islands option"), but not by most other colonial governors, and was effectively shelved after Attlee's defeat in the 1951 British election.[18]

In 1955, the conservative government took up the issue of small dependent territories once again. The secretary of state proposed the development of a new concept of statehood; a state could be self-governing domestically, but dependent

on the United Kingdom for defense and foreign policy. It would also be represented in the House of Commons. The idea of "full integration," which was first
applied to Malta, was taken up by one of the Gambian political parties, the
Gambia Muslim Congress (GMC), but fell into disfavor after its eventual rejection
by the Maltese political parties in 1958.[19] By 1960, another option—that Gambia
and Sierra Leone might form a federation—had also been effectively abandoned
because of the distance between the two countries, Sierra Leone's financial difficulties, and a lack of enthusiasm for the suggestion except from a few Creoles in
Freetown.[20]

Because the Colonial Office still considered that independence was out of the
question for Gambia, only one other option, that Gambia be joined in association
with Senegal, remained. This course of action was also favored by the Foreign Office,
by Governor Sir Edward Windley of Gambia, and by President Senghor of Senegal.[21]
To facilitate the negotiations (and in accord with the recent precedent of British
Somaliland), the Colonial Office believed that Gambia might need to proceed to
independence even if only for a few days; indeed, in December 1962, Duncan
Sandys, the secretary of state for the colonies, stated in the House of Commons that
if a satisfactory basis for association with Senegal could be worked out, then independence would be granted to Gambia.[22] A United Nations team of experts arrived
in Bathurst in October 1963 to examine the question of association; its report, which
was submitted in April 1964, recommended that a Senegambia Federation be established. However, after discussions between the Senegalese and Gambian governments in May, only a loose association was actually implemented.[23] Nevertheless, even
though the British government had made association a precondition for Gambian
independence, it permitted the constitutional process to continue. A conference in
London in July 1964 agreed a post-independence constitution and the colony
achieved independence within the Commonwealth (as The Gambia) in February
1965 with D. K. (later Sir Dawda) Jawara as prime minister.[24]

Nine months after independence, Jawara organized a referendum to decide
whether The Gambia should become a republic. This was required; similarly to
the Sierra Leone constitution of 1961, the monarchical form of government was
protected under an "entrenched" provision of the 1964 constitution. Entrenched
provisions in the Gambian constitution could only be amended if supported by
two-thirds of the elected members of Parliament (MPs) and confirmed by a two-
thirds majority in a subsequent referendum.[25] Most participants in the referendum supported the establishment of a republic, but the government failed by
fewer than 800 votes to achieve the required two-thirds majority. To the surprise
of many observers, Jawara accepted his defeat graciously and, when he tried again
in April 1970, the constitutional change was approved.[26]

Jawara, as the leader of the majority party in the House of Representatives,
automatically became the country's first president and replaced Queen Elizabeth
II as head of state. A vice president was also appointed to lead government business in the House of Representatives. At first, the presidency was decided by a simple majority of directly elected MPs (who were obliged to declare their preference

at the time of their own election). However, between 1982 and 1992, a separate presidential election was held at the same time as the parliamentary election, although this was not a constitutional requirement. No limitations were placed on the number of terms a president could serve. Presidential elections were held in 1982, 1987, and 1992; all were won by Jawara.[27]

In July 1994, the Jawara government was overthrown in a military coup by a small group of Gambian National Army (GNA) officers led by Lieutenant Yahya Jammeh. These officers subsequently termed themselves the Armed Forces Provisional Ruling Council. The GNA had been gradually built up in the 1980s, following an attempt in July 1981 by a group of radical civilians and disaffected members of the paramilitary Field Force to overthrow the state. This putsch had been defeated after armed Senegalese intervention on behalf of the legitimate government. However, in 1994, there was minimal internal resistance to the coup (there were no reported casualties) and no external intervention on behalf of the Jawara government. This was partly because the Senegambia Confederation, which had been established between The Gambia and Senegal in 1982 to promote closer cooperation between the two countries, had been wound up in December 1989.[28] Direct military rule continued until 1996 when a new constitution was introduced; the first presidential election conducted under the new constitution was won by Jammeh in September 1996. His newly created political party, the Alliance for Patriotic Re-orientation and Construction, subsequently won the first election to the new National Assembly in January 1997. Jammeh went on to win a further presidential election in October 2001 and, at the time of writing, remains president.[29]

The Machinery of Government in the Colonial Period

The Letters Patent of June 1843, which established Gambia as a separate colony, also provided it with the now customary structures of government, an Executive and a Legislative Council. In 1791, Canada became the first colony in which the undifferentiated governor's advisory council, which contained both official and unofficial members, had been abolished and replaced by two separate councils with differing functions. A similar process had been adopted in several West Indian colonies and in Ceylon in the 1830s and 1840s, although not in Sierra Leone, where the advisory council established in 1811 remained in operation until 1863. Moreover, in a number of newly established colonies after 1820, an Executive and a Legislative Council had been provided from the outset and Gambia duly fitted into this pattern.[30]

The Executive Council: 1843–1963

The function of the Gambian Executive Council (as described in the Letters Patent) was "to advise and assist the Governor . . . in the administration of the

Government." A governor was required to consult with his councilors over the performance of all his official duties unless government service would be materially prejudiced by consultation; he considered the matter to be too unimportant to merit consideration; or the issue was so urgent that there was insufficient time to convene a meeting. A governor did not have to abide by the advice he received, but if he acted against the opinions of the Executive Council, he was required to inform the Colonial Office.[31]

The Royal Instructions given to the first governor, Commander Henry Seagram, laid down the composition of the Executive Council, which held its inaugural meeting in October 1843. Apart from the governor, it was to contain two other officials, the colonial secretary and the collector of customs. A fourth official member, the queen's advocate, was added in 1845. No unofficial members were appointed initially, but a British merchant, Thomas Brown, was added to the council in 1853; he served again on the council in his official capacity as acting queen's advocate or acting chief justice in the 1860s.[32] As noted, the Gambian Executive Council was abolished on the establishment of the West African Settlements in 1866; it was not restored until 1888 when Gambia once more became an independent Crown Colony. The reconstituted Executive Council at first comprised only official members, although unusually for West Africa in this period, it did have one unofficial member (James Topp) between 1890 and 1896. However, the experiment was not considered a success by Administrator Llewelyn (or the Colonial Office) and after Topp's enforced retirement, no other unofficials were appointed to the Executive Council.[33] By the mid-1930s, the idea that an unofficial could serve on the council was considered an absurdity by the Gambian government (although not by the Nigerian government).[34]

In 1942, following an initiative by Governor Burns of the Gold Coast, African unofficials were appointed to the Executive Councils of the Gold Coast and Nigeria; Governor Stevenson of Sierra Leone reluctantly followed suit in 1943. Governor H. R. R. (later Sir Hilary) Blood of Gambia supported the idea in principle, but argued that there were no suitable candidates.[35] His successor, Andrew (later Sir Andrew) Wright, adopted a more positive approach. On his recommendation, three African unofficials, E. F. Small, the winner of the first direct election to the Legislative Council, Seyfu (Chief) Tamba Jammeh and J. C. (later Rev. J. C.) Faye, were appointed to the Council in November 1947.[36] After the second Legislative Council election of October 1951, Wright's successor, Percy (later Sir Percy) Wyn-Harris, added a fourth unofficial to the Executive Council (there were also six officials, plus the governor) and appointed two of these, Faye and I. M. Garba-Jahumpa, to be "members of the government." They were permitted to offer advice to the governor on a range of selected subjects, but were not granted specific portfolios. Garba-Jahumpa remained a "member of the government" during the life of the constitution, but Faye was dismissed in 1953.[37]

Prior to the third election to the Legislative Council in 1954, a new constitution was introduced by Wyn-Harris. This was based on the recommendations of a Consultative Committee, which met six times in April and May 1953.[38] There were now to be at least six unofficial members of the Executive Council, who should be appointed after consultation with the Legislative Council. Two of these were also to be offered specific portfolios and termed "ministers." However, as they were required to work with Advisory Committees (which were to include the European heads of departments), they were not to receive full ministerial responsibility.[39] After the 1954 election, the three elected candidates in Bathurst, P. S. N'Jie, Faye, and Garba-Jahumpa, were appointed to ministerial posts and four others (including two Protectorate Chiefs) joined the Executive Council. Faye and Garba-Jahumpa retained their portfolios until 1960, but P. S. N'Jie was dismissed in January 1956 and was not replaced.[40]

Following a series of constitutional conferences in 1958–59, a new constitution was drawn up in September 1959 and introduced after the first national general election of May 1960. The Executive Council now consisted of the governor (Sir Edward Windley, who had succeeded Wyn-Harris in 1958); four officials and six ministers (who no longer depended on Advisory Committees). Four ministers—D. K. Jawara, A. B. N'Jie, H. O. Semega-Janneh, and Seyfu Omar M'Baki—were granted portfolios, and the other two posts were offered to S. S. Sisay and P. S. N'Jie; when the latter declined the invitation, he was replaced by Andrew Camara.[41] Despite not being a member of the Executive Council at the time, Windley selected P. S. N'Jie to be Gambia's first chief minister in March 1961; this entitled him to advise the governor on the selection of ministers and the allocation of portfolios. In protest at P. S. N'Jie's appointment, Jawara, Sisay, and A. B. N'Jie all resigned from the council.[42] Because the Executive Council was now no longer representative of the outcome of the 1960 election, Windley was forced to convene a fresh constitutional conference in Bathurst in May 1961. This paved the way for a second constitutional conference in London in July, when it was agreed that the next election should be held by May 1962 and that, after it, a premier (who would take over the responsibility for selecting ministers) should be appointed. In addition, the number of ministers should be increased to eight and the official membership reduced to two.[43]

In October 1963, Gambia progressed to the next constitutional stage, full internal self-government. As was customary, the Executive Council was abolished and replaced by a cabinet headed by a prime minister. Unusually, the cabinet retained European representation until as late as 1968 in the form of the attorney general, Phillip (later Sir Phillip) Bridges.[44] When The Gambia became a republic in 1970, President Jawara took charge of the cabinet, which remained small by African standards; for example, the cabinet appointed after the 1992 election contained only fourteen members.[45]

The Legislative Council: 1843–1960

The function of the Legislative Council, as laid down in the Letters Patent, was "to make and establish all such laws, institutions and ordinances as may from time to time be necessary for the peace, order, and good government of our subjects and others within the said present or future settlements in the River Gambia and in its dependencies."[46] In practice, the powers of the Legislative Council were restricted by a number of clauses in the Royal Instructions given to the governor on his appointment. The most important of these were that the council could enact no law or ordinance that had not previously been proposed by the governor; could pass no ordinance that would have the effect of diminishing the revenue that would accrue to the crown; and could not pass legislation designed either to increase or to decrease the salaries of public officers. Finally, the crown reserved to itself the right to disallow any law or ordinance passed by the council.[47]

The original members of the Legislative Council, which met for the first time in November 1843, were the governor (who presided over council meetings); the colonial secretary (who presided in his absence); the chief justice; and the officer commanding the troops. On the instructions of the secretary of state for the colonies, and in keeping with the precedent of the Gold Coast and Sierra Leone, the Legislative Council also contained unofficial representation from the outset, through a prominent British merchant, William Henry Goddard. Two other merchants, Richard Lloyd and Thomas Brown, were added to the council in 1847 and 1850, respectively.[48] Africans were appointed to the Gold Coast and Sierra Leone Legislative Councils from their establishment in 1850 and 1863, respectively, but there were no African members of the Gambian Legislative Council until the 1880s. Indeed, Africans were even represented on the Legislative Council of Lagos (which had only been established as a colony as recently as 1861) before that of Gambia.[49]

After the establishment of the West African Settlements in 1866, the Legislative Council was downgraded in Gambia as on the Gold Coast. Its membership was cut from eleven to three, these being the administrator, the collector of customs, and a magistrate (Thomas Brown, the sole unofficial).[50] It was not until 1883 that a second unofficial was appointed. This was J. D. Richards, a merchant, who thus became the first African member of the council.[51] Two other commercial men, S. J. Forster (an African merchant) and H. H. Lee (the agent of J. F. Hutton, a Manchester magnate) were appointed in 1886 and 1887, respectively. However, in 1889, the council was reconstituted with unofficial representation being cut to two (Forster and H. C. Goddard, the agent of the Bathurst Trading Company). At first, no time limit was placed on their term of service, but in 1895, the secretary of state decreed that unofficials in West Africa should henceforth be appointed for renewable five-year terms. After a process of consultation, both men were reappointed in November 1895 and again in November 1900.[52]

Goddard resigned from the council in January 1905 before completing his second term.[53] Forster was reappointed that November, but died in October 1906. His successor was another African merchant, Samuel Horton Jones; in March 1907, Samuel Forster (the son of the late councilor) became the second African member. The younger Forster, who was a barrister, was the first African professional to serve as an unofficial member of the council.[54] Henri Staub, the agent of the French firm, Compagnie Française de l'Afrique Occidentale, had (like Jones) been appointed in June 1906; he thus became the first Frenchman to serve on the council. He was reappointed in 1911, but after his death in December 1912, the number of unofficials was cut to three (one European and two Africans). Jones was replaced by an African medical practitioner, Dr. Thomas Bishop, in 1916; consequently, for the first time since 1843, mercantile interests were not represented on the council.[55]

Forster was reappointed for further terms in 1917 and 1922, but Bishop's appointment lapsed after November 1921. He was succeeded in March 1922 by Ousman Jeng, a prominent Wolof trader, who thus became the first Muslim member of the council (and the first Muslim "commoner" to sit on any legislative council in West Africa).[56] The Bathurst Chamber of Commerce (which, although originally open to African merchants, was an exclusively European organization) was also permitted to nominate one of its members to the council; its choice was William Yare, the agent of the Bathurst Trading Company.[57] All three were reappointed in 1927; Forster was also persuaded to accept a sixth term in 1932, but Jeng and Yare were replaced by Sheikh Omar Fye, another Wolof Muslim trader, and James Howie, the manager of the Bank of British West Africa, respectively.[58] A year later, in May 1933, unofficial representation rose to four, the highest total since 1912. There were three Africans, Forster, Fye, and Forster's nephew, W. D. Carrol, another barrister. Carrol was nominated (unanimously) by the members of the Bathurst Urban District Council (BUDC), a partially elected body established in 1930 as the first organ of municipal government in Gambia.[59] Forster and Fye were reappointed once again in 1937; in May 1938, Carrol retained his seat on the nomination of the Bathurst Advisory Town Council (BATC), which replaced the BUDC in 1935.[60]

Forster died in 1940 and Carrol in 1941 before completing their terms of service; the BATC chose E. F. Small, a journalist and political leader, to replace him, and Forster was succeeded by Small's brother-in-law, J. A. Mahoney, a commercial clerk. Both took their seats for five-year terms in January 1942; Fye was reappointed for two more years in March 1942.[61] The Gambian government now considered that the time was ripe for the concession of the franchise, which had been granted to the other three West African colonies in the 1920s. One member should be directly elected to the council and one Protectorate chief should be appointed by the governor, and the BATC should lose its right to nominate a councilor and the Muslim community its special representation.[62] The secretary of state gave his formal consent in October 1943, but owing to a series of delays, it was not until November 1946 that the revised constitution was finally drawn up and the first direct election did not take place until November 1947. The electorate consisted of British subjects or natives of the Protectorate resident in Bathurst or Kombo St. Mary aged 25 or over; the Protectorate was entirely excluded from the process. No property, income, or literacy qualifications were imposed on voters, which in this respect placed Gambia ahead of its sister colonies in West Africa.[63]

Shortly before the 1947 election, the secretary of state conceded the principle of an unofficial majority, an important milestone which placed Gambia ahead of

Sierra Leone, where Creole opposition to the 1947 Stevenson Constitution meant that an official majority was retained until 1951.[64] The number of unofficials was increased to seven (compared with six officials) and the governor lost his original (although not casting) vote. The Protectorate secured unofficial representation for the first time (by three chiefs and the headmaster of an Anglican mission school, J. C. Faye), but unlike in Nigeria and the Gold Coast (or in Sierra Leone as proposed by Governor Stevenson), all its members were nominated and not indirectly elected.[65] The other unofficials were the elected member (E. F. Small); the member for commerce, the United Africa Company's manager, C. L. Page; and A. W. M'Bye, a trader, who represented the Muslim community (because a Christian had won the election).[66]

The second election to the Legislative Council in October 1951 was conducted under a new constitution introduced by Wright's successor, Percy Wyn-Harris. This increased the number of elected members to three, two for Bathurst and one for Kombo St. Mary, and also allowed for the appointment of a Gambian as vice president of the Legislative Council. The successful candidates in Bathurst were Faye and I. M. Garba-Jahumpa, who was a school teacher at the time; Henry Madi, a Gambian businessman of Lebanese extraction, was victorious in Kombo St. Mary. J. A. Mahoney (the former unofficial member) was appointed vice president of the council.[67]

These constitutional reforms were modest, but the second Wyn-Harris Constitution of 1954 was more radical. The number of unofficials was increased to sixteen, of whom three were to be directly elected in a multimember constituency in Bathurst and one in Kombo St. Mary and seven were to be indirectly elected by the Conference of Protectorate Chiefs or the (Protectorate) Divisional Councils. These eleven councilors would then act as an electoral college to select three others from a panel submitted jointly by the Bathurst Town Council and the Kombo Rural Authority. The remaining two members were to be a "well-known citizen" and a person "skilled in commerce," who would be nominated by the governor after consultation with the Legislative Council. A speaker would also be appointed, thereby allowing the governor finally to withdraw from the council. The Bathurst poll was headed by a relative newcomer, politically, P. S. N'Jie (a barrister), with Faye and Garba-Jahumpa also being returned. Madi won again in Kombo St. Mary.[68] This was the last election to the Legislative Council, which ceased to exist when the Windley Constitution came into operation in May 1960. It was replaced by the House of Representatives.

Administration of the Protectorate

Financial and manpower constraints (of the twelve commissioners who were appointed between 1893 and 1903, three died of illness, two were killed, and one was invalided out of the service) meant that, particularly initially, the British relied heavily on appointed African district and village chiefs to manage the day-to-day affairs of the Protectorate.[69] A number of existing indigenous kingdoms retained their boundaries as administrative districts and loyal traditional leaders remained as district chiefs. Jihadist states were overthrown, which allowed a number of pre-Islamic ruling families (Soninkes) to reestablish their authority under British hegemony, although this did not prevent a continuing expansion of Islam itself.[70] With only two "travelling commissioners" at first for the whole of the Protectorate and little desire to achieve more than the establishment of law and order, imperial rule was "felt very little if at all in many regions of the old Mandingo states . . . and to a considerable extent administration of the river states during the first ten years of the Protectorate remained under the control of Africans."[71] Although the slave trade in the Protectorate was abolished in 1894, local slavery was not abolished fully until the 1930s, because the British could not afford to antagonize slave-holding local chiefly allies.[72]

In addition to these considerations, the Protectorate remained isolated from national political life because there was little economic and social development before the 1950s. Protectorate society was deliberately insulated from the new political activities in Bathurst and the Colony; the chiefs, and their senior advisers were regarded, as elsewhere in British Africa at this time, as the authentic voice of the rural majority. Reforms began in the early 1930s under Governor H. R. Palmer, regarded as one of the major architects of the policy of indirect rule in Northern Nigeria where he had previously served as lieutenant governor. Native Administration Ordinances, which created Native Authorities and Treasuries, but left these controlled by local chiefs, under the overall direction of divisional commissioners (whose number varied between four and five), were intended to start the process of modernizing local government in the interior.[73]

Although our knowledge of the dynamics of local Protectorate politics between the 1930s and 1950s remains fragmentary, it is evident that the same chiefly families (and, in some cases, the same individuals) tended to remain in power in their localities.[74] Moreover, elective politics was not introduced until the constitutional reforms of the 1950s, when the impact of social and economic changes up river brought about a growth in the number of partially educated young men, eager to challenge both the dominance of traditional elites in the Protectorate and urban-biased political movements in the capital city claiming to speak for the whole of Gambia. Even then, the annual Chiefs' Conference with the governor, which had begun in 1944, together with the nomination of some chiefs to the Legislative Council, as indicated, remained the major means of transmitting rural "opinion" to government.[75]

Political Assemblies: 1960–94

As noted, the Legislative Council was abolished in 1960 and replaced by the House of Representatives. Initially, it met three or four times a year, but later, according to Wiseman, it met up to eight times a year, with sittings lasting up to eight days. It was responsible for the enactment of legislation. Even though, as Wiseman has pointed out, government bills were invariably accepted by the House, it performed an important function as a forum for political debate and for the representation of constituency interests. It certainly played a more important role than most other postcolonial African legislatures.[76]

As constituted in 1960, the House of Representatives consisted of thirty-four MPs (twenty-seven elected and seven nominated), plus a speaker. Nineteen were elected by universal suffrage in single-member constituencies by those aged 21 or over and the other eight were selected by the Chiefs' Conference. The Protectorate now possessed the majority of elected seats (twelve out of nineteen), but it remained underrepresented in terms of population. All its MPs had either been born or appeared on the electoral register in the Protectorate or were recognized as being from Protectorate families.[77] In theory, all MPs were supposed to speak English "well enough to take part in the proceedings of the House" (this remained a requirement subsequently).[78]

Some alterations to this structure were agreed at the constitutional conference held in London in July 1961 and implemented after the 1962 election. The number of directly elected members was increased from nineteen to thirty-two; all the additional seats were granted to the Protectorate, with the Colony's representation remaining unaltered at seven, but the geographical restrictions on where candidates could stand were dropped, thereby permitting Bathurst parties to campaign openly in the rural areas. The chiefs were marginalized by their representation being halved; there was to be only one ex officio member (the attorney general) and up to two nominated members, and neither they, nor the speaker, were to be given voting rights.[79] The amendments to the constitution agreed at the 1964 constitutional conference in London did not alter the composition of the House. However, the new constitution did allow for the appointment of a Constituency Boundaries Commission, which would be required to ensure, as far as was reasonably practicable, that each constituency should have an equal number of inhabitants. The commission could, however, depart from numerical equality to ensure adequate representation for sparsely populated rural areas and could also take account of the means of communication, existing geographical areas and the boundaries of administrative areas.[80]

Relatively few changes were made to the structure and composition of the House after independence, prior to the military coup of 1994. In 1966, the number of Bathurst constituencies was reduced to three and the existing Jarra and Kombo constituencies were further sub-divided. The number of elected seats remained the same until 1977, when three additional constituencies were granted to Serrekunda (Serekunda), the Kombos, and Niumi. One more seat was created in 1987 with the division of Wuli into two constituencies. The lack of large-scale creation of constituencies meant that an MP represented about 28,000 constituents in 1993, compared with only about 10,000 in 1966.[81] All MPs were still elected in single-member constituencies by the first-past-the-post system (a movement to proportional representation having never been seriously considered); the voting age remained 21.[82]

The representation of the chiefs increased by one to five in 1982 (and remained at five at the time of the coup); the chiefs continued to be elected from among themselves, but after 1962, they had little power. However, the number of nominated members rose more dramatically from two in 1962 to eight in 1992. According to Wiseman, President Jawara used nomination to increase the number of women (the first of whom was appointed as early as 1968), Christians, and professionals in the House; a trade union leader was also added to the House in 1987. The government did not, however, use nomination as a means to increase its voting power, because nominated members were denied any voting rights.[83] As noted, since the establishment of the republic in 1970, the Leader of the House had been the vice president, because the president was not a member; after the 1992 election, there was speculation that the post of vice president might be abolished and a prime minister once more appointed, but this did not materialize before the coup.[84]

Seven general elections took place in The Gambia between 1960 and 1992. The People's Progressive Party (PPP) led by Jawara won most seats in the 1960 election, but not an overall majority; however, it achieved a comfortable overall majority in all subsequent elections after 1962. Even so, opposition parties retained a continuous presence in the House until the coup. In the 1992 election, the PPP won twenty-five seats; the leading opposition party (the National Convention Party) won six seats and the Gambia People's Party two seats. Three Independents were also elected. Although there were two by-elections in 1993, party representation in the House remained unchanged at the time of the coup.[85] Following the coup, the House of Representatives was abolished; it was replaced by the National Assembly in 1997.[86]

Senegambia Confederation: 1982–89

As noted, the Senegambia Confederation operated between 1982 and 1989. The confederal parliamentary institutions consisted of a confederal executive, with the Senegalese president, Abdou Diouf, as president and Jawara as vice president; a Confederal Assembly with sixty members, of whom twenty were Gambians; a nine-member Council of Ministers (four of whom were Gambians), and a confederal secretariat. The members of the Confederal Assembly were indirectly elected by the elected representatives of the Senegalese and Gambian national Parliaments.[87]

Summary

Initially a small British trading settlement under the jurisdiction of Sierra Leone, The Gambia became an independent British colony for the second (and final) time in 1888 and eventually, in 1965, an independent nation. During the colonial period, Gambia was governed through typical administrative bodies, an Executive Council, and a Legislative Council, the composition of which changed, as

European officials were gradually replaced by Gambian unofficial and elected members. In 1960, the Legislative Council was succeeded by the House of Representatives; changes to its structure and composition, prior to its sudden, unexpected, demise in 1994, are summarized. Later chapters indicate how the nature of domestic politics has often been shaped by these wider constitutional and institutional developments.

3

MERCHANTS AND RECAPTIVES

THE ORIGINS OF MODERN POLITICS, 1816–86

The essence of politics in Gambia during the greater part of the nineteenth century was the interaction between three different interest groups: the officials of the Gambian government; the resident British merchants; and the politically conscious portion of the African population of Bathurst, which consisted largely of Liberated Africans (Recaptives) and their descendants and freeborn Africans from other parts of West Africa. These were not independent political actors, because domestic politics was affected by the views of the Colonial Office, and the opinion of the Sierra Leonean government was also relevant before 1843 and again after 1866.

Until the 1860s, Africans played only a peripheral role in local politics, which was dominated by merchants and officials. The merchants were generally very influential; indeed, in the mid-1860s, they were described as "the ruling power" of Gambia.[1] Thereafter, however, their influence was in decline. In contrast, Bathurst's African population had improved its relative position. This was recognized when a prominent Aku, J. D. Richards, was appointed to the Legislative Council in 1883.

Politics in the Sierra Leone Era: 1816–43

Administration by Commandants: 1816–29

The settlement at St. Mary's had originally been founded as a military post to suppress the slave trade and at first its administration was the sole responsibility of the commandant of the fort, Captain Alexander Grant. Grant was himself answerable to Governor Charles MacCarthy of Sierra Leone.[2] However, as noted in Chapter 1, a civilian population was soon established by the transfer of a dozen or so merchants of British origin from Gorée, following the resumption of French rule in 1817, and from Sierra Leone. Most of these merchants headed small (and frequently unsuccessful) family firms that they ran themselves from Africa. A good example of a (successful) family firm was the one started by Thomas Chown, a former naval captain who remained in Bathurst until his death in 1845; the family business was then taken over by his son, also Thomas, and subsequently by his grandson, Thomas C. Chown. Other merchants who settled in the settlement in its early years included Edward and Richard Lloyd, former military officers who had been stationed at Gorée in the early years of the century; Charles Grant, a cousin of Alexander Grant who arrived from Sierra Leone in 1819; and W. H. Goddard, who moved to Bathurst from Gorée in 1819.[3] There was also one larger commission house, Forster and Smith, which was to develop extensive trading interests in West Africa by supplying goods on credit to individual correspondents. Its agent in Bathurst, William Forster (the younger brother of the firm's senior partner, Matthew Forster), who moved to Bathurst in 1817, appears to have been the political leader of the mercantile community until his death in 1849. Mercantile policies, which were presented as a unanimous expression of opinion, were apparently decided at meetings in his house.[4]

The British merchants had been accustomed at Gorée to shaping government policy in conjunction with the military commandant. They therefore welcomed the decision by Governor MacCarthy, during a visit to Bathurst in 1818, to devolve legislative, executive, and judicial powers to the new settlement. MacCarthy established a Settlement Court, composed of the commandant and five merchants, which was empowered to pass regulations for the peace, welfare, and good government of the settlement (subject to his disallowance) and to authorize the collection of revenue and its expenditure. MacCarthy also created a formal judicial structure; the Court of Police and Equity was empowered to try minor civil cases, and the Settlement Court was permitted to deal with appeals from the lower court and also to try criminal cases.[5]

In conjunction with the commandant, the merchants used their executive powers to authorize the construction of public buildings in the town, including Government House, the gaol and the barracks, and the clearing and draining of a large part of Bathurst.[6] Nevertheless, when Gambia and the Gold Coast were formally placed under the authority of Sierra Leone in 1821, all local customs and regulations were repealed; in practice, this meant that the Settlement Court was abolished, leaving Gambia without any judicial or legislative machinery. Some limited magisterial powers were subsequently restored, with the justices of the peace being drawn from the ranks of the merchants, but all important cases had to await the infrequent visitations of the chief justice of Sierra Leone.[7] The legislative and executive powers of the Settlement Court were not restored at all, even though, at the instigation of the merchants, a parliamentary commissioner, Major James Rowan, recommended in 1827 that Gambia be granted a council to make regulations on trade and internal affairs. In contrast, in 1828, the Colonial Office agreed to hand over control of the Gold Coast forts to a committee of three London merchants, which included Matthew Forster.[8]

Gambian merchants resented the loss of formal legislative and executive powers after 1821, because they could no longer exercise control over revenue and expenditure; it also made it harder for them to resist undesirable government policies.[9] Nevertheless, in practice, merchants and officials tended to share the same goals, particularly in matters of commerce; there was a common awareness that the prosperity of the settlement entirely depended on trade. One key demand of the merchants was that they and their agents should be able to trade up river in safety. It was for this purpose that Grant purchased an island (which he renamed MacCarthy Island) in 1823 and established a small garrison on it. The "Ceded Mile" was also acquired from the King of Barra in 1826 for commercial reasons; the king had demanded custom duties from all trading vessels that entered the river and had disrupted trade in other ways.[10]

Unfortunately for the merchants, the commandants were not free agents and on several occasions, their endeavors to promote commerce were frustrated by the Colonial Office. In 1824, Major Alexander Findlay, Grant's successor, was prevented from taking action against French vessels, which had taken advantage of the establishment of a trading post at Albreda to smuggle contraband goods up river beyond James Island. Findlay had responded to persistent complaints by the merchants by prohibiting all French vessels from entering the river unless they paid import duties at Bathurst. The secretary of state for the colonies decided, however, that this would be in violation of the Treaty of Paris (which had brought the Napoleonic Wars to an end) and repudiated Findlay's action; it was not until 1848 that decisive action was taken to curb smuggling by French traders.[11] The Colonial Office also proved reluctant after 1826 to sanction the annexation of further territory, as the merchants demanded, because this might lead to unwanted commitments and expenditure. One treaty signed by Governor Campbell of Sierra Leone in 1827, which would have resulted in the annexation of land at Brikama, was allowed to remain a dead letter; another, signed by the acting lieutenant governor, William Hutton, and the King of Wuli in 1829, was repudiated by the secretary of state for the colonies.[12]

Administration by Lieutenant Governors: 1829–43

The commandant, Lieutenant Colonel Alexander Findlay, was appointed as the first lieutenant governor of Gambia in 1829, but, in February 1830, he was promoted to the same post in Sierra Leone. He was succeeded by the first civilian lieutenant governor, George Rendall, a former acting chief justice of Sierra Leone.[13] Rendall was very sympathetic to the merchants, being particularly anxious to promote trade, and the decision to transfer Liberated Africans from Sierra Leone, discussed in Chapter 1, was taken partly for commercial reasons.[14]

Nevertheless, the merchants remained discontented because of their lack of legislative and judicial powers. In 1834, they protested against the anomaly of having to accept inappropriate legislation from Sierra Leone and demanded the establishment of a Legislative Council; they also called for a separate Gambian judiciary. Rendall supported this petition, but the secretary of state still rejected it. In 1840, another lieutenant governor pointed out the difficulties caused by the colony's lack of legislative power, but again to no avail.[15] A year later, however, Dr. Robert Madden was sent by Parliament to examine the condition of all British possessions in West Africa. He recommended that Gambia should become independent of Sierra Leone and that the crown should resume direct control of the Gold Coast forts; both recommendations were subsequently endorsed by a Parliamentary Select Committee, which met in the summer of 1842 and in June 1843, Gambia became a separate Crown Colony.[16]

The merchants involved in the Gambian trade could claim some of the credit for this decision. Matthew Forster, the senior partner of Forster and Smith who had been the member of parliament (MP) for Berwick-on-Tweed since 1841, was a leading member of the Parliamentary Select Committee and one of the most persuasive witnesses who was called to give evidence. John Hughes, a Mulatto merchant resident in Bathurst, also gave evidence to the Committee.[17] The officials of the Gambian government also welcomed the severance of the connection with Sierra Leone, but in other respects, the relationship between merchants and officials had deteriorated markedly since the death of Rendall from yellow fever in September 1837.[18]

The merchants, who could count among their number the wealthiest and most experienced members of Bathurst society, had expected to have some say in the selection of the new lieutenant governor.[19] They were therefore most displeased when the position was offered to an individual who had been involved in the Gambian trade in the early 1820s, but had failed in business and had returned to Britain. They duly remonstrated with Lord Glenelg, the secretary of state, apparently successfully, for the appointment was eventually cancelled. The position was then offered in September 1838 to Major William Mackie and again the merchants objected; Mackie had once been employed as a clerk by a Bathurst merchant and the mercantile community presumably objected to the fact that one of their former employees would now head the administration.[20] The merchants soon had further grounds for complaint. Mackie first ignored their advice in the construction of a market house (which promptly collapsed) and then made a disastrous attempt to drain the island, which left the town inundated for three days. This led to an outbreak of fever to which Mackie himself fell victim in February 1839.[21]

The post of lieutenant governor then passed (on an acting basis) to the acting colonial secretary, Thomas Ingram, who was even more unpopular with the merchants. Ingram had apparently been an "insolvent trader" before entering government service in 1835 in the comparatively lowly guise of clerk of customs and of the Police Court; he owed his rapid rise to the high death toll among officials during the yellow fever outbreak of 1837.[22] According to the later account of Governor MacDonnell, Ingram had agreed, prior to Mackie taking office, that he would never assume the administration of the colony without the consent of the merchants. But after Mackie's death, he promptly took over the government on the grounds that, as (acting) colonial secretary, he was the most senior official. In 1840, he secured confirmation of his position as colonial secretary, whereas the recently appointed queen's advocate, Richard Pine, who shared the merchants' distrust of Ingram, was dismissed from government service.[23]

In April 1840, Captain H. V. (later Sir Henry) Huntley was appointed the substantive lieutenant governor. The merchants were pleased that Huntley endorsed their criticisms of the Sierra Leonean connection, but in other respects they were unhappy with his decisions. Huntley was accused of pursuing an "uncertain and fluctuating policy" toward the chiefs of the interior and of wasting the colonial revenue, particularly on "an injudicious and . . . unnecessary" attempt to improve Government House.[24] The merchants were critical of any perceived misuse of government funds; as noted in Chapter 1, the duty they paid on imported goods remained the major source of government revenue.[25]

Ingram again assumed the administration after Huntley's promotion to the post of lieutenant governor of Prince Edward Island in 1841. This so incensed the merchants (whom Ingram, perhaps not surprisingly, declined to consult over policy matters) that in 1842, they sent one of their number, John Hughes, to London to outline their views to the secretary of state. Hughes presented a petition to Lord Stanley in which the merchants called for the appointment of officials of integrity and specifically attacked Ingram. Shortly afterward, the merchants accused Ingram of exerting official pressure in the courts through his brother, Alexander, who was an assistant judge. They also called for the removal of John Mantell, who had been appointed queen's advocate in succession to Pine despite apparently being without legal qualifications; Mantell was another of Ingram's allies.[26]

Some of these petitions were signed not only by the European and Mulatto merchants, but also by a number of African clerks and traders. This was of some significance; prior to 1842, Africans had apparently not participated in the political process. However, it should be noted that these men were mainly employed by the merchants and may even have been instructed to sign. The petitions were in any case rejected by the secretary of state, an indication of the limitations to the merchants' influence, and Ingram and Mantell remained in office.[27]

Even after the establishment of the independent Crown Colony in 1843, relations between Ingram and the merchants remained difficult; indeed, it was not until Ingram had been dismissed as colonial secretary in 1849 that they began to improve. The merchants predictably objected to Mantell's promotion to chief justice in 1847 and also disliked the fact that Ingram frequently assumed control of the administration in the mid-1840s in the absence of the substantive postholder. For his part, in May 1844, Ingram was driven to complain to the secretary of state that three merchants were the instigators of "a party highly inimical to the Authorities at the Gambia."[28] The three were Charles Grant, the long-established merchant; James Finden, who had been trading at Portendick since the 1830s; and Thomas Brown. Brown, who was to remain a key figure in Gambian politics for the next three decades, arrived in Bathurst in 1829 at the age of 18 to work as a clerk for Forster and Smith (initially combining this role with employment in government service). In the early 1840s, he worked as the agent of Thomas Hutton of Watling Street, but when the latter abandoned the coastal trade (after 1843), he established his own firm, Thomas Brown & Co.[29]

Interest Group Politics in an "Independent" Gambia: 1843–66

The creation of Gambia as an independent Crown Colony in 1843 automatically increased the theoretical powers of the British merchants. The establishment of a Legislative Council, on which they were represented from the outset, meant that for the first time since 1821, they had a forum in which to discuss government policies. It also allowed them to debate and vote on the annual budget estimates. Their periodic representation on the Executive Council was a further source of influence. In contrast, as noted in Chapter 2, no Africans served on the Legislative Council until the 1880s, even though the Madden Report had recommended that "one or two of the respectable class of coloured residents" should be appointed to it.[30] This exacerbated the political weakness of the Liberated Africans and meant that their most effective weapon remained the sympathy of the colonial governor. In practice, as we shall see, some governors were to prove more sympathetic to their cause than others. Between 1843 and 1847, there were three different governors (all of whom were naval officers); because the first two rapidly succumbed to the climate, only the last of these, Commander Charles Fitzgerald, remained in office long enough to have any impact on domestic politics.[31] Fitzgerald appears to have been popular with Liberated Africans, probably because he made a determined attempt to complete the draining of Bathurst and thereby prevent the flooding which was so detrimental to the health of the poorer inhabitants of the town. In 1846, he imported granite blocks from England to construct a lock with sluice gates at the Malfa Creek, but before the project could be completed, he left office.[32]

Governor MacDonnell: The Merchants' Ally

Fitzgerald was succeeded in October 1847 by Richard MacDonnell, the first civilian governor, who had been appointed chief justice in 1843 when aged only twenty-eight.[33] MacDonnell immediately abandoned the Malfa Lock project on the grounds that the colony possessed insufficient funds to complete such an expensive project. The decision, which may have been taken after pressure from the British merchants, was strongly resented by the African population, particularly as MacDonnell continued to spend money on making alterations to Government House. In 1849, the rains were heavy and when these resulted in the flooding of the greater part of Bathurst, a petition protesting against MacDonnell's administration and calling for his removal from office, which was signed by 139 of the self-proclaimed "principal Black Inhabitants" of Bathurst, was dispatched to the secretary of state, Earl Grey.

The petition was organized by a "Committee of the Black Inhabitants," which was headed by Providence Doyery, a Liberated African Anglican convert, and Reme Lome. Its other members included Daniel Prophet, a clerk of Egba (a Yoruba subgroup) origin who had signed one of the anti-Ingram petitions of 1842, and John Bocock, a Liberated African trader originally from Popo in modern Togo. The petition, which received no support from the British merchants, was dismissed by MacDonnell, who claimed that it had been instigated by the disgraced Thomas Ingram. The governor also argued that many of the petitioners were ignorant of its contents, and others had been forced to sign by the headmen of a despotic (friendly) society based in the Soldier Town area of the town. Not surprisingly, the petition was subsequently rejected by the secretary of state.[34]

The friendly societies were to adopt a political role again in the 1860s and it is therefore necessary to describe their origins. The first such society had been established in 1842 by Thomas Reffles (or Reffell), a Liberated African of Ibo origin. A former soldier, Reffles apparently was sent to Bathurst in 1821 at the age of twenty-six by Governor MacCarthy of Sierra Leone to help with the construction of a clock. He remained in Gambia thereafter, was wounded while fighting in the Barra War of 1829 (for which he was granted a pension in 1838), and was probably involved in trading with Freetown in the 1830s and 1840s.

According to Joseph Reffles (his son), the Ibo Society was founded on the initiative of a Wesleyan missionary (presumably William Fox). Fox was approached by a group of European magistrates, who were concerned by the misconduct of the Liberated Africans who were transferred to Bathurst during the 1830s, without adequate provision being made for their welfare; because they lacked alternative means of making a living, many of them apparently turned to crime. At a meeting of Wesleyan church leaders in 1842, it was agreed that a "Workmen's Club" should be founded to assist unemployed Liberated Africans and Reffles had led the way by forming a society for his fellow Ibo.[35] Once the benefits of the Ibo society had been demonstrated, Yoruba Recaptives followed suit and established their own societies (as they had in Freetown); around 1850, a Protestant Wolof shipwright named Senegal Fye established a "Shipwrights' Society," which catered for carpenters and masons, as well as shipwrights. The principal function of most societies appears to have been to ensure that their members could afford their burial expenses. The headmen also exercised a degree of social control over the members.[36]

Governor MacDonnell left office in 1852 with an enhanced reputation. He remained popular with the British merchants because he adopted an aggressive policy to protect their commercial interests against the predatory actions of hostile tribes. He was, for example, publicly thanked by the merchants for leading a successful expedition against the people of Kunnong and Bambako who had been attacking trading posts. He was also the first administrator since Findlay to take decisive action against the French traders at Albreda. In 1848, he enforced a blockade to prevent smuggling; as a consequence, trade from Albreda was reduced by a quarter by 1852.[37] MacDonnell was, however, much less popular with

Liberated Africans. Beside abandoning the Malfa Lock project and failing to take adequate measures to prevent the floods of 1849, he also introduced a. Rates Ordinance of 3 to 4 percent per annum on property in 1850. Although merchants and Africans alike were required to pay this tax, in relative terms the burden was much greater on the latter. Not surprisingly, Liberated Africans condemned the ordinance prior to its introduction.[38] As indicated, they were also to call for its repeal in 1862.

Governor O'Connor: The Promotion of Liberated African Interests

When MacDonnell's designated successor, A. E. (later Sir Arthur) Kennedy, was promoted to the post of governor of Sierra Leone without ever having set foot in Bathurst, the position was offered to Colonel L. S. O'Connor of the First West India Regiment.[39] At first, O'Connor followed the policies of his predecessor and British merchants continued to exercise a great deal of influence. Indeed, in 1853, he appointed Thomas Brown to the Executive Council.[40] The mercantile members were equally effective on the Legislative Council and it was their pressure that persuaded O'Connor (who had previously declared that he intended to remain neutral) to intervene in the civil war in the Kombo.[41]

By the mid-nineteenth century, the Mandinka were divided into two groups, the Soninkes and the Marabouts. The former were animists, or Muslims who failed to observe Islamic practices, most notably by consuming alcohol; in practice, they consisted of the rulers and aristocracies of the kingdoms and their followers. The latter, members of the Tijani Islamic confraternity, were often traders and clerics and strictly avoided alcohol. They were excluded from land ownership and offices of state in all Mandinka states; additionally, Marabouts were often given the poorest land by the Soninke rulers and were heavily taxed. These grievances eventually persuaded the Marabout-dominated town of Sabajy (or Sabaji, modern Sukuta) to rebel against their Soninke king, the Mansa Kombo, in the late 1840s.[42]

The beginning of the civil war in the Kombo alarmed both MacDonnell and the British merchants, who favored the Soninke party in the Kombo. This was partly because any political instability was likely to threaten the production of groundnuts (now the colony's main export crop) from the Kombo. Moreover, Lieutenant Governor Huntley had purchased a portion of Upper Kombo in 1840 (it became British Kombo) and merchants (and officials) had acquired large plots of land there, which might be threatened by instability; furthermore, the Mansa Kombo had promised to cede more land if Sabajy (Sabiji) were to be destroyed. MacDonnell had requested permission to intervene in 1852, but the Colonial Office denied his request. Nevertheless, spurred on by the merchants, O'Connor marched into Sabajy in May 1853 and completely destroyed the town. He then signed a treaty with the Mansa Kombo, who duly ceded Sabajy and other parts of Upper Kombo to the British.[43]

Although the British merchants pushed O'Connor into action in 1853, they were dismayed by the consequences. Because O'Connor attacked Sabajy without prior consultation with the Colonial Office, the secretary of state refused to foot the bill and the cost had to be met from the colony's revenue. To make matters worse, O'Connor attempted to distribute the newly acquired crown land to Liberated Africans and African small farmers, rather than allowing the merchants to purchase even larger plots. He then tried in 1856 to ban the sale of gunpowder, a source of lucrative trade, along the river.[44]

The merchants were able to use their influence to prevent the implementation of both these policies. However, their attempts to resist other undesirable government actions were less successful. First, they were not able to prevent the signing of the Anglo-French Convention in March 1857. Under its terms, Britain was ceded Albreda, in return for renouncing all rights to participate in the gum trade at Portendick. There had been virtually no trade with Portendick for a decade and so the merchants were willing to give up their trading rights. However, in addition, French ships had been granted free and legal access to the river above James Island, thereby permitting them to establish businesses in Bathurst for the first time. The British merchants, who feared the prospect of additional competition, protested strongly through their three representatives in the Legislative Council in August 1858, all of whom actually resigned over the issue. But the governor, who was a convinced free trader, strongly endorsed the agreement, which gave the Gambian government the right to charge customs duties on French ships for the first time.[45]

Second, they were unable to prevent O'Connor pushing two bills, which sought to protect the interests of Liberated African artisans against their mercantile employers, through the Legislative Council. The "truck" system, by which merchants had paid their employees partly in cash and partly in goods, which they valued well above the normal retail price in Bathurst, was abolished in 1856.[46] Moreover, certain clauses in the Grumetta Act, which had allowed magistrates (who were usually merchants) to impose punishments (including hard labor) on artisans who refused to work for wages offered by employers, were repealed in 1858. Both bills were strongly opposed by the merchants and two of their number actually resigned from the magisterial bench in protest.[47]

According to a later account, O'Connor introduced the two bills as a result of a meeting he had with Harry Finden in 1856. A Liberated African Methodist church member who had received no formal education and was virtually illiterate, Finden apparently succeeded Thomas Reffles as leader of the Ibo community in Bathurst after Reffles' death in 1849. He was the owner of a "grog" shop in Bathurst and was also involved in the riverine trade; he appears to have been reasonably successful in these ventures, for in 1870, he was said to be the owner of property worth an estimated £350 and to have total assets of £600.[48]

Governor D'Arcy: The Rule of the "Great Mercantile Interest"

O'Connor was succeeded in 1859 by another army officer, Colonel G. A. K. D'Arcy, under whom the merchants were to regain their influence. Indeed, by the mid-1860s, the "great mercantile interest" was said to have become the ruling power in the colony, and in 1869, Thomas Brown was described as having acquired "an influence which in a peculiar mixture of antagonistic races might prove dangerous."[49] Two factors help to explain these developments. First, because the colony was in severe financial straits—there was a budget deficit every year between 1859 and 1865—the governor could not afford to antagonize the main providers of revenue, the merchants.[50] Second, the governor could not rely on a secure majority in the Legislative Council. Whereas he was at odds with some of his long-serving senior officials, who were sympathetic to the merchants' cause, the three unofficial members of the council, Thomas Brown, W. H. Goddard, and Thomas F. Quin, a long-serving former government official turned merchant who had joined the council in 1860, tended to work together. D'Arcy could not even be certain of control over the Executive Council. This was dominated by Brown, who had been appointed acting queen's advocate in 1861, because of a lack of officials following a yellow fever outbreak in 1859, and was to retain an official position until 1866. He was therefore an ex officio member of the Executive Council.[51] The result was the passing of a series of ordinances which strengthened the position of the merchants at the expense of both the Liberated African community and the French business houses which, as noted in Chapter 1, had begun to move into Bathurst since 1860.[52]

First, the burden of taxation was shifted away from the merchants. In 1861, a tax was imposed on the importation of kola nuts for the first time. This fell squarely on Liberated African traders who controlled the trade with Freetown. In 1863, the ad valorem duty of 4 percent on all duties was abolished. It was replaced by an export duty on groundnuts and hides, which fell principally on French merchants, who by offering cash for groundnuts (whereas British merchants continued to use a complicated credit system), had hitherto avoided paying import duties. Finally, in 1865, a new tariff, which had been drawn up by Thomas Brown in his guise as acting queen's advocate, introduced heavier duties on commodities (such as sugar) that were imported by the French houses and those (like kola nuts and palm wine), that were controlled by Liberated Africans. A license was also imposed on retailers of spirits, who were again mainly Liberated Africans.[53]

Second, the various attempts made by Governor D'Arcy to uphold the interests of Liberated Africans were resisted. In 1862–63, for example, the merchants prevented any amendments being made to the 1850 Rates Ordinance. A large group of African petitioners, headed by Harry Finden, had argued that because only British merchants derived any advantage from the ordinance (the districts in which they resided acquired street lamps and were now patrolled by policemen), they should pay more for their privileges. D'Arcy sympathized with the petitioners, but the merchants did not and they were able to persuade the Legislative Council to reject D'Arcy's attempt to repeal the ordinance in 1863. Similarly, in 1865, strong mercantile opposition forced Governor D'Arcy to withdraw a proposed Bankruptcy Bill. Under the existing legislation, debtors could be imprisoned without trial even where there was no evidence of fraud or misappropriation. Consequently, Africans trading up river for European merchants were sometimes jailed for making losses on their trading account. The measure was not finally passed until 1873 and then only after the Colonial Office pressured the administration.[54]

Third, the merchants persuaded D'Arcy to pass the Friendly Societies Ordinance in June 1865. In 1864, the headmen of the societies had imposed a boycott on the Colonial Surgeon, Dr. W. H. Sherwood. Sherwood, who was widely considered to be racist, a drunkard, and incompetent, illegally seized a hearse from a society to bury a white sailor. For several months afterward, Sherwood was unable to find any carpenter or mason who would carry out any work for him. Similar action was taken in January 1865 against the Liberated African gaoler, John Campbell, who was accused of being too pro-European. These actions provoked Thomas Brown, in his role as a magistrate, to impose a heavy fine on the carpenter who had refused to work for Campbell. Brown then persuaded D'Arcy to introduce an ordinance into the Legislative Council that required the registration of all societies and permitted a magistrate regularly to investigate their subscription books. This ordinance was clearly designed to destroy the power of their headmen. The merchants (and Chief Justice Mantell) considered that the bill did not go far enough, because it did not outlaw strikes, and voted against it. Nevertheless, it was passed by the council and became law in September. The headmen of both the ethnic societies and the craft societies, led by Harry Finden, protested to the secretary of state for the colonies, but to no avail.[55]

The policies D'Arcy initially adopted, which included placing Finden in command of a large detachment of African troops during the Baddibu War of 1861 and provisionally selecting Thomas Johnson as one of the first two African magistrates, were welcomed by Liberated Africans.[56] Indeed, as late as 1864, a large number of them signed a petition to the secretary of state calling for D'Arcy's term of office as governor to be extended and generally extolling his virtues.[57] But by 1865, the Liberated African community increasingly resented the governor's pro-merchant stance. Matters reached a climax that December, when the French Consul in Bathurst informed D'Arcy that a plot had been hatched by Finden to kill all the Europeans in the town. D'Arcy took various precautionary measures, although he did not follow the advice of Hastings Kneller, the collector of customs, and declare martial law. His actions were fully supported by the executive councilors, including Brown. However, the other two unofficial members of the Legislative Council, Quin and Goddard, were skeptical about the rumors of a plot and martial law was not in fact declared.[58]

Politics under the West African Settlements: 1866–86

Establishment of the Settlements

At this critical juncture in Gambian public life, the political balance in Bathurst was altered by developments in London. In July 1864, following a disastrous war between the Gold Coast government and the Asante, C. B. Adderley, the

Conservative MP for Staffordshire North, had proposed that another Parliamentary Select Committee be established to examine the condition of the West African colonies. Adderley, who considered the colonies to be a drain on imperial resources, hoped to achieve a British withdrawal from the Gold Coast and perhaps also from the other colonies.[59] The Colonial Office, which was anxious to ensure that the Select Committee made its recommendations on the basis of up-to-date information, commissioned Colonel H. St. George Ord (the governor of Bermuda) to provide the necessary evidence. However, contrary to Adderley's hopes, the Ord Report did not recommend withdrawal from any of the settlements, but suggested that they should be placed under one centralized administration as a way of saving money.[60]

This recommendation was unpopular with the merchants (who had of course welcomed Gambian independence from Sierra Leone in 1843) and they petitioned the secretary of state for the colonies against the restoration of the link with Freetown. In contrast, the Liberated African community welcomed centralization as a means to curb mercantile power. In particular, it was thought that an independent governor-in-chief would be more likely to administer justice impartially than a pro-merchant chief justice like Mantell.[61] Unlike in 1842, the merchants had no powerful allies on the Parliamentary Select Committee and they also failed to put forward their case effectively.[62] Consequently, their views were ignored and in February 1866, the West African Settlements were established. The post of governor was abolished and replaced by that of an administrator; the Executive Council was abolished and the Legislative Council downgraded, with only one unofficial (Brown) being retained. D'Arcy initially served as administrator, before being succeeded by Rear Admiral Charles Patey in October 1866.[63]

Patey Administration: 1866–69

The avowed intention of the new administrator was to check "a reckless expenditure" and thereby to reduce the colony's growing budget deficit.[64] This aim could only be achieved by firm action against the merchants. In 1867, Patey brought a case against Brown for an infringement of customs regulations, but the case was dismissed. Two years later, he ordered an investigation into the operation of the Customs House. This found that merchants had often avoided paying duty on goods because of the "gross errors" in the account books of the collector of customs (Hastings Kneller); procedures were subsequently tightened.[65] Customs revenue increased, but the merchants, who were already resentful that Patey preferred to follow the advice of the first writer, Henry Fowler, rather than consult the Legislative Council and had also abolished the right of merchants to serve as magistrates, were further alienated from his government.[66]

Matters were brought to a head in 1869 by a cholera epidemic that killed over 1,100 Africans in Bathurst alone.[67] The merchants blamed Patey for failing to take adequate precautions to prevent cholera reaching the town, arguing that this was due to his "parsimonious economy." They were also critical of the measures he had subsequently adopted and urged the Colonial Office to remove both him and Fowler. Some Liberated Africans, including Finden, who were alarmed by Patey's alleged ill treatment of prisoners, supported their petition.[68] However, others were unwilling to join forces with the merchants over any issue and offered their support to Patey. This second group included Thomas Reffles' son, Joseph, who was to become a key figure in the resistance to the cession of Gambia in 1870.

Joseph Reffles served as barracks sergeant and clerk in the Ordnance Department in Bathurst for six years before he was dismissed from the service. He then found employment trading up river for Thomas Brown. But he was an unsuccessful trader and Brown fired him for incurring losses. He was then employed by William Goddard, the agent of Forster and Smith, but again incurred losses and was dismissed. Despite these setbacks, Reffles' abilities were recognized by prominent Liberated Africans who raised sufficient funds to enable him to travel to London in 1865 to acquire a legal training. Their aim was that he should be able to defend their interests in Gambian courts. Reffles returned to Bathurst in 1867 and applied to be admitted to the Sierra Leone bar as a practicing attorney and advocate, but his request was rejected. He then took advantage of an ordinance permitting him to act as a legal agent for clients on their written authority, but this ordinance was repealed in December 1867 by Kneller, who was then acting administrator; according to Reffles, Kneller acted at the instigation of his former employer, Thomas Brown. Reffles returned to London in 1868, presumably to acquire more legal training, and remained there until 1870. Under the circumstances, it was not surprising that Reffles bore a grievance against both the merchants and their allies among the officials.[69]

Predictably, the merchants' petition against Patey and Fowler was dismissed by Earl Granville, the secretary of state for the colonies, who soon afterward promoted Patey to the post of governor of St. Helena and also praised Fowler for his actions during the epidemic. In contrast, the officials who had sided with the merchants over the affair, such as Kneller and Dr. J. H. Jeans, the colonial surgeon, were punished. The former was forced to resign, and the latter was dismissed.[70] The administration then passed on an acting basis to Major Alexander Bravo, the police magistrate of Sierra Leone, who was in office when news of the proposed cession of Gambia to France broke in 1870.[71]

Resistance to Cession: 1870–76

In 1870–71, and again in 1875–76, domestic political issues were temporarily superseded by the issue of the proposed transfer of Gambia to France. The course of events has been examined in detail elsewhere, especially by Hargreaves; our focus is on the opposition to exchange from two separate quarters, the British merchants and the Liberated Africans.[72]

Although, as early as March 1866, the French government had proposed that Gambia be exchanged for corresponding French territory, it was not until February 1870 that the British government finally decided to accept the offer. This was not because the Colonial Office was anxious to retain Gambia; on the contrary, it wished to be rid of a settlement in severe financial difficulties, particularly because the situation was unlikely to improve in the near future. The problem was that the British government was unable to find any corresponding French territory it actually wanted; it did not desire the three French settlements on the Ivory Coast, Grand Bassam, Assinie, and Dabou, that were originally offered, nor Gabon (added by France to the equation in 1867). But in 1869, the Colonial Office was persuaded by the governor-in-chief of the West African Settlements, Sir Arthur Kennedy, that an acceptable price for Gambia would be the renunciation by France of any claim to the disputed Mellacourie region north of Freetown. This offer was put to the French government in 1870.[73]

First Attempt: 1870–71

The British proposal was accepted in principle by France at the end of March and, as Hargreaves puts it, "All seemed clear for a rapid conclusion."[74] However, when news of the impending deal broke, it was fiercely opposed by merchants and Liberated Africans alike. Their resistance was effective, since it helped delay the process to such an extent that in July 1870, the secretary of state for the colonies in the liberal government, the Earl of Kimberley, was forced to announce that it would not be possible to proceed in the current Parliamentary Session. Since Kimberley subsequently decided that the idea of exchange was inappropriate, this effectively ended the matter until the return of a Conservative government in 1874.[75]

During 1870, all four British business houses in Bathurst publicly announced their opposition to exchange. The first to do was the firm headed by Thomas Quin; in January 1870, he declared that he viewed the proposal "with horror."[76] The three other firms (Forster and Smith, Thomas Brown and Co., and the Chown family firm) did not declare their hand until July, perhaps because they were carefully preparing support for their cause in advance. At the beginning of July, Brown persuaded the Manchester Chamber of Commerce to protest against exchange; later that month, Forster and Smith organized a memorial supported by forty-one other London merchants, manufacturers, and traders. The merchants' principal argument was that exchange would force them to abandon the Gambian trade, because the French authorities would pressure them to leave. In support of their arguments, they cited French policy in Gorée after the resumption of colonial rule in 1817 as an indication of what was likely to happen.[77]

The merchants also demanded compensation for the loss of capital, property, and trade goods, if they were forced to give up the trade and set out in detail what this would cost.[78] Indeed, Governor Kennedy was convinced that their real aim in stirring up opposition to exchange was not to prevent it going ahead, but rather to force up the price. Hargreaves argues that "there is much evidence to support his interpretation"; in particular, Thomas Brown stated in the Legislative Council in May 1870 that he did not object to the transfer, "provided equitable terms" were arranged. In contrast, Mahoney considers that the merchants' opposition was genuine and it should be noted that the Liberated African community subsequently thanked Brown and Quin (although not the Chowns or Forster and Smith) for their "untiring efforts" to prevent the transfer from proceeding.[79]

If the motives of at least some of the merchants were ambiguous, there is no reason to suppose that the opposition of Liberated Africans to exchange was anything other than genuine. Their initial response was in April 1870, when a petition signed by over 500 traders, mechanics, and other black inhabitants was dispatched to Kennedy for onward transmission to the secretary of state. A second petition was sent at the end of May and a third, which contained 120 signatures, was sent to Queen Victoria in October. All prominent Liberated Africans who were not in government employment appear to have opposed exchange. Indeed, Administrator Bravo commented that the petitioners represented "whatever intelligence, respectability, property or feeling there may be in the natives of these settlements."[80]

The April petition was headed by Harry Finden, although Governor Kennedy believed that it was drawn up by William Chase Walcott, a controversial lawyer originally from Barbados who had recently arrived from Sierra Leone; Kennedy had a very low opinion of Walcott, who had recently been in prison in Freetown, and this increased his hostility to the opponents of cession.[81] Finden, together with eight other members of the Liberated African community, John Bocock, Daniel Prophet, John T. Barber, Abraham Goddard, Providence Joof, Charles Pignard, Joseph D. Richards, Samuel J. Forster, and a leading member of the small West Indian community in Bathurst, Thomas King, headed a deputation to Governor Kennedy in May.

These men, together with Reffles, who was probably still in London at the time, can be regarded as the leaders of the Liberated African opposition to exchange. All except Joof, a shipwright, and Pignard, who was probably also an artisan, were engaged in commerce and trade. Judging by their estimated assets, most were reasonably successful; King (who had headed the list of petitioners calling for D'Arcy's period of office to be extended in 1864) was generally considered the wealthiest of the non-European merchants with property of an estimated value of £2,500 and total assets of an estimated £4,000. Two members of the group, Bocock and Prophet, were veteran leaders of the local community, having signed the petition against Governor MacDonnell in 1849; all were Protestants (Wesleyan Methodists, except for Barber and King, who were Anglicans) and at least three—Finden, Bocock, and Barber—were Liberated Africans. The leaders also represented the range of ethnic groups within the Liberated African community; by origin, Richards and Goddard were Aku, Forster and Finden were Ibo, Prophet an Egba, Bocock a Popo, and Joof a Wolof.[82]

Two members of this group, Richards and Forster (whose early career is described in Chapter 5), were to remain prominent politically for the next thirty years. A Methodist, whose parents were Liberated Africans of Aku origin, Richards was born in Freetown in December 1843, but moved with his mother (a prosperous kola nut trader) to Gambia as a child and attended the Wesleyan School in Bathurst. Since at least 1864, he had been active in the riverine trade and he may also have become involved in the kola nut trade with Freetown (which was to be his main commercial activity in later years). He was clearly successful; by 1870, he was said to be the owner of a property worth £500 and to possess total assets of £800. Indeed, along with Thomas King, he was described as a "merchant" rather than as a "trader" in the April 1870 petition, a sign of his enhanced status.[83]

The majority of the people who signed the petitions were Protestants (mainly Methodists), but a few Roman Catholics and a larger number of Muslims also supported the campaign. It may be assumed that many of the artisans and mechanics who added their names were instructed to do so by the headmen of societies; indeed, one of the leaders of the anti-cession campaign, Providence Joof, was the leader of the Carpenters and Shipwrights' Society, which had been at the forefront of the protests against the Friendly Societies Ordinance of 1865.[84]

One significant feature of the Liberated African opposition to exchange was that it united the "Gambian" and "Sierra Leonean" wings of the Liberated African community. In April 1868, Governor Kennedy of Sierra Leone introduced competitive examinations for junior clerical posts in the civil service throughout British West Africa, thereby enabling Africans to apply for promotion in any colony. Because Sierra Leoneans tended to be much better educated than the locally born inhabitants of the other three colonies, they began to fill the available posts in increasing numbers, including in Gambia. This caused great resentment in Bathurst and in 1871, a petition, which criticized the influx of Sierra Leoneans and argued that clerical posts in Bathurst should be reserved for Gambians, was addressed to Kennedy (a similar petition to Governor Hennessy of Sierra Leone called for the dismissal of these Sierra Leoneans and their replacement by Gambians). The 1871 petition was headed by Reffles and apparently drawn up by Walcott; it was also signed by Forster, among many others. However, it would appear that Finden, Barber, Richards, and King were all satisfied by the appointments and refused to sign the petition, which was ignored by the Colonial Office.[85]

The Liberated Africans, unlike the British merchants, were primarily worried about the threat posed by French colonial rule to their way of life. As evidence, they cited the military system of government practiced in the neighboring French colonies of Gorée and St. Louis. It was feared that the French would not respect the property rights of Liberated Africans, nor allow them to practice their Protestant religion. So great was their concern that many of them were prepared to sell their property and leave the colony; alternatively, they were ready to accept increased taxation if this would ensure the continuation of British administration.[86]

Second Attempt: 1875–76

The threat to withdraw from Gambia was of course never put to the test; negotiations with France were broken off in July 1870. It was not until the Conservatives regained power at Westminster in February 1874 that the issue resurfaced on the political agenda. In April 1874, the French government proposed that both the Ivory Coast and the Mellacourie should be exchanged for Gambia. Although this was an improved offer on that of 1870, the new secretary of state for the colonies, Lord Carnarvon, still held out for more; in July 1875, he instead proposed that France should renounce all political influence between the borders of Gabon in the south and "the northern limit of the existing French possessions." This would have been accepted by the French, but before the issue could be discussed by Parliament, it was announced (erroneously) that negotiations had been completed; Carnarvon was forced into a denial and to announce in the House of Lords that nothing would be done until the next parliamentary session in February 1876. During the period between parliamentary sessions, opposition to cession revived both in Britain and Gambia. This weakened Carnarvon's resolve, which collapsed entirely in March when it appeared possible that he might be accused of having misled Parliament. He therefore abruptly broke off negotiations.[87]

Since 1870, the Gambian trade had been in decline. One of the four British firms, Forster and Smith, had been taken over by an American company, Lintott and Spink, probably following the death of W. H. Goddard in 1873. Of the remainder, only the Chowns seem to have been doing much trade; indeed in 1874, Thomas Brown began negotiating the sale of his business and property to a French house.[88] The administrator, C. H. Kortright, predicted that there would be little opposition to cession from the merchants, but in fact all the British firms resisted the proposal. Brown led the way in a letter to Carnarvon in September 1875 and subsequently sent further letters of protest. In addition, with the assistance of the Manchester merchant, James F. Hutton of Hutton & Co., he persuaded the Manchester Chamber of Commerce to raise formal objections once again. He also organized a further petition from Bathurst in February 1876. Brown's son, David, together with Quin and Thomas C. Chown, also served as a member of the newly formed Gambia Committee, which sent a deputation to Carnarvon in February 1876 to condemn cession and Chown protested separately in a letter to the secretary of state. Only Lintott and Spink stayed aloof, although its agent in Bathurst, James Topp, did sign the petition of February 1876.[89]

Once again the British merchants emphasized that French rule would discriminate against their trading interests. Brown, for example, pointed out, as an indicator of French intentions, that the merchants of Senegal were currently seeking the imposition of discriminatory tariffs on British goods. Other arguments were added in 1876, including the threat to the Protestant religion and (by Chown) the adverse impact that cession would have on the Liberated African population. It seems unlikely, given the vehemence of the opposition, that the merchants were simply interested in maximizing their compensation and so their protests should probably be accepted as genuine.[90]

Liberated African hostility to cession was also as strong as in 1870. The first protest petition, drawn up in October 1875, received 152 signatures; a second in

December 1875 attracted over 500 names; and the third (sponsored by Thomas Brown) in February 1876 over 100. The first two petitions were both headed by J. D. Richards. Richards probably supplanted Finden as leader of the campaign partly because of his literacy and partly because, contrary to the opinion of the Gambian government, his commercial interests were continuing to expand (he imported goods worth £1,817 in 1875) and he was now one of the wealthiest men in Bathurst.[91] He became secretary of the Gambia Native Association (GNAssocn), a newly established committee of traders and shopkeepers which coordinated the resistance in 1875–76. Its other committee members were Finden, Barber, and Forster, the leaders of the 1870 resistance; George N. Shyngle, a Sierra Leonean who was one of the wealthier Liberated African entrepreneurs; and H. G. Dodgin, the leader of the Liberated African traders on MacCarthy Island. It will be noted that, once again, the campaign united "Gambians" and "Sierra Leoneans."[92] Joseph Reffles, the other key figure in 1870, was not active in 1875–76; his wife had recently died and he had become a lay preacher in the Methodist Church. He later became embroiled in a bitter public quarrel with one of the European missionaries in Gambia, Rev. George Adcock, but was not prominent politically thereafter. He died in 1886.[93]

Rank-and-file petitioners were mainly employed as artisans, traders, or clerks, although the signatories of the second petition included headmen of settlements in the Kombo.[94] Most were Wesleyan Methodists (as were five of the six GNAssocn committee members) and, unlike in 1870, the European leaders of the local Wesleyan Church actively supported the protests. Rev. Adcock signed the October 1875 petition and may even have chaired the meeting to draw it up, and all three missionaries later wrote to the general secretary of the Wesleyan Methodist Missionary Society to urge the Missionary Committee to oppose cession.[95]

The petitioners of October, like those of 1870, emphasized their firm attachment to British government and a corresponding aversion to French military rule, especially as demonstrated at St. Louis and Gorée; it was argued that French rule would "materially interfere with their social and religious rights."[96] They also argued that transfer would threaten their property rights and once again expressed their willingness to accept additional taxation to avoid transfer to France. The December 1875 petition was more comprehensive. It compared the advantages of Gambia with the French settlements with which it was to be transferred and, not surprisingly, concluded that Gambia was of greater intrinsic value than all of them put together. It also emphasized the value of Bathurst's public buildings, houses, and merchants' stores and pointed out that the employment prospects of clerks and artisans would be adversely affected by cession because they could not speak French. Finally, the petition noted that Liberated African entrepreneurs involved in the Freetown trade (such as Richards, who specialized in the kola trade) would also suffer, because the steamboat service between Bathurst and Freetown would cease to operate.[97]

The abandonment of the negotiations in March 1876 was by no means the final chapter of the story. Lord Salisbury, Carnarvon's successor at the Colonial Office, would have liked to reopen negotiations in 1879–80, but the idea was resisted by his own more cautious officials; in any case, a Liberal government returned to office in March 1880. There was further discussion within the British government in 1883 and again in 1888, but no firm proposals were put forward.[98] Even after the boundary of Gambia was settled in 1889, the possibility of territorial exchange remained; indeed, three further overtures were made by the French government between 1904 and 1911, but all came to nothing.[99]

Toward African Political Representation: Domestic Politics, 1870–86

Three separate, but interconnected, themes shaped the course of internal Gambian politics in the 1870s and early 1880s. First, during the early 1870s, there was a realignment of political forces with merchants and Liberated Africans, who had been mutually antagonistic under Governor D'Arcy, adopting a united front on most political issues. Second, despite their key role in preventing cession, the political influence of the merchants gradually declined, so that, by the 1880s, they ceased to be an independent force in local politics. Third, the Liberated African community, its confidence increased by the part it had played in the campaign against cession, completed the process of establishing an independent political identity and achieved representation on the Legislative Council. These three themes are examined in turn.

Relations between Merchants and Liberated Africans

Although the rapprochement between the mercantile and the Liberated African community had begun under Administrator Patey, the process was accelerated by the campaign against cession, which "bridged the gap created by racial antipathy" in the 1860s.[100] Indeed, after 1870, the political interests of the two groups were very similar. The merchants opposed the idea of the West African Settlements from the outset and their hostility to rule from Sierra Leone was strengthened during the 1870s. Liberated Africans, who had originally favored centralization, now turned against it because of the role played by the governor-in-chief, Sir Arthur Kennedy, in trying to force through cession. Kennedy was regarded as the villain of the piece, not only because he had been the main advocate of exchange, but also because he had adopted a highly dismissive attitude toward the legitimate objections of the Liberated African community; it may also have been known that he had tried to revive the issue in 1871.[101] Both groups also resented Kennedy's apparently deliberate attempt "to make things difficult in the Gambia" by withdrawing the small garrison and blocking the purchase of either a gunboat or an armed steamer. Kennedy also exacted an annual subsidy for the cost of a new mail boat service, which was better suited to the needs of Freetown than of Bathurst.[102]

Merchants and Liberated Africans were also critical of the Gambian government, which was headed by a considerable number of administrators and acting administrators between 1869 and 1877.[103] Successive administrators were condemned for wasting money on unnecessary items, such as repairs to Government House, while more important matters, such as the drainage of Bathurst, were neglected. There was also irritation that heavy expenditure was incurred without the sanction of the Legislative Council and large sums of money were then voted retrospectively to pay for it.[104] Moreover, there was a general belief that the civil establishment was overstaffed and could be reduced (and salaries cut) without any corresponding loss of efficiency. Brown and Quin even suggested in August 1869 that, in view of the heavy expenditure on the establishment, it might be desirable to replace the crown colony system of government with a consular system similar to that practiced since 1849 in the Bights of Biafra and Benin; as Dike points out, this system served the interests of British merchants well. Subsequently, Brown and Quin appear to have modified their view; they argued, in September 1870, that the civil establishment should be retained, but at reduced levels. Certain prominent members of the Liberated African community (including Reffles and Finden) endorsed the revised proposal although, unlike Brown and Quin, they stressed the necessity for the retention of a chief magistrate, an indication of continued concern about mercantile "justice."[105]

Decline of the British Merchants and the Rise of the Gambia Native Association

Although the British merchants (particularly Brown) continued to voice their opinions on a range of subjects, they were much less effective in achieving their aims in the 1870s than in the 1860s. By the end of 1873, Brown was the sole remaining resident British merchant; W. H. Goddard had died, and Thomas Quin and Thomas C. Chown had retired to England.[106] Brown remained on the Legislative Council, but his views were often disregarded by the administrators (some of whom clearly regarded him with disdain) and because, unlike in the D'Arcy era, official members now supported government policy, he was invariably outvoted. In addition, he was sometimes absent from the colony for long periods, which also weakened his influence.[107] In May 1874, his political influence in Bathurst was further reduced, when he was forced to resign from the Legislative Council over his role in the Mrs. Anna Evans scandal. Acting on behalf of the latter, Brown had in the previous year accused his old enemy (and fellow council member), Henry Fowler, the First Writer, of administering noxious drugs to Mrs. Evans to procure a miscarriage of a child of whom he was the father; the colonial surgeon, Thomas H. Spilsbury, was accused of supplying the drugs for the purpose. Both actions were criminal offences at the time. However, after an investigation, the queen's advocate, D. P. Chalmers, concluded that it was doubtful that a conviction could be secured in either case and the matter was dropped.

Despite the secretary of state's evident disapproval of his general conduct, Fowler was promoted to the post of receiver general in Bermuda, whereas Brown lost his seat on the council. Thereafter, although he remained in Bathurst until his death from bronchitis at the age of seventy in December 1881, he did not serve on the council again except for a brief period in 1879 when he was acting chief magistrate.[108] He was succeeded in 1875 by Henry Helm, a naturalized Prussian who acted as agent for the Chowns and later for the French firm, C. A. Verminck, but Helm was no more successful.[109]

The decline of the British merchants did have one important side effect; it smoothed the way for the Liberated African community to assume a more important role in local politics. This opportunity was seized by the GNAssocn, the organization established to oppose cession in 1875–76. In 1877, the colony acquired a new substantive administrator, Dr. Valesius S. Gouldsbury, when the nominal holder of the post, Dr. Samuel (later Sir Samuel) Rowe, was finally promoted to the post of governor of Sierra Leone.[110] Gouldsbury, like Patey a decade before, came into office determined to reduce expenditure, which had risen from £16,662 in 1871 to £21,489 in 1876.[111] This resulted in a large budget deficit.

Gouldsbury (like Patey before him) soon found that his attempts to raise revenue and cut expenditure made him unpopular, both with the European merchants and the wider Liberated African community. He alienated the merchants by tightening up the laws and regulations of trade, which he claimed were being abused, and by raising the customs tariff on certain commodities in 1878. This was despite the vehement objections of James Topp (who had succeeded Helm as the unofficial member of the Legislative Council in April 1876) and other merchants (including Brown).[112] He angered the Liberated Africans by his cost-cutting measures. Public works were curtailed, the streets of Bathurst were not cleaned and the drains were not repaired, and no satisfactory steps were taken to prevent the encroachment of the sea. In the poor sanitary conditions that prevailed, it was not surprising that there was an outbreak of fever in October 1878 that resulted in the deaths of several Europeans and Africans. Liberated Africans blamed the colonial engineer, J. C. Bauer, for his "culpable neglect" and "great ignorance" in permitting such a state of affairs and even sent a petition to the Colonial Office, which called for a board of inquiry into the Engineering Department. Gouldsbury was also widely criticized for defending Bauer, who was said to be his right hand man.[113]

Gouldsbury's other policies were no more popular. These included the passing of an ordinance to abolish the right to a trial by jury when traders were accused by their employers (the merchants) of fraud; this meant that cases were to be tried before the chief magistrate and two assessors, because the merchants considered that no jury in Bathurst would convict.[114] Gouldsbury's unpopularity was demonstrated by articles both in the *African Times* and the *Bathurst Observer and West Africa Gazette*; the latter had been established as Bathurst's first substantive newspaper in 1883 by W. C. Walcott (the alleged author of the Finden anti-cession petition of April 1870).[115]

Liberated African opposition in Bathurst to Gouldsbury was led by the GNAssocn. Four of its leading members signed the anti-Bauer petition of 1878.[116] The GNAssocn itself presented an anti-government memorial to the governor-in-chief, Samuel Rowe, during one of Rowe's rare visits to Bathurst in 1879 and sent other memorials to the secretary of state for the colonies (for example, to protest against the abolition of trial by jury). The association was by now headed by Jeremiah D. Jones, a shopkeeper and trader originally from Sierra Leone. Jones was a controversial figure in Bathurst, having incurred the wrath of the European merchants by running up large debts with them, failing to pay his bills, and then escaping justice (as they saw it) in the courts; he was also said to use dubious tactics to ensure support for his anti-government petitions.[117] However, the GNAssocn did not possess a monopoly on public opinion; at least two leading African traders, S. J. Forster and J. D. Cole (as well as the major European merchants), apparently refused to sign the petition against Bauer in 1878.[118] These internal differences within the Liberated African community were to reemerge in the 1880s over the appointment of a second unofficial member of the Legislative Council.

Legislative Council Representation

As early as May 1873, the secretary of state for the colonies, the Earl of Kimberley, informed a deputation from the Manchester Chamber of Commerce (which included other interested parties such as Thomas Quin and T. C. Chown) that he would be pleased to see greater mercantile representation on the various West African Legislative Councils. Nothing concrete had resulted in Gambia, primarily because the official view was that there were very few eligible candidates, a decision that may not have displeased Liberated African opinion.[119]

In 1878, William McArthur, the MP for Lambeth (and a member of the Gambia Committee in 1876), persuaded the secretary of state to direct that a second unofficial be appointed. A naturalized Swedish merchant, Peter A. Bowman, was duly selected on Gouldsbury's recommendation, but for unknown reasons did not take his seat. Because the administrator was unable (or unwilling) to find an alternative candidate, James Topp remained the sole unofficial councilor.[120] There the matter rested until July 1882, when Gouldsbury received a deputation of Bathurst merchants. The merchants criticized several aspects of the governor's policy and also called for the appointment of more unofficial members of the council, one of whom should be an African. Gouldsbury was willing to comply with this request, not apparently through any desire to promote Liberated Africans per se, but rather to find "a foil" to Topp, who frequently attacked government actions and policy (including Gouldsbury's own pioneering expedition to explore the River Gambia to its source in 1881).[121]

In November 1882, Gouldsbury recommended to the secretary of state that the former secretary of the GNAssocn, J. D. Richards, be appointed to the council. This suggestion was accepted and, after a delay for technical reasons, Richards took his seat in March 1883. The selection was perhaps surprising, given that Richards previously joined the attacks on Gouldsbury's protégé, Bauer. More recently, however, Richards had apparently avoided taking sides too overtly over the abolition of the jury trial in fraud cases.[122] The appointment met with a mixed reaction in Bathurst. On the one hand, the GNAssocn, which had previously been critical of Gouldsbury, complimented him on the choice of Richards, whom it claimed enjoyed "the confidence and esteem of the community." On the other hand, W. C. Walcott, editor of the *Bathurst Observer*, condemned the choice. He claimed that Gouldsbury persuaded Richards to stand surety for Bauer when the latter was appointed acting collector and treasurer in 1882, following the death of the colonial secretary, W. H. Berkeley; his reward was his appointment to the council. Walcott also named a number of candidates (including S. J. Forster and Harry Finden) whom he considered more deserving of the appointment because they were wealthier than Richards.[123]

If Gouldsbury hoped that Richards would prove a more compliant member of the Legislative Council than Topp, he was soon disillusioned. In practice, the two unofficial members disagreed over only one major issue, taxation. Richards, as the chief importer of kola nuts into Bathurst, consistently opposed any rise in customs duties on that commodity, whereas Topp equally determinedly resisted any increase in the duty on spirits (which he mainly imported).[124] Generally speaking, however, the two men acted in concert and neither hesitated to attack the government. Both criticized excessive expenditure on certain items in the estimates of 1883 and 1884; condemned the Tariff Ordinance of 1883; and objected to its repeal in 1886. In addition, Richards opposed the removal of restrictions on foreign ships trading in the River Gambia in 1885, which so irritated Gouldsbury's successor, Captain C. A. Moloney, that he accused him of putting the sectional interests of the small African ship owners before those of the wider community.[125]

By 1886, therefore, the Gambian government was so concerned with the opposition of Topp and Richards that it was looking to ways to strengthen its position on the council. The response of the new administrator, Captain J. S. Hay, was to make two further appointments, one official and one unofficial, S. J. Forster. As we shall see in Chapter 4, Forster's elevation was to mark the beginning of a political dynasty, since there was to be a Forster on the Legislative Council for the next fifty-four years.

Summary

The key political groups in Gambia in the nineteenth century were the Gambian government, the British merchants, and the Liberated African community. Until the 1860s, the merchants, who were the main providers of the colony's revenue and highly influential on the Legislative Council, were generally the dominant force in local politics; and were able to ensure that most decisions made by the government met with their approval. In contrast, the Liberated African community remained weak and politically ineffective until the 1870s, when largely as a result of the successful campaign against cession, it increased its political authority, while the power of the merchants began to decline. In 1883, this development received official recognition when the first Gambian African was appointed to the Legislative Council.

4

PATRICIAN POLITICS IN THE ERA OF THE FORSTERS, 1886—1941

Gambian politics in the late nineteenth and early twentieth centuries may be characterized as conforming to a "patrician" model. It was dominated by a handful of educated Aku and Wolof who lived in Bathurst. This political elite was linked in a clientelist relationship with a larger number of Aku and Wolof in the Colony, but the Protectorate was largely excluded from the political process. The elite was by no means homogenous, but was divided into factions which were drawn up on the basis of personal and family connections, social and religious status, political ambition, and ethnic identity.[1] The rivalry between these factions was the essence of politics, particularly after World War I.

The Forster family headed the dominant faction throughout this period. The first Samuel John Forster was appointed to the Legislative Council in 1886 and remained a member of it until his death in 1906. One of his sons, also called Samuel John, filled the vacancy and continued to serve until his death in 1940. The younger Forster was assisted by a network of relatives, friends, and clients, the most important of whom was his nephew, W. Davidson Carrol. Carrol was expected to become his political heir, but his untimely death in 1941 brought the Forster political dynasty to a close. This enabled the main rival faction in Bathurst politics, headed by Edward Francis Small, to secure representation on the Legislative Council for the first time.

The Rise of the Forsters: 1886–1900

Samuel J. Forster was born in Bathurst, probably in the 1830s or 1840s. His father was a freeborn Ibo trader who traveled to Freetown from Nigeria with two of his brothers to make a living and had then moved on to Gambia. A Wesleyan Methodist (either by birth or conversion), S. J. Forster worked as a clerk in the Commissariat Department in Bathurst in the 1860s before resigning to concentrate on commerce. He specialized in trading in rice and, thanks to family connections in the interior, he prospered; by 1875, he was said to be the owner of a house and land worth some £300, which made him one of the wealthiest men in Bathurst.[2] As indicated in Chapter 3, he was a leading opponent of cession in the mid-1870s, but does not appear to have been involved in the Gambia Native Association (GN Assocn) in the late 1870s and early 1880s.

Given his wealth (by the mid-1880s, he was importing clothing and other goods from Europe) and political moderation, Administrator Gouldsbury might have been expected to appoint him as the first African member of the Legislative Council in 1883, but as noted earlier, he was passed over in favor of J. D. Richards. Gouldsbury's successor, C. A. Moloney, however, appointed Forster as a justice of the peace in 1884, a sign of official favor. Forster had earlier earned the plaudits of the Gambian government, but incurred criticism from a part of the Liberated African community, by signing the petition from the merchants which called for the abolition of jury trial when traders were arrested for debt. A year later, he was appointed a deputy sheriff and in 1886, he was finally added to the Legislative Council by Moloney's successor, J. S. Hay. Administrator Hay described Forster as "highly respected and esteemed by the community, he is very intelligent and thoroughly conversant with native affairs."[3] No doubt he also calculated that Forster would prove more willing than either Richards or James Topp to support government policy on the council.

Legislative Council Politics: 1888–1900

Two years after Forster's appointment, in November 1888, the administrative ties between Gambia and Sierra Leone were severed for the final time. Unlike in 1843, the decision was taken by the Colonial Office, rather than by Parliament. Gambia was coming under increasing threat from French expansion in the 1880s and it was considered that the colony required the presence of an administrator able to take immediate decisions without having to consult the governor-in-chief in Freetown in advance. There was a growing realization that the centralized system caused delays and these were likely to be exacerbated if, as anticipated, the mail service between Bathurst and Freetown became less regular. The Colonial Office was also aware that the linkage with Sierra Leone had been criticized by both the mercantile community in Bathurst and by merchants involved in the West Africa trade in England. Similar protests had helped to bring about the independence of Lagos from the Gold Coast in 1886 and no doubt helped to sway opinion on this occasion also.[4]

One important consequence of Gambian independence was that it provided an opportunity for the Gambian government to reconstitute the Legislative Council. In January 1887, H. H. Lee, the agent of the Manchester merchant, J. F. Hutton (who had taken over the business of the late Thomas Brown), had become the third unofficial member of the council. As noted in Chapter 3, Hutton played an important role in resisting cession in the mid-1870s and subsequently served as president of the Manchester Chamber of Commerce and as the member of Parliament for Manchester North. He remained an influential figure in British politics and was able to persuade the secretary of state for the colonies that the English merchant houses needed to be directly represented on the Gambia council. Administrator Hay disagreed (although he had no other objection to Lee), but was overruled by the Colonial Office.[5]

Lee's appointment meant that the council now had five official members and four unofficials. However, in 1888, the death of the collector of customs and the abolition of the post of queen's advocate meant that the official majority was lost. This was considered unsatisfactory by the government and so the new administrator, Gilbert T. Carter, proposed that Lee (who had in the meantime been appointed to an official position) should not be replaced and that Richards should be removed. Carter objected to the latter's attacks on government policy, particularly over the proposed withdrawal of the subsidy to the company running the mail service. Richards, who depended for his commercial success on the maintenance of a regular steamer service with Freetown, helped to organize the opposition in Bathurst to the proposal and had also persuaded the merchants of Liverpool to join the protest. Carter also disapproved of Richards' close links with J. D. Jones (the former leader of the GNAssocn), whom he described as "a dishonest agitator." Above all, he resented the criticisms Richards had made about the standard of conduct of European officials in West Africa. These arguments were accepted by the secretary of state and Richards left the council in December 1888.[6]

Carter had a higher opinion of Forster and Topp, both of whom generally endorsed government policy in recent years (including the mail subsidy). He awarded the former the lucrative contract to supply the government with provisions, and he rewarded the latter by appointing him postmaster in November 1888 (and in March 1890 persuaded the secretary of state to appoint him to the Executive Council as an its "unofficial" member).[7] Because Topp could no longer serve on the Legislative Council in his unofficial capacity, Carter appointed Henry Charles Goddard, the agent of the Bathurst Trading Company, to fill the vacancy in January 1889. Goddard was a member of the small Mulatto community, but seems generally to have been regarded as a European.[8]

R. B. Llewelyn (who became administrator in 1890) shared Carter's faith in Forster and regularly asked him (and/or Goddard) to attend the Executive Council as an "extraordinary" member. Both men were present in February 1894 when the Executive Council discussed the question of groundnut duty and again in December 1894 when it considered the proposed imposition of a yard tax in the Protectorate. Forster was also invited in November 1895 to give his views on a recent disturbance in Bathurst against the Frontier Police.[9] When Forster was made a justice of the peace in 1884, one Bathurst correspondent of the *African Times* had complained that Forster was too willing to support any and every government measure, whatever the public interest.[10] But his actions both in the Legislative Council and outside it showed that this was unfair. His stance was in fact not dissimilar to that of Sir Samuel Lewis in Sierra Leone, the most famous African legislative councilor of the day. Lewis believed that unofficial members should give the government "frank support" whenever they could honestly do so, but should reserve "the right to criticize government policy whenever they considered it necessary."[11] Like Lewis, Forster was quick to denounce unnecessary expenditure, particularly on the salaries of officials; in 1894, he even opposed a proposed salary increase for Llewelyn, an action an official deemed tantamount to a vote of censure in the administrator.[12]

Forster was also ready to defend the commercial interests of the merchants to the hilt. For example, in 1894, both unofficials declared their opposition to the proposed establishment of a government wharf in Bathurst; they expressed irritation that the mercantile community had not been consulted in advance of the purchase of the site and argued that the expenditure on it had been exorbitant. Similarly, they objected to the Customs Tariff Ordinance of 1896 and, after Forster had received a petition from the leading African and European merchants against the bill, opposed its reenactment in 1898.[13] Finally, according to Grey-Johnson, Forster used his position as the interim editor of a newly established (but short-lived) Gambian newspaper, *The Gambia Intelligencer*, to criticize the Gambian government, particularly with regard to its actions in the Protectorate.[14]

1895 and 1900 Legislative Council "Elections"

It appears that Forster was an effective spokesman for the merchants. Whether he was also considered an effective representative of Liberated African interests is harder to ascertain.[15] The only clues to his standing in the African community were provided by two indirect elections to the Legislative Council in 1895 and 1900.

In March 1895, the secretary of state for the colonies, Lord Ripon, issued a circular dispatch to the governors of the four West African territories in which he stated that unofficial members should henceforth be appointed for renewable five-year terms. Unofficial members had previously only been appointed for fixed terms in Lagos Colony (since 1886).[16] The Sierra Leone Executive Council decided that the existing African unofficial members, Samuel (soon to be Sir Samuel) Lewis and Theophilus Bishop should be retained.[17]

The response of the Gambian Executive Council was mixed. The nominated "unofficial" member, James Topp, argued that an election should be held to choose the unofficial members of the Legislative Council, but Llewelyn and his officials considered this too radical a solution. Instead, Llewelyn invited the special jurors, magistrates, and "professional men" of the colony confidentially to nominate three candidates for the council; they were given only a day to respond. In total, ninety-one confidential circulars were issued, with sixty-nine being returned. Goddard and Richards each gained forty-nine votes to head the poll; Forster and Edmund Thomas, an Aku merchant originally from Sierra Leone, who had been resident in Bathurst since the early 1870s, each received thirty-four votes. No one else gained more than eight votes. It is probably reasonable to assume that Goddard's candidature was endorsed by most European (and probably some African) merchants. Moreover, the fact that Richards polled more votes than Forster no doubt indicated that the Liberated African community was somewhat dissatisfied with Forster's performance as a councilor.[18]

The outcome of the consultative exercise was embarrassing for Llewelyn who, like his predecessor, had a low opinion of Richards regarding him as "bumptious" and "conceited" and of being "extremely suspicious even for a native of every act of the Government." In 1892, Llewelyn refused to increase the executive powers of the Board of Health (established in 1887) because he feared that Richards could use these powers to strengthen his authority within the African community.[19] Similarly, he had no desire to have a "troublesome member" on the Legislative Council. Consequently, he ignored the outcome of the "election" and persuaded the secretary of state that Goddard (whom he considered "immeasurably the most intelligent man here") and Forster (whom he termed "agreeable . . . with no extreme views or fads") should be reappointed for further five-year terms, a decision that took effect in November 1895. There seems to have been no public protest against the exclusion of Richards, perhaps because not even the Executive Council was informed that he had received more support than Forster.[20] Soon afterward, in April 1896, Topp (whom Llewelyn no longer trusted) ceased to be the "unofficial" member of the Executive Council; he was not replaced and it appears from the minutes that neither Forster nor Goddard were subsequently invited to attend the Executive Council as "extraordinary" members.[21]

In November 1900, Forster and Goddard's terms of service expired. Acting Administrator H. M. Brandford Griffith decided to follow the precedent set by Llewelyn in 1895 and issued fifty-seven circulars to the leading members of the community, with each person being asked to put forward three nominations. Fifty ballots were returned and Goddard again headed the poll, this time with forty-two votes. Richards gained thirty-three votes, Forster thirty-two, and Thomas sixteen; Zachariah T. Gibson, a solicitor originally from Freetown, received six votes. Nine others received four nominations or fewer. Goddard was duly returned to the council, but despite once again outpolling Forster, Richards was passed over. Griffith described Forster as "much more useful than Mr. Richards would be" (albeit not very active); in contrast, he considered Richards to be "faddy" and "a stumbling block" who was likely to oppose all measures introduced by the government, without being able to suggest any practical alternatives.[22]

It also appears that on this occasion (and perhaps also in 1895), Richards' prospects were harmed by his connections with Freetown. In the 1890s, there was growing prejudice against Creoles in West Africa, particularly in the Gold Coast. In one celebrated case, Dr. J. F. Easmon, the chief medical officer of the Gold Coast, was subjected to sustained criticism by the local African population for being a Sierra Leonean and, indirectly, this led to his dismissal in 1897. Sierra Leoneans were also excluded from the Gold Coast Legislative Council as a matter of policy. Before his appointment as treasurer of Gambia in 1894, Griffith, who was the son of a former governor of the Gold Coast, Sir William Brandford Griffith, had spent most of his career in the Gold Coast and it is likely that he shared the anti-Creole prejudice of many Gold Coast officials. It is therefore significant that even though he had spent most of his childhood and all his adult life in Bathurst, Richards was described as more or less representing the "Sierra Leonean portion of the community in Bathurst" by Griffith because of his commercial and family connections with Freetown. In contrast, despite being of Ibo descent, Forster was considered to represent the "Gambian portion" of the local community.[23] Whether either man would have approved of their categorization is not known, although it should be noted that Forster had signed the 1871 petition that criticized the influx of Sierra Leoneans into Bathurst, but Richards had apparently refused to do so.[24]

Unchallenged Forster Dominance: 1900–20

Despite increasing infirmity, Forster was reappointed to the council by Governor Sir George Denton in November 1905. The local community was not consulted in advance, nor was it to be again over subsequent appointments until the 1920s. Forster did not complete his term; in June 1906, he left Bathurst for the Canary Islands to try to recover his health, but died at Las Palmas that October. On Forster's departure from Gambia, Denton invited Samuel Horton Jones, an Anglican merchant originally from Sierra Leone who had lived in Bathurst since 1874, to represent African commercial interests (an indication that Denton did not share the anti-Creole prejudice of Griffith). Forster's old rival, J. D. Richards, was not considered for the position, having retired from business in 1900; he remained a leading member of the Aku community until his death in November 1917.[25] A month after Jones' selection, Denton appointed Forster's second son (also Samuel John) on a provisional basis. This appointment, which was formally confirmed in March 1907, marked the beginning of the longest unbroken spell of an African on any colonial Legislative Council; the second Forster served for thirty-three years, until his death in July 1940.[26]

Legislative Council Politics: 1900–20

Samuel Forster, the younger, was born in June 1873. He was educated at the Wesleyan Boys' High School (WBHS) in Bathurst and the C. M. S. Grammar School in Freetown, before traveling to Rhyl in North Wales in 1889 to attend Epworth College. It was at this time highly unusual for Gambians (unlike Sierra Leoneans) to be educated in Britain and this clearly demonstrated the wealth of the Forster family. He then attended the Liverpool Institute before going up to Merton College, Oxford, in 1893, to read law. He graduated in 1896 and two years later became the first Gambian (excluding the Bathurst-born resident of Lagos, J. E. Shyngle) to qualify as a barrister at the Inner Temple. He returned to

Bathurst in 1899 to practice both as a barrister and a solicitor, and in March 1901, his talents (and family background) were recognized by his appointment as acting colonial registrar and public prosecutor. Governor Denton was very satisfied by his performance although, because Forster was an African native of Bathurst and "much mixed up in the internal politics of the place," he would not recommend his substantive appointment as colonial registrar. Nevertheless, in the circumstances, it was no surprise when Denton appointed him to the Legislative Council for a five-year term in succession to his father.[27]

During his first term of service, Forster adopted a low-key approach, although (like his father before him) he was sometimes critical of government expenditure plans.[28] Perhaps inevitably he was reappointed to the council in March 1912 by Governor Sir Henry Galway, who had only been in Bathurst a few months and claimed to be in no position to make any other recommendation. Besides, Galway had been informed that Forster was "the leading member of the native community of Bathurst" and that no one else could take his place.[29] Soon after his reappointment, Forster demonstrated his independence of government by attacking certain clauses of the Rates and Public Health Ordinances. The Rates Ordinance (which amended an earlier ordinance of 1891) imposed a 5 percent rate on every lot valued at £5 or over; Forster called for the retention of the previous 3 percent rate and the continuation of the system whereby lots valued at less than £5 were excluded. He was supported by the two European unofficial members of the council, but the official majority was invoked to ensure the bill's safe passage at the cost of only a minor concession. The official majority was also used to defeat opposition led by Forster to the Public Health Ordinance.[30]

Forster's willingness to support popular grievances (albeit unsuccessfully) was doubtless appreciated by Bathurst's African population and his prestige was further strengthened when he founded the Reform Club for "upper-level elite" (patrician) Aku in 1911. Forster became the first president of the club, a position he was to hold for virtually the rest of his life. It is probable that the Committee of Gentlemen, an informal organization established around this time (and certainly by 1917) over which Forster also presided, was made up of Reform Club members.[31]

S. H. Jones was reappointed to the Legislative Council in 1911, but was not active in the opposition to the two ordinances. This may have been because his health was poor and at the end of his second term in May 1916, he left the council. He was succeeded in the following November by another Sierra Leonean, Dr. Thomas Bishop, who had been in medical practice in Bathurst since 1904 and had been active in public affairs.[32] Even though the secretary of state had previously stated that an unofficial member should serve three terms only in cases of necessity, Forster was reappointed by Galway's successor, Sir Edward Cameron, in March 1917.[33] His predominance seemed assured for the foreseeable future, but by 1920 his position was under threat from a new quarter. The challenge was posed by E. F. Small, who was to become not only Forster's most dogged opponent, but also Gambia's most famous proto-nationalist. His background is now considered.

E. F. Small and the Congress Movement: 1920–28

Small's Entrance into Politics

Edward Francis Small was born in Bathurst, probably in January 1890.[34] His father, John W. Small, was an Aku tailor, who had perhaps inherited the family business from his father (a Sierra Leonean) in the 1870s. J. W. Small built up a successful enterprise; by the mid-1880s, he was doing sufficiently well to advertise as a "general tailor and outfitter" in the *Bathurst Observer* and by the early 1900s, he was considered one of the leading artisans of Bathurst. He was also by now a prominent lay member of the Methodist Church in Bathurst.[35] However, E. F. Small's mother was not Ellen Small (J. W. Small's wife), but Annie Eliza Thomas, a Jola, who apparently worked as a "basket woman" (petty trader) in the town. Thus, he was illegitimate.[36]

After initial education at the Wesleyan Day School in Bathurst, E. F. Small, who was thought to be of above-average intelligence, received a government scholarship, thus enabling him to attend the WBHS in Freetown for two years. But unlike the younger Forster, for example, he was unable to go on to higher education and instead started work in Freetown in 1910. Possibly because his father had died, he returned to Bathurst in January 1912 to work as a cost clerk in the Public Works Department (PWD). But that October, he resigned from government service after an application for promotion was refused. He then worked until 1915 for the French firm, Maurel et Prom, before resigning and accepting a substantial cut in salary to become a teacher at the WBHS in Bathurst.[37] It was around this time that he decided to enter the church. It is clear that his talents were already widely recognized, for the leading lay members of the Wesleyan Church (including Forster) offered in January 1916 to raise the money to enable him to train for holy orders.[38] The Rev. P. S. Toye, the European chairman of the Wesleyan mission, was also impressed by Small's abilities and agreed that he should be appointed as a mission agent on a probationary basis. He was therefore sent to a Methodist mission station at Ballanghar in MacCarthy Island Province.[39]

Unfortunately for Small, early in 1918, he became involved in an acrimonious dispute with James Walker, a European trader based in the town. The incident was initially a trivial one. Small ordered the bell of the mission chapel at Ballanghar to be tolled to herald the Watchnight service on New Year's Eve; this disturbed Walker's sleep and the two men eventually came to blows. However, it became more serious when Small subsequently denounced the province's (European) commissioner, J. L. McCallum, who sided with Walker. McCallum thereupon insisted on Small's removal from the town and when his stance was upheld by both the administration in Bathurst and the Wesleyan authorities, Small was withdrawn from Ballanghar and sent to another mission station at Sukuta in the Kombo. All might have been well if Small had apologized but, resentful of the treatment he had received, he attacked the clerical authorities and was eventually dismissed from mission employment. This ended his hopes of a career in the church, and his overt criticism of government officials meant that he could not expect to regain a position in the civil service. Small's conduct was also condemned by the leading African lay and clerical members of the Methodist Church, including Forster, a fact that Small may never have forgiven.[40]

Small then found employment at Kaur, a trading depot on the River Gambia, as a trader for one of his previous employers, Maurel et Prom. But he was discontented and in early 1919, founded the Gambia Native Defensive Union (GNDU) at Kaur to expose "blatant flaws in the administration of the Central Government."[41] Small became its secretary; among its other known members were Benjamin J. George, a former clerk in the Treasury Department, who probably now worked as a commission agent; Cyril J. D. Richards, the son of the former legislative councilor, J. D. Richards; and Samuel S. Davis, who was employed as a trader by the Bathurst Trading Company. It is probable that other members of the GNDU included the ill-fated Ebenezer MacCarthy (another trader at Kaur) and Henry M. Jones, the son of the former councilor, Samuel Horton Jones, who was now running the family business on his father's behalf. The GNDU members were thus mainly educated Aku from Bathurst who were involved in commerce; most were probably in their late twenties or early thirties. Moreover, Small was not the only one nursing a grievance; George, for example, had recently been dismissed from government service for refusing to work in the Protectorate. Indeed, it may have been his sacking that provided the catalyst for the establishment of the GNDU.[42]

This connection between an individual's alleged mistreatment by the colonial authorities and subsequent political radicalism was far from uncommon in West Africa. For example, the "father of Nigerian nationalism," Herbert Macaulay, resigned from government service in Lagos in 1892 over what he considered to be racial injustice, and Thomas Hutton-Mills, the first president of the National Congress of British West Africa (NCBWA), was dismissed as a government clerk in the Gold Coast in 1886. Another early leader of the NCBWA, the Nigerian doctor and journalist, Dr. R. A. Savage, was radicalized by the loss of his position as medical officer to the Cape Coast Castle when the post came under the control of the Gold Coast government in 1913.[43]

Establishment of Gambia Section

The GNDU would, in all probability, have remained in obscurity had it not been for developments elsewhere in British West Africa. In 1914, Savage and the prominent Gold Coast lawyer and journalist, J. E. Casely-Hayford, invited some of the leading figures in Accra, Freetown, and Lagos to consider the desirability of holding a conference of educated West Africans. No contact seems to have been made either with Forster or with anyone else in Bathurst.[44] The scheme was put on ice at the outbreak of World War I, but was revived in 1917 and by the end of 1918, preparations had reached an advanced stage, particularly in Freetown and

Accra. Because the conference organizers deemed it essential that all four colonies be represented, Casely-Hayford and Professor Orishatukeh Faduma, a leading member of the Sierra Leone conference committee, asked Isaac J. Roberts, an Aku solicitor in Bathurst, in late 1918 to drum up support. Roberts did little about it, but when Small heard about the proposed conference, he converted the GNDU into its Gambia committee in October 1919. He also launched an appeal so that a Gambian delegation could be sent. More than £100 was raised, which was sufficient to enable one Gambian to attend. Forster provided the largest contribution of ten guineas and Small, as secretary of the conference committee, was the obvious delegate. He therefore resigned from his job and traveled to Accra where the conference took place in March 1920.[45]

The most important of the eighty-three resolutions adopted at Accra called for the concession of the franchise. It was resolved that half the seats on Legislative Councils should be reserved for Africans. Moreover, these should be directly elected by the people and no longer nominated by colonial governors. The conference also resolved itself into a permanent NCBWA to be composed of the committees that had already been established in the four colonies. Consequently, on his return to Bathurst in May 1920, Small converted the conference committee into the Congress' Gambia Section.[46] Most members of the branch were Aku and Christians, although a handful were Wolof and/or Muslims. They were mainly drawn from the "lower-level" elite, being employed as clerks, artisans, or traders by mercantile firms. A few civil servants attended meetings, but were probably put under pressure not to do so and stronger sanctions may have been taken against active members.[47] As far as can be ascertained, the branch's entire membership was drawn from Bathurst and, like the other Congress committees, had only tenuous links with the Protectorate. Indeed, just as a section of the Gold Coast chiefs led by Nana Ofori Atta I supported the rival Aborigines' Rights Protection Society (ARPS) in opposition to the Congress, so Gambian Protectorate chiefs apparently repudiated any connection with the Bathurst branch in January 1921.[48]

At first the Gambia Section was directed by two separate bodies, a "Working Committee," which was dominated by Small (the overall branch secretary) and other former GNDU activists, such as George and Cyril Richards, and a "General Committee," which Forster chaired. The General Committee almost certainly included other members of the patrician elite, such as the former unofficial member of the Legislative Council, Thomas Bishop, M. J. R. Pratt (a barrister from Sierra Leone) and the Aku merchant, Edmund Thomas (one of the unsuccessful candidates in the 1895 and 1900 Legislative Council "elections"). The two committees were soon at odds over both the tactics and the policies which the branch adopted. The inevitable conflict between the two factions was precipitated when Small called a "mass" (public) meeting in the town to endorse the resolutions of the Accra Conference without consulting Forster. This alarmed the latter who feared a more "populist" approach to politics might threaten the control he had hitherto exercised over community affairs. Forster was also concerned about the implications of the main Accra resolution, the demand for the franchise; he seems to have feared that in any election in Bathurst, the minority Christian community would be swamped by the majority Muslim population.[49]

Because it appeared that he could not control the Congress from within, Forster decided to resign from the branch and attack it from without. He remained a staunch opponent of the Congress thereafter. Bishop also resigned and so, in all probability, did Pratt and many other patricians.[50] This lowered the Congress' prestige and removed many of its wealthiest supporters; moreover, it meant that the Gambian government, which had initially recognized that the Congress contained most of the leading figures of Bathurst society, quickly turned against it. The Gambian branch was not alone in being opposed by an influential conservative elite. The Lagos Committee was opposed by the Reform Club, whose members (led by a barrister, Sir Kitoyi Ajasa) were "drawn from the well-to-do and intellectual middle-class crust of Lagos." The Gold Coast patrician elite tended to support the Congress, although not exclusively so; a section of it favored the ARPS. In contrast, with few exceptions, the Sierra Leonean elite strongly supported the Congress and these exceptions stayed aloof, rather than actively opposing it.[51]

In the longer term, the defection of Forster and his colleagues proved very damaging to the Congress, but its immediate effect was to strengthen the hand of Small and his more radical colleagues. Consequently, in July 1920, Small and Henry Jones were selected at a meeting of the branch's Executive Committee (which replaced the earlier General and Working Committees) to represent Gambia as part of a Congress delegation to London. This choice was then apparently "unanimously agreed" at a mass meeting and the two delegates traveled to London in August.[52] Small did not return to Bathurst until early 1922, but in the meantime the branch was apparently controlled by his associates.[53] Moreover, despite the loss of the patrician elite, the branch's finances remained healthy and it was claimed in July 1920 that it had cash funds of £580. One-third of this sum was provided by the solicitor, I. J. Roberts (who remained loyal to the Congress despite his high social status); another third was raised from the Muslim community of Bathurst; the Christian community provided only £80.[54]

Given the dominance of the branch's leadership by Christians, the extent of the support of the Muslim community at this time may seem surprising. In fact, as constituted in June 1920, the branch did include a few prominent Muslim members, among them three traders, Ousman N'Jie, the son of Gormack N'Jie, a former Almami (Imam) of Bathurst; Saloum N'Jai; and Ousman Jeng. Omar B. Jallow, the secretary of the Almami's Advisory Committee in the early 1920s, and Omar Sowe (a future Almami) were probably also supporters.[55] The Congress also attracted the tacit support of the Muslim spiritual hierarchy, headed by the aged Almami of Bathurst, Momadu N'Jai, who personally contributed £10 toward the cost of sending Small and Jones to England in 1920. Although the Almami was apparently regretting his generosity by 1921, he nevertheless sent three of his leading advisers to attend a Congress meeting in June 1921 as his official representatives.[56]

The most important of these early Muslim supporters for the Congress was Ousman Jeng, who was to become the first prominent Muslim politician in Gambia. Jeng was born in Bathurst in 1881. He was a Wolof and probably also a Tijani (a member of one of the three main Muslim Sufi brotherhoods in West Africa). It is likely that he was among the minority of Muslims who were educated in the mission schools in Bathurst in the late nineteenth and early twentieth centuries; he was said to be able to speak and write English fluently. By 1920, he was working as a trader for S. H. Jones at Salikene in the Baddibu district of the North Bank.[57] Although initially not on the Executive Committee of the Gambia Section, he apparently served as branch treasurer for a short period between 1920 and 1922.[58]

1922 Legislative Council "Election"

Despite the defection of Forster, the position of the Gambia Section appeared promising at the beginning of 1921. By the end of 1922, matters were very different. First, Governor Captain C. H. (later Sir Cecil) Armitage reappointed S. J. Forster to the council for a fourth term in March 1922, even though his predecessor, Sir Edward Cameron, who was apparently angered by Forster's failure to attend the official Peace Celebrations to mark the end of World War I, had given him to understand that he could not expect further nomination. But Armitage considered him the only articulate and useful unofficial member of the council. He also described him as the "most enlightened native member of the community," presumably because of his steadfast opposition to the Congress, and was therefore unwilling to lose his services.[59]

Second, and perhaps more importantly, Bathurst's Muslims in large part turned against the Congress following the appointment of Ousman Jeng as the first Muslim member of the Legislative Council in March 1922. The catalyst for this important moment in Gambian politics was the appointment of Armitage as governor in December 1920. Armitage had been chief commissioner of the Northern Territories of the Gold Coast where he was known as a strong advocate of chiefly institutions.[60] He was determined to bolster chieftaincy in Gambia and decided that when Bishop's term on the Legislative Council expired in November 1921, he should be replaced by a Muslim Chief. However, unlike in the Gold Coast, where chiefs had been represented on the Legislative Council since 1916, or Nigeria, where they served on the Nigerian Council, there was no Gambian chief with sufficient education to be able to participate effectively.[61] Consequently, Armitage decided to appoint a member of Bathurst's Muslim community, but to consult with the chiefs prior to making his choice; this would therefore comprise a rare example of the Protectorate participating in the political process.

By November 1921, the governor's plans had become public knowledge and two rival candidates had emerged. One was Jeng, whose cause was championed by Momadu N'Jai, the current Almami of Bathurst; a "Committee of Bathurst Muslims" led by Yerim N'Dure, the president of the Almami's Advisory

Committee; and the future Almami, Omar Sowe (Jeng's father-in-law), who was also a member of this Advisory Committee.[62] The other candidate was Sheikh Omar Fye, who played a key role in Gambian politics until the late 1940s. Fye was born in Bathurst in 1889 and was therefore younger than his rival. He was a Wolof and a Tijani; like Jeng, he was able to speak and write English as well as Arabic, having presumably been educated at a mission school. He was also engaged in trade, being employed as a dealer (possibly by the Bathurst Trading Company) at Njawara in the Baddibu area of the Protectorate.[63] His supporters in the contest included two other members of the Advisory Committee, Cherno Jagne and Ebriema Bobb, as well as two prominent artisans in government employment, Harley N'Jie, the head carpenter in the PWD, and N'Jagga Cham, the head black-smith in the PWD.[64]

Fye based his claim to a seat on the Council on the fact that his father, Ebriema (a shopkeeper), was a leading member of the Muslim community in Bathurst. Ebriema Fye had been invited (along with Almami Momadu N'Jai) to attend the Legislative Council as an "extraordinary" member in July 1905 to discuss the Mohammedan Law Ordinance. He had also been appointed one of the trustees of the Mohammedan School established in 1903, a position he retained until his death in 1925.[65] Unfortunately for Fye, this advantage was more than outweighed by the fact that, as Jeng's supporters pointed out, the Fyes were griots, a low status social caste within traditional African society.[66] Consequently, when Armitage toured the Protectorate in February 1922 to ascertain the views of the chiefs, the latter either openly declared for Jeng or stated that they would be content to leave the choice to the governor; none apparently supported Fye's candidacy. Armitage (who was presumably aware that Samuel Forster strongly supported Jeng) then convened a meeting of Bathurst's Muslims in March and asked any objectors to Jeng's appointment to state their reasons; when there was no response, he announced that he would select Jeng, a decision that he claimed "was received with the greatest enthusiasm."[67]

Immediately after his appointment to the council was confirmed, Jeng con-vened another public meeting of Bathurst's Muslims at which, he claimed, it was unanimously agreed that the community would have no further dealings with the Gambia Section. Although this was an exaggeration, a number of other former Congress supporters, including Omar Sowe, Omar Jallow, and Ousman N'Jie, also turned against the branch around this time.[68] Jeng's tactics were shrewd, not only because they enabled him to capitalize on growing Muslim disillusion with the Congress, but because they also improved his standing with the Gambian govern-ment. Armitage made his opposition to the Congress, in general, and its local branch, in particular, abundantly clear on his arrival in Gambia. In his inaugural address to the Legislative Council in January 1921, he denounced the "monstrous institution" of the Congress and ridiculed the "absurd and pretentious" claims of its "self-appointed" leadership to represent public opinion.[69] Within a few months, Armitage's hostility to the Congress increased considerably. He disapproved of the personal conduct of various Congress leaders, including Henry Jones, the second

Gambian delegate to London, and strongly resented any criticism that they made of his policies.[70] Not surprisingly, therefore, he welcomed Jeng's defection from the local branch. Meanwhile, after his defeat in the 1922 "election," the disappointed Sheikh Omar Fye, who had hitherto stayed aloof, temporarily threw in his lot with the Congress and even attempted unsuccessfully to persuade the new Almami, Wakka Bah (who succeeded Momadu N'Jai in August 1922) to give it his support.[71]

Decline of Gambia Section: 1922–28

The appointment of Jeng, the reappointment of Forster, and the refusal of the new Almami to endorse the Congress were all setbacks for the movement. Given the hostility of the Christian patrician elite and the reduced support from the Muslim Wolof community, the government's jibe that the Congress represented only the unrepresentative "Sierra Leonean" element of Bathurst society had some justification.[72] The current weakness of the branch may have been one reason why E. F. Small (who returned from England in early 1922) resigned as its secretary and left Gambia later that year to live in Rufisque, where he remained for up to a year. Situated about twelve miles east of Dakar, Rufisque was one of the Quatre Communes, which enjoyed significant constitutional privileges, particularly the right, with the three other communes, to elect a deputy to the French Chamber of Deputies.[73] It was during this period that Small produced the first edition of *The Gambia Outlook and Senegambian Reporter*, the first Gambian newspaper to be produced for twenty-six years, which was published in Dakar in May 1922.[74] Much to the irritation of Governor Armitage, he continued to take a keen interest in Gambian affairs and to criticize government policies. His activities also caused the British consul-general in Dakar "a great deal of bother."[75]

It is likely that while resident in Rufisque, Small made contact with a group of Sierra Leone Creoles (or other West Africans of Creole descent) who established a branch of Marcus Garvey's Universal Negro Improvement Association (UNIA) in the town in 1922; the leader of the group, Wilfred A. Wilson, and three others were deported from Senegal in July 1922, but other members of the small branch remained.[76] Small may have stayed in contact with at least one member of the UNIA group in Rufisque, whom he met again in 1930.[77] But he was never an active supporter of the movement. There is no evidence that he ever made direct contact with Garvey, or openly espoused his radical political program. His response to Garveyism may have been similar to that of a number of Congress leaders elsewhere in West Africa, who were reluctant to yield control of African political advancement to non-West African Negroes. Indeed, it may well have been because of Small's failure to associate himself with it that no UNIA branch was ever established in Bathurst.[78]

By July 1923, Small moved on again, this time to London.[79] Relatively little is known of his activities over the next few years. He did try (albeit with little success) to relaunch his newspaper and he also made a vain attempt to interest both

Governor Armitage and former Governor Galway in a scheme to build a railway in the colony. He also ran up debts. Indeed, it may have been because he was short of money (and/or to escape his creditors) that he returned to Bathurst in late 1926.[80] Meanwhile, in his absence, the leadership of the Congress branch had passed first to B. J. George and then to another Aku Methodist, John A. Mahoney. The son of the late J. E. Mahoney, a leading Gambian merchant before World War I, J. A. Mahoney was a former government clerk who had risen to the post of chief clerk of the French firm, Maurel et Prom. Moreover, his wife, Hannah, was one of Small's half sisters and Governor Armitage believed that the latter in fact continued to direct the affairs of the branch from England.[81]

Since its foundation in 1920, the principal aim of the Congress had been to secure the franchise and there was a breakthrough in 1922 when the elective principle was formally conceded (on a limited basis) in Nigeria and Sierra Leone, and a few years later in the Gold Coast.[82] These reforms spurred the Gambian branch into action and in July 1923, a petition calling for direct elections to the Legislative Council was presented to Governor Armitage. Given his past opposition to the Congress, it was not surprising that Armitage rejected the petition out of hand. He did so on the grounds that the Congress was quite unrepresentative even of the people of the Colony (let alone of the Protectorate) and that, in any case, sufficient representation was provided by Forster, Jeng, and the Chamber of Commerce member, William Yare. In an echo of the anti-Creole attitudes shown by Acting Governor Griffith in 1900, Armitage also considered it "absurd" that some of the petitioners had either been born in Sierra Leone, or in Bathurst of Sierra Leonean parentage.

The Congress leaders disputed the validity of these arguments; they argued, with some justification, that the selection of Jeng "did not carry the essentials of fair electioneering" and suggested that it was unfair to allow Muslims to elect their own representative, while the "indisputably more competent" Christian community had to be content with nomination. They also pointed out that Forster was of Ibo descent and Bishop was a Sierra Leonean. But their complaints were simply ignored by the government.[83] Consequently, in May 1924, Mahoney drew up a fresh petition, which this time was sent directly to J. H. Thomas, the secretary of state for the colonies in the first Labour government. Thomas was not unsympathetic, but was reluctant to go against the strongly expressed views of Armitage, even though these were at odds with the opinions of Governors Clifford (Nigeria), Slater (Sierra Leone), and Guggisberg (Gold Coast), all of whom were prepared to accept the franchise. In any case, Thomas allowed himself to be persuaded by his officials that the Colony and Protectorate could not easily be separated in any constitutional arrangement. Because there were very few (if any) chiefs who possessed the standard of education to be able to sit on the council, he stated that he would make no further concessions to Bathurst aspirations.[84]

The rejection of its petition was a major setback for the Gambian branch. It was due to host the Third Session of the NCBWA in May 1925, but following the rejection of the petition, it became so ineffective that the session had to be postponed until the following December.[85] In the meantime, the branch attempted to revive its popularity by pursuing a number of local grievances. In 1924, it tried to persuade Governor Armitage to reduce the rates in the poorer areas in the town, which suffered from flooding. Unlike in 1912–13, its appeal was not supported by Forster (a sign, perhaps, of his growing conservatism) and Governor Armitage was less sympathetic than Galway had been a decade before.[86] It also petitioned the secretary of state to restore the jury system in criminal cases in 1924 and campaigned against the unpopular Licensing Bill in 1924–25. This issue was of concern to Wolof as well as to Aku and even Omar Sowe (who had succeeded Wakka Bah as Almami in 1923) was prepared to sign the petition. But once again the branch's efforts were in vain.[87]

Despite these earlier setbacks, the Congress Session of 1925–26 proved to be a success. The most important development (at least in the view of the Gambian hosts) occurred when Governor Armitage informed a Congress deputation led by J. E. Casely-Hayford that when Forster's term of office on the Legislative Council expired in March 1927, he would recommend to the Colonial Office that "the African member of the Legislative Council" be elected rather than nominated as hitherto. The Gambia would therefore gain the franchise.[88]

In view of his previous hostility to the Gambia Section, Armitage's decision appears surprising. By 1926, however, he had come to believe that the local Congress branch, which was now under the leadership of the elderly solicitor, I. J. Roberts (who, as noted, was originally asked to promote the Congress in Bathurst in 1918), was a far more moderate organization than hitherto. Moreover, Armitage insisted that candidates must meet strict qualifications with only those who were "native of the Gambia" being eligible. It is not certain what Armitage meant by this; if the only qualification for candidates was to have been born in Gambia, then most leading members of the Gambia Section would have been eligible to stand. If, however, Armitage envisaged the exclusion of all those with close family links with Sierra Leone, then many local Congress leaders (including Small and Henry Jones) would have been barred. In any case, as an additional safeguard, Armitage resolved that Forster should not lose his seat, but rather should be retained on the council for life; the elected member would be an additional member, thereby increasing the number of unofficial representatives to four (the same number as in 1912). This would still leave an official majority of one.[89]

Unfortunately for the Congress, the Colonial Office rejected Armitage's recommendation. In part, this was because of developments elsewhere in West Africa, which had made Colonial Office officials reluctant to introduce further constitutional reforms in the region. Earlier in 1926, a major railway strike in Freetown had been strongly supported by the Freetown elite, including the elected African members of the Sierra Leone Legislative Council, H. C. Bankole-Bright and E. S. Beoku-Betts. This so incensed the Sierra Leonean government that some had called for the suspension of the 1924 constitution.[90] Consequently, there was no desire to create further problems by drawing up a constitution for Gambia.

Meanwhile, in February 1926, a new political organization, the Gambia Representative Committee (GRC), had been established, with John A. N'Jai-Gomez, a retired civil servant of mixed Wolof and Manjago origin, as its secretary. According to N'Jai-Gomez's later account, this followed a mass meeting in Bathurst, which took place shortly before a visit to the colony by the under-secretary of state, W. G. A. Ormsby-Gore. The meeting endorsed a list of issues to be presented to Ormsby-Gore by a delegation led by Forster, whom Ormsby-Gore subsequently termed "the outstanding personality in Bathurst." The issues raised ranged from the need for legal reforms, including the abolition of trial by assessors, to a call for improved roads and the establishment of schools in the main Protectorate districts. However, significantly, the delegation made no demands for the franchise and thus the GRC can be regarded as a more politically conservative organization than the NCBWA.[91]

In these circumstances, it was inevitable that the secretary of state for the colonies should reject Armitage's suggestion. Instead, Governor Sir John Middleton, who had only recently arrived in Bathurst and was therefore dependent on the advice of his colonial secretary, C. R. M. Workman (a longstanding critic of the Congress), reappointed both Forster and Jeng in 1927 without any prior consultation with either the Christian or the Muslim communities.[92]

The failure to secure the franchise in 1927 was a bitter blow for the Congress, which functioned only intermittently thereafter and apparently ceased to exist after the end of 1928.[93] But, as demonstrated in the next section, Forster and Jeng were by no means safe from attack. Opposition to both men began to build up in 1929 and although Forster ultimately survived the challenge, Jeng was to lose his place on the council in 1932 due to factionalism within the Muslim community.

The Revival of an Anti-Forster Party: 1929–41

Intra-Muslim Conflict and the Fall of Ousman Jeng: 1929–32

During his first term on the Legislative Council, Ousman Jeng managed to consolidate his hold over Bathurst's Muslim population, but in so doing he created many enemies. The most important of these was a group of Muslim "elders" led by Momodu Jahumpa, an aged former shipwright who was now an owner of four river cutters. Jahumpa and the other elders had been influential in the Muslim community since the early years of the century and Jahumpa himself had been one of the original trustees of the Mohammedan School.[94] The Juma Society, the society of the elders, also claimed to have nominated all successive Almamis since the 1880s and to have played the decisive role in securing Jeng's appointment to the Legislative Council in 1922.[95]

Jahumpa and his allies had no doubt expected to retain their influence after Jeng's appointment. It had therefore come as an unpleasant surprise when Jeng "aspired to set himself up as a dictator," presumably by ignoring the Almami's

Advisory Committee (on which the elders were strongly represented). The disgruntled elders intended (or so they later claimed) to oppose Jeng's renomination to the Legislative Council in 1927 in favor of Sheikh Omar Fye, but were given no opportunity to express their opinion. A year later, however, their chance for revenge arose when Jeng (who already had three wives) had a child by an adulterous relationship with a fourth woman. This, according to Jahumpa, constituted a "capital offence" under Islamic law and rendered Jeng unfit to serve on the Legislative Council. Jahumpa also insisted that Jeng's father-in-law, Omar Sowe, be "disqualified from being a Muslim leader in any capacity" for condoning Jeng's action by permitting him to marry the woman after the baby was born.[96] When neither Jeng nor Sowe resigned from their respective positions, the Jahumpa party—perhaps with the covert encouragement of Fye—sought an injunction to prevent Sowe from officiating in the mosque. This did not succeed; in March 1929, Judge Aitken ruled that the Supreme Court had no power to intervene in a religious dispute.[97]

After much further public argument, both parties finally agreed to the appointment of Muslim arbitrators to settle the dispute in October 1929. But when the arbitrators proceeded to dismiss the charges against the Almami, Jahumpa refused to accept the verdict and the conflict within the community continued unabated.[98] The battleground now shifted from the mosque to the Mohammedan School; both factions sought control over its Managing Committee. Momodu Jahumpa's claim was based on the fact that he alone of the original trustees was still alive; but his opponents (generally supported by the Gambian government) argued that this did not give him the right to control the school. Neither side would compromise and, in April 1931, Governor H. R. Palmer lost patience and imposed a three-member school Managing Committee (which included Fye) on the warring parties.[99]

The ill feeling between Jeng and Jahumpa persisted even after the appointment of a "neutral" Managing Committee. Consequently, when Jeng's second term on the Legislative Council expired in 1932, the Gambian government concluded that it would be unnecessarily provocative to reappoint him. He was replaced by Fye, who had twice previously tried to gain a place on the council, but had been deemed unsuitable. In August 1924, the Almami of Bathurst had recommended to Governor Armitage that a second Muslim be appointed to the Legislative Council (or as a justice of the peace) and that Fye should be selected. However, when Jeng was consulted, he alleged that Fye had bribed the Almami to nominate him for the post. In addition, Fye was considered an unsuitable candidate because he had been placed on the "Black List," which contained the names of traders and dealers who made losses for which they were deemed responsible by the European firms. The fact that Fye had also joined the Gambia Section probably also counted against him. In April 1928, Almami Omar Sowe had requested the new governor, John Middleton, to appoint Fye as a second Muslim member of the council, but again the request was turned down.[100] In 1932, Fye was now more acceptable to the Gambian government because he had managed in recent years to avoid identification with either of the Muslim factions. Moreover, he had severed his past links with Small and may even have privately indicated to Governor Palmer that he was now an opponent of Small and his political associates.[101]

Trade Unionism and Radical Politics: 1929–33

In the meantime, S. J. Forster, the other African member of the Legislative Council, faced difficulties of his own. As in the early 1920s, his main opponent was Small, who returned to Gambia in 1926, determined to make a name for himself. He revived his newspaper, the *Gambia Outlook*, in 1927, apparently thanks to the financial backing of a leading trader at Kaur, John M. Roberts, who had been a relatively unimportant member of the Gambia Section since 1920.[102] Early in 1929, he also established the Gambia Planters' Syndicate (initially in partnership with Sheikh Omar Faye), which sought to increase the production of groundnuts on a collective basis. It was later renamed the Gambia Farmers' Co-operative Marketing Association (GFCMA) and assumed wider aims, with Small seeking to find an overseas buyer prepared to offer a higher price for groundnuts than the members of the "Unilever Combine" cartel (which included the United Africa Company (UAC) and other mercantile houses). The GFCMA was also one of the first organizations to seek to establish direct links between the Colony and the Protectorate.[103]

Small probably also became involved in the factional conflict within the Muslim community, as an ally of Jahumpa against his old enemy, Ousman Jeng. Soon afterward, in May 1929, he helped to found the first Gambian trade union, the Bathurst Trade Union (BTU). This was a trade union for artisans, whose leaders included Jahumpa and other members of the anti-Jeng party, some of whom were former members of the Congress; a number of Small's Christian associates from the Congress days were also involved in the BTU, but Sheikh Omar Fye was not.[104]

Shortly after its founding, the BTU became involved in a dispute with the European private sector employers. The employers, meeting as the Chamber of Commerce, decided in April to reduce the wages of the artisans and sailors they employed, but when the cuts became operative in October, the union organized effective resistance. Successive groups of artisans were called out on strike in October and early November, with employers trying in vain to break the strike. By mid-November, employers were ready not only to withdraw the wage cuts and recognize the union, but also to increase wages. Before a settlement could be reached, there was a violent clash between a detachment of armed police and a group of strikers. A number of civilians were injured and the incident caused an outcry in Bathurst. Indeed, after the matter had been reported in the British press, questions were asked in the House of Commons. The day after the clash, the employers hurriedly convened a "round table conference" with the union and substantial wage increases were conceded.[105]

The successful outcome to the strike (which was almost unheard of in British West Africa between the wars) made Small a hero in Bathurst.[106] On the other hand, Forster "almost entirely lost his influence" in the town. This was because both African councilors had been instructed by Governor Sir Edward Denham to declare their opposition to the strike in public. Forster, for example, was required on the day of the clash with the police to berate an angry crowd for its folly.[107] This response did not go down well with the local population and, as indicated, was in marked contrast to the reaction of the African members of the Sierra Leone Legislative Council during the 1926 Freetown railway strike. The Bathurst strike also had far-reaching consequences for the development of trade unionism in the British colonies. It seems clear that it provided the catalyst for the Passfield Memorandum, the famous circular dispatch issued by Lord Passfield (the former Sidney Webb) to all colonial governors in September 1930, which called for "the compulsory registration of Trade Unions."[108]

The initiative therefore lay with Small, but he did not make effective use of his advantage. There were several reasons for this. First, he spent a large part of the next two years abroad, trying vainly to secure financial assistance for the BTU and the GFCMA. He left Gambia in February 1930 to travel via Dakar to Marseilles to purchase a new printing press for his newspaper; he later moved on to London to try to attract financial backing for the GFCMA. He did not return to Bathurst until mid-May and then left again in mid-June, again to travel to Europe; he did not arrive home until late November.[109] Although he was generally resident in Gambia during 1931, he did stay in Senegal between June and August 1931, having earlier visited Accra in the Gold Coast.[110] During this period, he left control of the BTU in the hands of its general secretary, Thomas Collingwood Fye, but he proved a disastrous choice as lieutenant.[111]

Second, Small further alienated an already hostile Gambian government and the Colonial Office by associating with two "subversive" organizations, the League Against Imperialism (LAI) and the International Trade Union Committee of Negro Workers (ITUC-NW). The LAI was founded in 1927 as an organization dedicated to combating imperialism. It had a number of sections, including one in Britain, which was headed by its secretary, Reginald Bridgeman. During 1929, the LAI moved sharply to the left following the expulsion of one of its founder members, the leader of the Independent Labour Party, James Maxton, and the subsequent resignation of other non-Communists. Indeed, in November 1929, the Labour Party's national executive declared the LAI to be an organization "ancillary or subsidiary to the Communist Party and that it was ineligible for affiliation to the Labour Party." Some members of the LAI, including Bridgeman and Glyn Evans, were also members of the Labour Research Department (LRDept).[112] The LRDept was founded by one of the luminaries of the Labour Party (and wife of Sidney Webb), Beatrice Webb, in 1912, but was taken over by members of the British Communist Party by 1924.

Small may have first come into contact with the LRDept during his visit to London in 1920–21 (he certainly established links with the Parliamentary Labour Party (PLP) at this time) and in 1929 he revived these links by affiliating the BTU to the LRDept.[113] This proved a fortuitous development, for during the 1929 strike, both the LRDept and the LAI mobilized support in Britain for the BTU and sought to force the Colonial Office to instruct the Gambian government to make concessions to the union. It is possible, although there is no clear evidence of this, that financial assistance was also offered to Small during or after the strike. What is certain is that Small greatly appreciated the external support he received from these organizations.[114]

The LAI was also closely associated with the ITUC-NW, which was permanently established in Hamburg in 1930 through the combined efforts of the LAI and the trade union affiliate of the Comintern (the Third International)—the Profintern or Red International of Labour Unions (RILU). George Padmore, a prominent political activist originally from Trinidad, was the RILU's secretary and the editor of its journal, *The Negro Worker*.[115] The two men probably met during the first of Small's two visits to Europe in 1930; this may have been in London or in Berlin, because Small allegedly went to Germany to attend a meeting of the European Congress of Working Peasants, a Comintern-front organization.[116] At the end of April, while Small was still in England, Padmore traveled to Gambia at the start of a wider African tour under his real name, Malcolm Nurse. His aim was to recruit delegates for an International Conference of Negro Workers that the ITUC-NW was organizing in Hamburg in early July. He returned to Bathurst on June 13, at the end of his West African trip; four days later, Small himself left Gambia to travel first to Dakar and then to Europe, possibly on the same ship, the *S. S. Abinsi*.[117] Small duly made his way to Hamburg, where he delivered a fiery denunciation of "capitalist and imperialist exploitation" and made exaggerated claims of the strength of his trade union. He was subsequently elected to the ITUC-NW Executive and was appointed an associate editor of the *Negro Worker*. He may have been one of the Hamburg Conference delegates who subsequently attended the Fifth Congress of the RILU in Moscow in August 1930.[118]

Prior to 1930, the authorities saw Small as more of an irritant than a subversive threat; even as late as December 1928, Governor Denham granted him an interview in which he reported Small as praising government advertising support for the *Gambia Outlook* and providing it with correct information.[119] But Small's connections with the LAI and LRDept, as well as the fact that various articles from the *Negro Worker* were reprinted in the *Gambia Outlook* in March and April 1930, were more than sufficient to persuade the Gambian government that Small was a Communist sympathizer, if not necessarily a member of the Communist Party.[120]

Not surprisingly, Small strongly denied the charge that he had become a Communist.[121] Nevertheless, this official belief had a number of immediate repercussions. It resulted, for example, in increased harassment by government officials. His baggage was searched after his return to Gambia in November 1930 when, according to the French Consul in Bathurst, "bolshevik [*sic*] propaganda" was seized.[122] Much to his annoyance, his details were subsequently circulated to other West African governments, with the result that his brother, William A. Small (a clerk, who was apparently not involved in Small's political activities), had his baggage searched on his arrival in Freetown.[123] In October 1931, Small and Babucarr Secka, his agent in Senegal, were served with expulsion orders from the colony, albeit in Small's case, in absentia.[124] Finally, on the advice of Acting Governor Workman, the Colonial Office also ensured that the Liberian government withdrew an invitation to Small to become its honorary consul in Bathurst; Small must have greatly resented the loss of this prestigious appointment.[125]

At the same time, the colonial authorities also sought to undermine Small's various organizations. First, alarmed by no doubt exaggerated claims by Small that some 2,000 farmers had paid the one shilling membership fee to join the GFCMA, the Gambian government permitted the commissioners in the Protectorate to stir up opposition to it in 1930–31. For example, R. W. Macklin, the commissioner of MacCarthy Island Province, urged the chiefs in his area to persuade farmers not to join the association and "pointed out . . . the grave challenge to their authority should they allow outsiders to gain influence over their people." Meanwhile, the Colonial Office attempted to persuade the potential backers of the scheme in Europe to withdraw their support. Partly as a result of these efforts, the GFCMA collapsed in early 1932.[126] Second, as discussed in the next section, the Gambian government used its legislative powers to weaken Small's position; the Licensing Ordinance was designed to make it more difficult for Small to publish the *Gambia Outlook* and the Trade Union Ordinance aimed to destroy his hold over the labor movement in the colony.

The colonial authorities continued to be suspicious of Small's political beliefs until at least the mid-1930s. For example, in March 1934, Acting Governor Oke considered that Small could be regarded as a "link subversive," a term used by Sir Philip Cunliffe-Lister, the secretary of state for the colonies, to describe individuals who were thought "to spread Bolshevik propaganda in the colonies."[127] One modern commentator, Edward Wilson, who, in the 1970s, examined the Comintern's activities in Black Africa in detail, indeed argued that Small had been engaged in "revolutionary activity" in West Africa during this period. But another, J. A. Langley, considered that he was essentially "a black Edwardian, though slightly more radical in his politics."[128] In fact, a careful review of the evidence and some of its contradictions suggests that, at most, Small's flirtation with Communism was short-lived and that he was primarily interested in the practical benefits his external contacts could offer him. Small recognized the value of the support offered by the LRDept and LAI during the strike; between 1930 and 1933, he also regularly requested one or other organization to intercede with the British government on his behalf and on at least one occasion he openly solicited funds from the LRDept.[129] Another of his lieutenants, Richard S. Rendall, a retired Aku and Methodist civil servant, even tried (albeit unsuccessfully) to develop a relationship with the right-wing British Conservative Party. Assuming that Small approved of Rendall's approach, this was hardly the action of a committed Communist![130]

The hostility of the colonial authorities was not the only problem facing Small and his supporters in the early 1930s. They also faced renewed opposition from Forster and his supporters among the patrician elite; this is discussed in the next section.

The GRC and the RPA: 1930–36

In October 1930, the moribund GRC was revived. The GRC (like the earlier Committee of Gentlemen or the Reform Club of Lagos) represented the interests of the patrician elite. It was headed by the increasingly conservative Forster. Forster's services to the government, which had already been recognized by his appointment as acting police magistrate in 1928 and coroner of the Island of St. Mary in 1929, received further acknowledgement when he was awarded the OBE in 1930. He was subsequently knighted in 1933, the first Gambian to receive this honor.[131] J. A. N'Jai-Gomez remained as the GRC's general secretary and other members included Forster's Aku nephews, Henry D. Carrol (the head of the Bathurst family firm of H. R. Carrol and Co.), and his younger brother, W. Davidson Carrol. The latter, like his uncle, was a graduate of Oxford University and a barrister. He had returned to Bathurst to practice law in the mid-1920s; while in England, he was elected the first president of the West African Students Union (WASU) but, unlike some other WASU pioneers, he was in no sense a radical. These men were all Methodists, but the GRC also included prominent Muslims such as Almami Sowe and Jeng (but not Fye).[132]

The purpose of the revived organization was to ensure that Forster's allies were elected to the Bathurst Urban District Council (BUDC), which Governor Palmer was about to establish as a replacement for the now moribund Board of Health. The BUDC, which was entitled to discuss such municipal matters as roads, markets and sanitation, comprised four ex officio and four other nominated (European) members. In addition, to the irritation of the Colonial Office, Palmer abandoned his original aim to nominate Africans to the new body (African members of the old Board of Health were also nominated). Instead, he decided that each of the wards of the town (Half Die, Soldier Town, New Town, Joloff Town North, Joloff Town South, and Portuguese Town) should be permitted to elect one councilor. The franchise was to be restricted to persons on the rating list (i.e., owners rather than occupiers) and to government employees. Moreover, the ballot was to be open and the assistant colonial secretary was to oversee the election.

Governor Palmer probably calculated that, in these circumstances, government employees would vote for pro-government candidates and the position of Forster and his allies would be strengthened, and Small's influence would be reduced and calls for the franchise weakened.[133] This proved to be the case; the GRC won at least five out of six seats in the inaugural election held in January 1931. The successful candidates included the two Carrols and N'Jai-Gomez; Gabriel M. N'Jie, a retired Wolof civil servant who was their staunch ally in 1932–33; and J. Francis Senegal, a commission agent who established a short-lived newspaper, *The Gambia Public Opinion*, in 1932, which provided a "sweeping endorsement" of Forster's policies. All bar Senegal (who was replaced by another GRC man, an Aku, Noble J. Allen) were reelected to the council a year later.[134] Indeed, when the GRC persuaded Forster to postpone his planned retirement and accept another term of office on the Legislative Council in March 1932, it appeared that the patricians had regained the political ascendancy.[135] In contrast, as noted, Small's position was weakened by the collapse of the GFCMA, and a dissident faction (which Small termed the "dissenting society") led by a shipwright, Joseph Lemu N'Jie, and two carpenters, Marie Kebbeh and John L. Owens, emerged within the BTU leadership.[136]

Two months after Forster's reappointment, the political pendulum began to swing once more toward Small. Governor Palmer came into office determined to reform the system of government both of the Colony and the Protectorate. His first move was to codify the laws of the Colony, a step recommended by Judge Aitken as early as 1929. In September 1931, Judge Horne, Aitken's successor, agreed to draw up a Criminal Code and a Criminal Procedure Code, which would be based on those in operation in Kenya. The draft version was completed by May 1932 and a committee was appointed to consider it.[137]

Codification was a controversial issue in West Africa; for example, a proposal to codify the laws of Sierra Leone provoked widespread protest in Freetown between 1918 and 1920, which ultimately succeeded in preventing its implementation.[138] Similarly, the announcement that the government was to introduce the codes into Gambia met with fierce resistance. Small launched a vigorous and sustained press campaign against codification. This was portrayed as a retrogressive step which would bring about the introduction of "new offences and new penalties" and would sweep away existing legal safeguards.[139] Simultaneously, a Committee of Citizens and Ratepayers (a typical Creole organization), held a series of well attended public meetings to denounce codification.[140] Nevertheless, opposition to the codes was not universal. Forster, who was a member of the Codes Committee, was strongly committed to their implementation; W. D. Carrol and all other elected members of the BUDC also declined to attack them.

Their refusal to do so (which may be contrasted with the attitude adopted by the elected African members of the Gold Coast Legislative Council toward the Criminal Code Amendment Ordinance of 1934), was resented by Small, Rendall, and their allies, who became increasingly critical of Forster and the elected councilors.[141] In July 1932, they founded the Bathurst Ratepayers' Association (RPA), which sought (like other West African ratepayers' associations) to organize municipal elections. Unusually, however, the RPA's aim was to bring about the removal of existing councilors; it was more customary for ratepayers' organizations to be founded before any elections had taken place.[142]

Despite its title, the RPA was not restricted to the approximately 1,500 persons on the rating list. Any owner and occupier of property in Bathurst was entitled to be a member and it was therefore theoretically a "mass" organization, unlike the exclusive GRC.[143] In practice, however, the RPA was dominated by its executive and ward committees. Rendall was its first secretary, and its other members included former Congress activists and leaders of the faction within the BTU who had remained loyal to Small. It contained both Christian and Muslim members, among them Momodu Jahumpa. Small may not himself have been an executive member of the RPA; indeed, he was probably not even a ratepayer.[144] However, he exerted an overriding influence on proceedings through the Committee of

Citizens.[145] Indeed, the Gambian government believed that Rendall (the committee's secretary) was "a man of straw" and that Small was really responsible for writing the many petitions Rendall presented.[146]

At first the RPA met with limited success and its protest meetings and petitions failed to deflect Governor Palmer from the general tenor of his reform program. Apart from the codes, Palmer introduced new Rates and Licensing Ordinances and a Trade Union Ordinance and, in January 1933, passed three ordinances that aimed to transform the basis of administration in the Protectorate. These three ordinances—the Native Authority, Native Tribunal, and Subordinate Courts Ordinances—are collectively termed here the "Protectorate Ordinances."[147] Some concessions were made before these passed through all their readings in the Legislative Council, but only because of interventions by Forster or the elected councilors. At the request of the African members of the BUDC (supported by Forster in the Legislative Council), Palmer agreed that the level of increase of rateable value should be held in check, at least for 1933. After appeals and a petition from the councilors, the license fee for hawkers (under the Licensing Ordinance) was also halved; the newspaper license slightly reduced from £5 to £4 and, most important of all, a number of amendments were made to the Protectorate bills that had caused alarm in Bathurst.[148] In contrast, the efforts of the RPA were much less successful. For example, a petition calling for the disallowance of the Protectorate Ordinances was rejected out of hand by the Colonial Office.[149]

Two of these measures—the Licensing Ordinance and the Trade Union Ordinance—were clearly designed to weaken Small's influence. Small, who was now deeply in debt, could not afford to pay the new Licensing Ordinance and the *Gambia Outlook* was forced to close in February 1933 and was not published again until June 1934.[150] The Trade Union Ordinance, which Forster supported, stemmed from the Passfield Memorandum of September 1930 that, as noted, called for the registration of colonial trade unions. Unlike most colonial governments, which were opposed to the legislation, the Gambian government saw it as an opportunity to weaken Small's influence. The Legislative Council passed the ordinance in December 1932 and it received the Royal Assent one month later.[151] At the beginning of March, N'Jie, Owens, and Kebbeh asked the register general, A. G. B. Manson, to register their faction under the ordinance as the Bathurst Trade Union. Manson consented and, despite Small's bitter complaints, the Gambian government eventually confirmed this decision in July.

Small's political opponents were directly involved in the dispute. W. D. Carrol acted as the lawyer for the dissident faction and threatened Small with legal proceedings if he did not hand over certain items to his clients; N'Jai-Gomez allowed Small's opponents to meet at his home and was elected as honorary secretary of the BTU in February 1933; and Forster, who was asked to adjudicate on the rival claims in June, not surprisingly announced that the dissident faction "had a superior authority and a legal right of preference, as it were to call meetings." Small subsequently petitioned the Colonial Office for redress, but the secretary of state

(Cunliffe-Lister), on the advice of the Gambian government and clearly mindful of Small's political reputation, refused to intervene.[152]

The RPA was thus unable to deflect Governor Palmer from his legislative course of action. It was also unable to displace the GRC at the forefront of local politics. Rather surprisingly, it failed to mount an effective challenge in the 1932 BUDC election; only one seat was contested (N'Jai-Gomez was challenged by two candidates, both of whom were probably Independents) and this was won easily by the GRC secretary.[153] The RPA paid dearly for its failure to oust the incumbent councilors. In March 1933, Governor Palmer granted the BUDC the right to nominate a candidate to the Legislative Council in recognition of the support it had offered his reform program in the face of much public criticism. The unanimous choice of European and African councilors alike was W. D. Carrol. His nomination was welcomed by Palmer, who valued the role he had played over the codes and no doubt also welcomed the legal advice that Carrol was giving to Small's opponents within the BTU; Carrol was appointed for a five-year term in May 1933.[154]

In December 1933, the RPA did manage to field three candidates, Rendall, Cecil S. Richards (a trader, who was another of the sons of J. D. Richards), and Edward Lloyd-Evans (a Mulatto writing clerk) against G. M. N'Jie and the two Carrols. But the three won only eleven votes between them and all were comfortably defeated in very low polls.[155] The incumbents were able to claim as an achievement that they had secured an additional unofficial seat on the Legislative Council. Their position was further strengthened when, a few days before the election, Acting Governor Parish agreed to make a number of significant amendments to the codes' bills. These had been revised by the Colonial Office for the sake of uniformity with a proposed new code for East Africa; as a result, a number of punishments, including corporal punishment, had been increased. After an appeal by the councilors, Parish agreed to remove these new punishments. The elected members could therefore argue, with some justification, that their private interventions had achieved something tangible, whereas the public protests organized by Small and Rendall had fallen on deaf ears.[156]

The omens did not seem good for the RPA, particularly when the Carrols, N'Jai-Gomez, Allen, and others established *The Gambia Echo* in Spring 1934. Supported by the European manager of the UAC, Lionel Ogden, the syndicate intended that their newspaper should take the place of the currently defunct *Gambia Outlook* and promote the GRC cause.[157] However, in the December 1934 election, the RPA at last made a significant breakthrough when four of the existing councilors, W. D. Carrol, N'Jai-Gomez, G. M. N'Jie, and Allen, were defeated by RPA candidates. Although the turnout remained low (a total of 441 votes were cast in the four constituencies, a 33 percent turnout), this election did attract much greater public interest than any since 1931.

It was also the most controversial to date; for example, W. D. Carrol was roundly condemned for appealing to the votes of "scavengers" (low-paid government employees who were not ratepayers, but who, as noted, were permitted to vote), and the RPA candidate in New Town accused police officers of instructing policemen to vote for Allen.[158] The incumbents were again criticized for their association with the codes, which were finally introduced in October 1934, following the rejection of one last call for their non-enforcement. Unlike in 1933, the councilors were unable to claim any last-minute concessions; their subsequent fate can be compared with that of Dr. F. V. Nanka Bruce (the sitting member) who was defeated in the 1935 Gold Coast Legislative Council election by the more radical Kojo Thompson primarily because he had failed to oppose the Sedition Bill with sufficient vigor. The councilors were also blamed for failing to demand the introduction of a proper town council (with an elected majority) and for doing nothing to reduce unemployment in Bathurst.[159] Finally, there was irritation that the councilors refrained from attacking the sweeping quarantine regulations that had been imposed after an outbreak of yellow fever. These were highly unpopular, especially because the disease primarily affected Europeans rather than Africans.[160]

This proved to be the last election to the BUDC, for in May 1935, it was replaced by the Bathurst Advisory Town Council (BATC). The new body was responsible for a wider range of functions than its predecessor, but possessed no executive authority (not that the BUDC's potential powers had ever been exercised in practice). In addition, the voting rights of government servants were removed and only ratepayers were now permitted to vote or stand for election.[161] Small, who had called in the previous year for the replacement of the BUDC by a municipal council with an elected majority, welcomed the changes, although he argued that they did not go far enough. However, Rendall (who was not a ratepayer) disliked the fact that only ratepayers could now stand for election.[162] The first election to the BATC was held in May 1936 and the RPA won all the elected seats; it was perhaps indicative of the declining power of the GRC that only two wards (Half Die and New Town) were contested and then only because of dissension within the RPA.[163] This proved to be the last contested municipal election until 1943. In the meantime, all the elected African members of the municipal council were returned unopposed, having been nominated by RPA executive and ward committee meetings.[164]

Legislative Council Appointments: 1937–38

In the 1936 BATC election, Ousman Jeng, the former Muslim member of the Legislative Council, won the New Town ward election. Not long after his removal from the council in March 1932, Jeng had joined the RPA and had become president of its New Town ward committee. As early as 1933, the Committee of Citizens had hoped to persuade him to stand for election to the BUDC, but he declined the invitation. If he had done so, there might well have been objections from Momodu Jahumpa, a prominent figure in the RPA in Half Die. However, in September 1935, Small at last effected a reconciliation between the two key figures in the dispute within the Muslim community and a few days later, a Mohammedan Society was founded "to find the verdict of the community on any common interest."[165] Its members included Jeng, Jahumpa, and Almami Omar

Sowe but, significantly, not Sheikh Omar Fye. Indeed, one of the main aims of the society was to secure Fye's removal from both the Board of Management of the Mohammedan School and the Legislative Council.[166]

The Mohammedan Society hoped that when Fye's term on the council expired in March 1937, it would not be renewed. The Gambian government accepted that Fye was not popular, but because the only alternative candidate was Jeng (and his selection would be seen as a victory for Small's party), he was offered a second term. Sir Samuel Forster was also reappointed for an unprecedented seventh term.[167] The RPA could not seriously have expected that one of its candidates would replace Forster, but had high hopes of ousting W. D. Carrol when his term expired in May 1938, because all the elected members of the BATC were now RPA supporters. Nevertheless, when the question was put to the vote during a meeting of the BATC in March 1938, Carrol defeated his challenger, E. F. Small, by seven votes to four. He owed his victory to the intervention on his behalf by Governor Sir Thomas Southorn. Like his predecessors, Southorn was concerned about Small's political beliefs and connections and so instructed the four officials to vote for Carrol. The three nominated European unofficials also voted for him. Because all four elected members who were present voted for Small, the RPA protested to the secretary of state about the propriety of allowing nominated members to vote, but its petition was ignored by the Colonial Office.[168]

In common with unofficial members of Legislative Councils throughout West Africa, both Forster and Carrol strongly supported the Allied cause when war was declared in September 1939. However, Carrol did oppose the Gambian government on one domestic issue, the proposed introduction of income tax, in May 1940. Similar proposals often met with resistance in West Africa. The conservative Lagos Reform Club opposed the introduction of income tax in 1920, and resistance in the Gold Coast was so strong that Governor Slater's Income Tax Bill of 1931 had to be abandoned. Governor Jardine also dropped plans to introduce income tax in Sierra Leone in 1940 in part because of objections from unofficial members of the Legislative Council. In Forster's absence because of ill health, Carrol took the lead in opposing income tax in Gambia; indeed, he voted against the bill, as did the Chamber of Commerce member, L. De V. Bottomley (the manager of the UAC) and even Sheikh Omar Fye. But the unofficial members were outvoted by the official majority and a "silent protest" led by Small and the elected members of the BATC was equally ineffective.[169]

This intervention by Carrol suggests that he (like his uncle and great uncle) cannot simply be dismissed as a government stooge. It is true that neither Forster (the barrister) nor Carrol criticized the government very frequently or very hard and they were not prepared to make common cause with more radical elements (except possibly over income tax). It is also reasonable to argue that Forster became more conservative as he grew older. Nevertheless, a useful description of Forster (which may also be applied to his nephew) is that he was good example of a "shock absorber," who absorbed and toned down agitations to the government and performed a similar function with government policies.[170]

Neither Sir Samuel Forster nor W. D. Carrol lived to complete their terms of service on the council. Forster died in July 1940 (aged sixty-seven), and Carrol, who suffered from ill health for some years, died at the age of only forty-one in October 1941.[171] This brought the political dynasty of the Forsters to a close and, as we shall see in Chapter 5, allowed their old enemy, E. F. Small, at last to gain a seat on the Legislative Council.

Summary

Gambian politics between the mid-1880s and the early 1940s were dominated by a single family, the Forsters. Under their influence, representatives of the African community on the Legislative Council increasingly adopted a pro-government political stance, but after World War I, a more radical political movement, led by E. F. Small, inspired by events in other British West African colonies, arose to challenge the dominant patrician elite. Despite its use of populist techniques—"mass meetings" and vigorous criticism of government policies in Small's newspaper—and its dismissal as "subversive" by the government and its conservative opponents, the radical faction always acted constitutionally in criticizing government and demanding political reform. Indeed, some of its objectives were shared more widely in the African community. By the mid-1930s, despite the hostility of the Gambian government and various setbacks, it secured control over local politics in Bathurst by forming a new alliance between the Christian and Muslim communities, with which to oppose the patricians. Yet it failed to displace them from the Legislative Council so that its influence remained very limited.

5

THE ESTABLISHMENT OF PARTY POLITICS, 1941–59

One of the most important developments in West Africa in the late 1940s and early 1950s was the sudden proliferation of political parties. Both before and immediately after World War II, most political organizations were of the "congress" type. They had loose-knit structures and sought to embrace all shades of political opinion to achieve specific (and limited) reforms, or to block undesirable legislation. Often as a result of an internal split, these congresses then gave birth to political parties that aimed to mobilize the mass of the population, both for immediate electoral purposes and to hasten the process of decolonization. As the political stakes became higher, rival parties, which often adopted a communal or regional complexion, were formed to challenge the monopoly of the dominant party.[1]

This chapter shows how this transition from the broadly based congress to the more narrowly focused party occurred in The Gambia as elsewhere. Although the Bathurst Ratepayers' Association (RPA), a typical congress organization, managed to win the first direct election to the Legislative Council in 1947, it was swept aside in the 1951 election by the colony's first genuine political party, the Gambia Democratic Party (GDP). Two other parties, the Gambia Muslim Congress (GMC) and the United Party (UP), were established by the time of the 1954 election. Nevertheless, party politics remained in a fledgling state at the end of the 1950s. Political parties remained undeveloped, with each depending on the personality and actions of its leader. They could therefore be described as "elite" or "patron" parties.[2] Moreover, all parties continued to draw their support exclusively from the urbanized area in and around Bathurst, with the Protectorate remaining very largely excluded from the national political process.

Legislative Council Politics: 1941–47

The death of W. D. Carrol in October 1941, following that of Sir Samuel Forster in 1940, meant that for the first time since 1883, the African Christian community was not represented on the Legislative Council. Governor Southorn did not seek to fill the vacancy left by Forster's death, because he believed that Carrol could adequately represent Christian interests.[3] However, after Carrol's death, Southorn invited the members of the Bathurst Advisory Town Council (BATC) to nominate a successor. Two candidates emerged, Simeon A. Riley, a retired Aku civil servant and petty trader who served on the BATC since 1936 and was a leading member of the RPA, and E. F. Small, the defeated candidate in 1938, who was actually proposed by Riley! Riley was in fact only nominated because some councilors were under the mistaken impression that the choice must be made from one of their number. When the error was pointed out, his supporters tried to withdraw his name. But they were persuaded to allow it to go forward and he was defeated by only one vote. The outcome hinged on a decision by Southorn—who was impressed by Small's staunch loyalty to the Allied cause since the outbreak of the war—to instruct the official members to abstain, whereas he had ordered the official members to vote for Carrol in 1938. Riley probably received the support of the two European unofficial members; the nominated African member, J. A. N'Jai-Gomez (an old enemy of Small) and one of the elected African members, but the other five elected RPA members voted for Small to ensure his victory.[4]

Small took his seat in January 1942, and Southorn simultaneously appointed J. A. Mahoney to fill the vacancy caused by Forster's death. Mahoney had been secretary of the Gambian branch of the Congress in the mid-1920s, but had not been active in local politics in recent years and does not appear to have been a member of the RPA.[5] Both men were appointed for the customary five-year terms; in March 1942, Southorn also reappointed Sheikh Omar Fye for a further two years. Southorn had hoped to be able to replace Fye with a younger man, but reluctantly concluded that no other eligible Muslim candidate was both sufficiently knowledgeable in English and held in high enough esteem by Bathurst's Muslims to merit selection.[6]

Southorn also intended to introduce the franchise during his period of office, but pressure of work caused by the war prevented him from doing so. It was therefore his successor, H. R. R. (later Sir Hilary) Blood, who drew up firm proposals in February 1943. Whether constitutional reform in West Africa in the 1940s occurred because of popular pressure or imperial initiative has been fiercely debated, but it is clear that, at least in Gambia, the impetus came from above. Calls for the franchise had been infrequent in the past few years and the unofficial members of the Legislative Council were not united on the issue; whereas Small and Mahoney were anxious to achieve the franchise, Fye preferred to maintain the status quo and the Chamber of Commerce representative, L. de V. Bottomley (a European), was opposed to the idea. Nevertheless, Blood was keen to make concessions before there was any real necessity to do so and so pressed ahead.[7]

After the secretary of state approved the principle of constitutional reform, Governor Blood appointed a Franchise Committee in December 1943 to examine the electoral basis of the proposed constitution. The committee unanimously recommended that there should be universal suffrage for any British subject or native of the Protectorate resident in Bathurst or Kombo St. Mary aged at least twenty-five, and persons literate in English or Arabic should have the vote at twenty-one. Candidates had to be aged at least twenty-five; be able to read, write, and speak English; and not be in receipt of a salary from the public revenue (which excluded civil servants). E. F. Small, who was selected by the other unofficial members to represent them on the committee, also persuaded the majority of its members that until the predominantly rural Kombo St. Mary developed as "a live suburb" of urbanized Bathurst, there was "no practical basis" for the two areas to form a single constituency. Consequently, there should be two distinct constituencies, each of which should elect its own member. Mahoney adopted the same line when the Legislative Council considered the Franchise Committee's report, but Fye, together with the European officials, argued that Bathurst and Kombo St. Mary should form a single constituency.

No doubt both Small and Fye took account of the likely electoral consequences. The chances of the former would be improved by the separation of Bathurst and Kombo St. Mary, because almost all his potential supporters lived in the capital. In contrast, Fye, who because of his farming interests liked to pose as the Protectorate's representative on the council, probably calculated that the predominantly rural, Wolof and Muslim voters of Kombo St. Mary would vote for him.[8] His view prevailed, because Blood considered that the population of Bathurst was too small to support its own member of the council and that it would be a mistake "to fortify the political, social and cultural barriers," which already existed between Bathurst and the rest of the colony. He also hoped that in a single constituency, the influence of the educated Aku elite (whom he disliked) would be nullified and, for the same reason, endorsed the recommendation of the Franchise Committee that there should be universal suffrage. The Colonial Office was unhappy about the idea of universal suffrage, but was reluctantly prepared to accept it, provided that the voting age was raised to twenty-five for the whole electorate.[9]

Beside being at odds over constitutional reform, the Gambian unofficial members also periodically adopted differing positions over issues debated by the Legislative Council. Small and Mahoney (who tended to act in concert) frequently criticized government policy, whereas Fye usually supported the government. For example, Small and Mahoney (as well as Bottomley) opposed a proposal to increase income tax in 1942; voted against the Registration of Newspapers and the False Publication Ordinances of 1944; and attacked government plans to reduce overcrowding and vagrancy in Bathurst in 1943. In contrast, even though Fye had opposed the introduction of income tax in 1940, he supported the raising of its level in 1942. He also voted with the officials over the Customs Tariff Amendment Ordinance in 1945, even though, according to Mahoney, the new duty would result in a 300 percent increase in taxation.[10]

Apart from their political differences, Small and Fye were also personally on bad terms. As shown in Chapter 4, Small and Fye fell out in the early 1930s and remained at odds thereafter. During the 1940s, the mutual antagonism of the two men was exacerbated by the Mohammed Faal affair. Faal was a Mauritanian cattle dealer who held a lucrative contract to supply cattle to the army for most of the war. In 1944, the contract was transferred to Fye even though, according to Small, Service Regulations prohibited a member of the Legislative Council from undertaking such work. Moreover, in early 1945, the controller of supplies decided to allocate cloth—which was in short supply—to cattle dealers in proportion to the number of cattle they provided for slaughter. Fye apparently received his full quota of cloth, which left Faal an insufficient amount to meet his commitments. Small, who was asked by Faal to take up the case with the authorities, alleged that Fye exerted undue political pressure on the controller to secure his quota, a charge that did nothing to improve their relationship.[11]

Garba-Jahumpa and the Bathurst Young Muslims Society

As noted, after the demise of the Gambia Representative Committee, the only political organization operating in Bathurst was the RPA. However, in 1945–46, several new political organizations were established. These included such ephemeral creations as the New Town Democrats and the People's Party (whose Chairman was R. S. Rendall, Small's colleague of the 1930s).[12] But the Bathurst Young Muslims Society (BYMS) was a much more substantial body. It was founded as early as August 1936 as an offshoot of the Mohammedan Society and intermittently functioned thereafter as a cultural association for younger Muslims. In May 1946, it was revived as a political organization by Momodu Jahumpa's son, Ibrahima M. Garba-Jahumpa. This conversion of a cultural association into a political organization was fairly common in West Africa in this period; a comparison may be drawn, for example, with the formation in Nigeria in 1951 of the Action Group out of the Yoruba cultural society, the Egbe Omo Oduduwa, and the Northern People's Congress out of the predominantly Hausa Jam'iyyar Mutanen Arewa.[13]

I. M. Garba-Jahumpa, who was born in Bathurst in 1912 and attended the Mohammedan School, was one of a new breed of educated young Muslims. He qualified to be a teacher in 1936 and, except for a short period during World War II, was employed in this profession until 1951. Momodu Jahumpa had been a key member of the RPA's ward committee in Half Die (Bathurst South) and his son apparently began his career in public life in the 1930s as an assistant secretary of the RPA. Garba-Jahumpa's promise was recognized when Governor Southorn appointed him to the BATC, as a nominated member, in succession to J. A. N'Jai-Gomez (who had become the first nominated African member in 1941).[14] A year later, he became secretary of the Gambia Labour Union (GLU, a trade union founded by Small in 1935) and it seems clear that Small, who had deliberately selected a Muslim rather than a Christian protégé, was grooming Garba-Jahumpa to be his trade union and political heir. Consequently, he invited the younger man to attend the prestigious World Trade Union Conference in London in February 1945 as his secretary.[15]

A few months later, however, the two men quarreled. Ostensibly, the cause appears to have been that both wished to attend the Sixth Pan-African Congress in Manchester in October 1945. Garba-Jahumpa almost certainly attended the preliminary conference for delegates in March 1945 and certainly signed the manifesto, drawn up by the Pan-African Federation and other bodies, which was presented to the United Nations in April 1945. Small, in contrast, neither signed the manifesto nor showed much prior interest in the Congress. Shortly after Small's departure to Paris to attend a second World Trade Union Conference, a Pan-African Congress Committee was established in Bathurst to raise funds to enable a delegation to be sent to Manchester. This committee was dominated by its joint secretaries, Garba-Jahumpa and the editor of the *Gambia Echo*, C. W. Downes-Thomas, and not surprisingly these two were chosen to be the Gambian delegates. Perhaps because Downes-Thomas was thought to be a supporter of Sheikh Omar Fye, Small's supporters in Bathurst led by Abdou Wally M'Bye, a prominent Wolof trader, protested strongly and a telegram was despatched to London to urge him to attend the Congress. A second telegram was then despatched by Rendall of the People's Party and others to cancel the first and Downes-Thomas and Garba-Jahumpa did eventually go to Manchester.[16]

There was also a broader reason for the conflict between Small and Garba-Jahumpa. Small believed that, in view of his extensive political experience, he was still best equipped to lead Gambia to the next stage of constitutional reform. But Garba-Jahumpa considered that he had served his apprenticeship in the GLU and, fired by the experience of rubbing shoulders with some of Africa's most prominent nationalists at the Manchester Congress, considered it was now time for him to be allowed to make his mark. A parallel may be drawn with the conflict between J. B. Danquah and Kwame Nkrumah in 1949, which led to the split in the United Gold Coast Convention (UGCC) and the formation of the Convention People's Party. Small, like Danquah, was part of the pre-war generation of politicians who expected to retain the political mantle for the foreseeable future; Garba-Jahumpa, like Nkrumah, was part of a younger, more radical, group who believed that their turn had now come. Danquah regarded Nkrumah as a traitor for turning against the UGCC, which had given him employment as its general secretary. Small's view of Garba-Jahumpa was probably not dissimilar.[17]

The new organization appealed specifically to the "Youth" of Bathurst and was therefore in the tradition of the political movements and leagues of the later 1930s. Indeed, it actually received the blessing of the founder of the West African Youth League (WAYL), I. T. A. Wallace-Johnson, who happened to make a fleeting visit to Bathurst in June 1946 while en route to an international trade union conference in Moscow.[18] There was, however, one fundamental difference between the WAYL and the BYMS; whereas the WAYL was predominantly a Christian body that had tried to attract Muslim support, the BYMS appealed exclusively to Muslims.[19] This narrowly sectarian approach was completely at odds with the approach of the RPA, which had always contained Muslim, as well as Christian, members and had sponsored candidates of both religious persuasions in municipal elections. Indeed, the foundation of the BYMS greatly alarmed Small, who feared that it might make use of the inbuilt Muslim majority in Bathurst to sweep the RPA (and the Christian community in general) out of political life.

The formation of the BYMS meant that the municipal election of that year was the first to be contested by rival political factions since 1934.[20] The political atmosphere was intensified by the fact that in July 1946, Bathurst had at last been granted a Town Council, which enjoyed much greater powers than its predecessors; all fifteen elected seats were at stake in the inaugural election, with each voter possessing three votes in one of five three-member constituencies. The potential electorate, estimated to be 8,000 strong, was also much larger than before.[21]

Before the election, the RPA had become alarmed at the prospect of losing its control over municipal politics and concern had been expressed by Small and others that the voting qualifications had been made too liberal, an interesting reaction from the prime mover for constitutional reform in the 1930s. The relevant ordinance enfranchised the husbands and wives of all qualified voters, which in the RPA's view, gave an unfair advantage to Muslims (and perhaps therefore to the BYMS).[22] Nevertheless, although the RPA lost its monopoly of the elected seats, it still emerged victorious in the election, winning six seats and securing representation in four out of the five Bathurst wards. Moreover, it is probable that most of the five civil servants who were elected were sympathetic to the RPA rather than to the BYMS. Despite this, the outcome was not an unqualified success for the RPA; its defeated candidates included J. W. Kuye, the deputy chairman of the Bathurst Temporary Local Authority (the forerunner of the Bathurst Town Council [BTC]) and S. P. Gibbs, the chairman of the RPA's Executive Committee. Indeed, Governor Blood interpreted the outcome as a severe setback for the organization.[23]

Three BYMS candidates were elected, including Garba-Jahumpa, but the BYMS' overall showing was disappointing. Not one of its three successful candidates headed the poll in their respective constituencies, with even Garba-Jahumpa being defeated in the family stronghold of Half Die.[24] Indeed, Garba-Jahumpa may have concluded that to fulfill his ambition of achieving a place on the Legislative Council, he would have to broaden the base of his support, which was too narrowly restricted to a segment of the Muslim community in Bathurst. One way of doing this would be to control the Gambian labor movement. Consequently, in January 1947, he persuaded a number of trade union leaders to join with him in founding the Gambia Amalgamated Trade Union (GATU) as a rival of Small's GLU. Garba-Jahumpa became general secretary of the new organization. There can be little doubt that this was a deliberate maneuver designed to secure him votes in the forthcoming Legislative Council election; indeed, Garba-Jahumpa fits the stereotype outlined by Berg and Butler of ambitious politicians who used the trade union movement as "one of many organizational channels . . . in their rise to power."[25]

Political Role of Ex-Servicemen

If the establishment of a political organization that appealed specifically to younger Gambians was not untypical of West Africa in this period, The Gambia was unusual in that ex-servicemen appear to have played no significant, collective role in postwar politics. Gambians served in substantial numbers in the imperial war against Japan.[26] Elsewhere in West Africa, in Senegal, Nigeria, and particularly the Gold Coast, demobilized veterans played a key political role in the development of an anticolonial coalition, which in turn helped to bring about political change. In contrast, there is no evidence that war veterans adopted a distinctive political voice in Gambia after 1945. There were two main reasons for their political passivity. First, the majority seemed to have returned fairly quickly to their homes in the Protectorate. By March 1947, 4,000 servicemen had been demobilized. Of these, 2,500 returned to the Protectorate and therefore effectively removed themselves from national politics, given that the franchise was restricted to the urban areas. Second, employment, albeit of a seasonal nature, appears to have been found for most of the veterans who remained in Bathurst and Kombo St. Mary under the Employment of Ex-Servicemen Ordinance of 1945; by 1948, only an estimated 500 were not employed.[27] Gambian ex-servicemen therefore lacked the economic grievances of their Gold Coast counterparts and although individual veterans doubtless became involved in domestic politics after 1945, they did not do so as a collective entity.

1947 Legislative Council Election

Although the revised constitutional instruments had been agreed in principle in 1944, the first election to the Legislative Council did not take place until November 1947. The Colonial Office blamed the delay on legal problems, a lack of staff, and an overload of constitutions requiring revision. It is clear, however, that the lack of popular pressure for reform was also a factor, because resources tended to be concentrated on more volatile colonies.[28] The new constitution was eventually finalized in November 1946. However, the election was then further delayed because the new governor of Gambia, Andrew (later Sir Andrew) Wright, wished to appoint a number of Africans to the Executive Council (including the winner of the first direct election to the Legislative Council), and it took time for the details to be worked out with the Colonial Office.[29]

Candidates

Five candidates competed in the November 1947 election: Small, Fye, Garba-Jahumpa, R. S. Rendall, the leader of the People's Party, and John Finden Dailey, the editor of the *Gambia Weekly News*, who was allowed to contest the election despite being a convicted felon.[30] Small described himself as a journalist, rather than as the leader of the RPA, which conceivably ceased to function after 1946, and Garba-Jahumpa stood as a trade union, rather than the BYMS, leader. The other three candidates were Independents. Only the first three could entertain any serious hope of victory. Rendall, Small's main lieutenant in the early 1930s, won only twenty-seven votes in the 1946 BTC election to finish tenth out of eleven candidates in Soldier Town ward and just twenty-three votes in the 1947 election, whereas Finden Dailey was largely discredited because of his espousal of unpopular causes.[31] A few years before, Small would have been the clear favorite; indeed, the concession of the franchise was held up in the 1930s because it was assumed that he would automatically win any election. Now the outcome was much harder to predict. An anonymous correspondent to the *Crown Colonist*, writing at the beginning of September, even argued that Fye was the favorite, with Garba-Jahumpa likely to be his nearest challenger.[32]

This prediction that Fye would defeat Small seemed justified because the former possessed three important advantages over the latter. First, he was a Wolof in a predominantly Wolof constituency, whereas his opponent was an Aku. The Wolof made up just under half of the African population of Bathurst and about a sixth of the African population of Kombo St. Mary; the Aku accounted for only 12 to 13 percent of the African population of Bathurst and 2 percent of the African population of Kombo St. Mary. Second, he was a Muslim, like most of the electorate, whereas Small was a Christian. Approximately three-quarters of the Bathurst population—and 80 percent of the population of Kombo St. Mary—were Muslim; only 13 percent of the population of Bathurst, and 3 percent of the population of Kombo St. Mary, were either Anglicans or Methodists.[33] Fye could also count on the support of Bathurst's Islamic spiritual leader, Almami Mama Tumani Bah. Third, as a prosperous merchant and contractor, Fye had much greater financial resources at his disposal than Small, who by all accounts was of modest means.[34] Fye could even conceivably claim that he possessed more political experience than Small, having been a member of the Legislative Council since 1932. Finally, Small was now a recluse who was rarely seen on the streets of Bathurst—certainly he did not actively campaign.[35]

The suggestion that Garba-Jahumpa was likely to be Fye's nearest challenger also seemed plausible. Like Fye, Garba-Jahumpa was a Wolof and a Muslim. He could also claim to be the leading Gambian trade unionist; the European labour officer D. Barrett (who admittedly was sympathetic to him and hostile to Small) claimed in 1947 that the GATU possessed between 250 and 1,000 members and the GLU less than 50. If converted into votes, this could prove a decisive factor. In addition, Garba-Jahumpa might even be able to turn his relative lack of political experience to his advantage. In the 1938 Nigerian Legislative Council election, for example, the Nigerian Youth Movement successfully countered the claims of the Nigerian National Democratic Party to possess the greater experience by suggesting that in its fifteen years of representation on the Legislative Council, it had accomplished little.[36]

Election Results

Despite these apparent disadvantages, Small comfortably headed the poll. The turnout was lower than might have been anticipated, given the importance of the

occasion and the presence of three serious candidates; out of a potential electorate of perhaps 10,000, only 5,580 electors registered and 3,195 actually voted
(although this was a higher turnout than for the 1946 BTC election). This level of
participation compared poorly with the inaugural election to the Sierra Leone
Legislative Council in 1924 when 89 percent of those registered had cast their
votes, but quite favorably with the inaugural elections to the Nigerian and Gold
Coast Legislative Councils. Nevertheless, the outcome was decisive. Small gained
1,491 votes (47 percent of those cast) to the 1,018 of Fye (32 percent), and the
679 of Garba-Jahumpa (21 percent); Rendall and Finden Dailey polled a mere
seven votes between them.[37] Small was consequently appointed to the Legislative
Council for a three-year term, as well as to the Executive Council. The reasons for
his success are considered below.

First, and most important, it is clear that the electorate did not vote along rigid
religious or ethnic lines. No doubt Small received the votes of most Aku and of
most Protestants, but he must also have been supported by a substantial number
of Muslims. To demonstrate that he was not solely a Christian Aku candidate,
Small was careful to select the Muslim Wolof trader, A. W. M'Bye (his ally in the
controversy over the Pan-African Congress meeting in 1945), as one of his three
nominators. No doubt he (or his supporters) also emphasized that Muslims were
always placed in leading positions within the trade union and political organizations he established and that, throughout his career, he had been willing to take
up the cases of Muslims (as well of Christians) with the authorities.[38] Behind the
scenes, Small also used Ousman Jeng, the still influential former legislative councilor, to stir up latent hostility to Fye within parts of the Muslim community in
Bathurst. Jeng probably also sought to persuade Muslim voters that the overtly
sectarian stance adopted by Garba-Jahumpa was out of keeping with Gambian
political traditions.[39]

Second, it is likely that the electorate considered that Small had been responsible for the achievement of the franchise. As noted, the initiative was in fact taken
by the Gambian government, although of course Small had been pressing the case
for more than twenty years and had recently been the leading member of the
Franchise Committee. Consequently, Bathurst opinion appears to have been that
it would be an act of ingratitude to deny Small the honor of being the first elected
member of the Legislative Council. Small's supporters probably also pointed out
that, contrary to the wishes of the representatives of Bathurst and Kombo St. Mary
on the Franchise Committee, Fye was opposed to the idea of having two separate
constituencies.[40]

Third, since his appointment to the Council in 1942, Small had proved more
responsive to the needs of his constituents than Fye. He was willing to take up
their grievances and also to criticize unpopular legislation. In contrast, Fye's main
concern appeared to have been to further his own business interests by using his
influence to obtain the army cattle contract or to secure his full quota of cloth.
Such actions were probably resented, particularly because Fye apparently made little attempt to take up the grievances of Bathurst citizens with the authorities

(although he did show greater concern for prominent inhabitants of the Protectorate). This suggests that the belief of the *Crown Colonist*'s correspondent, that Fye enjoyed "a wide influence and popularity amongst all sections of the community" was wide of the mark.[41]

Finally, it is at least conceivable that, in the last stages of the campaign, Garba-Jahumpa encouraged some of his supporters to switch their allegiance to Small to prevent Fye winning the contest. In an interview with one of the authors in 1984, Garba-Jahumpa claimed that when it became clear shortly before polling day that he could not hope to win, his supporters in Kombo St. Mary were asked to vote for Small to ensure that Fye was defeated. Although on the face of it, this version of events seems unlikely, given the known enmity between Small and Garba-Jahumpa at this time, it should be noted that an independent source made a similar suggestion in separate interviews (and at different times) to both co-authors.[42]

It should also be noted that some of the disadvantages Small faced may have been more real than apparent. It is probable that many of Garba-Jahumpa's supporters were under the age of twenty-five and therefore ineligible to vote. Furthermore, some farmers of Kombo St. Mary may have viewed with skepticism Fye's claim to be their natural representative, whereas others may have failed to register because registration took place at the height of the farming season. Small may also have benefited from the support of the Kombo chiefs, who conceivably instructed the "commoners" under their jurisdiction to vote for him. Small later claimed that, in 1947–48, he had been asked by these chiefs to be their representative on the Legislative Council.[43]

Small's victory in the 1947 election proved to be his crowning political achievement. After 1947, he was much less politically active than hitherto and spent a great deal of time abroad attending international trade union conferences on behalf of the GLU. Fye also retired from politics after his electoral defeat, and Garba-Jahumpa left Bathurst in 1949 to work as a teacher in Georgetown.[44]

1950 Wyn-Harris Constitution

Because Small had been appointed to the Legislative Council for a three-year term in November 1947, the second direct election should have taken place no later than November 1950. But it was delayed by the introduction of the first Wyn-Harris Constitution. In May 1950, Percy Wyn-Harris, who succeeded Sir Andrew Wright as governor in 1949, proposed to the Colonial Office that the number of elected members of the Legislative Council be increased to three. Two of these should be elected in a single two-member constituency in Bathurst, the third in Kombo St. Mary. Wyn-Harris also argued that each voter in Bathurst should be granted only one vote (even though two candidates were to be elected). He hoped that this mechanism would protect minority interests and help to prevent the development of "a party system of Government in the Gambia." This novel idea caused some concern in the Colonial Office, but the governor's proposals were formally accepted in September 1950.[45] This was too late for the changes to be implemented before the November election, a fact that was once again blamed on the volume of work. However, as Wyn-Harris (echoing Blood) caustically pointed out, "political advancement appears more likely to be expedited in places where there is political disturbance than where the people behave in a peaceful, loyal and orderly manner."[46] Indeed, the amended Order-in-Council was not prepared until June 1951 and, owing to Wyn-Harris' absence from the colony, the election did not take place until October.

Prior to the promulgation of the new constitution, Wyn-Harris had also discussed the future composition of the Executive Council with the Colonial Office. He suggested that a fourth unofficial be added to the council and that two of the four should be appointed "members of the government." They would be permitted to tender advice to the governor on a range of subjects, including development, education, and public works, but would not be offered specific portfolios. Each "member of the government" would also be expected to support any government measure in the Legislative Council on a subject for which he was the adviser and to resign if in disagreement with the government over a major issue. It should be emphasized that Wyn-Harris did not regard the appointment of "members of the government" as the first step toward a full ministerial system, which was "not a practical policy here." His proposals were accepted by the secretary of state at the beginning of August 1951 and published in the *Gambia News Bulletin*.[47]

1951 Legislative Council Election

Candidates

Seven candidates contested the second direct election to the Legislative Council in Bathurst. Three of these, Small, Garba-Jahumpa, and Finden Dailey, had competed in the 1947 election; the other four, Rev. J. C. Faye, P. S. N'Jie, Mustapha Colley, and J. Francis Senegal, had not done so, although one of them (Faye) was already a nominated member of the council.

The first of the new candidates, John Colley Faye, was born in 1907 of a Serere father (who was a storekeeper in the Public Works Department) and a Wolof mother. Faye was a fluent Wolof speaker and is best regarded as a "Wolofized" Serere. He was educated at the (Wesleyan) Methodist Boys' High School (MBHS) before becoming a teacher in the early 1930s. Following a period of training in England at the University of Southampton, he was appointed headmaster of St. Mary's Anglican School, Bathurst, in 1939. In 1942, he became the first headmaster of a recently established Anglican mission school at Kristikunda in Upper River Division (URD). Two years later he assumed full control of the mission station. In February 1947, he became the first Gambian to be ordained as an Anglican deacon and, having served his curacy at Kristikunda, he returned to Bathurst in 1949 to serve as curate of St. Mary's Cathedral. It was in recognition of his educational work in the area, which had also brought him an MBE, that he was appointed to the Executive Council by Governor Wright in November 1947, on the recommendation of the commissioner of the URD.[48]

Although Faye does not seem to have been particularly active in politics before World War II, the RPA persuaded him to stand for election to the BATC for the Portuguese Town Ward in 1940. Elected unopposed, he transferred to the Joloff Town North ward in 1941 and retained his seat until November 1942, when he resigned from the BATC on his transfer to Kristikunda. He continued to follow political events during his sojourn in the Protectorate and, on his return to Bathurst, soon became active in local politics once again.[49]

To improve his prospects in the forthcoming election, Faye first pioneered a trade union, the Motor Drivers' and Mechanics' Union (MDMU); like Garba-Jahumpa in 1947, he seems to have viewed trade unionism primarily as a source of votes. Under the auspices of a "Committee of Union and Progress," he then set about establishing a new, broadly based, political organization by inviting a variety of cultural groups and trade unions to a series of committee and "mass" meetings to discuss his ideas. These meetings attracted an enthusiastic response and the process culminated in the public proclamation of the Gambia Democratic Party in June 1951; Faye was appointed party leader.[50] The bulk of the GDP's support was derived from the Aku and Wolof communities and consisted of civil servants, traders, and commercial clerks, as well as some of the more elderly former supporters of Small, such as Henry Jones and Cyril Richards. Many GDP supporters were Christian, but the party also attracted support from a significant number of educated Muslims.[51]

Two other new candidates stood as Independents. One of these, J. F. Senegal, an ex-journalist turned auctioneer, had been a founding member of the Bathurst Urban District Council in 1931 and was currently an elected member of the BTC. He therefore had a bedrock of support in his Soldier Town ward.[52] But it was most unlikely that he would manage to capture "Protestant" votes from either Faye or Small.

The other Independent, Pierre Sarr N'Jie, was a political newcomer, but seemed a much stronger candidate. A Wolof then aged forty-two, P. S. N'Jie had been brought up as a Muslim, before converting to Roman Catholicism at the age of twenty. He began his career as a teacher at St. Augustine's School in Bathurst before entering the civil service in 1929. After working in a series of government departments, he transferred to the Judicial Department as assistant clerk of the courts in 1932, where he remained until 1943.[53] Until then, he appeared to follow a not untypical civil service career. However, in February 1943, he was suddenly arrested on a charge of forgery in a complicated case involving the eviction of two tenants from a property owned by one of his cousins and in which N'Jie himself had an interest. Following a five-day trial, he was acquitted by the local magistrates on the grounds of a lack of evidence. He then tried to institute civil proceedings for false imprisonment and malicious prosecution against the two European police officers who had arrested him, but was refused permission to pursue the case by Governor Blood. N'Jie later claimed that one of the officers, Assistant Police Superintendent Cyril Roberts, was a notorious racist and womanizer who bore him a grudge; he also alleged that Roberts received Blood's support because he was a European, and he was an African, and that the colonial secretary, Rex Ward, used Sheikh Omar Fye to threaten him about his future career prospects if he pursued the action. Despite his acquittal, N'Jie in the meantime was transferred to another government department, but his career in the civil service soon came to an end when a Medical Board ruled in June 1943 that he was suffering from "cardiac trouble." He was therefore allowed to retire on medical grounds with a pension and a gratuity.[54]

Three months later, in September 1943, having concluded that the chances that he would find suitable employment in Gambia were slim, he traveled to England to begin training as a barrister at Lincoln's Inn in London. Having become the first Wolof to be called to the bar in 1948, he returned to Bathurst in early 1949 to set up a law firm. Almost immediately, he petitioned first the Gambian government and then the secretary of state for compensation for the damage done to his health and reputation as a result of his arrest and prosecution and the financial losses he had incurred from leaving the civil service. The Gambian government remained unsympathetic to his plight, and although the Colonial Office believed that Blood had been wrong to deny N'Jie access to the courts, the secretary of state finally ruled in February 1950 that he was not entitled to any compensation.[55]

P. S. N'Jie's treatment by the Gambian government was not dissimilar to that experienced by E. F. Small some twenty years earlier. Both men felt that they were treated unfairly by the colonial authorities, with their sense of grievance heightened by the fact that their respective European opponents soon afterward fell foul of the colonial authorities.[56] It is therefore reasonable to assume that, as in the case of Small in 1919, N'Jie's personal experience was a catalyst for his decision to enter politics. He was encouraged to do so by two disparate groups within Bathurst society. First, the Roman Catholic community, which was critical of a government proposal that the four existing secondary schools in the colony be replaced by a single, nondenominational, school, was keen for its interests to be defended at the highest levels by one of its own. Second, a section of the Muslim community was willing to support N'Jie (who remained on good terms with many Muslims) because of their distrust of Garba-Jahumpa's sectarian approach to politics.[57]

The other newcomer to politics was one of the joint editors of the *Gambia Weekly News*, Mustapha Colley. Colley stood in conjunction with his co-editor, John Finden Dailey, the two having established the Common People's Party a few weeks before the election. Colley assumed the post of secretary of the Bathurst Trade Union earlier in the year in the hope of capturing the trade union vote, but his chances seemed remote; only a week before the poll, he was defeated (albeit narrowly) in Half Die in the BTC election. Finden Dailey had even less chance, having won only four votes in the 1947 Legislative Council election and twenty-five in the recent BTC election.[58]

The two remaining candidates in Bathurst, Garba-Jahumpa and Small, were supported by political organizations (rather than by political parties). The former, who was now headmaster of Bakau School, apparently helped to draft the political program of the GDP. Nevertheless, in August 1951, he announced that he would stand for election, once again as the candidate of the BYMS.[59] Small did not enter the contest until mid-September, much later than most of his rivals, and it is probable that he originally intended to retire and throw his weight behind Faye. Faye had been regarded as his political protégé since his quarrel with Garba-Jahumpa in 1947; the two men worked closely together at the Africa Conference in London in 1948 and coordinated the protests in Bathurst against the transfer of the popular Governor Wright in 1949. Faye was also a former member of the RPA and the main Protestant candidate. But the two men fell out after the unofficial members of the Legislative Council selected Faye to represent Gambia at the Festival of Britain celebrations in London in July 1951. Small had assumed that, as the "senior unofficial" member of the council, he would be the automatic choice and was clearly resentful that Faye declined to withdraw in his favor. Perhaps in a fit of pique, he therefore decided to stand for election once again, this time as the candidate of the Gambia National League, a new creation that incorporated the Committee of Citizens (which had not functioned since the 1930s) and other largely ephemeral organizations.[60]

The separate election in Kombo St. Mary attracted three candidates: Henry Madi, a naturalized Gambian of Lebanese extraction, who was the scion of the leading commercial family in the colony and said to be "incomparably the richest man in the Gambia"[61]; J. W. Kuye, an Aku accountant; and Howsoon O. Semega-Janneh, a wealthy businessman prominent in the transport industry. Semega-Janneh, whose family originated from Mauritania, was a Serahuli who was "Wolofized" by residence in the Colony.[62]

Election Results

Despite the increased number of candidates and the protracted nature of the campaign, only 2,262 votes were cast in Bathurst and a further 1,075 in Kombo St. Mary. The very low turnout surprised the public, but was easily explained; the many errors and omissions in the registers effectively disenfranchised a large number of voters, including many who were able to vote in 1947. Faye headed the poll in Bathurst, and he gained 905 votes (40 percent of those cast), with Garba-Jahumpa, who received 828 votes (37 percent), also being elected. Both men were subsequently appointed to the Executive Council as a "member of the government" by Wyn-Harris. N'Jie was the best placed of the unsuccessful candidates with 463 votes (20 percent); Small picked up only forty-five votes and the remainder just twenty-one votes between them. Meanwhile, in Kombo St. Mary, Madi easily defeated Kuye and Semega-Janneh; after the election, he was also appointed to the Executive Council.[63]

Faye probably owed his victory to four factors. First, the GDP was much the best organized participant in the election. It began campaigning before its rivals and apparently cornered the market in drummers (i.e., griots), whose role was to call people to Faye's public meetings. The GDP may also have used the taxi drivers enrolled in the MDMU to ferry pro-GDP voters to the polls.[64] Second, like Small in 1947 and to demonstrate that he was not just a "Christian" candidate, Faye invited a prominent and wealthy Muslim businessman in Bathurst to be one of his nominators. This was Momodou Musa (M. M.) N'Jie, an import/export merchant originally from the URD, who was to continue to play an important, if indirect, role in national politics for several decades.[65] Faye's tactic paid off; a number of educated Muslims (as well as many Christians) appear to have voted for him. Third, the GDP was the most trenchant critic of the unpopular Wyn-Harris government. It criticized the fact that each voter was allowed only a single vote in a two-member constituency (and therefore in practice possessed only half a vote) and it disliked the constraints that were to be imposed on the "members of the government." It also attacked the slow pace of Africanization under the Wyn-Harris administration.[66] Finally, Faye was reportedly the first (but by no means the last) Gambian politician to seek to boost his electoral support by distributing free bags of rice to the electorate.[67]

Garba-Jahumpa, the other successful candidate, fared much better than in 1947, probably because he enjoyed the support of most Muslims, including Almami Mama Bah.[68] This more than compensated for the loss of trade union votes brought about by the winding up of the GATU in 1948. The BYMS also benefited from its attacks on the limitations of the new constitution (it called for the creation of a full ministerial system), and Garba-Jahumpa's long experience in municipal politics stood him in good stead. Its major disadvantage was that it was perceived by most Christians and many Muslims to be a sectarian party.[69]

Although unsuccessful, N'Jie fared respectably, considering that he had no prior base in municipal politics, nor any formal organization behind him, although he did enjoy the support of the *Gambia Echo*. He managed to pick up a fair share of Muslim votes, in part because of the endorsement of the still influential Ousman Jeng, and he might have fared even better if he had attacked the Wyn-Harris constitution.[70] Finally, unlike the Colonial Office, the Gambian government was not surprised by Small's poor performance. Not only were his supporters "moderate and rather out-moded," they also tended to concentrate exclusively on Small's past record, particularly his pre-war record, rather than looking to the future. To compound his difficulties, Small openly endorsed the new constitution, which he suggested should be accepted "without reserve."[71] After his humiliating defeat, Small retired from active politics. However, after the 1954 election, he was appointed to the Legislative Council by Governor Wyn-Harris as the "nominated unofficial" member. Unlike most of his predecessors, Wyn-Harris greatly admired Small and had already been instrumental in securing him the award of an OBE. in 1953. Small retained this position on the council until his death in January 1958.[72]

Small's retirement marked the end of an era, because it meant that all the leading politicians of the 1920s and 1930s had either died or ceased to be actively involved in politics. His defeat in 1951 also signified the demise of the Aku minority as an independent force in Gambian politics, just as the failure of the National Council of Sierra Leone (NCSL) in the 1957 election was to end an independent Creole role in Sierra Leonean politics. Except temporarily (as after the death of W. D. Carrol), the Aku had enjoyed unbroken representation on the Legislative Council since 1883, but after 1951, the community provided few prominent politicians. Like the Creoles in Sierra Leone, the Aku community did, however, continue to play an influential role, through its continued domination of the upper ranks of the civil service and the professions.[73]

1954 Wyn-Harris Constitution

The third election to the Legislative Council in 1954 was fought under a new constitution. As noted, Wyn-Harris was anxious to prevent the evolution of a ministerial system of government. He argued that, outside the ranks of the civil service, there were too few Gambians capable of serving as ministers and that even these were not of ministerial caliber; that all the potential candidates hailed from the Colony and would therefore be likely to disregard the interests of the Protectorate; and that the territory could not afford the cost of establishing ministries or paying ministerial salaries.[74] Recognizing that there would be disappointment in Bathurst that Gambia was not to progress down the normal constitutional path to self-government, Wyn-Harris set up a Consultative Committee in April 1953 to draw up proposals for a revised constitution. The committee consisted of thirty-four prominent citizens of the Colony, all but two of whom were Africans. Its members were selected after the governor had consulted two of the three unofficial members of the Executive Council, Garba-Jahumpa and Henry Madi. Faye, the third unofficial member of the Executive Council, was absent from the colony but, according to Wyn-Harris, he stated that he would accept the nominations and, on his return, "tacitly" did so.[75]

The Consultative Committee, which met six times in May 1953, recommended that unofficial representation on the Legislative Council be increased to sixteen. Four members should be directly elected in Bathurst and Kombo St. Mary. Seven should be indirectly elected (three by the Chiefs' Conference and four by a Divisional Electoral Conference) to represent the Protectorate and three should be chosen by the previously elected councilors from a pool of candidates put forward by the BTC and the Kombo Rural Authority. There should also be two appointed members: a person "skilled in commerce" should be appointed by the governor "after consultation with" the Legislative Council and one unofficial should be appointed "after approval by" the Council. A speaker should also be appointed "after approval by" the council. The three Bathurst members should all be elected in a single constituency but, as in 1951, each voter should possess only one vote. This device would enable the three main segments of Bathurst society—Muslims, Protestants and Catholics—each to have a chance of getting one of its number elected. Finally, the Consultative Committee called for the concession of an unofficial majority on the Executive Council. Moreover, at least two of the six nonofficial councilors should be called "ministers" and given responsibility for specific departments.[76]

Wyn-Harris accepted most of the recommendations of the Consultative Committee and they were eventually incorporated into the revised constitutional instruments. But various changes were made to the report, mainly at the insistence of the Colonial Office. First, the Colonial Office objected to the writing into the constitutional instruments of a requirement for consultation. Whereas the Consultative Committee had proposed that the "nominated unofficial" member of the Legislative Council and the speaker should be appointed by the governor "after approval by" the Legislative Council, the secretary of state opposed the writing into the constitutional instruments of a formal requirement that these appointments should be made "after consultation with" the council. Second, and more important, the Colonial Office modified the Consultative Committee's proposals about "ministers." The committee suggested that, if requested either by the minister concerned or by an official member of the Executive Council, an Advisory Committee would be set up to help the minister to carry out his duties. However, the secretary of state insisted that ministers should be required to work with the Advisory Committees, a potentially significant diminution of their authority.[77] As indicated below, these changes to the Consultative Committee's proposals were to become a factor in the election.

The 1954 Legislative Council Election

Candidates and Parties

The third Legislative Council election was held in October 1954. Four candidates competed for three seats in Bathurst: Faye, Garba-Jahumpa, P. S. N'Jie, and George St. Clair Joof, a barrister and former member of the BTC.[78] The three candidates who had stood in 1951 all now headed political parties: Faye led the GDP, Garba-Jahumpa, the Gambia Muslim Congress and N'Jie, the United Party.

The GMC, which was founded in January 1952, was an amalgamation of about forty Muslim organizations, including the BYMS. The new party was endorsed not only by Almami Mama Bah and the Assistant Almami, Momadou Lamin Bah, but also by Sheikh Omar Fye and other Muslim dignitaries. Its support was drawn exclusively from Muslims and very largely from Muslim Wolof; it had few non-Wolof leaders, except for the "Wolofized" Serahuli brothers, H. O. and B. O. Semega-Janneh. The GMC's leading members included the growing number of educated Muslims employed in the civil service or as commercial clerks and the party was pledged to end the discrimination faced by Muslims in the provision of educational facilities. But its critics argued that it enjoyed little popular support outside Half Die, Garba-Jahumpa's stronghold.[79]

According to Gailey (and most subsequent commentators), the UP was founded as early as October 1951, immediately after N'Jie's defeat in the second Legislative Council election. But this seems very unlikely. The Political Intelligence Report (normally a reliable source of information) for April 1953 stated that there were only two parties in Bathurst, the GDP and the GMC, and Fletcher notes that she was told by P. S. N'Jie that the UP was founded about six months before the 1954 election, which is consistent with this evidence.[80]

The UP, like the GMC, drew its support mainly from the Wolof community, in particular from Wolof associated with the Saloum District of Central Division; N'Jie claimed to be descended from the kings of Saloum and the "Saloum Kheet (or Het)" or "Saloum-Saloum" factor (i.e., quintessential Wolofness) seems to have been an important element in the UP's development. Moreover, like the GDP, the UP was not confined to one religious group. Roman Catholics welcomed the formation of a party led by one of their number, but Muslims were also well represented. The latter were no doubt assured that the UP would not be converted into a "Catholic" party by the fact that many of P. S. N'Jie's relatives, including his half-brother E. D. (a future party leader), remained Muslim. Finally, the UP attracted strong support from (Wolof) women, many of whom were organized in women's societies presided over by "Yayi Kompins", in which N'Jie's sister, Yadicone, played a prominent role.[81]

Election Results

Since 1951, the electoral registers had undergone a wholesale revision and the number of registered voters in Bathurst had risen to 6,286. Owing to the introduction of a new system of voters' cards, many of the problems that beset the 1951 election were eliminated and 94 percent of all registered voters went to the polls. According to the later report of the chief superintendent of police, public order was maintained effectively throughout the period of the campaign and on polling day, although party feelings ran high and there was some animosity between the parties on occasions. All three candidates who competed in 1951 substantially increased their total vote. More surprisingly, the order of the three candidates changed, with N'Jie rising from third to first by picking up 2,123 votes (36 percent of those cast). Faye gained 1,979 votes (33 percent), and Garba-Jahumpa 1,569 votes (26 percent), but St. Clair Joof won only 252 votes (4 percent).[82]

Several factors help to explain the remarkable progress made by N'Jie in the Bathurst constituency since 1951. Then, he stood as an Independent, whereas in 1954, he had the support of a party behind him. Fletcher considers this very important, but it should not be given too much weight; at the time of the 1954 election, the UP probably had a very undeveloped structure. It is likely that the role played in the campaign by the party's informal network of Yayi Kompins was more significant; indeed, the UP may have derived the bulk of its support from women. An official in the Colonial Office subsequently claimed that N'Jie was elected "primarily by the women," and a British academic, J. H. Price (who was in

Bathurst at the time of the election), cryptically suggested that "a great deal of P. S. N'Jie's electoral success . . . could be attributed to his undoubted ability to be all things to all women at all times."[83] In addition, N'Jie probably had much greater resources at his disposal than his opponents. Since 1951, his law practice had expanded considerably, primarily because he played a key role in a series of transactions in which land in Bathurst had been transferred from Africans to Lebanese. This had apparently made him "very wealthy" and no doubt enabled him, when the time came, to spend heavily on securing his election. It may be no coincidence that both the governor and the GDP subsequently claimed that many votes had been purchased during the election, although admittedly neither specifically charged the UP with this offence.[84] Finally, unlike his opponents, N'Jie was not associated with the increasingly unpopular Wyn-Harris administration (other than through participation in the 1953 Consultative Committee).[85]

Rev. J. C. Faye, who headed the poll in 1951, more than doubled his vote in 1954, but saw his share of the vote fall to 34 percent. Since the previous election, Faye had faced financial difficulties because of the failure of his business concerns, notably the Pilot Produce Syndicate. Indeed, one of his creditors brought a judgment writ against him in March 1953, and others appear to have held off taking action only because of his political influence.[86] It is likely that these difficulties weakened his chances in the 1954 election, if only because it made it harder for him to mount an effective campaign.

Faye had also encountered political problems, having twice been dismissed from the Executive Council. In mid-June 1952, the three elected members of the Legislative Council, Faye, Garba-Jahumpa, and Henry Madi, informed the secretary of state, Oliver Lyttleton, during a visit to Gambia that there was popular pressure for further constitutional reform. Wyn-Harris was furious that they had done so without discussing the matter with him first and told the three men that his confidence in them as members of the Executive Council was badly shaken. A fortnight later, Faye made remarks at a public meeting on June 26 that were interpreted by Wyn-Harris, on the basis of a police report, to be a statement that he had lost confidence in the governor. Faye was ordered to confirm or deny the accuracy of the report, but refused to do so. Wyn-Harris then instructed him to resign from the Executive Council, and when Faye also refused this course of action, he dismissed him on July 4.

This decision provoked outrage in Bathurst and a "mass meeting" was called to protest against Faye's treatment, the intention apparently being to march on Government House and throw stones at the windows. However, the meeting was abandoned because of torrential rain. Before it could be reconvened, the Anglican bishop, Roderic N. Coote, headed a deputation of "responsible and well thought of citizens of all denominations" to the governor to seek Faye's reinstatement. Eventually, after further lengthy negotiations between Wyn-Harris, Coote, and Faye, Wyn-Harris agreed at the end of July to reinstate Faye after the latter had assured him that he did not intend to convey the impression that he had lost confidence in him.[87]

The political effect of this first confrontation with Wyn-Harris is hard to gauge. Wyn-Harris argued that "the general wish of Bathurst" was that unofficials should work with government and so there was disapproval of Faye's conduct. However, it seems likely that many people in Bathurst considered that Wyn-Harris had acted unreasonably and Faye's position may actually have been strengthened, particularly as he refused to apologize to the governor for his actions.[88] Indeed, the main effect of the incident may have been to weaken the position of Garba-Jahumpa, who seems to have been blamed for engineering Faye's downfall; certainly, Garba-Jahumpa had been very quick to confirm to Wyn-Harris that Faye had stated at the public meeting on June 26 that he had lost confidence in him.[89]

Faye's second dismissal from the Executive Council in September 1953 officially occurred because of his prolonged unsanctioned absence from the colony. Faye claimed, however, that he was a "political martyr," who was removed for attacking the proposed new constitution (the principles of which were published in July 1953). He had argued that the proposals of the 1953 Consultative Committee had been "very tame, and come short of what any other body, elected by the people, would have demanded"; indeed, according to Wyn-Harris, Faye stated publicly that he had only signed its report "in the interests of a peaceful solution and not because he believed in it." He was even more critical that some of the Consultative Committee's recommendations had been watered down, in particular over the Advisory Committees. Faye was not alone in expressing dissatisfaction with the new constitution; a committee formed in November 1953 endorsed the recommendations made by the Consultative Committee and criticized the changes made to its report. Although Faye's opposition to the constitution was undoubtedly in tune with the popular mood, he could be criticized for having failed to adopt this position on the Executive Council.[90]

The third major candidate, Garba-Jahumpa, also substantially increased the number of votes he received, but saw his share of the vote fall from 37 to 27 percent. Garba-Jahumpa had remained a member of the Executive Council and a minister throughout the life of the constitution. This gave him powers of patronage that he used to good effect; he was in fact accused in June 1952 of using his official position to secure employment for his relatives and friends.[91] But it also meant that he was closely associated with the unpopular administration. Perhaps his fate was sealed when he also welcomed the new constitution.[92] His support ebbed and a large number of Muslim notables (including the assistant Almami, Momadou Lamin Bah, a key supporter in 1951) declined to endorse him; there was even a demonstration outside Government House after his subsequent appointment as a minister.[93]

Meanwhile, in the separate election in Kombo St. Mary, the incumbent, Henry Madi, defeated S. J. Oldfield, a retired Aku civil servant turned manufacturer of mineral water, by 984 votes to 650; the turnout was again extremely high, at 97 percent.[94] The election of the Protectorate representatives took place earlier; the Chiefs' Conference selected three senior Seyfolu (none of whom could speak English well), and the Divisional Electoral Conference chose one younger chief,

Seyfu Omar M'Baki, and three "commoners" to represent the four Gambian Divisions. A Tukulor, who had been Seyfu of Sami District in MacCarthy Island Division since 1949, M'Baki was much better educated than most other chiefs, having attended the MBHS. He was trained at the Njala Teacher Training College in Sierra Leone and worked as a school teacher, including at Armitage School, before his appointment as a chief. Yet despite these appointments, the chiefs remained a peripheral element in Legislative Council politics until the late 1950s.[95]

Post-Election Appointments

Immediately after the election, the eleven newly elected members of the Legislative Council formed an electoral college to choose three more members from a list of candidates put forward by the two urban local authorities. H. O. Semega-Janneh, the defeated candidate in the 1951 Kombo St. Mary election; Jacob L. Mahoney, an Aku barrister and close relative of J. A. Mahoney; and Alieu O. Jeng, a Wolof trader, who was the son of Small's old lieutenant, were selected in this way.[96] These fourteen elected councilors (together with the nominated unofficial member, E. F. Small) were then asked by Wyn-Harris to nominate three candidates for the Executive Council and two "ministers." There was unanimous agreement that N'Jie and Garba-Jahumpa should be appointed to the Executive Council; Faye received thirteen out of fifteen votes. N'Jie received thirteen or fourteen votes, and Garba-Jahumpa twelve votes in the "ministerial" poll, but Faye was supported by only four councilors. Nevertheless, even though he had previously intended to appoint only two ministers, Wyn-Harris agreed to offer all three men specific port-folios once he received an assurance from Faye that he would cease to be active in business and would resign if there were any further judgments against him for debt. Presumably he anticipated that there would be an unfavorable reaction in Bathurst if Faye were to be denied a portfolio, given that he had polled more votes than Garba-Jahumpa in the Legislative Council election. N'Jie was offered respon-sibility for education and social welfare, Faye for public works and transport, and Garba-Jahumpa for agriculture.[97]

Party Alliances and Party Conflicts: 1954–59

We suggested that one of the underlying purposes behind both constitutions pro-moted by Governor Wyn-Harris was to prevent the evolution of a party political system in Bathurst. His strategy of allowing each voter only one vote in a three-member constituency appeared to be vindicated by the outcome of the 1954 elec-tion. All three major interests in the town secured representation on the Legislative Council and no one party could dominate proceedings. Nevertheless, during the second half of the 1950s, partisan rivalries intensified, even though the three parties remained "patron" parties and failed to develop the characteristics of "mass" parties.[98] One consequence was that, as elsewhere in West Africa in the 1950s and 1960s, political alliances were formed, broken, and reformulated by politicians anxious to outflank their rivals.[99] The UP and GDP formed a loose political alliance between the end of 1955 and mid-1959 to isolate the GMC. The GDP then joined forces with the GMC in a last-minute attempt to prevent the UP dominating Gambian politics, and eventually signed a merger in 1960. Meanwhile, a fourth party, the Gambia National Party (GNP) was formed in 1957 as a pressure group ostensibly above party politics. This was a somewhat outdated concept and the GNP was unsuccessful; by 1960, one section of its leadership had joined the UP and another the GDP.

The first sign of party conflict occurred in October 1955 when the UP and the GDP formed an electoral pact for the BTC election; each party was to be given a free run in two wards. The pact was directed against the GMC, which held Half Die and hoped to oust the UP in New Town East.[100] Both parties in fact retained their respective seats, but ill feeling was stirred up between the parties and the day after the election, there was an affray between GMC and UP supporters near Garba-Jahumpa's house in Bathurst. Several UP supporters were arrested (including P. S. N'Jie's nephew) and this provoked the UP leader to accuse Garba-Jahumpa of being "the principal participant in this fight" and of having imported a consignment of whips from Senegal to be used to attack UP supporters. N'Jie urged the attorney general to charge Garba-Jahumpa and, when he declined to do so, accused the chief superintendent of police of suppressing crimes of violence and of treating lightly an "averted massacre of innocent people."[101]

Governor Wyn-Harris responded by announcing the appointment of a commission of inquiry to examine N'Jie's allegations against the police. The commissioner, a retired senior puisne judge in the Nigerian government, F. H. Baker, concluded that there was no evidence to support the charges and strongly criticized N'Jie's conduct.[102] Wyn-Harris then instructed N'Jie to resign from the Executive Council and as minister of education but, like Faye in 1952, he refused to do so. He was therefore first suspended and then dismissed in January 1956. A memorial, containing over 4,000 signatures, was presented to Wyn-Harris to protest against the Baker Report. However, unlike in 1952, the governor refused to compromise and N'Jie remained outside the government for the rest of the life of the constitution.[103] The UP was convinced that Garba-Jahumpa had engineered the whole affair to discredit N'Jie and thereafter, there was "deep and bitter enmity" between the two men.[104] Public opinion generally sympathized with N'Jie and in the next BTC election in October 1956, Garba-Jahumpa—who had been returned unopposed in 1953—held on to his seat in Half Die by only eight votes, after a record turnout.[105]

Pressure for Constitutional Change: 1957–60

According to Wyn-Harris, the UP and GDP now decided to band together to press for constitutional reform "to place effective political control of the Gambia in

their joint hands."[106] By 1958, developments elsewhere in West Africa were beginning to have an impact. The Gold Coast achieved independence as Ghana in
March 1957, and in Sierra Leone, Sir Milton Margai was appointed premier in 1956
and became prime minister on the attainment of full internal self-government in
1958.[107] Inspired by these events, the two parties drew up constitutional proposals
in 1957, which differed in detail, but were not dissimilar in overall approach. For
example, both criticized the allocation of only one vote to each voter in a three-
member constituency, which had prevented parties fielding more than one candidate in 1954; the indirect methods of election that were used; and the enforced
dependence of ministers on Advisory Committees. They also called for direct elections throughout the Colony and Protectorate to an enlarged Legislative
Assembly; the division of Bathurst into five single-member constituencies; the abolition of Advisory Committees; and the replacement of the Executive Council by
a council of ministers under a chief minister (GDP) or a cabinet headed by a
prime minister (UP).[108]

When he returned from leave in November 1957, Wyn-Harris offered to meet
Faye and N'Jie to discuss their proposals informally, but both men declined to do
so.[109] In the previous month, it had been announced that Wyn-Harris would retire
in mid-1958 and, given both his attitude to constitutional reform and his obvious
dislike of them, the two party leaders preferred to await the arrival of his successor. Wyn-Harris was increasingly unpopular in Bathurst and when he left Gambia
in April 1958, he quietly slipped across the border into Senegal with little fanfare.
According to one former government official, this was to avoid embarrassing
demonstrations.[110]

He was succeeded by Sir Edward Windley who, like his predecessor, had spent
most of his career in Kenya, his most recent appointment having been as chief
native commissioner and minister for African affairs.[111] Unlike Wyn-Harris,
Windley (who arrived in Gambia in June) was quite willing to listen to Gambian
demands for further constitutional change. He therefore convened a series of
constitutional conferences at Brikama (October 1958), Georgetown (January
1959), and Bathurst (March 1959) to discuss the issue.[112]

Even before Windley's arrival, the UP and GDP had drawn up a resolution in
April to the secretary of state, which called for the concession of self-government
in 1959.[113] This resolution was also endorsed by the GNP. The GNP had been
founded the previous July by the leading figures in an informal "Committee of
Gentlemen." It had no overall party leader, but rather a collective leadership
which included Edrissa J. Samba, a "firebrand" Wolof trader; Melvin B. Jones, an
equally fiery Aku journalist; John W. Bidwell-Bright, a well known Aku businessman; and Kebba W. Foon, a Wolof chartered accountant, who had returned to
Gambia in 1955 after living in Britain for ten years.[114] Its leaders frequently
attacked the policies and the personnel of the Gambian government and the performance of the existing ministers in public meetings and through the columns
of a Bathurst newspaper established in early 1958, *The Vanguard*, which was owned
by Bidwell-Bright and edited by Jones. They also urged the existing parties to press

more strongly than hitherto for constitutional reform but, at least initially, did not seek to challenge the other parties in BTC elections.[115]

The call for self-government was not, however, supported either by the third Bathurst party, the GMC, or by the Protectorate chiefs who, in the absence of any Protectorate parties, remained the dominant element in the countryside (see Chapter 6). Although the GMC put forward constitutional proposals that were not dissimilar to those of the other parties in February 1958, it remained at odds with them. According to Wyn-Harris, the GMC was "basically conservative," notwithstanding Garba-Jahumpa's earlier flirtation with Pan-Africanism, and feared that unless a future constitution (like the present one) protected minorities, the party would be pushed aside by the more powerful UP and GDP. The GMC therefore attempted to stem the tide of reform. It refused to adopt the common negotiating policy agreed by the UP and GDP at the start of 1958 and then declined to sign the April 1958 resolution.[116] Meanwhile, the GDP and UP did not even bother to consult the chiefs about the April resolution, even though there were clear signs that the chiefs were beginning to play a greater role in national politics; for example, at the annual Chiefs' Conference in February 1958, they called for an increase in the Protectorate membership of the Executive and Legislative Councils. Had they done so, the parties would have found that the chiefs did not approve of the proposals.[117]

Realizing the weakness of the GMC's position, Garba-Jahumpa sought to make political capital of the situation. He was confident that he could do so; apart from religious affinities with the overwhelmingly Muslim Protectorate, Garba-Jahumpa had served as minister of agriculture since 1954 and this, he believed, gave him a special rapport with the chiefs. Consequently, at the Brikama Conference, he supported the argument of the chiefs that only "yard owners" (heads of families) and their senior wives should be enfranchised, even though the political parties had previously agreed that there should be universal adult suffrage throughout the territory. He also suggested that the chiefs should be offered government grants and even be built houses at government expense. Similarly, at the Georgetown Conference in January 1959, he seems to have accepted the view of the chiefs that no Bathurst resident should be allowed to stand as a candidate in the Protectorate, even though this was at odds with a fundamental principle of the Bathurst parties.[118]

Unfortunately for Garba-Jahumpa, the chiefs (who in fact were not at all impressed with his performance as minister of agriculture) did not believe he was acting in good faith and ignored his overtures.[119] At the final constitutional conference held in Bathurst in March 1959, the GMC therefore changed sides, a characteristic of Garba-Jahumpa's political style on future occasions as well, and indicative of the primacy of personal advancement over political principles on his part, and generally supported the UP and the GDP.[120] This brought the GMC back into the political mainstream and raised the possibility that it might be able to take advantage of any breakdown in the relationship between the UP and the GDP. Despite their common strategy over constitutional reform, which had been maintained at the three constitutional conferences of 1958–59, the two parties had drifted apart since 1955; certainly in 1957, and possibly also in 1958, their candidates stood against each other in BTC elections, which strengthened the hand of the GMC.[121] But until June 1959, when the UP disassociated itself from a demonstration organized by the GDP against the secretary of state, Alan Lennox-Boyd, there was no overt disagreement between the parties.

During a visit to Gambia, Lennox-Boyd held a meeting with the March confer-ence delegates, which the GDP considered unsatisfactory. Although not ruling out any of the conference recommendations, Lennox-Boyd expressed reservations about a number of proposals.[122] Consequently, two of the most active GDP leaders, Alieu E. Cham-Joof (its secretary) and Councilor Crispin R. Grey-Johnson, together with M. B. Jones (general secretary of the GNP), convened a public meeting in Bathurst. The meeting was addressed by Rev. J. C. Faye, who claimed that the sec-retary of state intended to reject three-quarters of the conference recommenda-tions. Faye was then asked to leave the meeting and a large crowd headed by Cham-Joof and Jones marched on Government House to protest against the visit of the secretary of state and had to be dispersed by force. Ironically, Lennox-Boyd had just arrived from Freetown where he had faced another demonstration, but this time by Creoles protesting *against* constitutional reform.[123] As an example of politi-cal unrest, the Bathurst "riot" was small beer when compared with the disturbances in Sierra Leone or the Gold Coast in the 1950s. Nevertheless, it had a profound effect on public opinion in Bathurst, which was quite unused to such events, and the next day the UP, the GMC, and K. W. Foon, the president of the GNP, all disassoci-ated themselves from both the meeting and the demonstration.[124]

The GDP's willingness to organize a demonstration against Lennox-Boyd sug-gested that it intended to repeat the tactic adopted before the 1951 and 1954 elec-tions of posing as the most radical party. The publication of the new constitutional instruments in September 1959 provided it with good ammunition, because the proposals put forward at the Bathurst Conference in March were watered down considerably. This conference, which was attended by delegates from all four Bathurst parties, together with several independents, recommended the estab-lishment of a House of Representatives of 34 elected and nominated members and a speaker. Nineteen members of Parliament (MPs), seven in the Colony and twelve in the Protectorate, should be elected by universal suffrage, which would mean that, for the first time, ordinary residents of the Protectorate would partici-pate in the political process. The conference also called for an enlarged Executive Council, with an increased number of ministers under a chief minister, as well as the abolition of the unpopular Advisory Committees, which would enable minis-ters to be fully responsible for their departments.[125]

Windley Constitution

Governor Windley accepted most of these proposals, including universal suffrage for the Protectorate, which he considered the most important development; the abolition of the Advisory Committees, which he believed had failed to serve a useful purpose; and an enlarged legislature. These reforms were approved by the Colonial Office, although not without reservation; its preference would have been for only "yard owners" in the Protectorate to be enfranchised.[126] However, Windley (supported by the Colonial Office) insisted on various alterations being made to the conference proposals.

First, the constitutional instruments merely permitted, but did not require, the appointment of a chief minister, Windley arguing that it could not be assumed that "the new franchise would produce anyone able to count on a stable majority or, that if such a person did emerge, he would be qualified to head the administration either as leader of any one party or coalition of several." The rejection of a chief minister meant that, in effect, Gambia had yet to reach the constitutional stage achieved in Sierra Leone as early as 1954.[127]

Second, the new constitution allowed for the appointment of up to six ministers, whereas the conference delegates had sought nine. Windley argued that the colony could not afford the cost in staff, buildings, and facilities for a greater number; he was also anxious that certain key posts (attorney general and financial secretary) should be filled by Europeans, because it was unlikely that suitably qualified persons would be elected to the House of Representatives.

Third, Windley accepted the argument of the Protectorate chiefs (who feared that otherwise they would be swamped by better-educated "carpet-baggers" from Bathurst) that candidates for Protectorate constituencies must either have been born in the Protectorate, or be on the electoral register there, or be recognized as hailing from Protectorate families. In contrast, the Bathurst Conference had proposed that no geographical restrictions should be imposed on candidates.[128]

Fourth, Windley strongly disagreed with the proposal that MPs should be paid salaries, given that the House would probably meet only three or four times a year. He was also concerned that this measure would create a class of professional politicians, which he considered undesirable. He therefore argued that MPs should receive allowances only when the House was in session.[129]

Finally, the governor disliked the proposal that English be made the compulsory language of the House; he feared that this would enable Bathurst politicians to dominate proceedings. He was, however, prepared to compromise on this matter by allowing the Legislative Council to decide the matter and in November 1959, it resolved that English should indeed be adopted as the language of the House.[130]

Immediately after the publication of the new constitution, a Committee of Citizens (which had no connection with Small's organization of the 1930s) was established to oppose it. Its members included Garba-Jahumpa who, having failed to achieve his ends by conservatism, turned to radicalism, and other GMC leaders; E. J. Samba of the GNP; and the leaders of the recently formed Gambia Workers' Union, Momodou E. Jallow and Henry J. Joof (who was also a member of the GNP). But it was dominated by the GDP secretary, A. E. Cham-Joof (who also became its secretary) and by other GDP leaders.[131] In mid-October, a petition criticizing the constitution was presented to Windley, but it had no effect. A subsequent petition to the secretary of state was also rejected.[132]

According to Senghor, all four Bathurst parties were involved in the Committee of Citizens. In fact, even though the UP and GDP delegates had expressed similar opinions at the Bathurst Conference, the UP (and some GNP leaders, including Foon and Jones) were opposed to it. Moreover, after returning from England (where he had gone to prepare an appeal to the Privy Council against being disbarred from the legal profession), P. S. N'Jie publicly endorsed the new constitution.[133] Two factors may help to explain the UP's position. First, acceptance of the constitution would mollify Protectorate opinion and facilitate its efforts to pick up votes in the rural areas. Second, even in Bathurst, public opinion seemed to be rejecting radicalism and the GDP had faced criticism "for leading people astray" by organizing the June demonstration.[134] Indeed, in the October 1959 BTC election, the UP unexpectedly won three seats. It retained New Town East and also won New Town West (defeating the GDP) and Half Die (where the GMC leader, Garba-Jahumpa, lost his seat). The UP also helped its new ally, M. B. Jones of the GNP, to defeat another incumbent, the GDP's secretary, C. R. Grey-Johnson, in Soldier Town. The GMC won only one seat and both GDP candidates were defeated.[135]

By the end of 1959, therefore, the UP seemed to be in the ascendancy, and the GDP and the GMC were in decline. The GNP was hopelessly divided, particularly over the new constitution, and soon ceased to exist, with its leaders joining other parties.[136] Moreover, in contrast to Sierra Leone, where the major party since 1951 had been the Sierra Leone People's Party (SLPP), which drew the bulk of its support from the Protectorate, none of the parties had yet attracted meaningful support outside the Colony.[137] This was to prove fatal because, as will be shown in Chapter 6, the Bathurst parties were soon to be outflanked by a new party, which appealed explicitly to voters in the countryside, the Protectorate People's Party (later the People's Progressive Party).

Summary

Postwar constitutional reforms provided the impetus for the establishment and growth of urban political parties, which were usually set up either to fight Legislative Council elections or in response to their results. These Bathurst parties were dominated by their particular leaders, whose personal alliances and quarrels shaped the nature of politics and overrode sectarian or ethnic divisions within the Colony. Protectorate society still remained largely excluded from the political events of this period.

6

THE "GREEN UPRISING"

THE EMERGENCE OF THE PEOPLE'S PROGRESSIVE PARTY, 1959—65

Until the end of the 1950s, Gambian politics was essentially an urban pheno-menon with the four-fifths of the population that lived in the Protectorate being excluded from national politics. However, the promulgation in 1959 of a new con-stitution, which allocated twelve out of nineteen directly elected seats to the Protectorate, transformed the situation. The People's Progressive Party (PPP), which was specifically founded to give a voice to rural society in national affairs, won more seats than any other party in the first nation-wide election in 1960. Despite suffering a setback when P. S. N'Jie of the rival United Party was appointed chief minister in 1961, it achieved an overall majority in the 1962 election and its leader, D. K. Jawara, was appointed premier. The party strengthened its position after the election, so that by independence in February 1965, it controlled three-quarters of the House of Representatives. The urban parties, in contrast, were by now in terminal decline. Consequently, a "green uprising," a term coined by Huntington to describe the seizure of power by a rurally based political movement opposed to urban based parties, had taken place in Gambia.[1]

The Origins of the People's Progressive Party

During the 1950s, the number of Mandinka living permanently in Bathurst (and Kombo St. Mary) increased significantly, with the recorded Mandinka population of the Colony rising from 4,115 in 1951 to 6,657 in 1963 (see table 1.5). Most Mandinka remained poorly educated and employed in low status jobs as laborers, petty traders, or domestics, but an increasing minority were now better educated and ambitious to advance themselves in the face of the economic ascendancy and

134

social disdain of the urban literate community. Some of these were alumni of Georgetown's Armitage School. As noted in Chapter 1, Armitage was established in the 1920s to cater for the sons and close relatives of Protectorate chiefs, but after World War II, it increased its enrolment.[2] Others had been "adopted" by Christian or Muslim families in Bathurst and had attended secondary schools in the capital, before obtaining clerical posts in the civil service or in the private sector.[3]

To cope with the vicissitudes of urban life, Mandinka immigrants founded a number of welfare and social associations in the 1950s. These included the Lillahi Warasuli (Arabic for "For God and his Messenger Society"), which was founded by Sanjally Bojang. A wealthy but unlettered Mandinka born in 1910, Bojang joined the United Africa Company (UAC) in the late 1920s and had risen to become its head labor contractor by the 1940s. The original aim of the society (which initially was called the Kombo–Niumi Friendship Society) was to ensure that provincial Mandinka who died in the capital received appropriate funerary rites, by arranging for the proper return of their bodies to their home villages. Bojang may have supported P. S. N'Jie in the early 1950s, but by the late 1950s, apparently oscillated between the Gambia Muslim Congress (GMC) and the Gambia Democratic Party (GDP).[4] A similar society was the Janjang Bureh Kaffo, which was founded by Ebrima N'Jie. N'Jie, who was the head of Bathurst Mandinka's community, was a confirmed United Party (UP) supporter.[5]

Apart from the frustrations and unresolved aspirations of provincial youths living in the Colony, British officials noticed a growing unrest among the younger generation in the Protectorate itself as early as the mid-1950s. A study of the Western Division in 1955 identified a "spread of restlessness among young men."[6] This perceptive analysis identified several areas of discontent: youths had no opportunity to become head of their own "yard" (household) until they were forty; chiefs and elders were described as corrupt and reactionary, manipulating the district tribunals to their own advantage, while at the same time adopting a critical attitude towards the young men. The latter's restlessness was also fanned by proximity to Bathurst, with their economic grievances increasingly stirred by new political ideas deriving from the capital. The British themselves felt that some kind of reform of local administration in the Protectorate was required. Gerald Smith, the report's compiler, noted that the jealous protection of their existing powers by the chiefs, local councilors and elders ". . . was not matched in many cases by an equivalent determination to give good and progressive government to a common people."[7]

Early in 1957, a new organization, the Protectorate People's Society (PPS) began to establish itself in Bathurst. The PPS was founded at a meeting on December 30, 1956 at the Bathurst residence of Mamadi B. Sagnia (also known as Momodou Sanyang), a government health inspector in the Medical and Health Department, who was the son of the Seyfu of Kantora in the Upper River Division (URD). Sagnia became its first chairman; other leading figures in the organization included Baro Sanyang, an interpreter at the Magistrates Court, who was originally from Kiang; Bakary K. Sidibeh, a teacher at Yundum College, who became its vice chairman; and B. O. Fofana, then probably an architectural draughtsman in the Public Works Department, who served as its honorary secretary (and later became an ambassador). Other members included Farimang Singhateh, a government pharmacist, who was later the first Gambian governor general and his future wife, Mrs Fanta Basse Sagnia; and M. F. Singhateh, who worked in the Audit Department.[8]

Three future PPP ministers, Sheriff S. Sisay, Lamin B. M'Boge, and Kebba N. Leigh, were also members of the PPS in the late 1950s. All three were from MacCarthy Island Division (MID) and were members of chiefly families. The son of the late Seykuba Sisay, a long-serving Seyfu of Niamina District, Sisay was employed as a clerk in the Education Department; by October 1958, he had succeeded Fofana as honorary secretary of the PPS. M'Boge, who was employed as a records clerk in the Public Works Department, was a close relative of Seyfu Lamin Bakoto M'Boge of Niamina Dankunku, and Leigh (who was a carpenter) was related to Seyfu Koba Leigh of Fulladu West (who was one of the representatives of the chiefs on the Legislative Council).[9] Many (although by no means all) of the most active members of the PPS were young,[10] educated (primary education in many instances), and resident in Bathurst. Most were of Mandinka origin.[11]

At first the PPS made little impact, but in October 1958, it unexpectedly merged with Bojang's Lillahi Warasuli society. This followed virulent criticism of Bojang (and the Protectorate people as a whole) by the Bathurst pressure group, the Committee of Gentlemen, in part because Bojang had organized a petition seeking an extension to Governor Wyn-Harris' term of office. The merger with Bojang's society greatly enhanced the status of the PPS within the Mandinka community. Bojang was appointed president and Sagnia vice president; Sisay became general secretary. The organization's stronghold was the Kombos, where Bojang wielded great influence.[12] Shortly afterward, the PPS resolved to convert itself into a political party, the Protectorate People's Party (ProtPP), to enable it to participate more effectively in the ongoing discussions about a new constitution.[13] The formation of such a party was welcomed by the Protectorate chiefs and, significantly, the establishment of the ProtPP was formally announced at the annual Chiefs' Conference at Basse in February 1959.[14] Over the next few months, some chiefs offered considerable assistance to the fledgling party and in some districts helped to coordinate its fund raising.[15]

During the first few months of its existence, the ProtPP was led by Sanjally Bojang, who devoted considerable time and resources to canvassing support for the new party in the Protectorate.[16] However, by the end of 1959, the ProtPP had chosen a new "party leader," David Kwesi (later Dawda Kairaba) Jawara. Born in 1924 at Barajally in MID, Jawara was the son of a prosperous, but low status—his father was a "nyamalo," a member of the leatherworker caste—Mandinka Muslim trader and farmer. He was brought up by a prominent Muslim family in Bathurst and educated initially at its Mohammedan School (where he was a student of I. M. Garba-Jahumpa) and subsequently at the Methodist Boys' High School (MBHS).

After working for two years as a nurse at the Royal Victoria Hospital in Bathurst, he obtained a part scholarship in 1947 to study nursing at the prestigious Achimota College in the Gold Coast. In the following year, he secured a place at Glasgow University's Veterinary School, again on a part scholarship, becoming the first Mandinka to gain a university degree. On his return to Gambia in January 1954, he entered the veterinary department and by 1958, following a further period of training in Scotland, this time at Edinburgh University, he had become principal veterinary officer, the highest position in the civil service yet obtained by a Mandinka.[17] In 1955, he converted to Christianity, apparently so that he could marry Augusta Mahoney, a nursing sister in the Protectorate, who was the daughter of the Aku speaker of the Legislative Council, John (later Sir John) Mahoney. This was a very prestigious marriage for a provincial Mandinka.[18]

Jawara's appointment as leader of the ProtPP may appear surprising for several reasons. First, although he apparently joined the PPS around October 1958, he did not become an office holder of the society. Second, as noted, his family was of relatively low status in Mandinka society. But these disadvantages were more than outweighed by other factors. Jawara was one of only two Mandinka graduates at this time; he was the head of a government department; and his standing as an effective "cow doctor," in a society where cattle were highly prized, meant that he was a very popular figure in the Protectorate. He was therefore selected as "party leader" ahead of other candidates, such as B. K. Sidibeh and the only other Mandinka graduate, the director of agriculture, Dr. Lamin J. Marenah. At the same time, Bojang was confirmed as the ProtPP's national president and Sisay resigned from government service in early 1960 to become its full-time administrative secretary.[19]

The ProtPP thus acquired a foothold in the Protectorate by the end of 1959, but it had little or no support in Bathurst (it had not even bothered to contest the 1959 Bathurst Town Council (BTC) election). As part of its attempt to widen its appeal, particularly in the urban areas, the party dropped its formal identification with the Protectorate in December 1959 when it was renamed the People's Progressive Party (originally the Progressive People's Party) (PPP). It was now ready to prepare for the first nation-wide election in 1960.

The 1960 Election

The election took place over a two-week period between May 18 and 30, 1960.[20] It was contested by the PPP, P. S. N'Jie's United Party and a new party, the Democratic Congress Alliance (DCA), which was formed through a merger of the GDP led by Rev. J. C. Faye and the GMC headed by I. M. Garba-Jahumpa. Each is considered in turn. The fourth urban political party, the Gambia National Party (GNP), did not formally contest the election, although, as noted, its general secretary, M. B. Jones, did stand as an Independent. The GNP was always a loose coalition of individuals and its internal divisions were widened by the Windley Constitution, which, as noted in Chapter 5, some founder members had welcomed and others had opposed. These internal disagreements remained and it now ceased to function. There was also a separate indirect election for Protectorate chiefs, which was held at the Chiefs' Conference at Georgetown in May.

One complicating factor for this election was that, unlike in later Gambian elections, candidates were not required in 1960 to declare their party allegiance before polling day and many of them in fact chose not to do so. Although nominally Independent, a number of these candidates received the endorsement of one party or another without actually standing under its colors. Appendix table C.1 provides our assessment of the political affiliation (and ethnic origin) of all fifty-five candidates in the election, but it is not possible to be certain about either factor in all cases.

People's Progressive Party

Undoubtedly, the PPP fielded more candidates of its own than either the UP or DCA. Indeed, the central leadership of the party made strenuous efforts to find candidates in all twelve Protectorate constituencies (although, as discussed below, these efforts were thwarted in Basse). The main factors in selecting candidates were an individual's record of political activity within the PPS and/or the PPP; their occupational status; and the local importance of their families.[21]

At least three candidates, M. B. Sagnia (Kantora); Sheriff Sisay (Niamina); and K. N. Leigh (MacCarthy Island) had been members of the PPS; a fourth, B. K. Sidibeh, was initially offered the party nomination in MacCarthy Island, hesitated over accepting, and was replaced by Leigh.[22] Two others, Jawara (Kombo) and Sheriff M. Dibba (Baddibu), had been prominent in the PPP in 1959–60. Dibba, who was the twenty-three-year-old son of a Mandinka farmer from Salikene in Central Baddibu, was educated at Armitage School and the MBHS. Formerly a clerk for the UAC, he had served as a PPP assistant secretary since 1959.[23]

Several PPP candidates in the Protectorate were either civil servants or school teachers. The former were required to resign to stand for election, but could apply to be reappointed if they were defeated at the polls (and could expect to regain their jobs). This group included Jawara, who was the most senior Protectorate-born civil servant; Sisay; and Jerreh L. B. Daffeh (Kiang), who was a junior employee in the Veterinary Department. The latter group included Michael Baldeh (Basse) and Musa S. Dabo (Wuli-Sandu).[24]

In Michael Baldeh's case, a more important consideration than his occupational status (or, indeed, his limited involvement in Bathurst politics in the 1950s), was that the Baldehs of Mansajang Kunda were one of the two families who contested the chieftaincy of Upper Fulladu East. Baldeh's endorsement by the PPP, which was enforced by Sanjally Bojang and other PPP militants, meant that their bitter rivals, the Kruballys of Koba Kunda, promptly turned against the party and, as noted below, three of the sons of Seyfu Jewru Krubally were to stand against the

PPP as Independent candidates. But the selection of Baldeh backfired, for although the PPP paid his election deposit, he appears to have secretly defected to the UP even before the election.[25] Several other PPP candidates were related to, or endorsed by, incumbent chiefs. Daffeh, for example, was apparently the nephew of Seyfu Karamo K. Sanneh of Kiang West, and Omar Jame Sise (Niani-Saloum) was the son of the Seyfu of Upper Saloum, Matar Sise. Moreover, Kalilu S. Dabo, the son of Seyfu Soro Dabo of Jarra East, was initially chosen as the PPP's candidate in Jarra, but was later dropped for supporting the idea of an alliance with the DCA and replaced by a young policeman from Sankwia, Yaya Ceesay.[26]

The PPP's rudimentary organization meant that it contested only two out of seven seats in the Colony. Alphonso M. (Fansu) Demba, another civil servant, was selected to fight Kombo East, and Augusta Jawara, the wife of the party leader, became the first Gambian woman to contest a Legislative Council/Parliamentary election. She stood in Soldier Town, Bathurst, a constituency in which her fellow Aku made up one-quarter of the Gambian population.[27] The PPP also endorsed the candidature of an Independent, A. S. C. Able-Thomas (a retired Aku headmaster), in another Bathurst seat, New Town West.[28] Perhaps as many as 11 of the 14 candidates who were originally selected by the PPP (i.e., including Baldeh) were Mandinka. These were D. K. Jawara, Sisay, Dibba, Daffeh, Demba, Sagnia, Leigh, Dabo, Yaya Ceesay, O. J. Sise (Niani-Saloum) and Famara B. Manneh (Niumi-Jokadu). There was also one Jola, Momodou N. Sanyang (Foni); one Fula Firdu (Baldeh); and one Aku (A. Jawara). Apart from the Jawaras, who were Methodists, and Baldeh, who was a Roman Catholic, it is probable that all were Muslims as well.[29] Many of them were in their 20s or 30s and were to remain politically active for two decades or more. One had a criminal record, which did not prevent him from standing for election.[30]

United Party

The UP fielded fewer candidates of its own than the PPP, but appears to have endorsed a number of others who were nominally Independents. It is possible that as few as six candidates—five in the Colony and one in the Protectorate—openly declared for the UP at the time of their election.[31] Four of these—the party leader, P. S. N'Jie (New Town East), Joseph H. Joof (Half Die), Ishmael B. I. Jobe (New Town West), and J. E. Mahoney (Jolloff/Portuguese Town)—sought seats in Bathurst. All bar N'Jie had a background in local politics in the capital; indeed, in the equivalent wards in the 1959 BTC election, Joof and Jobe were elected and Mahoney (who was the party's general secretary) was defeated. N'Jie's half-brother, Ebrima D. N'Jie, was selected to fight Kombo West (the modern Serrekunda West). A former welfare and labor officer, who had retired from the civil service in 1955, E. D. N'Jie had qualified as a barrister in February 1958 and worked in his brother's law firm. He often served as party leader during P. S. N'Jie's many absences from the Colony. Two of the five UP candidates in the Colony were lawyers (the two N'Jies); Mahoney was a retired school teacher; Jobe worked as a writer for the shipping line, Elder Dempster; and Joof was a clerk.[32]

The party's only definite candidate in the Protectorate was Alasan N. Touray, a Wolof, who fought Niani-Saloum.[33] However, according to the party chairman, M. B. N'Jie, the UP fielded two other candidates in the Protectorate. One of these was certainly Michael Baldeh, and the other was probably Numukunda M. Darbo, a trader from Bansang, who contested MacCarthy Island.[34] If this assessment is correct, then the UP probably fielded five Wolof candidates (P. S. and E. D. N'Jie, Joof, Jobe, and Touray), one Aku (Mahoney), one Fula (Baldeh), and one Mandinka (Darbo). Thus the ethnic origin of the UP and PPP candidates differed considerably with the overrepresentation of the Wolof and the underrepresentation of the Mandinka among UP candidates being particularly striking. UP candidates also differed from their PPP counterparts in terms of religious persuasion; four out of the eight (Mahoney, Joof, P. S. N'Jie, and Baldeh) were Christian.[35]

M. B. N'Jie also asserted that the UP had "adopted" the GNP's general secretary, M. B. Jones (another Aku Christian), as its candidate in Soldier Town, Bathurst, and supported seven other Independent candidates in the Protectorate. He also claimed that, in total, the UP's own candidates and those it supported received just under 24,000 votes in the election. Although there is no doubt that the UP assisted Jones, as indeed he had been in the equivalent ward in the 1959 BTC election, the suggestion that the UP also endorsed candidates in most Protectorate constituencies where it did not have a candidate of its own is more controversial. N'Jie's argument was put forward to refute the colonial secretary's view that the UP gained only 6,000 votes out of a possible 69,000 in the election; he therefore had every incentive to exaggerate the degree of UP support in the country.[36] N'Jie provides no indication of the nature or extent of UP endorsement of the Independent candidates and it is doubtful whether it amounted to much in areas where the UP had only a rudimentary party structure. Nevertheless, we have taken N'Jie's claim at face value and have endeavored, therefore, to ascertain which candidates might have received the UP's assistance.

On the basis of the limited contemporary evidence, the reflections nearly four decades on of Assan Musa (formerly Andrew D.) Camara, one of the candidates in 1960, and the political stance adopted by individuals in the 1962 and 1966 elections (not always a reliable guide, of course, to their political leanings in 1960), our view is that the UP supported the following eight Independent candidates: Jones; A. D. Camara (Kantora); Omar J. Ceesay (Niamina); Saihou Biyai (Foni); Kantora Juwara (Wuli-Sandu); Kalilu S. Dabo (Jarra), after he had lost the PPP nomination; either B. or L. Sanneh (Kiang); and Landing Omar Sonko (Niumi-Jokadu). The ethnic origin of these candidates differed from the main UP candidates; four were Mandinka, the others being a Fula Firdu, an Aku, a Jola, and a Serahuli.[37] The eight presumed UP candidates—Jones and the seven candidates the party supported in the Protectorate—in total received more than 23,500 votes (irrespective of the identity of its candidate in Kiang), which would be consistent with M. B. N'Jie's claim. If this interpretation is correct, then the UP failed to nominate or support a candidate in only two constituencies, Kombo and Baddibu.

Democratic Congress Alliance

The DCA was established only a month before the election, following the amalgamation of the GDP and GMC. Faye became "Leader of Alliance," and Garba-Jahumpa was appointed its secretary general. Other posts were divided up between the two parties.[38] Tactical expediency largely explained the merger for, as we have seen, the two leaders had a past history of intense personal rivalry. A joint Christian–Muslim leadership, and Faye's presumed good standing in the Protectorate (particularly in the URD), were seen as potential vote winners. Even so, the merger was not universally welcomed by GMC supporters and, as discussed below, three leading GMC members were in fact to stand as Independents in Bathurst, having failed to secure the Alliance's nomination.

The DCA nominated candidates in all five Bathurst seats. Like the UP, it relied on individuals with a background in municipal politics. Alieu B. N'Jie (Joloff/Portuguese Town) and Alieu E. Cham-Joof (New Town East) were serving members of the BTC, and Garba-Jahumpa (Half Die) and Crispin R. Grey-Johnson (Soldier Town) were former members, having been defeated in the 1959 election. The DCA's other definite candidate in Bathurst was Momodou D. Sallah, a former headmaster of Armitage School (New Town West); it is also possible that the party supported an Independent, S. J. Oldfield, who had been a candidate in the 1954 Legislative Council election, in Kombo East.

A. B. N'Jie's decision to accept the DCA nomination is particularly interesting. A Muslim Wolof in his mid-fifties who had reached the senior position of registrar of the Supreme Court before his retirement from the civil service in 1958, N'Jie had represented the Joloff/Portuguese Town ward on the BTC as an Independent since 1949. He was not listed as a DCA office holder in April 1960 and may have been persuaded to stand as a candidate for the Alliance at the last moment.[39] Meanwhile, the party leader, Rev. J. C. Faye, perhaps surprisingly, contested Kombo West. He had apparently intended to stand in the Protectorate (presumably in the URD), but was prevented from doing so by the regulation that candidates in such seats must either have been born in the Protectorate or be recognized as originating from Protectorate families (the intention of the British, as noted in Chapter 5, being to prevent "carpet baggers" from Bathurst gaining a presence in the interior). This ruling in fact appears to have prevented the DCA nominating any candidates in the Protectorate at all.[40] Three of the known six DCA candidates, A. B. N'Jie, Cham-Joof, and Garba-Jahumpa, were Wolof; Faye was a "Wolofized" Serere; Grey-Johnson was an Aku; and Sallah was a Tukulor. Two were Christian and four were Muslim.[41]

Independents

Party formation was of course still in a fledgling stage in 1960 and there was a considerable number of Independent candidates both in the Colony and the Protectorate. In the Colony, Jones, Able-Thomas, and perhaps Oldfield, received the overt or tacit endorsement of a political party, whereas, as noted, seven

Independents were supported by the UP in the Protectorate. In addition, according to Governor Windley, three GMC members who lost out when the DCA divided constituencies between the GMC and GDP, also stood as Independents.[42] These were H. O. Semega-Janneh, a member of the Legislative Council in the 1950s, who stood in his home area of Kombo West against the DCA party leader, Faye; I. A. S. Burang-John, an employee of the Marine Department and a GMC councilor for the Half Die ward, who opposed Garba-Jahumpa in the same constituency; and Sulayman B. Gaye, the cashier of the UAC and until recently the general secretary of the GMC, who opposed A. B. N'Jie in Joloff/Portuguese Town.[43]

At least two of the Independent candidates in the Protectorate, B. K. Sidibeh and Kalilu Dabo, were initially offered the PPP nomination, but later were replaced and then stood against the PPP candidate. Another, Andrew Camara, claimed that he was wooed by both the PPP and UP, but rejected the overtures of both parties at the behest of his constituents. Originally from Mansajang in the Basse area of URD, and a Fula Firdu, Camara was the son of a farmer and cattle breeder and was educated in Bathurst. An Anglican, he was then aged thirty-seven and, having taught at the Kristikunda mission school since 1948, latterly as headmaster, was a well-respected figure in the URD.[44]

Other Independents may have been encouraged to stand for election by individual Protectorate chiefs who were anxious to secure a voice in the new House of Representatives. For example, three of the sons of Seyfu Jewru Krubally of Fulladu East stood in Basse, Kantora, and Wuli-Sandu; Landing Omar Sonko, the son of Seyfu Landing Omar Sonko of Upper Niumi contested Niumi-Jokadu; and Kalilu B. Jammeh, the son of Seyfu Tamba Jammeh of Upper Baddibu, stood in Baddibu.[45] The best educated chief, Omar M'Baki of Sami, even toyed with the idea of standing as an Independent, but in the end decided not to.[46] Some of the remaining Independent candidates were probably genuinely unattached to any party or grouping; certainly, unlike in some neighboring French West African colonies where pro-government parties were encouraged by the colonial power to try and curb radical anti-colonial movements, there is no evidence of any official sponsorship of candidates by the Gambian government, although some officials clearly disliked the more disruptive elements in the PPP.[47]

Trade Union Neutrality

Finally, it is worth noting that the trade union movement remained neutral in the election; unlike elsewhere in West Africa, active Gambian trade union leaders neither stood for election themselves nor endorsed a particular party.[48] We saw in Chapter 5 that the Gambia Labour Union (GLU) and the Gambia Amalgamated Trade Union played a small role in the 1947 Legislative Council election, and Faye established the Motor Drivers' and Mechanics' Union to try to improve his prospects in the 1951 election. The labor movement was in a moribund state in the mid-1950s and did not play a significant role in the 1954 election. However, in

February 1960, only a few months before the election, a new general workers' union, the Gambia Workers' Union (GWU), led by M. E. Jallow, organized the first successful general strike in The Gambia since 1929. In the immediate aftermath of the strike, Governor Windley gained the impression that Jallow and other union leaders would try to capitalize on their success by seeking power at the ballot box.[49] But in fact Jallow, who realized the danger of disruption to the union if the GWU were to participate in the election (particularly given the varied political allegiances of its leaders and rank-and-file members), chose to remain neutral. The GWU instead preferred vociferously to denounce all parties as ineffective and open to manipulation by the colonial government and demanded further constitutional reform.[50]

Election Process

Prior to this election, a unique "drum and marble" method of voting was specially devised by two colonial officials. Under this system, a voter used a marble rather than a ballot paper to cast a vote. The marble was dropped through a narrow tube into an empty, sealed steel drum, which contained a bicycle bell; as it fell to the bottom of the drum, it struck the bell which made a sound audible to the presiding officer and the party agents outside the ballot box. One source of confusion was that the marbles used were blue—the party color of the PPP! This system was intended not only to make it easier for illiterate voters to participate (each drum bore the name, photograph, and chosen symbol of the candidate), but also to prevent electoral fraud. Multiple voting was not feasible; if a voter tried to drop two marbles into the drum, two sounds would be heard. This method (which has been used in all subsequent Gambian elections), together with the close checking of voters' credentials, was completely successful and ensured that the contest would be uncommonly honest by the standards of the region.[51]

The election was noteworthy, not only because it was free and fair, but also because it was not marred by any significant violence. Unlike in other pre-independence elections elsewhere in British West Africa, notably the elections in the Gold Coast in 1956 and Nigeria in 1959, there was very little unrest during the election campaign. Only two serious incidents were reported, both in the URD at Fantumbu and Basse, and only in the latter was there serious fighting between supporters of different parties and rioting.[52]

Election Results

The election was hard fought throughout Gambia. There were thirty-five candidates for twelve seats in the Protectorate, only one of which (Kombo) was not contested, and twenty candidates for seven seats in the Colony.[53] The turnout was high in the Colony where more than 90 percent of the registered electorate voted. The turnout was much lower in the Protectorate, at 51 percent, in part because the registers prepared in 1959 proved defective. The registers were initially prepared in Arabic script and many errors occurred when they were transliterated into Roman script. This made it difficult to identify individual names and quite a number of people who registered correctly were turned away at the polling stations as their names could not be found.[54]

The confusion over the party affiliation of candidates means that external commentators have not agreed about the detailed results. However, after a careful analysis of the evidence, including Colonial Office files released in the 1990s, our conclusion is that the PPP won nine seats, the UP five, and the DCA one. Four Independents, one of whom was allied with the UP, were also elected. This assessment differs from other accounts.[55] An initial report in the *Gambia News Bulletin* (*GNB*) at the beginning of June 1960 stated that the PPP had gained 27,521 votes (44 percent of those cast); the UP, 14,190 votes (22 percent); the DCA, 3,525 votes (6 percent); and the various Independent candidates between them, 17,368 votes (28 percent). This analysis of the performance of the various parties has been generally accepted by secondary sources; however, a comparison of these figures with the final results published later in the *GNB* show that they are incomplete, because a total of 69,048, rather than 62,604, votes were actually cast. It is not possible to account for the discrepancy between these figures. Our assessment is that the PPP won 25,490 votes (36.9 percent); the UP, 12,497 votes (18.1 percent); and the DCA, 3,526 votes (5.1 percent). The various Independent candidates gained 27,535 votes (39.9 percent) in total.[56]

Although the PPP gained fewer votes than the Independents, it won most seats. Moreover, its share of the vote would have been even greater had Jawara faced any opposition in the safe seat of Kombo. Not surprisingly, it fared particularly well in the Protectorate, where it was successful in eight out of twelve constituencies. This was an impressive achievement, given that the party was still in its infancy, and occurred for a number of reasons. First, as noted, the party often managed to persuade powerful local political leaders, like Michael Baldeh, to accept the party symbol. This pragmatic approach to candidate selection reaped rich dividends. Second, the party was much better organized than its rivals. In the months before the election, it set up a basic party structure in the countryside with PPP branches being established in many areas.[57] Third, it campaigned vigorously in the Protectorate, making extremely effective use of the traditional election techniques of drumming and dancing; the "osiko" drum, introduced from Senegal, served as the rallying point for young men and women. The highlight of the campaign was a grand tour of the whole Protectorate organized by Sanjally Bojang shortly before the election.[58] Fourth, its party leader, Jawara, was well-known and respected in the Protectorate because of his veterinary work (e.g., he had recently helped to control an outbreak of cattle rinderpest), whereas the leaders of the Bathurst parties were neither as familiar nor as well-regarded.[59] Fifth, the PPP was regarded at grassroots level as a farmers' party—its emblem was the hoe (the UP's was an umbrella), symbolic of the party's struggle for farmers' rights as well as independence.[60] Finally, the PPP was also considered to be a Mandinka party and it could thus capitalize on the built-in Mandinka majority in the Protectorate. It is no coincidence that it won seven out of the eight Protectorate constituencies (Baddibu, Jarra, Kiang, Kombo, MacCarthy Island, Niamina, and Wuli-Sandu) in which the Mandinka comprised the largest ethnic group. The only exception was Niumi-Jokadu (where the successful Independent, L. O. Sonko, was himself a Mandinka). The PPP's other victory in the Protectorate was in Foni. The Jola comprised three-quarters of the Gambian population in this constituency and the PPP candidate, M. N. Sanyang, was a Jola.[61]

One other factor probably on balance also helped the PPP secure victory. During the election campaign, some PPP activists adopted a militant anti-chieftaincy stance. This probably brought the PPP more support from Protectorate "commoners," who were dissatisfied with the activities of their chiefs, than it cost it in the loss of votes from the more conservatively minded. A few chiefs who had originally supported the establishment of the PPP, were already turning against the party as early as October 1959, but there is no evidence that they campaigned as a group against the PPP. Their collective opposition to the PPP was rather to manifest itself a few months after the polls.[62]

In striking contrast to its success in the Protectorate, the PPP won only one seat in the Colony. This was Kombo East, where Fansu Demba defeated S. J. Oldfield by twenty-three votes. Because Oldfield was a much better known candidate, it is likely that ethnicity tipped the balance in Demba's favor; he was a Mandinka in a predominantly Mandinka constituency, whereas Oldfield was an Aku.[63] But Augusta Jawara was a well-beaten third in Soldier Town, her family ties having proved ineffective against two prominent local politicians, both of whom were Aku like herself. Indeed, the PPP would not be able to win a seat in Bathurst in any general election until 1972.

The UP won three Bathurst seats, New Town East, New Town West, and Half Die and was defeated only in Joloff/Portuguese Town. M. B. Jones was also successful in Soldier Town with UP support. This confirmed the UP's good showing in the 1959 BTC election when it won the same three wards and also helped Jones to win Soldier Town. It also demonstrated the personal popularity of the party leader, P. S. N'Jie, who continued to have a particularly strong following among women in the capital, and made effective use of their neighborhood associations (the "kompins"), which strengthened his party's ward organization in Bathurst. The UP also benefited from Roman Catholic support.[64] The party was also relatively well financed. The financial resources of the leader and other party candidates were augmented from funds raised by ward and neighborhood associations and by donations from richer members of the business community, in particular the merchant, M. M. N'Jie. A key supporter of Rev. J. C. Faye in the early 1950s, M. M. N'Jie, who was described in the mid-1960s as the richest man in The Gambia, had begun to support P. S. N'Jie in the late 1950s.[65]

Alasan Touray easily defeated the PPP's O. J. Sise in Niani-Saloum. This was not surprising, because this was the one Protectorate constituency in which the Wolof made up the largest single group of the population. In addition, the UP emphasis on its "Wolofness" ("Saloum Het"), with N'Jie making great play of the fact that he was the nephew of Semu Joof, the last king of Saloum, was of course particularly effective in this constituency.[66] Michael Baldeh also won comfortably in Basse. However, E. D. N'Jie was defeated in a four-cornered contest in Kombo West and Darbo was defeated in MacCarthy Island.

The sole DCA winner was A. B. N'Jie. Elsewhere, the party's failure confirmed its poor showing in the 1959 BTC election, when the GMC won only one ward out of five and the GDP none. Although possibly a surprise to contemporaries, the defeat of the party's leaders, Faye and Garba-Jahumpa, was not unpredictable. Faye contested a seat (Kombo West) where he had no significant electoral base against Semega-Janneh, a wealthy candidate with strong local connections, and Garba-Jahumpa had been defeated by the same candidate, J. H. Joof, in the equivalent ward in the 1959 BTC election. This did not prevent Garba-Jahumpa publicly claiming that Joof had bribed the electorate to ensure his narrow victory (he won by sixty-six votes), a charge that was subsequently rejected by the Supreme Court.[67]

Apart from Jones and Sonko, two other Independents, Semega-Janneh and Camara, were successful. Jones joined the UP immediately after the election and although Semega-Janneh had defeated the UP's candidate, E. D. N'Jie, he also quickly joined forces with the UP (although nominally remaining an Independent for the time being). The other two GMC rebels, Burang-John and Gaye, also joined the UP soon after the election.[68]

At least seven defeated candidates from differing parties (or their supporters) petitioned the Supreme Court to have the results overturned, but only O. J. Sise was successful. The court ruled in October that the UP's A. N. Touray was not on the register in Niani-Saloum at the time of the election and he was unseated. But, as noted below, the UP retained the seat in the subsequent by-election in January 1961.[69]

Five of those elected in the separate election of chiefs had served in previous Legislative Councils, including their most prominent member, Tamba Jammeh of Upper Baddibu and the much younger, but better educated, Omar M'Baki of Sami, who to became their political spokesman.[70]

Ministerial Appointments: 1960–61

July 1960 Appointments

A few days after the election, Governor Windley appointed six of the newly elected members of parliament (MPs) as ministers. This followed discussions with various MPs including Jawara, P. S. N'Jie, A. B. N'Jie, and Camara, all of whom submitted nominations for ministerial office. Jawara's list consisted of PPP MPs and the DCA's A. B. N'Jie, but excluded UP MPs, Independents, and the Protectorate Chief MPs. A UP deputation submitted a list that included UP MPs (and Semega-Janneh) only. According to Windley, A. B. N'Jie and Camara presented a "coalition" list and promised to cooperate in any government, particularly with the chiefs.

Governor Windley's own preference was to appoint members of all parties and groups to the Executive Council after the first nation-wide election. Because no party achieved an overall majority, he was able to choose a representative of each of the parties (Jawara, P. S. N'Jie, and A. B. N'Jie); a chief (M'Baki); and two of the three remaining Independents, Semega-Janneh and Camara. Semega-Janneh was one of the few elected members with prior legislative experience, and Windley regarded Camara (erroneously) as a strong supporter of the chiefs. Windley did not, however, appoint a chief minister. All except P. S. N'Jie and Camara were offered specific portfolios and all bar the former accepted their preferment.[71]

Windley was reluctant to grant P. S. N'Jie full ministerial responsibilities for two reasons. First, his record as a minister in the mid-1950s had been far from satisfactory and Windley, who appears to have regarded him as "unbalanced," considered that he needed to reestablish himself in a minor post.[72] Second, there was a danger that the original decision of the Gambian Supreme Court to disbar N'Jie from the legal profession might be upheld by the highest court, the Judicial Committee of the Privy Council. On the eve of the election, the Privy Council allowed the attorney general of Gambia to lodge an appeal against a decision by the West African Court of Appeal to overturn N'Jie's disbarment. It would be a cause of some embarrassment to the government if the original verdict were to be upheld while N'Jie was serving as a minister. N'Jie, who apparently confidently expected to be appointed chief minister after the election, reacted with "pained surprise" when informed that he had not been offered a portfolio and immediately declined to serve on the Executive Council. Consequently, Windley appointed a second PPP MP, Sheriff Sisay, to fill the vacancy.[73]

UP MPs were angered that their leader was not offered a specific portfolio and that they did not receive more posts in the coalition government. They therefore staged a walk out from the House of Representatives during its official opening on June 15 and, following subsequent demonstrations in Bathurst, a memorial was sent to both Windley and the secretary of state for the colonies. This memorial, which was organized by the UP Executive Committee, expressed dissatisfaction with the election, the subsequent ministerial appointments, and the current government. Even though P. S. N'Jie had accepted the 1959 constitution before the election, the UP memorial also called for its abrogation and demanded that Gambia become fully self-governing. The UP's request for further constitutional change was rejected by the Gambian government and the party was henceforth effectively at odds with the governor.[74]

Meanwhile, although the PPP had in the end secured more seats on the Executive Council than the other parties, it remained dissatisfied with the coalition government that had denied it the fruits of its victory at the polls. At the beginning of October, its opposition to the policies of the Gambian government became overt when it issued its "Independence Manifesto." This manifesto, which was finalized by Jawara during a visit to Lagos to celebrate the granting of independence to Nigeria, called for internal self-government by May 1961, which should be followed by independence during 1962.[75] Because the DCA remained committed to independence, all three political parties were now seeking further constitutional change.

Appointment of a Chief Minister

Governor Windley was reluctant to revise a constitution that had come into force so recently, but realized the need to make further concessions to the political parties. After securing the approval of the Colonial Office, he therefore announced to the House of Representatives in December 1960 that he would shortly appoint a chief minister. The composition of the House meant that Jawara, P. S. N'Jie, and M'Baki each had a bloc of support, and A. B. N'Jie was a possible compromise candidate who might be able to command a majority if all else failed. Windley held discussions with the various candidates in January and February of 1961 and ascertained that Jawara and P. S. N'Jie would not serve under each other and that neither would serve under M'Baki or A. B. N'Jie. Effectively this meant that the chiefs (who were acting in concert) held the balance of power; their eight votes would be enough to give either the UP or the PPP the fourteen votes necessary for an overall majority of the elected members.[76]

Once the chiefs realized that M'Baki would not be selected for the post of chief minister, they made clear their preference for P. S. N'Jie over Jawara. In July 1960, they complained to Acting Governor Smith that their status in rural society was being "seriously threatened" by members of PPP. They noted that the public was being advised by PPP MPs to disobey their lawful orders and court summonses and instead to take their complaints to the MPs to resolve. They also claimed that PPP MPs were stirring up hatred in the rural areas. Jawara subsequently agreed to tell his supporters not to try to usurp the customary and statutory powers of the Seyfolu, but the chiefs remained suspicious of his party's intentions.[77] In contrast, the UP appeared willing to allow the chiefs free rein in the rural areas and was also prepared to give them a permanent role in national politics through the establishment of a separate House of Chiefs.[78]

By March 1961, Windley ascertained not only that the Protectorate chief MPs preferred P. S. N'Jie to Jawara, but that all the Independent MPs (and A. B. N'Jie) supported the UP leader.[79] This was sufficient for N'Jie to command a majority. Several other factors were in N'Jie's favor. First, Windley appears to have modified his previously unfavorable opinion of the UP leader, whom he considered to have steadied down and to have given up alcohol.[80] Second, the governor believed that, in both the Colony and the Protectorate, public opinion was moving toward the UP. This view seems to have been based on the result of a by-election in Niani-Saloum, which was called after the unseating of Touray; E. D. N'Jie comfortably retained the seat for the UP.[81] Finally, Windley believed that P. S. N'Jie was more likely than Jawara to have influence over the leader of the GWU, M. E. Jallow, who he regarded as a dangerous militant with radical political connections.

The GWU had called another general strike in January 1961. This strike, which paralyzed the country and resulted in a substantial wage increase, firmly established Jallow's reputation and Windley was now convinced that Jallow would use his success as a stepping stone for power on a slogan of Independence for Gambia and a fair deal for Gambians vis-à-vis Europeans. The 1961 strike revealed that the PPP had little influence over the GWU; Jawara and Sisay, the PPP members of the Executive Council, were powerless either to prevent the strike or to help bring it to a rapid conclusion, and had indeed "remained rather on the sidelines." In contrast, Windley believed that the GWU received considerable support from P. S. N'Jie and the UP during the strike. Because Windley was aware that many GWU members were UP supporters, the governor hoped that the GWU leader would be reluctant to undermine a UP-led administration by further militancy.[82] Consequently, on March 14, he informed the Executive Council of his decision to appoint P. S. N'Jie as chief minister.

Although Jawara was not surprised by this turn of events, he naturally complained about the decision, arguing that the chiefs should be required to support the largest party and claiming that three of the Independent MPs would have supported him if he had been nominated. When Windley refused to change his mind, he resigned from the Executive Council; Sisay followed suit later that day. A. B. N'Jie also resigned on March 21, not apparently out of sympathy with the PPP ministers, but rather at Windley's request when it became clear that he was unacceptable to the UP. The three ministers were replaced by P. S. N'Jie, E. D. N'Jie, and Baldeh, which meant that the council now comprised three UP MPs, two Independents (both of whom were closer to the UP than to the PPP), and one chief.[83] Because the majority party in the House was no longer represented on the Executive Council, Windley convened a new Constitutional Conference in Bathurst in May, which was attended by three representatives of each of the political parties, three chiefs, and three independents, Jallow, Henry Madi, and Rachel Palmer (a doctor's wife who was selected to represent Gambian women). The Bathurst Conference called for full internal self-government as the next stage of the constitutional process, which should be followed within nine months by independence. These views were then reiterated two months later at a follow-up Constitutional Conference in London attended by representatives of the various political parties and of the chiefs and by other independent individuals.[84]

It was agreed at the London Conference that a new constitution should be drawn up. This constitution (which would come into operation after a new election) reduced the powers of the governor, who was now required to act on the advice of the Executive Council in all areas of internal affairs except security and the public service. The composition of the Executive Council was also revised; its membership now consisted of the governor, the deputy governor, and eight ministers. The composition of the House of Representatives was also altered significantly. The number of elected members was increased to thirty-two, with twenty-five seats being allocated to the Protectorate and seven to the Colony; the representation of the Protectorate chiefs was reduced to four. The leader of the majority party in the House was to be appointed as premier by the governor and would then advise the latter on the appointment of the other ministers. Finally, it was agreed that a new general election should be held by May 1962.[85] This election is discussed below.

1962 Election

Three parties, the PPP, the UP, and the DCA, contested the next election which took place between May 22 and 31.[86] In marked contrast to the 1960 election, there was only one Independent candidate, Karamo Kinteh, in Lower Baddibu (see Appendix C.2). Two of the three parties, the PPP and DCA, formed an electoral pact, and the UP received the support of a new political organization, the Gambia National Union.

People's Progressive Party/Democratic Congress Alliance

The DCA and PPP had tended to coordinate their activities in opposition to the UP since the resignation of A. B. N'Jie from the Executive Council in March 1961. The two parties adopted a common position on key issues at the London Conference and (along with the GWU leader, M. E. Jallow) met privately with the secretary of state to express their dissatisfaction with the political situation in Gambia. They also jointly tabled a vote of censure against P. S. N'Jie in the House of Representatives and formed an electoral pact to fight the 1961 BTC election; this helped the DCA win four out of five wards and thereby challenge the UP's predominance in municipal politics.[87] Under the terms of a general election pact, which was signed shortly before the 1962 election, the PPP agreed to support DCA candidates in four of the five Bathurst seats and in Serrekunda and the DCA to support the PPP in the twenty-five Protectorate constituencies and the remaining two seats in the Colony, Bakau and Soldier Town, Bathurst.[88]

Although there was no doubt that the PPP was the stronger party in the pact, both sides anticipated that they would benefit from it. No doubt encouraged by its success in the 1961 BTC election, the DCA hoped that Mandinka and Jola votes might help its candidates, particularly the party leaders, Garba-Jahumpa and Faye, to win marginal constituencies in Bathurst. Moreover, if the PPP were to win the election, the DCA could expect to be rewarded with one or more ministries in the first Gambian cabinet. For its part, the PPP expected to benefit from the DCA's financial resources for its own campaign; if the rumors were true, the DCA received money from the Ghanaian government because of Garba-Jahumpa's personal ties with Kwame Nkrumah.[89] If the UP lost any seats in Bathurst, the PPP's chances of securing an overall majority would also be improved.

The PPP reselected all nine of its current MPs, again for the same or similar constituencies, and gave two of its unsuccessful candidates in 1960, F. B. Manneh (Niumi) and M. B. Sagnia (Kantora), another chance. Three Independents who had been defeated in 1960, A. S. C. Able-Thomas (Soldier Town), Bangally Singhateh (Wuli), and Kebba J. Krubally (Basse), also received the party nomination.[90]

Its remaining thirteen candidates, who had not stood for election previously, had a range of backgrounds. As in 1960, some had come to prominence through their party activities. For example, Lamin M'Boge (Illiassa) and Famara Wassa Touray (Western Kombo) were active in the early days of the PPP, but did not gain the party nomination in 1960; the latter played a major part in building up support for the party in 1959 and succeeded Bojang as national president in 1960. Similarly, Baba M. Touray (Jokadu) had become well known as a result of his role in the PPP's Youth Wing.[91] Several were civil servants, including Touray, M'Boge, Kalilou F. Singhateh (Lower Baddibu), and Demba S. Cham (Niani)[92]; others, including Amang S. Kanyi (Eastern Kiang) and Yusupha S. Samba (Sabach Sanjal), were involved in commerce. The candidate in Lower Fuladu West, Paul L. Baldeh, had a particularly interesting background. A Lorobo Fula, he was the son of one of the biggest cattle owners in the Fuladu West district, who was a member of the Native Tribunal and a supporter of a former Seyfu of Fuladu West, Cherno Kady Baldeh. Like a number of other educated Fula, Baldeh was a Roman Catholic. Very unusually, he was also a university graduate, having recently gained a degree from Trinity College Dublin, and before the election, he was employed as a teacher at St. Augustine's School in Bathurst.[93]

Four of the five DCA candidates had contested the 1960 election. A. B. N'Jie defended his seat in Joloff/Portuguese Town; Garba-Jahumpa and Cham-Joof again challenged J. H. Joof and P. S. N'Jie in Half Die and New Town East, respectively; and Faye, having realized the folly of competing against H. O. Semega-Janneh in Serrekunda, stood in his old stamping-ground of New Town West (succeeding M. D. Sallah).

United Party/Gambia National Union

The UP was supported in the election by the Gambia National Union (GNU), a somewhat shadowy organization that appears to have been in existence between 1960 and 1962. The driving force behind it was Sanjally Bojang, the former PPP national president. In September 1960, while Jawara was in Lagos to attend the Nigerian Independence celebrations, Bojang conspired with Garba-Jahumpa and other leaders of the DCA and the former GNP to achieve a merger of all the existing parties. The aim was to establish a new party, the Gambia Progressive Union (popularly known as the "Gambia Solidarity Party"), which would press the colonial authorities for constitutional change. P. S. N'Jie attended a meeting called by Bojang to discuss the idea, but the return of Jawara (strongly opposed to it) ensured that the common front proved abortive.[94] Bojang was subsequently expelled from the PPP and with K. W. Foon (formerly of the GNP) later established the GNU, which by early 1962 could probably count on the support of L. O. Sonko (MP for Niumi-Jokadu until his elevation to the chieftaincy of Upper Niumi in 1962). M. E. Jallow may also have joined the new party (although the

GWU again remained neutral in the election), and Seyfu Omar M'Baki perhaps also endorsed it. It is unclear if the GNU and UP signed a formal electoral pact; however, the GNU certainly campaigned actively for the UP during the election campaign.[95]

Unlike in 1960, the UP nominated candidates in all constituencies except Western Kiang, where its candidate apparently failed to appear at the appointed time.[96] Eight of these, including H. O. Semega-Janneh, who apparently joined the UP soon after the 1960 election, and Andrew Camara, who joined the UP on the eve of the 1962 election to meet the wishes of his local constituents, were sitting MPs.[97] All were nominated for the same (or similar) constituencies. In addition, A. N. Touray, who had won Niani-Saloum in 1960 before being unseated on an electoral petition, was selected in Niani, and N. M. Darbo, who had been defeated in MacCarthy Island, this time stood in Upper Fulladu West. Five other UP candidates of diverse ethnic background had contested the 1960 election as Independents. These were the former GMC rebel, S. B. Gaye (Joloff/Portuguese Town), who was now a leading member of the UP; Kebba C. A. Kah, who had recently been dismissed as a clerk in the post office (Jokadu); Saihou Biyai (Western Foni); Mafode Sonko (Niumi); and Kalilu Jammeh (Illiassa).[98]

The remaining sixteen UP candidates had not stood for election previously. These included the GNU's Kebba Foon and two Basse-born civil servants who were to remain prominent in politics for the next two decades, Momodou C. Cham (Tumana) and Momodou C. Jallow (Wuli). A twenty-five-year-old Tukulor, Cham was the son of a respected elder and trader in Basse; prior to the election, he was a civilian clerk in the police department. The latter, who was the son of a prominent religious leader in Basse, Cherno Abdoulie Jallow, was a forty-two-year-old Fula who, after a career in the Veterinary Department, retired from the civil service as a first grade veterinary assistant just before the election.[99]

The three political parties differed considerably in terms of the ethnic background of their candidates. The PPP remained dominated by the Mandinka, who perhaps supplied twenty out of its twenty-six candidates. Two were Jola and two were Wolof from the rural areas, the others being a Fula and a Tukulor. The DCA was predominantly a Wolof party. Four of its candidates were Wolof, the others being a Wolofized Serere and an Aku. The UP was the most ethnically diverse party. Our estimate is that it had ten Mandinka, ten Wolof, five Fula, two Serahuli, two Tukulor, one Jola, and one Aku candidates.[100]

Election Issues

Some contemporary observers found it difficult to distinguish between the parties in terms of issues,[101] but in four respects, the UP's policies differed from that of the PPP/DCA coalition. First, as at the London Conference, its approach to constitutional change was more conservative. In the view of the new governor, John (later Sir John) Paul, it emphasized the need for orderly economic and political development toward independence in close association with the British government, whereas the PPP, and particularly the DCA, wished the pace to be quickened and were less concerned about assistance from Britain.[102] Second, it adopted a different stance toward Senegal. The UP remained more strongly in favor of eventual political, as well as economic, links with Senegal than either the PPP or the DCA; indeed, Faye went so far as to claim that Britain intended to sell Gambia to Senegal. Ironically, however, in a short space of time, N'Jie would excoriate the PPP for allegedly compromising Gambian independence, and the UP would stage demonstrations in Bathurst against the visit of the Senegalese leader, Léopold Senghor.[103] Third, it held a different view over the future role of the chiefs. The UP emphasized the value of chieftaincy, whereas the PPP attacked the "overbearing authority" of the chiefs and denounced them as "tools of imperialism" and "exploiters of the people." The PPP also criticized P. S. N'Jie for his failure, while serving as chief minister, to bring about the establishment of Area Councils, which would serve as an alternative source of authority in rural districts. It is difficult to say whether N'Jie's respect for the chiefs was born of his own aristocratic pretensions, or merely a ploy to forge a coalition against the PPP in the countryside.[104] Finally, the PPP emphasized that, compared with the Colony, the Protectorate, in general, and the Mandinka areas, in particular, continued to receive a lesser distribution of funds and services.[105]

These policy differences were exacerbated by the mutual ill-feeling between the parties. Both major parties accused the other of corruption.[106] In a party broadcast, P. S. N'Jie went further and allegedly likened "the PPP machine" to an "organisation of the devil . . . Here is a gang of political upstarts operating on the well-known totalitarian principles of terrorism and coercion." N'Jie apparently also accused the PPP of "compelling their lukewarm supporters into taking secret and frightful oaths of allegiance to the party."[107] Perhaps more important, both parties accused the other of "tribalism." The UP accused the PPP of using anti-Wolof slogans, while apparently adopting an anti-Mandinka stance itself, even though almost one-third of its candidates were Mandinka. Not surprisingly, in this volatile atmosphere, some unrest occurred in the Protectorate (although, as in 1960, compared with elections elsewhere in British West Africa in this period, it was of a very minor nature) and F. W. Touray, the PPP candidate in Western Kombo, was arrested and bound over to keep the peace.[108]

Election Results

Unlike in 1960, the outcome of the election was clear cut and has not been disputed. The PPP won eighteen seats, the UP thirteen, and the DCA one. The PPP gained 56,343 votes (57.7 percent of those cast) in twenty-six directly contested seats (and would have won a higher percentage of the vote if Western Kiang, a safe PPP seat, had been contested); the UP won 37,016 votes (37.9 percent) in thirty-one seats; and the DCA, 4,180 votes (4.3 percent) in the five seats it contested in the Colony. The sole Independent candidate won a mere 108 votes. The polling was high, with an estimated 65 to 70 percent turnout in the Protectorate and a turnout of 85 percent in the Colony. Despite the earlier unrest, the Gambian government reported that, as in 1960, the polling was "orderly and well-conducted."[109]

The PPP won seventeen out of twenty-five seats in the Protectorate. Its eight existing Protectorate members of Parliament were safely returned, all with comfortable majorities; indeed, only four of the seventeen gained less than 60 percent of the vote in their constituencies; six gained over 80 percent.[110] The PPP captured all four seats in the Western Division; seven out of nine in the Lower River Division (LRD); and four out of six in MID. But despite polling just over 50 percent of the divisional vote, it won only two out of six seats (Wuli and Sandu) in URD. The PPP also retained Bakau through A. M. Demba, but A. S. C. Able-Thomas, its candidate in Soldier Town, was defeated.

The UP retained the four seats it held in Bathurst at the time of the election, and Semega-Janneh comfortably won in Serrekunda. It also won Jokadu and Niumi in LRD; Saloum and Upper Fulladu West in MID; and Jimara, Basse, Tumana and Kantora in URD. However, it won a number of seats by narrow margins; only two UP candidates were elected with more than 60 percent of the ballot.[111] As we shall see, several of those who won narrow victories in 1962 were to defect to the PPP by the end of 1964.

The DCA gained one-third of the total Colony vote, but captured only one seat, Joloff/Portuguese Town, where A. B. N'Jie defeated the UP's S. B. Gaye by fifty-three votes. The electoral pact with the PPP did not bring the anticipated benefits to its party leaders, because both were narrowly defeated; Faye lost to I. B. I. Jobe by sixty-nine votes and Garba-Jahumpa to J. H. Joof by just eleven votes.

A number of factors helped to bring about the victory of the PPP. First, and most important, the redistribution of seats in 1961 favored the PPP. All the additional seats were awarded to the Protectorate where the PPP was powerful and none were given to the UP's stronghold in the Colony. Moreover, many of the new seats in the Protectorate were in predominantly Mandinka areas. Second, the UP's close links with the chiefs were counterproductive; by now the latter were largely discredited. Third, the UP's position as the party of power brought it little material advantage, but did make it appear responsible for unpopular government policies. Fourth, the PPP remained much better organized than the UP, particularly in the rural areas, and (outside Bathurst) conducted a much more vigorous and effective campaign.[112] Fifth, it is likely that the PPP had greater financial resources at its disposal than the UP; for example, P. S. N'Jie's income was declining by 1962 because he was still barred from directly practicing law (and this was probably not offset by his increased salary as chief minister). Finally, Jawara had greater personal qualities than N'Jie; the latter's behavior during the election campaign seems to have been a mixture of excessive self-confidence and indolence.[113]

It appears that fourteen out of eighteen directly elected PPP new MPs were Mandinka, the remainder being a Jola, a Fula, a Tukulor, and a rural Wolof. The UP's thirteen members of Parliament were more ethnically diverse: four urban Wolof, two Fula, two Tukulor, two Serahuli (one of whom was Wolofized), two Mandinka, and one Aku. The sole DCA member was an urban Wolof.

Four chiefs were elected separately in a keenly contested election in which four ballots were held over consecutive days in May. All, including Omar M'Baki of Sami (the only one to be elected unanimously), were known to be UP supporters, but were subsequently warned by Governor Paul that they would be dismissed if they voted against the PPP government.[114]

Ministerial Appointments

The PPP thus achieved an overall majority and Governor Paul duly appointed Jawara as premier. On the latter's recommendation, eight other ministers were selected. Six of these, Sisay, Dibba, Paul Baldeh, Dabo, Daffeh, and Samba, were PPP MPs and the other posts were filled by A. B. N'Jie and M'Baki. A. B. N'Jie owed his seat in the cabinet to the PPP's electoral pact with the DCA and to the lack of experience amongst PPP MPs. Indeed, Jawara originally intended to appoint both Faye and Garba-Jahumpa as ministers. Following their defeats at the polls, he asked Governor Paul to appoint them as "nominated" MPs so that they could then be selected as ministers, but Paul considered that this would infringe the spirit of the constitution (if not the letter of it) and refused the request. Jawara therefore submitted a new ministerial list three days later, which excluded Faye and Garba-Jahumpa, but contained M'Baki, who was presumably included as a sop to the chiefs. Governor Paul accepted the recommendations.[115] Consequently, the first PPP cabinet contained five Mandinka (Jawara, Sisay, Dibba, Dabo, and Daffeh); one urban Wolof (N'Jie) and one rural Wolof (Samba)[116]; one Fula (Baldeh); and one Tukulor (M'Baki). Thus non-Mandinka were more strongly represented in Jawara's cabinet than their representation among PPP MPs merited, an indication that Jawara was seeking to accommodate non-Mandinka elements within the party and to shift the PPP from a Protectorate movement to a national political party, in substance as well as in name.

Establishment of the Gambia Congress Party

Apart from the appointment of A. B. N'Jie, the DCA gained a number of other benefits from its alliance with the PPP. Sallah was rewarded for standing aside for Faye in New Town West by being appointed (along with T. D. Mallinson, the European manager of the UAC) as a "nominated" MP on Jawara's recommendation.[117] Moreover, another DCA activist, Alieu S. Jack, the manager of the Madi groundnut mill and former member of the BTC, was elected speaker of the House with the support of the PPP; Faye was sent to London to head the colony's Liaison Office in Britain.[118] Nevertheless, the co-leader of the Alliance, Garba-Jahumpa, who was acutely disappointed that he had again failed to secure a seat in Parliament, considered that he had gained little from the electoral pact. Frustrated by the turn of the events, he broke away from the DCA and founded the Gambia Congress Party (GCP) in October 1962, remaining as its general secretary until its merger with the PPP in 1968. Some DCA leaders joined the new party, but most seem to have remained loyal to the Alliance.[119]

The GCP, like the former GMC, appealed primarily to Muslim Wolof from Bathurst. It was also closely associated with the GLU, E. F. Small's old union, which was now a bitter rival of the much more powerful GWU. Garba-Jahumpa served as vice president of the GLU for a short period from September 1962 and was succeeded in this post by the GCP's chairman, A. K. John. It seems clear that, as in the 1940s, Garba-Jahumpa was hoping to make use of organized labor to build an effective power base in Bathurst.[120] The new party was initially on good terms with the UP and the two parties signed an electoral pact in October 1962 that gave Garba-Jahumpa a free run in Half Die in the BTC election. This helped to establish a GCP presence in local government in the capital and, at independence, the GCP held four out of the fifteen seats on the BTC (compared with seven for the UP and four for the PPP/DCA); however, by the end of 1964, there were signs that relations between the two parties were strained.[121] Somewhat incongruously, the GCP adopted a radical foreign policy stance, which enabled its leader to engage in a series of visits to socialist countries and also provided much-needed funds for the party, but increased suspicions about Garba-Jahumpa's integrity.[122]

Election Petitions

In 1960, the result in a number of constituencies was challenged and the election of A. N. Touray was overturned. Similarly, after the 1962 election, election petitions were brought against at least eighteen elected MPs; sixteen of these were brought by defeated UP candidates and only two (against the N'Jie brothers) by losing PPP candidates. The first eight petitions (including one against Jawara) were dismissed by the Supreme Court, but the ninth was upheld. This was brought by the UP's Mamadi Sabally against the PPP's Yusupha Samba in Sabach Sanjal (LRD). This constituency had witnessed one of the closest contests in the Protectorate; Samba had won by only 147 votes. Samba won the resulting by-election in October 1962, but the court's verdict threatened to undermine the whole election, because it called into question the legality of the election not only in LRD, but in the whole Protectorate.[123]

As noted, the 1962 election was fought under a new register of voters in the Protectorate. A bill, supported by both the UP and the PPP, was passed in 1961 to allow the compiling of fresh registers to replace those drawn up in 1959, which had proved unsatisfactory. However, the UP's lawyers (P. S. N'Jie's brothers, E. D. and Sheriff, and Berthan Macauley, a prominent Sierra Leonean barrister) argued that the revised registers had been compiled by a method differing from that laid down in explicit terms in electoral legislation. Their arguments were rejected by the Gambian Supreme Court in March 1963, but the West African Court of Appeal declared the registers in LRD invalid a month later. P. S. N'Jie promptly traveled to London to ask the British government to dissolve the House and call a fresh election. However, at the end of May, the secretary of state for the colonies,

Duncan Sandys, announced that the registers would be validated retrospectively by Order-in-Council to allow progress to be made toward full internal self-government. His decision incensed N'Jie and was condemned in the House of Commons by the opposition Labour Party, but Sandys dismissed their demands for a fresh election. The UP launched one final legal challenge, arguing that the Order-in-Council was not legally valid, but this was rejected by the High Court of Chancery in July 1964.[124] Nevertheless, P. S. N'Jie remained unchanging in his opinion that he had been badly treated by the British.[125]

The PPP Consolidates: 1962–65

Between 1962 and 1965, the PPP strengthened its political position. It ended any threat to its control of the Protectorate from the chiefs, who ceased thereafter to play any significant role in national politics. It made solid progress both inside and outside Parliament at the expense of the UP and it improved its standing in Bathurst through developing closer ties with the DCA. These developments are discussed below.

Weakening of the Chiefs

The Protectorate chiefs generally supported the UP (albeit covertly) in the 1962 election. They were spared the embarrassing dilemma of declaring for one party or the other after the election because the PPP achieved an overall majority.[126] Nevertheless, some members of the PPP, particularly the new minister of local government, Sheriff Dibba, were determined that the chiefs would never again side with its opponents. Consequently, between July 1962 and March 1965, the PPP either dismissed or forced to retire at least fourteen chiefs, who were either UP sympathizers or were considered to be too independently minded or too old. Those removed in 1962–64 included Tamba Jammeh, who was appointed Seyfu of Upper Baddibu as early as 1928, first sat on the Legislative Council in 1947, and had long been regarded as the most powerful and influential of the Protectorate chiefs. Two leading UP supporters, Jewru Krubally of Fulladu East (a chief since at least 1924) and Silla Ba Dibba of Central Baddibu (appointed in 1945), were also removed (the latter being replaced by Mustapha Dibba of Salikene, who was the father of Sheriff Dibba). Seven more chiefs were either forced to retire or were dismissed in March 1965. Four of these were apparently UP supporters and three were considered pro-PPP. Perhaps not surprisingly, their successors were quick to declare their allegiance to the PPP.[127]

The former group of chiefs included two MPs, Omar M'Baki of Sami and Seykuba Jarjussey of Jarra West. Both men were consequently also forced to resign from the House of Representatives. M'Baki's fall from power was gradual; he lost his specific portfolio as minister of communications in October 1963 and was then forced to resign from the cabinet in September 1964. No chief thereafter served as a minister during the Jawara period.[128]

Defection of United Party Members of Parliament

As noted, the UP gained a respectable thirteen seats in the 1962 election. However, by October 1964, its parliamentary strength had fallen to five. K. C. A. Kah, who only joined the UP on the eve of the 1962 election, defected to the PPP almost immediately after his election.[129] By the end of 1963, Andrew Camara, Michael Baldeh, and probably also Mafode Sonko and I. B. I. Jobe, had crossed the carpet.[130] Demba Jagana and H. O. Semega-Janneh defected to the PPP during 1964, and M. B. Jones, having previously sought membership of the PPP, joined the DCA in 1964.[131]

UP MPs apparently joined the PPP for a combination of reasons. First, they were disillusioned by P. S. N'Jie's failure to provide an effective leadership. N'Jie was frequently absent from Gambia after 1962 and rarely attended the House of Representatives. He spent a great deal of time in London attempting vainly to persuade the British government that another election was necessary before independence could occur.[132] Second, they hoped to obtain office. In November 1962, only a few months after he joined the PPP, Kah was appointed a parliamentary secretary in the Ministry of Finance; in November 1963, Camara replaced his fellow Fula, Paul Baldeh, as minister of education.[133] Other UP defectors may have hoped that they would receive similar rewards. Third, some of the defectors secured relatively small majorities in the 1962 election and no doubt feared that they would lose their seats next time round.[134] Finally, some may have been encouraged to join the PPP by influential supporters in their constituencies. MPs were expected to look after the interests of their constituents and opposition MPs were unlikely to share in any government patronage as the PPP came to take over from the British administration.

The hemorrhaging of its parliamentary strength encouraged some UP leaders (particularly E. D. N'Jie, who was effectively the UP leader in his brother's absence) to consider overtures from the PPP for the establishment of a government of national unity. Preliminary discussions were initiated in November 1963, but were quickly abandoned by the UP when P. S. N'Jie, who remained implacably opposed to the PPP, returned home. They were resumed in September 1964 (while P. S. N'Jie was again in England) and in December, the UP, DCA and PPP agreed to cooperate over the election of a chairman and deputy chairman to the BTC. Consequently, the PPP's B. O. Semega-Janneh was elected chairman of the BTC and became mayor of Bathurst in February 1965; the UP's I. A. S. Burang-John was appointed deputy chairman. The two parties also agreed in principle to form a coalition government after independence.[135] Some UP supporters, probably including P. S. N'Jie (although he publicly avoided commenting on the issue), were opposed to the coalition, as were some PPP supporters in the Protectorate; nevertheless, only a fortnight after independence, Jawara announced his first cabinet reshuffle with E. D. N'Jie, who had brokered the deal, being appointed minister of health. However, as discussed in Chapter 7, N'Jie was to be dismissed and the coalition to collapse only three months later.[136]

Closer Links with the Democratic Congress Alliance

If attempts by the PPP to establish a better relationship with the UP proved abortive, the party was able to work closely with the DCA. This process was facilitated by A. B. N'Jie's continued membership of the Jawara cabinet and by the common opposition of the two parties to the UP. The DCA endorsed the PPP's stance over election petitions and even challenged P. S. N'Jie's claim to Gambian citizenship in the courts; the PPP supported DCA candidates in the BTC election and organized a joint congress with the DCA in April 1963. The two parties also adopted a similar stance toward constitutional reform in the run up to independence. Eventually, as noted in Chapter 7, the DCA was to be absorbed into the PPP in August 1965.[137]

The Gambia therefore entered independence as a parliamentary democracy with two main political parties. It was certainly conceivable that the decline of the opposition since 1962 would continue after independence and that The Gambia would in time become yet another African one-party state (de facto, if not de jure). Yet it was equally possible that its multiparty tradition would survive. Although the PPP was clearly the major party at independence, controlling the central government and holding two-thirds of the seats in the House of Representatives, its dominance was not complete and the possibility remained that the UP might mount an effective challenge to its sway in the future. The PPP/DCA alliance now held two of the five Bathurst parliamentary constituencies, but this was only because I. B. I. Jobe and M. B. Jones had changed parties, and it was likely that the bulk of the urban electorate still favored the UP (or possibly the GCP); moreover, the PPP's overreliance on the Mandinka vote in the countryside seemed to offer the UP the continued opportunity to mobilize non-Mandinka ethnic groups in the interior. Chapter 7 examines political developments in the post-independence period.

Summary

In the early 1960s, constitutional changes resulted in a permanent shift in the balance of power away from existing urban-centered parties to a new rural-based political movement, the PPP. A detailed examination of the 1960 and 1962 general elections reveals how the PPP mobilized political and economic discontent in the Protectorate to become the dominant political force by 1962; before further strengthening its position, at the expense of its political opponents, in the run up to independence.

7

ELECTORAL POLITICS, 1965—81

The first year or so of independence appeared to confirm the viability of the two-party political system in The Gambia: an early prospect of a one-party state through a coalition of the two major parties foundered; an attempt by the People's Progressive Party (PPP) to introduce a republican constitution by means of a national referendum in November 1965 was narrowly defeated; and even though the PPP easily defeated the United Party (UP) in the parliamentary election of Spring 1966, the latter won sufficient seats and achieved a large enough share of the vote to provide a credible opposition. However, over the next few years, the PPP steadily eroded UP support in Parliament and the country at large, culminating in its near annihilation in the general election of 1972. At the same time, the PPP overcame splits within its own ranks in 1968–70, which resulted in the formation of the People's Progressive Alliance (PPA) and succeeded a second time round, in April 1970, in winning a republic referendum, transforming Dawda Jawara from the prime minister to an executive president of the new republic.

The ruling party, as far as the established opposition was concerned, seemed invincible and any threat to its position now depended on further internal frag-mentation. Such a prospect reemerged twice in the 1970s, first with the Independents in 1972 and then with the National Convention Party (NCP) in 1975; but these threats were also successfully countered.

This chapter examines the course of Gambian politics in the first fifteen years of independence and offers explanations for the transformation from a working two-party system to de facto single-party government. It also places Gambian post-inde-pendence politics within a broader context, by examining some of the similarities and differences between its experience and those of other African countries.

1965 Republic Referendum[1]

Two months after independence, in April 1965, Jawara informed the governor general, Sir John Paul, that he was contemplating replacing the monarchy with a

160

republic on the first anniversary of independence in February 1966.[2] The decision was formally approved by the cabinet in mid-May and made public soon afterward; in a speech to the House of Representatives on June 1, Jawara outlined the reasons for the proposed constitutional change. He argued that Gambians were unable to understand the distinction between the formal authority possessed by the governor general and the real power exerted by the prime minister; that the head of government required the more extensive powers of a president to carry out his duties effectively; that some countries doubted that a monarchy could be truly independent; that it would be easier for a fellow president than a prime minister to develop closer links with President Senghor of Senegal; and finally, that the constitutional change would reduce administrative and staffing costs.[3]

As noted in Chapter 2, the existing form of government was protected under an "entrenched clause" of the 1964 constitution and could only be amended if endorsed by two-thirds of the elected members of Parliament (MPs) and confirmed by a two-thirds majority of those voting in a subsequent national referendum. Given the PPP's control of Parliament, the support of MPs was inevitable and the Republic Bill duly passed its first reading on June 1. Although the UP MPs abstained on this vote, they made their opposition to the republic clear. P. S. N'Jie (who had returned to the country in January 1965) argued that the monarchy was working well, that fundamental human rights would not be protected by the new constitution, and that it was dangerous to give "too much power to one man" (i.e., Jawara). He also claimed that Jawara had only introduced the bill to avoid having to call an election (which he would lose), although ironically Jawara originally hoped to use an election victory as the means to establish a republic.[4] No doubt N'Jie also calculated that if the government were to be defeated in the referendum, the UP's prospects at the next general election would be improved. It was also rumored that he wished to succeed Sir John Paul as governor general and thus had a personal motive for ensuring the monarchy was retained.[5]

The Gambia Congress Party (GCP), which had no representation in the House of Representatives, also opposed the bill, albeit for slightly different reasons; it argued that a republican constitution would give too much power to the president, enable the government to imprison opposition politicians and trade unionists, and do nothing to alleviate more pressing economic problems. It also suggested that the establishment of a republic would allow Senegal to "swallow up" The Gambia. Perhaps as important, the GCP leader, I. M. Garba-Jahumpa, was determined to remain on good terms with the UP to ensure a clear run for himself in a Bathurst constituency in the next general election and so had no choice but to oppose the referendum.[6]

In contrast, the bill was supported by the Democratic Congress Alliance (DCA), which helped to strengthen the already close relations between it and the PPP, and in August the DCA was formally merged into the PPP with members of its Executive Committee being absorbed into an enlarged PPP Executive. The absorption of the DCA was not welcomed by all PPP members, however. Indeed, one leading PPP member, Abdoulie (Ablai) Fadia, protested so strongly that he was expelled from the party.[7]

One immediate consequence of the UP's opposition to the Republic Bill was the ending of the coalition pact that, as noted in Chapter 6, was reached with the PPP in February. On June 7, E. D. N'Jie was dismissed as minister of health (subsequently to be replaced by the former UP MP, K. C. A. Kah) and a day later, the PPP rescinded the pact. This was on the grounds that P. S. N'Jie had been unwilling to cooperate with the government and that certain members of the UP (including E. D. N'Jie) had been working actively against it. P. S. N'Jie, who showed little enthusiasm for the coalition, probably did not regret this development.[8]

Both the UP and the GCP campaigned actively against the referendum, as did two prominent politicians, the Independent MP for Illiassa, Lamin M'Boge, and the former DCA leader, Rev. J. C. Faye. Since his election in 1962, M'Boge had been one of the most outspoken PPP MPs. He was critical of the government's domestic policies and, together with two other PPP MPs, Kalilou Singhateh and Paul Baldeh, also attacked its pro-Western foreign policy.[9] He was also on close terms with the leader of the Gambia Workers' Union (GWU), M. E. Jallow, which caused Jawara further concern.[10] Following an inflammatory speech at a GWU May Day rally in the capital, M'Boge was expelled from the PPP and sacked as the deputy speaker. Consequently, he now sat in Parliament as an Independent.[11] Faye had only reluctantly signed the merger agreement with the PPP in August and resigned from the PPP in September over the republic issue.[12]

The referendum was also opposed by the main trade union, the GWU. Although in favor of a republic in principle, the GWU feared that its establishment might be followed by a crackdown on trade unions and strikes (as had occurred in Ghana); at least as importantly, the union needed to restore its reputation, which was badly tarnished. Moreover, after failing to make his name in the wider African trade union movement, the GWU leader, Jallow, was seeking to revive his flagging career at home.[13] Finally, at least some of the Protectorate chiefs who were removed from office in March sought to rally opposition to the referendum in the rural areas behind the scenes.[14]

The second and third readings of the Republic Bill received the assent of Parliament on November 9, with the referendum being held between November 18 and 26.[15] The result was extremely close: there were 61,568 votes in favor of the bill and 31,921 against, which meant that the government failed by only 758 votes (or 0.8 percent) to achieve a two-thirds majority of the votes cast. Votes were counted in two centers—Georgetown (covering the Upper River [URD], MacCarthy Island [MID], and Lower River [LRD] Divisions) and Bathurst (covering Bathurst, Kombo St. Mary, and the Western Division [WD])—with the government failing to secure its required majority by 535 votes in Bathurst and, much more surprisingly, by 203 votes in Georgetown. The overall turnout was only 60.6 percent, lower than in either the 1962 or 1966 elections and although it was as high as 90 percent in Bathurst, it was as low as 30 percent in some provincial areas.[16]

The result was "a considerable shock" to Jawara and his ministers, although not to the governor general. Paul argued that two main factors accounted for the outcome. First, the PPP government was overconfident. It failed to make sufficient efforts to explain the purpose of the referendum to the electorate (especially in the rural areas) and also did not bother to campaign effectively in the Provinces (formerly the Protectorate); for example, Jawara himself did not leave Bathurst to tour the Provinces until November 16, only two days before the referendum began. Second, it failed to counter opposition arguments about the dangers of an executive presidency. Paul believed that this accounted for the low turnout in URD and MID among Fula and Serahuli who had a close knowledge, or direct experience, of the Guinean or Malian states. He also felt that the specter of the Ghanaian regime influenced "a number of the more thinking members of the electorate."[17]

Although Paul tended to discount its importance, the anti-republican coalition did make a difference. It campaigned strongly in Bathurst, which ensured a good turnout of UP and GCP supporters in the capital. Its campaigning in the rural areas was more limited, but did have some impact, and the still influential ex-chiefs managed to persuade a number of PPP supporters to vote no (or at least abstain).[18] In addition, the timing of the election in November—a very busy time for farmers—may have reduced the turnout in the Provinces.[19]

Although the PPP gained almost two-thirds of the vote, the result was regarded as a defeat for the ruling party and a victory for the UP and its allies. Many PPP supporters reacted angrily and some ministers, apparently including Sheriff Dibba, Sheriff Sisay, and A. B. N'Jie, called for the result to be ignored and for the republican constitution to be introduced anyway. Jawara refused to consider this option, but instead, without consulting the cabinet or the party executive, decided unilaterally to call an early general election in May 1966 to test his party's continued popularity.[20] Soon afterward, he requested that Sir John Paul (who was due to leave the country in early 1966) be replaced as governor general (initially on an acting basis) by Farimang Singhateh. A retired civil servant who had established a pharmacy at Farafenni in 1963, Singhateh was a justice of the peace and a member of the Public Services Commission (the body responsible for all civil service appointments). More important, he was a Mandinka and a longstanding PPP supporter, so his appointment was designed to placate Jawara's cabinet critics.[21]

Meanwhile, their success in the referendum brought the two opposition parties, the UP and the GCP, closer. This culminated, in February 1966, in an electoral pact between them. As far as the UP was concerned, the main aim of the pact was to prevent the PPP taking any Bathurst seats; Garba-Jahumpa's motive was to regain the parliamentary seat he had lost in 1962.[22]

1966 General Election[23]

The first post-independence election was held between May 17 and 26, 1966. As in 1962, a total of thirty-two directly elected seats were contested. Before the election, the Madi Commission redistributed seats in accordance with recent population changes; consequently, the number of Bathurst seats was reduced from five to three, an additional seat was granted to the Kombos, and the Jarra constituency was divided into two. These changes seemed certain to benefit the government, given that both the Jarras and the Kombos were strongly PPP, whereas Bathurst of course remained an opposition stronghold.[24] The number of registered voters had also increased considerably since the 1965 referendum, an indication perhaps of a renewed popular interest in politics.[25] The election was contested by the PPP, the UP, the GCP, and several Independents. Each is considered in turn.

People's Progressive Party

The PPP not surprisingly nominated candidates in all constituencies. All except two of its successful candidates in 1962 were reselected for the same (or a similar) constituency, the exceptions being Lamin M'Boge (Illiassa) and A. M. Demba (Bakau), who were replaced by Baba M. Touray and Abdoulie K. N'Jie, respectively. Touray had been the unsuccessful PPP candidate in Jokadu in 1962, but had since made his name as a pro-PPP (and anti-GWU) trade union leader.[26]

Five of the losing PPP candidates from 1962, M. B. Sagnia (Kantora), F. B. Manneh (Niumi), Malick Lowe (Saloum), Noah K. Sanyang (Tumana), and Alieu Marong (Upper Fulladu West), were also replaced, the first two by the sitting MPs, Andrew Camara and Mafode Sonko. Three other defectors from the UP, K. C. A. Kah (Jokadu), M. B. Jones (Bathurst Central) and H. O. Semega-Janneh (Serrekunda), also gained the PPP nomination. However, in Jimara, M. B. Sillah, the PPP's candidate in the same seat in 1962, was chosen rather than the incumbent, Demba Jagana; M. Harley N'Jie was preferred to I. B. I. Jobe in Bathurst North (which incorporated Jobe's old constituency of New Town West).[27] Because the remaining ex-UP MP, Michael Baldeh, had died in July 1965, the PPP selected Kebba J. Krubally, who won the subsequent by-election in Basse the following October by more than 500 votes.[28] Apart from Jones, it appears that only one former DCA leader was selected by the PPP; this was A. B. N'Jie, who transferred from the Joloff/Portuguese Town constituency in Bathurst (which now formed part of the new Bathurst Central constituency) to the much safer seat of Northern Kombo. The ethnic origin of some of the PPP candidates is disputed, but our estimate is that it fielded nineteen Mandinka, four Wolof, three Jola, two Fula, two Tukulor, one Aku, and one Serahuli candidates. Thus the PPP remained a predominantly Mandinka party, although its ethnic base was widening.[29]

United Party

Buoyed by its recent success and already geared up for campaigning from the recent referendum, the UP was confident of exploiting the anti-republican sentiment, or perhaps more accurately, the continuing fear among the electorate of the PPP and Jawara exploiting their control of the state; for example, P. S. N'Jie informed the British high commissioner that he expected to win eighteen seats.[30] The party fielded twenty-nine candidates in total, of whom eleven were joint UP/GCP candidates; the other eighteen represented the UP only; the UP also endorsed the sole GCP candidate, Garba-Jahumpa, in Bathurst South. Thus, it failed to contest only Southern Kombo and Western Kiang.[31]

Four of the UP's five remaining sitting MPs (P. S. N'Jie, E. D. N'Jie, N. M. Darbo, and M. C. Cham) were reselected for the same or similar constituencies. However, the MP for Half Die, J. H. Joof, was forced to retire, to enable his old adversary, Garba-Jahumpa, to stand in the new constituency of Bathurst South. This appears to have been resented by some UP activists, including its energetic General Secretary, I. A. S. Burang-John, who harbored ambitions of winning the constituency nomination; Burang-John instead contested the much less promising seat of Jokadu.[32] In addition, the MP for Jimara, Demba Jagana, having rejoined the UP (after failing, as noted, to gain the PPP's nomination), was punished for his earlier disloyalty by being moved from his relatively safe seat to face certain defeat against Sheriff Dibba in Central Baddibu (he was to obtain only 262 votes). He was replaced in Jimara by M. C. Jallow, who had come within forty-four votes of defeating Bangally Singhateh in Wuli in 1962, but had lost more heavily to Kebba Krubally in the Basse by-election; nevertheless, with the rural connections he had developed through his work as a veterinary assistant, he seemed a stronger candidate than Jagana.[33]

Apart from Jallow, only two other unsuccessful UP candidates from the previous election were reselected by the party.[34] Most UP candidates were therefore standing for the first time. These included John R. Forster in Bathurst Central and Gibril (Gibou) M. Jagne in Serrekunda. As the eldest son of Sir Samuel Forster (and a nephew of E. F. Small), the former was a member of Bathurst's leading Aku family. He was also a highly respected retired civil servant, a Methodist lay preacher, and a former Bathurst town councilor. Having been elected to the Bathurst Town Council (BTC) in 1955 for the GDP, he had joined the UP in 1959, but had never before stood for Parliament.[35] Our calculation is that ten of the thirty UP and UP/GCP candidates were Wolof, nine were Mandinka, four were Tukulor, three were Serahuli, two were Fula, one was an Aku, and one was a Jola.[36] The main differences between the ethnic background of these candidates and the PPP's were that the Wolof were much more strongly represented among the opposition and the Mandinka among the PPP.

It is evident that the UP was in no shape to challenge the PPP nationally. Fletcher, discussing the state of the party after independence, rightly saw its weakness deriving from its "patron" structure system, with a consequent inability to convert itself into a mass party outside the Bathurst area.[37] Such a system depends on the personal appeal, organizational ability, and personal financial resources of the patron and his close supporters—in the UP case, P. S. N'Jie and a small coterie of urban businessmen and rural notables. "Leaders gave little attention to the development of a cohesive philosophy or party program as such . . . although the party was clearly more than an amalgamation of independent units, it was less than a centralized, hierarchical organization."[38] As P. S. N'Jie increasingly failed to provide effective leadership and wealthy patrons began to back away, party organization and morale in the Provinces was further undermined.

Gambia Congress Party

As noted, the sole GCP candidate was Garba-Jahumpa. This was an indication of the unequal nature of its alliance with the UP and showed that it was an even more atrophied version of a patron party, lacking even the loose network of support in the Provinces still enjoyed by the UP. Moreover, the party was in some internal disarray, having recently witnessed the defection to the PPP of several of its leading members, including two of its four representatives on the Bathurst City Council (BCC).[39]

Independents

Finally, six Independents fought the election. These included Rev. J. C. Faye, who stood in his home area of Bathurst Central, Lamin M'Boge, who contested Illiassa; and M. E. Jallow. Jallow had expected to win the UP/GCP nomination in Bathurst Central, as a reward for helping defeat the referendum, but instead was offered the hopeless seat of Western Kiang, where Amang Kanyi had been elected unopposed in 1962. In a fit of pique, he chose to challenge P. S. N'Jie in Bathurst North.[40] M'Boge, Jallow, and Fabakary Jatta (Southern Kombo) all adopted the same symbol of a ladder, an indication that they were working in tandem.[41]

Election Issues

Some indication of the issues animating the election may be gleaned from radio broadcasts made by government and opposition leaders.[42] The PPP was given three slots, including the first by Sisay, another by A. B. N'Jie, and the last by Jawara. A common theme was the achievements of the young PPP over the past seven years. It was argued that the PPP served the needs of the rural populace in particular, while remaining mindful of the need to represent all the people under a democratic government. Although Sisay confined himself to an unspecified claim of the gains made under the PPP (which had been fighting for "independence and the farmers") and dismissed the three Bathurst parties for ignoring the needs of the rural electorate, A. B. N'Jie spelled out in greater detail his party's accomplishments, but expressed criticism of his Aku "friends." While praising their past record, he regretted a recent "decline in the public spiritedness of this community." Finally, Jawara, as prime minister, speaking in Wolof, Mandinka, and English, stressed the unity of the country under his party, epitomized by the abolition at independence of the divisive names of the Colony and the Protectorate. He also gave a lengthy account of his government's achievements, again stressing the benefits to the countryside, but not ignoring improvements in the urban areas. He also denounced opposition claims of a "sell out" to Senegal in respect of an agreement for the joint development of the Gambia River basin.

The opposition were given at least two broadcasts, one each for the UP and GCP leaders. N'Jie gave the second broadcast, but this was a short address confined to general and unspecified denunciation of PPP rule. He extolled the UP for its stand on personal liberty and freedom from hunger and made the unusual claim that his party was not for kicking the British out and bringing in Americans (although, as noted in Chapter 10, the United States installed a resident consul in Bathurst, there was no indication that the PPP was advocating such a move).[43] N'Jie mentioned that three other UP speakers would broadcast on May 11, but, if they did, the *Gambia News Bulletin* never reported them. Garba-Jahumpa's was the fourth broadcast, coming after that of A. B. N'Jie. He made a longer address than the UP leader, providing both a lengthy criticism of PPP rule and an outline of the GCP's alternative policies. The PPP was attacked under seven headings: "imprudent tribalism"; "to Mandinkanise the country"; rampant "Nepotism and curry-favouring"; coercion and improper use of chiefs; disastrous economic policies, particularly with regard to rural development; a political defeat in a referendum to establish "a bigoted Republic"; subordinating Gambian interests to those of Senegal in respect of exploiting the common resources of the River Gambia; and failing to pursue a "non-alignment policy." Garba-Jahumpa's residual commitment to his earlier Nkrumahist pan-Africanism was therefore at odds with the pro-British stance of his electoral ally, P. S. N'Jie.

Garba-Jahumpa also put forward a package of measures to stimulate the economy, in general, and agriculture, in particular; but these were little different from government policies. He suggested increasing the price of groundnuts to promote farming; the promotion of trade and foreign investment; more overseas aid to modernize infrastructure; and free education for those under fifteen within two years. He also stated that he was against an executive president and that he wished to bring in Mali and Guinea, together with Senegal, to help develop regional economic links and a free trade zone. As demonstrated below, the overwhelming majority of Gambians felt the PPP was performing satisfactorily and were not convinced by the combined opposition case.

Election Results

The election was keenly contested, with a turnout of 70.8 percent, considerably higher than in the 1965 referendum, although slightly below the 72.4 percent of 1962. It was won by the PPP, which gained 65.3 percent of the vote (81,313 votes). The UP and the GCP between them received 41,549 votes (33.4 percent); the UP candidates standing alone won 17.4 percent and the UP/GCP alliance a further 15.9 percent. The Independents won only 1.3 percent of the vote.[44] The UP/GCP alliance share of the vote thus turned out to be remarkably similar to its performance in the 1965 referendum. The PPP benefited from the first-past-the-post electoral system to win three-quarters of the seats (twenty-four); the UP gained seven seats and the GCP one. All the PPP incumbents in the Provinces were returned, but its two ex-UP MPs in the urban areas, H. O. Semega-Janneh in Serrekunda and M. B. Jones in Bathurst Central, were easily defeated by the UP's J. R. Forster and G. M. Jagne.[45] Most PPP victories were by comfortable margins, with fourteen candidates polling more than 70 percent of the vote. If our estimate is accurate, after the election, the PPP had seventeen Mandinka, two Wolof, two Tukulor, two Fula, and one Jola MPs.[46]

The regional distribution of the UP/GCP vote confirmed its strength in the Bathurst-Kombo St. Mary area, where it won four out of five seats and two-thirds of the vote. Despite his erratic leadership of the party in recent years, P. S. N'Jie won 75 percent of the vote in Bathurst North, and Forster and Jagne gained 60 and 68 percent of the vote in Bathurst Central and Serrekunda, respectively. Garba-Jahumpa's victory in Bathurst South was even more emphatic: thanks to the support of UP, as well as GCP, adherents, he won 80 percent of the vote.[47] In the Provinces, the UP retained the three seats (Saloum, Upper Fulladu West, and Tumana) it held at the dissolution of Parliament and regained Jimara through M. C. Jallow, an indication that it retained support among the non-Mandinka in MID and URD. Significantly, however, only E. D. N'Jie in Saloum won more than 60 percent of the vote and, in all four constituencies, the UP share of the vote was lower than it had been in 1962. Moreover, although polling around two-fifths of the vote in each constituency, it failed to regain any of the other seats (Basse, Jokadu, Kantora, or Niumi) that it had won in 1962, but then lost through the defection of their MPs to the PPP. Elsewhere, the party gained more than 40 percent of the vote only in Lower Fulladu West and Wuli.

All the Independent candidates were soundly defeated. Fabakary Jatta was the most successful, gaining 18 percent of the vote in Southern Kombo, but Jallow, Faye, and M'Boge each coincidentally won only 4 percent of the vote in their respective constituencies. Jallow returned to trade union activities, but, as noted below, sought election again as an Independent in 1972.[48] Faye did not stand for Parliament again after his humiliating defeat (although he was an unsuccessful UP candidate for the BCC in 1968); ordained as a priest in 1973, he thereafter concentrated on working for the Anglican Church until his death in December 1985.[49] In contrast, as discussed below, M'Boge moved openly into political opposition in 1967, before rejoining the PPP in 1968.

Several factors serve to explain why the PPP enjoyed a more comfortable victory than in 1962. First, the PPP and its leader, Dawda Jawara, enjoyed considerable prestige as "the bringer of independence," perhaps particularly because the UP could be portrayed as the party that had sought to delay independence through its legal maneuvers after the 1962 election. Second, obtaining control of the post-colonial state allowed the PPP to control the material and psychological resources of political office. PPP supporters (particularly in the Provinces) could still confidently expect that the distribution of political patronage, already begun after the granting of internal self-government in 1963 and extended after independence, would continue unabated; disillusion with the PPP had yet to set in. In contrast, the opposition had little patronage to offer. Third, the PPP could undoubtedly make more effective use of state resources, such as government vehicles or the local radio station, during this election period than in 1962.[50] Fourth, having learned from the bitter experience of its referendum "defeat," the PPP campaigned much more vigorously; for example, Jawara traveled extensively in the rural areas.[51] Fifth, given the willingness of the PPP since the 1962 election to accommodate important non-Mandinka politicians, such as the Fula, Andrew Camara and Michael Baldeh, and the Tukulor, K. C. A. Kah, it was now much more difficult for the UP to portray the PPP as a Mandinka party; conversely, P. S. N'Jie did little to conceal his contempt for Mandinka, which was unlikely to endear him to wavering Mandinka voters.[52] Finally, the support provided the UP by Protectorate chiefs was much less significant in 1966 than it had been in 1962. As noted in Chapter 6, some of the most open supporters of the UP had been dismissed in March 1965 and replaced by PPP loyalists; others were doubtless wary of giving open support to the UP, fearing that they too might be dismissed after the election.

Jawara made few cabinet changes after his latest election victory. Paul Baldeh, who was said to be "desperately ill," lost his position as minister of education for the second and final time, and Sheriff Dibba was shifted to Works and Communications. In addition, Jawara requested that Sir Farimang Singhateh be confirmed as governor general, having proved to be, according to local British officials, a surprisingly effective choice.[53]

The Decline of the Urban Opposition: 1966–70

After the euphoria of its "victory" in the 1965 referendum, the UP's performance in the 1966 election was a bitter disappointment for P. S. N'Jie and one he found difficult to accept; insisting that the UP had won the election, he challenged the results in the courts, but his claim was, not surprisingly, dismissed out of hand.[54] Yet he was still hopeful that the UP would build on its alliance of Bathurst and rural non-Mandinka to extend its support in the countryside by the next election, because the PPP failed to deliver on its promises to the electorate, and so remained confident of ultimately replacing Jawara. Whether the other MPs shared his confidence is less certain. Unlike after the 1962 election, no UP MP defected to the ruling PPP in the first four years of the new Parliament, but as early as July 1967, a group of UP leaders, including M. C. Cham and M. C. Jallow, opened talks with the PPP about a coalition. But Jawara offered few concessions and the talks broke down. They were revived in February 1968, with P. S. N'Jie this time meeting Jawara, but again came to nothing, because the UP's demands were too high.[55]

During 1968–69, the UP experienced a series of setbacks. First, it lost one of its shrinking band of financial backers, the extremely wealthy Bathurst businessman, M. M. N'Jie (who was also very influential in URD), following the marriage of Jawara to his sixteen-year-old daughter, Chilel. Jawara had been on bad terms with his Aku Christian wife, Augusta, for some time. He successfully filed for divorce in January 1967, but the Supreme Court's verdict was challenged by the Mahoney family and overturned by the Court of Appeal in May. The government then swiftly passed the Marriage Bill (Special Circumstances) Act of 1967, which allowed an automatic divorce if one partner converted to another religion (as of course the prime minister had done) and also permitted a polygamous marriage. It was under this legislation that Jawara (who did not divorce Augusta and, indeed, remained formally married to her) was able to marry Chilel.[56] The arranged marriage was clearly undertaken for both political and financial reasons; Jawara was under pressure from leading figures in the PPP to get rid of his Christian wife and marry a Muslim, and M. M. N'Jie's money provided a very welcome new resource for both himself and his party.[57] One side effect of the marriage was that some of N'Jie's Bathurst's clients, including the Almami of Bathurst, Momadou Lamin Bah, and his deputy, Ibrahima Ndow, apparently also joined the PPP, although his rural protégé, the UP MP for Tumana, M. C. Cham, stayed loyal to his party.[58]

Second, also in March 1968, the UP lost its electoral ally when, despite the past differences between the GCP and the PPP, particularly on foreign policy, Garba-Jahumpa suddenly dissolved his GCP and joined the victorious PPP; this was not the first time that this peripatetic politician abandoned an alliance that was no longer of use to him.[59] By early 1968, Garba-Jahumpa realized his party was moribund. In the 1968 BCC election, the GCP won only one seat (his own) with the UP's Burang-John securing one more vote than he did in Bathurst South[60]; his chances of retaining his parliamentary seat at the next general election therefore seemed slim. Garba-Jahumpa probably also demanded a ministerial post as the price for crossing the floor; certainly, less than a month after the dissolution of the GCP, he was appointed minister of health in a cabinet reshuffle, which was to have far-reaching consequences.[61] Nevertheless, he was taking a risk by merging his party with the PPP; the loss of UP support automatically made his Bathurst South constituency a marginal.

Jawara's reasons for accepting Garba-Jahumpa into the fold may have been more complex. Certainly he must have welcomed the chance to regain a foothold in Bathurst, which had been lost after M. B. Jones' defeat in the 1966 election. As Nyang suggests, he probably wished to benefit from Garba-Jahumpa's experience or, at least, as the British high commissioner argued, silence his most damaging critic.[62] But in addition, as discussed in Chapter 6, Jawara had made a conscious decision even before independence to open up the victorious party to former opposition elements, in the pursuit of a policy of national reconciliation or integration between the former Colony and Protectorate and between the potentially antagonistic ethnic groups in the country. From this perspective, Garba-Jahumpa, as both a leading Bathurst politician and a Wolof, made an ideal convert.

Third, the UP suffered further setbacks during 1969, when three of its parliamentary candidates in 1966, Baboucar B. Cham (Northern Kombo), Karamo Kinteh (Lower Baddibu), and Jallow Sanneh (Eastern Kiang), defected to the PPP. Sanneh, the son of Karamo K. Sanneh, the deposed Seyfu of Eastern Kiang, was undoubtedly the most significant acquisition by the PPP.[63]

The decline of its urban opponents strengthened the PPP's position, but from 1967 onward, it faced new challenges from its former supporters. It is these intraparty challengers to its predominance that are next examined.

Intraparty Challenges

The PPP, as shown in Chapter 6, was not entirely free of personality rivalries and factional intrigue, but the pursuit of political power on behalf of the economically neglected and politically ignored Protectorate, and the anticipated redistribution of national resources consequent on winning independence, provided its leaders and supporters with a common set of objectives. Once independence was secured and the formal opposition entered a period of political decay, elements within the PPP renewed their opposition to the new direction of party policy, the neglect of grassroots activists as a result of growing complacency, and the increasing power of the prime minister, Dawda Jawara. The first serious challenge to the party and its leadership was made by the PPA in 1968. Their lead was followed by the Independents in 1972 and, finally and more dangerously, by the NCP from 1975.

These challenges took place over fifteen years and involved different political actors, but they had several themes in common. The most important of these was the perceived departure in party policy away from the primacy of provincial and Mandinka interests to a more inclusivist approach embracing the old Colony and Protectorate, the Mandinka and other ethnic groups, in a shared national community. This involved a greater extent of power sharing within the senior ranks of the party and in the government with non-Mandinka, and the balancing of Mandinka aspirations in respect of party and state patronage with the need to reward opposition elements who increasingly crossed over to the ruling party.[64] The power sharing can be seen in the steady growth of urban Wolof in the cabinet and the National Executive Committee of the PPP. A. B. N'Jie had been in the cabinet since 1965. Those promoted to cabinet rank in 1968 included Garba-Jahumpa and, as discussed below, Momodou Lamin Saho, who replaced the expatriate, Phillip (later Sir Phillip) Bridges, as attorney general in September 1968, after Bridges was appointed chief justice.[65]

To achieve such a delicate equilibrium, the PPP had to promote sufficient economic development to justify its claims to rule the new state and create the necessary opportunities for all key political players and their supporting communities to feel a benefit. Given the high degree of expectation, particularly among the provincial heartland of the party, the post-independence PPP government faced recurrent criticism of its development policies. The essentially patron–client nature of politics, in which political loyalties were rewarded with opportunities for self-enrichment through public office, had the effect of undermining government development policies aimed at improving living conditions in the Provinces and threatened the legitimacy of the ruling party.

The government's critics focused their attacks on Jawara. Not only was he the architect of the new inclusivist party policy, he was also at the center of the patronage system. Critics expressed mounting concern over the growth in his personal power, both within the ruling party and in government. In a matter of a few years, Jawara extended his authority from that of first among equals of a new generation of politically inexperienced provincial politicians to an astute and determined executive president, displaying the leadership style of a "prince," as typologized by Jackson and Rosberg.[66] Their depiction of the "prince" as "an astute observer and manipulator of lieutenants and clients . . . [who presides] . . . over the struggle for preferments . . . but not to let it get out of hand, nor to let any leader emerge as a serious challenger" fits Jawara's evolving presidential rule well. It was thus not only the UP that would question his motivations for moving from a constitutional monarchy to an executive presidency.

National Convention Party: 1967–69[67]

The first of these intraparty challengers, the National Convention Party, was founded in May 1967 by Noah Sanyang. As noted, Sanyang had been the PPP candidate in Tumana in 1962, but was replaced in 1966 by A. S. Kandeh, who fared only marginally better than he against the UP's M. C. Cham.[68] Its other leaders were two former PPP MPs, A. M. Demba and Lamin M'Boge, and two radical journalists, "Ba" (Baboucar) M. Tarawale and M'Backe N'Jie. Tarawale was the PPP's former political secretary and editor of the initially pro-PPP newspaper, *The New Gambia*, who resigned from the PPP in July 1966, following the closure of its Political Bureau, which he headed. N'Jie was the editor of *The Progressive*. Significantly, all save N'Jie were Mandinka. But the party was an ephemeral creation; by August 1967, M'Boge and Tarawale had left, allegedly to establish the even more obscure Gambia People's Party. Sanyang, who probably earlier merged his party into the PPA, rejoined the PPP in August 1969.[69]

The People's Progressive Alliance: 1968–72[70]

The second challenger to the PPP, the PPA, posed a much more serious threat. It was launched in October 1968 by four dissident PPP ministerial MPs, Sheriff Sisay (Niamina), K. C. A. Kah (Jokadu), Paul Baldeh (Lower Fulladu West), and Yusupha Samba (Sabach Sanjal), all of whom nursed real or imagined grievances against the PPP leadership. They were assisted by B. M. Tarawale, the PPP's former political secretary, who, as noted, flirted with the National Convention Party, and by the former UP parliamentary candidate, Jallow Sanneh, who helped to draft the party's constitution, but soon after defected to the PPP. Tarawale had once been extremely close to Jawara, but was subsequently a persistent gadfly who used the columns of his *New Gambia* newspaper to expose corruption in government circles and attack Jawara's leadership style.[71] It should be noted that only three of the six original PPA leaders (Sanneh, Sisay, and Tarawale—the last-named a "Mandinkanized" Bambara) were Mandinka; Samba was a rural Wolof; Baldeh a Fula; and Kah a Tukulor.

The PPA leader was Sisay, one of the founders of the PPP and its secretary general, who ever since 1962 had held the position of minister of finance. This was generally regarded as the second most important post in the cabinet after the prime minister. However, in December 1967, Jawara decided to reshuffle his cabinet. He appointed Sheriff Dibba as minister of finance in succession to Sisay, who was instead offered the less prestigious external affairs portfolio. Although the move was apparently designed in part to get rid of the discredited A. B. N'Jie, it was rumored in Bathurst that Sisay was plotting against Jawara and the prime minister was keen to cut his overambitious subordinate down to size. Sisay at first accepted the new post, but when Jawara confirmed that he was now ranked third in the cabinet behind himself and Dibba, he changed his mind and resigned from the cabinet in January 1968 with the vacancy being filled by Andrew Camara.[72] He remained as secretary general of the party until June when he was relieved of his post and replaced by Jawara himself.[73]

Meanwhile, in April, Kah, the minister of health, was ousted to make room for Garba-Jahumpa on the merger of the GCP with the PPP. He was apparently offered a position as a parliamentary secretary, but declined it and returned to the back benches. At the same time, Samba was dismissed as parliamentary secretary to the minister of local government, lands and mines; he was replaced by Demba S. Cham, possibly to retain a Tukulor presence in the cabinet after Kah's departure, although Samba's lifestyle certainly contributed to his loss of office.[74] Baldeh had a longer standing grievance. He had twice served as minister of education, but, as noted, had not received any ministerial portfolio after the 1966 election, again in part because of disapproval of his lifestyle.

During the summer of 1968, the disagreement between the party leaders took on a more serious complexion. This was in part because the deposed ministers interpreted their political demotion as evidence of a growing neglect of provincial interests in the government, as demonstrated by the prime minister's desire to open up party and government to non-Mandinka, and his nascent authoritarianism in respect of policy initiatives and cabinet appointments. There was undoubtedly, as well, a degree of rivalry between Jawara, better educated but of low social caste, and Sisay, of more limited schooling, but the son of a chief, dating back to the PPP's decision to choose the former as its leader and the country's first prime minister.

Matters began to move to a head in August 1968 when the dissident MPs joined forces with the UP to attack the government in Parliament. All four voted against an attempt to increase the number of "nominated" MPs and a bill to ministerialize the post of the attorney general. Both bills were associated with Jawara's desire to have M. L. Saho in the cabinet. To be a minister, Saho had first to be a MP, but there were no convenient vacancies and Jawara was unable to persuade any existing PPP MP to stand down. Because he did not wish to replace either of the existing "nominated" MPs (both of whom represented commercial interests), he decided to increase their number to four, which would also allow him to appoint the first female member of Parliament. This would not have been enough in itself to allow him to appoint Saho to the cabinet because, as a recent member of the Public Services Commission, the latter was barred from holding a ministerial post for three years. The second bill was therefore designed to allow Jawara to circumvent this restriction. When the bills were put to the vote, the PPP won, but by only twenty votes to eleven; this was less than the two-thirds majority that the opposition claimed was necessary on the grounds that the constitution was being amended. Eventually the British government concurred with Jawara's view that a simple majority only was required, but their enactment was delayed for several months.[75]

The willingness of the dissident MPs to join forces with P. S. N'Jie (who was unusually effective in Parliament over the issue), greatly angered Jawara. The prime minister first acted skillfully to prevent the rebellion from spreading by using patronage to exploit the factional tendencies and personal ambitions of second-tier PPP leaders. As the main beneficiary of the first reshuffle, Sheriff Dibba, who would later challenge Jawara, on this occasion strongly supported the prime minister. Indeed, he pressed for Sisay's expulsion from the PPP. Other beneficiaries of the cabinet reshuffles also supported the prime minister. To prevent the rebellion spreading outside the party, Jawara enticed back Lamin M'Boge, perhaps with a promise of Sisay's Niamina constituency at the next election; M'Boge rejoined the PPP in October.[76] Once Jawara was sure of the backing of his party, he acted decisively; on September 1, the PPP's National Executive Committee endorsed his recommendation to expel the four MPs from the party "for persistent and consistent indiscipline and disloyalty."[77]

A month later, the expelled MPs formed the PPA.[78] The deliberate overlapping of the new movement's name with that of the ruling party was part of an attempt by the dissidents to claim to speak for the unadulterated rural movement of the past; a going back to the PPP's original roots of a Mandinka provincial-centered organization under collective leadership (although, as noted, only three of the six original PPA leaders were Mandinka or "Mandinkanized"). This was in contrast to what had evolved under Jawara's imperious leadership, an interethnic and transregional party, in danger of selling out on its historic mission and native constituency (a theme to be brought up again by a new group of rebels in the mid-1970s).

The PPA leaders were supported by many of their constituents (including Sisay's brother, the chief of Niamina at this time) and a handful of urban political figures from the distant past, including two members of the defunct Gambia National Party, Edrissa Samba and Alexander Jobarteh. But support for the PPA remained local and it was never able to establish a national organization.[79] Moreover, despite its carefully thought-out appeal to the rural electorate, it failed to undermine Jawara's personal ascendancy or displace the PPP in the affection and loyalties of the rural populace. This was not least because it could offer no tangible benefits to an electorate that had come to view political power as the means to distribute state largesse to constituencies. Many Mandinka may also have distrusted Sisay personally. Its difficulties were compounded by a lack of money. This was a reflection of its failure to attract any important patrons in the rural constituencies, or any mass following to provide sufficient income from membership dues to enable it to expand its organization beyond the constituencies of the rebel ministers.[80] Instead, it came to rely on the insufficient profits of Tarawale's newspaper. A further setback occurred when Paul Baldeh, who retained a following among the Fula community of MID, died in December 1968 at the age of only thirty-one.[81]

The PPA was therefore doomed to remain, at best, a minority party, with no prospect of winning more than a handful of rural seats, and, more remotely, achieving a successful electoral pact with the UP at the next general election. As noted, Jallow Sanneh joined the PPP in early 1969, and Kah did so in July. The latter claimed that this was due to pressure being exerted on him by his constituents, but dissatisfaction with the PPA was probably the root cause.[82] However, he did not enjoy his good fortune for long; in October 1969, he (together with the UP's N. M. Darbo) was charged with fraud involving passport irregularities. He was subsequently convicted and sentenced to a two-year term of imprisonment. He automatically forfeited his parliamentary seat, as a result of failing to appeal against the Court of Appeal's upholding of the sentence. He was expelled from the PPP in February 1971 and subsequently disappeared from political life.[83] The two remaining PPA MPs, Sisay and Samba, struggled on somewhat half heartedly. For example, the PPA did not contest any of the seven by-elections that occurred between 1968 and 1971, even in Baldeh's old seat of Lower Fulladu West.[84]

1970 Republic Referendum[85]

The first real opportunity for both the UP and the PPA to challenge the ruling party nationally since the 1966 election was in April 1970, when Jawara and the PPP felt sufficiently emboldened to hold a second republic referendum. After failing to secure the required two-thirds majority in 1965, Jawara apparently put his plans to establish a republic on hold for two or three years. He may then have been deterred by the rise of the PPA, which initially seemed to threaten the PPP's dominance and would certainly enable the opposition to block any bill to amend the constitution in the House. But Paul Baldeh's death, together with the by-election victories of the PPP's Abdul M'Ballow and Della Singhateh in Lower Fulladu West and Wuli in February and March 1969, respectively, changed the political arithmetic; it meant that the PPP once again could be certain of achieving the twenty-two votes in the House it required.[86] Consequently, no doubt with Jawara's approval, in May 1969, the PPP's Executive Committee unanimously resolved that it would seek to establish a republic, a decision made public a few days later. The Republic Bill was eventually published in November 1969 and considered by the House. The new bill was broadly similar to that put forward in 1965, although in a number of respects the power of the president was strengthened.[87]

Once again, the UP opposed the bill on the familiar grounds that the new constitution would vest absolute power in the president and that Jawara had introduced the bill to avoid having to call a general election in 1971. But apart from trying (unsuccessfully) to persuade Margaret Thatcher, then an opposition Conservative MP, to take up his cause, P. S. N'Jie did little to mobilize resistance to the bill.[88] Unlike in 1965, the referendum was not opposed by the GWU (which remained neutral), and the GCP was of course no longer in existence; it was also now much harder for dissident chiefs (or ex-chiefs) to foment opposition to the bill. However, this time the opposition to the bill included the PPA (even though its leaders had all supported the referendum in 1965); it argued that the abolition of the monarchy was undesirable and also objected to several specific clauses in the Republic Bill, particularly that a "yes" vote would effectively mean a vote for Jawara to be the first president.[89] But its tactical alliance with the UP backfired; the government succeeded in undermining grassroots Mandinka support for the PPA, by playing on the latter's alliance with the UP, the historic opponent of the former Protectorate. The PPP also discredited the PPA by accusing it of going against the social consensus of Mandinka society and threatening it with a damaging disunity.[90]

Even with the cooperation of the PPA, the UP was unable to prevent a determined PPP, which presented its case more effectively than in 1965, from forcing through a "yes" vote on this occasion. The government obtained 84,968 "yes" votes to the 35,638 "no" votes of the opposition; this meant it won 70.5 percent of the vote and achieved 4,163 votes more than the required two-thirds majority. The very high turnout (90 percent) reflected not only the government's determination and improved organization, but also the much improved electoral register.[91] Six of the seven constituencies with UP MPs in 1970 voted "no," the exception being Jimara (where the "yes" majority was one); the "yes" majority was also relatively small in two other constituencies in URD, Kantora and Wuli. The only other constituency to record a majority for the "no" camp was Niamina, Sheriff Sisay's home area, although there was solid support for the referendum in Yusupha Samba's constituency of Sabach Sanjal. Of the third of the electorate that was against the government, a clear majority, it could be claimed, were UP sympathizers. At the same time, when compared with the outcome of the 1965 referendum, the result could be interpreted as further evidence of the shrinking of the UP's rural vote.[92]

After the referendum, Sir Farimang Singhateh (whose role during the campaign was controversial) stepped down as governor general.[93] Jawara was automatically sworn in as president on April 24, and the Parliamentary seat he vacated in Eastern Kombo was inherited by Lamin Kitty Jabang, a twenty-nine-year-old Mandinka head teacher, in an uncontested by-election. Jabang, who was to become a leading political figure in the 1980s and 1990s, was the first of a new wave of younger and generally better educated PPP politicians to enter Parliament.[94] But if the result was a triumph for the PPP, the outcome marked the beginning of the end for the PPA. In July 1970, Sisay and Samba initiated discussions with Jawara and the PPP Executive Committee, but it was not until December 1971, a few months before the next general election, that they were finally readmitted to the party. The PPA was subsequently formally dissolved in February 1972.[95]

Despite returning to the fold, neither man was selected for the PPP in the next general election. Although some of his constituents tried to persuade him to stand as an Independent, Sisay supported the PPP and was subsequently rewarded for doing so by being appointed governor of the Central Bank of The Gambia in

December 1972.[96] He even made it back to his old post of minister of trade and finance in 1982. His brother was not so fortunate; he was removed from office in June 1971.[97] The Sisay episode throws an instructive light on Jawara's leadership style and his understanding of the mentality of his colleagues in the government. Both as prime minister and president, he manipulated their usually selfish aspirations against each other. Rebels were rarely cast from office for long; instead Jawara used periods of political "exile" to sanction them, often bringing them back into government later to be used against new challengers to his authority.

Unlike Sisay, Samba did not regain his former position and faded out of politics. Meanwhile, although Tarawale was readmitted to the PPP in July 1970, his rapprochement with the PPP was short-lived; in 1971, the government pressed charges of seditious libel against him for defaming the president in a series of articles. He was convicted in May 1971 and served eight months of a two-and-a-half year sentence, but on his release in 1972, the government prevented him from recommencing his newspaper, the *New Gambia*.[98] It would be another ten years before he and the PPP leadership would be reconciled. Tarawale's treatment was evidence of the coercive, as well as the patron clientage, approach adopted by the PPP in dealing with its political opponents; although dismissals and exclusion were the preferred means.

The 1971 Area Council and 1972 General Elections

The next test of the PPP's ascendancy came on June 16, 1971 when Area Council (local government) elections took place.[99] On the basis of their outcome, when the PPP won sixty-eight seats out of seventy-two, it had every expectation of sweeping the polls in the general election some nine months later. In Kanifing Urban District Council (the authority for the capital's mainland suburbs), the PPP stood unchallenged in six of the eleven seats; of the other three, it won two and lost one to the UP. The situation was repeated in the Provinces. In Brikama Area Council (WD), it won all twelve seats unopposed and in Mansakonko Area Council (LRD), it again took all twelve seats, facing only a handful of Independent candidates. In Kuntaur Area Council (MID), despite a tradition of UP support, the party managed to contest only six seats out of twelve, winning only Ballanghar in Lower Saloum. In Kerewan Area Council (North Bank Division–NBD), only one UP candidate was put up; the PPP won twelve seats and Independents the other three. The same story was repeated in Georgetown (MID), again an area where the UP might have hoped to retain seats, having won three in 1967, but it failed to put up any candidates; the PPP took nine seats unopposed and defeated Independents in the remaining three. In addition, the PPP swept the board in Basse Area Council (URD), even though there had been previously strong support for the UP in this area. The results painfully exposed the organizational weaknesses of the UP as well as a fatalistic acceptance of PPP hegemony on the part of most voters. Yet, despite these depressing results, the UP refused to give up the struggle and put up a renewed, if hardly more successful, challenge to the government in the general election held the following March.

The second post-independence general election took place over two days, March 28–29, 1972.[100] It was contested by the PPP, the UP and by a large group of Independent candidates. Each is considered in turn.

People's Progressive Party

At the dissolution of Parliament, the PPP held twenty-eight seats and was confident of retaining all of these. Not surprisingly, almost all its sitting MPs, including M. C. Cham (Tumana) and M. C. Jallow (Jimara) who, as discussed below, joined the PPP from the UP in 1970, were renominated. There were only three exceptions: Della Singhateh (Wuli) and the former PPA leaders, Sheriff Sisay (Niamina) and Yusupha Samba (Sabach Sanjal). Singhateh was replaced by Sana Saidy; Sisay by the PPP's administrative secretary, Lamin M'Boge, who was now fully rehabilitated; and Samba by a young Radio Gambia technician from Kataba, Saihou Sabally.[101] In addition, the PPP could reasonably expect to win back Jokadu (which had been lost in a by-election to an Independent candidate in 1971), having replaced its inappropriate by-election candidate, Abdoulie M. Drammeh (a Bathurst lawyer and a Wolof), by Landing Jallow Sonko, a Mandinka teacher from Sika in Niumi, who was, more importantly, a member of the Sonko ruling family. The PPP also shrewdly chose Omar A. Jallow, a young cooperative inspector and former official of the GWU, who was well known as a local youth leader, to challenge Gibou Jagne in Serrekunda. Along with Lamin Kitty Jabang, Sabally, Sonko and Jallow represented the second wave of PPP politicians who were to come to prominence in the 1970s and 1980s.[102]

The PPP also nominated strong candidates in its two target seats in Bathurst: I. B. A. Kelepha-Samba in Bathurst North and Horace R. Monday (senior), in Bathurst Central. The former was a career civil servant who had retired as senior accounting officer in the Marine Department shortly before the election; the latter was a former accountant general and Gambian high commissioner in London who, in recent years, had served as the chairman of the Public Services Commission. Their selection demonstrated that senior civil servants of an Aku and Wolof background, previously identified with the UP, were now confident that their positions would not disappear under a wave of provincial Mandinka aspirants.[103] Similarly, Christians were reassured by key civil service appointments that they would not be displaced by Muslims.[104] The Bathurst elite discovered that the relatively inexperienced PPP government needed its professional and administrative experiences to run the new state and the promotion of provincial Mandinka in the public service was checked by a combination of their lack of training and by government prudence.

The choice of Kelepha-Samba, who was mayor of Bathurst between 1967 and the sudden dissolution of the BCC in June 1971, also illustrated how far the PPP's presence in local government in the capital had increased since independence. As early as 1967–68, control of the BCC and Kanifing Urban District Council had passed to the PPP, by means of a combination of election victories and the appointment of nominated councilors to achieve overall majorities.[105]

In the Provinces, the PPP revived its dormant party structure, sending senior PPP MPs to head campaign teams in their home areas: Sheriff Dibba concentrated on NBD; B. L. Kuti Sanyang was in charge in WD; Yaya Ceesay took on LRD; Kebba Leigh managed the MID campaign; and Andrew Camara ensured that there was no UP revival in URD.[106] Seven PPP candidates, including Sanyang and Ceesay, were returned unopposed. This reflected the success of the ruling party in discouraging opposition candidates from standing through a combination of inducements and veiled sanctions. This allowed the PPP to redeploy financial resources and MPs to help out in other constituencies.

United Party

Since its defeat in the 1970 republic referendum, the UP had suffered a series of further setbacks (apart from its poor performance in the 1971 Area Council elections). First, on the eve of the referendum, the party's general secretary (and editor of the *Gambia Echo* since 1968), I. A. S. Burang-John, joined the PPP, taking the party's records with him. Burang-John's justification for changing sides after ten years' service to the UP was that he had despaired of ever achieving the unity between the UP and PPP, which he had long sought; he had also previously tried in vain to persuade P. S. N'Jie not to oppose the referendum, which he considered the UP could not win. Second, in August 1970, M. C. Jallow, the MP for Jimara, defected to the PPP; Jallow also mentioned the cause of unity, but interestingly added that his decision met with the approval of his constituents.[107]

Third, in October 1970, M. C. Cham, the MP for Tumana, joined the PPP. His decision to join the PPP seems to have been a direct consequence of a fourth blow to the UP's prospects, the death of E. D. N'Jie. On May 8, the party's Executive Bureau had dismissed P. S. N'Jie as leader and replaced him with his more pragmatic brother, with Cham as deputy leader. P. S. N'Jie had refused to accept the legitimacy of the referendum or the establishment of the republic and in protest had withdrawn from the House of Representatives (even before then his attendance was erratic and his frequent absences attributed to a serious drink problem, which he subsequently overcame). Initially, he even refused to handle the new currency with Jawara's portrait on it. He also failed to attend meetings of the party's Executive Committee. This was the final straw for the other UP MPs who ousted him in the hope that E. D. N'Jie would provide a more effective leadership style. P. S. N'Jie initially challenged their decision, but in July, E. D. N'Jie was formally confirmed as UP party leader in the House of Representatives.[108] However, on October 19, E. D. N'Jie died from injuries sustained in a car accident and the party was obliged to reinstate P. S. N'Jie because no alternative leader could be found. This led almost immediately to the defection of Cham, who had strongly supported the replacement of

P. S. N'Jie, which not only effectively destroyed the UP's prospects in URD, but also meant that the UP lost one of its most active spokesmen.[109] As discussed, both Cham and Jallow were to fight the 1972 election under the PPP banner.

A further blow to the UP cause was the loss of two of its seats in by-elections. In October 1970, a by-election was held in Upper Fulladu West because the sitting UP member, N. M. Darbo, had been sentenced to a two-year term of imprisonment in the previous November; the PPP candidate, Kebba Jawara, a relative of the president, who had lost to Darbo in 1966, this time defeated the UP's Sheikh Samba Jobe with 70 percent of the vote. Even more significantly, in January 1971, the UP rural stronghold of Saloum, which E. D. N'Jie had won with 61 percent of the vote in 1966, was lost when K. W. Foon was defeated by the PPP's Kebba A. Bayo by 178 votes.[110]

These by-election defeats meant that the UP held only three seats at the dissolution of Parliament, all in the former Colony area: Bathurst North through P. S. N'Jie, Bathurst Central through J. R. Forster, and Serrekunda through Gibou Jagne. Moreover, the loyalty to the UP of both Forster and Jagne was open to question; according to the British high commissioner, both men were ready to defect to the PPP if they could find a means of doing so without alienating their constituents.[111] In addition, in at least one constituency (Wuli) and possibly elsewhere, a potential UP candidate was persuaded by intimidation to withdraw. In view of these problems, the UP was able to field only fourteen candidates in total, compared with the twenty-nine it had put forward in 1966.[112] Four of these were newcomers to national politics, but only Momodou (Dodou) M. Taal, who represented the Bathurst South ward on the BCC and had been the president of the Gambia National Youth Council, was in any way known to the general public.[113] It was also evident that the UP's regional base had shrunk considerably since the previous election; although it contested four out of five seats in Bathurst/Kombo St. Mary and five out of six in Georgetown Administrative Area, it could contest only three out of six seats in URD and only two out of fifteen seats in the three other administrative areas combined (Brikama, Mansakonko, and Kerewan).

The Independents[114]

As we have seen, there had been Independent candidates in each Gambian general election since 1960. However, in the 1962 and 1966 elections, their presence was token: there were only two Independent candidates in 1962 and six in 1966 and none came remotely close to winning a seat. In contrast, in 1972, there were no fewer than nineteen Independents and they stood in every Administrative Area except Kombo St. Mary. That so many Independents were to contest a general election was most unusual in post-independence Africa; where competitive party politics continued after independence, almost all candidates represented a political party.[115]

One Independent candidate, Maja Omar Sonko, was a sitting MP. The nephew of Landing Omar Sonko, a former MP who was now the Seyfu of Upper Niumi, Maja Sonko had won the Jokadu by-election in March 1971, which was brought about by the downfall of K. C. A. Kah. Sonko, who thus defeated the government's attempt to impose an outsider on a reluctant constituency organization in his home area, almost immediately applied to rejoin the PPP, but was turned down. L. O. Sonko, who had been dismissed as Seyfu in February 1971 for supporting his relative, also stood as an Independent, in Niumi.[116] Two candidates, the GWU leader, M. E. Jallow (Bathurst North) and Momodou K. Sanneh (Western Kiang), had been unsuccessful Independent candidates in the 1966 election; M. B. Sagnia (Kantora), one of the original founders of the Protectorate People's Society, had contested the 1960 and 1962 elections for the PPP. It is also probable that Yaya Dabo had fought Jarra for the UP in 1962.[117] All the rest appear to have been political newcomers who had not previously stood for Parliament.

All save one (M. E. Jallow) of the Independents were PPP supporters and constituency-level office holders. The PPP received over 200 applications for the thirty-two parliamentary seats and a number of those who were rejected chose to stand as Independent candidates.[118] Many were opposed to the virtually automatic re-adoption of existing MPs by the ruling party; as noted, twenty-five out of twenty-eight sitting members were renominated. Even Musa Dabo, who had been accused in January 1970 of aiding and abetting the obtaining of money by false pretences and forced to resign as minister of health, was reselected in Sandu.[119] This is a common problem with newly created political parties in the Third World, whose initial cohort of MPs are unusually young (compared with the age profile of MPs in developed countries) and consequently remain relatively youthful and unprepared to give up office, even after ten years of power. Consequently, a new generation of party activists find it difficult to displace their seniors, whose livelihood now derives from political office.

Many, although not all, of the Independents were young.[120] As will be seen in Chapter 8, youths in The Gambia were no different from their counterparts elsewhere in Africa in being critical of the party in power for personal, as well as for ideological, reasons. In seeking to exercise some control over them, the PPP reorganized its own youth wing in 1971, but it was from this same organization that most of the Independent candidates in 1972 were to emerge.[121] Personally ambitious to advance socially and economically through parliamentary office, they sought to mobilize kinship and locality support for their rebellious challenge to the party hierarchy, while at the same time claiming to be loyal to the PPP. This was not as inconsistent as it sounded: the bulk of the Independents saw themselves as loyal party members and their opposition was to the selection process, not to the PPP's manifesto and policies or leader. They even sought to adopt party leader Jawara as their presidential preference, but in a move designed to isolate them from rank-and-file party loyalists, who were strongly attached to him, he refused to accept their support.[122]

Typically, the Independents were drawn from the lower ranks of the public service and commerce—such as teachers and clerks. In fact their socioeconomic backgrounds were no different from other candidates, save that PPP candidates now described themselves as "politicians" and enjoyed an improved standard of

living as a result of their new livelihoods. Although all had to be sufficiently conversant in English to pass the simple linguistic and literacy tests applied by divisional commissioners at the time of their adoption, the competence of a number
of them was limited.[123]

Nine of the nineteen candidates, including many of the most active, contested
seats in the Kerewan Administrative Area of the LRD[124]; five stood in the three
seats in the Baddibu districts, with a tradition of youth unemployment and migration to the capital city in search of work and social betterment. Baddibunku (those
from Baddibu) in the Bathurst area supported their kinsmen at home and two of
the leading organizers of the Independent group were from Salikene in NBD:
Momodou S. K. Manneh and Lamin K. Saho. Both men, who were in their twenties, had recently returned home with doctorates, following higher education in
the United States and West Germany, respectively. Prevented by the electoral residency regulations from standing himself against Sheriff Dibba in Central
Baddibu, Saho sponsored his brother, B. K. Saho, as well as providing wider leadership for the Independents in Baddibu and more generally. Manneh was also
prevented from standing by the residency regulations.[125] Baddibu discontent, an
amalgam of economic grievances and resistance to PPP central office attempts to
enforce sitting MPs on local constituencies, persisted after the collapse of the
Independents' challenge in 1972 and helped to fuel a more serious challenge to
the government a few years later.

Linked to the Independents' attacks on the selection process for parliamentary
candidates was their criticism, often shared more widely, of incumbent MPs for
neglecting their constituents. This was usually expressed in terms of the MPs keeping away from their constituencies, save at election time; failing to secure sufficient development projects for their home areas (infrastructural and health
provisions, in particular); and not providing work opportunities for local youths
at a time of rising unemployment among school leavers. At the same time, they
enjoyed the perceived benefits of office, legitimate or otherwise, in the distant
capital.[126]

It has to be said that attitudes toward political corruption in The Gambia have
always been ambiguous[127]; anti-corruption rhetoric is part of the opposition's
attacks on government, but it does not take long for the same critics, should they
achieve office themselves, to engage in the very same practices earlier condemned.[128] There appears to be a general perception of the corrupting nature of
power, but a relatively indulgent attitude toward those enjoying it, provided the
benefits are either spread about more widely or circulated among competing sections of the aspiring political elite. The improper use of state resources or private
money to "buy" votes is a case in point. The practice dates back to late colonial
times in Bathurst[129]; yet the PPP and later critics of such irregularities readily
resorted to the same methods in pursuit or defense of their own political power.
It is more the lack of equal access to such patronage, rather than its use, that fuels
such criticism. Independent candidates, lacking the means to engage in "vote buy-
ing," were understandably quick to condemn it.

Although the Independents' criticisms of MPs struck a chord with many voters, their chances at the polls were limited. First, the Independent candidates had very little in common other than their (generally) shared PPP background and frustrated ambitions, and no central organization to convert them into a new political party. Emblematically, this was seen in the adoption by Independents of a variety of symbols (such as a lantern, ladder, or key) from an official list, rather than a shared one, which would have at least lent them a cosmetic unity. Indeed, in three constituencies (Illiassa, Niumi, and Lower Baddibu), Independents stood against each other.[130] Attempts were made to couch their grievances in terms of issues of principle and M. E. Jallow, the veteran trade union leader and anticolonial nationalist standing as an Independent in Bathurst North, and with the assistance of some of the Baddibu dissidents, did produce short, duplicated, communiqués which sought to identify common criticisms of the government. But at heart, nearly all the candidates were driven by ambition to hold elected office, a factor successfully exploited by the PPP leadership. Moreover, attempts to campaign as a group largely foundered, save for an initial rally in Banjul and limited joint campaigning in Niumi and the Baddibus. A promised joint campaign tour of the country was shelved, because the Independent candidates were forced to focus on their own localities.[131]

Second, the fact that nearly all Independents saw themselves as only temporarily in dispute with the PPP meant they could not form an alliance with the UP, still remembered as the political enemy in most rural areas. The UP, on its part, claimed to have offered limited financial support to some Independent candidates, but remained suspicious of them.[132] Such support would have been justified tactically, because Independents stood against the government in eleven constituencies in which the UP failed to put up candidates of its own. It would have had to have been offered discreetly, because PPP propaganda sought to present the Independents as covert allies of the UP. In five constituencies (Bathurst North, Upper Fulladu West, Niumi, Sandu, and Sabach Sanjal), Independents stood against the UP, but only in Sabach Sanjal did this allow the PPP to win on a minority vote.

Third, the Independents failed to attract the backing of local rural notables. Unlike with the PPA, and later the NCP or Gambia People's Party, no prominent political leader or powerful opinion leader in the provinces, save for chiefly close relatives of candidates, was prepared to come out openly for Independents. However, the father of Batapa Drammeh was removed as Seyfu of Sandu for campaigning for his son.[133] Independents were instead forced to rely on other, and ultimately less successful, stratagems. The principal ones were community-based extended family networks, village and locality loyalties and an appeal to youth (except that few of the latter were registered electors, given the 21 voting age requirement).[134] These tactics were not restricted to the Independents; they were, and are, the stuff of Gambian politics. All candidates, including party nominees, sought to mobilize local networks to command a majority of votes in their constituencies. Family pedigree and social standing were of great political value, as had been the case in earlier elections. The PPP proved adept at door-to-door canvassing of heads-of-family in the interior, appealing to traditional notions of deference to age and social standing. This reliance on personal contacts helps explain the limited role of the news media and party political literature in the campaign, and, indeed, in other elections.

Fourth, the Independents, like the UP, lacked the financial resources to bolster their campaigns. Funding was the responsibility of each candidate, but PPP candidates enjoyed the financial support of the party and additional assistance from sections of the business community. The latter had nothing to gain, and much to lose, by supporting anti-government candidates. Likewise, local communities, eager to tap into albeit limited government development funds, put these at risk by voting for an opposition candidate.[135]

Finally, because the PPP regarded the Independents as a much more serious challenge to it than the long-established UP, it addressed its formidable resources, including its divisional campaign teams, to defeating them. Jawara, who took the opposition of the Independents very seriously, himself traveled the country "indefatigably" to bolster the support of PPP candidates.[136] The PPP also proved adept at dividing the support base of the Independents. The parochial nature of their activities allowed ruling party activists to play on family, ethnic, personal, generational, geographical, and, in one case, gender, divisions within constituencies. The more Independent candidates sought, in default of alternative resources, to mobilize local social networks, such as family, locality or age–grade ties, the easier it was for the PPP to counter these by appealing to rival constituency affinities. In Eastern Kombo, for example, the PPP effectively undermined a potentially serious challenge by Mrs. Ya Fatou Sonko, a twenty-four-year-old PPP party official from Brikama and the only female contestant, by playing on a combination of male prejudices against women holding office; generational hostility of elders to youths seeking to displace them; and geographical rivalry between Brikama town, from where Sonko drew much of her support, and the villages in the eastern half of the constituency, from where the PPP candidate, Lamin Jabang, hailed.[137] These strategies were in addition to the familiar pressure on chiefs and village headmen to keep out of the battle, or to support the government candidate, and financial inducements.[138]

Election Results

The interest generated by the campaign of the Independents was probably the main reason why the turnout was much higher than in 1966 at 76.1 percent.[139] The PPP comfortably won the election, winning twenty-eight seats out of thirty-two. Its share of the total vote actually fell from 65.3 percent in 1966 to 63.0 percent, but this was mainly due to the fact that seven of its candidates were returned unopposed and it would certainly have expected to gain an above-average vote in these constituencies. For the same reason, its total vote fell from 81,313 in 1966 to 65,388.[140] The UP won three seats, but it gained only 17,161 votes (compared with 41,549 for the UP/GCP coalition in 1966) and its share of the poll, at 16.5 percent, was its lowest to date. The Independents won only one seat, but nevertheless performed unusually well when all the disadvantages they faced are considered. They polled 21,302 votes, 20.5 percent of the total cast; a remarkable achievement for a disparate group of inexperienced and underfunded political novices.

All the PPP incumbents, except Musa Dabo in Sandu, were returned; Dabo was defeated by the Independent, Batapa Drammeh, who was elected with 53 percent of the vote. The PPP also regained Jokadu through Landing Jallow Sonko and, for the first time, won a seat in an election in the capital, with Garba-Jahumpa narrowly defeating the UP candidate in Bathurst South, M. M. Taal. All three current UP MPs, N'Jie, Forster, and Jagne, retained their seats, but saw their majorities sharply reduced. Meanwhile, although N'Jie overcame his customary lethargy in one last burst of campaigning in March, when he undertook a demanding eighteen-day tour of the Provinces, no mean achievement for a man of his years (he was sixty-two) and at the hottest time of the year, the UP failed to recover any of the seats it had lost through defections or by-elections. Indeed, only K. W. Foon in Saloum came even relatively close to winning and even in Jimara, which the UP had held until 1970, it managed only 14 percent of the vote. The bogey of Mandinka supremacism among the lesser ethnic communities had been laid to rest by the PPP's redefinition of itself and its effective use of patronage. Apart from Drammeh, Independents polled over one-third of the vote in four other constituencies. Only three won less than 10 percent of the poll.

There were various reasons for the UP's poor performance. First, as noted, its regional base was dwindling, thanks to the defection of its MPs and its declining role in rural local government. Second, the UP's financial resources were much reduced since 1966, particularly following the loss of support from M. M. N'Jie; P. S. N'Jie was probably also less able than in the past to fund the party out of his own pocket.[141] Third, the UP's organization was always weaker than the PPP's, but by 1972, the party had no effective propaganda machinery, nor any newspaper of its own to put across such views as it had. Although N'Jie did address the electorate (for the last time) in 1972, when he issued a press release of his radio election broadcast, entitled "Political Dark Ages of the Gambia," this was a poorly argued rant against the iniquities of the PPP, and with no clearly set out alternative policy. Typical of N'Jie's procrastination was his failure to send another election "press release" (a rather better argued one in which he rightly criticized antidemocratic acts on the part of the PPP government, such as dismissing chiefs whose sons stood against the ruling party) to *The Nation* newspaper until after the election![142] Not surprisingly, the overwhelming majority of voters rejected an increasingly idiosyncratic N'Jie and his party. A skeptical electorate questioned the capacity of defeated or inexperienced opposition leaders to improve on the existing government; by the 1970s, there was little memory of N'Jie's brief administration in the early 1960s, and nothing in his current pronouncements, to suggest he could do any better than Jawara and the PPP.

N'Jie also conceded defeat for the presidency, even before the election took place. Under the indirect system of choosing the head-of-state, operative in 1972 and 1977, the president was selected by a college of electors made up of the directly elected MPs in the House of Representatives. These were required to state their presidential choice at the time of standing for parliamentary election. Whereas all PPP candidates opted for Jawara, UP candidates nominated as their presidential choice not P. S. N'Jie, the party leader, but Percy H. Coker, a charming, but politically quite obscure and ineffective, Aku government pensioner.[143] N'Jie faced a dilemma in that he had campaigned against a presidency in 1965 and 1970, so could hardly stand for it in 1972. At the same time, his refusal to stand undermined his party's credibility and left Jawara as the most likely president even in a hung parliament.

Post-Election Cabinet Changes

Following his latest election victory, Jawara made only minor changes to his cabinet. Dibba remained as vice president and minister of finance, Camara as minister for external affairs, and M. L Saho as the attorney general; only one minister, H. O. Semega-Janneh (agriculture), was sacked. However, there were two newcomers to the cabinet: Sir Alieu Jack, who had been speaker of the House of Representatives since 1962, became minister of works and communications, and M. C. Cham was appointed minister of state, with responsibility for information, broadcasting, and tourism. The appointment of Jack (who was appointed as a "nominated" MP to permit this), together with the reappointment of A. B. N'Jie (who replaced Semega-Janneh) and Garba-Jahumpa, meant that there was now a bloc of powerful urban Wolof politicians in the cabinet. Both former UP MPs, Cham and M. C. Jallow, were rewarded for defecting to the PPP; the latter was appointed a parliamentary secretary.[144]

Impact on the United Party and Independents

Meanwhile, the UP survived its humiliation in 1972 to contest two further elections in 1977 and 1982. But although officially remaining leader of the party, the election marked the end of P. S. N'Jie's active political career. He again boycotted Parliament and was consequently expelled from the House in August 1972 for nonattendance for two consecutive meetings.[145] By 1974, he had developed the bizarre notion that the British high commissioner in Banjul had been instructed by his superiors in London to call on him to take over the reins of government, but was refusing to do so; after several meetings in London, in which he tried in vain to disabuse N'Jie of this notion, one official concluded that he was "mentally unbalanced" on the subject.[146] The UP retained Bathurst North through Musa A. Jobe, a retired civil servant, in the subsequent by-election held in December 1972, but only just; the PPP candidate, Kelepha-Samba, lost by fifty-seven votes in a hard-fought and bitter contest.[147] As noted below, on his third attempt, in 1977, the latter was to take the seat.

Despite its good performance, the Independent challenge quickly dissolved after the elections and a number of the defeated candidates sought to rejoin the ruling party in 1972–73, as had been the case with the earlier PPA defectors.[148] These did not include Batapa Drammeh (as Nyang claims); Drammeh was in fact unseated in August 1973 for failing to attend Parliament, probably on medical grounds, with Dabo regaining the seat in the subsequent by-election in November.[149] However, other Independent candidates were to stand for the new political opposition that emerged on the political scene in the mid-1970s, the NCP, which was to provide the next, and most serious, challenge to the PPP.

The Emergence of the National Convention Party

Parties such as the PPP, with their weak ideological bonds and loose organizational structure, are particularly prone to internal leadership fissures. The fresh round of schism in the mid-1970s echoed the earlier one of the PPA era, in that a senior party leader once again challenged the dominance of the party leader (and now head of state) and sought to regroup the party around himself. Sheriff Dibba, as noted in Chapter 6, was a founding member of the PPP and its leading figure in NBD, where he had held the seat of first Baddibu and then Central Baddibu since 1960. He played a major part in the early successes of the PPP and was rewarded with high office in the new African administration. He was appointed minister of labor in 1964, then took up the strategic post of minister of local government in 1965; he became minister of works and communications in 1966 and then replaced Sisay as minister of finance in 1968. Finally, he became vice president and leader of government business in the first republican Parliament in 1970, while remaining minister of finance.[150] These key offices of state ensured him a crucial and public role in managing parliamentary affairs. At the same time, they placed him next in the political succession, a position that caused Jawara anxiety. Moreover, over the years, Dibba had acquired many powerful political enemies, who viewed him as a determined and ruthless operator.

In September 1972, Dibba's situation suffered a major reversal, which left him in the political cold and embittered. The "butut affair" was a scandal involving his businessman brother, Kutubo. At the end of August, a government Landrover flying the Gambian flag was stopped at a Senegalese customs checkpoint en route to Dakar. It was carrying a quantity of contraband goods and its occupants were subsequently charged with illegally importing transistor radios and copper Gambian currency (bututs) to Senegal (where they were recycled for their metal content). They were found guilty and fined heavily. It later transpired that the chief culprit was Kutubo Dibba, who was running the operation from No. 1 Marina, Dibba's formal residence as vice president, and that Sheriff Dibba raised the money to pay the fine. Although rumors about his involvement were already circulating in Bathurst, the pressure increased on Dibba when the disgruntled former minister, H. O. Semega-Janneh, publicly attacked him in a speech in the House of Representatives. Although Dibba continued to deny any personal knowledge of what had been taking place, the political and diplomatic embarrassment was too much for Jawara who, egged on by Dibba's rivals in the cabinet and the party hierarchy, forced him to resign as vice president two days later; he was replaced by Andrew Camara.[151] He remained temporarily as minister of finance, but was no longer in Jawara's confidence, and on October 9, Jawara reshuffled his cabinet, with Garba-Jahumpa succeeding him as minister of finance. As compensation, Dibba was appointed The Gambia's first envoy to the European Economic Community at Brussels, but this sidelining only served to stoke up his resentment. It also failed to pacify his predominantly Mandinka supporters, who were becoming increasingly disgruntled at their weakened representation in the cabinet.[152]

In July 1974, Jawara reshuffled and enlarged his cabinet. A key change involved Dibba, who was brought home to head the new Ministry of Economic Development and Industrial Planning (MEPID). Dibba had apparently been angling to return to political life in The Gambia for some time and had been seeking to build up his grassroots support. Thus while the appointment was perhaps an indication that he had been partially rehabilitated, Jawara may also have considered that it would be easier to keep an eye on him if he was in the cabinet.[153] Certainly if Dibba and Jawara were reconciled, it was not for long; Dibba's relations with Jawara and his ministerial rivals deteriorated to the extent that on July 29, 1975, he was accused of seeking to unseat the president through a cabinet revolt and was dismissed. The British high commissioner, J. R. W. Parker, stated that he had been informed by Eric Christensen (the secretary to the cabinet) that the atmosphere in the cabinet had become "intolerable," with Dibba "constantly voicing his criticism of some of his colleagues and attempting to split off the others." Parker further suggested that there had been rumors for some time that dissident groups were intending to form a new political party to challenge the PPP at the next general election and that some ministers believed "that Dibba was in touch with, or attracting support from these groups." President Jawara also told Parker that Dibba had been seeking to take advantage of a general strike which had broken out on July 28 and that his "appeal was essentially to the hard-line Mandinka tribalists who wanted a dominant say in all the affairs of the country, to the virtual exclusion of other ethnic groups." For his part, Dibba later claimed that his expulsion was engineered by three principal cabinet opponents: A. B. N'Jie, the minister of external affairs; Sir Alieu Jack, the minister of works; and M. L. Saho, the attorney general. Significantly, as noted, all three men were Banjul Wolofs.[154]

Dibba was subsequently expelled from the PPP in August and on September 7, 1975, he launched his own party, the National Convention Party (which should not be confused with the earlier, and now defunct, party of the same name), at a rally at Busambala in Northern Kombo constituency.[155] The new party drew most of its support from Dibba's own political heartland (the Baddibu districts of NBD) and from migrants from these districts to Banjul, Serrekunda and the Brikama area. It had a particular appeal for those experiencing economic difficulties as a result of rising inflation and unemployment. Many of these blamed the PPP government for failing to prevent the breakdown of existing trading networks and to stop profiteering by wealthy businessmen.[156]

Dibba's brother, Abdoulie, had succeeded their father as the Seyfu of Central Baddibu since 1969, naturally joined the NCP, but the government acted swiftly, first suspending him from office and later deposing him.[157] However, only one other PPP MP, Kebba A. Bayo (Saloum), together with the UP MP, Gibou Jagne (Serrekunda), joined the new party, with the other two Baddibu MPs, Baba Touray (Illiassa) and Kalilou Singhateh (Lower Baddibu), remaining loyal to the PPP. Thus, unlike in 1968, there were no other defections of cabinet ministers. One reason for this was that Jawara reacted swiftly to the crisis; after Dibba's expulsion from the PPP, he toured the Provinces extensively, speaking at up to ten meetings per day, to condemn the former vice president for tribalism and disloyalty.[158]

Not surprisingly, the NCP was in many ways a clone of its parent organization, differing principally in its leadership. Dibba hoped to build on Mandinka resentment at Jawara's successful policy of turning the PPP into a national trans-ethnic party through power sharing with the Bathurst/Banjul and non-Mandinka provincial elites. As early as 1973, this gave rise to protest meetings: a rally in Gunjur and a public meeting in a cinema in Banjul, at which disaffected sections of Mandinka society, most notably in the Baddibus, played a prominent role.[159] The perceived denial of opportunity for educated Mandinka youth later merged with the alleged discrimination against Dibba, seen as still loyal to his Mandinka origins. Yet the NCP could not hope to gain power solely on the basis of a Mandinka section of the PPP, as had been demonstrated in the short-lived history of the PPA, particularly if this rested on opposition to Jawara's trans-ethnic initiatives. The defection to the NCP of Gibou Jagne, a Wolof, and the later adoption of several other non-Mandinka parliamentary candidates, was insufficient entirely to dispel the new party's "tribalist" image.

Consequently, like Sheriff Sisay before him, Dibba sought to portray Jawara as a dictatorial leader, overthrowing the collective leadership principles of the PPP in pursuit of personal power. He further accused Jawara of presiding over a corrupt and incompetent administration to consolidate his position and undermine his critics within the party leadership.[160] The NCP focused on the past two years of the government's record, so as to avoid personal embarrassment to Dibba, who of course had held senior positions in the party and then the government since the early 1960s. Dibba, in contrast, projected himself as true to the old party ideals and as an honest and effective alternative to Jawara. The electorate would not be impressed with this selective interpretation of recent history.

As far as policies were concerned, the NCP's "Farafenni Declaration," which was issued in 1976, was a rehash of the PPP's original manifesto. Its eleven-point program revealed both a damaging lack of credible alternative policies on the new party's part and any evidence of its ability to usher in a more honest and efficient administration. Both its domestic and international policies were, in large part, those that the PPP was already pursuing. Perhaps not surprisingly, there was no mention of trying to reestablish the Mandinka hegemony, the decline of which had led to the formation of the NCP in the first place.

As part of its endeavor to be regarded as a national party, it adopted as its emblem the groundnut "cutter," seen as an equally potent symbol of the Gambian rural populace and economy as the hoe (the PPP emblem); although by then this sailing vessel, which was used to transport groundnuts from the Provinces to the oil mills near Banjul, was largely defunct. Less explicable were the new party's color—white—and its Latin motto, "Semper Fidelis" ("always faithful"); the latter was perhaps an attempt to emulate the earlier adoption of a Latin tag by the PPP ("vox populi, vox dei"—"The Voice of the People is the Voice of God") and to avoid the potentially divisive use of a motto in an indigenous language.[161]

Because no by-elections were held between the foundation of the NCP in September 1975 and the next general election in April 1977, the latter would be the first opportunity to test the popularity of the new party.

1977 General Election[162]

Prior to the 1977 election, which was held on April 4–5, the number of parliamentary constituencies was increased from thirty-two to thirty-five to reflect the increase in The Gambia's population since the last revision of the constituency boundaries in 1966: the Serrekunda and Niumi constituencies were both divided into two, and a fourth constituency was added to the Kombos (Central Kombo). Partly as a result of the population increases, there had also been a substantial rise in the number of registered voters since the early 1970s; the total was now well over 200,000.[163] Four parties contested the election: the PPP, the NCP, the UP and another new party, the National Liberation Party (NLP). These are considered in turn.

People's Progressive Party

The PPP held twenty-seven of thirty-two seats at the dissolution of the House. As usual, virtually all its incumbent MPs were reselected, with only Sana Saidy in Wuli being deselected. He was replaced by Seni Singhateh, a civil servant from the area who was employed in the Social Welfare Department until the election. The party selected five other new candidates. The two NCP defectors, Sheriff Dibba (Central Baddibu) and K. A. Bayo (Saloum), were replaced by Dr. Lamin Saho (one of the leading Independents in 1972) and Amulai Janneh (a pharmacist), respectively. Another leading Independent in 1972, Dr. Momodou Manneh, was chosen in Jokadu, thereby allowing the incumbent, Landing Jallow Sonko, to transfer to his home constituency of Upper Niumi. The two new seats of Central Kombo and Serrekunda West were filled by Dembo Jatta and Abdoulie A. N'Jie (who had recently retired from the civil service as the lands officer), respectively. The PPP also once again chose its unsuccessful candidates in the 1972 election in Bathurst North and Bathurst Central; and O. A. Jallow transferred from Serrekunda to the new seat of Serrekunda East.[164]

Apart from its customary election broadcasts and limited support in the local Banjul press, the PPP once again relied on its personal network of political influentials and patronage to obtain electoral support. It produced no fresh propaganda literature, relying instead on its earlier manifesto and campaigned on the slogan, "Peace, Progress and Prosperity"—emphasizing the success of its rural development program, which initially focused on URD and MID, but was extended before the election to LRD and WD. In contrast, it paid very little attention to the economic problems of the urban areas.[165]

National Convention Party

The NCP selected candidates in thirty-one seats, including Dibba in Central Baddibu and Jagne in Serrekunda West, allowing the UP a free run in the three Banjul seats and, more surprisingly, in Saloum, which it held through K. A. Bayo (who decided not to stand). Bayo was replaced by K. W. Foon, who had previously, and unsuccessfully, contested the seat for the UP. At least two of its other candidates, Foday A. K. Makalo (Lower Baddibu) and Maja Sonko (Upper Niumi), had stood as Independents in 1972; Badara K. Sidibeh (Tumana) also had some political experience, having been a PPP staff member.[166] However, most of the remaining candidates were political novices. Importantly for the future, these included an obscure young Jola named Kukoi Samba Sanyang, who stood in the PPP stronghold of Eastern Foni.[167] Prior to the election, the NCP received an important boost when Solo Darbo, a high-profile PPP financial patron in URD and a relative by marriage of President Jawara, joined the party, apparently because the PPP chose Seni Singhateh rather than his brother, Mohammed S. Darbo, as its candidate in Wuli. He was to remain one of the major sources of NCP finance until the early 1990s.[168]

In its campaign, the NCP stressed that the PPP government was guilty of corruption, extravagance, and inefficiency and had failed to deal with rising urban inflation and unemployment. It also condemned the failure of the PPP to implement its rural programs effectively and argued that the government had sought to undermine the institution of chieftaincy, in which Dibba himself had played a prominent part.[169]

United Party

The other two parties had fewer candidates. The UP contested each seat in the capital: M. A. Jobe and J. R. Forster defended Banjul North and Banjul Central, respectively, the latter standing even though he was terminally ill, and M. M. Taal again took on Garba-Jahumpa in Banjul South. It also fought Upper Niumi on its own. In the absence of any direction from the party leader (who would surely have disliked a pact with the "revolutionary" NLP, given his conservative outlook) and with no national selection process in place any more, local activists formed an electoral pact with the NLP to fight six other seats; a UP candidate was selected in four of these seats (Niani, Saloum, Lower Fulladu West, and Upper Fulladu West).[170] Thus the party had no candidates at all in Kombo St. Mary, Basse, Brikama, or Mansakonko Administrative Areas. Perhaps not surprisingly, given that it was now almost entirely an urban party, the UP emphasized the economic problems of Banjul, even suggesting that the Five Year Development Programme was a political gimmick designed to pacify the rural electorate and prevent improvements in the capital.[171]

National Liberation Party

The NLP was established at a meeting in Banjul on October 4, 1975, following an earlier meeting in the capital on April 27, 1975.[172] It adopted a collective leadership, but the driving force was certainly Pap Cheyassin Ousman Secka, who was elected as its interim chairman. A Wolof from Banjul in his early thirties, who may have been the first Gambian to graduate from an American university, Secka returned to The Gambia in 1973 to practice law, having been very active in radical politics while at university in the United States. He was now determined to make his mark in local politics. Sam Sillah, a former lieutenant colonel in the Nigerian Army who had fought in the Biafran War and subsequently worked for a security company in the diamond-mining area of Sierra Leone, became the NLP's vice chairman; Alasan N'Dure, the former GCP national propaganda secretary, who later represented the PPP on the BCC, was its organizer; and Henry Baldeh from Basse was treasurer. One of its supporters in Banjul was Alieu Kah who, like Secka, was to participate in the 1981 coup. The party adopted a radical socialist viewpoint, but remained a largely ephemeral creation.[173]

Only two NLP candidates stood in the election, both in nominal alliance with the UP. Secka contested Sabach Sanjal and N'Dure stood in Jokadu. However, the latter was killed in a car crash on the eve of the polls and when the postponed Jokadu election was held a month later, no NLP candidate was put forward. The NLP also appears actively to have campaigned in only four constituencies.[174]

Independents

In contrast with 1972, there were only two Independent candidates: Lamin Waa Juwara, a nephew of President Jawara and a well-known divisional commissioner, who had tried and failed to secure selection by the PPP, contested Sabach Sanjal, and the ex-chief of Sami, Omar M'Baki, stood in Sami.[175]

Election Results

The election was hotly contested. There was a very high turnout, variously estimated at between 82 and 84 percent,[176] and the result was another comfortable victory for the PPP. It received 125,233 votes (69.7 percent of the total cast) and won twenty-eight seats. The NCP, with 40,668 votes, gained 22.6 percent of the vote, some 2 percent more than that won by the Independent candidates in 1972, but fared better, winning five seats to the one of the Independents. Even so, because of the first-past-the-post system, it took nearly twice as many votes to return a NCP MP as a PPP one; hence the NCP's demands for a proportional representation system. The four UP candidates who stood in Banjul and Upper Niumi between them gained only 3.0 percent of the vote nationally, but won two seats. The five UP/NLP candidates and the two Independents each took 2.3 percent of the vote, but no seats.[177]

The PPP won both the Niumi constituencies, Central Kombo, and one of the two Serrekunda seats (Serrekunda East). In addition, it regained Saloum from the NCP through Amulai Janneh and also at last captured the former UP stronghold of Banjul North through I. B. A. Kelepha-Samba, who narrowly defeated M. A. Jobe. But these gains were offset by the loss of three seats to the NCP and one to the UP. Many of its victories were by large margins; eighteen candidates polled more than 70 percent of the vote, although a number of the results in Kombo St. Mary and WD were much closer.

The NCP retained two of the three seats it held at the dissolution and gained three seats from the PPP. However, it failed to break out of its original geographical heartland—the Baddibus and the Kombos, where Baddibu migrants were an important element of the population. Support for the NCP decreased in an easterly direction. In Kombo St. Mary, it won Bakau, where a newcomer, Bakary B. Camara, defeated the sitting PPP MP, A. K. N'Jie, and Serrekunda West, through G. M. Jagne. It also obtained 47 percent of the vote in Serrekunda East, a seat it claimed it lost through electoral irregularities on the part of the government.[178] In NBD, across the Gambia estuary, it also did very well, taking 38 percent of the vote and winning all three Baddibu seats. Dibba withstood the challenge of Lamin Saho in Central Baddibu, albeit with a reduced majority, while Foday Makalo and Fodayba Jammeh ousted the sitting members of Parliament, Kalilou Singhateh (who was minister of health, social welfare and labour at the time of the election) and Baba Touray in Lower Baddibu and Illiassa respectively.[179] It did less well in the Niumi, Jokadu, and Sabach Sanjal seats. In WD, it also won over one-third of the vote (34 percent), but failed to win any of the six seats. With a more even playing field, it could well have won Northern Kombo and Central Kombo, where it polled 48 and 43 percent, respectively. NCP support largely evaporated in the interior divisions: in LRD, it was just over 30 percent, but in MID and URD it was only 8 to 9 percent.

The NCP's failure to achieve a political breakthrough was due to a number of factors. First, despite Dibba's efforts to present himself and his party as genuinely inter-ethnic—as many as nine of its thirty-one candidates were non-Mandinka[180]—the early history of the NCP dogged it; at the same time the PPP skillfully portrayed it as antagonistic to non-Mandinka and Dibba as an unscrupulous, disloyal, and ungrateful individual. Unlike in the Baddibus, the majority of Mandinka remained loyal to Jawara in MID and URD, whereas Fula, Serahuli, and Wolof voters had little reason to abandon a party that had so consciously opened up its ranks to them to join an opposition party, which fed off Mandinka particularism.

Second, it was evident that the NCP was very much a personalist movement, and overdependent on its leader and his limited financial and organizational resources. Despite its efforts to contest every seat (save where it supported UP candidates), it was evident that a number of its candidates were nominal only, and most of its efforts had to be concentrated on the North Bank and the Kombos.[181] In contrast, however unimpressive the PPP organizational structure was between elections, it was still able to marshal its much greater human and material resources to good effect during election campaigns and to appeal to ancient solidarities among an electorate which still preferred the government that it knew to the uncertainties of a tyro administration under the NCP. Dibba recognized, in retrospect, these fatal weaknesses. He himself faced impossible logistical problems and enormous physical strain in trying to provide support for his almost entirely novice fellow candidates across the length of the country, while at the same time facing a major PPP onslaught on his own Central Baddibu constituency.[182] His undoubted political skills and energy were insufficient to contend with the divisional campaign teams of the PPP, led by senior ministers, backed by the resources of the state and reinforced by frequent personal visits to rural constituencies and appeals for loyalty by President Jawara.

Third, there was a huge disparity between the NCP and PPP in terms of material resources. As Dibba himself identified, two particular areas of weakness related to the party's lack of finance were transport and a newspaper of its own. M. B. Jones' little duplicated news sheet, the *Gambia Outlook* came out in support of the NCP, but its impact was very limited. In contrast, the official (and supposedly neutral) *Gambia News Bulletin*, as well as Radio Gambia, ensured a full coverage of government campaigning. Neither did the NCP have sufficient funds to purchase more than a handful of vehicles, so that hiring additional transport for campaigning and getting voters to the polls in the countryside presented serious difficulties. This was not helped by the reluctance of some private taxi and lorry owners to be seen to be renting their vehicles to the opposition. Despite the financial backing of Solo Darbo of URD and some other donations, membership subscriptions and the personal savings of Dibba and other NCP candidates were the principal sources of finance for the party and, although sufficient to establish a NCP presence throughout the Provinces, were unable to deliver the national victory claimed at the start of the election.

Fourth, the PPP benefited from the support of the chiefs, who campaigned openly for the government; moreover in some constituencies, such as Serrekunda East, there may well have been electoral irregularities. Nevertheless, there was no evidence of systematic vote rigging by the PPP, as Dibba himself accepted after the election.[183]

The UP won Banjul Central, where J. R. Forster slightly increased his share of the vote to 56 percent, but died almost immediately after the election,[184] and Banjul South, which M. M. Taal unexpectedly regained with 54 percent of the vote, defeating the minister of finance, I. M. Garba-Jahumpa. This, in ending the political career of his arch rival of the past, offered P. S. N'Jie some consolation, but probably occurred because of Garba-Jahumpa's unpopularity among trade unionists and other working class voters, rather than because UP fortunes in the constituency were reviving. Garba-Jahumpa subsequently blamed his defeat on the machinations of Sir Alieu Jack, the minister of works, whom he accused of working against him covertly in the constituency where Jack also enjoyed some standing by virtue of family connections and his position as the former speaker of the House of Representatives. After this latest political setback, Garba-Jahumpa, who was now sixty-five, retired from politics; he died in September 1994.[185] However, the UP lost Banjul North in a tight contest, and in the Provinces, its opportunistic alliances, particularly with the NLP, not surprisingly met with little success. It did best in its old Saloum stronghold, where it managed to get 22 percent of the vote. Even this was a bitter disappointment, seeing that this was less than half the share of the vote that Foon achieved in 1972.

The UP's poor performance at the polls was not unexpected. Since its defeat in the 1972 election, its decline had continued unabated and by 1977, the party organization had virtually broken down, even in Banjul. Although still nominally party leader, P. S. N'Jie refused to take part directly in the election, or indeed to advise his followers on what to do, leaving his influential elder sister, Yadicone, to continue to rally female supporters in Banjul. Moreover, in contrast to 1972, N'Jie was also no longer physically up to the rigors of campaigning in the Provinces and he left it to those remaining party activists in the field to continue the struggle. Finally, unlike in past elections when the central party provided financial assistance with some of the election costs, candidates now had to rely even more on their own limited resources (especially as P. S. N'Jie could no longer bankroll the party); these were no match for their PPP rivals.[186]

The UP suffered a further blow a few weeks after the election, when its candidate, the luckless K. W. Foon, was defeated by 120 votes in the Banjul Central by-election brought about by Forster's death. The PPP candidate, H. R. Monday, thus finally achieved what Jawara's first wife (and also an Aku), Augusta, failed to bring about in the first national election in 1960, a PPP victory in the very heart of UP territory. The by-election also represented another humiliation for the NLP leader, Pap Secka, who gained only 123 votes.[187] M. M. Taal was left as the last remaining UP MP until November 1978, when he gave up the unequal struggle and defected to the PPP.[188] As noted in Chapter 9, the UP was to field three candidates in the 1982 election, but all were unsuccessful and although Jabel Sallah retook Banjul South for the UP/NCP alliance in 1987, he was probably a member of the NCP at the time. Meanwhile, the UP leader, P. S. N'Jie, lived on until the age of eighty-four, dying in December 1993. In his latter years, he seldom ventured out of his home on Buckle Street except to attend daily Mass at the Roman Catholic Cathedral, and he played no part in political life after 1977.[189]

Neither Independent was successful, although both performed well; Lamin Juwara gained 39 percent of the vote in a four-way contest in Sabach Sanjal, and Omar M'Baki won 35 percent in a three-way battle in Sami.[190] In contrast, the performance of the NLP's sole candidate, its leader Pap Cheyassin Secka, was very poor; he gained only 226 votes (4 percent) in Sabach Sanjal.

Post-Election Cabinet Changes

After the election, Jawara was reelected as president, with only the five NCP MPs and the two UP MPs among the electoral college of directly elected members of the House of Representatives voting for Dibba. He reshuffled his cabinet, appointing A. B. N'Jie as vice president and Lamin M'Boge as minister of finance (who lost the position to Camara within a few days), but apart from Kalilou Singhateh and Garba-Jahumpa, who lost their seats, only one other minister, Sir Alieu Jack, was dropped. Jawara also restored the veteran MP, H. O. Semega-Janneh, to the cabinet and promoted two parliamentary secretaries, M. C. Jallow and Lamin Jabang, to health and external affairs, respectively.[191] But Jabang was the only member of the cabinet who entered national politics in the 1970s and the age profile of the ministers was continuing to rise.[192]

Despite their overwhelming defeat at the polls and the advantages, legal and otherwise, enjoyed by the PPP, both Dibba and the NCP remained strongly committed to electoral politics and sanguine about their prospect in five years' time, seeing the 1977 election as the beginning only of their political odyssey. As a result, they vigorously contested a key by-election in the new Parliament, which was held in Bakau in June 1978 following the death the previous March of Bakary Camara in a car accident; their candidate, Dembo Bojang, won a hard-fought contest against the PPP's Famara S. Bojang, with voters among the locally based Field Force perhaps playing a crucial role in the outcome.[193]

The NCP, in alliance with the UP in Banjul, also put up a substantial number of candidates in the next local government election, which was held in March 1979, following the dissolution of all the Area Councils save Basse on grounds of corruption and incompetence. Its share of the popular vote, just under 40 percent, was up considerably on its 1977 general election result, but once again, it made few gains outside its established heartland. All councils remained under PPP control, even Banjul, where the NCP won half of the ten seats as a result of UP support. Overall, it won eighteen seats to the sixty-seven of the PPP. Although party leader Dibba was pleased with a presence in the Foni wards of Mansakonko Area Council, it made no impact in MID, where it could only field six candidates for the twenty-four seats on the Kuntaur and Georgetown Area Councils, all of whom lost. Dibba blamed the poor performance on the failure of the UP leader, P. S. N'Jie, to endorse NCP candidates outside of Banjul, some unwise choice of candidates, and a lack of money.[194]

The very success of the PPP in 1977, created a new and more dangerous threat to its predominance. Two of the defeated candidates in 1977, Kukoi Sanyang of the NCP and the NLP leader, Pap Secka, interpreted the overwhelming defeat of yet another opposition party by the ruling party as conclusive proof that there were no constitutional means of defeating the PPP. Instead, they came to believe that the only way to replace Jawara and his administration was by insurrection.

Summary

During the first fifteen years of independence, the PPP defeated challenges from the UP; from the large group of Independent candidates in 1972; and from two internal schisms within its ranks led by former senior ministers—Sheriff Sisay and the PPA in the late 1960s and Sheriff Dibba's NCP from 1977. Loyalty to Jawara personally and to the PPP, together with the president's opening of the party to all ethnic groups, reinforced by judicious use of state patronage, ensured the party's success. At the same time, its overwhelming parliamentary strength, although not leading to presidential dictatorship or a one-party state, so common elsewhere in Africa in these years, gave rise to a much more threatening nonparliamentary challenge.

8

RADICAL AND INSURRECTIONARY POLITICAL CHALLENGES, 1965–81

As Chapter 7 showed, the People's Progressive Party (PPP) successfully maintained its political hegemony in the first fifteen years after independence, despite severe internal divisions and the emergence of the National Convention Party (NCP) in the mid-1970s. Yet its position remained insecure. The longer it stayed in power, the more it suffered from political sclerosis with its attendant neglect of important sections of the political community.

President Jawara also came to be seen as tolerating a persistent and growing incidence of cronyism and downright corruption on the part of his ministers and senior civil servants identified with the PPP administration. Even when it became necessary to remove such transgressors, the almost ritualistic process, which usually avoided any legal investigation or penalty, came to be his political Achilles' heel and contributed to the undermining of his legitimacy in radical political circles. Jawara's own personal finances also came under suspicion. In addition, his "one nation" approach, involving the creation of patron–client networks to link the political centre with its periphery, came with a price. Although it had clearly helped The Gambia avoid the intercommunal strife that wracked so many other African states after independence, the system was denounced by his radical critics.

The first wave of post-independence dissidents were won over with scholarships and accelerated promotions. But a second wave came close to overthrowing The Gambia's democratic political system by violent means in 1981. The Gambian coup was unusual in sub-Saharan Africa, where coups were then commonplace, in being organized and led by disaffected civilians rather than by soldiers, although the support of disaffected members of the paramilitary Field Force was crucial to the success of the operation. The coup, which resulted in several hundred deaths, was eventually defeated after the intervention of Senegalese forces.[1]

Ideological and Economic Dimensions of Radical Political Opposition

Radical political dissent in The Gambia after independence centered principally on urban youths, whose opposition to the status quo rested on a mixture of ideological idealism and personal frustration (although, as indicated below, the opportunities for career advancement were in practice much greater for this group than for the second wave of dissidents). This is in line with the experience of other African countries; in Ghana, for example, economically and socially ambitious, but undereducated youths known as "verandah boys," or "Standard VII" boys, have rightly been identified as a crucial element not only in the nationalist struggle, but also in the drive for state socialism.[2] It does seem to be the case that youthful elements in Africa in general, particularly in urban areas, are frequently drawn to revolutionary rhetoric with its promise of simplistic answers to the complex problems of underdevelopment, and the prospect of enhanced opportunities for personal advancement (both in respect of employment and social recognition) through the adoption of a collectivist Marxist–Leninist state. Latent xenophobia, rooted in colonial experiences and the continued marginalization of postcolonial African states, also formed part of African radicalism, informing attacks on "white" Western capitalism and its allies among moderate African governments; the latter being dismissed as "neocolonial stooges or puppets."[3]

At the regional level, Gambian radicals were attracted to the political ideas of such first-generation radical-nationalist African leaders as Kwame Nkrumah of Ghana and Sékou Touré of Guinea. From 1957, when Ghana obtained its independence until well beyond his death in 1972, Nkrumah's eclectic ideology, combining elements of Marxist–Leninism with pan-Africanism, offered politically disaffected young Gambians a persuasive critique of their country's underdevelopment and an exciting vision of an independent and unified African continent. The Ghanaian leader also offered scholarships in 1962 to more than 100 young Gambians to study and intensify their revolutionary outlook in Ghana, primarily at the Kwame Nkrumah Ideological Institute at Winnebah. These scholarships were organized by I. M. Garba-Jahumpa, who had first met Nkrumah at the Pan-African Congress in 1945, through the Young Pioneers youth movement.[4] Ironically, however, by the time that many of the Gambians returned home, Garba-Jahumpa had moved back to the political center ground, merging his party, the Gambia Congress Party, with the PPP in 1968. Touré, although a francophone African, was admired for standing up to the French and his equally vigorous denunciation of neocolonialism and advocacy of a socialist united Africa. But apart from providing some funds to the Gambia Workers' Union (GWU) in the late 1950s, we found no evidence that the Guinean government offered any financial assistance to Gambian organizations.[5]

Further afield, Soviet, Chinese, and Cuban Marxism also had an impact on the political thinking of the first wave of Gambian dissidents. Among the second wave of dissidents were elements more strongly influenced by the more ideologically idiosyncratic Libyan leader, Colonel Muammar Qaddafi.[6] Radio stations from the Communist bloc also broadcast to sub-Saharan Africa and Marxist literature was not banned, although in December 1970, the Gambian government did proscribe the Gambian–Soviet Friendship Society, which had been set up by the "radical" anti-colonialist journalist, M. B. Jones and others a few months earlier, ostensibly for distributing anti-Israeli literature.[7] The authorities were also concerned about the number of young Gambians being granted scholarships in the 1970s to study at the Patrice Lumumba Friendship University in Moscow. These were apparently either directly granted by the Russians or were allocated by the Gambia Labour Union (GLU). The GLU, which had adopted a Marxist ideology since the mid-1960s, reaffiliated with the World Federation of Trade Unions (WFTU), the trade union international supported by the Soviet bloc, in 1967, and particularly admired the North Korean leader, Kim Il Sung.[8] Poorly educated Gambian youths faced severe difficulties in getting scholarships to, and enrolment at, established British and North American universities, or Commonwealth higher education institutions (a consequence in part of the limited senior schooling facilities available in The Gambia). Sponsored further education in eastern bloc countries was therefore attractive, even to individuals not immediately drawn to Communist ideology. As elsewhere in Africa, not all those trained in Soviet bloc countries or China returned home convinced revolutionaries, notwithstanding the expectations of their educational mentors; although, as noted below, several important radical leaders did study in Eastern Europe.

A parallel ideological attraction was radical race assertion associated with "black power" movements in the United States, the writings of the francophone West Indian Frantz Fanon and the anglophone West Indian Walter Rodney and, in the 1970s, the ideas of Steve Biko, the black consciousness leader in South Africa. The radical pan-Africanism of Gambian dissidents consequently combined, often in a vulgarized way, aspects of racial assertion with Marxist critiques of neocolonialism. The result was a continuous denunciation of the moderate PPP government as a "tool" of Western imperialism.[9]

Economic factors also played a part in stimulating urban radicalism, at least in the case of second wave dissidents, in two ways. First, the gradual Africanization of the civil service before and after independence meant that in the 1960s and early 1970s, educated young radicals could be bought off with the offer of jobs. But by the late 1970s, there were far fewer opportunities for career progression for this group; it may be significant that, as noted below, two of the better educated individuals involved in the 1981 coup, Kukoi Sanyang and Tijan ("Koro") Sallah, were both unemployed at the time. Second, as noted in Chapter 1, one consequence of the economic and social modernization of The Gambia was a substantial increase in the urban population in the 1960s and 1970s, particularly in Serrekunda and other parts of Kombo St. Mary, but also in Brikama, the administrative centre of the Western Division. Population growth was fuelled by internal migration from impoverished rural areas by an overwhelmingly youthful and male migrant community which experienced rising inflation and unemployment from the mid-1970s and a consequent deterioration in living standards. As Wiseman has shown, a significant number of young people in Serrekunda had become alienated from the political system by the early 1980s and some of these would participate in the 1981 coup.[10]

Radical Political Opposition Groups

First-Wave Dissidents

Prior to independence, politicized youths in The Gambia tended either to be involved in the struggle for independence or in the trade union movement. Some joined the youth wings which the various political parties established during the 1950s. They could be mobilized to campaign and vote for party candidates in elections; to participate in organized demonstrations; and occasionally to become involved in violent clashes with political opponents.[11] Other young Gambians were rank-and-file members, or at least supporters, of the GWU, which reached the peak of its power when it organized a successful general strike in January 1961. But by independence, there were fewer alternative outlets for Gambian youths; the youth wings of the political parties were perhaps less active than hitherto, and the GWU, although still a force to be reckoned with, had been in gradual decline since 1961.[12] There was also a new central organization of youth bodies, the Gambia National Youth Council (GNYC), which was established in November 1963, but this claimed to be both nonpolitical and nonsectarian.[13] Thus, those who were dissatisfied with the political status quo after independence turned to more radical politics.

The earliest radical groups in the capital were often formed on the basis of neighborhood associations, known as "vous" (said to be a shortened form of rendezvous) or among politically conscious teachers, students, and senior secondary school pupils.[14] Their meetings and other activities were usually not covered by the local press, even by older "left-wing" journalist critics of the government, such as M. B. Jones or W. Dixon-Colley, or discussed by outside observers and their own news sheets tended to have an ephemeral existence. As far as is known, they also did not publish the names of their leaders and office holders. Thus only fragmentary information about their activities has survived from written sources and we have had to rely more heavily on oral sources than for other topics.[15] One consequence of this is that it is often difficult even to date their foundation and demise with any precision.

It appears that the first of the radical organizations was Tonya (Mandinka for truth), which was certainly functioning by 1965.[16] This was organized among sixth-form students in Bathurst, probably with the support of militant teachers at the Gambia High School and students at the Yundum Teachers' Training College, but had a provincial membership and focus.[17] Like other radical groups, which succeeded it, Tonya eschewed formal electoral politics, preferring to attack the PPP administration in its occasional news sheet. Its militants also toured the rural areas to try and educate the people in their political rights, as well as denounce the government. According to our informants, among its leaders were O. G. Sallah, Mousa G. Bala-Gaye, Adama M'Boge, and Gibou Semega-Janneh. Tonya dissolved within a few years as its activists either entered the civil service directly or obtained government awards to study overseas, after which they often ended up in government or professional careers. Sallah entered the civil service as early as 1965 and Bala-Gaye (after graduating from Legon University in Ghana in 1970) did so in 1971; both ended up as senior civil servants. Meanwhile, M'Boge became a lecturer at a Nigerian university and Semega-Janneh a barrister in Banjul and an unsuccessful aspirant for selection as a PPP parliamentary candidate.[18]

The Kent Street Vous (KSV) was formed around 1967, and met in the open in Kent Street in Banjul. Its leaders included Sulayman Samba and various members of the Taal family, including the future United Party and PPP member of Parliament (MP), M. M. Taal, and his brother, Sheikh Omar Taal. The latter had been sent to Ghana by Garba-Jahumpa and, as a consequence, had absorbed much of Nkrumah's Pan-Africanism; the vous apparently met near their home.[19] It also included others from what were deemed low-caste families in the Half Die area of Bathurst South. The KSV attracted some provincial as well as urban members, although it is probable that the majority were urban Wolof. It deliberately rejected ethnic identity and drew heavily on members of the teaching profession, themselves drawn from different sections of the community, for its members and leadership. Membership of this and other radical groups was small and loose, with individuals moving between them. Some twenty-five to thirty individuals regularly attended its informal political discussion meetings.

The KSV differed from the usual informal neighborhood youth groups, in engaging in socialist as well as social activities. From the outset, it adopted a critical position toward the government, and, like Tonya, adopted a similar left-wing critique of domestic and foreign policy and published its own occasional "newspaper," in which to attack the government. For example, in an issue produced in 1969, it argued that independence brought benefits only to the privileged few and called for a reduction in the salaries and allowances of ministers, MPs and civil servants and demanded the introduction of a "socialist development programme" to end "the legacy of extreme poverty."[20]

The KSV was also able to mobilize support in Bathurst for public demonstrations. Thus, in February 1971, possibly with the backing of the GNYC, which had also condemned the Senegalese, it organized a demonstration in the capital against the presence of the Senegalese head of state, Léopold Senghor, following recent Senegalese infringements of Gambian territorial integrity (see Chapter 10). The demonstration was led by Sheikh Omar Taal. The KSV first presented a petition to Jawara, who was so incensed by its tone that he refused to speak to the KSV leaders or view their banners; they then organized an attack on the Senegalese High Commission and the properties of Senegalese traders.[21] When a

KSV leader (or possibly the leader of one of the other radical groups) appeared in court in March 1971, there was also some minor rioting in Bathurst.[22] But this perhaps marked the high point of the KSV's popularity and soon afterward it fell into decline. As with Tonya, it appears that many of its key members (including Samba, as discussed below) were absorbed into the political establishment following state awards to study abroad and civil service positions on their return.

The Black Brotherhood Movement (BBM), likewise, was founded in the mid-1960s. Its leading lights are said to have included Moussa Battaye, Lamin Lanha, Ndeckem Ngueye, Sehou Taal, Pa Omar N'Jie, Dawda Faal, and two men who were to remain very active in radical politics, Ousman Manjang and Koro Sallah. At least two of these, Battaye and Sallah (as well as another member, Tamsir Jallow), apparently received scholarships to Ghana. On his return, Sallah may have been employed as a teacher at the Crab Island (secondary) School for a time, as well as becoming a well-known local footballer.[23] Membership of the BBM overlapped with that of the KSV (again, many members were of low caste). It also attacked the government from a radical position, in this case Nkrumahist pan-African socialist. Again, it had a monthly news sheet, "Fansoto" (Mandinka for "self-freedom"), containing frank and aggressively anti-government articles (it also had a cartoon feature in which Jawara was depicted as a pig—a particularly offensive image in a Muslim society).

The BBM's membership also overlapped with another more obscure organization, the Black Panthers, whose leaders included Dawda Faal, which adopted the name and reflected the influence in the late 1960s of African-American activists such as Stokely Carmichael. Carmichael, who was then resident in neighboring Guinea, paid a four-day visit to The Gambia in December 1969 and led a symposium in Bathurst. The British high commissioner subsequently blamed him for the growth of xenophobia, which he detected during 1970.[24] As well as sharing some of the political vocabulary of African-American militants, their Gambian emulators also dressed in a similar manner, namely, black berets and dark glasses. The Black Panthers were perhaps more radical than the BBM and also apparently contained a clandestine group, the Black Scorpions, which engaged in direct action; this included the desecration of what was regarded as the opulent grave of the former minister, Amang Kanyi. It is thought that the leader of the 1981 coup, Kukoi Samba Sanyang, was a member of the latter group.[25]

As in the case of Tonya and the KSV, many of the BBM's members drifted from radical politics once they obtained scholarships and jobs from the government or went abroad to study, although as noted below, two notable exceptions to this trend were Manjang and Sallah. Others turned increasingly to heavy drinking and endless arguments among themselves, thereby discrediting and further undermining the movement. One of these arguments concerned the fate of proceedings of a concert given in Bathurst by Carmichael's wife, Miriam Makeba, the internationally renowned South African singer and anti-Apartheid activist, during their joint visit in December 1969. It is also probable that some BBM members moved into the PPP youth wing in 1969–70. According to Bakarr, Alasan Jaye, one of the leaders of the Black Power Movement, joined the PPP youth wing in October 1969, and in December 1969, *West Africa* reported that a group of youths from the Black Power Movement had applied to join the PPP youth wing. Given the similarity between the names, it seems likely that the BBM and the Black Power Movement were one and the same organization.[26]

The Kwame Nkrumah Memorial Foundation (KNMF) was established following the death in exile (in Rumania) of the former Ghanaian leader in April 1972. Radical youths organized a symbolic funeral in Banjul, processing from Allen Street via Lasso Wharf and Anglesea Street to the Guinean embassy in Hagan Street. The coffin was taken into the building and a young Aku teacher, Femi Peters, gave an address from the roof. The Guinean ambassador also spoke. This event was followed by a symposium on the achievements of the late Ghanaian head of state at the National Library on Independence Drive, chaired by Sulayman Samba, a former member of the KSV.[27] The KNMF was set up as a result of the symposium. It issued membership cards and held monthly meetings at the Allen Street Youth Centre. It had over twenty members including Peters; two former members of the BBM in Ousman Manjang and Koro Sallah; Sam Osseh Sarr (who was probably then employed as a teacher); Wassa Fatty; and Coumba Marenah who, as a woman, stood out in the male-dominated environment of the radical groups.[28] Sidia Jatta, another who was to remain active in radical politics thereafter, may also have been a member of the KNMF for a short period. Jatta, a Mandinka from Wuli Sukutoba in Upper River Division, attended Yundum Teachers' Training College between 1964 and 1966 (where he may well have been radicalized) and was subsequently employed as a primary and secondary school teacher.[29]

The PPP government was attacked from a Nkrumahist or Pan-African/Marxist-Socialist position. The KNMF sought financial assistance from overseas and distributed books for the radical PANAF press to raise funds and disseminate radical ideology. It even wrote to the inspector general of police for funding! Internal problems quickly arose. The chairman, Sulayman Samba, soon afterward traveled to the United States to study for a higher degree and on his return to The Gambia in 1977 entered the civil service, like many radical activists before him; he eventually rose to become permanent secretary to the Office of the Chairman under President Jammeh in 1995.[30] Peters was asked to take over after Samba's departure, but claimed that the organization was usurped by Sam Sarr and Koro Sallah, at which point he left it to run a radical bookshop. By 1975, the KNMF had apparently broken up.[31]

Sallah, who had influential family ties (his brother, Captain Baboucarr Sallah, was managing director of the Gambia Ports Authority) went abroad to study as an engineer, reportedly first at Harvard University in the United States and thereafter at the Patrice Lumumba University in Moscow.[32] Manjang too went abroad to study, probably also to the Soviet Union; Jatta certainly went to France to study in 1972.[33] Meanwhile, Peters turned first to trade unionism and later entered constitutional politics; after the 1994 coup, he became a leading member of the

United Democratic Party (UDP), the principal opposition to the Jammeh Government, serving as the UDP's campaign manager in the 1996 election.[34] Marenah would later become a senior official in the Department of Community Development and secretary to the National Women's Council and even served briefly as minister of health, social welfare and women's affairs in the Armed Forces Provisional Ruling Council administration.[35]

These early radical groups were limited in membership, generally fractious in organization and viewpoints, and short-lived as their leading activists moved on to other things. According to the British high commissioner, the various "black power" groups did combine to form the Gambia Socialist Party in October 1972, but the new party was refused registration by the government and seems to have disappeared from the political scene thereafter.[36] Their political impact at this time was practically negligible. Their extreme political views, predominantly youthful and urban membership and urban-focused activities, in a rural and conservative Muslim society, largely account for this. It was only the later groups that realized the necessity to address their policies to the rural and poorly educated majority of the populace or to take up feminist interests, in a belated recognition of the double disadvantage facing rural women. Generally, though, they remained male dominated and arguably less interested in promoting women's interests than the PPP.[37]

The radical groups also failed to make alliances with more effective bodies. They did not join forces with any of the political parties opposing the PPP in the 1960s and early 1970s. Moreover, they did not develop close ties to Gambian trade unions which, unlike their counterparts elsewhere in sub-Saharan Africa and the Third World, did not feature prominently in stimulating or organizing radical opposition to the government in The Gambia.[38] Neither the GWU nor its rival, the GLU, sought to establish links, let alone provide much-needed financial assistance, to more radical youth groups. After independence, the GWU continued to focus more on industrial rather than political grievances and its leader, M. E. Jallow, did not seek to form a labor party, although he did stand for Parliament twice as an Independent in 1966 and 1972; in any case, there were ideological differences between the radicals, with their Marxist leanings, and the GWU, which formally affiliated with the pro-Western international labor movement, the International Confederation of Free Trade Unions in March 1963.[39] Although the GLU seemed a more likely ally for the radicals, its commitment to left-wing socialism was questionable and its critics dismissed this as little more than an attempt to obtain funding from Soviet bloc countries and free trips to various Communist-funded jamborees.[40]

Finally, the radical groups had little money with which to pursue their cause and there is no evidence of funding from Socialist bloc countries. This did not prevent internal quarrels over money. The history of Gambian political radicalism reveals that "bourgeois" politicians had no monopoly on financial impropriety, only that they had access to more money from their control of the postcolonial state and so could misappropriate larger amounts of it than their radical critics.

Second-Wave Dissidents

As the earlier grouplets broke up, new organizations emerged in the late 1970s to continue radical and direct forms of political protest. Three new political organizations were established in the late 1970s, two of which shifted political opposition into more violent directions. The first of these was a shadowy, neo-Marxist, organization, the People's Movement for Independence against Neo-Colonialism and Capitalism in The Gambia (known popularly as "Red Star") which, according to the subsequent allegation by the government, began to operate in 1975.[41] The government also alleged that its leaders included the former KNMF activist and teacher, Sam Sarr; Halifa Sallah (another graduate, who was employed as a social worker in the Social Welfare Department); Sarr's wife, Amie Sillah (a health inspector in the Ministry of Health); Adama Bah; Momodou Sarho; and Louis Sambou. This group was widely suspected of editing and distributing a free underground newspaper, *The Voice of the Future* (which probably first appeared in late 1978), around the streets of Banjul and the Kanifing area. Sarho, who, as noted below, was a member of another radical organization, was accused of distributing *The Voice* and put on trial in 1980, as were all six leaders in 1984, but all were acquitted.[42]

The Voice specialized in highly personalized and virulent attacks on individuals within the PPP government and on exposing examples of corruption in political life.[43] No doubt some of its accusations were more accurate than others. However, it does appear that corruption was becoming more widespread in The Gambia by the late 1970s, in part because of the increased opportunities for graft brought about by the expansion of the public sector under the first Five Year Plan (although when compared with Nigeria, for example, it remained negligible).[44] Yet there was little evidence that the government took the issue seriously. Jawara did periodically reshuffle his cabinet at least in part to remove individuals suspected of corruption (although this was never stated as the reason for a dismissal), but no further action was taken against either the politicians or senior civil servants. For example, Pap Cheyassin Secka, the leader of the National Liberation Party (NLP), claimed that when it was found that a minister and an ambassador had received bribes from a French firm, the former was dismissed and the latter was transferred to another post, but that no prosecutions took place.[45] The president did apparently set up an inquiry into all ministries after the sacking of Yaya Ceesay in September 1978, but nothing more seems to have come of this.[46] Indeed, suspect ex-ministers continued to find comfortable sinecures for themselves after leaving office.[47] On at least one occasion before the coup, Jawara set up a formal commission of inquiry to investigate corruption, in this case into the infamous Rural Development Project (RDP) I. But the long-awaited report did not appear until after the coup and even then, despite the recommendations of the commission, the senior civil servants who were implicated escaped serious punishment.[48]

Whether Jawara was personally corrupt is difficult to assess. *The Voice* claimed that the reason that "Fafa" (the president) was loath to act against his ministers was because he himself was culpable. Secka noted that there were rumors circulating about Jawara's business interests abroad and property in The Gambia, but admitted that there was no evidence that the president was personally implicated in corruption.[49] After Jawara's overthrow in 1994, however, a number of allegations about his conduct were made before the various commissions of inquiry set up by the Jammeh government.[50]

The Voice also condemned the PPP government for its authoritarian response to nonparliamentary opposition. It highlighted the sacking of a number of employees of the Gambia Utilities Corporation (GUC) in November 1976; the suppression of the general strike called by the GWU to support the GUC workers in the same month; the subsequent deregistration (portrayed as banning) of the GWU in January 1977; and the unjustified public accusations of sabotage that the minister of works and communications, Kuti Sanyang, leveled at GUC workers in October 1978.[51] All these incidents served to strengthen the opposition of urban radicals to the regime. However, it should be recognized that the government was acting within the framework of the law, both in its response to the general strike and the actions it subsequently took against the GWU. The Trade Union (Amendment) Act of October 1976 had made strikes illegal without twenty-one days' notice in essential services and fourteen days' notice in nonessential services, yet the GWU leadership (which naturally condemned the legislation) called its supporters out on strike without any prior notice at all. Moreover, the GWU and four other trade unions were deregistered for their persistent failure to submit their accounts for inspection to the registrar general. Annual submission of accounts had been a requirement of the Trade Union Act since the colonial period, but the GWU, along with other trade unions, often failed to comply and had still not submitted its accounts for 1974 and 1975 at the time of its deregistration, despite a number of warnings from the registrar general.[52]

The second organization, the Movement for Justice in Africa—The Gambia (MOJA-G, more commonly MOJA), was formed in 1979 and operated in the Greater Banjul area.[53] Two of its prominent spokesmen were Koro Sallah and Ousman Manjang; both men, along with another leader, Wassa Fatty, were previously active in radical political organizations, and another member, Momodou Sarho, was a member of the NLP between 1975 and 1978. Unlike earlier educated activists, Sallah apparently was not offered a civil service job on his return from higher education and remained unemployed.[54] MOJA-G was doubtless inspired by the original Movement for Justice in Africa (MOJA-L), which was founded by a small group of Liberian academics based at the university in Monrovia in the late 1970s, although there is no evidence of closer ties between the two bodies. The Liberian MOJA had played an important role in undermining the standing of President William Tolbert and his True Whig Party in the late 1970s by denouncing corruption and misgovernment. Although MOJA-L leaders do not seem to have participated directly in the bloody coup in Monrovia in March 1980 that overthrew Tolbert, they subsequently attempted to provide ideological guidance to the semi-literate army leadership headed by Master Sergeant Samuel Doe. However, their efforts proved short-lived and several were forced to flee abroad.[55]

MOJA-G, which strongly endorsed the views expressed in *The Voice* about government corruption and authoritarianism,[56] refused to convert itself into a formal political party, presumably because it did not accept the legitimacy of the electoral process. However, it did not preach the violent overthrow of the government. Instead, it adopted similar tactics to earlier radical groups, pamphleteering against the government and seeking to undermine its legitimacy by similar exposures and "consciousness-raising" campaigning in rural areas; pro-MOJA graffiti also appeared on walls in Banjul.[57] Even so, after the events in Liberia in March 1980, the authorities became increasingly anxious about its role and in the wake of the disturbances involving the Field Force (see below), MOJA was declared an unlawful society under the Societies Act of 1971 and banned on October 30, 1980. The following day, six of its members, Koro Sallah, Fakebba Juwara, Momadou M'Boge, Solomon Tamba, Bekai Jobe, and P. Modu Jobe, were arrested at Sallah's house.[58] They were subsequently charged with managing an unlawful society and possessing firearms and ammunition; the case eventually came to trial in December 1980. Four of the defendants were acquitted on both charges in April 1981, although Sallah and Juwara were convicted on the first charge of managing an unlawful society in July; they were each fined D500 and released. Sallah appealed against his conviction, but the appeal had not been heard by the time of the coup.[59] Amnesty International's observer concluded that the trial was conducted fairly, but criticized the fact that there was no evidence that MOJA was operating as a political society between the banning order appearing in the *Gambia Gazette* and the arrests. The defendants were therefore effectively being tried for their activities *before* October 30 when MOJA was not illegal.[60]

The principal MOJA defense lawyer was Pap Cheyassin Secka, the former leader of the now defunct NLP, who may recently have returned to The Gambia after a spell living abroad following his party's poor performance in the 1977 general election.[61] In interviews he gave to *West Africa* and the *New African* following the banning of MOJA, Secka made it clear that he strongly sympathized with its aims and supported its attacks on PPP corruption, but he did not apparently join the organization.[62] It should also be noted that in December 1980, the Gambia Court of Appeal ruled that Secka would be imprisoned unless he repaid a sum of D89,000 to a client; having apparently repaid only D25,000, he absconded to Dakar to avoid arrest. This incident may have increased his alienation from the political system, which was to manifest itself the following July.[63]

If the government hoped to curb MOJA's influence by the ban, it was soon disappointed, for it appears that its supporters now turned to political vandalism. This involved the destruction in late 1980 or early 1981 of two government-owned vessels, Jawara's yacht, the *Barajali* and the presidential river boat, the *Mansa Kilaba*; the latter was an independence gift from West Germany.[64] As discussed below, some MOJA members subsequently participated in the 1981 coup.

The third organization, an apparently harmless radical movement, announced itself to the Gambian public in early 1980. The Gambia Socialist Revolutionary Party (GSRP) was led by "Dr." Gibril L. ("Pengu") George, an unsuccessful small businessman, seemingly with a grudge against the former inspector general of police, Harry Lloyd-Evans, and a purchased doctorate to lend him intellectual standing. Of itself, George's small odd-ball group of political malcontents (its only other known member at this stage was another businessman, the former NLP member, Alieu Kah) posed no visible threat to the state, which tolerated it at first. Indeed, it was seen as rather ludicrous; George's interview with S. A. Bakarr in *The Sun* in July 1980, certainly reinforced such a judgment. The GSRP was also declared an unlawful society on October 30, although George was not arrested. It continued to exist in clandestine form, adopting the new name of the Gambia Underground Socialist Revolutionary Workers Party (GUSRWP). It was now committed to the violent overthrow of the Jawara government.[65]

Unrest in the Field Force

As noted, there was also serious unrest within the country's paramilitary police, the Gambia Field Force, in October 1980. Since the abolition of the Gambia Company of the old intercolonial Royal West African Frontier Force for financial reasons, the country had had no regular army. Instead, the Gambia Company had been replaced in 1958 by a cheaper backup force for the civil police in the form of the Field Force, which was based outside the capital at Bakau (with a small pioneer detachment stationed up river at the strategic crossing point of Farafenni). Originally, the Field Force had 140 men.[66] According to Momodou N'Dow N'Jie, who became its new commander after the coup, it had 358 members at the time of the coup, but in fact the figure may have been closer to 500.[67]

During its twenty years' existence, the Field Force had remained politically quiescent, although there had been unsubstantiated rumors of internal discontent in 1967.[68] It was therefore a considerable shock to all Gambians when the deputy commander, E. J. "Eku" Mahoney, was murdered by an insubordinate soldier, Mustapha Danso, at the Bakau Depot on October 27, 1980. Although initially explained as a solitary murderous act of mutiny by a drug-intoxicated constable, the government's rapid reaction to the incident suggested otherwise. Invoking a mutual assistance treaty of 1965 (see Chapter 10), the government called in 150 Senegalese soldiers on October 30, ostensibly as a joint training exercise, "Operation Foday Kabba I," to protect key installations and prevent the disaffection spreading among Field Force ranks. The Senegalese forces remained for a week, after which time the Gambian government felt sufficiently secure to have them recalled home.[69]

Another measure taken in the wake of Mahoney's murder, which contributed to the insurrection of July–August 1981, was the government's decision forcibly to retire Assistant Commander Ousman Bojang of the Field Force. Bojang was suspected of involvement in Field Force disaffection; his resentment at his dismissal undoubtedly led him to participate in the subsequent coup attempt. Bojang had no particular sympathy with the revolutionary aspirations of Gibril George and Kukoi Sanyang, but he held a lasting grudge against what he claimed to be a Wolof/Aku dominance of the Field Force leadership. As a senior provincial Mandinka, he believed that this led to his ousting.[70]

A final step the government took after the murder of Mahoney was to break off diplomatic relations with Libya on October 29 and shut down its embassy. Relations with Libya were friendly in the mid-1970s (see Chapter 10), but then deteriorated sharply. This was principally because of the growing size of the Libyan embassy in Banjul and its alleged support for local dissidents (the Gambian authorities believed that it was funding *The Voice*). In addition, the government was concerned about the adventurist foreign policy in the West African region of the Libyan leader, Colonel Qaddafi, a policy regarded as seeking the overthrow of pro-Western governments in the subcontinent. Indeed, as early as July 1980, the Libyan government was accused of providing military training to Gambian nationals who were recruited by the Senegalese dissident, Sheikh Ahmed Niasse of Kaolack.[71]

Insurrectionary Politics:
The Attempted Coup of July 1981

As long as civilian leftist groups largely confined themselves to limited forms of political opposition—pamphlets, demonstrations, graffiti, vandalism—and enjoyed little support outside urban circles, the PPP could breathe easily. However, in July 1981, an attempt was made to overthrow the government by force. Although some details remain unclear and some of the evidence is contested, enough information is available to provide a general explanation of the origins and execution of The Gambia's first coup attempt and a reasonably informed reconstruction of the events of July–August 1981.[72]

The coup was led by Kukoi Samba Sanyang, who in recent years had been engaged in constitutional mainstream politics, rather than in any of the radical political organizations. Born in December 1953 and in his childhood called Dominique (or Dominic) Samba, Sanyang came from a Catholic Jola family living in Somita in Eastern Foni in the Western Division. He initially intended training for the priesthood, like two other revolutionaries, Joseph Stalin and Kwame Nkrumah. After completing his primary education, he therefore spent three years at a Roman Catholic seminary in Casamance, but was rejected as a candidate. He then enrolled at St. Augustine's High School in Bathurst, but achieved only one O level.[73] He became involved in radical politics while still at school, joining the Black Scorpions and the abortive Gambia Socialist Party; but he had not yet abandoned the constitutional path.[74] Although he was ineligible, on residential grounds, to stand himself as a candidate in the 1972 general election, he sponsored his elder brother, Momodou L. Sanyang, as an Independent candidate against the incumbent PPP member of Parliament, Momodou N. Sanyang, in Eastern Foni constituency and took an active part in his campaign. Like most of the Independents, M. L. Sanyang was defeated, gaining only 23 percent of the vote and he seems to have withdrawn from electoral politics thereafter.[75]

After the election, Sanyang apparently went abroad once again to Libya and then to the Soviet Union, possibly having tried and failed to secure employment as a teacher.[76] He returned to The Gambia in time to contest the next general election in 1977. By now, he had reverted to his original name of Samba Sanyang and added the Kukoi prefix.[77] Like his brother, Kukoi stood in Eastern Foni, albeit as a NCP candidate. He, too, was defeated, losing to the PPP's Ismaila Jammeh and winning a mere 15 percent of the vote. After this, he disappeared from the political scene and thereafter again traveled overseas, allegedly on a scholarship given him by the GLU, during which time he may have visited Libya among other countries.[78]

Sanyang apparently returned home in June 1980.[79] By now, he had certainly abandoned the constitutional politics of the opposition NCP for a woolly revolutionary Marxism. He joined George's party, turning a comic opera outfit into a more sinister organization and, within six months of coming back to The Gambia, was actively plotting to overthrow the government. This was presumably in conjunction with other members of the outlawed GUSRWP, while by January 1981, the NLP leader, Pap Cheyassin Secka, had also been drawn into the conspiracy.[80] Whether others were involved at this stage is unclear. Simon Talibeh Sanneh, one of the coup leaders, claimed at his trial that in mid-July, Sanyang showed him a list of the names of ten civilians and thirty-six Field Force officers who had sworn on the Koran to overthrow the government at a meeting at George's house at Fajara. He added that the civilians on the list included George; Secka; and five of the six MOJA activists who had been tried in December 1980, including Koro Sallah, and two other MOJA members, Ousman Manjang and Momodou Sarho.[81] But the list was never produced in court and we cannot be certain that all those who were (allegedly) named were involved in any such meeting. Sallah, for example, later claimed that the MOJA activists were added to the list to implicate the organization; stating that he was opposed to the coup and only became involved to resist the Senegalese invasion.[82] Nor do we know when the alleged meeting took place.

According to Secka's later account, it was originally intended to stage the coup on January 31, 1981, but for reasons that remain unclear, it was postponed.[83] Secka later claimed that he withdrew from the plot thereafter, but Sanyang remained determined to act and, in the summer of 1981, the plans were reactivated. Together with a small group of about fifteen civilians and Field Force personnel, he was responsible for planning the details of the coup attempt during a series of covert meetings in Serrekunda at the end of July.[84] Most of this group of conspirators were from the same ethnic group as Kukoi himself, the Jola, which were long regarded as one of the most marginalized ethnic groups. Apart from their generally common ethnic identity, the group was closely connected socially, lived in Talinding-Kujang, the Jola quarter of Serrekunda, and was largely illiterate.

At least four of them (Jerreh Colley, Junkung Sawo, Momodou Banda, and Kantong Fatty) were currently in the Field Force; another, Dembo Jammeh, was a former member. Moreover, a number were employed as taxi drivers—hence the labeling of the plot as a "taxi drivers' coup."[85] Reliance on a Jola social network also led to claims that the coup was part of a wider Jola conspiracy, involving fellow Jola living across the border in the Senegalese Casamance region and beyond in Guinea-Bissau. The Senegalese authorities feared what was referred to as the three Bs—Banjul, Bignona (the centre of Jola population in Casamance), and Bissau—and their prompt response to Jawara's new call for military assistance was partly influenced by this perception of a wider conspiracy. Although as noted in Chapter 10, Jola secessionism in the Casamance would not become a serious problem until after the defeat of the Gambian insurrection, there was a long-established sentiment for greater autonomy in this Senegal's remotest and in many ways, most problematic region.[86]

It should be noted that not all the alleged plotters were Jola and so the popular view that this was a Jola coup was only partially correct. For example, George was an Aku Marabout (a Muslim Aku from Banjul), Secka was an urban Wolof, and Bojang was a Mandinka. Moreover, the thousand or more detainees held after the suppression of the coup included many Mandinka and Wolof, as well as Jola. Another opinion that was widely held was that all the rebel plotters were illiterate, semiliterate, or of low social standing. But Secka, although of low caste, was a graduate of an American university and a barrister (a high-status profession since the days of Sir Samuel Forster).[87] Meanwhile, Kukoi received a modicum of higher education overseas, although exactly to what level and in what subjects, have never been established; his part exposure to elements of political science were evident in the few broadcasts that he made during the rebels' brief control of Radio Gambia. Koro Sallah, if indeed he plotted with the GUSRWP, was believed to be a graduate of an Eastern European university.

Rebel ideology, as revealed from press interviews with Gibril George and the handful of radio broadcasts by Kukoi, suggested some familiarity with Marxist and radical pan-Africanist thinking, although in a woolly and vulgarized form. Marxist jargon and revolutionary sloganeering concealed a poverty of concrete policies and realistic objectives. Kukoi's broadcasts were certainly not those of an assured or authoritative speaker and it was later claimed in court (and accepted by the trial judge, despite Secka's denials both at the time and later on) that the latter wrote his "take over" speech. The insurgents spoke of "Victory for the Gambian revolutionary struggle under the dictatorship of the proletariat and the leadership of a marxist–leninist party" and of "Death to neocolonialism, racism and fascism," familiar if inappropriate revolutionary battle calls.[88] Beyond that, little could be discerned. M'Bemba Camara claimed that all ministers and senior officials and police officers were to be arrested, together with the president's relatives. Those supporting the coup were to be reinstated to advise the new government; the others were to be dismissed.[89] Nowhere in the evidence of the accused were political executions mentioned; the killing (noted below) of Assistant Commander of

Police Kikala Baldeh and others during the insurrection appeared to have been carried out independently by rebel elements.

Given the brevity of their seizure of power, the rebels proceeded no further than formally suspending the constitution and the judiciary, abolishing Parliament and political parties (measures that would also be taken by the military putschists of 1994), closing all financial institutions, and announcing the creation of a "Supreme Council of the Revolution," a "National Liberation Army," and a "National Revolutionary Redressing Committee." It will never be known who would have been appointed to such exalted positions. However, these were well beyond the abilities of virtually all GUSRWP cadres and might well have been filled by MOJA-G leaders, with Secka as the judicial supremo and with the assistance of any acceptable member of the previous administration.

The rebels promised "brilliant ideas" for the future running of the country, but what these were to be, beyond some collectivist, state-managed framework, were never disclosed. It was suggested at the time that the houses of the rich in the Fajara area were not destroyed because the "revolutionary" leadership had earmarked them as their own.[90] According to M'Bemba Camara, Kukoi's explanation for the coup was that, "the Government is not straightforward, the Ministers and top civil servants have enrich [*sic*] themselves from the Government money" and that the revolutionary state would seize their "ill-gotten assets . . . including property and cars."[91] Neither the majority of the people of The Gambia, nor revolutionary or socialist governments abroad, showed any belief in the desirability or attainability of such a political future. Atheistic Marxist slogans were particularly repugnant as well as mystifying to a poorly educated, but intensely religious, rural Muslim populace, the alleged beneficiaries of revolutionary changes.

In any event, the insurgents were never given the opportunity to implement their self-proclaimed revolutionary program. The plotters' timing was shrewd in that they waited until President Jawara was away in England on a private visit (which included attendance at the wedding of the Prince of Wales) before launching their assault. Given the highly personalized nature of the political system, the rebels hoped that in the absence of the president, those left in charge of the country would be paralyzed with indecision and confusion and that Jawara might be discouraged from seeking to return home to try and quell the insurrection. The plotters also, on this occasion, had the advantage of surprise, suggesting a degree of unwarranted complacency on the part of government intelligence and security forces, which thought that any threat had been rooted out the previous October.[92]

The coup began in the early hours of Thursday July 30, when Kukoi and ten civilian accomplices made their way on foot from the house of Momodou Sanyang in Talinding-Kujang at 2:00 AM to the military base some five miles away. They were armed only with five shotguns and a revolver, the former obtained from villagers in the conspirators' home district of the Fonis, and a pair of wire cutters for cutting their way through the perimeter fence of the Field Force Depot. Once inside the camp unobserved, they made contact with a fellow conspirator in the Field Force—Momodou Sonko—who took them to the armory, which they seized without resistance. Once armed with Kalashnikov rifles from the armory, the rebels then took over the Depot and collected the former assistant commander of the Field Force, Ousman Bojang. Some disaffected Field Force men joined them, and others were coerced into supporting the coup, possibly when they learned of the fate of certain loyalists, such as Assistant Commander Kikala Baldeh, who was murdered in front of his family.[93] The greater number of Field Force personnel, judging from the lists of those arrested after the collapse of the coup, melted away, neither loyal to the government, nor throwing in their lot with the conspirators.[94]

Once the Depot was secured, the rebels quickly moved on to other targets of military or symbolic value, achieving almost complete success by dawn. Their objectives included the capture of the Radio Gambia buildings, which were nearby, and Yundum airport and State House in Banjul, which were further afield. The seizure of the airport was a well-considered move, for in the previous October, Senegalese paratroops had been dropped over it. On repeating the same tactic, this time the Senegalese suffered casualties. Civilian supporters of the coup, who now included elements of MOJA-G, and indeed anyone who could produce a voter's card, were given guns at the Field Force Depot.

Despite these initial successes, the insurgents quickly ran into serious difficulties and began to disintegrate into uncoordinated elements. Bojang, of whom much was expected, was killed in the fighting and the inexperienced Kukoi was unable to provide military leadership. Bloody infighting also took place within the rebel leadership and the GUSRWP leader, George, was killed by his own side at the Field Force Depot on July 31, perhaps because he tried to seize control from Sanyang. Another of the earliest actions of the coup makers was to take over the prison at Mile Two on the outskirts of Banjul to release Mustapha Danso, whose appeal against the death sentence for the murder of Deputy Commander Mahoney had recently been rejected.[95] All other prisoners were released as well. Some acquired weapons and turned what the rebels intended as a popular insurrection into personal vendettas and criminal forays. Although this added to the general confusion facing those trying to resist the coup, the activities of armed criminals further undermined the patriotic credentials of the rebels and lost them popular support. At the same time, widespread looting and criminal activity helped to justify renewed Senegalese intervention on the Gambian government's behalf.

The rebel leadership hoped that with Jawara unable to intervene, the security forces fragmented and demoralized, and the capital city and surrounding area under their control, the president would reluctantly accept his fate and seek asylum in Britain, where he had a home. That would mean the Senegalese government would not become involved, so enabling the rebels to consolidate their control over the whole country and mop up any further resistance. But events turned out differently. Two key ministers, the attorney general, M. L. Saho and the vice president, Assan Musa Camara, had managed to escape to the Central Police Station in Banjul which, as discussed below, remained in the hands of pro-Jawara forces. Saho suggested that Camara invoke the mutual assistance treaty of 1965 once again to secure Senegalese assistance. The Senegalese government was persuaded to intervene and as early as the afternoon of the first day of the coup; reconnaissance aircraft were reported over the Banjul area and Senegalese forces went into action the following day. In total, perhaps as many as 3,000 soldiers were committed to "Operation Foday Kabba II," including airborne and sea assault units.[96] Meanwhile, with the backing of the British government, Jawara flew back to the Senegalese capital, Dakar, in an official Senegalese aircraft three days after the start of the coup. There he dissuaded President Abdou Diouf from withdrawing his troops because of mounting costs and casualties.[97]

During the ensuing week, in addition to air drops over Yundum, Senegalese seaborne forces landed behind the enemy "lines" at Bijilo. The main ground force attacks were from northern Senegal to Barra, across the Gambian estuary from Banjul and from Casamance toward Brikama and through the Foni districts of the Western Division, where the Jola population is concentrated and where provincial support for the rebels might have been expected to be greatest.[98] In the event, despite being poorly equipped and untrained in comparison with their opponents, rebel elements did inflict casualties in ambushes on the advancing Senegalese forces, but could not prevent them from advancing on the Greater Banjul area and recapturing key locations.

The rebels also underestimated local resistance to their surprise attacks. In Banjul, the Central Police Station, manned by some twenty-one loyalist police under Inspector General of Police A. S. M'Boob and reinforced on the second day of the coup by a force of twenty men from the Farafenni Field Force Pioneer Unit Depot, led by the seconded British army officer in command of the unit, held out until relieved by Senegalese forces on the Sunday after the coup. Shortage of weapons was overcome by taking those from dead rebels; in addition, a rebel "leader," in a vehicle full of guns and ammunition, was captured. The area around the police station, which included the Senegalese and American embassies (both of which provided radio telephone links to the beleaguered government ministers), was secured by using police and fire service vehicles to form road blocks, and several rebel attacks were repulsed at great cost to the latter. Vice President Assan Musa Camara took charge of the government in the president's absence, operating from the Senegalese embassy once cooperation was obtained. He was joined by Saho and the ministers of finance and external affairs, Saihou Sabally and Lamin Jabang. Together, they demonstrated to other Gambians and the international community that the government had not capitulated to the insurgents. After the coup, M'Boob and the leader of the Senegalese intervention force were given national honors, but M'Boob's "promotion" to the new post of minister of the interior in November 1981 might have been for reasons other than his heroic role during the coup.[99]

Sanyang also overestimated the extent of popular support for the coup and subsequent rebel claims about the coup being a national insurrection against Jawara and the Senegalese were not borne out by events during the insurrection. The overwhelming majority of Gambians tried to avoid the fighting, showing little willingness to take up arms against the government, but at the same time, understandably refusing to come out in support of the administration. Survival was the principal and immediate concern of most people. Among those who did join the coup in significant numbers, however, were dockers employed in the port at Banjul; between thirty-four and sixty of these were dismissed for alleged involvement.[100] But the trade union movement as a whole was opposed to the coup and several unions, notably the GLU and the Gambia Dock Workers' Union, denounced it (admittedly after its suppression) and prudently contributed to the Government's Relief Programme Fund. The coup was also opposed by the leadership of the GWU (which was still banned); partly as a result of this, the ban was provisionally lifted after the 1982 election, although for reasons unconnected with the events of July 1981, ultimately it was not reregistered.[101]

Although it is not inconceivable that some militant NCP members joined the insurrection, Kukoi's attempts to recruit the leader of the main opposition party, Sheriff Dibba of the National Convention Party, were unsuccessful. According to the latter's subsequent account, Kukoi twice called at his house to urge him to join the Supreme Council of the Revolution, to broadcast on Radio Gambia in favor of the coup, and to get Colonel Qaddafi's telephone number. But Dibba refused his requests (although neither did he publicly denounce the coup) and also cautioned Sanyang about the inevitable Senegalese response.[102] Nevertheless, soon after the coup, Dibba was arrested on charges of supporting the insurrection. Gibou Jagne, the NCP MP for Serrekunda West, and other NCP activists, including the party's administrative secretary, Badara Sidibeh, were also arrested, although at least two of the other three NCP MPs, Foday Makalo and Dembo Bojang, were not even questioned, let alone detained.[103]

Jagne and Sidibeh were eventually released without charge, but Dibba was put on trial after a lengthy detention. He was accused of conspiring with Sanyang, George, and Solo Darbo (the financier of the NCP) and of giving money to Ousman Bojang. But the prosecution case was very weak and one of its main witnesses, Sanjally Bojang, discredited. In June 1982, Dibba was rightly found not guilty and freed. As a constitutional and moderate politician, who considered himself the only experienced alternative to Jawara, and who still had faith in the electoral system, Dibba had nothing to gain from throwing in his lot with a bunch of naive and anarchic self-styled revolutionaries.[104]

Inevitably, given the military superiority of the Senegalese and the failure of the rebels to obtain external recognition and assistance, or widespread local support, the coup was doomed to failure. By the morning of Sunday, August 2 (day four of the coup), Banjul and its approaches from Yundum airport had been cleared of rebel forces and Jawara was able to return to State House with a Senegalese escort and resume command of the government. Driven back toward the Bakau Field Force Depot, there was a fear that the remaining rebels would engage in a suicidal last stand, killing the estimated 105 hostages taken during the insurrection. Among these was one of the president's two wives, Lady Chilel, and ten of his children; Dembo Jatta, the minister of education; the deputy inspector general of police, Commander M. B. ("Tex") Khan; Momar Faal, an official in the Senegalese High Commission; and Seydou Nourou Bah, the executive secretary of the

Senegalo-Gambian Permanent Secretariat.[105] Several of these were forced to make pro-rebel broadcasts over Radio Gambia to try and whip up support for the coup and deter the Senegalese from invading; some were perhaps thought to have done so rather too willingly and faced sanctions after the coup as a result. For example, Sanjally Bojang, one of the founders of the PPP, who had been district chief of Brikama since 1975, was dismissed a few weeks after the coup. Similarly, both Jatta and Famara Wassa Touray (the parliamentary secretary in the Ministry of Information) resigned from the government in August, although both were retained as PPP candidates for the 1982 election.[106]

As it turned out, and unknown to the government forces, Kukoi and nine accomplices left Bakau three days before the final rebel collapse. They traveled across the Kombos to Kartong, where they stole a boat to take them to eventual sanctuary in Guinea-Bissau. Koro Sallah, who was wounded by security forces, also escaped, thanks to the assistance of his family.[107] Meanwhile, at the Bakau Depot, a small team of the British Special Air Service (SAS), who were flown into the country, successfully infiltrated the camp and sought out and rescued the hostages without any casualties.[108]

Although all the hostages were safely rescued, the week of mayhem and its suppression resulted in numerous human casualties and substantial financial losses. No accurate figures were ever released of the fatalities; the Gambian government's estimation that 500 lives were lost appears reasonable, although it is possible that the real figure was higher.[109] The Senegalese army admitted to losing thirty-three men, but the rebels claimed that more were killed.[110] A measure of their sacrifice was the Gambian government's decision to give a million dollars from its external relief fund to the Senegalese forces in recognition of their contribution to the defeat of the rebels. One of the tragedies of the coup was that a considerable number of civilians uninvolved in the fighting ended up as casualties, victims of accidental shootings or deliberate killing by criminal elements armed by the rebels. There was economic damage as well; the local economy was paralyzed for a week with markets being shut and places of work closed. Several stores and property were looted and there was additional gunfire damage.[111] Although the scale of the violence and damage was beyond the experience and comprehension of the Gambian population, the destruction of life and property seemed modest by the standards of sub-Saharan coups, and damage and disruption was limited to a small, if important, part of the country. In the Provinces, support for the rebels was very limited and confined to nonmilitary acts of sympathy.[112]

In the wake of the coup, more than 1,100 individuals were detained under the State of Emergency, which the government declared on August 2.[113] An analysis of the gazetted notices of detention revealed that more than 90 percent of those detained came from Banjul/Kanifing and the Western Division (which comprised the Kombo and Foni districts), and over half were resident in the Kanifing Urban District Council area (which included the Jola settlement of Talinding-Kujang). Some of these were doubtless migrants from further up river who were now resident in the coastal area. Over the next twelve months, all detainees were processed and over 800 were released without legal prosecution. It was evident that the government had used a fine-tooth comb to search out suspects. Conditions in the detention centers—ironically, most were held at the Bakau Depot—were not ideal and there were undoubted incidents of human rights violation during the initial stages of arrest and internment. To the government's credit, it allowed in Red Cross representatives and an Amnesty International team was permitted to visit and report critically on the situation.

Equally important, the government determined to avoid summary justice of the kind accompanying failed coups elsewhere on the continent and allowed the ordinary law courts, rather than military tribunals, to try the remaining detainees. At some expense, senior legal luminaries from other Commonwealth countries were recruited to conduct the trials and ensure proper legal procedures were observed. Most of those put on trial were let off or given light sentences and relatively few were given death sentences. Among these were Secka, who had been extradited from Senegal to where he had escaped; Kukoi and other leading plotters who were charged with treason, mostly in absentia; and some other individuals who were accused of committing murder during the rebellion. All save one of those sentenced to death had their sentences commuted to life imprisonment and were eventually released. These included Secka, who was released in 1991, resumed his legal practice and re-entered politics after the 1994 coup, supporting the bid of Jawara's successor, Yahya Jammeh, for the presidency and serving as attorney general and secretary of state for justice in 2000–2001. The exception was Mustapha Danso (already facing the death sentence), who was shot at the Mile Two prison in October 1981.[114]

Political recovery after the coup was hastened by the nonvindictive policies of President Jawara, who, despite the unprecedented threat to his position and the lives of his family, determined to return the country to political normality, although this could never entirely be achieved. As discussed in Chapter 9, constitutional politics restarted even before the lifting of the State of Emergency in February 1985. The 1982 election went ahead as planned, with the NCP being allowed to participate, despite the government's suspicions about its role in the coup.

In contrast, radical political activists were barred from participation in political life. The Kukoi group was destroyed or scattered and its moral and political credentials totally undermined. Sanyang himself did not give up his opposition to the Jawara government and, after residing in Cuba for a number of years following his expulsion from Guinea-Bissau (see below), he returned to Africa. He moved initially to Libya where he continued to seek the violent overthrow of the Jawara government; for example, in May 1988, two Gambians, Musa Sanneh and Ousman Sanneh, and two Senegalese from Casamance, Adrien Sambou and Amadou Badjie, were accused of conspiring with Sanyang and others between January 1984 and January 1988 to overthrow Jawara. All bar Sambou were later convicted and sentenced to lengthy terms of imprisonment.[115] Sanyang later went to Burkina Faso, where he plotted against both Jawara and his successor, Yahya Jammeh.[116]

Some MOJA leaders also went into exile after the coup, with Koro Sallah, Manjang, and others successfully seeking asylum in Sweden. Other activists remained in The Gambia and in May 1984, three were arrested.[117] MOJA sought to distance itself from Kukoi, denouncing his coup attempt as infantile (indeed, years later Sallah would confide to a senior former member of the PPP administration his regret at having joined in the 1981 coup at all) and even allegedly passing information to the PPP government about him.[118] It no longer sought the violent overthrow of the PPP government, but tried to undermine its democratic credentials through propaganda activities from exile. Eventually, in November 1992, the ban on the movement was lifted, but even before then some of its activists had returned home.[119] In the meantime, the physical destruction or involuntary exile of the insurrectionary leadership left in The Gambia forced other Gambian radicals to review their position. Momodou Sarho was detained after the coup, but was not charged.[120] As outlined in Chapter 9, several of those alleged to have been behind *The Voice* were subsequently to establish a new constitutional political party, the People's Democratic Organisation for Independence and Socialism, which contested the 1987 election. The great hope now was that the terrible excess of the radical rebellion of 1981 had permanently turned away Gambians both from radical and insurrectionary politics.[121]

Economic recovery after the coup was speeded up by generous domestic and external contributions to government relief appeals. International support for the Jawara government was widespread and socialist countries as well as capitalist states condemned the coup, notwithstanding rebel attempts to attract international sympathy through their revolutionary rhetoric. The Soviet bloc and China rejected the coup-makers, as did leftist African states such as Algeria, Guinea (Conakry), and Tanzania. Moreover, a wide band of countries, headed by Saudi Arabia, made generous financial donations to the Gambian government—one-third of the U.S. $30 million received came from the Saudi government. The international response indicated continuing support for the Jawara government, despite its shortcomings.[122]

In contrast, no country publicly supported the coup, with the partial exception of Guinea-Bissau, which criticized Senegal for sending its army into The Gambia, interpreting the action as an invasion, rather than as a legitimate response to a request for assistance, and gave temporary shelter to the rebel leaders. This was probably because the Vieira government contained pro-rebel individuals of Gambian extraction. But its embassy in Banjul kept its distance from the rebels during the coup. Moreover, President Vieira determined to mend fences with the Gambian and Senegalese governments as soon as possible; a special envoy was sent to Banjul in August and although he declined to return the rebels to The Gambia, Vieira deported them to Cuba in April 1982. By December 1982, good relations between the two countries had been restored.[123]

Whether the Libyan government supported the coup has remained in dispute since 1981. The Libyans denied any involvement, but allegations of Libyan assistance to Kukoi and his supporters were later made both by the Gambian and Senegalese presidents, who had every reason to be suspicious of Colonel Qaddafi. But many years later, President Jawara admitted that no concrete proof of Libyan involvement in the 1981 coup had been established.[124] According to Diene-Njie, a meeting had been scheduled to take place in London on July 30, 1981, between representatives of the Gambian and Libyan governments to discuss the restoration of diplomatic ties between the two countries; if this is correct, it seems improbable that the Libyans would have supported the coup at the same time. Kukoi's two unsuccessful attempts to acquire Qaddafi's telephone number from Sheriff Dibba also suggest that their previous contact had been minimal. Nevertheless, diplomatic relations with Libya were not restored until 1984, and there were no ambassadorial exchanges until after the 1994 coup.[125] In addition, the North Korean embassy was also closed down after the coup, although there is no evidence that North Korea was involved in the coup.[126]

The most important external consequence of the failed coup was the short-term reliance of the Jawara government on its neighbor, Senegal. Relations with Senegal are discussed in Chapter 10, but the necessity of a Senegalese security shield in the wake of the coup led to the creation of the Senegambia Confederation and the permanent stationing of Senegalese security forces on Gambian soil. Their presence, however controversial and unpopular in certain quarters, allowed the Jawara government to reestablish itself and return to electoral politics. It also enabled Jawara to reorganize his security forces totally. Out of the ashes of the discredited paramilitary police force emerged two countervailing military formations, whose recruits were carefully vetted for political reliability. The first of these, the Gambian National Army, was set up in 1983–84 by a small British military training team; it consisted of the remnants of the Field Force, together with new recruits. This was replaced by a much larger Nigerian mission in 1991. The other, a National Gendarmerie, constituted a paramilitary second line of support for the civil police. Established in 1986, it was based on the francophone model and trained by the Senegalese.[127]

The consolidation through the new binding defense and security protocols of the Senegambia Confederation and the reconstruction of the country's internal security forces by means of "cleansed" and binary replacement formations seemed to assure Jawara and the PPP government long-term political security. Although it is true that these innovations strangled the insurrectionary left, at the same time they brought into being a more familiar form of insurrectionary challenge to those in power, the military, which was to overthrow the PPP in 1994.

Summary

In the post-independence period, the Gambian government faced various forms of left-wing challenges to its rule, deriving their inspiration from Marxist and "black consciousness" sources and fuelled by worsening economic conditions by the early 1980s. These culminated in the failed coup attempt of Summer 1981. Ideological, financial, and factional factors, together with rapid Senegalese military intervention when radical protest turned insurrectionary, limited these challenges and electoral politics returned within a year.

9

ELECTORAL POLITICS, 1981–94

Even though the State of Emergency, which was introduced immediately after the end of the attempted coup of July–August 1981, had not yet been lifted, the government decided to honor the constitutional requirement to conduct five yearly elections in May 1982.[1] Further rounds of elections took place in 1987 and 1992. On all three occasions, the People's Progressive Party (PPP) reaffirmed its dominance over the legislature, resorting to familiar techniques of patronage and the mobilization of state resources to ensure success at the polls against the National Convention Party (NCP) and a variety of other opponents. However, the PPP was much less successful in dealing with more deep-seated political problems. There was accumulating evidence over the next decade of a renewed complacency and an unwillingness or incapacity to undertake the kind of fundamental political and administrative changes needed to dissuade future extra-constitutional adventures of the kind launched by Kukoi Samba Sanyang. In the end, this proved fatal; three years before the next scheduled election in 1997, the PPP government was overthrown in a second, and this time successful, coup in July 1994.

1982 Parliamentary and Presidential Elections[2]

The government's decision to proceed with the elections despite the coup showed that it was determined to reestablish The Gambia's reputation as a parliamentary democracy both at home and abroad. It also enabled the PPP to measure its support among the electorate soon after the traumatic events of the previous summer. Furthermore, in the absence of a separate referendum, the elections demonstrated the extent of public support for the decision to establish a confederation with Senegal, which went into effect in February 1982 (see Chapter 10).[3]

One important constitutional innovation in 1982 (which was endorsed by both the NCP and the PPP) was that conjointly elections were held for the office of president as well as for the House of Representatives. Each elector voted twice at the same polling station, but at different booths. The number of "nominated"

221

members of parliament (MPs) was also increased from five to eight to widen the president's scope when making appointments to the cabinet.[4] Three parties fought the election: the PPP, which held thirty-two seats at the dissolution, the NCP, which held the remaining three seats, and the United Party (UP), which had been unrepresented in Parliament since 1978. As noted in Chapter 8, the only other party that contested the 1977 election, the National Liberation Party, was now defunct and its leader, Pap Cheyassin Secka, was in prison; the Movement for Justice in Africa—The Gambia (MOJA-G) remained banned.

People's Progressive Party

As usual, the PPP contested every seat. As in 1972, there was strong competition for selection as a PPP candidate, with a total of 137 aspirants seeking the thirty-five nominations.[5] However, unlike in 1972 and 1977, existing PPP MPs were not automatically reselected as candidates. At the Third Ordinary Congress of the PPP, which was convened in Banjul in March 1982, it was agreed that a three-man Selection Committee should be established to vet the candidate selection process in every constituency. The increased centralization of the selection process resulted in the biggest turnover of PPP candidates since independence; it appears that four incumbents were persuaded to retire and another four were deselected.[6] The retiring MPs certainly included Mafode Sonko (Lower Niumi) and the former vice president, A. B. N'Jie (Northern Kombo), the others probably being H. R. Monday (Banjul Central) and D. S. Cham (Niani).[7] Since resigning as vice president in August 1978, N'Jie had been a backbencher; although he was now in his late seventies, he was persuaded to lead the PPP election campaign, but tragically was killed in a helicopter crash in April.[8] H. O. Semega-Janneh (Western Kiang) was definitely among those who were deselected, with the other three probably being Famara Wassa Touray (Southern Kombo), Abdul (formerly Andrew) M'Ballow (Lower Fulladu West), and Ismaila Jammeh (Eastern Foni).[9] All except Monday (elected in 1977) and Jammeh (elected in 1973) had been in the House of Representatives for more than a decade; N'Jie and Semega-Janneh first became MPs in 1960, and Sonko, Cham, and Touray in 1962.[10] Four of the losing PPP candidates from 1977 were also replaced.[11]

Most of the former MPs were replaced by younger and better educated newcomers to national politics. At least two were senior civil servants before the election. Mathew Yaya Baldeh, a graduate and son of the former Seyfu of Fulladu West, Cherno Kady Baldeh, was assistant education officer before resigning to fight Lower Fulladu West, and Mbemba Jatta, formerly the senior statistician, stood in Southern Kombo. In addition, a prominent businessman from Kuntaur, Talib Omar Bensouda, was nominated in Niani, and Mrs. Nyimasata Sanneh-Bojang, a former teacher who had worked for the PPP Women's Bureau since 1980, replaced A. B. N'Jie in Northern Kombo; she was the only female candidate in the election. All four were standing in their home constituencies.[12] One exception to this influx of new blood occurred in Banjul Central, where Monday's successor was the attorney general and minister of justice, M. L. Saho; Saho had served as an ex-officio MP since 1968, but this was his first attempt to win a seat at the ballot box.[13]

The most controversial deselection of an incumbent occurred in Western Kiang where Semega-Janneh, who had been a cabinet minister as recently as October 1981, was replaced by a thirty-five-year-old Mandinka civil servant and diplomat, Bakary Bunja Dabo, who was selected as the PPP candidate for his home constituency. Dabo was educated at the Gambia High School before graduating with a degree in modern languages from the University of Ibadan in Nigeria in 1967. He was then employed in various civil service posts in the capital and Provinces, before being appointed manager of the commercial operations of the Gambia Commercial and Development Bank (GCDB) in Banjul in 1974. In March 1979, he was appointed Gambian high commissioner to Senegal and, during the coup, he helped to mobilize Senegalese support for the Jawara government. He was subsequently rewarded by being appointed as a "nominated" MP and minister of information and tourism in September 1981.[14] Since the 1970s, Dabo had been a leading member of the Teeri Kafoo (a Mandinka phrase meaning "group of friends"); these were Mandinka intellectuals who criticized Jawara for not having a greater Mandinka presence in the government and, like its other members, he was rumored to have been a covert supporter of the NCP. He apparently did not join the PPP until after the coup.[15]

Semega-Janneh deeply resented being replaced by such a candidate and seems to considered standing as an Independent for the seat, although ultimately he decided not to. But he remained embittered and when he was arrested and charged with theft (although later acquitted) a few months after the election, it was alleged that this was to stop his criticisms of the PPP. Whatever the truth of the claim, this incident may have been the cause of his final break with the PPP; in December 1982 he stood against the official PPP candidate in the Banjul City Council (BanCC) election. He thereafter effectively ceased to be a PPP member.[16]

National Convention Party

The NCP contested nineteen constituencies. Ten of its candidates stood for the party in the 1977 election; the other nine were newcomers.[17] Although the NCP fought fewer seats than in 1977, this was not surprising under the circumstances. As noted in Chapter 8, Sheriff Dibba and the NCP MP for Serrekunda West, Gibou Jagne, along with perhaps as many as 800 NCP party officials and supporters (including Badara K. Sidibeh and Kemeseng S. M. Jammeh, the party's candidates in Tumana and Western Jarra respectively), were detained following the abortive coup. Jagne was released from prison only a week or so before the election, whereas Dibba (and Sidibeh) was not released until July 1982 and so had to fight the parliamentary and presidential elections from his prison cell.[18] In addition, the NCP, until the acquittal or release of its leading representatives, faced accusations of complicity or support for the coup attempt from government supporters, which may have made aspiring politicians reluctant to stand for it. Some leading NCP members had also rejoined the PPP in recent years, including Lamin Waa Juwara, an Executive Committee member, who claimed that he had resigned because the NCP was "all a Mandinka affair" and Dembo Sanneh, the party's candidate in Central Kombo in the previous election; there was evidence as well of loss of support in other areas, such as Serrekunda.[19]

United Party

The UP contested only three constituencies, all in Banjul, where it retained a modicum of influence despite the retirement of P. S. N'Jie; its candidates were supported by the NCP, which did not stand in the capital. The veteran politician, K. W. Foon, having lost in Saloum in the previous election, now stood against M. L. Saho in Banjul Central in the hope of capitalizing on the attorney general's unpopularity. Another defeated candidate in 1977, Jabel Sallah, transferred from the hopeless seat of Niani to the much more promising Banjul South to challenge M. M. Taal. The party's third candidate, M. L. N'Jie (Banjul North), was fighting his first election.[20]

Independents

The other striking feature of the 1982 general election was the return of Independent candidates in significant numbers. There were only two Independent candidates in 1977, but there were thirteen in 1982; a fourteenth withdrew shortly before the election.[21] As in 1972, nearly all were young men who were frustrated applicants for the PPP nomination. In many cases, the local constituency party organization seems to have supported their nomination, but was overruled by the national Selection Committee. Twelve of the Independents in fact declared themselves to be "PPP Independents," as many of their predecessors had done ten years earlier, but this did not save them from being expelled from the PPP shortly before the election.[22]

Five of the Independents sought election in the Upper River Division (URD). These included Bubacarr M. Baldeh, the son of the late MP for Basse, Michael Baldeh. Baldeh, who was both the secretary general of the PPP youth wing and the head of a nongovernmental organization in the URD, the Freedom from Hunger Campaign, clearly expected to gain the party's nomination in Basse. When the PPP's Selection Committee instead reselected the ageing incumbent, Kebba Krubally, Baldeh decided not only to oppose his father's old opponent, but also to support Independent candidates in three other constituencies: Tumana, Jimara, and Sandu. As an indication of their alliance, all four adopted the same electoral symbol (a dairy cow), whereas the symbols chosen by the other Independent candidates were all different.[23] It was widely rumored at the time (and later openly asserted by Jawara) that the vice president, Assan Musa Camara, a close relative of Baldeh, offered him active, if discreet, support, a charge that Camara vigorously denied.[24]

Election Results[25]

Although there was a substantial increase in the number of registered voters from around 213,000 in 1977 to 285,000, there was an unusually low turn out in the parliamentary election (65 percent compared with 82.3 percent in 1977).[26] This was understandable given the prevailing political and security situation. Ousman Manjang subsequently claimed that the turnout was low because voters had heeded a call by MOJA-G to boycott the election, but this can be discounted; his organization had very little influence outside the urban areas.[27]

The election passed with very little disruption, but not without familiar opposition claims of intimidation and electoral irregularities, although the expected election petitions either failed to materialize or were rejected by the courts.[28] With the electorate still traumatized by the excesses of the insurrection and the NCP laid low, the results of both elections could never be in doubt. The PPP gained 102,545 votes (61.7 percent of the total) and won twenty-seven seats, including two gains from the NCP: Serrekunda West, where Abdoulie A. N'Jie ousted Gibou Jagne, and the crucial seat of Central Baddibu, where Dr. Lamin K. Saho defeated his old rival, Sheriff Dibba, by just 120 votes. No doubt both the defeated candidates were severely handicapped by being in prison for most, or all, of the election campaign. Saho was rewarded by being appointed a parliamentary secretary at the Ministry of Agriculture after the election.[29] Elsewhere, Nyimasata Sanneh-Bojang became the first woman ever to be elected to Parliament. Although its share of the vote was eight percentage points lower than in 1977, the PPP would have achieved a higher figure had four of its candidates not been elected unopposed.[30] Moreover, fourteen of its candidates won overwhelming victories by taking more than 70 percent of the vote.

The NCP received 32,634 votes (19.6 percent), three percentage points less than in the more favorable circumstances of the 1977 polls, and retained three seats: Lower Baddibu, Illiassa, and Bakau. Although the defeats of Dibba and Jagne were major setbacks, the NCP retained most of its core support in the Baddibu districts of North Bank Division (NBD) and the Greater Banjul area; whereas most NCP supporters in the Baddibus were Mandinka, Wiseman has shown that in Serrekunda, they came from a wide range of ethnic groups.[31] However, the party revealed its same weaknesses with regard to regional support as in 1977, failing to make any impact in MacCarthy Island Division (MID) and URD. As noted, the "personalist" nature of the NCP meant that it suffered particularly badly from being deprived of its leader under the State of Emergency. In addition, the NCP found it difficult to campaign given the security arrangements in force. The party also derived no tangible advantage from its electoral alliance with the UP; although the contests in Banjul Central and Banjul South were hard fought, all three UP candidates in the capital were defeated. In total, the UP gained only 2.9 percent of the national vote (4,782 votes).

Although the number and share of the vote of the Independents, 15.7 percent, was down on 1972, their total vote of 26,141 was some 5,000 more. More important, five of them defeated the official PPP candidates, whereas only one had succeeded a decade earlier. In the URD, where Jawara's campaigning was cut short by the helicopter crash that killed A. B. N'Jie, Bubacarr Baldeh won Basse and helped A. K. Touray to victory in Sandu. Meanwhile, in the predominantly Jola constituency of Eastern Foni, Henry M. Jammeh, a graduate teacher and a Jola, who was fighting a seat in his home area, not surprisingly defeated the PPP candidate, Alkali James Gaye, another teacher, who was not only less well-educated but, more importantly, not a Jola. In the Lower River Division (LRD), Kebba O. Fadera and Saihou Barrow were victorious in Eastern Kiang and Eastern Jarra, respectively. Although Basse and Sandu were not part of the PPP "heartland," the other seats had returned government candidates since national elections were first held in 1960. The defeat of the PPP's candidates reflected serious local discontent with the selection process and the record of incumbent MPs. This evidently counted for more than the attempts of the president and the PPP to appeal to the electorate's patriotism in the wake of the recent failed coup.[32]

Presidential Election

Not unexpectedly, the president won the first direct presidential election handsomely with 137,020 votes to Dibba's 52,095 in a straight contest. Both men performed far better than their parties (explained by the size of the Independent vote in the parliamentary polls); Jawara won 72.5 percent of the vote and Dibba 27.5 percent. Although Dibba's performance was a creditable one, he was defeated in all seven Administrative Areas and in all save three constituencies. He even lost in his former seat of Central Baddibu. It was evident that the recent foiled insurrection worked very much to Jawara's advantage and against the opposition leader.[33]

Post-Election Cabinet Changes

After the election, Jawara sought to revitalize his government by a wide-ranging cabinet reshuffle. The most important changes involved the appointment of Bakary Dabo as vice president in succession to Assan Musa Camara; the restoration of Sheriff Sisay to the position of minister of finance in place of Saihou Sabally; and the replacement of M. L. Saho as attorney general and minister of justice by Fafa M'Bai.[34]

By 1982, Camara was the most senior politician in the government apart from Jawara himself and, except in 1962–63, he had held ministerial office continuously since 1960. He served as vice president between 1972 and 1977 and then again after the resignation of A. B. N'Jie in August 1978 until the election.[35] Moreover, as noted in Chapter 8, Camara played a key role in resisting the coup in central Banjul until the arrival of the Senegalese army. His stock seemed to be high, based as it was on his role in resisting the coup as well as on his longer established record as an honest and principled politician. Yet he soon slipped from favor with Jawara and was not only replaced as vice president by Dabo, but was dropped from the cabinet altogether.[36] As discussed, he was suspected, unfairly and without any obvious advantage to himself, of having conspired with the Independent candidates in URD to defeat the PPP. But it certainly was the case that he failed either to anticipate, or deal effectively with, the rebellion in the URD that resulted in the loss of two seats in the division.

Since his election to the House of Representatives in 1972, Saihou Sabally's career had blossomed. A Mandinka from Kataba in Upper Baddibu, who was then thirty-four, Sabally was appointed a parliamentary secretary for the first time as a result of the cabinet reshuffle of July 1974. He entered the cabinet in December 1978 when he became minister of economic planning and industrial development. In January 1981, he succeeded M. C. Cham as minister of finance and trade when the latter was sacked.[37] But Sabally failed to halt the country's economic decline and so his replacement by Sheriff Sisay, who returned to the cabinet after a gap of fourteen years, was not surprising.[38] Since the collapse of the People's Progressive Alliance (PPA) in 1972, Sisay had not been actively involved in politics; he gained a postgraduate degree in economics at an American university, served as governor of the Central Bank of The Gambia between 1972 and 1977, and later worked for the International Monetary Fund. No doubt it was hoped that his appointment would encourage The Gambia's external creditors to provide increased financial assistance.[39] Unlike Camara, Sabally received a new cabinet post, being appointed minister of agriculture.

A Wolof law graduate, who previously held a number of legal appointments in The Gambia, as well as holding office in the PPP, Fafa M'Bai seems to have been charged by Jawara with the task of eradicating corruption in political and public life.[40] To that end, he established an Assets Evaluation Commission in March 1983 to investigate the origins of apparently unearned wealth. But somewhat bizarrely, M'Bai was the first victim of its probings. He was forced to resign in June 1984 over his involvement in a foreign exchange scandal in which a controversial London-based Nigerian businessman, Chief Alfred Nzeribe, was also implicated. He was subsequently arrested and put on trial, but was acquitted and returned to private practice in Banjul.[41] M'Bai was apparently the sole casualty of the commission before it wound up; although seventeen cases were reported, it appears only to have investigated those involving M'Bai and the managing director of the Gambia Produce Marketing Board, Kabba Jallow, who retained his job.[42]

Although Saho no doubt realized that he would be replaced as attorney general, he and his supporters confidently expected that he would be appointed vice president as a reward for organizing the post-coup treason trials. But he was deliberately overlooked, despite his seniority in the party and close links to the new protecting power, Senegal. It seems that his pro-Senegalese feelings were a little too pronounced for Jawara who, instead, turned to his fellow Mandinka, Dabo, perhaps because of the latter's nonpolitical background (and despite the rumors that Dabo was sympathetic to Dibba and the NCP). Saho was instead offered the decidedly inferior position of minister of local government. At first he accepted the position, but, on the following day, he resigned from the cabinet and was replaced by a nephew of the president, Kebba Jawara. To make matters worse, he then launched a fierce public attack in *The Nation* on President Jawara for establishing a government that was "openly tribalistic," consisted of "known supporters" of the NCP, and included an individual (Dabo) who had only recently joined the party. Saho subsequently apparently apologized to the party, but did not return to favor.[43]

It appears that of the fourteen members of the new cabinet (including Jawara), no fewer than seven were in their thirties. These were Dabo, Sabally, M'Bai, Lamin Kitty Jabang (External Affairs), Omar A. Jallow (Water Resources and Environment), Landing Jallow Sonko (Information and Tourism), and Dr. M. S. K. Manneh (Economic Planning and Development). Another minister, Kebba Jawara, was forty. In marked contrast to the position in the mid-1970s, there was now only one minister (M. C. Jallow, the minister of health), who was over sixty.[44] In addition, Jawara sought to strengthen the position of women within the government. The "nominated" MP, Mrs. Louise N'Jie, the sister of Jawara's first wife, Augusta, had been the parliamentary secretary for health since 1979; now the newly elected MP, Nyimasata Sanneh-Bojang, was appointed parliamentary secretary for education. Apart from Sisay, one other "nominated" MP held ministerial rank; this was A. S. M'Boob, the former inspector general of police, who continued as minister of the interior.[45]

Nine members of the new cabinet were Mandinka, three were Wolof, and two were Fula but, unlike after the 1977 election, there were no Jola or Serahuli representatives. The ethnic composition of the new cabinet was broadly representative of PPP MPs.[46]

Consolidation and Fragmentation: 1982–87

In the first three years after the 1982 election, the PPP further strengthened its political position. It initiated internal party reforms designed to increase popular involvement in the party and its decision-making processes; these were at least partially successful. It had also seen off the threat of the Independents by the end of 1985 and prevented the NCP making any significant progress. However, the emergence in 1986 of two new parties, the Gambia People's Party (GPP) and the People's Democratic Organisation for Independence and Socialism (PDOIS— generally referred to as DOI),[47] posed new challenges, particularly if they could benefit from the adverse economic situation.

PPP Party Reforms

At the PPP party congress held shortly before the 1982 election, President Jawara gave his public blessing (albeit not entirely wholeheartedly, because if the reforms were too thorough they would weaken his patronage networks and enhance Dabo's standing) for a program of internal party reforms. The intention to revitalize the party was also signaled by the holding of a seminar on "The Political Party as an Instrument of Change" in October 1982. This was funded by the West German organization, the Friedrich Ebert Stiftung (Foundation).[48] Vice President

Dabo was put in charge of the reform process, which was backed by other "young Turks" within the party. The reformers attacked corruption and undemocratic practices within the party; they also sought to strengthen the PPP's youth and women's wings, which were given separate National Executive Committees and established a Political Education Unit, under Dabo's control. The party reformers also assumed editorial control of *The Gambia Times*, the PPP's party newspaper, to give direction and publicity to their program.[49]

Parallel to this process, the reformers also achieved the further demotion of "old guard" elements in the PPP leadership. As noted, H. O. Semega-Janneh was ousted before the 1982 election and M. L. Saho fell soon afterward; subsequently, in June 1983, Sir Alieu Jack was forced to resign the speakership of the House. This was after he was exposed for trying to get an opposition MP to ask a question in Parliament designed to embarrass the new minister of justice, Fafa M'Bai, a leading member of the reform group.[50] Although the reforms were not entirely successful (and the power of the "old guard" was not decisively broken), they did help to improve the PPP's image and may well have contributed to the dearth of Independent candidates in the 1987 election noted below.

The Decline of the Independents and the National Convention Party

The government responded to the group of Independent MPs in the new legislature in two ways. First, it refused to recognize them as a distinct political grouping, so that they were not able to become the official parliamentary opposition; this remained the NCP, now under the effective parliamentary leadership of Foday Makalo, MP for Lower Baddibu; Sheriff Dibba was no longer in the House.[51] Second, the ruling party brought its patronage to bear on the disparate group of Independent parliamentarians; it refused to readmit any back into its fold unless they first resigned and then sought the PPP nomination in a subsequent by-election.[52] One of the five, Saihou Barrow, went through this process a few months after the election and duly won the Eastern Jarra by-election in April 1983. Kebba Fadera, the member for Eastern Kiang, also resigned as an Independent MP, but, unlike Barrow, was not accepted back by the PPP. Instead the party selected Jallow Sanneh, who had been a "nominated" MP since 1970 and a parliamentary secretary since 1977, as its by-election candidate. Sanneh, who was standing in his home area and was the son of a former Seyfu of Eastern Kiang, was subsequently elected in July 1983.[53]

A third Independent MP, Bubacarr Baldeh, the member for Basse, of whom much was expected in the new Parliament, was expelled for repeated nonattendance in 1985, his prolonged absences cynically attributed to government inducements by some Gambians.[54] For the subsequent by-election in December 1985, the PPP replaced its unpopular previous candidate, Kebba Krubally, with the younger and better educated Omar B. A. Sey, the director of youth, sport and culture. Sey was opposed by a cousin of Bubacarr Baldeh, Ousainou Baldeh, who having originally announced his intention of standing as an Independent, perhaps unwisely joined the NCP a few weeks before the poll; this may have been an important factor in Sey's victory by less than sixty votes.[55] This left only two Independent MPs, Henry Jammeh and A. K. Touray, in the House of Representatives.

The NCP also failed to make any significant progress nationally after the election and effectively ceased to exist as a force in local government. In the BanCC elections held in December 1982, the PPP won all seven contested seats against UP/NCP candidates, an eighth against an Independent (H. O. Semega-Janneh), and a ninth uncontested seat. The NCP then boycotted the Area Council elections of May 1983, which allowed the PPP to achieve a virtual clean sweep at the polls.[56] In addition, during 1984, a substantial number of NCP supporters publicly rejoined the PPP at a series of political rallies.[57]

The Emergence of the Gambia People's Party

As was the case a decade earlier with Sheriff Dibba and the NCP break-away from the PPP, the rupture that resulted in the foundation of the GPP at the end of March 1986 focused on a former vice president. Since losing his cabinet seat in 1982, A. M. Camara had kept a low profile within the PPP. Although he retained his position in the party's central committee, he was dropped from the party secretariat and was snubbed during the twenty-fifth anniversary celebrations of the PPP's foundation in 1984.[58] Nevertheless, it was not until February 1986 that he finally resigned from the PPP's central committee. There was no obvious catalyst for breaking with the PPP at this time, although the discontent caused by the austerity measures, growing social unrest, and perhaps specific incidents, such as the burning down of the Albert Market in Banjul in January 1986, may have persuaded him that the time was propitious to act. A few days later, two other ex-ministers, H. O. Semega-Janneh and M. L. Saho, followed suit.[59] Saho seems to have been preparing to defect from the PPP for some time; in the previous December, he launched a blistering (and widely publicized) attack in the House of Representatives on the "Banjul Mafia," a group of big businessmen and parastatal heads closely connected to the PPP whom he deemed most responsible for corruption in the public sector.[60]

A month later, on March 29, the GPP was formally launched. Camara was selected as party leader and a draft constitution and manifesto were adopted.[61] The new opposition within the PPP seemed unlikely, based as it was on the political frustration of three quite different individuals. Semega-Janneh, a Banjul Serahuli, was a political has-been by the 1980s with no real standing in the party or the country. Saho, despite his services to the president and ruling party, was deeply unpopular and distrusted, particularly because of his role in the political trials before and after the coup (see Chapter 8). Camara, in complete contrast, was a widely respected senior politician, if out of favor with Jawara. In retrospect, Camara recognized that a political party based on an alliance with Semega-Janneh and Saho could neither defeat the PPP nor replace NCP as the official opposition.[62]

However, in 1986, these doubts were suppressed and the GPP was launched as a challenge to the existing two-party setup.

To try to establish some ideological and policy differences from the existing mainstream parties, the GPP claimed to be "more socialist" in its orientation than the PPP. Camara also attacked the PPP as a one-man band and argued that it had misused the foreign aid it had received after the coup. Like Dibba and the NCP, the GPP also made familiar promises to clean up corruption and attend to the needs of the people; it also announced that it would reduce the powers of the presidency by amending the constitution so that the president could serve for two terms only. In addition, it claimed to be vaguely Islamic in that it adopted a Muslim-Arabic motto, "La haula wala huata ila bilah" ("Power and Might are in the hands of God"), rather than the Latin ones favored by the PPP and NCP. The GPP's emblem was the plow.[63] All three leaders were practicing Muslims (Camara converted to Islam in 1974),[64] but so were the leaders of the other two parties.

In reality, the GPP's program differed little from that of the two main parties. Indeed, it should be emphasized that the GPP, like the PPA and NCP before it, essentially arose from personality differences rather than policy divisions. There was little evidence to support any suspicion that the party was a bid for power by the Fula, the country's second largest ethnic group, but allegedly politically underrepresented, on account of its main leader, Camara, being a Fula, as the two other leaders were a Banjul Wolof (Saho) and a Wolofized Serahuli (Semega-Janneh). However, the party undoubtedly hoped to do well in MID and URD where most Gambian Fula lived. In reality, the Fula did have two other cabinet ministers at this time and both were strongly to support the PPP in the 1987 elections.[65] Neither was there any truth in the fanciful suggestion that the GPP was some kind of mutation of the virtually defunct UP and the long-dead Gambia Muslim Congress, because two of its leaders (Camara and Semega-Janneh) once belonged to these parties and the GPP flag incorporated the colors of these two parties—red and green.[66] Given the tactical alliance between old UP elements and the NCP, there was no truth to this claim.

The GPP gained a third MP when the Independent, Henry Jammeh, joined the party in June 1986 and another important recruit when Suntu Fatty, a former secretary of the Cooperative Society who was apparently a founding member of the PPP, defected from the NCP.[67] It also appeared to acquire an important financial backer when, following negotiations in Lagos at the end of May, an agreement was allegedly reached with Chief Alfred Nzeribe (whose lawyer in Banjul was Saho), whereby pre-election financial support would be traded for far-reaching financial concessions to the latter in The Gambia in the event of a GPP win. Unfortunately for the GPP, the PPP got wind of these discussions (probably when Suntu Fatty rejoined the party in October 1986) and published what was purported to be the correspondence between Nzeribe and Saho.[68] The news that the GPP seemed to be reliant on foreign financial support proved very damaging to the new party, not least because Nzeribe already had a very poor reputation in The Gambia because of his involvement in the downfall of Fafa M'Bai in 1984.[69]

The Foundation of People's Democratic Organisation for Independence and Socialism

The second party to be established before the 1987 election, PDOIS, was very different from the GPP and all earlier Gambian political parties. It was founded in August 1986 by a number of those who, as noted in Chapter 8, were accused (but acquitted) of managing the People's Movement for Independence against Neo-Colonialism and Capitalism in The Gambia and distributing *The Voice*, including Halifa Sallah, Sam Sarr, Amie Sillah, and Adama Bah. Another cofounder of PDOIS was Sidia Jatta. Although, as noted in Chapter 8, he may have briefly been a member of the Kwame Nkrumah Memorial Foundation in the early 1970s, Jatta was less active in radical politics. Arguably the most intellectual of any Gambian politician, he completed an undergraduate and master's degrees in linguistics at the University of Grenoble in France in 1973–77. After briefly returning to The Gambia in 1978, he accepted a research fellowship in African linguistics at the International African Institute in London in 1980–82, before returning to The Gambia as senior curriculum development officer. Sallah and Jatta resigned from government service in 1985–86, in protest against official policies and performance, and to work full time to achieve their political goals.[70]

PDOIS was formally launched in August 1986 following a three-week long congress in Banjul. The new organization, which had a collective leadership rather than an official individual leader, attacked the PPP for its corruption, bankrupting the economy, and, perhaps in particular, for compromising the sovereignty of The Gambia by entering into an unequal relationship with Senegal.[71]

Prior to deciding to contest the 1987 elections, PDOIS was principally engaged in radical political education of the masses by means of its turgidly didactic newspaper, *Foroyaa* (a Mandinka word with a range of positive meanings: freedom, truthfulness, bravery, trustworthiness, and moral purity) and public meetings. It also worked through several self-help organizations, all of which were in the Greater Banjul area. PDOIS continued to criticize the PPP from a radical Pan-Africanist position. It played down any Marxist and revolutionary ideology, which its activists may have espoused previously, partly in response to the need to court a non-leftist electorate and because of the global collapse of Marxist regimes, but also because of a great deal of candid reflection on their earlier political positions. PDOIS leaders certainly brought a new element of earnestness, personal probity and intellectual engagement and a rejection of any leadership cult in favor of grassroots democracy, previously largely absent, to Gambian political life.[72]

The Economic Context

Despite the emergence of the GPP and PDOIS, the PPP appeared still to be in a strong position politically. But there remained a danger that the electorate would react badly in the election to the Economic Recovery Programme (ERP) that, as discussed in Chapter 1, was introduced in August 1985. This resulted in a range of austerity measures, including the dismissal of several thousand civil servants in 1986, as well as increases in petroleum prices, transport fares, and utility charges. In some African countries, notably the Côte d'Ivoire, Congo, Nigeria, and Zambia, attempts at implementing economic reforms led to widespread popular protests.[73] These had not occurred in The Gambia.[74] Nevertheless, the experience of some small democracies, notably Mauritius in 1982, was that the introduction of austerity measures before an election cost the ruling party dearly.[75] It remained to be seen whether there would be a similar outcome in The Gambia.

The 1987 Parliamentary and Presidential Elections[76]

The parliamentary elections, which were held in March 1987, were contested by four parties: the PPP, the NCP (in alliance with the UP), the GPP, and PDOIS. In sharp contrast to 1982, there were only two Independent candidates, Dodou Ceesay in Eastern Jarra and Alasan Jaye in Banjul South, an indication perhaps, as noted, of the success of the PPP's internal party reforms.[77] The PPP, NCP and GPP also nominated candidates for the presidential election which was held on the same day; the UP supported the NCP's candidate (as in the 1977 and 1982 elections); PDOIS nominated no one. One additional parliamentary seat was created prior to the election through the subdivision of the Wuli constituency, although the size of the registered electorate had, rather surprisingly, fallen since 1982 to 263,000, despite the continuing rise in the national population.[78]

People's Progressive Party

The PPP, which held twenty-eight seats at the dissolution of Parliament, as usual contested every constituency, but unlike in 1982, almost all of its candidates from the previous election (as well as all four MPs who elected in by-elections) received the party nomination. Only one incumbent MP, Dr. M. S. K. Manneh (Jokadu), was deselected. Manneh was sacked from the cabinet in January 1985 after being accused of harassing NCP supporters in the Baddibu area, amassing illicit wealth, bullying and showing disrespect to elders in his constituency, and speaking against the president. He remained out of favor with his party and was replaced by a Serere newcomer, Dodou A. S. Jome, a former civil servant subsequently employed as a commercial assistant in the American Embassy in Banjul.[79] The losing PPP candidates from 1987 in Illiassa and Sandu were also replaced (although James Gaye, who was defeated in Eastern Foni, was given another chance). In addition, Pa Mandu Sagnia (a Serahuli from the area who had been living in Liberia) and Ebrima A. B. ("Pesseh") N'Jie (a son of A. B. N'Jie) were selected to replace Camara and Saho in Kantora and Banjul Central, respectively.[80] Jawara was naturally once again selected as the party's presidential candidate.

National Convention Party

The NCP held four seats at the dissolution of Parliament through Dembo Bojang (Bakau), Foday Makalo (Lower Baddibu), Fodayba Jammeh (Illiassa), and the former Independent MP, A. K. Touray (Sandu), who now joined the party.[81] This time round, the NCP also contested every parliamentary seat (three in alliance with the UP in Banjul seats) and Dibba expected to win at least twenty-one of them, thus giving him control of Parliament.[82] If its three UP allies, M. L. N'Jie, Kebba Foon, and Jabel Sallah, are included, half of its thirty-six candidates had experience in fighting a general election. Dibba was once again selected as the party's presidential candidate. The NCP made no attempt to form an electoral pact with the other main opposition party, the GPP; this reflected the extent of the antipathy between Camara and Dibba, dating back to their clashes when both served in the PPP government, as well as Dibba's confidence in his party's ability to win without an alliance. Indeed, it was argued that the differences between the two main opposition parties were greater than between either opposition party and the PPP.[83] An alliance with PDOIS would have been electorally insignificant and would have been impossible given the ideological differences between the two parties.

Gambia People's Party

The GPP nominally held three seats at the dissolution, through Camara, Saho, and Henry Jammeh. In fact, Saho had by now deserted the party that he helped to establish. In October 1986, he was arrested in London on fraud charges. While in prison awaiting trial, his health deteriorated and he had to have a leg amputated, with the government providing the funds for his family to visit him. He was eventually convicted, but soon released on compassionate grounds. He then abandoned the GPP and in January 1987 tried to rejoin the PPP, but his application was rejected. Nevertheless, his defection left Camara to bear most of the burden of the campaigning and its costs.[84]

Surprisingly, the GPP put up as many as thirty-four candidates across the country.[85] This was an unwise decision, given the strains that this put on its limited finances and organizational resources; but, like the NCP, to resist the government's accusation of it being nothing more than a disaffected regional–ethnic minority, it felt the need to demonstrate its national credentials and territorial spread by standing in as many constituencies as possible.[86] Five of its candidates apart from Henry Jammeh had stood as Independents in 1982: Jain Coli Fye (Lower Niumi), Malick Sabally (Niamina), Nganyie Touray (Saloum), Mbemba Tambedou (Tumana), and Sulaymen Sumbundu (Basse). In addition, Mrs. Ya Fatou Sonko (Central Kombo) had stood as an Independent in 1972. However, the GPP failed to secure the backing of another former Independent MP, Bubacarr Baldeh, as it had perhaps anticipated doing.[87] The party's other candidates, apart from Boto B. Camara (Western Kiang) who was a recruit from the NCP, and the veteran ex-minister, H. O. Semega-Janneh (Banjul South), were newcomers to national politics. A. M. Camara was nominated as the GPP's presidential candidate as well as the party's nominee for his home constituency of Kantora.

People's Democratic Organisation for Independence and Socialism

The decision by PDOIS to contest elections took everyone by surprise; certainly it was in no position to challenge the political order. As a left-wing collectivity previously opposed to the prevailing electoral politics, and also hostile to the concept of a formal political party, it was even less experienced and organized than the other opposition parties. Although it enjoyed a measure of respect for its integrity and intellectual position, its sympathizers were not formally organized into a political organization, were mainly found in the Greater Banjul area, and tended to be drawn from the ranks of disaffected junior civil servants, teachers, and students.[88] Despite a lack of electoral experience, an established political leader, and adequate funds, and a disdain for the parochial and mercenary nature of Gambian politics, PDOIS put up five candidates. Four of these were in the Greater Banjul area, where its prospects appeared to be best; these included Halifa Sallah, who contested Serrekunda East. The fifth constituency was at the eastern extremity of the country, Eastern Wuli, but was the home area of Sidia Jatta, who stood for the movement there.[89] PDOIS stood more to try to educate the Gambian public about political issues and to familiarize them with a less personalist and corrupt form of politics, than to win seats.[90] After all, if the Gambian left were to engage in constitutional rather than agitational politics, a start had to be made at some time. For the PDOIS activists, this was to be an important experience in mainstream political organization and in seeking to win over the Gambian electorate by force of moral argument and personal example.

Election Results

The election was keenly contested, with a much higher turnout than in 1982 of 80 percent, providing further evidence that The Gambia usually had one of the higher turnouts among parliamentary democracies.[91] The parliamentary election confirmed the dominance of the PPP once again. For the fifth time since independence, it gained an overwhelming victory in a general election, at least as expressed in terms of parliamentary seats won. Indeed, it managed to increase the number of seats it won from twenty-seven in the 1982 election to thirty-one in 1987, by regaining all the five seats lost to Independents in the previous election and taking the new seat of Western Wuli, to offset the loss of two seats to the NCP/UP coalition. The PPP gained 119,248 votes, but its share of the popular vote was, however, down to 56.4 percent, a decline from its 62 percent share of the vote in 1982 and 70 percent in 1977.[92] Once more, the ruling party benefited from the "first-past-the-post" electoral system, a distortion increased by the presence of three opposition parties. PPP candidates won on a minority vote in six constituencies (and NCP in one).[93]

Several factors helped to account for the PPP's success. First, the PPP made strenuous efforts to shore up its support in the rural areas. The president undertook a series of "Meet the Farmers" tours in 1986–87, which, although ostensibly intended to explain the ERP to farmers, were in reality designed to bolster support for his party. Other ministers also toured the provinces; moreover, for the first time, the party organized its congress outside Banjul (it took place in Basse) as a demonstration of its commitment to rural voters.[94]

Second, the PPP skillfully attacked the credibility of its opponents, particularly the GPP. Once it learned about Camara's financial links with Chief Nzeribe, it not only questioned Camara's patriotism, but also attacked his moral reputation; his party was now denounced, unfairly and somewhat hypocritically by the PPP, as the "Greedy People's Party."[95] In addition, government propaganda sought to present the GPP as the stalking horse of the Senegalese (even though, as noted in Chapter 8, it was the PPP who called in the Senegalese army in 1981 and continued to rely on the presence on Gambian soil of Senegalese military detachments). By 1987, there was growing evidence, within the ruling party and among the populace at large, of dissatisfaction with this new and humiliating relationship. Senegal's desire to bring about closer political and economic union, as a quid pro quo for military protection, was also opposed by the majority of Gambians and skillfully resisted in negotiations by Jawara (see Chapter 10). Yet without any real evidence, other than Saho's maneuverings and a broadly worded statement of support for Senegambian unity (virtually no different from the PPP's formal position) in the party's manifesto, the GPP was castigated as unpatriotic by the PPP.[96]

Third, the all-too-familiar application of state power and financial patronage played a decisive part in its victory. As in previous elections, the PPP undoubtedly used government vehicles (including even United Nations vehicles) to transport candidates and voters alike and Radio Gambia to help get across its messages; it also directed the chiefs to use their influence on its behalf.[97] Opposition parties also alleged that certain ministers distributed presents of money and goods to the electorate in advance of voting. They also suggested that there was double registration of PPP supporters (voter registration cards were distributed by the village head, the alkalo, who was almost always a PPP supporter) and evidence of multiple voting and voting by aliens.[98] As a result of the opposition complaints, a total of nineteen election petitions were presented to the courts by the NCP and GPP, but all were rejected in July by Chief Justice Ayoola on the grounds that they were filed incorrectly.[99] Although the complaints were not substantiated, the turnout in some key constituencies, particularly Illiassa, was perhaps suspiciously high.[100]

Finally, and perhaps rather surprisingly, the government may actually have benefited politically from the introduction of the ERP. Certainly, at the very least, the ERP did the PPP very little political damage. The key policy reforms of the ERP, which included an increase in the price paid to farmers for their groundnuts and the liberalization of the rice trade, coupled with the end of the drought that had blighted the agricultural sector in the early 1980s, are estimated to have increased per capita rural income by approximately 12 percent between 1985 and 1988.[101] Thus, some farmers continued to support the PPP because their economic position improved in recent years, and others stayed loyal because they accepted any reform program endorsed by Jawara, even if few of them understood its details.[102] The response of the electorate in the Greater Banjul area to the ERP was of course very different; urban voters experienced most of the hardships, such as the retrenchment of civil servants and the floating of the currency, associated with the program. But this did not matter greatly, because they comprised a relatively small proportion of the electorate.[103]

The NCP/UP coalition won five seats and with 58,461 votes increased its share of the vote to 27.6 percent. NCP candidates gained the great majority of these (55,251 votes) and its electoral strength remained much as before—63 percent of the coalition's votes still came from Kombo St. Mary, North Bank Division (NBD), and Western Division (WD), where it held on to Lower Baddibu, Illiassa and Bakau. It also managed to recapture the marginal seats of Serrekunda West through the veteran MP, Gibou Jagne (who subsequently replaced Foday Makalo as the NCP's parliamentary leader) and Banjul South through Jabel Sallah. Its success in Banjul South was in part due to UP support, but perhaps a more important factor was that urban resentment at the costs of the ERP resulted in registered voters who were PPP supporters not bothering to go to the polls; the turnout in this constituency (51 percent) was almost certainly the lowest in the country.[104] However, once again, Dibba failed to recapture Central Baddibu, where he was overstretched in trying to recover his former constituency, while trying to assist a greater number of NCP candidates across the land. Dr. Lamin Saho's small majority of ninety-five inevitably raised questions about the veracity of the result, although it should be noted that Saho was regarded as a good constituency MP because he secured substantial external developmental aid for the area.[105] Elsewhere, as before, support tailed off sharply further inland. The NCP managed only 17 percent of the vote in URD and A. K. Touray lost Sandu. Whereas the PPP received at least 37 percent of the vote in every constituency (and its highest share was 79 percent), the NCP share ranged from just over 2 percent to 59 percent. The PPP's portrayal of the NCP as a Mandinka "tribalist" party and Dibba as an ethnic champion, rather than as a genuine national leader, all his efforts to project a trans-ethnic image notwithstanding, was still widely accepted by the electorate.[106]

The GPP fared far worse, completely failing to defeat the PPP or replace the NCP as the official opposition. Its hopes of winning at least seventeen seats were totally dashed for, although the GPP polled 31,604 votes (14.9 percent), it failed to win a single seat.[107] Its vote ranged from barely 1 percent to a best of 44 percent in Lower Niumi. Its candidate in this seat, Jain Coli Fye, a Serere teacher, also came closest of all to winning; in a three-cornered contest, he lost to the PPP's Dodou N'Gum by only fifty-one votes.[108] Even the party leader, Camara, seemingly secure in his Kantora constituency, where he had won every election since 1960, was overwhelmed by a PPP blitz to unseat him and so deliver a crippling blow to this latest challenger. He was defeated by the PPP's Pa Mandu Sagnia by more than 500 votes. The outcome was therefore very different from 1982, when he was elected unopposed for the PPP. The GPP did best, predictably in MID and URD, where it won 53 percent of its votes, thanks mainly to Camara's family and social connections as a Fula from the Basse area (Mansajang), as well as his personal reputation. Yet, in too many constituencies, its presence was almost of a token nature for seventeen of its candidates lost their deposits. Only in five constituencies (Eastern Foni, Kantora, Lower Niumi, Niamina, and Tumana) did it win one-third or more of the votes.

There were several reasons, apart from the PPP's effective attacks on it, for the GPP's poor performance. First, despite its ambitious decision to try to contest every parliamentary seat, the GPP entered the campaign with very little money. It is doubtful whether the party ever received any money from Nzeribe, and Camara also found it difficult, like other opposition politicians before him, to persuade local businessmen to back him financially.[109] Because he had never been a wealthy man (because of his modest circumstances and probity in public life), Camara could not afford to bankroll his party himself (as P. S. N'Jie had done for the UP, for example). As a consequence, the GPP found it impossible to provide its candidates with sufficient funds to engage in the financial bargaining that had traditionally played such an important part in winning elections in The Gambia. Camara's reputation for integrity, skillfully undermined by PPP propaganda, was insufficient to offset these deficiencies.[110]

Second, Camara's social and political networks in the eastern half of the country were no match for the combination of financial inducements, administrative pressures, and appeals for personal loyalty to Jawara, that the PPP campaign teams once again marshaled. The PPP was also able to exploit his presence in Kantora, which was necessary if he was to hold on to his threatened seat, to demolish his party's candidates elsewhere in the country, while at the same having the resources to target his constituency and wrest the seat from him. Although Camara himself refused financial inducements to stand down, key supporters were persuaded to change sides for material benefit, as well as in response to appeals to remain loyal to Jawara and the PPP as the historic bringers of independence.[111] GPP candidates were largely left to themselves as the campaign progressed and Camara was forced to concentrate on his own constituency.

Not unexpectedly, PDOIS won only 2,069 votes (1.0 percent), with all its candidates losing their deposits. Halifa Sallah did best in Serrekunda East, where he won 9.8 percent of the vote in a four-cornered fight. It was evident that even in the urban constituencies, the Gambian electorate, although recognizing a number of the issues raised by PDOIS, found its leftist jargon incomprehensible and its "solutions" unconvincing.[112] At the same time, anti-PPP voters had the choice of two other political parties, led by experienced senior politicians, to choose from and, in the urban areas, disaffected voters still preferred Dibba and the NCP to the radical left. On the whole, as in previous post-independence elections, the overwhelming majority of voters still clung to Jawara and the PPP, a more familiar and thus more reassuring choice, however flawed their record.[113] Finally, the two Independent candidates between them gained only 233 votes.

Presidential Election

Meanwhile, in the second direct presidential election, Jawara headed the polls, again as generally predicted. He gained 123,385 votes (59.2 percent), considerably fewer than in 1982, when he secured over 137,000 votes (72.5 percent) even though the number of those voting in the presidential election increased from 189,115 in 1982 to 208,479 in 1987. The drop in his share of the vote could in part be attributed to the less emotional and politically uncertain situation in the country; in 1982, as noted, he benefited from a surge of support for himself and the PPP in reaction to the trauma of the failed coup of the previous year. A second explanation was the presence of a third presidential candidate, Camara of the GPP, who came in third with 27,751 votes (13.3 percent). Jawara's lost votes went to Camara, for the other candidate, Sheriff Dibba of the NCP, although increasing his number of votes (from 52,095 to 57,343), again won 27.5 percent of the vote. Despite the fall in the size of his vote, Jawara remained the only candidate to enjoy nation-wide support. He headed the polls in all save four of the thirty-six constituencies; he was narrowly beaten by Dibba in Central Baddibu, but had a clear lead over Camara in Kantora. He also once again achieved a higher share of the total vote than his party did in the parliamentary elections. Dibba gained more votes than Camara in five Administrative Areas, the exceptions being Banjul and Basse, and in twenty-five out of thirty-six constituencies.[114]

Post-Election Cabinet Changes

After his latest victory, President Jawara again reshuffled his cabinet. Two veteran ministers, M. C. Jallow (Health) and Lamin M'Boge (Works and Communications) were dropped, the latter being replaced by another PPP stalwart, M. C. Cham; Cham owed his unexpected restoration to office in part to his effectiveness as a backbencher since 1982, which included strong attacks in the House on M. C. Jallow and the minister of education, Louise N'Jie.[115] In addition, Omar Sey was promoted to the Ministry of External Affairs, no doubt in recognition of his success in holding Basse with an increased majority and in helping to deliver URD; he replaced Lamin Kitty Jabang, who was appointed minister of the interior. In addition, the position of the vice president, Bakary Dabo, was strengthened as he acquired a specific portfolio (Education, Youth and Culture) as vice president for the first time; the previous minister, Louise N'Jie, faced criticism for her tough stand on student protests in February 1987, but nevertheless kept her cabinet seat because she replaced M. C. Jallow at Health.[116] Other key posts remained unchanged; Sheriff Sisay continued as minister of finance, Hassan Jallow as attorney general, and Saihou Sabally as minister of agriculture. Sabally was by now regarded as the mouthpiece of the "old guard," who were opposed to Dabo's program of PPP internal reforms.[117]

The Succession Crisis: 1989–92

A further significant cabinet change occurred in February 1989, when Sisay retired on grounds of ill health (he died the following month) and he was replaced by Sabally.[118] This was despite the fact that Sabally was one of four ministers who had been named by Sanna "Ticks" Manneh, the editor of a radical news sheet, *The Torch*, in an article in October 1988, which alleged widespread corruption in public life. The others were Dr. Lamin K. Saho, the minister of information and tourism, who had so forcefully denounced the failings of the PPP government back in 1972 when a leader of the Independent candidates; Landing Jallow Sonko, the minister of local government and lands; and M. C. Cham, the minister of works and communications. Sabally, Saho, and Sonko (but not Cham) sued Manneh for libel and defamation, but when the case came to court in April 1989, only Sonko was successful. The magistrate, W. G. Grante, concluded that Saho was guilty of customs evasion with regard to the importation of drugs from Germany, while Sabally had been unable to prove his innocence in connection with "dubious rice deals" with Momodou M. Dibba, the manager of the Gambia Cooperatives Union (GCU). Manneh was therefore cautioned and discharged.[119] The attorney general, Hassan Jallow, subsequently appealed against the findings of the earlier trial and in June 1990, his appeal was upheld by the chief justice. But this was not enough to save Saho; he was sacked in May 1990 even before the verdict was announced. Cham, who had not contested the allegation in *The Torch*, was sacked in June 1990, which effectively ended his long ministerial career. Manneh appealed against the second verdict to the Court of Appeal, which eventually found in his favor, albeit on technical grounds, in December 1991.[120]

Unlike Saho, Sabally retained his ministerial position, but his reputation was certainly damaged by the trial. A charitable view is that he was certainly more reluctant than his predecessor to clamp down on corruption; for example, whereas Sisay had made a determined effort to eradicate customs fraud in 1986–87, Sabally took no action to prevent it increasing again in the early 1990s. In addition, the widespread embezzlement within the GCU, which was detected in 1993, took place while Sabally was minister of agriculture and many people shared the view of Manneh (and Grante) that he was personally implicated.[121] His political survival suggested that the PPP government remained reluctant to deal firmly with the persisting issue of political corruption.

Despite his very poor reputation, Sabally continued to prosper politically. Indeed, by the early 1990s, he came to be regarded as the main rival to Bakary Dabo as the most likely successor to Jawara as party leader and head of state; a third faction may have supported the claims of Lamin Kitty Jabang, the minister of the interior.[122] Jawara's attitude to a possible successor was previously similar to that of leaders of other personalist regimes in Africa: not to declare a "dauphin" or new leader in waiting and to circulate favors and expectations among lesser rivals in the party hierarchy.[123] At first, Dabo appeared to have the upper hand in the internal power struggle within the PPP, but by late 1991, he found himself being gradually eclipsed by the Sabally faction as the president began to favor his rival. Either because of this policy of deliberately encouraging rivalry and uncertainty, or because he was having second thoughts about his vice president, Jawara began to take more notice of Dabo's enemies who had long accused him of pro-NCP sympathies from his time as a civil servant.[124]

Matters came to a head at the closing ceremony of the fifth PPP national congress in Mansakonko in December 1991.[125] On December 4, shortly before a motion proposing the reselection of Jawara as the PPP's presidential candidate was put to the congress, the president suddenly announced his intention of giving up power before the Spring elections in 1992 (although he stated that he would remain as leader of the PPP). His motives for so doing were disputed, with some commentators considering it a ploy by Jawara to test his popularity and the loyalty of his lieutenants.[126] Certainly the announcement appeared to take everyone by surprise and caused consternation in the ranks of the party faithful, who feared that without Jawara to head the campaign, the party would split once again between rival contenders and Sheriff Dibba could take advantage to win the election.

The first to respond to Jawara's speech was Sabally who pleaded with the president not to retire; with the support of other "old guard" PPP politicians, including M. C. Cham, M. C. Jallow, and I. B. A. Kelepha-Samba, he subsequently organized a campaign among PPP activists to persuade Jawara to stay on. Sabally had much to lose if Jawara stood down; as noted, the extended Sanna Manneh case was finally concluded in Manneh's favor and the vice president may have feared that if Dabo came to power, he would sack him as a way of gaining immediate popularity.[127] In contrast, Dabo made no public appeal to Jawara to change his mind. Instead, immediately after the congress, he apparently held a series of meeting with his supporters to work out a strategy to make him Jawara's successor and then announced his availability to head the party in the event of Jawara standing down. This was a not unreasonable gesture on his part, but was politically dangerous. The Sabally faction seized on this statement to persuade the president, who was never quite sure of his lieutenants in light of past history, that Dabo's leadership aspiration was a threat. Following a mass demonstration at the airport to greet Jawara's return from attending the Organisation of Islamic Conference summit and then another large rally in Banjul (organized by M. C. Cham), at which Sabally was lauded by the gathering, Jawara announced on December 17 that he would lead the ruling party into the next election.[128] But in the campaign arrangements, Dabo was dropped from any prominent role, unlike in 1987, when he played an important part in coordinating the party's provincial campaigning.[129]

The 1992 Parliamentary and Presidential Elections[130]

All four parties that contested the 1987 election—the PPP, the NCP (again in alliance with the UP), the GPP and PDOIS, together with a new party, the People's Democratic Party (PDP)—contested the next elections which took place in May

1992. Unlike in 1987, all the parties nominated candidates for the presidential election. There was a substantial increase in the number of registered voters to 338,739, which meant that it was estimated that more than four-fifths of the eligible population had registered.[131]

People's Progressive Party

A record number of 145 individuals sought the PPP nomination, a much higher total than in 1987. The PPP, which held thirty-one seats at the dissolution, replaced eight of its 1987 candidates, including six MPs. The senior ex-ministers, M. C. Jallow (Jimara) and Lamin M'Boge (Niamina), retired before the election. Jallow, who was seventy-two, agreed not to stand again and was given a "nominated" seat in Parliament as compensation. He was replaced by the ex-Independent MP, Bubacarr Baldeh, who was now reconciled with the party. The latter was replaced by a newcomer, Malanding Ceesay, a well-connected relative of the late Sheriff Sisay. Belatedly, M'Boge had resought the nomination, and his disaffection may have contributed to the loss of the seat to the more dynamic Independent candidate.

The other four former MPs were deselected. In at least two other constituencies, local opposition to the incumbent MPs was sufficient to bring about their deselection. In Eastern Kiang, Jallow Sanneh, who made himself increasingly unpopular by his autocratic manner, was replaced by Wally Sanneh, the former NCP candidate, who was fighting the seat for the third time. In Eastern Jarra, following opposition from the youths in the constituency, Saihou Barrow was deselected, but a controversial selection process resulted in the front runner to succeed him, Saide Wasse, being rejected by the National Selection Committee in favor of Fafanding Dabo. The other two MPs who were deselected were Dodou Jome (Jokadu) and Mrs. Nyimasata Sanneh-Bojang (Northern Kombo). Jome, a reform-minded MP who was disillusioned with the nature of Gambian politics subsequently claimed that he did not wish to stand again and was relieved when replaced. Sanneh-Bojang later asserted that she was ousted because she told Jawara that he was right to resign and openly championed the cause of Bakary Dabo. On the other hand, the sacked minister, Dr. Lamin Saho, was retained in Central Baddibu in the absence of a strong rival candidate.[132]

The unsuccessful PPP candidates in 1987 in Bakau and Illiassa, A. K. N'Jie and Abdoulie Jammeh, were also replaced. The former was succeeded by Lieutenant Colonel Sam Sillah, one of the founders of the National Liberation Party in 1975 and the latter by Kebba T. Jammeh. A son of the powerful and controversial former Seyfu of Baddibu, Tamba Jammeh, Kebba Jammeh was also a former Seyfu of Upper Baddibu; a former NCP stalwart, he rejoined the PPP in 1990.[133] However, three others who had lost in the last election, M. M. Taal (Banjul South), A. A. N'Jie (Serrekunda West), and Kebba F. Singhateh (Lower Baddibu), once again faced NCP opponents. Finally, some incumbent MPs were retained despite local opposition. These included Dodou N'Gum in Lower Niumi, who was supported by the party hierarchy, despite a challenge from A. B. Fye; Omar Sey in Basse; and M. C. Cham in Tumana. In Banjul, I. B. A. Kelepha-Samba refused to stand down in Banjul North despite his age (he was seventy-seven) and the discredited "Pesseh" N'Jie was able to retain the party's nomination for Banjul Central, despite having been dismissed as a parliamentary secretary for persistent dishonesty and in spite of the strong claims of Abdoulai Dandeh N'Jie, an educated Wolof griot and businessman. Likewise, in Banjul South, Momodou Taal fought off a rival, Momodou Sallah, with the aid of what was described as the "Banjul Mafia" of powerful businessmen.[134]

The PPP once more felt confident of victory, regarding the increase in the number of rival parties as further dividing an already fragmented opposition. It stood on its record of past political and economic achievements, promising to uphold democracy and work for greater economic diversification and improvement in living standards and social provision.[135] A tactical innovation was a promise to review the 1970 constitution to bring it more in line with popular expectations (an assumption here, in light of Jawara's retirement intention, was the reduction in the powers of the presidency and the creation of an executive post of prime minister). As before, President Jawara's personal standing featured prominently in the campaign and he engaged in customary provincial tours to rally loyalist forces.

National Convention Party

Since the 1987 election, the NCP faced a number of internal difficulties. First, two of its candidates in 1987, Momodou P. Gaye (Sabach Sanjal) and Wally Sanneh (Eastern Kiang), along with a number of other NCP members, joined the PPP.[136] Second, the MP for Lower Baddibu, Foday Makalo, one of its most experienced leaders, was arrested in London in November 1990 for possession of a large quantity of cannabis and subsequently sentenced to a three-year term of imprisonment.[137] Third, and probably most important, the politically peripatetic Solo Darbo, who was the NCP's principal financial backer since its establishment in 1975, was suddenly expelled from the party in July 1991, following a bitter dispute with Sheriff Dibba. The latter claimed that Darbo was trying to use his financial weight to dominate the party, which he resisted; for his part, Darbo claimed that Dibba was too authoritarian and mismanaged party funds. In addition, the two men clashed over the selection of the NCP candidate in Eastern Wuli. The NCP candidate (in Wuli) in both 1977 and 1982 was Mohammed S. Darbo, Solo Darbo's brother; now, following a family quarrel, Solo Darbo wanted to replace M. S. Darbo with his nephew, but this was resisted by Dibba. As discussed below, Solo Darbo along with two NCP MPs, Jabel Sallah and A. K. Touray, were to join the newly established PDP in September 1991.[138] It was probably in recognition of the weakness of his party that Dibba (and other NCP leaders) held several meetings with Jawara between 1990 and 1992 to discuss the possibility of the two parties forming a coalition or an alliance. However, on each occasion, the stronger PPP rejected both options.[139]

Despite these setbacks, the NCP fielded candidates in thirty-three constituencies, including the three Banjul seats in alliance with the rump UP. These included its three remaining sitting MPs, Gibou Jagne (Serrekunda West), Fodayba Jammeh (Illiassa), and Dembo Bojang (Bakau), as well as twenty-one new candidates. It did not contest Kantora, having reached agreement with the GPP that it would not oppose Camara in his constituency, in return for the GPP not contesting Dibba's Central Baddibu seat, and also withdrew from Tumana to help Mbemba Tambedou defeat M. C. Cham. It may also have deliberately withdrawn from Niamina to improve the chances of an Independent, Lamin Waa Juwara. If the three candidates in Banjul (who were probably UP members) are included, fourteen out of thirty-three candidates had prior experience of contesting an election, all in the same seats as in 1987.[140]

In its campaigning, the NCP attacked the government much as it had done in previous elections. Political corruption and economic and social stagnation ("the lost decades") featured prominently in its manifesto and public declarations; likewise its solutions for these political ills were a repetition of earlier ones and it failed to set out a significantly different set of policies to those of the PPP.[141] Despite fighting to regain his lost seat in Central Baddibu, Dibba visited the thirty-two other constituencies where his party stood, and paid particular attention to Lower Niumi and Western Foni, where he rightly thought his party stood a good chance of winning.[142]

Gambia People's Party

Since the 1987 election, there had also been some high profile GPP defections to the PPP, including at least four parliamentary candidates, Mbemba Tambedou (Basse), Ya Fatou Sonko (Central Kombo), Yero B. A. K. Mballow (Jimara), and William S. Mendy (Serrekunda West).[143] Perhaps because of this, the GPP this time fielded only seventeen candidates, although the party may also have learned from its experience of 1987 when it overstretched itself by fighting all the seats. Its predominantly rural support was demonstrated by the fact that it did not stand in any seats in either Banjul or Kombo St. Mary.

Despite the fact that it only contested half the number of seats it had fought in 1987, only five of its candidates from 1987 were nominated again; one of these, Mbemba Tambedou, rejoined the GPP, having earlier failed to gain the PPP's nomination. Moreover, several of those who performed relatively well in the previous election, such as Henry Jammeh and Jain Coli Fye, did not stand again.[144] Only one of its original leaders stood for election; M. L. Saho had of course long since abandoned the GPP and was in any case in poor health, and H. O. Semega-Janneh was not selected, after performing very poorly in 1987. However, the GPP did persuade one of the founders of the PPP, Bakary K. Sidibeh, to stand in Sami, and M. J. M. ("Babung") Phatty, who had been commissioner of the WD until his recent retirement from the civil service, contested Upper Fulladu West after being turned down by the PPP. Both men regarded themselves essentially as Independent candidates who had only a nominal affiliation with the GPP.[145]

The party brought out a partly revised version of its 1987 manifesto. It again attacked the government's record in the social and economic fields, as well as corruption in political life and set out its own remedies as before, including that "discipline should apply at all levels of endeavour."[146] Interestingly, foreign affairs did not feature in the 1992 manifesto (perhaps to avoid any reference to the sensitive relationship with Senegal) and a new entry on poverty was included. Like other opposition parties, the GPP found it difficult to present policies that were different from those being pursued by the PPP; at least to convince the electorate that they would be any more successful given the economic realities of the country. As in 1987, party leader Assan Musa Camara faced a particularly hard fight to try and regain his lost seat of Kantora, while at the same time trying to offer support to his colleagues, all on inadequate financial and organizational resources.

People's Democratic Organisation for Independence and Socialism

PDOIS fielded fourteen candidates in 1992, claiming it did not have sufficient time to stand in all thirty-six constituencies, a delay caused by the time-consuming egalitarian process adopted by the organization to arrive at democratically chosen candidates. These included Halifa Sallah in Serrekunda East and Sidia Jatta in Eastern Wuli. Half of its candidates contested seats in Banjul and Kombo St. Mary, with the remainder being scattered around provincial constituencies. The anticipated setback in 1987 sharpened its political skills, rather than driving it back to a passively critical position. One practical lesson learnt by PDOIS was to ensure that all its candidates had a set of the election regulations and a tape measure, to try and prevent PPP candidates from breaching them; particularly with regard to entering the proscribed area of the polling booths to attempt last-minute canvassing of voters.[147] But its political messages remained unchanged and its perception for the future was still "sometime utopian."[148] It found it hard to live down its Marxist past and other parties still condemned it as a communist and godless movement.[149]

People's Democratic Party[150]

The PDP was launched at Bakau on September 28, 1991 by a thirty-eight-year-old Mandinka private medical practitioner from Brikama in the Kombos, Dr. Lamin "Bolong" Bojang, a newcomer to national politics. In an interview with Hughes after the election, Bojang stated he was moved to take up politics by conditions in The Gambia on his return home from Cairo, in 1982, where he had studied medicine. Although influenced by Islam—the cow emblem of his party had Islamic connotations, as well as being the symbol of the farming community—he rejected fundamentalism when in Egypt. Still in government service in 1987, he kept out of that year's election. He considered joining PDOIS, but found its socialist politics unacceptable. Instead, he founded his own party in September 1991, with financial assistance from Solo Darbo, who, as noted, had been expelled from the

NCP in July. Darbo's financial backing was crucial to the fledgling and impecunious PDP. Having previously quarreled with President Jawara and the PPP as well, Darbo's involvement with Bojang might have been nothing more than score settling with the other parties. But he did provide sufficient financial backing for the PDP to put up a total of seventeen candidates and for Bojang to contest the presidential elections, as well as standing for Parliament in Central Kombo.

Although Bojang claimed that many key supporters came from other parties, the PDP's leading figures were former NCP members. Apart from Darbo, it recruited Jabel Sallah, the MP for Banjul South, to be its secretary general, and the MP for Sandu, A. K. Touray. Moreover, one of Bojang's many complaints about the PPP government was its alleged domination by Wolof, a charge that echoed criticisms made by the NCP on its foundation in the mid-1970s. Both Sallah and Touray stood for election; the former rather surprisingly chose to stand in Saloum, claiming that Banjul constituents were politically "backward" and dominated by local political bosses.[151]

According to the new party's brief manifesto, its political objectives differed little from those of other opposition parties (or even PDOIS) in that it claimed to be fighting for a democratic and corruption-free Gambia and to promote the social and economic well-being of its people within a market economy and liberal democratic system of government. However, it did condemn the NCP and GPP as parties of "PPP extraction" and therefore unlikely to be free of the ruling party's shortcomings. Yet the PDP joined GPP to publish a "petition" for electoral reform ahead of the elections, even threatening to boycott the polls if these were not carried out, and advised its supporters in constituencies where no PDP candidates were standing to vote for PDOIS or GPP. The PDP even avoided standing in Kantora to give Camara a better chance of recovering, even though the GPP put up a candidate in Central Kombo. Given its newness, inexperience, and lack of an original or realizable program, its prospects were not good. However, this did not stop Bojang from claiming that the PDP would win ten to fifteen seats.[152]

Independents and Women

As in 1972 and 1982, there was a marked increase in the number of Independent candidates to eleven. Several of these had stood previously for other parties or were rejected as candidates on this occasion. The best known of these were the former minister of economic planning and development, Dr. M. S. K. Manneh, and Lamin Waa Juwara. The former, who served as MP for Jokadu between 1977 and 1987 before being dropped by the PPP (as noted earlier) was attempting a comeback in his old constituency. The latter, who had unsuccessfully attempted to secure the PPP nomination, not only hailed from Niamina, but served as a divisional commissioner for fifteen years until being sacked as commissioner of the LRD in 1990. He was thus a well-known figure in the rural areas.[153]

Finally, three women stood for Parliament in 1992. Although still lamentably few, this was the largest number in any election. Amie Sillah stood for PDOIS in Banjul

South; Fatou Sanneh Colley represented GPP in Central Kombo; and a Banjul newspaper editor, Anna Frances Thomas, declared herself a feminist Independent in Banjul Central. Not surprisingly, given their gender and political affiliations, all fared poorly: Sillah won 236 votes; Sanneh Colley 142; and Thomas 63.[154]

Election Results

Although the PDP and GPP had originally threatened to boycott the election, all the opposition parties (as well as both local and international observers) considered it to have been the fairest in the country's history.[155] Certainly some of the odds against the opposition were evened out as far as access to the media was concerned, with opposition candidates being given equal access to Radio Gambia.[156] In addition, President Jawara agreed to stop PPP candidates using government vehicles for campaigning purposes and instructed divisional commissioners to stop chiefs acting partisanly toward the ruling party.[157] As a result, there were fewer opposition post-election accusations of electoral irregularities; only seven defeated candidates filed election petitions and five of these were from the PPP.[158] However, the usual mixture of Jawara's standing, sentimental appeal, and patronage led to the PPP's sixth victory. The election did see some inroads into the PPP's parliamentary majority, but Jawara's personal popularity remained high, even if reduced. On a turnout of 61.5 percent, well below that in 1987 (which perhaps reflected the increase in the registered electorate), the PPP gained 109,059 votes and won twenty-five seats. This was six fewer than in 1987 and its share of the vote also fell to 54.2 percent.[159] Indeed, on this occasion, the turnover of seats was much greater than in any election since independence. The government lost nine seats: four to the NCP, three to Independents, and two to the GPP. But it also recovered three seats from the NCP. The decision to retain M. M. Taal in Banjul South and A. A. N'Jie in Serrekunda West paid dividends as the PPP regained both constituencies; in addition, Kebba Jammeh defeated Fodayba Jammeh in Illiassa to end fifteen years of unbroken NCP control of this seat.

The NCP/UP coalition won six seats, one more than in 1987, but saw its number of votes fall to 48,845 and its share of the vote decline to 24.3 percent. Rather surprisingly, it managed to hold on to only two of the five seats it held at the dissolution of Parliament. Moreover, in both of these, its majority was cut; Dembo Bojang defeated Sam Sillah in Bakau by only 294 votes, and Foday Makalo's successor, Majanko Samusa, took Lower Baddibu by the even smaller margin of 191 votes. But to offset its losses elsewhere, Sheriff Dibba at last regained Central Baddibu, with a reasonably comfortable margin of victory over Dr. Lamin Saho; Ibrahim J. F. B. Sanyang, who mounted a strong challenge in the same seat in 1987, this time overcame the veteran PPP MP, Kuti Sanyang, in Western Foni[160]; and the party took advantage of the divisions within the local PPP constituency parties to win Eastern Jarra and Lower Niumi through a former PPP supporter, Momodou Saidywane and Jerreba Jammeh, respectively.[161] Although the NCP's successes were more evenly spread than in the past, with victories being achieved in four out of the seven

Administrative Areas, the results suggested that its support was diminishing in its core areas of the Baddibus and the urban areas around the capital.

The GPP won two seats, its first victories at the ballot box, despite a sharp fall in its total number of votes to 13,937 and its share of the vote to 6.9 percent. Mbemba Tambedou finally defeated M. C. Cham on his third attempt in Tumana, having successfully exploited Cham's errant behavior and poor record as a constituency MP, and Babung Phatty defeated Kebba Jawara in Upper Fulladu West. Despite these victories, the GPP generally performed poorly and failed even to rally MID and URD to its cause; Camara could manage only 43 percent of the vote in a two-way contest in Kantora and only one other candidate (Sidibeh) won more than 15 percent of the vote. Moreover, ominously for the GPP's future, both Tambedou and Phatty (along with the NCP's Momodou Saidywane) attempted to rejoin the PPP a few months after the election, but all the requests were rejected by the PPP's Central Committee. Cham appealed against Tambedou's victory and in March 1993, the Supreme Court ruled that Tambedou had failed to meet the six-month residential qualification to stand in Tumana. A by-election was subsequently conducted in June 1993, which Tambedou won again, with a greater majority.[162]

The failure of Dibba and Camara to merge their parties, or at least form an electoral coalition, as the NCP did with rump UP elements in Banjul, certainly weakened both parties, although how many additional seats could have been gained is hard to determine. Any further cooperation beyond a willingness to stand aside in a few selected seats was prevented in part by Dibba's continuing belief that he could take on the PPP unaided and by Camara's persisting distrust of him. Dibba still suffered from a public perception of tribalism and unbridled ambition on his part, fanned as in the past by government propagandists.

Neither PDOIS nor the PDP won any seats and gained only 2.3 percent (4,632 votes) and 4.6 percent (9,291 votes) of the vote, respectively. PDOIS's best result was in Banjul North, where Baboucarr Sise won 19 percent of the vote, but still placed only third in a four-cornered contest. One of the movement's founders, Sidia Jatta, was the runner up in Eastern Wuli, but took only 16 percent of the vote; Halifa Sallah gained just 11 percent in Serrekunda East to finish well behind both the PPP and NCP candidates. Clearly, therefore, the electorate found PDOIS's manifesto promises unconvincing. Meanwhile, the PDP's best result was in Sandu, where A. K. Touray won 34 percent of the vote without seriously threatening to unseat the PPP's Musa Drammeh. The PDP leader, Lamin Bojang, gained only 7 percent of the vote in his home constituency, Central Kombo.

The Independent candidates between them gained 7.6 percent of the vote (15,331 votes) and three were elected. Despite his problems at national level, Dr. M. S. K. Manneh secured more than twice as many votes as the PPP's Amadou Lowe, and Lamin Waa Juwara won Niamina. A newcomer, Almamy Abubacar Touray, narrowly defeated the PPP incumbent, Talib Bensouda, in Niani. The Supreme Court later ruled that a number of tokens from the presidential contest in Jokadu were incorrectly added to Manneh's total. However, he won the subsequent by-election in June 1993.[163]

An unusual aspect of the 1992 general elections was the high number of candidates who won on a minority vote—nine out of thirty-six—perhaps suggesting a degree of tactical voting as well as a profusion of aspirants; only in four constituencies were there two-cornered fights and in one constituency (Eastern Kiang), six contested. All three major parties benefited from this: PPP won three seats, NCP two, and GPP one; and all three Independent candidates won on a minority share of the vote.

Presidential Election

At the same time, the presidential election resulted in another easy victory for Jawara, who gained 117,549 votes (58.5 percent of those cast).[164] Although his share of the vote was marginally higher in 1987 at 58.7 percent, there were two fewer candidates in that election. Jawara continued to enjoy strong support across the country; he topped the poll in thirty-three out of thirty-six constituencies, including in eight where the PPP parliamentary candidate was defeated. In contrast, Dibba gained only 44,639 votes (22.2 percent), a decline of more than five percentage points from 1987, and headed the poll only in his home constituency of Central Baddibu and in Bakau and Lower Baddibu. Camara's share fell to 8.1 percent and Jawara defeated him by more than 600 votes even in Kantora. The remaining votes were won by Lamin Bojang, who did surprisingly well to win as much as 6.0 percent of the vote and Sidia Jatta, who took 5.2 percent. Although PDOIS determined to carry on the struggle, Bojang retreated from the political scene after his defeat.

Post-Election Cabinet Changes

After the elections, Jawara proceeded once again to reshuffle his cabinet. There were two major surprises. First, he brought in only one newcomer, Bubacarr Baldeh, who became minister of education, youth and culture and restored several "old guard" ministers, most notably Yaya Ceesay who returned to the cabinet for the first time since 1978 as minister of local government and lands. Second, Bakary Dabo was replaced as vice president by Saihou Sabally. Sabally's power base was further strengthened by being made minister of defense, the first time since the 1981 coup that anyone other than Jawara himself had held this office. To avoid alienating Dabo (as he had A. M. Camara after the 1982 election), Jawara appointed him minister of finance.[165] Presumably with Jawara's approval, Dabo soon established an Assets Management and Recovery Commission, which aimed to recover the huge loans given to prominent PPP politicians, senior civil servants, and leading businessmen by the now defunct GCDB and other government parastatals. But his efforts were hindered by powerful figures in the PPP and were largely unsuccessful, a sign perhaps that the president was no longer seriously interested in eradicating corruption.[166]

Prior to the 1992 election, there was speculation that Jawara would retire midway through the next Parliament and announce his chosen successor.[167] Whether that was indeed his intention is not clear; certainly he made no public decision regarding an heir before his overthrow in a military coup led by Yahya Jammeh in July 1994, which abruptly ended nearly thirty years of parliamentary democracy in The Gambia. Chapter 11 briefly discusses the reasons for the coup and then provides an assessment of the Jawara legacy.

Summary

Jawara and the PPP, having narrowly survived overthrow in the abortive coup of 1981, enjoyed over another decade of political success; this time defeating not only the established NCP, but three new parties and a new group of Independent candidates, in three elections. However, they failed again to tackle the deep-seated problem of political corruption, opening themselves up to a second and successful illegal seizure of power; this time from the very institution they had created to protect themselves with—the Gambian National Army.

10

THE GAMBIA'S EXTERNAL RELATIONS, 1965–94

At independence in February 1965, the Gambian government, like its counterparts in many other small states created out of randomly constructed former colonial dependencies, faced three major immediate and longer term challenges: to defend the country's national sovereignty, to promote economic and social development, and to ensure its own survival. An effective foreign policy was seen as an essential tool by which these challenges could successfully be met.[1]

Despite its unpromising political and economic situation at independence, Prime Minister (later President) Sir Dawda Jawara skillfully ensured that The Gambia achieved its primary foreign policy objective of retaining its sovereignty, albeit with difficulty in the 1980s. Moreover, by gradually developing good relations with a wide range of countries, including fellow African and fellow Muslim states, as well as with developed countries and communist states, Jawara made a major contribution to The Gambia's limited resources through securing substantial external aid; thus the second foreign policy aim was also fulfilled. To some extent, the third objective was also achieved, since the government's foreign policy making generally buttressed its domestic political standing and, more specifically, ensured that Senegal despatched troops to suppress the 1981 coup. But ultimately this objective was not met, since Jawara's high standing internationally failed to secure external intervention the second time his government was confronted by a coup in July 1994.

Characteristics of Decision Making in Foreign Policy[2]

Before independence, only a few Gambians had any experience of foreign policy making. As early as November 1960, Jawara, P. S. N'Jie and Omar M'Baki held discussions with the new Senegalese president, Léopold Senghor, in Dakar.[3] When chief minister in 1961, N'Jie initiated talks with the Senegalese government, and Jawara extended these responsibilities when the colony obtained internal self-government

251

in 1963. He was able to develop the process of establishing links with other African leaders, but it was only in 1965 that decision making became an entirely Gambian responsibility. Even then, inexperience and lack of resources led the new Gambian administration to turn to the British government and its local representative (the British high commissioner) for both formal and informal advice and assistance.[4] In addition, in December 1966, Jawara appointed K. W. J. (Winton) Lane (a British expatriate who was previously his permanent secretary) as his special adviser. Because Lane was also employed as the United Nation's (UN) regional association adviser between 1967 and 1970, he was in a particularly good position to counsel Jawara on relations with Senegal.[5]

Although the formal organizational structure of foreign policy decision making was based on the British system, in practice both the determination and conduct of external relations reflected new African political realities. As in domestic politics, so in external affairs; the drift toward presidentialism gave increasing power to Jawara.[6] Even when prime minister, he assumed a key role both in setting out his country's foreign policy and in conducting diplomacy. The Ministry of External Affairs (MEA) was initially located in the Office of the Prime Minister, with Jawara holding the ministerial portfolio himself, while A. B. N'Jie acted as minister of state and Gambian high commissioner in Dakar. It was only in April 1967 that N'Jie took over the foreign ministry (but only until January 1968, although he served again between 1974 and 1977). Moreover, he, like his successors, Andrew (Assan Musa) Camara (1968–74), Lamin Kitty Jabang (1977–87), and Omar Sey (1987–94) had any influence on decision making limited by the dominant role of Jawara and a handful of other advisers outside the MEA.[7] Chief among the latter was the head of the civil service—the secretary general. The first secretary general, Eric Christensen, was also secretary to the cabinet and permanent secretary in the MEA, and was widely credited with enjoying considerable influence on external relations during the early years of independence.[8] After 1970, the new Office of the President came to rival the cabinet and individual ministries in decision making, as access to the head of state helped to determine influence on decision making. Jawara's political longevity also contributed to his ascendancy; whereas ministers and senior civil servants came and went, Jawara remained in power throughout the period.

Apart from the personalization of power around the president, the other feature of official decision making was its elitist and bureaucratic nature. Foreign policy, in particular, was limited to a small group of ministers and non-elected officials. The relative remoteness of foreign policy issues (with some important exceptions, such as relations with Senegal) and the higher level of specialist knowledge required to permit informed participation, strengthened the hand of unelected officials. Ministers, both in cabinet and in those departments of state that impinged on external relations, were involved in decision making—policy matters were brought to cabinet by ministers as well as the president—and decisions were taken on a consensual basis. But these usually reflected options that had already been determined by the head of state and an inner clique of advisers;

the wider political community had very little influence. Even the central organs of the ruling party, the People's Progressive Party (PPP), rarely strayed into foreign policy matters, preferring to leave matters to their secretary general, Jawara.

The same was true of the House of Representatives. It was not solely the overwhelming majority enjoyed by the PPP and the absence of backbench criticism that accounted for this. As an analysis of parliamentary debates revealed, both PPP and opposition members of Parliament (MPs) were principally interested in domestic issues, particularly the needs of their constituencies.[9] The former were usually, although not invariably, content to leave the more arcane area of foreign policy to the head of state and his advisers.[10] The latter (with rare exceptions, notably Garba-Jahumpa before 1968)[11] generally preferred to scrutinize government domestic policy, particularly in respect of access to developmental resources, to raising foreign policy issues. This approach satisfied the electorate, which viewed political participation as largely to do with extracting resources from the government to satisfy local wants.

Outside Parliament, the relatively underdeveloped nature of civil society meant that organs of public opinion did not exist to the same degree as in the developed world. The indigenous press was limited largely to a handful of under-resourced roneo-ed newspapers; there were few pressure groups with an interest in foreign policy issues and these were principally concerned with African liberation themes. Even the overwhelmingly Islamic character of Gambian society did not immediately influence government attitudes. The Gambian populace was prepared to be led, rather than to demand a defining role, with respect to external affairs, which gave the executive considerable latitude in determining and conducting foreign policy.[12]

Foreign Policy Objectives[13]

The principal objectives of the Gambian government's foreign policy under Jawara and the PPP may be summarized as follows. First, it was determined to defend the newly gained sovereignty of The Gambia, particularly given the country's straitened resources. This involved demonstrating its independence of Britain, its former colonial metropole, and defining an effective relationship with Senegal, The Gambia's only contiguous neighbor and one whose interests were already closely entwined with its own. Second, the government sought to pursue the interlinked goal of economic and social development, both to overcome the potentially fatal resource weaknesses of The Gambia, and to consolidate public support for ruler and party. Third, it aimed to ensure the stability and survival of the regime. Given its strong identification with the achievement and defining of nation-statehood, this objective closely overlapped with the first. Calvert would go further in arguing that foreign policy in new states is little more than the means to project the image of rulers internationally, to satisfy their egos and enhance their prestige at home.[14] Jawara, certainly, mixed with the internationally power-ful and had many opportunities to be photographed with them at international gatherings and on official visits abroad, but the purpose of such opportunities was more to serve the second objective of foreign policy as outlined.

These related foreign policy objectives required flexibility and adaptability in their pursuit and the avoidance of extreme, restricting, or inflexible posturing. Moderation and pragmatism came to characterize the Gambian leadership's approach to issues. Although Jawara was steadfastly committed to such moral or ideological issues as African liberation, anti-racism, third-world development, and human rights (at a time when few other African leaders were prepared to denounce the oppressive policies of many of their fellow rulers), the "ethical dimension" of foreign policy was tempered with a large measure of pragmatic self-interest; a concern driven by the new and vulnerable small country's uncertain future.[15] Jawara was to demonstrate great diplomatic skills and considerable suc-cess in "punching above his weight" in the international arena, even if his critics regularly complained about his frequent absences from Banjul and the high costs of overseas forays. Such an approach, then, was more than the reactive foreign policy attributed to micro-states; as also argued by Denton, foreign policy was as much a proactive instrument to serve national and leadership needs.[16] The skilful use of diplomacy would make it an additional national resource; in certain cir-cumstances, the very smallness of The Gambia could be exploited to advantage.

Gambian External Relations

In the period immediately after independence, Gambian foreign policy was focused on the country's relationships with Britain and Senegal; indeed, initially The Gambia only had permanent diplomatic missions in these two countries through high commissioners.[17] However, Jawara and his government gradually developed a wide range of other external ties. Politically, The Gambia's most important rela-tionship was with Senegal, although its connections with other West African states were also significant at different times, not least so that these countries could act as a counterbalance to Senegalese influence. Economically, The Gambia's relations with Britain and other Western countries were the most important, although its ties to Arab states became of much greater significance in the 1980s.

The following section examines these relationships in turn, beginning with The Gambia's relations with Senegal and with other West African countries. This is fol-lowed by a discussion of its relations with Britain and other Western powers; with the Islamic world (including Libya and Morocco); and finally with the Communist bloc.

Relations with Senegal before Gambian Independence: 1960–65[18]

Once Senegal gained independence from France in 1960 (initially between June and August 1960, as part of the Mali Federation), the question of its future political and economic relationship with Gambia became a critical issue for all parties concerned: the British government, the Senegalese government under President Senghor, and Gambian political leaders who were influenced, at least to some extent, by local public opinion.

The British government's position was firmly established by 1960. Once the two alternative proposals of "full integration" and federation between Sierra Leone and Gambia had been ruled out, the Colonial Office, the Foreign Office, and both governors of Gambia before independence, Sir Edward Windley (1957–62) and John Paul (1962–65), all favored some form of close association between Gambia and Senegal within "Senegambia." Although there was a genuine belief that Gambia could not be economically viable as an independent state, other considerations also played a part; the British government was clearly reluctant to take on what it was assumed would be a long-term financial commitment to the new country.[19] Initially, it was hoped that association would occur before the end of colonial rule, but in December 1962, Duncan Sandys, the secretary of state for the colonies, stated in the House of Commons that if a satisfactory basis for association could be agreed, then independence would be granted to Gambia.[20] However, by early 1964, the British position had shifted: it was now willing to offer independence whether or not such an agreement had been reached.[21]

The position of the Senegalese government was also clear-cut in 1960–64: it desired the eventual merger of Senegal and Gambia. The latter would become Senegal's eighth province, while retaining a high degree of internal autonomy (for example, Gambia would retain its own laws, education system, and Parliament and English would remain as the official language).[22]

There were a number of ideological, economic and strategic reasons why the Senegalese sought a merger with their smaller neighbor. First, Senghor was a leading advocate of African unity and had been the driving force behind the formation of the Mali Federation in April 1959 as a means of retaining the union of French-speaking West Africa. Despite its collapse in August 1960, Senghor remained committed to the concept of African unity, although understandably his experiences of precipitate political merger dissuaded him from forcing the pace over Gambia. Perhaps unlike other Senegalese ministers, he was certainly never prepared to use force to achieve this end.[23]

Second, the Senegalese considered that closer ties with Gambia would produce a number of practical economic advantages. The most important of these would be a reduction in the re-export trade (or "smuggling" as the Senegalese authorities preferred to call it) from Gambia. This served to reduce the revenue from customs that the Senegalese government derived from its own imports. Since the 1920s, goods imported into Bathurst had subsequently been exported into Senegal and other colonies in West Africa because of their availability and lower cost.[24] This trade was particularly extensive in the early 1960s because of the marked differences in the import policies of the two countries. Whereas Gambia encouraged free trade (including from low-cost producers such as Japan) and had relatively low import charges, the Senegalese government imposed import quotas,

payment restrictions, and high import tariffs. The cost of living was also conservatively estimated to be 30 to 50 percent higher in Dakar than in Bathurst.[25] It was
estimated in the mid-1960s, that smuggled imports amounted to less than 1 percent of Senegal's total imports and that the value of customs duties lost by smuggling represented only 2 percent of its revenue from import duties.[26]
Nevertheless, smuggling remained an irritant to the Senegalese government,
which considered that an economic union, either as part of an overall political
union or as a precursor of it, would lead to common economic borders and the
elimination of the tax differentials that allowed the contraband traffic to flourish.
It should also be noted that groundnuts were smuggled across the border,
although the direction of this trade tended to vary according to whether the price
paid to farmers was higher in one country or the other and whether payment was
by cash or credit. Thus, this factor was less important as a reason for Senegal to
seek economic union.[27]

The eradication of smuggling was not the only probable economic benefit to
Dakar of an economic union. The export of its groundnut crop, which was rendered more difficult by the loss of access to Malian railways following the break up
of the Mali Federation, would be facilitated by fuller use of the River Gambia.
Gambia might also prove to be a useful market for Senegalese manufactured
products.[28] But these advantages might be offset by the likelihood that at least part
of the considerable French financial assistance to Senegal might be diverted to
Gambia. Indeed, the Senegalese government preferred publicly to present economic union as a cost, rather than as a benefit, to itself.[29]

The final, and undoubtedly the most important, reason in the view of the
Senegalese government was that closer political ties with Gambia would ease its
security concerns. These were threefold. First, it feared that an independent
Gambia might develop close ties with more radical governments in West Africa
(Ghana, Guinea, and Mali under Kwame Nkrumah, Sékou Touré, and Modibo
Keita, respectively) with which it was at odds politically. It was therefore determined to prevent Gambia from developing an independent (and possibly hostile)
foreign policy.[30] Second, it was worried that it might provide a haven for its own
internal dissidents, such as the supporters of its imprisoned former prime minister, Mamadou Dia.[31] Third, a political association would help the Dakar government to deal with any future challenges posed by the predominantly Dioula (Jola)
people living in its southern province of Casamance. The shortest and quickest
route from northern Senegal to Casamance lay through Gambian territory via the
Trans-Gambia Ferry at Farafenni (in the absence of a bridge across the river). This
avoided the long detour around the eastern half of Gambia. Political union would
allow direct Senegalese control of the river crossing, so that military convoys could
be given priority.[32]

Gambian calculations of the benefits of closer ties with Senegal were somewhat
different. Gambian political leaders recognized that there would be some economic advantages from closer integration with Senegal; these included, in the
short term, the sharing of diplomatic missions in countries where Senegal was

already represented and, in the longer term, the integrated development of the Gambia River basin. For example, a report prepared by the Food and Agricultural Organisation in 1964 somewhat optimistically suggested that construction of a dam in the upper river could permit the irrigation of thousands of acres and the generation of several hundred million kilowatts of electricity.[33]

These advantages were, however, more than outweighed by the likelihood that the cost of living in Gambia would increase considerably if tariff structures were equalized at Senegalese levels through a customs union and the loss of customs revenue on imported goods would be considerable if the re-export trade ceased. It was estimated in the early 1960s that goods imported into Gambia and then smuggled into Senegal represented between 10 and 15 percent of Gambian imports and produced about 15 percent of Gambia's total revenue from import duty. It therefore made a significant contribution to Gambian revenue; import duties were second only to the levy imposed on groundnut exports.[34] In addition, local businessmen in Bathurst who were involved in the re-export trade, such as Momodou Musa N'Jie, had no desire for it to cease.[35]

There was even less enthusiasm for any kind of political union. It was assumed that this would adversely affect the position of Gambian political leaders, who would be denied the full fruits of independence; English-speaking civil servants, who feared that they might lose out to French speakers if closer relations were established; and lawyers and other professionals, who were concerned that the value given to their status and qualifications would be reduced.[36] Political union would also almost certainly prevent Gambia joining the Commonwealth after independence, a goal desired by all political parties.[37]

Domestic political calculations also affected the responses of Gambian politicians during the first half of the 1960s. The Wolof United Party (UP) leader, P. S. N'Jie, initially favored closer links with the predominantly Wolof-dominated Senegalese state. When briefly chief minister in 1961, following the granting of limited power sharing, he had initiated discussions with the Senegalese prime minister, Mamadou Dia, on future relations between the two countries in the hope of improving his precarious political position. Dia and Valdiodio N'Diaye, the Senegalese minister of interior (a cousin of N'Jie's) visited Bathurst in April 1961, the main outcome being the establishment of an Inter-Ministerial Committee, which met for the first time in 1962.[38] But the committee achieved little and N'Jie derived no tangible political advantage from his pro-Senegalese stance. After the UP's defeat in the 1962 election, he turned against the idea of closer ties with Senegal; thereafter he sought to castigate Jawara for trying to "sell" the country and the UP (partially) boycotted an official visit by Senghor to Bathurst in March 1964. His party's stance was in part influenced by its disproportionate support in the Bathurst area, particularly from businessmen and civil servants who feared for their livelihoods.[39]

The PPP leader, D. K. Jawara, was initially more wary of Senegalese intentions, not least because of their perceived support for P. S. N'Jie.[40] However, the Senegalese government allegedly provided some financial assistance to the PPP prior to the 1962 election. After the election, Jawara openly expressed support for closer political links with Senegal in the form of a confederation, although he was determined that this should not be at the expense of the country's impending political independence.[41] It was on his initiative that in October 1962, the UN was jointly invited by the Gambian and Senegalese governments to examine the possible forms of political relationship between their two countries. After some delay, the UN team of Swiss and Dutch experts, headed by Dr. H. J. van Mook, arrived in West Africa in October 1963 and submitted its report to the Gambian and Senegalese governments in April 1964.[42]

The van Mook report identified three options: political and economic union through the complete integration of Gambia into an enlarged Senegal; a Senegambia federation, which would initially be limited to defense, foreign policy, and external representation and would gradually be extended; or a looser entente, which would promote political integration gradually by means of closer functional cooperation. The UN team's preference was for the second option, but accepted that, in the existing climate of opinion, probably only the third was feasible. It also recommended the establishment of a customs union and an import quota system.[43]

The UN report was discussed by the two governments in Dakar and Bathurst in May and June 1964. The Gambian government first proposed the establishment of a confederation that would be responsible for handling all matters of defense (including internal security), foreign policy, and overseas representation for both countries; the new body would be headed by a Council of Ministers with an equal number of Gambian and Senegalese ministers, with Senghor as president and Jawara as vice president. This suggestion was apparently not wholeheartedly supported by all PPP ministers. However, the proposal was rejected by the Senegalese government, which feared that the Gambian solution might create as many problems as the ill-fated Mali Federation. It therefore proposed the establishment of a powerful unitary central government, which would be responsible for all Gambian affairs except for its civil service and its legal and educational systems. This in turn was rejected by the Gambian side, which also rejected both the customs union and import quotas.[44]

Although the negotiations were generally unsuccessful, the two sides did eventually sign two treaties to cover defense and security and foreign policy. It was agreed that foreign and defense policies would be harmonized, with Jawara discussing all matters of external representation in Gambia with the Senegalese before reaching a decision, and the Gambians would share Senegal's diplomatic missions in nine countries. Senegal also raised no objections to Gambia joining the Commonwealth and promised to provide military training and technical assistance for the Gambian Field Force should Jawara request it.[45] P. S. N'Jie subsequently argued that the treaties should only be ratified if supported by a referendum (as well as approved by Parliament) on the grounds that they implied a loss of Gambian sovereignty, but his arguments were rejected by the secretary of the state for the colonies and the treaties duly came into force in February 1965.[46]

Both governments seem to have been reasonably satisfied with the outcome of the talks in Dakar. Senghor remained sanguine about an eventual political union; his view was that Gambia's economic difficulties would ultimately lead its government to establish closer ties. Jawara, on the other hand, was disappointed by the Senegalese attitude toward confederation.[47] However, because the British government was now willing to grant independence in any circumstances, the Gambian government's rejection of the more constrictive political options would ensure the country's sovereignty; it would also permit it to retain links with Britain and pursue additional relationships with other newly independent countries in the region.

Relations with Senegal from Independence to Confederation: 1965–82

In the first few years after independence, some progress was made in developing the economic links between the two countries, but the unexpected improvement in the Gambian economy, as described in Chapter 1, made these links less pressing. During a visit to The Gambia by Senghor in April 1967, Senegal and The Gambia entered into a somewhat vague Treaty of Association that aimed at extending coordination and cooperation between the two countries in all fields.[48] As a result of this treaty, a Senegalo-Gambian Permanent Secretariat (which was based in Bathurst/Banjul, but had a Senegalese secretary general) was eventually established in 1968 to make a reality of the broad agreements that were reached.[49] A trade agreement followed in 1970, and a treaty in 1973 granted Senegalese manufactured goods a preferential margin in The Gambia. There were also a number of other technical and cultural agreements that aimed at improving relations between the two states. However, according to Denton, few of these were actually ratified.[50]

Progress would have been greater if the relationship of the two countries had not deteriorated in the late 1960s and early 1970s. In January 1969, the Senegalese minister of finance and economic affairs, Jean Collin, announced that the increased level of smuggling by Gambians was an act of "economic aggression"; in reiterating this line, Senghor added that this constituted a "mortal peril" to the Senegalese state.[51] This was despite the fact that Senegalese traders (particularly politically well-connected merchants from the Mouride stronghold of Touba) were preeminent in the cross-border contraband trafficking.[52] Subsequently, Senegalese border guards violated Gambian sovereignty by crossing the border from Casamance to seize Gambian citizens who were believed to be involved in the trade. The Gambian populace reacted furiously. During a periodic heads-of-state visit to Banjul in February 1969, President Senghor had to face the anger of Gambian crowds; Senegalese flags were burnt, tear gas was used for the first time since 1961 to curb a demonstration, and Senghor subsequently stated that he never wished to visit The Gambia again.[53] The Senegalese responded first by trying (unsuccessfully) to persuade Jawara to accept a customs union and import quotas and then by tightening up the border to such an extent that the legitimate border trade between the two countries virtually ground to a halt. As noted below, this in turn persuaded Jawara to seek a defense agreement with Britain as a counter to Senegal.[54]

In January 1971, trouble flared up again. First, two Senegalese customs officers pursued a lorry carrying groundnuts from Casamance into Gambian territory and allegedly threatened a group of Gambian villagers. Second, and more seriously, a fortnight later, around 150 Senegalese troops entered the village of Jiborah (located just inside The Gambia), arrested three Gambians and took them to Ziguinchor before releasing them. As noted in Chapter 8, the radical organization, the Kent Street Vous, organized a demonstration in Bathurst which resulted in some damage to Senegalese properties; in addition, the Gambian government protested strongly to the Senegalese and made a formal complaint to the United Nations.[55]

Once again, relations between the two countries subsequently improved, but three years later, the issue resurfaced when Senegalese forces arrested around twenty Gambians in two separate incidents in July 1974; this led to strong protests by the Gambian government.[56] In addition, there was a dispute over ownership of some twenty-eight border villages in the Kantora area. Senghor eventually diplomatically yielded on the boundary dispute and all save two of the contested villages were recognized as part of Gambian territory by a border commission in 1976 (although it was to be 1979 before both countries ratified the new boundary).[57]

In 1975, the improving relationship between the two countries led to the establishment of a Coordinating Committee to develop the Gambia River basin. This committee was upgraded in 1978 into the Gambia River Basin Development Organisation (L'organisation pour la mise en valeur de la fleuve gambienne [OMVG]), along the lines of the earlier OMVS (for the Senegal River). It was charged with devising and implementing plans for the joint exploitation of the river resources, including the construction of a barrage and/or a bridge in the Yelitenda area of Central Gambia, adjacent to the existing, but inadequate, Farafenni ferry crossing (which was prone to breaking down). The aim was to make the two oil-dependent countries self-sufficient in hydroelectric power and to bring an additional 24,000 acres of irrigated land under cultivation (mainly to grow rice) in central Gambia, at a time when drought was increasingly becoming a problem. The exploitation of iron ore deposits in Eastern Senegal would also be facilitated. The Gambian preference was for a bridge/barrage to facilitate rice cultivation, and the Senegalese favored a bridge for improved communication with the Casamance. But the project faced a number of delays.[58]

If progress toward economic integration was slow, in the early years of independence, the Gambian government did consult with the Senegalese government over foreign policy matters and also, on at least one occasion, handed over its internal dissidents to it.[59] Indeed, security ties between the two countries were generally strengthened during this period. As early as August 1965, the Senegalese government was seeking to persuade the Gambians to suggest conditions under which it would intervene militarily in the case of internal disturbance. The Gambians were reluctant to do so at this stage; they were concerned that if the Senegalese sent in troops, they might be unwilling to pull them out. However, at a meeting of the Inter-Ministerial Committee in Dakar in June 1967, an agreement was reached. The Senegalese government then confirmed that it would intervene in the event of internal Gambian disorder and specified which Gambian ministers and officials could appeal for Senegalese assistance.[60] As discussed in Chapter 8, this agreement was to be invoked twice by the Gambian government, first in October 1980 after the assassination of Eku Mahoney and second, and more important, following the 1981 coup.[61]

Senegal was particularly willing to accede to Gambian appeals for help in the early 1980s because of its own security concerns. Following the overthrow of Kwame Nkrumah in 1966 and Modibo Keita in 1968, the threat from these sources had receded, but new dangers emerged in the late 1970s, particularly from Libya. As discussed in Chapter 8, the Senegalese now feared that the Gambian government would be overthrown by Marxists backed by Libya, with which it severed diplomatic relations in 1980. It was also concerned by the threat posed by Muslim fundamentalists, particularly Sheikh Ahmed Niasse of Kaolack, who was himself backed by Libya, and was alleged to have recruited Gambians working in Nigeria for military training in Libya.[62] A further security issue became more pressing from 1980 when the underlying tensions between separatists in the Casamance and the Senegalese government in Dakar flared up into open conflict between the Mouvement des Forces Démocratiques de la Casamance (MFDC) and Senegalese security forces. Violent clashes were to become a serious problem and continued into the post-Jawara period, despite several attempts at peace talks and cease fires.[63]

Senegambia Confederation: 1982–89[64]

Perhaps not surprisingly, the relationship between the two countries changed dramatically as a result of the coup and the subsequent Senegalese intervention. The Gambian government's total dependence on the Senegalese military, which was symbolized by the fact that, as noted in Chapter 8, Jawara returned to Banjul in early August 1981 with a Senegalese security escort,[65] provided President Abdou Diouf (who had succeeded Senghor in January 1981) with the opportunity to advance more rapidly the cause of interstate union between the two countries. In fact, it appears to have been Jawara who proposed that a confederation be established at a meeting in Dakar on August 19, perhaps to deflect the pressure from the Senegalese government for a federation.[66] During a visit to The Gambia by Diouf in November 1981, only a few months after the suppression of the coup, the two presidents announced their intention to form a Senegambia Confederation at Kaur. On December 17, the Confederal Agreement was duly signed by the two presidents in Dakar and on December 29, it was simultaneously endorsed by near unanimous votes in the Gambian House of Representatives and the Senegalese National Assembly. The confederation came into effect on February 1, 1982.[67]

The Treaty of Confederation laid down that the Senegalese and Gambian heads of state should respectively become president and vice president of the new body. They were to be served by an administrative office headed by a Senegalese secretary general and assisted by nine ministers. All five Senegalese ministers in the inaugural Council of Ministers, which met for the first time in January 1983, were full ministers, whereas two of the four Gambians were deputies; however, a Gambian, Sheriff Sisay, did hold the important position of confederal minister of finance. An indirectly elected confederal Parliament, whose sixty members were chosen by the two national Parliaments, also met for the first time in January 1983; forty of these were nominated by the Senegalese National Assembly and twenty by the Gambian House of Representatives. Because any decision by the confederal Parliament had to be passed by a majority of three-quarters of its members present and voting, this imbalance did not matter greatly.[68] The funding of the confederal institutions was also constituted according to the same two-thirds/one-third formula. Although this meant that The Gambia was overrepresented in relation to its population, which was little more than one-tenth that of Senegal, it bore a disproportionate share of the costs, given its much smaller economy and revenues.[69]

The Confederal Agreement stipulated that the confederation would be based on the development of an economic and monetary union; the coordination of policy in external relations; the coordination of policy in communications and other technical areas; and the integration of the armed forces and security forces of The Gambia and Senegal.[70] This final protocol, which was signed by the two presidents in January 1983, essentially legalized the Senegalese military presence in The Gambia. A substantial number of Senegalese security forces personnel remained in The Gambia after the suppression of the 1981 coup and were eventually reconstituted as Senegambian or confederal soldiers and gendarmes in 1986. The confederal security establishment was meant to be made up of Senegalese (two-thirds) and Gambians (one-third). It was also intended that the costs be divided in the same proportion. Political control of these forces was again, technically, the responsibility of the confederal executive in Dakar. The decision to deploy the confederal security forces, including the right to declare a state of emergency in any part of the confederation (which challenged the rights of the Gambian head of state and Parliament, where such powers resided) thus lay with the Senegalese president, advised by the Gambian head of state; both were ultimately subject to the confederal Parliament.[71]

Undoubtedly, the terms of the treaty favored Senegal. Yet, it was the best agreement that the Gambians could have obtained under the circumstances of total military dependence on Dakar in 1981–82. Government and party propaganda sought to minimize the inevitable erosion of sovereignty implicit in the protocols of confederation, with Jawara emphasizing the difference between a confederation and a federation. They also justified their necessity by means of familiar appeals to the "natural" unity of the two peoples and the "unquestionable" advantages to be gained from a pooling of resources and a convergence of policies in respect of developing the Senegambia region.[72] Indeed, as outlined below, the structure and powers of the confederation came to represent more closely the preferences of the Gambian leadership and people than those of Senegal, despite Jawara being in the weaker bargaining position.

As both ruling parties enjoyed enormous parliamentary majorities and the decision was taken at a time of national crisis in The Gambia, it is not surprising that opposition to confederation was muted and limited to the modalities of its implementation, rather than to the decision itself. Initially, in fact, the PPP rallied strongly behind Jawara's decision to proceed way beyond what previously had been regarded as the limits to any loss of national sovereignty in respect of Senegal. PPP MPs appear to have supported the president from the same mixture of pragmatism and idealism that Jawara himself expressed, with all thirty-two who were present in the House voting for the establishment of the confederation in December 1981 and at least twenty of these speaking in favor of the motion.[73] PPP MPs also apparently welcomed the development of closer ties with the ruling party in Senegal, the Parti Socialiste, through the formation of a joint committee.[74]

The main opposition party, the Parti Démocratique du Sénégal (PDS), which probably held fourteen seats in the Senegalese National Assembly at the time, apparently voted for the confederation in December 1982.[75] In contrast, the three National Convention Party (NCP) MPs who remained in Parliament, Foday Makalo, Fodayba Jammeh, and Dembo Bojang, all walked out of the House before the vote was taken, condemning the rapidity of the action and the failure to consult the opposition over the issue; they did not, however, explicitly condemn the idea.[76] In the absence of a referendum, it is difficult to gauge the extent of public support for the confederation, although the PPP's overwhelming victory in the 1982 election perhaps suggested that at the outset there was at least qualified acceptance of it. But there was certainly little enthusiasm for confederation, or even much interest in it; it was noticeable how little public attention was paid to the deliberations of the confederal assembly, even though attempts were made to create interest through official publications and newspaper reporting.[77]

The confederal Parliament and the Council of Ministers met for the first time in January 1983 and thereafter held meetings twice a year.[78] But despite this, little progress was made on the economic front. Joint commissions of experts were set up in the aftermath of the 1981 coup to try and work out acceptable conditions for an economic union and the issue was clearly of particular concern to Diouf,[79] but nothing had been achieved by the time of the dissolution of the confederation in 1989.

The two principal sticking points were the extent of economic integration and the future of the Gambian currency—the dalasi. On the first issue, Senegal favored the establishment of a full customs union to reduce or eliminate the re-export trade of manufactured goods from The Gambia, whereas The Gambia preferred a looser free trade agreement. On the second, the Senegalese government insisted that the two countries should jointly seek membership of the West African Monetary Union, the regional currency and banking system based on the

CFA franc, which was linked to the French franc. The Gambian government, on the other hand, wished to enter the monetary union as a separate member, so emphasizing rather than diminishing its sovereignty.[80] As a result of the failure to achieve economic integration, there was no evidence of any reduction in smuggling, which was estimated in this period to cost Senegal CFA 20 billion a year.[81]

Moreover, despite the signing of a range of confederal protocols in the fields of defense and security, foreign policy harmonization, technical cooperation, and the creation of the political institutions, nothing substantial was achieved by 1989 in these or other areas.[82] Even the proposals to develop the Gambia River basin came to nothing. Despite a succession of proposals which sought to refine the projects to make them environmentally and financially attractive, potential external financial backing for the scheme was limited. It was subsequently put off altogether by a negative environmental audit by a team from the University of Michigan in 1985, which voiced concerns about the environmental damage resulting from such a project and rising estimated costs.[83] Moreover, at least in the view of the Senegalese press, which alleged that the MFDC had bases in Brikama and Serrekunda and that The Gambia acted as a transit point for shipment of arms to the MFDC, the confederation did little to improve Senegal's security situation.[84]

One reason for the slow progress toward closer union was that Jawara, conscious of Senegal's longer term unificationist objectives, and mindful of the long-standing distrust toward their next-door neighbor among his own people, sought to prolong the negotiations to implement them.[85] Given the initial weakness of his position, he proved remarkably successful in fashioning the relationship so that it reflected Gambian priorities more than those of Senegal. Another factor may have been that by the later 1980s, The Gambia's economic situation had improved markedly as a result of the Economic Recovery Programme (ERP) and so its government felt much more confident about its future economic viability.[86]

The general lack of progress did, however, result in mounting disenchantment with the Senegambia Confederation among both Gambians and Senegalese. At the establishment of the confederation, the Senegalese had had expectations of using the existing agreement as the means to complete economic, and eventually political, union. The Senegalese leadership (and press, in particular) found it increasingly hard to restrain their criticism of what they regarded as Gambian prevarication and evasion, particularly as Senegal was footing most of the bill.[87]

Gambians, in turn, became more and more disenchanted with even the limited concessions made and both the process and details of confederation led to a revision of their earlier more positive attitudes. Some PPP leaders increasingly criticized the imbalance within the confederation and argued that economic and social benefits to the country were not as certain as had been previously assumed.[88] Specific issues also contributed to the growing disillusionment of Gambians. Many were unhappy about the permanent relegation of their head of state, despite his seniority in age and length of political office, to the vice presidency of the confederation. They expected that, after a while, the posts of president and vice president would rotate between the two countries.[89] Clashes between

Senegalese soldiers and Gambian civilians contributed further to Gambian disenchantment. The most damaging incident occurred at the National Stadium in Bakau in 1985, when the Senegalese high commissioner in Banjul ordered Senegalese forces to quell disturbances at a football match by force. This unilateral action outraged the Gambian public, painfully reminding them of the subordinate nature of their relationship with Senegal, and led the government to insist on the diplomat's recall.[90]

Public opposition to confederation, at least in the urban areas, was fuelled first by the Movement for Justice in Africa—The Gambia (MOJA-G) and then by the People's Democratic Organisation for Independence and Socialism (PDOIS) through its *Foroyaa* newspaper. PDOIS' pamphlets (including a long one denouncing the nature of the relationship with Senegal) extended its radical critique of PPP foreign policy to include dependence on, and subservience to, Senegal; confederation was portrayed as politically demeaning and economically disadvantageous to the Gambian people. Although the NCP and the Gambia People's Party (GPP) were generally careful not to make their stance on confederation clear, the latter was regarded as too pro-confederation and this explains in part its unexpectedly poor performance in the 1987 election. However, PDOIS' strongly anti-Senegalese stance did not markedly improve its political fortunes, although its critique gave added arguments to those ministers who were critical of Senegal.[91]

The Collapse of the Senegambia Confederation and Beyond: 1989–94

Although opposition to the confederation had grown during the 1980s, its sudden collapse in 1989 still surprised many observers. In May 1989, border conflict erupted between Senegal and its northern neighbor, Mauritania. Mutual attacks on each other's citizens led the Senegalese to strengthen their forces on the border and Mauritanian citizens to flee across the Gambian boundary to seek refuge. The Senegalese government was critical of The Gambia's failure to rally to its support, seeing it as inconsistent with the protocols and spirit of the confederation.[92] The tension between the two countries increased when, on August 1, 1989, Jawara demanded that the posts of confederal president and vice president be rotated between the two countries. This proposed change to the confederal Agreement was interpreted by Dakar as a delaying tactic to closer union and as a "disloyal" act given the crisis. A few weeks later, on August 18, the Senegalese government, without consultation with the Gambian government, withdrew its troops, ostensibly to reinforce its forces on the border with Mauritania.[93] Four days later, Diouf announced that confederation would be put "on ice" until The Gambia displayed greater enthusiasm for extending economic integration.[94] Jawara responded to this situation by initiating the necessary legal measure to dissolve the confederation in September and it was formally wound up in December by the Gambian Parliament.[95]

In the wake of the collapse of the Senegambia Confederation, relations between Dakar and Banjul cooled once again. Although both governments spoke still of the historic fraternity existing between their two peoples and the necessity of maintaining practical links, the Senegalese authorities adopted a policy that challenged both these assumptions. Tight restrictions were placed on interstate trade, and Gambian travelers to Senegal experienced considerable bureaucratic harassment. These measures, which were justified by the Senegalese as necessary to combat smuggling, were regarded by many Gambians as a form of "punishment" for abandoning the confederation. They also demonstrated the vulnerability of the Gambian economy to Senegalese economic sanctions; both in respect of its vital regional re-export trade and some key imports, such as bottled gas for commercial and domestic use.[96] It was only in January 1991 that a new Treaty of Friendship and Co-operation was signed by the two countries, which, although providing for annual meetings of the two heads of state and the creation of a new joint commission to handle matters of common concern, effectively turned the clock back some thirty years in respect of the ties between them.[97]

Two years later, in September 1993, relations between the two countries took a sudden downturn when the Senegalese government reinforced its border and transit trade controls. As discussed in Chapter 1, the effect was to lower the value of The Gambia's re-export trade between 1992–93 and 1993–94 by 22 percent and thus considerably reduce its foreign exchange earnings.[98] The overthrow of the Jawara government in July 1994, when the Senegalese government pointedly failed to intervene, did not automatically end the strains in the relationship, because the Senegalese continued to maintain their trade controls.[99]

Regional Diplomatic Initiatives

Gambian uncertainty about Senegalese intentions encouraged Jawara to broaden his external relations from the late 1960s and seek friendship, although not defense agreements, with other countries in the West African region as a counterweight to Senegalese influence.

One natural direction lay toward the three other English-speaking and former British dependencies: Sierra Leone, Ghana, and Nigeria. In each case, a number of historical and cultural affinities could be claimed. As outlined in Chapter 1, The Gambia's small, but influential, Aku community had strong family and educational links with Freetown in Sierra Leone and a number of Gambians still pursued higher education at Fourah Bay University.[100] However, although The Gambia established full diplomatic relations with Sierra Leone in 1969 and established a Treaty of Friendship with it in 1970 following a state visit by President Siaka Stevens, it could not realistically expect a great deal from what was itself a small and weak state.[101]

Ghana, the first West African colony to achieve independence, appeared a better prospect, at least in the early 1960s. Jawara, who had firsthand experience of Ghana (having studied at Achimota College, Accra) and probably initially a certain respect for its eminent leader, Kwame Nkrumah, welcomed Ghanaian interest in his country. Although not subscribing to Nkrumah's pan-African social-ist ideology, he benefited from Ghana's ideological rivalry with Senegal. In particu-lar, President Senghor's fear of Ghanaian intentions regarding The Gambia, encouraged him to outbid the Ghanaian president.[102] But Jawara disliked Nkrumah's financial handouts to the opposition leader, I. M. Garba-Jahumpa (see Chapter 6) and probably had reservations about him more generally.[103] Following the military coup of February 1966, which overthrew Nkrumah, Ghana ceased to be as important to Gambian foreign policy.[104] Although relations with the civilian government headed by President Hilla Limann (1979–81) were good, Jawara dis-trusted his successor, Jerry Rawlings; the latter's overthrow of Limann, his links with Libya, and his radical political views (seen as encouraging youthful militants in The Gambia) caused concern. Rawlings was also opposed to the Senegambia Confederation.[105]

In the 1970s, Nigeria, the remotest of The Gambia's anglophone neighbors, became its most important regional contact apart from Senegal. This was partly because of Nigeria's emergence as regional hegemon after the successful conclu-sion of the Biafran war in 1971, following which the Nigerian head of state, General Yakubu Gowon, carried out his own version of a regional good neighbor policy.[106] In addition, Nigeria emerged as a major oil-producing country in the early 1970s. Jawara, who had sided with the federal government during the civil war, had reason to expect diplomatic and even economic assistance from a grate-ful Gowon. Indeed, within weeks of the Biafran surrender, Gowon was guest of honor at The Gambia's Independence Day celebrations in February 1971 when a Treaty of Friendship was signed between the two countries; moreover, in July 1973, The Gambia decided to establish an embassy in Lagos.[107] Unlike Senghor, Jawara was also a willing subscriber to the proposal by Gowon and Togo's leader, Gnassingbé Eyadema, that a West African regional grouping—the Economic Community of West African States (ECOWAS)—be established.[108] The Gambia's cultivation of Nigeria, on this and subsequent occasions, while never leading to a defense pact, was undoubtedly noted with irritation by the Senegalese govern-ment, and was the subject of extreme attacks by sections of the Senegalese press.[109] Again, Jawara was able subtly to exploit Senegal's rivalry with an assertive Nigeria, which shared Nkrumah's earlier criticisms of Senegal for its "demeaning" pro-French foreign policy, while at the same time promoting himself and his little country as a bridge between the region's two language blocks.[110]

Although Jawara's attempt to maintain good relations with Nigeria was compli-cated by its rapid turnover of governments, he continued to pursue his country's national interests by means of friendship with successive regimes, even when Nigeria lapsed into undemocratic military rule. An accord was signed between Jawara and General Muhammadu Buhari (Nigerian head of state between December 1983 and August 1985) in 1984 and Buhari visited The Gambia on an official visit in February 1985. Relations were even better during the administra-tion of General Ibrahim Babangida (Nigerian head of state between August 1985 and August 1993), who twice graced Gambian Independence Day celebrations.[111] As discussed in Chapter 11, one consequence of these good relations was the decision to replace the small British military training mission with a much larger and politically controversial Nigerian one in 1991 (there were probably also financial savings for the Gambian government); ironically, this would be a key factor leading to the coup that overthrew Jawara in 1994.[112]

At the same time as pursuing closer relations with anglophone West African states, Jawara more selectively cultivated other countries in the region, in particular, at various times, Guinea (Conakry), Mauritania, and Guinea-Bissau. Under its charismatic radical leader, Sékou Touré (who was Guinean president between its independence in 1958 and his death in 1984), Guinea had a long political and ideological rivalry with Senghor's Senegal. Touré, very much the personification of the ideological anti-neo-colonial spirit in francophone West Africa, was the antithesis of the pragmatic pro-French Senegalese leader and had nothing in common with Jawara either.[113] Although Jawara by temperament, style, and policy was much closer to Senghor, the deterioration in relations with Senegal in the early 1970s encouraged him to establish contacts with Conakry for the first time. In September 1970, the Gambian government detained thirty-eight Guinean exiles who were accused of planning to overthrow Touré (probably as part of a wider invasion plot launched from Portuguese Guinea in the following month); the group was deported to Conakry in December on the grounds that the government was supporting the principle of (Guinean) territorial sovereignty.[114] This action aroused considerable controversy in The Gambia, particularly because it was assumed that the exiles would face a bleak fate in Guinea; indeed, much to the dismay of the Gambian government, which had received assurances from the Guinean government that the exiles would not face capital punishment, they were put to death. Nevertheless, his actions won Jawara the friendship of the Guinean government, which established an embassy in Bathurst.[115] It was also yet another signal to Dakar of Gambian autonomy, particularly because the Senegalese government refused to hand over any of its Guinean exiles, a decision that led to a severe deterioration in the relations between Senghor and Touré.[116]

By 1978, Jawara was able to build on his new relationship with the isolated and politically paranoid Touré to help effect a reconciliation between him and Senghor. Furthermore, in 1980, Jawara persuaded the Senegalese to extend membership of the OMVG to Guinea, from which country the River Gambia originated and without which no effective joint development of its river basin was possible. Jawara's reward came in 1981, when, as noted in Chapter 8, the "revolutionary" Touré denounced the leftist coup in Banjul and stood aside while Senegalese forces entered The Gambia to suppress it.[117]

Jawara also strengthened ties with another of Senegal's vexatious neighbors, Mauritania, following the collapse of the Senegambia Confederation in 1989. Religious and business ties already existed between The Gambia and Mauritania. Since at least the 1960s, Muslim spiritual leaders (marabouts) in the latter country had enjoyed a high reputation in The Gambia, and Mauritanian traders were dominant in the lower levels of the retail and distribution trade in The Gambia (although periodically they had earned Gambian resentment).[118] The Gambian government established diplomatic accreditation in Mauritania as early as 1969 and state visits were paid to The Gambia by Presidents Mokhtar Ould Daddah in November 1976 and Mohammed Khouna Haidalla in August 1980. In addition, a joint committee was set up in 1980 to promote economic, scientific, and technical cooperation.[119] The difficult relationship between Banjul and Dakar after the end of the confederation, when Senegal pursued a policy of causing economic difficulties for Gambians, naturally led the Gambian government publicly, if again symbolically, to affirm its good relations with Mauritania.[120]

During its long struggle against colonial rule in the former Portuguese Guinea, the liberation movement, the PAIGC (Partido Africano da Independência da Guiné e Cabo Verde), was recognized by The Gambia as the legal government of the contested territory and its office in Banjul had been afforded diplomatic status in 1973.[121] The independence of Guinea-Bissau in 1974 was welcomed by Banjul and Gambian trade with Bissau developed apace.[122] As noted in Chapter 8, relations between the two countries deteriorated sharply in 1981–82, over the reaction of the Vieira government to the coup, but had been restored by the end of 1982. Indeed, The Gambia strongly supported the adherence of Guinea-Bissau to OMVG in August 1983, although it was not a riparian state, given that its economy was closely integrated already with that of its three other member states. Politically, from a Gambian perspective, there was also some advantage from enlarging the OMVG, in that it further lessened Banjul's dependency on Senegal for subregional development projects.[123]

The Gambia also cultivated support at a regional level in West Africa. An early supporter of the idea of a regional economic organization, Jawara not only led his country into ECOWAS in 1975, but later emerged as an "elder statesman" within it, serving as its chairman in 1988.[124] His long-established relations with leaders across the ideological and linguistic divide, as well as the unthreatening nature of his country, allowed him to act effectively at a time when ECOWAS was threatened with fissure over support for rival factions in the Liberian civil war. It was following a round table conference of Liberian interest groups in Banjul in August/September 1990 that an Interim Government of National Unity was formed under Dr. Amos Sawyer. The Gambia also sent a small army detachment to join the ECOWAS Cease-Fire Monitoring Group (ECOMOG), in Liberia.[125] However, as discussed in Chapter 11, later events suggest that this decision, although welcomed by Nigeria and the other West African states participating in ECOMOG, led to disaffection among Gambian rank and file soldiers on their return.[126]

The Gambia also participated in other regional activities. These included not only the OMVG, which, with its rotating chairmen and venues for heads-of-state and panels of experts meetings, helped to promote Jawara's standing as an astute international statesman, but also the Comité permanent intre-états de la lutte contre la sécheresse dans le Sahel (CILSS). When it was set up in 1973, CILSS was originally limited to the francophone countries that were suffering from the worsening effect of drought in the West African interior. The Gambia joined in

December 1973, with Senegalese backing, but it was only after the severe drought of 1977 that it took a more prominent part in its activities. Following a conference in Banjul in September 1977, Jawara was appointed chairman of CILSS (from January 1978) and in 1978–79, he spent much time traveling around the region (and further afield) assessing the needs of the nine CILSS members and putting requests for assistance for the Sahel Development Programme to the United States and Western European and Arab countries. He then extended his activities to the United Nations and the Organisation of African Unity (OAU), taking up the drought issue on a continental as well as at a regional level.[127] Although Jawara ceased to be CILSS chairman in January 1980, The Gambia remained active in promoting its cause. The results varied in respect both of donor commitment and local interest, but both The Gambia and Jawara met with some success: some U.S. $67 million aid was pledged to CILSS by donors and Jawara's reputation as an international statesman was greatly enhanced.[128]

Wider African Relations

Jawara and The Gambia's identification with the cause of African liberation and continental unity cannot be attributed solely to personal, regime, or national self-interest. Jawara expressed support for the anti-colonial liberation movement even before his country's independence from British rule.[129] After its own independence, the Gambian government supported attempts to achieve independence, or black majority rule, in those parts of the African continent that remained under European rule—by the mid-1960s, this consisted primarily of Portuguese-held territory, together with South Africa, South West Africa (Namibia), and Rhodesia (Zimbabwe), where the prime minister, Ian Smith, announced a Unilateral Declaration of Independence (UDI) in November 1965. Jawara regularly criticized the British government over Rhodesia,[130] but where The Gambia differed from some other countries was in the means to be adopted to speed up decolonization. For example, it refused to join the group of nine independent African states that obeyed a 1965 OAU resolution to break off diplomatic relations with Britain over its failure to use force to put an end to the Smith regime.[131] Nor would it engage in other than diplomatic statements criticizing British and other western involvement in South Africa.[132] Jawara thus associated his country with the moderate bloc of countries within the OAU in respect of the means to achieve both the liberation of remaining European-held territories in Africa and the substance and pace of continental unity.

The Gambia's cautious approach was also seen in the matter of recognition of liberation movements. Where, as in Namibia or South Africa, one organization emerged clearly to command the liberation struggle, Banjul gave it unequivocal recognition. But where resistance was fragmented among several movements, as in Angola and Zimbabwe, The Gambia refused, at least initially, to give precedence to any one organization, and was critical of the OAU for taking such sides.

However, the Movimento Popular de Libertação de Angola (MPLA) was recognized in January 1976, immediately after it became clear it had achieved military control; and the Zimbabwe African National Union–Patriotic Front government was recognized immediately after its victory in the 1980 Zimbabwean election.[133]

The Gambian government was similarly hesitant in respect of the claims by the Sahrawi Arab Democratic Republic (SADR) to autonomy for the Western Sahara (the former Spanish Sahara). Following the Spanish withdrawal in 1976, the territory was annexed by Morocco (and for a time, Mauritania), but Moroccan rule was challenged by the military arm of the SADR, the Polisario Front. The Gambia urged a cease fire between the two sides and a referendum to decide the territory's future. However, when, in February 1982, the OAU council of ministers voted by the narrowest of majorities to recognize the SADR as the legitimate government of the disputed territory ahead of the promised, but much delayed, referendum, The Gambia, together with eighteen other largely conservative states, walked out of the meeting in Addis Ababa. The same countries subsequently boycotted the next council of ministers meetings in July/August and November 1982. Banjul's reluctance to support the SADR's claims was based on more than a correct interpretation of the OAU charter's condition of entry for new members; it also reflected its relations with the states of the Maghreb.[134]

Despite its small size, The Gambia refused to play a subservient role in the continent's affairs. The Gambia was an active member of the OAU from independence.[135] Moreover, Jawara took the lead in seeking zealously to persuade often indifferent and hostile fellow African heads of state to take environmental protection and the promotion of African human rights more seriously. His efforts in the first area were largely responsible for the OAU adopting the "Banjul Declaration" on environmental conservation in 1977.[136] Jawara, who had previously condemned the brutality of the Idi Amin regime in Uganda in the 1970s,[137] also hosted the two sessions of the OAU Ministerial Conference on Human and People's Rights that resulted in the OAU's adoption of the African Charter on Human and People's Rights (known as the "Banjul Charter" in recognition of The Gambia's role) in Nairobi in 1981. The Banjul Charter eventually came into force in 1986 after being ratified by OAU members and a commission was established in Banjul to take it forward. In further recognition of The Gambia's pivotal role in bringing about the charter, the headquarters of the African Centre for Democracy and Human Rights Studies were established at Fajara, near Banjul, in 1989.[138]

Relations with Western Countries and Financial Institutions

Relations with Britain

The Gambian government remained on good terms with Britain even after independence while avoiding supine dependence on its former colonial master (notwithstanding the accusations to the contrary of its left-wing critics).[139] British tact and Gambian assertiveness thus gave their relationship a more even character than was the case in a number of former Francophone colonies in West Africa, where the dominance of France remained in visible and contentious forms. Given its tiny economic resources and no realistic prospect of radically enlarging them, some form of external dependency was the only means for the state to survive. Jawara's skill was to diversify or multilateralize reliance on other countries or agencies, so as not to remain dependent on Britain. Until June 1967, The Gambia relied on a British grant-in-aid of £1.1 million to balance its budget. But in 1968 (much earlier than skeptics forecast), its modest spending and an upturn in the volume and value of the groundnut crop, the principal source of private wealth, state revenue, and export earnings, allowed the government to dispense with grant-in-aid and even pay back some of the surplus it had accrued.[140]

Although there was a surplus in recurrent expenditure because of increased revenue, this was not true of development expenditure. For political and moral reasons, the PPP government was compelled to pursue a program of social and infrastructural development, particularly in the Provinces, where the bulk of its supporters resided and where expectations and needs were highest. Although modest by the scale of development programs elsewhere in postcolonial Africa, The Gambia's projects still required far more funds than could be generated locally. In practice, all the development programs and plans adopted and implemented from 1965 onward required substantial external funding.[141] Britain was the leading donor until the mid-1970s and, as late as 1975–79, provided over one-quarter of bilateral foreign aid. Its aid was spread across a range of activities: agriculture and rural development, transport and communications, and technical training.[142] Britain continued to provide extensive financial assistance in the 1980s. It contributed £3 million as a grant to the World Bank's Structural Adjustment Credit (SAC) as part of the ERP and gave further grants of £10.5 million in fuel between 1986 and 1989 and in 1991–92.[143]

Few issues caused difficulties between London and Banjul, a situation quite different from Britain's relations with a number of its other former African dependencies. Neither changes of government in Westminster; nor Britain's contentious presence in South Africa; nor even, as discussed, its failure to put an end to UDI in Rhodesia, threatened the "special relationship." Jawara's moderate stance in inter-African affairs and his pro-Western position in the Cold War context, as well as the absence of any legacy of animosity arising from the colonial transition, ensured an amicable relationship.

Apart from much-needed British economic assistance, The Gambia saw Britain as yet another counterweight to Senegal. Indeed, prior to independence, Jawara hoped to persuade the British government to sign a formal defense agreement; that he failed to do so was due to the latter's reluctance to enter into an agreement with a Commonwealth member in Africa.[144] In 1969, in the light of his country's deteriorating relations with Senegal, Jawara tried once again to secure a defense agreement with Britain or persuade it to guarantee The Gambia's territorial integrity, but again his efforts were unsuccessful.[145] Nevertheless, the two countries maintained a number of low-key agreements in the area of military training. For a number of years, small numbers of British soldiers undertook tropical acclimatization exercises in the Kiang area and RAF fighter aircraft operated training flights between Gibraltar and Yundum airport, near Banjul. Officers in the Gambian civil and paramilitary police were trained in Britain, which also provided the limited military equipment required by Banjul.[146]

Sensitive to radical accusations of neo-colonialism, the Gambian government eventually phased out these limited arrangements. However, the value of the links between the two countries was evident when both governments faced quite different security threats in the early 1980s. As noted in Chapter 8, during the 1981 coup, Britain quietly despatched a small team of Special Air Service men to rescue members of President Jawara's family and other hostages seized by the insurgents and whose lives were threatened. The Gambian government reciprocated during the Falklands War of 1982, when it allowed British military tanker aircraft to refuel at Yundum en route to the distant Falklands (the Senegalese authorities provided a similar facility at Yoff airport, Dakar). Britain also sent a small training mission to Banjul in 1984 to help set up the Gambian National Army; this mission remained until 1991.[147] This was a good example of the counterbalancing principle in practice: as outlined, Senegal provided a security umbrella during this reconstruction and was responsible also for training the other successor to the discredited Field Force, a National Gendarmerie.

Relations with Other Developed Industrial States

Apart from Britain, with its residual, but decreasing, obligations to its former colony, no other Western country had much interest in the little country's survival. After all, The Gambia was but one of many new states struggling for international attention in the post-imperial era. Moreover, hampered by financial and organizational deficiencies, The Gambia had to be selective in its overseas representation. Initially, as noted, it was represented directly only in Britain and Senegal. Moreover, only these countries had resident ambassadors in Bathurst from 1965; the United States and France were represented by resident consuls, and other countries were represented by nonresident ambassadors based in Dakar.[148]

In these circumstances, it was difficult for the Gambian government to attract the favorable international attention that would result in external support from developed countries. This was essential for its survival and the achievement of development goals, which in turn legitimized the Jawara administration's claims to rule. Nevertheless, by the mid-1970s, a considerable amount of Western aid was flowing into The Gambia; indeed, between 1975 and 1985, foreign aid to The Gambia averaged U.S. $80 per capita per year, one of the highest levels in Africa, with the amount being particularly high at U.S. $120 per capita in 1980–81 because of the drought and attempted coup.[149]

Much of the credit for this should go to Jawara, who learned to use foreign policy, linked to domestic policies, to create attention and sympathy for his country.

His moderate and pragmatic foreign policy, with its pro-Western interpretation of non-alignment during the years of Cold War, earned his country a positive image in Western decision-making circles. This was reinforced by his liberal democratic political reputation at home, and his avoidance of excessive state interference in economic management. Both parliamentary democracy and free market economies went into sharp decline during the first two decades of African independence and so, however limited or flawed these domestic achievements were (as his critics would maintain), they undoubtedly helped to single out The Gambia and its leader as worthy of support.

By the end of the 1970s, the main sources of external aid (apart from Britain) were the European Economic Community (EEC), West Germany, and the United States. When Britain joined the EEC in 1972, The Gambia, together with other former British dependencies, joined as an associate member and rapidly appointed an ambassador to Brussels (Sheriff Dibba).[150] Unlike some other African political leaders, Jawara was eager for The Gambia to join the EEC and his approach soon paid dividends; both the EEC itself, through the European Development Fund, and individual EEC members provided support for the Gambian economy. The Gambia benefited from a range of disbursements under the Lomé I, II, and III treaties, with funding being allocated to a number of infrastructural projects (water supply, drainage, and roads).[151] The country also obtained support for its export prices, as these dipped on the world market, from EEC STABEX (price support) funds; these grants were particularly important in the 1980s, because they helped to support the ERP.[152] Meanwhile, West German financial assistance increased sharply in the late 1970s, as it became the second most important European donor after the UK.[153]

During the 1980s, Western financial assistance increased considerably. Both individual Western countries, in particular the United States, West Germany, and France (as well as Britain), and the EEC responded positively to Gambian attempts to sort out its economic difficulties. By the second half of the decade, America had become The Gambia's largest donor. American aid averaged U.S. $10 million a year during this period, the increase being due directly to The Gambia's political record and its determined efforts to sort out its economic difficulties through the ERP.[154] However, repeated attempts to interest American businessmen in The Gambia, and to attract African-American support by capitalizing on the "Roots" phenomenon (an attempt to drum up tourism and investment from among the African diaspora) were less successful.[155] France also increased its bilateral assistance. This aid consisted of a combination of grants and loans, again mainly in infrastructure and communications provision; for example, the contract to upgrade the Gambian national telephone network was given to the French.[156]

As well as receiving increasing aid from these countries, The Gambia developed closer political links with many of them. In 1983, Jawara paid his first state visit to France since independence, as part of his new diplomacy "sans frontières linguistique."[157] As with other diplomatic initiatives, the cultivation of France demonstrated Jawara's adaptability and dynamism in the field of external relations. Good relations with the United States were cemented further when the Americans were permitted in 1989 to extend the Yundum airport runway to allow emergency landings of space shuttles, while Jawara was also well received on a state visit to Washington in 1990. It was therefore a bitter irony that in July 1994, the United States refused to deploy marines to put down the coup that toppled Jawara and Gambian democracy.[158]

Relations with International Financial Institutions

Although direct aid from Western countries remained important, by the 1980s, the International Monetary Fund (IMF) and the World Bank (through the International Development Association) had assumed the dominant role in Gambian economic management. In February 1984, the Gambian government negotiated a stand-by agreement with the IMF but, as outlined in Chapter 1, it soon breached the expenditure targets of the program and fell into arrears to the IMF, which cancelled the programe in January 1985. The government was then forced to allow the fund to oversee its ERP in return for an emergency aid package and medium-term financial support. The World Bank was also directly involved in the ERP through provision of a SAC of SDR 29 million in 1985–86 and a second SAC of SDR 41 million in 1989, much of which was funded by the Bank itself.[159]

Because The Gambia's international creditworthiness was determined by the IMF, the government supported and implemented the tough recovery measures demanded of it. Its actions cost it some political support at home although, as discussed in Chapter 9, the austerity measures did little damage to the PPP's prospects in the 1987 election. Within two years of the initiation of the ERP, a significant measure of financial control and recovery was established and The Gambia was regarded as one of the IMF/World Bank's success stories. By the early 1990s, however, there was increasing evidence of slippage in the strict management of public sector finances, as old habits, such as corruption and mismanagement, reappeared to undermine the moral authority of Jawara and his administration.

Relations with the Islamic World

Despite its population being overwhelmingly Muslim, Islam has only had a limited impact on Gambian foreign policy. Until the oil price crisis of the 1970s, the Gambian government did not develop an Islamic dimension to its foreign policy. In the 1960s, it had good relations with Israel, with which it signed a Treaty of Friendship in 1966 and it was not until the Arab–Israeli War of 1973 that relations were broken off (and were not restored until 1992).[160] However, the worsening economic situation facing The Gambia from the 1970s led to the strengthening of ties with oil-rich Muslim states, most notably Libya, Saudi Arabia, and Kuwait.

Gambian ties to Libya dated back to 1974 when, following a visit by Jawara to Tripoli, a Treaty of Friendship and three agreements were signed between the two countries. Subsequently, joint business ventures were set up, notably the Gambian–Libyan Public Transport Corporation. In addition, Libya promised financial assistance for road building in the more inaccessible north bank areas and for the building of a new central mosque in Banjul. However, The Gambia was to be disappointed with the limited extent of Libyan aid (and its reluctance to provide the aid it promised) and became increasingly alarmed at what it considered to be the adventurist policy of Colonel Qaddafi in West Africa; this view was shared by Senegal and by several other governments in the region. As noted in Chapter 8, diplomatic relations were broken off in 1980 and, although partially restored in December 1984, full ambassadorial ties were not restored until November 1994 after the overthrow of Jawara and the PPP.[161]

The unhappy experience with Libya naturally drew The Gambia toward more moderate and conservative Arab Muslim states. In North Africa, The Gambia found a ready friend in Morocco, itself feeling threatened by Qaddafi's brand of populist radicalism. This, as Touray argues, helped to define The Gambia's position with regard to SADR claims over the Western Sahara. Although not among the wealthier group of Arab states, Morocco did provide The Gambia with assistance after the failed coup of 1981.[162]

Further east, Jawara carried out a policy of personal diplomacy, with the aim of obtaining some of the oil surpluses being piled up during the 1970s, principally by Saudi Arabia and Kuwait. In November 1974, a Gambian embassy to Saudi Arabia was opened in Jeddah. Subsequently, Jawara reaffirmed his Muslim credentials by intensifying the teaching of Arabic and Islamic studies in Gambian schools. He also undertook the hajj (the pilgrimage to Mecca which all Muslims, who can afford it, are expected to take at least once in their lifetime) as part of a tour of Middle East countries in 1976.[163] The Gambia also allowed the Palestine Liberation Organization to set up an office in Banjul, following a visit by its chairman, Yasser Arafat, to The Gambia in 1984.[164] In addition, Jawara formally attached his country to the Organisation of Islamic Conference (OIC), where The Gambia supported radical positions on such issues as the status of Jerusalem and the national rights of the Palestinian people and, as discussed below, condemned the Soviet invasion of a fellow Muslim state, Afghanistan. There is no doubt that a key aim of these pro-Arab and pro-Islamic acts was to secure aid though, in fairness to Jawara, his support for national self-determination was long established. The policy was very successful; Touray notes that in the period 1975–80, Arab states (basically Saudi Arabia and Kuwait) accounted for 27 percent of international aid received by The Gambia.[165]

Diplomatic and financial support from Arab states was also evident after the failed coup of 1981. Saudi Arabia gave the Gambian government U.S. $10 million as part of the relief efforts. A tour of the Middle East by the minister of external affairs, Lamin Kitty Jabang, resulted in over U.S. $12 million being offered towards reconstruction. Indeed, in 1980–85, Arab countries provided no less than 70 percent of The Gambia's international aid and although the Kuwaiti contribution fell as a result of the Gulf War in 1990, it remained a significant source of overseas aid. Predictably, The Gambia supported Kuwait and its Western allies during the Gulf War. This was not merely because of the extent of Kuwaiti aid (compared with this, Iraqi aid, a U.S. $10 million loan, was insignificant), but because of broader moral considerations—the invasion of a small state by a powerful neighbor and the brutal nature of Saddam Hussein's regime. Nevertheless, the economic response was swift. In 1992, Saudi Arabia wrote off a D150 million loan for development projects and numerous projects continued to be funded from Arab sources.[166]

Aid from Arab countries was obtained both bilaterally from Kuwait and Saudi Arabia and through agencies such as the Arab Bank for Economic Development in Africa and the Islamic Development Bank. Arab contributions were also channeled through other international institutions, such as the Organisation of Petroleum Exporting Countries, which provided one-third of Arab loans. Saudi Arabia, the largest donor, concentrated its aid on such schemes as Yundum Airport Phase II, a number of important road projects, and a national water supply scheme to provide capped hand-pump wells in every village. Kuwaiti aid was also largely committed to infrastructure development. This aid continued to 1994.[167]

Unquestionably, Gambian oil diplomacy paid handsome dividends. Not only did it result in much-needed overseas aid, it also enhanced Jawara's stature as an international statesman further. For example, in 1984, following the death of President Sékou Touré of Guinea, he took over the chairmanship of the Peace Committee of the OIC, which was set up in 1980 to try and resolve the Iraq–Iran war. This was described in an official publication as being, "Perhaps the most significant manifestation of his standing in the international community."[168]

Relations with the Communist Bloc

Relations with the Communist world never featured prominently in The Gambia's foreign policy. Nevertheless, as suggested, Jawara and the Gambian government regarded such diplomatic contacts as a mark of their autonomous international position and as a possible means of diversifying foreign economic assistance. On the other hand, The Gambia's Lilliputian size and global marginality meant that the country could not expect extensive aid from the Socialist bloc. But as with the West, small crumbs from a donor's table could be sizeable for a micro-state such as The Gambia. No Gambian embassy was set up directly in any Communist country, and only the People's Republic of China and North Korea (for a time) set up embassies in Banjul; instead, representation was established via diplomatic missions in neighboring countries.

The Gambia established diplomatic relations with the USSR in November 1965. It was represented in Moscow by the Senegalese ambassador, but resisted Russian requests to be allowed to establish an embassy in Bathurst.[169] An Agreement on Cultural and Scientific Co-operation having been signed in March 1973, Jawara's invitation to visit Moscow in 1975 raised prospects of further Russian aid. But in reality, links between the two countries remained limited. Moreover, the awarding of scholarships to Gambians to study in the Soviet Union, which formed part of the Soviet aid package, caused the Gambian government concern, because it was feared (correctly, as it turned out; see Chapter 8) that some of these students would engage in radical politics on their return. But it was only in 1978 that formal relations worsened, when The Gambia denounced the Soviet Union's invasion of Afghanistan. Even then, only the 1973 agreement, and not diplomatic relations, was broken off.[170] Except in the case of a few urban radicals, Gambian society remained impervious to Soviet (or other Communist) propaganda. Although some links were also established with a number of other East European Communist states (as well as Cuba), these were of no practical significance, merely an extension of The Gambia's nominally even-handed foreign policy during the Cold War years.[171] Local self-styled Marxist attempts to overthrow the government in 1981 made the Jawara administration even more wary of closer ties with Eastern bloc states and non-alignment, in reality, was exercised in a pro-Western way.

Prior to December 1974, when the Gambian government unexpectedly established diplomatic relations with mainland China and broke off those with Taiwan, Jawara had pursued a "two-China" policy, but had limited formal diplomatic relations to Taiwan. These were established in November 1968, with the first resident Taiwanese ambassador arriving in February 1972.[172] In return, The Gambia received modest amounts of assistance with rice cultivation.[173] Beijing's "one-China" policy, and the general extension of recognition of mainland China by African states in the mid-1970s, partly explain the Gambian government's volte face, but expectation of a greater amount of economic assistance is likely also to have influenced Gambian thinking. Certainly, within a month of the establishment of diplomatic relations, a high-powered Gambian mission had winged its way to Beijing and a valuable Agreement on Economic and Technical Co-operation was signed in February 1975. A loan worth more than D25 million was provided by the Chinese, together with a larger team of rice experts. Jawara visited Beijing in June 1975 and further Chinese aid to build a hospital and sports facilities was obtained. Within five years, Chinese exports to The Gambia had trebled, suggesting that the benefits were not entirely in one direction. The Gambia remained on good terms with China throughout the Jawara era.[174]

During the 1960s and early 1970s, The Gambia had no diplomatic relations with North Korea, but only with South Korea.[175] But in March 1973, in accordance with his government's non-aligned policy, Jawara extended recognition to North Korea, although it would be 1975 before a mission arrived in Banjul, where it rented space in the ruling party's headquarters building. Neither of the Koreas objected to dual representation and the Gambian government publicly supported the peaceful unification of the two states. A Gambian mission visited both Koreas in 1973 and modest amounts of aid were received from both, with South Korea providing the most. In return, whereas The Gambia received virtually no exports from North Korea, imports from South Korea nearly quadrupled between 1975 and 1980. The North Korean mission was subsequently shut down, without explanation, after the 1981 coup attempt.[176]

Summary

Gambian foreign policy was principally determined by President Jawara and specialist advisers and combined "ethical" considerations with a strong dose of pragmatism. Foreign policy successfully evolved to sustain the country's autonomy, to promote development objectives and to reinforce the standing of the Jawara government, at home and abroad. While The Gambia extended its range of overseas contacts, both within Africa and further afield, its interpretation of non-alignment was undoubtedly pro-Western. But it was the government's decision to become involved in the Liberian civil war in the early 1990s and, in particular, to invite a Nigerian military mission into the country, which precipitated Jawara's downfall in 1994.

11

THE 1994 COUP AND THE JAWARA LEGACY

On Friday July 22, 1994, President Jawara and the People's Progressive Party (PPP) government were overthrown in a bloodless coup by a group of young junior officers of the Gambian National Army (GNA) who subsequently established the Armed Forces Provisional Ruling Council (AFPRC) government. The first part of this chapter analyses this coup in detail. As pointed out both by Wiseman and Vidler and by Saine, it marked the demise of the longest continuously surviving multiparty democracy in Africa and ended the period in office of the longest serving national leader in Africa; it also meant that The Gambia was traveling in the opposite direction to many sub-Saharan states, which were moving toward some kind of multiparty political system.[1] The ending of the Jawara era was a particularly significant moment in Gambian history and the second part of the chapter assesses his overall contribution to Gambian public life.

1994 Coup

The coup has previously been examined by a number of authors writing from a range of perspectives.[2] These published sources have more recently been supplemented by a series of Internet articles written by a GNA officer of the time, believed to be Captain Sheriff Samsudeen Sarr (using the pseudonym "Ebou Colly").[3] As outlined below, there are some differences between the sources. However, two common themes have been the internal grievances of the military and the problems of civil society at the time of the coup. These are considered first, before the course of events during the coup and its immediate aftermath are described. In this chapter, a number of comparisons are made with the failed coup of 1981 and also with other successful military coups in Africa.

Gambian National Army

Chapter 8 pointed out that, following the suppression of the 1981 coup, the discredited Field Force was disbanded in 1982. It was initially replaced by a Senegalese-trained confederal army, staffed mainly by Senegalese soldiers. Subsequently, two separate forces were established: the GNA, which was created in 1983–84 under the command of a Gambian, Colonel Momodou N'Dow N'Jie, and the Gambian National Gendarmerie (GNG), which was gradually built up from 1982. In 1992, the GNG was integrated into the Tactical Support Group (TSG), composed of former members of the GNG and former civilian police officers. The GNA received British military assistance (until 1991), and the GNG was trained by Senegalese officers. Some officers and rank and file in the two forces were drawn from the old Field Force, but many were new recruits.[4] At the time of the coup, the GNA numbered about 800 men, some of whom had seen active service, having been part of the Gambian contingent of 105 soldiers that had served in the larger Economic Community of West African States Cease-Fire Monitoring Group (ECOMOG) force in Liberia in 1990–91; there they came into contact with soldiers from a number of other African countries, including Ghana, Nigeria, and Sierra Leone, where military interventions had become commonplace.[5] The TSG was a smaller force than the GNA and also had inferior weaponry, which reduced its effectiveness as its counterweight.[6]

It was noted in Chapter 10 that in the early 1990s, relations between Nigeria and The Gambia improved considerably. One consequence of this was that in 1992, the Nigerian government agreed to supply the GNA with military personnel and assistance. Jawara presumably assumed that his government's security would be enhanced by increased cooperation with Nigeria; if so, this proved to be a grave miscalculation.[7]

A total of sixty-nine officers and men of the Nigerian Armed Forces Training Group were assigned to assist in the command, training and development of the GNA, and a Nigerian, Colonel (later Brigadier General) Abubakar Dada, was appointed its commander. By 1993, Nigerians also held all the other senior positions in the army. In April/May 1994, Dada was replaced as the head of the Nigerian mission by another Nigerian, Colonel Lawan Gwadabe, against his will; it was his refusal to accept his demotion and give up his official residence that resulted in a fatal breakdown of the chain of command.[8]

All the junior officers (of whom there were said to be forty-six at the time of the coup) were Gambians, with the most senior Gambian officers being of major rank.[9] These included the four men who were to organize the coup and initially to comprise the AFPRC: Yahya A. A. J. J. Jammeh, Sadibou Hydara, Sana B. Sabally, and Edward D. Singhateh. Jammeh, who is currently (at the time of writing) the Gambian Head of State, was then head of the army Military Police at Yundum Barracks. Twenty-nine at the time of the coup and a lieutenant, he had been born in Kanilai in the Foni Kansala District of the Lower River Division of a Jola Muslim family and began his military career in the GNG in 1984. He was commissioned as an officer (second lieutenant) in 1989 and transferred to the GNA in August 1991. He was promoted to lieutenant in February 1992; his earlier duties had included serving as presidential escort in the Presidential Guard in 1989–90.

Like Jammeh, Hydara, a Gambian Muslim (of Mauritanian origin) from Dippakunda near Banjul, who was thirty at the time of the coup, joined the GNG in 1984. He transferred to the army in 1993, having apparently worked his way up through the ranks to become second lieutenant. Sabally, a twenty-nine-year-old Fula Muslim from Kasakunda, a village near Brikama in Western Division, worked in a supermarket before joining the GNA, thus following the footsteps of his elder brother who was a sergeant in the Field Force. Sabally was a second lieutenant and a platoon commander at the time of the coup. The youngest member of the group was Singhateh, a twenty-five-year-old from Banjul of mixed Gambian (Mandinka) and English parentage who, unusually, was of a Christian background. He entered the army as an officer cadet in January 1991, having previously worked as an electronic technician in the Civil Aviation Department, and was commissioned as a second lieutenant (platoon commander) in January 1992.[10]

Far from being marginal elements in society, as Kandeh suggests, some junior officers were relatively well educated (e.g., Jammeh attended Gambia High School and Singhateh, St. Augustine's High School) who, at a time of economic decline and reduced public sector employment in the 1980s, regarded the army as a good source of employment.[11] In addition, some had attended officer training courses in America or Britain.[12] As Wiseman points out, there have been no analyses of the ethnic composition of the GNA before (or after) the coup, but it is clear that, unlike in many coups elsewhere in Africa, ethnicity was not a factor in the decision to intervene.[13]

It is evident, however, that by 1994 there was significant discontent among the junior officer corps. Many Gambian junior officers disliked the Nigerian domination of the senior officer corps. According to Colly/Sarr, they resented the way that Colonel Dada had reneged on a promise to them to introduce proper evaluation procedures and speed up promotion for them. They also were resentful that their food and accommodation at Yundum Barracks were clearly inferior to those of their senior officers, and there were also wide differentials between their pay and those of the Nigerian officers. Gambian officers also lacked respect for Colonel Dada for his refusal to give up his command and for his attempt to persuade the government to act against *The Point* for publishing details of his demotion before they were officially announced.[14] Moreover, at least some junior officers had their own personal grievances; for example, it is known that Jammeh resented the fact that he was transferred from his prestigious position in the Presidential Guard in 1990 after only four months.[15]

The army rank and file also shared the grievances of the junior officers about their living conditions. Furthermore, those who had served with the ECOMOG forces in Liberia had an additional complaint that the government proved reluctant to pay the allowances due them for their Liberian service. On two occasions prior to the coup, a group of ECOMOG veterans took direct action to try to secure payment of these. In June 1991, around sixty marched on State House to demand their allowances; they were quickly persuaded to return to barracks and some of them were forced to resign or were retired. Another casualty of the incident was their commander, Colonel N'Dow N'Jie, who was forced to resign a week later. Another group of soldiers attempted a repeat performance in 1992, but were prevented from leaving their barracks by senior officers; thirty-five were subsequently court marshaled.[16]

Following the second incident, and in response to the increasing number of soldiers leaving the GNA, the PPP government took a number of steps to address the army's grievances. In particular, a number of officers and rank and file troops were promoted and new allowances were introduced. Improvements in accommodation and equipment were also promised. But it appears that these actions failed to satisfy the demands of the soldiers; the government perhaps also gave the soldiers the impression that it could be coerced into making concessions.[17]

Moreover, the small size of Gambian society, the permeability of civil and military boundaries,[18] and the openness of the political system, including the freedom of the press, meant that soldiers were very aware of the increasing problems of civil society. These are considered below.

Declining Government Legitimacy

Although the PPP comfortably retained power at the 1992 election, its popularity seems to have sharply declined thereafter.[19] This was for two reasons. First, there was a widespread belief that, after nearly thirty years in office, the PPP had become complacent and out of touch with public opinion, particularly with younger people.[20] As shown in Chapter 9, the reformist elements within the PPP led by Bakary Dabo lost ground to their opponents headed by the widely discredited Saihou Sabally, whose position was strengthened by his surprising appointment both as vice president and as minister of defense after the 1992 election.[21] Second, it was also generally believed that many, if not most, ministers, senior civil servants, heads of parastatal organizations, and leading pro-PPP businessmen were corrupt and that President Jawara was unwilling to take decisive action to check them.[22]

As Wiseman and Vidler pointed out, it is impossible to state whether or not the extent of corruption had increased in recent years.[23] But, as noted in Chapter 9, one major scandal came to light in September 1993, when the general manager of the Gambia Cooperatives Union (GCU), M. M. Dibba, and two other senior managers were sent on indefinite leave, having been accused of embezzling several million dalasis from union funds. Their homes were seized and subsequently put up for sale, but the government appeared reluctant to take any further action against the three men. The popular view was that Saihou Sabally was implicated in the scandal. It was not until June 1994 that a commission of inquiry into the GCU was established, but this did not present its findings until after the coup. On the basis of its report, Dibba and eleven other current and former employees of the GCU were found guilty and were ordered to repay a total of D23 million.[24]

Many Gambians were also dismayed by the ineffectiveness of the Assets Management and Recovery Commission (AMRC). The AMRC was established in December 1992 under Dabo to recover the bad debts of the Gambia Commercial and Development Bank (GCDB). But its efforts were resisted by powerful PPP supporters, notably Ousainou N'Jie, the GCDB's managing director, who was one of the sons of M. M. N'Jie and thus Jawara's brother-in-law, and Saihou Ceesay, a leading Gambian businessman, who reputedly owed the GCDB D131 million in unpaid loans. By the time of the coup, the AMRC had managed to recover only a fraction of the loans and Jawara was widely blamed for preventing it from being more effective.[25]

If these were the best known cases that had come to light by the time of the coup, they were certainly not the only ones.[26] After the coup, some former senior PPP figures, including Jawara, the former attorney general, Hassan Jallow, and the former minister of agriculture, O. A. Jallow, argued that the extent of corruption under the PPP was nothing like as great as claimed by the AFRPC.[27] However, the various commissions of inquiry that the Jammeh government established in November 1994 to investigate the conduct of the previous regime (and, as Wiseman points out, to undermine its legitimacy) did unearth considerable evidence of corruption and maladministration. The methods used for personal enrichment included nonpayment of taxes and government loans; irregular allocation of valuable plots of land in the Greater Banjul area; serious overpayment of travel expenses; and theft of state funds.[28]

Although, of course, not all the details of these cases were known to the public before the coup, they helped to ensure that, as Wiseman and Vidler put it, "public awareness and resentment of the problem was undoubtedly at an all time high."[29] It is perhaps reasonable to assume that the junior army officers genuinely shared the views of many civilians about the PPP; after seizing power, the coup-makers sought to justify their actions by accusing the PPP government of "rampant outrageous corruption" and "random plundering of the country's assets just to benefit a few people."[30] They were also very quick to take action against former PPP ministers and heads of parastatal organizations in particular.[31] Whether, before the coup, they considered that Jawara was personally corrupt is less clear; initially the new government did not condemn Jawara personally.[32] However, it soon became increasingly critical of Jawara, who headed those accused (and later found guilty) by the commission of inquiry into the crude and refined oil contracts entered into by the government between 1984 and 1994; the commission ruled that Jawara was responsible for the unaccounted balance of $41 million and should pay this to the AFPRC government.[33] Among the other accusations leveled against him were that he spent more than his allowance on overseas trips; did not pay tax on his private earnings; used foreign trips for his own personal benefit; and permitted employees of the Ministry of Agriculture to work on his personal farms at state expense.[34]

As a number of authors have pointed out, although the coup-makers may genuinely have condemned the corruption of the PPP government, they may have been at least equally determined to take personal advantage of the opportunities for personal enrichment that would accrue from control of the resources of the state. This is of course a common motive for military interventions in Africa.[35] This is obviously difficult to prove one way or another, although some of the actions taken by the AFRPC government since 1994 have certainly shed considerable doubt on the purity of their original motives.[36]

In its early pronouncements, the AFPRC government also condemned the PPP government for presiding over a sham democracy and for failing to alleviate the country's economic woes. But neither charge has much credibility. The Gambia, of course, was a functioning democracy at the time of the coup, although as we have seen, there were some flaws in the political process and the main complaint of the coup leaders seems to have been that there had been no independent electoral commission in place for any of the post-independence elections.[37] Moreover, despite the temporary dislocations caused by the closure of the border with Senegal in 1993, the economy was generally in a much healthier state than it had been at the height of the Economic Recovery Programme (ERP) and there was little direct relationship between the coup and the economic policy reforms. Certainly, unlike the civilian conspirators of 1981, the AFPRC had no desire to alter the country's basic economic policies.[38]

It seems most likely, therefore, that the leaders of the coup decided to act for a combination of reasons. They disliked the government's collective treatment of the GNA and the army's domination by Nigerians; they were critical of the behavior of the government and its leading supporters; they were seeking personal advancement within the GNA[39]; and they had expectations of personal enrichment through military intervention. They may also have been influenced by the "contagion effect" of military coups in neighboring countries, particularly Sierra Leone, where Captain Valentine Strasser seized power in May 1992 after President Momoh failed to alleviate the grievances of junior officers, and Nigeria, where full military rule was reimposed in November 1993 under General Sani Abacha.[40] Possibly the most direct model for Jammeh, however, was provided by Jerry Rawlings, then Ghana's president, who was certainly a strong influence on him after the coup.[41] Some sources also emphasize the importance of the "ECOMOG factor" (similarly, some of those who were involved in the Strasser coup in 1992 had served in Liberia). But in fact, despite later claims to the contrary, the coup leaders themselves had not actually done so.[42]

Yeebo suggests that the junior officers may have been encouraged to intervene by the U.S. government, which was dismayed by the growth of corruption, the government's failure to tackle it, and the marginalization of its preferred candidate as Jawara's successor, Bakary Dabo. But the evidence he supplies to support this theory is not convincing and the fact that the United States (as well as the European Union and other countries) imposed sanctions on the new government undermines its validity.[43] Nor is there any evidence that certain members of Jawara's presidential entourage participated directly or indirectly in the coup, as Diene-Njie reports was speculated at the time.[44]

Finally, though, it is quite conceivable that, as Touray suggests, the officers calculated that they could safely organize a coup because the chances of the Senegalese government once again sending troops to restore Jawara to power were remote. As noted in Chapter 10, relations between the two countries had not recovered from the demise of the Senegambia Confederation in 1989, despite the Treaty of Friendship and Co-operation in 1991; moreover, Senegal's border was closed to all Gambian re-export trade in 1993. The coup-makers may well have concluded that, in these circumstances, Senegal would not act provided that it was quickly reassured that its own security interests would not be threatened by the new government. Their assumption proved correct, although, as discussed below, it is possible that President Diouf did initially consider intervening.[45]

The Coup and Its Immediate Aftermath

It could be argued, therefore, that by July 1994, the conditions were ripe for a military intervention. Nevertheless, unlike in 1981, when the coup had been planned for a considerable period by the civilian radicals who led it, the coup was essentially spontaneous. The trigger was an incident on July 21. Colonel Akadjie (the Nigerian third in command in the GNA) and the Gambian director general of the National Security Service (NSS), Kebba Ceesay, ordered a public search for weapons of the guard of honor who had gone to the airport to greet Jawara on his return from a month's visit to London. This group of soldiers, which included Sabally and Singhateh (but not Jammeh), were disarmed and sent back to the barracks. Crucially, however, they were not placed under arrest and Singhateh and Sabally were able to convince a number of soldiers that this was a prelude to the government arresting them as coup suspects.[46]

Jammeh subsequently claimed that he planned the coup that night with other discontented lieutenants.[47] In fact, if the account by Colly is accurate, the ring-leaders were Sabally, Singhateh, and three other junior officers, Basiru Barrow, a lieutenant who was at the time in charge of the GNA's Motor Transport, and two other second lieutenants, Alhaji Kanteh and Alpha Kinteh. But at the last moment, Barrow (who was elected the leader of the coup), Kanteh, and Kinteh withdrew, apparently believing that the timing was not right for action; it was at this time that Jammeh and Hydara were brought in by Singhateh and Sabally to replace them.[48] Barrow's decision to withdraw proved to be a fatal error of judgment, for although he was appointed commander of the first Infantry Battalion immediately after the coup, he was distrusted thereafter by the AFRPC leadership. In November 1994, he and two other lieutenants, Abdoulie Dot Faal and Gibril Saye, allegedly attempted to overthrow Jammeh in a countercoup in which all three men were killed. In the view of some sources, including Colly, they (and others) were simply executed on the orders of Singhateh and Sabally.[49]

On the morning of July 22, the coup-makers took advantage of the fact that the GNA was due to take part in joint training exercises with U.S. marines to secure access, both to the armory and the necessary transport. They then seized control of the airport, the radio station, and State House.[50] A complacent Jawara was taken completely by surprise, having apparently initially assumed that the incident was no more than another protest by ECOMOG veterans about their allowances.[51] Shortly before the coup-makers took over State House, his family and various ministers, including Sabally and the minister of finance, Bakary Dabo, fled to a U.S. tank landing ship, *La Moure County*, which was moored off the coast in readiness for the planned training exercises with the marines.

The coup-makers faced some initial resistance from the TSG, which remained loyal to Jawara. Elements of the TSG were willing to fight, but would have been hopelessly outgunned, and were persuaded to lay down their arms; as a result, the coup was bloodless.[52] Some TSG officers were nevertheless subsequently detained for lengthy periods, as was Kebba Ceesay of the NSS.[53] The Nigerian senior officers also failed to take any action; Dada was absent and although Gwadabe apparently managed after some time to secure permission from President Abacha to intervene, it was too late and nothing happened. Some Nigerian officers were arrested, but were released after the coup and the Nigerian forces left The Gambia on August 18, with command of the GNA passing to Baboucarr Jatta, one of the five pre-coup Gambian majors, who was promoted to the rank of lieutenant colonel.[54]

Jawara appealed to the coup leaders to return to the barracks, but his plea was rejected. Apart from this, no senior PPP politician attempted to rally loyalist opposition to the coup, as A. M. Camara had done so effectively in 1981. A number of former PPP ministers were arrested soon after the coup and others escaped to Senegal, but none attempted to rally loyalist elements.[55] The fact that Jawara had left for the U.S. warship and the refusal of the United States to sanction the use of the marines to quell the coup undoubtedly tipped the balance in favor of the putschists in the hours following the coup.

Meanwhile, the National Convention Party (NCP) leader, Sheriff Dibba, gave his unqualified support to the coup, as did the Gambia People's Party (GPP) leader, Camara, initially. The People's Democratic Organisation for Independence and Socialism did not publicly denounce the coup, but did refuse to accept the two cabinet posts in the new government it was offered and also faced prosecution in bringing out editions of *Foroyaa* in defiance of the army prohibition.[56] Despite this evidence of the main political opposition supporting the military intervention, or at least remaining neutral, one of the first actions of the new government was to ban all opposition parties, as well as the PPP, and indeed all political activity under Decree No. 4. Even when the ban on political activity and some parties was finally lifted in August 1996 under Decree No. 89, the NCP and GPP, as well as the PPP, remained prohibited organizations.[57] Many leading figures in the NCP subsequently joined the United Democratic Party (UDP), which was founded in September 1996. At least seven NCP candidates in 1992 were nominated by the UDP in the first election to the National Assembly in 1997, with one other standing for the Alliance for Patriotic Re-orientation and Construction (APRC). Three former GPP candidates from 1987 and/or 1992, Mbemba Tambedou (Tumana), Musa Malang Sonko (Lower Niumi), and Saidi Amang Kanyi (Jarra East), also stood as UDP candidates in 1997; two others, Jain Coli Fye (Lower Niumi) and Sana Y. H. Jallow (Niamina Dankunku), stood as APRC candidates.[58]

Most commentators have asserted that the military intervention was generally welcomed by the Gambian civilian population. Kandeh, for example, stated that the coup was "internally popular." Radelet and McPherson argued, on the basis of media reports and their own discussions with Gambians, that "popular reaction to the coup was generally positive," although also noting that some Gambians decried the dissolution of democratic institutions or were worried about political or economic developments under the military. Saine also claimed that there was initially "euphoria and support" for the intervention from civil servants, and da Costa asserted that the coup was welcomed by many Gambians. Wiseman's view was somewhat different. He accepted that some sections of the population, especially the urban youth, undoubtedly welcomed the coup, but he noted that the imposition of military rule was later condemned by the Gambia Bar Association (GBA) and the Gambia Medical and Dental Association (GMDA). Wiseman also argued that the coup was opposed by leading trade unionists, notably Pa Modou Faal, the secretary general of the Gambia Workers' Confederation (GWC), but in fact the GWC was prepared to support the coup provided the new regime kept to the rule of law. Finally, he noted that many Gambians to whom he spoke in 1995, were privately opposed to the coup, but were too afraid to voice these criticisms publicly.[59]

While on board *La Moure County*, Jawara also called on the U.S. Ambassador, Andrew Winter, to deploy the marines to suppress the coup, but this was refused following discussions with the U.S. government, thus sparking off the unfounded rumors that the United States was behind the coup in the first place.[60] Jawara was taken to Dakar on July 24, where he sought to persuade President Diouf to intervene on his behalf once again.[61] However, although the Senegalese government quickly granted him and others, including Saihou Sabally, political asylum, it refused to send troops. According to Colly, who claims to have spoken to those directly involved, Diouf initially thought the coup was a radical lower ranks affair that could threaten Senegalese stability. But the plotters, with some difficulty, managed to speak with the Senegalese ambassador in Banjul, Moktar Kebe, and persuaded him that, unlike in 1981, the coup was led by more responsible junior officers. In turn, Kebe phoned Diouf to reassure him and the threat of intervention receded. Jammeh himself phoned Diouf on July 24, and, according to Colly, shrewdly suggested some form of reestablishment of confederal links to win over the Senegalese president. Diouf was persuaded that Jammeh and his colleagues posed no threat to Senegalese security and, in fact Senegal was the first country to recognize the new government.[62]

By the evening of July 22, the army was in complete control of the state and the establishment of the AFPRC was duly declared over the radio. It was also announced that the PPP government was dissolved, all political parties banned, and the (1970) constitution suspended.[63] The AFPRC's four-man membership (Jammeh, Singhateh, Sabally, and Hydara) was not announced until the following day, with Jammeh, as the most senior ranking officer, being elected leader. Lieutenant Yankuba Touray, a Mandinka, who was a training instructor at the

Army Training School at Farafenni, North Bank Division, was added to the AFPRC on July 25.[64] Second Lieutenant Alhaji Kanteh, one of the three original plotters who withdrew from the coup at the last moment, was added to the AFPRC on August 2, but was soon afterward dropped from it and detained; he was released on November 3, 1994, shortly before the alleged Barrow counter-coup.[65]

On July 26, Jammeh announced the names of his first cabinet, which was initially composed of seven soldiers and eight civilians. The AFPRC members retained the key positions: Jammeh was named as AFPRC chairman (and thus head of state), Sabally (the most senior second lieutenant of the original conspirators) as vice chairman, Singhateh as minister of defense, Hydara as minister of the interior, and Touray as minister for local government and lands.[66] Two more senior security officers, but non-AFPRC members, Captain Mamat Omar Cham and Captain Sheriff S. Sarr ("Ebou Colly"), also received less important portfolios. But they were dropped from the cabinet the next day, detained, and replaced by two more civilians.[67]

That the majority of post-coup governments were civilians was not unusual in Africa; in many cases, senior civil servants have been appointed to ministerial positions. One former permanent secretary, Bolong L. Sonko, was appointed minister of external affairs and another, more junior, civil servant, Musa Mbenga (a research scientist in the Ministry of Agriculture), was appointed its minister, but the remaining permanent secretaries were discarded and many of them were later forcibly retired.[68] More surprisingly, in view of the new government's attack on the PPP, one of its key appointments was that of the former PPP vice president, Bakary Dabo, who was persuaded to return from Dakar to assume his former position as minister of finance. His actions were criticized by many PPP supporters and Jawara later stated that he returned to Banjul without his blessing.[69] The AFPRC justified its decision by arguing that Dabo was not corrupt like other former PPP ministers, but its real motive for appointing him was to assure Western creditors that there would be no significant shift from the PPP's economic policies. It may also have believed that the appointment of Dabo, with his strong Senegalese connections, would pacify the Dakar government. However, as early as October 1994, Dabo was sacked from the cabinet for unspecified reasons and subsequently accused of being the main "civilian instigator" of the November coup. He fled into exile, first to Senegal, and later to Britain.[70]

Jammeh also appointed one opposition Member of Parliament (MP), Mbemba Tambedou, the GPP MP for Tumana before the coup, to his cabinet (even though his party was banned); Tambedou was to be sacked in September 1996 and, as noted, subsequently joined the opposition UDP.[71] In August, Jammeh made another surprising appointment, when the former PPP minister of justice and attorney general in the early 1980s, Fafa M'Bai, was persuaded to assume his old positions. As discussed in Chapter 9, M'Bai's downfall occurred in 1984 because he was accused of illegally transferring funds, so his appointment seems curious given the new government's attacks on corruption. He was sacked in March 1995 and once more accused of corruption.[72]

Most of the remaining civilian ministers were little known and certainly lacked an independent power base. Three of the more obscure ministers had family connections with either Jammeh or Sana Sabally, which probably explains their appointments. Both Mrs. Susan Waffa-Ogoo (information and tourism), who had been the deputy librarian at the Gambia College before the coup, and John P. Bojang (trade, industry and employment), who had previously been a school headmaster, were relatives of Jammeh; Mrs. Fatoumata Tambajang (health and social welfare) was reportedly Sabally's aunt.[73] Tambajang's period of office was short-lived; she was dismissed in February 1995 following the foiling of an alleged plot by two of the four original AFPRC leaders, Sabally and Sadibou Hydara, to assassinate Jammeh on January 27. Both men were arrested, with the former later being sentenced to a nine-year term of imprisonment; the latter died mysteriously in June 1995 before his trial could begin.[74]

To what extent, therefore, does the 1994 coup fit the wider pattern of coups in Africa? There is of course a vast literature on military interventions in Africa and many different theories about their root causes. Chazan et al., for example, suggest that the militarization of politics in Africa can be explained by reference to seven factors: economic stagnation; the loss of political legitimacy by the incumbent government; high levels of factional conflict within the state; the denial of access to the resources of the state to opposition groups; a military predisposition to articulate its corporate interest and to act to foster it; the personal ambitions of individual soldiers; and the contagion effect of successful coups in neighboring countries.[75]

The evidence presented here suggests that some, but not all, of these factors were present in the Gambian case. It is probable that the junior officers in the GNA were predisposed to foster the army's collective interest against what they perceived to be civilian neglect; considered that the government had lost its political legitimacy; were personally ambitious; and were influenced by successful coups elsewhere. It could also be argued that one of their motives was to rectify economic stagnation (or rather the failure of the PPP to achieve economic and social development), although this was a secondary motive at best. But it would be difficult to argue that the other two factors were present.

Over the coming months, Jawara made some efforts to persuade Western powers, particularly the United States, to intervene to persuade the Jammeh government to step down, but these achieved nothing.[76] Subsequently, he retreated into exile in England, but was granted an "amnesty" by Jammeh in late 2001 and returned home the next year to a nonpolitical life. He resigned the secretary generalship of the PPP and announced his retirement from public life in August 2002.[77] It is therefore appropriate to conclude by assessing the contribution he made to Gambian public life between the 1960s and the 1990s.

The Jawara Legacy

Sir Dawda Jawara first came to national prominence in Gambian politics when he was elected the leader of the PPP in 1959. As we have seen, he subsequently mobilized the rural electorate behind the PPP and led his party to victory in the first nation-wide election in 1960. He became prime minister after winning the hard-fought 1962 election, guided The Gambia to independence in 1965, and then led the PPP to six further general election victories after independence. Having played a key role in the establishment of the republic in 1970, he was reelected president on five occasions (three times after a directly elected national ballot). Thus, until his abrupt removal from power in July 1994, he dominated Gambian politics for three decades.

Jawara's formal political achievements make impressive reading. But what of his longer term political legacy? First, and perhaps most important, he ensured that The Gambia retained a competitive, multiparty democracy for nearly thirty years after independence, while almost all other African states experienced periods of military rule, civilian one-party government, or both. Throughout the Jawara period, all opposition parties that accepted the basic ground rules of the political system were allowed to operate freely and to contest elections and Jawara refused formally to outlaw rival parties. Although the PPP certainly enjoyed a number of unfair advantages and there were incidents of malpractice (to a greater extent in some elections than in others), the voting process itself was generally fair and opposition candidates could, and frequently did, win seats in the House of Representatives. It is also reasonable to suggest that where illegal electoral practices did take place, they were often carried out by PPP militants without Jawara's blessing.[78]

Of course, it could be argued that Jawara could adopt this tolerant attitude because, after 1962, the PPP was almost certain to win every election. Yet there is no reason to suppose that, had the PPP been defeated at the ballot box, Jawara would have tried to overturn the result; indeed, on the one occasion when the PPP experienced a major setback by failing to achieve the required majority in the 1965 republic referendum, Jawara calmly accepted the outcome against the wishes of some of his closest advisers.[79]

Second, Jawara extended his tolerance of his political opponents to other groups in society, including the press and, arguably to a lesser extent, to trade unions. There were opposition newspapers in existence for much of the Jawara era, including the pro-UP *Gambia Echo* in the 1960s and the pro-NCP *Gambia Outlook* in the later 1970s and 1980s, while the growth of an independent, and often critical, press in the early 1990s was permitted. This was in sharp contrast to the hostile attitude adopted toward the independent press by the Jammeh government.[80] The trade union movement was allowed to operate in an unfettered way as well. The only effective union of the time, the Gambia Workers' Union (GWU), was deregistered in 1977, but the action that the government took against the GWU was entirely legal and, arguably, justified.[81] The judiciary's independence was maintained and judges continued to make occasional judgments that were profoundly embarrassing for the government.[82]

Third, Jawara was largely responsible for ensuring that The Gambia was spared the ethnic conflicts which have been such a feature of so many other African states after independence. Having come to power largely on the basis of the support of the majority Mandinka ethnic group, Jawara made conscious efforts to accommodate all the minority ethnic groups within his government. If anything, he was almost too successful, for by doing so, he alienated a substantial portion of the Mandinka community, which turned to the NCP after 1975.[83] Jawara also maintained the long-standing Gambian tradition that religious differences did not result in ethnic conflict; although he himself reconverted to Islam after independence and most ministers were Muslim, Christians were not excluded from positions of influence and no anti-Christian policies were ever adopted.[84]

Fourth, having ensured that The Gambia achieved independence as a sovereign state against the wishes of the colonial power, he skillfully maintained its sovereignty over the next thirty years, despite considerable difficulty at times, notably in the aftermath of the 1981 coup. Even when he was forced to accede to Senegalese pressure for the establishment of the Senegambia Confederation in 1982, he ensured that Gambians by and large retained control over their own affairs. However, it could be argued in retrospect that Jawara became overconfident and misjudged the situation; by alienating the Senegalese, which led to the breakdown of the confederation in 1989, he ensured that there would be no attempt to restore him to power after the 1994 coup.[85]

Fifth, Jawara's personal commitment to human rights was far greater than almost all other African leaders and had a much wider impact than in The Gambia alone. Excluding those arrested and sentenced after the 1981 coup, following due legal process, there were never any political detainees in The Gambia; moreover, Jawara commuted all death sentences imposed by the courts, except in the case of Mustapha Danso after the 1981 coup, and also used his personal initiative to ensure that the death penalty was abolished in April 1993.[86] Coercion, when used by his administration, seldom took violent forms. Dismissals or denial of financial rewards, rather than the instruments of the police state, were the preferred options; and patronage was favored over repression, even if this compromised Jawara's moral integrity. Ever the pragmatist, his administration never suffered from the excesses generated in more ideological African political systems, where tyranny was exercised in the name of national or social equality. At an international level, he was instrumental in persuading the Organisation of African Unity to adopt the African Charter on Human and People's Rights and to set up monitoring institutions in Banjul, in recognition of his government's commitment to this goal.[87] Again, the comparison with the flawed record of the Jammeh government with regard to human rights is compelling.[88]

This is certainly an impressive record, which few post-independence political leaders in Africa can match. However, Jawara made mistakes and his record is far from flawless. First, in terms of his management of the economy, his overall record was mixed at best. It should be emphasized that the economic situation he inherited at independence was distinctly unfavorable, yet in the late 1960s and early 1970s, The Gambia fared surprisingly well. Subsequently, there was a sharp downturn in the later 1970s and early 1980s; although some of this could be attributed to external factors beyond his government's control, domestic policies certainly made matters worse and in 1984, The Gambia had to call in the International Monetary Fund (IMF). Yet once Jawara was persuaded that the ERP was necessary, he gave it his wholehearted support and helped to ensure that it became one of the more successful IMF Structural Adjustment Programmes in Africa.[89]

Second, Jawara signally failed to tackle the growth of corruption among his ministers, senior civil servants, and other key figures associated with the PPP. This became a problem in the late 1970s and early 1980s. Under ERP, the situation certainly improved, but as we have seen, it again became an issue in the early 1990s as the revelations of the commissions of inquiry established by Jammeh demonstrated. Jawara not only failed to take effective action against those who were widely suspected of corruption, but by appointing the notorious Saihou Sabally as vice president in 1992, he appeared to be declaring his public acceptance of it. Whether Jawara was himself personally corrupt remains a moot point, although the revelations made before the various commissions of inquiry after 1994 certainly damaged his reputation. Nevertheless, when compared with the revelations and accusations regarding his successor's far briefer rule and the flagrant excesses of many other African leaders, his shortcomings in this respect seem modest. Certainly, when in enforced exile in Britain, he lived a quiet life, which was totally lacking in ostentation, again in marked contrast to the opulent lifestyles of other exiled African rulers.

Third, like many other African political leaders, he crucially mishandled the issue of his succession. It appeared at the end of 1991 that he was doing all the right things by announcing that he would not stand again for president at the 1992 election. Unfortunately, he allowed himself to be persuaded to change his mind, a decision that he surely came bitterly to regret after the 1994 coup, despite his public statements to the contrary.[90]

Fourth, it could be argued that Jawara failed to bring about sustained social and economic development in The Gambia, in part because scarce resources were not used effectively or were misappropriated. As seen in Chapter 1, The Gambia remained near the bottom (161st out of 174 countries) of the Human Development Index at the end of the Jawara period. Moreover, poverty certainly remained an acute problem in the 1990s. However, it cannot be stated whether poverty increased or decreased between 1965 and 1994 and it is also worth reiterating that poverty in The Gambia increased considerably between 1992–93 and 1998, that is, after Jawara's downfall. It should also be recognized that under Jawara, literacy rates improved considerably and imbalances between males and females and urban and rural areas were reduced, if far from eliminated; life expectancy at birth also increased. There was also a growth in the number of schools and teachers and of rural medical facilities (if not of hospitals). The achievements were certainly modest, rather than spectacular, but it is unfair to claim that the Jawara government achieved nothing at all.[91]

Jawara's record is therefore flawed in a number of important respects. Yet it is clear that he made a greater contribution to Gambian political life than any of the other key political figures of the nineteenth and twentieth centuries whose careers have been described in earlier chapters. Men such as Thomas Brown, the two Samuel Forsters, I. M. Garba-Jahumpa, Rev. J. C. Faye, P. S. N'Jie, and Sheriff Dibba had long political careers,[92] but none could match Jawara's achievements. Perhaps only the journalist, trade union leader and politician, E. F. Small, who was of course operating in a very different political climate from Jawara, comes close to matching his overall contribution to Gambian public life. Despite the criticisms heaped on him by the Jammeh government, it is also evident that Jawara's overall record is a far more impressive one than that achieved to date by his successor. Although it is too early to attempt an overall assessment of Jammeh, who remains firmly in power at the time of writing, the major early analyses of his rule have been distinctly unfavorable.[93] Although it may be an exaggeration to say that the Jawara era will come to be regarded as a golden age in Gambian history, it is likely that future historians will judge him much more kindly than his successor.

APPENDIX A

MAJOR CONSTITUTIONAL CHANGES, 1816–1994

Table A.1. Major Constitutional Changes, 1816–1994

Date	Constitutional status	Executive body	Legislature
1816	Bathurst occupied. Joint control by Company of Merchants and Parliament	None	None
1821	Colonial rule resumes; Gambia placed under Governor of Sierra Leone with authority wielded locally by commandant		
1829	Commandant replaced by lieutenant-governor		
1843	Independence from Sierra Leone; first governor appointed	Executive Council founded. Contains governor and 3 officials; no unofficial members	Legislative Council founded. Contains governor, 3 officials and 2 European merchants
1866	West African Settlements formed. Governor replaced by administrator under governor of Sierra Leone	Council abolished	Council downgraded—only 1 unofficial remains
1883			First African member appointed

Table A.1. (*continued*)

Date	Constitutional status	Executive body	Legislature
1888	Independence from Sierra Leone. Crown Colony formed	Council restored. Official members only, except between 1890 and 1896	Council reconstituted with 5 officials and 2 unofficials (1 an African)
1889	Boundary of colony drawn—leads to establishment of Protectorate		
1901	Governor replaces administrator		
1907			Second African member appointed—now 4 unofficials
1922			Council reconstituted with 3 unofficials: 1 European to represent Chamber of Commerce and 2 Africans (1 to represent Muslims)
1933			Third African unofficial appointed to represent Bathurst Urban District Council
1947		Three African unofficials appointed	First African elected member; unofficial majority conceded
1951		Four unofficials appointed; 2 termed "members of the government"	Three members elected: 2 for Bathurst and 1 for Kombo St. Mary
1954		Unofficial majority conceded; 3 African "ministers" appointed, although dependent on officials	Unofficial membership increased to 16, 4 of whom are directly elected. Seven Protectorate representatives
1960		Council now contains governor, 4 officials, and 6 African ministers, 4 of	House of Representatives replaces Legislative Council. Contains 27 elected and 7 nominated

Table A.1. (*continued*)

Date	Constitutional status	Executive body	Legislature
		whom have portfolios	members. Seven directly elected in Bathurst/Kombo St. Mary and 12 directly elected in Protectorate; 8 chiefs indirectly elected
1961		Chief minister appointed	
1962		Chief minister upgraded to premier	Directly elected members rises to 32: 25 for the Protectorate and 7 for Bathurst/Kombo St. Mary
1963	Full internal self-government	Premier upgraded to prime minister. Executive Council replaced by cabinet	
1965	Independence		
1966			Bathurst seats reduced to 3; extra seats given to Provinces
1970	Republic established under an executive president		
1977			Directly elected members rises to 35
1982	Senegambia Confederation formed		
1989	Confederation ended		
1994	Suspension of constitution	Establishment of Armed Forces Provisional Ruling Council	House of Representatives abolished

APPENDIX B

LEGISLATIVE COUNCIL ELECTION RESULTS, 1947–54

Table B.1. Legislative Council Election Results: 1947

Constituency	Candidate	Ethnicity	Religion	Vote
Bathurst and Kombo St. Mary	**Edward F. Small**	Aku	Christian (Methodist)	1,491
	Sheikh Omar Fye	Wolof	Muslim	1,018
	Ibrahima M. Garba-Jahumpa	Wolof	Muslim	679
	John Finden Dailey	Aku	Christian	
	Richard S. Rendall	Aku	Christian (Methodist)	4
				3

Note: Winning candidate is noted in bold.

Source: Gambia Outlook, November 1, 1947.

Table B.2. Legislative Council Election Results: 1951

Constituency	Candidate	Ethnicity	Religion	Party	Vote
Bathurst	**John C. Faye**	Serere	Christian (Anglican)	Gambia Democratic Party	905
	Ibrahima M. Garba-Jahumpa	Wolof	Muslim	Bathurst Young Muslims Society	828
	Pierre S. N'Jie	Wolof	Christian (Roman Catholic)	Independent	463
	Edward F. Small	Aku	Christian (Methodist)	Gambia National League	45
	Mustapha Colley	Wolof	Muslim	Common People's Party	10
	J. Francis Senegal	Wolof?	Christian	Independent	6
	John Finden Dailey	Aku	Christian	Common People's Party	5
Kombo St. Mary	**Henry A. Madi**	Lebanese	Christian (Roman Catholic)	Independent	813
	Howsoon O. Semega-Janneh	Serahuli	Muslim	Independent	255
	John W. Kuye	Aku	Christian	Independent	7

Note: Winning candidates are noted in bold.

Source: Gambia News Bulletin, October 26, 1951.

Table B.3. Legislative Council Election Results: 1954

Constituency	Candidate	Ethnicity	Religion	Party	Vote
Bathurst	**Pierre S. N'Jie**	Wolof	Christian (Roman Catholic)	**United Party**	2,123
	John C. Faye	Serere	Christian (Anglican)	**Gambia Democratic Party**	1,979
	Ibrahima M. Garba-Jahumpa	Wolof	Muslim	**Gambia Muslim Congress**	1,569
	George St. Clair Joof	Wolof	Christian	Gambia People's Party	252
Kombo St. Mary	**Henry A. Madi**	Lebanese	Christian (Roman Catholic)	Independent	904
	Samuel J. Oldfield	Aku	Christian	Independent	650

Note: Winning candidates are noted in bold.

Source: Gambia News Bulletin, October 20, 1954.

APPENDIX C

GENERAL ELECTION AND BY-ELECTION RESULTS, 1960–93

Table C.1. General Election Results: 1960

Constituency	Candidate	Ethnicity[a]	Party[b]	Vote
Colony				
Bathurst			PPP	232
(total)			UP	3,075
			DCA	3,237
			Independent	973
New Town East	**Pierre S. N'Jie**	Wolof	**UP**	1,017
	Alieu E. Cham-Joof	Wolof	DCA	687
New Town West	**Ishmael B.I. Jobe**	Wolof	**UP**	617
	Momodou D. Sallah	Tukulor	DCA	559
	A. S. C. Able-Thomas	Aku	Independent (PPP)	185
Joloff/	**Alieu B. N'Jie**	Wolof	**DCA**	552
Portuguese	J. E. Mahoney	Aku	UP	432
Town	Sulayman B. Gaye	Wolof	Independent	102
Soldier Town	**Melvin B. Jones**	Aku	**Independent (UP)**	644
	Crispin R. Grey-Johnson	Aku	DCA	496
	H. Augusta Jawara (Mrs.)	Aku	PPP	232
Half Die	**Joseph H. Joof**	Wolof	**UP**	1,009
	Ibrahima M. Garba-Jahumpa	Wolof	DCA	943
	I. A. S. Burang-John	Wolof	Independent	42

Table C.1. (*continued*)

Constituency	Candidate	Ethnicity[a]	Party[b]	Vote
Kombo St. Mary (total)			PPP	647
			UP	415
			DCA	289
			Independent	1,256
Kombo East	**Alphonso M. (Fansu) Demba**	Mandinka	**PPP**	647
	Samuel J. Oldfield	Aku	Independent (DCA?)	624
Kombo West	**Howsoon O. Semega-Janneh**	Serahuli	**Independent**	562
	Ebrima D. N'Jie	Wolof	UP	415
	John C. Faye	Wolof/Serere	DCA	289
	M. A. Jobe[c]	Wolof	Independent	70
Protectorate Western (total)			PPP	3,362
			Independent	1,210
Kombo	**David K. Jawara**	Mandinka	**PPP**	Unopposed
Foni	**Momodou N. Sanyang**	Mandinka	**PPP**	3,362
	Saihou Biyai	Jola	Independent (UP)	1,210
Lower River (total)			PPP	10,496
			Independent	12,722
Kiang	**Jerreh L. B. Daffeh**	Mandinka	**PPP**	2,136
	B. Sanneh	Mandinka	Independent (UP?)	837
	L. Sanneh	Mandinka	Independent	786
Jarra	**Yaya Ceesay**	Mandinka	**PPP**	1,880
	K. Barrow	Mandinka	Independent	892
	Kalilu S. Dabo	Mandinka	Independent (UP)	804
Baddibu	**Sheriff M. Dibba**	Mandinka	**PPP**	5,020
	Kalilu B. Jammeh	Mandinka	Independent	3,994
	M. Gaye	Wolof	Independent	498
Niumi-Jokadu	**Landing O. Sonko**	Mandinka	**Independent (UP)**	2,371
	Kebba C. A. Kah	Tukulor	Independent	1,724
	Famara B. Manneh	Mandinka	PPP	1,460
	Mafode (Foday) F. Sonko	Mandinka	Independent	816

Table C.1. (*continued*)

Constituency	Candidate	Ethnicity[a]	Party[b]	Vote
MacCarthy			PPP	7,093
Island (total)			UP	4,446
			Independent	3,892
MacCarthy	**Kebba N. Leigh**	Mandinka	**PPP**	1,985
Island	Numukunda M. Darbo	Mandinka	UP	1,616
	Bakary K. Sidibeh	Mandinka	Independent	831
	G. O. M'Baki	Tukulor	Independent	591
	M. K. Sanyang	Mandinka	Independent	142
Niani-Saloum	**Alasan N. Touray**	Wolof	**UP**	2,830
	Omar J. Sise	Wolof	PPP	2,014
	B. A. Janneh	Mandinka	Independent	877
Niamina	**Sheriff S. Sisay**	Mandinka	**PPP**	3,094
	Omar J. Ceesay	Mandinka	Independent (UP)	1,451
Upper River			PPP	3,660
(total)			UP	4,561
			Independent	7,482
Basse	**Michael Baldeh**	Fula Firdu	**UP**[d]	4,561
	Muhammadou Krubally	Mandinka	Independent	1,550
Kantora	**Andrew D. Camara**	Fula Firdu	**Independent (UP)**	2,535
	Mamadi B. Sagnia[e]	Mandinka	PPP	1,154
	Kebba J. Krubally	Mandinka	Independent	634
Wuli-Sandu	**Musa S. Dabo**	Mandinka	**PPP**	2,506
	Kantora Juwara	Serahuli	Independent (UP)	1,505
	A. Krubally	Mandinka	Independent	797
	Bangally Singhateh	Mandinka	Independent	461

Notes: [a]See Chapter 6, notes 29, 35, and 41 for sources on ethnic origin.
[b]Party in brackets in thought to have "supported" candidate; see Chapter 6, 140.
[c]Or possibly M. N. Jobe; this is unlikely to have been Musa A. Jobe, a UP candidate in 1977.
[d]Nominated by the PPP.
[e]Also known as Momodou Sanyang.
Winning candidates are noted in bold.

Sources: Gambia News Bulletin, June 24, 1960; CO 554/2147, Windley to Eastwood, June 1, 1960 (Colony only); *The Vanguard,* June 4, 1960 (Protectorate results only).

Table C.1. (*continued*)

Constituency	Candidate	Ethnicity[a]	Party[b]	Vote

Table C.1. (*continued*)

SUMMARY OF RESULTS

Party	Number of votes	Percentage of votes
PPP	25,490	36.92
UP	12,497	18.10
DCA	3,526	5.11
Independents	27,535	39.88
Supporting UP	?11,357	?16.45
Total votes cast	69,048	100.00

Table C.2. General Election Results: 1962

Constituency	Candidate	Ethnicity[a]	Party	Vote
Colony				
Bathurst (total)			PPP	739
			UP	4,919
			DCA	3,582
New Town East	**Pierre S. N'Jie**	Wolof	**UP**	1,221
	Alieu E. Cham-Joof	Wolof	DCA	907
New Town West	**Ishmael B. I. Jobe**	Wolof	**UP**	893
	John C. Faye	Wolof/ Serere	DCA	824
Joloff/	**Alieu B. N'Jie**	Wolof	**DCA**	657
Portuguese Town	Sulayman B. Gaye	Wolof	UP	604
Soldier Town	**Melvin B. Jones**	Aku	**UP**	996
	A. S. C. Able-Thomas	Aku	PPP	739
Half Die	**Joseph H. Joof**	Wolof	**UP**	1,205
	Ibrahima M. Garba-Jahumpa	Wolof	DCA	1,194
Kombo St. Mary (total)			PPP	970
			UP	1,848
			DCA	598
Bakau	**Alphonso M. (Fansu) Demba**	Mandinka	**PPP**	970
	Kebba W. Foon	Wolof	UP	688
Serrekunda	**Howsoon O. Semega-Janneh**	Serahuli	**UP**	1,160
	M. O. Faal	Wolof	DCA	598
Protectorate				
Western (total)			PPP	12,190
			UP	2,844
Eastern Kombo	**David K. Jawara**	Mandinka	**PPP**	4,073
	Bakary K. Jabang	Mandinka	UP	721
Western Kombo	**Famara Wassa Touray**	Mandinka	**PPP**	3,262
	Baboucar B. Cham	Mandinka	UP	1,035
Eastern Foni	**Momodou N. Sanyang**	Mandinka	**PPP**	2,908
	Bernard Jamanka	Fula Firdu	UP	344
Western Foni	**B. L. Kuti Sanyang**	Jola	**PPP**	1,947
	Saihou Biyai	Jola	UP	744

Table C.2. (*continued*)

Constituency	Candidate	Ethnicity[a]	Party	Vote
Lower River			PPP	22,867
(total)			UP	10,855
			Independent	108
Eastern Kiang	**Jerreh L. B. Daffeh**	Mandinka	**PPP**	3,480
	Silla Sanneh	Mandinka	UP	972
Western Kiang	**Amang S. Kanyi**	Mandinka	**PPP**	Unopposed
Jarra	**Yaya Ceesay**	Mandinka	**PPP**	3,905
	Yaya Dabo	Mandinka	UP	713
Sabach Sanjal	**Yusupha Samba**	Wolof	**PPP**	2,273
	Mamadi Sabally	Mandinka	UP	2,126
Illiassa	**Lamin B. M'Boge**	Mandinka	**PPP**	3,175
	Kalilu B. Jammeh	Mandinka	UP	2,325
Central Baddibu	**Sheriff M. Dibba**	Mandinka	**PPP**	3,851
	Baboucar S. O. Jeng	Wolof	UP	313[b]
Lower Baddibu	**Kalilou F. Singhateh**	Mandinka	**PPP**	2,857
	Gabriel J. Faal	Wolof	UP	625
	Karamo Kinteh	Mandinka	Independent	108
Niumi	**Mafode F. (Foday) Sonko**	Mandinka	**UP**	2,243
	Famara B. Manneh	Mandinka	PPP	2,054
Jokadu	**Kebba C. A. Kah**	Tukulor	**UP**	1,538
	Baba M. Touray	Mandinka	PPP	1,272
MacCarthy			PPP	10,794
Island (total)			UP	7,908
Sami	**Kebba N. Leigh**	Mandinka	**PPP**	1,816
	Samba Jobe	Wolof	UP	1,086
Niani	**Demba S. Cham**	Tukulor	**PPP**	1,961
	Alasan N. Touray	Wolof	UP	758
Saloum	**Ebrima D. N'Jie**	Wolof	**UP**	2,099
	Malick Lowe	Wolof	PPP	1,129
Lower Fulladu West	**Paul L. Baldeh**	Fula Firdu	**PPP**	1,600
	Andrew M'Ballow	Fula Firdu	UP	1,126
Upper Fulladu West	**Numukunda M. Darbo**	Mandinka	**UP**	1,964
	Alieu Marong	Mandinka	PPP	1,501
Niamina	**Sheriff S. Sisay**	Mandinka	**PPP**	2,787
	Kebba F. Dampha	Mandinka	UP	875

Table C.2. (*continued*)

Constituency	Candidate	Ethnicity[a]	Party	Vote
Upper River			PPP	8,783
(total)			UP	8,642
Jimara	**Demba Jagana**	Serahuli	**UP**	1,511
	M. Baikoro Sillah	Mandinka	PPP	1,038
Kantora	**Andrew D. Camara**	Fula Firdu	**UP**	1,532
	Mamadi B. Sagnia	Mandinka	PPP	1,184
Tumana	**Momodou C. Cham**	Tukulor	**UP**	1,620
	Noah K. Sanyang	Mandinka	PPP	1,229
Basse	**Michael Baldeh**	Fula Firdu	**UP**	1,683
	Kebba J. Krubally	Mandinka	PPP	1,396
Wuli	**Bangally Singhateh**	Mandinka	**PPP**	1,354
	Momodou C. Jallow	Fula	UP	1,310
Sandu	**Musa S. Dabo**	Mandinka	**PPP**	2,582
	Kebba Dibba	Mandinka	UP	986

Notes: [a]See Chapter 6, note 100, for sources on ethnic origin.
[b]Given as 318 in *GNB*, but adjusted to be consistent with total results as shown in CO 554/2148, Paul to Eastwood, June 7, 1962.
Winning candidates are noted in bold.

Sources: Gambia News Bulletin, June 1, 1962 (in DO 195/382, Crombie to Greenhill, May 2, 1966).

SUMMARY OF RESULTS

Party	Number of votes	Percentage of votes
PPP	56,343	57.70
UP	37,016	37.91
DCA	4,180	4.28
Independents	108	0.11
Total votes cast	97,647	100.00

Table C.3. General Election Results: 1966

Constituency	Candidate	Ethnicity[a]	Party	Vote
Bathurst Administrative Area (AA) (total)			PPP	2,170
			UP/GCP	6,131
			Independent	219
Bathurst North	**Pierre S. N'Jie**	Wolof	**UP/GCP**	2,449
	M. Harley N'Jie	Wolof	PPP	688
	Momodou E. Jallow	Fula	Independent	115
Bathurst Central	**John R. Forster**	Aku	**UP/GCP**	1,564
	Melvin B. Jones	Aku	PPP	941
	John C. Faye	Wolof/ Serere	Independent	104
Bathurst South	**Ibrahima M. Garba-Jahumpa**	Wolof	**GCP/UP**	2,118
	Abdoulie M. Drammeh	Wolof	PPP	541
Kombo St. Mary AA (total)			PPP	2,060
			UP	1,553
			UP/GCP	889
Bakau	**Abdoulie K. N'Jie**	Mandinka	**PPP**	1,337[b]
	Kebba W. Foon	Wolof	UP/GCP	889
Serrekunda	**Gibou M. Jagne**	Wolof	**UP**	1,553
	Howsoon O. Semega-Janneh	Serahuli	PPP	723
Brikama AA (WD) (total)			PPP	15,078
			UP	1,537
			UP/GCP	481
			Independent	758
Northern Kombo	**Alieu B. N'Jie**	Wolof	**PPP**	2,402
	Baboucar B. Cham	Mandinka	UP	612
Southern Kombo	**Famara W. Touray**	Mandinka	**PPP**	2,599
	Fabakary Jatta	Mandinka	Independent	613
	Ebrima K. Janneh	Mandinka	Independent	145
Eastern Kombo	**Dawda K. Jawara**[c]	Mandinka	**PPP**	4,515
	Sillah Bojang	Mandinka	UP	589
Eastern Foni	**Momodou N. Sanyang**	Mandinka	**PPP**	2,826
	Paul Bojang	Jola	UP	336
Western Foni	**B. L. Kuti Sanyang**	Jola	**PPP**	2,736
	Ismaila K. N'Jie	Wolof	UP/GCP	481

Table C.3. (*continued*)

Constituency	Candidate	Ethnicity[a]	Party	Vote
Mansakonko AA			PPP	12,424
(LRD—South Bank)			UP	1,028
(total)			UP/GCP	611
			Independent	408
Eastern Kiang	**Jerreh L. B. Daffeh**	Mandinka	**PPP**	2,995
	Jallow Sanneh	Mandinka	UP	597
Western Kiang	**Amang S. Kanyi**	Mandinka	**PPP**	3,470
	Momodou K. Sanneh	Mandinka	Independent	408[b]
Eastern Jarra	**Kemo Sanneh**	Mandinka	**PPP**	2,812
	Kalilu S. Dabo	Mandinka	UP	431
Western Jarra	**Yaya Ceesay**	Mandinka	**PPP**	3,147
	Tairu A. K. John	Wolof	UP/GCP[d]	611
Kerewan AA			PPP	21,372
(LRD—North Bank)			UP	5,646
(total)			UP/GCP	2,517
			Independent	245
Sabach Sanjal	**Yusupha Samba**	Wolof	**PPP**	3,121
	Mamadi Sabally	Mandinka	UP	1,953
Illiassa	**Baba M. Touray**	Mandinka	**PPP**	4,578
	Sheriff Jammeh	Mandinka	UP	1,521
	Lamin B. M'Boge	Mandinka	Independent	245
Central Baddibu	**Sheriff M. Dibba**	Mandinka	**PPP**	4,319
	Demba Jagana	Serahuli	UP	262
Lower Baddibu	**Kalilou F. Singhateh**	Mandinka	**PPP**	3,656
	Karamo Kinteh	Mandinka	UP	489
Niumi	**Mafode F. Sonko**	Mandinka	**PPP**	3,522
	Alieu O. Jeng	Wolof	UP/GCP	2,517
Jokadu	**Kebba C. A. Kah**	Tukulor	**PPP**	2,176
	I. A. S. Burang-John	Wolof	UP	1,421
Georgetown AA			PPP	16,198
(MID) (total)			UP	2,685
			UP/GCP	9,217
Sami	**Kebba N. Leigh**	Mandinka	**PPP**	2,656
	Omar M'Baki	Tukulor	UP/GCP	1,541
Niani	**Demba S. Cham**	Tukulor	**PPP**	2,681
	Musa Cham	Tukulor	UP/GCP	1,403
Saloum	**Ebrima D. N'Jie**	Wolof	**UP/GCP**	2,706
	Kebba A. Bayo	Mandinka	PPP	1,737

Table C.3. (*continued*)

Constituency	Candidate	Ethnicity[a]	Party	Vote
Lower Fulladu	**Paul L. Baldeh**	Fula Firdu	**PPP**	2,702
West	Augustin A. Sabally	Fula Firdu	UP/GCP	1,862
Upper Fulladu	**Numukunda M. Darbo**	Mandinka	**UP**	2,685
West	Kebba K. Jawara	Mandinka	PPP	2,258
Niamina	**Sheriff S. Sisay**	Mandinka	**PPP**	4,164
	Sheikh S. Jobe	Mandinka	UP/GCP	1,705
Basse AA (URD)			PPP	12,011
(total)			UP	9,254
Jimara	**Momodou C. Jallow**	Fula	**UP**	1,607
	M. Baikoro Sillah	Mandinka	PPP	1,394
Kantora	**Andrew D. Camara**	Fula Firdu	**PPP**	1,648
	Momodou M. N'Jie	Serahuli	UP	1,249
Tumana	**Momodou C. Cham**	Tukulor	**UP**	2,103
	Abdou S. Kandeh	Mandinka	PPP	1,666
Basse	**Kebba J. Krubally**	Mandinka	**PPP**	2,207
	Bali Faal	Wolof	UP	1,685
Wuli	**Bangally Singhateh**	Mandinka	**PPP**	2,050
	Kantora Juwara	Serahuli	UP	1,536
Sandu	**Musa S. Dabo**	Mandinka	**PPP**	3,046
	Gibril M'Backe	Tukulor	UP	1,074

Notes: [a]See Chapter 6, note 100, for sources on ethnic origin.
[b]Results differ in Sagnia.
[c]Formerly David Jawara.
[d]Listed as an Independent by Sagnia.
Winning candidates are noted in bold.

Sources: Gambia News Bulletin, May 28, 1966; Bakarr, *Gambia Yesterday,* 81–82; Sagnia, *Gambian Legislature,* 61–64.

SUMMARY OF RESULTS

Party	Number of votes	Percentage of votes
PPP	81,313	65.31
UP (total)	41,549	33.37
UP only	21,703	17.43
UP/GCP	19,846	15.94
Independents	1,630	1.31
Total votes cast	124,492	100.00

Table C.4. General Election Results: 1972

Constituency	Candidate	Party	Vote
Bathurst AA (total)		PPP	3,828
		UP	4,231
		Independent	248
Bathurst North	**Pierre S. N'Jie**	**UP**	1,633
	I. B. A. Kelepha-Samba	PPP	1,320
	Momodou E. Jallow	Independent	248
Bathurst Central	**John R. Forster**	**UP**	1,361
	Horace R. Monday	PPP	1,170
Bathurst South	**Ibrahima M. Garba-Jahumpa**	**PPP**	1,338
	Momodou (Dodou) M. Taal	UP	1,237
Kombo St. Mary AA (total)		PPP	1,255
		UP	1,479
Bakau	**Abdoulie K. N'Jie**	**PPP**	Unopposed
Serrekunda	**Gibou M. Jagne**	**UP**	1,479
	Omar A. Jallow	PPP	1,255
Brikama AA (WD) (total)		PPP	9,662
		Independent	3,144
Northern Kombo	**Alieu B. N'Jie**	**PPP**	2,696
	Kebba F. Manneh	Independent	865
Southern Kombo	**Famara W. Touray**	**PPP**	Unopposed
Eastern Kombo	**Lamin K. Jabang**	**PPP**	4,383
	Ya Fatou Sonko (Mrs.)	Independent	1,518
Eastern Foni	**Momodou N. Sanyang**	**PPP**	2,583
	Momodou L. Sanyang[a]	Independent	761
Western Foni	**B. L. Kuti Sanyang**	**PPP**	Unopposed
Mansakonko AA (LRD—South Bank) (total)		PPP	4,838
		Independent	1,720
Eastern Jarra	**Kemo Sanneh**	**PPP**	2,761
	Yaya Dabo	Independent	352
Western Jarra	**Yaya Ceesay**	**PPP**	Unopposed
Eastern Kiang	**Jerreh L. B. Daffeh**	**PPP**	Unopposed

Table C.4. (*continued*)

Constituency	Candidate	Party	Vote
Western Kiang	**Howsoon O. Semega-Janneh**	PPP	2,077
	Momodou K. Sanneh	Independent	1,368
Kerewan AA		PPP	17,589
(LRD—NorthBank)		UP	1,955
(total)		Independent	10,716
Sabach Sanjal	**Saihou S. Sabally**	PPP	2,000
	Tairu A. K. John	UP	1,255
	Mustapha Jawara	Independent	1,242
Illiassa	**Baba M. Touray**	PPP	3,444
	Karamo Jadama	Independent	1,781
	Momodou L. Marong	Independent	555
Central Baddibu	**Sheriff M. Dibba**	PPP	2,931
	Baboucarr K. Saho	Independent	1,215
Lower Baddibu	**Kalilou F. Singhateh**	PPP	2,389
	Foday A. K. Makalo	Independent	1,043
	Kebba F. Singhateh	Independent	569
Jokadu	**Landing Jallow Sonko**	PPP	2,622
	Maja O. Sonko	Independent	1,540
Niumi	**Mafode F. Sonko**	PPP	4,203
	Landing Omar Sonko	Independent	1,822
	Jerreh Manneh	Independent	949
	Barra Jaiteh	UP	700
Georgetown AA		PPP	17,928
(MID) (total)		UP	8,013
		Independent	1,939
Sami	**Kebba N. Leigh**	PPP	2,459
	Kebba Touray	Independent	1,595
Niani	**Demba S. Cham**	PPP	3,042
	Gibril M'Backe	UP	1,029
Saloum	**Kebba A. Bayo**	PPP	3,046
	Kebba W. Foon	UP	2,481
Lower Fulladu West	**Abdul M'Ballow**[b]	PPP	2,849
	Augustin A. Sabally	UP	1,420
Upper Fulladu West	**Kebba K. Jawara**	PPP	3,078
	Harona Jallow	UP	1,678
	Samba Sidibeh	Independent	344

Table C.4. (*continued*)

Constituency	Candidate	Party	Vote
Niamina	**Lamin B. M'Boge**	PPP	3,454
	Ebrima N'Jie	UP	1,405
Basse AA (URD)		PPP	10,288
(total)		UP	1,483
		Independent	3,535
Jimara	**Momodou C. Jallow**	PPP	3,660
	Ebrima Manneh	UP	611
Kantora	**Andrew D. Camara**	PPP	2,222
	Mamadi B. Sagnia*c*	Independent	1,161
Tumana	**Momodou C. Cham**	PPP	Unopposed
Basse	**Kebba J. Krubally**	PPP	2,446
	Bali Faal	UP	746
Wuli	**Sana Saidy**	PPP	Unopposed
Sandu	**Batapa Drammeh**	**Independent**	2,374
	Musa S. Dabo	PPP	1,960
	Saloum Gaye	UP	126

Notes: *a*Result omitted in Sagnia.
*b*Formerly Andrew M'Ballow.
*c*Also known as Momodou Sanyang.
Winning candidates are noted in bold.

Sources: Bakarr, *Gambia Yesterday*, 84; Sagnia, *Gambian Legislature*, 65–68; FCO 65/1090, annex to Collins to Bambury, April 6, 1972.

SUMMARY OF RESULTS

Party	Number of votes	Percentage of votes
PPP	65,388	62.96
UP	17,161	16.52
Independents	21,302	20.51
Total votes cast	103,851	100.00

Table C.5. General Election Results: 1977

Constituency	Candidate	Party	Vote
Banjul AA (total)		PPP	4,783
		UP	5,285
Banjul North	**I. B. A. Kelepha-Samba**	**PPP**	1,727
	Musa A. Jobe	UP	1,623[a]
Banjul Central	**John R. Forster**	**UP**	1,731
	Horace R. Monday	PPP	1,435
Banjul South	**Momodou (Dodou) M. Taal**	**UP**	1,931
	Ibrahima M. Garba-Jahumpa	PPP	1,621
Kombo St. Mary AA (total)		PPP	7,150
		NCP	7,528
Bakau	**Bakary P. Camara**	**NCP**	1,831
	Abdoulie K. N'Jie	PPP	1,226
Serrekunda East	**Omar A. Jallow**	**PPP**	3,389
	Antouman (Antoine) Jatta	NCP	2,960[b]
Serrekunda West	**Gibou M. Jagne**	**NCP**	2,737
	Abdoulie A. N'Jie	PPP	2,535
Brikama AA (WD) (total)		PPP	18,422
		NCP	9,542
Northern Kombo	**Alieu B. N'Jie**	**PPP**	2,081
	Abdou K. Jatta	NCP	1,915
Southern Kombo	**Famara W. Touray**	**PPP**	2,655
	Ebrima Nyanko C. S. Bojang	NCP	1,698
Central Kombo	**Dembo A. S. Jatta**	**PPP**	3,034
	Dembo E. K. Sanneh	NCP	2,249
Eastern Kombo	**Lamin K. Jabang**	**PPP**	2,641
	Malang ("Prince") Sanyang	NCP	1,064
Eastern Foni	**Ismaila B. Jammeh**	**PPP**	4,532
	Kukoi S. Sanyang	NCP	708[a,b]
Western Foni	**B. L. Kuti Sanyang**	**PPP**	3,479
	Ibrahim J. F. B. Sanyang	NCP	1,908
Mansakonko AA (LRD) (total)		PPP	11,270
		NCP	4,889
Eastern Jarra	**Kemo Sanneh**	**PPP**	2,901
	Amang Kanyi	NCP	747
Western Jarra	**Yaya Ceesay**	**PPP**	3,235
	Kemeseng S. M. Jammeh	NCP	1,642

Table C.5. (*continued*)

Constituency	Candidate	Party	Vote
Eastern Kiang	**Jerreh L. B. Daffeh**	**PPP**	2,917
	Sitapha Sanyang	NCP	898
Western Kiang	**Howsoon O. Semega-Janneh**	**PPP**	2,217
	Momodou K. Sanneh[e]	NCP	1,602
Kerewan AA (NBD)		PPP	17,232
(total)		NCP	11,768
		UP	118
		NLP/UP	226
		Independent	2,034
Sabach Sanjal	**Saihou S. Sabally**	**PPP**	2,592
	Lamin W. Juwara	Independent	2,034
	Seku M. Sabally	NCP	314
	Pap C. Secka	NLP/UP	226
Illiassa	**Fodayba Jammeh**	**NCP**	3,763[b,d]
	Baba M. Touray	PPP[d]	2,044
Central Baddibu	**Sheriff M. Dibba**	**NCP**	2,604
	Lamin K. Saho	PPP	1,790
Lower Baddibu	**Foday A. K. Makalo**	**NCP**	2,765
	Kalilou F. Singhateh	PPP	1,263
Jokadu[f]	**Momodou S. K. Manneh**	**PPP**	Postponed
	Alasan N'Dure	NLP/UP	
Jokadu[f]	**Momodou S. K. Manneh**	**PPP**	2,116
	Maja O. Sonko	NCP	456
Lower Niumi	**Mafode F. Sonko**	**PPP**	4,578[b,c,d]
	Mustapha Manneh	NCP	1,087
Upper Niumi	**Landing Jallow Sonko**	**PPP**	2,849
	Maja O. Sonko	NCP	779
	Sarjo Darbo	UP	118
Georgetown AA (MID)		PPP	32,619
(total)		NCP	3,675
		UP/NLP	3,869
		Independent	2,140
Sami	**Kebba N. Leigh**	**PPP**	3,608
	Omar M'Baki	Independent	2,140
	Mamadi Sise	NCP	445

Table C.5. (*continued*)

Constituency	Candidate	Party	Vote
Niani	**Demba S. Cham**	**PPP**	5,330
	Jibbi Cham	NCP	607
	Jabel Sallah	UP/NLP	471
Saloum	**Amulai Janneh**	**PPP**	6,387[b,d]
	Kebba W. Foon	UP/NLP	1,815
Lower Fulladu	**Abdul M'Ballow**	**PPP**	5,768
West	Ansumana Saidy	UP/NLP	731
	Musumptu Sarr	NCP	708
Upper Fulladu	**Kebba K. Jawara**	**PPP**	5,963
West	Mawdo Suso	NCP	1,469
	Sheikh S. Jobe	UP/NLP	852
Niamina	**Lamin B. M'Boge**	**PPP**	5,563
	Lang Sanneh	NCP	446
Basse AA (URD)		PPP	33,757
(total)		NCP	3,266
Jimara	**Momodou C. Jallow**	**PPP**	6,825
	Bakary B. Sonko	NCP	158
Kantora	**Assan Musa Camara**[g]	**PPP**	5,243
	Momodou M. Sanyang	NCP	692[c]
Tumana	**Momodou C. Cham**	**PPP**	5,500
	Badara K. Sidibeh	NCP	84
Basse	**Kebba J. Krubally**	**PPP**	4,804
	Bakary Wally	NCP	472
Wuli	**Seni Singhateh**	**PPP**	4,839
	Mohammed S. Darbo	NCP	1,520
Sandu	**Musa S. Dabo**	**PPP**	6,546
	Saiku A. Camara	NCP	340

Notes: [a]Result differs in *GNB* (1977).
[b]Result differs in Bakarr.
[c]Result differs in Sagnia.
[d]Result differs in *GNB* (1982).
[e]Listed as M. L. Sanneh in the sources, but assumed to be M. K. Sanneh.
[f]Election postponed until May due to the death of N'Dure in a car accident.
[g]Formerly Andrew D. Camara.
Winning candidates are noted in bold.

Sources: Gambia Gazette, April 13, 1977; *Gambia News Bulletin,* April 7, 1977; May 7, 1982; Bakarr, *Gambia Yesterday,* 87–88; Sagnia, *Gambian Legislature,* 69–72; *West Africa,* June 13, 1977, 1182 (for the deferred Jokadu election).

Table C.5. (*continued*)

SUMMARY OF RESULTS

Party	Number of votes	Percentage of votes
PPP	125,233	69.74
NCP	40,668	22.65
UP	5,403	3.01
UP/NLP	4,095	2.28
Independents	4,174	2.32
Total votes cast	179,573	100.00

Table C.6. General Election Results: 1982

Constituency	Candidate	Party	Vote
Banjul AA (total)		PPP	6,436
		UP	4,782
		Independent	229
Banjul North	I. B. A. Kelepha-Samba	PPP	2,415
	M. L. N'Jie	UP	1,293
	Sanna ("Ticks") Manneh	Independent	229
Banjul Central	M. Lamin Saho	PPP	1,797
	Kebba W. Foon	UP	1,576
Banjul South	Momodou (Dodou) M. Taal	PPP	2,224
	Jabel Sallah	UP[a]	1,913
Kombo St. Mary AA (total)		PPP	10,084
		NCP	6,928
Bakau	Dembo Bojang	NCP	1,746
	Famara S. Bojang	PPP	1,488
Serrekunda East	Omar A. Jallow	PPP	4,858
	Idrissa O. I. Manneh	NCP	2,648
Serrekunda West	Abdoulie A. N'Jie	PPP	3,738
	Gibou M. Jagne	NCP	2,534
Brikama AA (WD) (total)		PPP	20,527
		NCP	10,667
		Independent	3,559
Northern Kombo	Nyimasata Sanneh-Bojang (Mrs.)	PPP	4,115
	Abdou K. Jatta	NCP	2,709
Southern Kombo	Mbemba Jatta	PPP	3,506
	Ebrima Nyanko C. S. Bojang	NCP	1,986
Central Kombo	Dembo A. S. Jatta	PPP	3,565
	Ebrima Sonko	NCP	2,466
Eastern Kombo	Lamin K. Jabang	PPP	3,399
	Tapha T. Sanyang	NCP	1,064
Eastern Foni	Henry M. Jammeh	Independent	3,559
	Alkali James Gaye	PPP	2,172
Western Foni	B. L. Kuti Sanyang	PPP	3,770
	Ibrahim J. F. B. Sanyang	NCP	2,442
Mansakonko AA (LRD) (total)		PPP	11,085
		NCP	2,422
		Independent	4,848

Table C.6. (*continued*)

Constituency	Candidate	Party	Vote
Eastern Jarra	**Saihou Barrow**	**Independent**	2,159
	Kemo Sanneh	PPP	1,760
Western Jarra	**Yaya Ceesay**	**PPP**	4,110
	Kemeseng S. M. Jammeh	NCP	1,456
Western Kiang	**Bakary B. Dabo**	**PPP**	3,676
	Boto B. Camara	NCP	966
Eastern Kiang	**Kebba O. Fadera**	**Independent**	2,689
	Jerreh L. B. Daffeh	PPP	1,539
Kerewan AA (NBD) (total)		PPP	19,354
		NCP	9,087
		Independent	3,206
Sabach Sanjal	**Saihou S. Sabally**	**PPP**	Unopposed
Illiassa	**Fodayba Jammeh**	**NCP**	3,846
	Karamo Jadama	PPP	3,187
Central Baddibu	**Lamin K. Saho**	**PPP**	2,372
	Sheriff M. Dibba	NCP	2,252
Lower Baddibu	**Foday A. K. Makalo**	**NCP**	2,361
	Kebba F. Singhateh	PPP	2,012
Jokadu	**Momodou S. K. Manneh**	**PPP**	2,727
	Yusupha Ceesay	Independent	643
Lower Niumi	**Dodou N'Gum**	**PPP**	4,811
	Jain Coli Fye	Independent	2,563
Upper Niumi	**Landing J. Sonko**	**PPP**	4,245
	Kebba F. Jatta	NCP	628
Georgetown AA (MID) (total)		PPP	19,716
		NCP	1,986
		Independent	4,628
Sami	**Kebba N. Leigh**	**PPP**	4,125
	Samba Sidibeh	NCP	697
Niani	**Talib O. Bensouda**	**PPP**	Unopposed
Saloum	**Amulai Janneh**	**PPP**	6,080
	Nganyie K. Touray	Independent	2,185
Lower Fulladu West	**Mathew Y. Baldeh**	**PPP**	Unopposed
Upper Fulladu West	**Kebba K. Jawara**	**PPP**	6,010
	Mawdo Suso	NCP	1,289
Niamina	**Lamin B. M'Boge**	**PPP**	3,501
	Malick B. Sabally	Independent	2,443

Table C.6. (*continued*)

Constituency	Candidate	Party	Vote
Basse AA (URD)		PPP	15,343
(total)		NCP	1,544
		Independent	9,671
Jimara	**Momodou C. Jallow**	**PPP**	4,245
	Momodou L. Drammeh	Independent	1,148
	Bakary B. Sonko	NCP	235
Kantora	**Assan M. Camara**	**PPP**	Unopposed
Tumana	**Momodou C. Cham**	**PPP**	2,982
	Mbemba M. Tambedou	Independent	1,986
Basse	**Bubacarr M. Baldeh**	**Independent**	2,720
	Kebba J. Krubally	PPP	1,173
	Sulaymen Sumbundu	Independent	624
Wuli	**Seni Singhateh**	**PPP**	4,463
	Mohammed S. Darbo	NCP	1,059
Sandu	**A. K. Touray**	**Independent**	3,193
	Musa S. Dabo	PPP	2,480
	Kissima A. K. Sillah	NCP	250

Notes: ^aListed as NCP by Sagnia.
Winning candidates are noted in bold.

Sources: Gambia Gazette, May 8, 1982; *Gambia News Bulletin,* May 12, 1982; Bakarr, *Gambia Yesterday,* 87–88; Sagnia, *Gambian Legislature,* 73–76.

SUMMARY OF RESULTS

Party	Number of votes	Percentage of votes
PPP	102,545	61.74
NCP	32,634	19.65
UP	4,782	2.88
Independents	26,141	15.74
Total votes cast	166,102	100.00

Table C.7. General Election Results: 1987

Constituency	Candidate	Party	Vote
Banjul AA (total)		PPP	4,218
		GPP	1,805
		PDOIS	486
		UP/NCP	3,210
		Independent	105
Banjul North	I. B. A. Kelepha-Samba	PPP	1,663[a]
	Amadou Taal	GPP	771
	M. L. N'Jie	UP/NCP[b]	708
	A. Baboucarr Gaye	PDOIS	301
Banjul Central	Ebrima A. B. ("Pesseh") N'Jie	PPP	1,275
	Kebba W. Foon	UP/NCP[b]	764
	I. Femi Peters	GPP	703
	Sam O. Sarr	PDOIS	185
Banjul South	Jabel Sallah	UP/NCP[b]	1,738
	Momodou (Dodou) M. Taal	PPP	1,280
	Howsoon O. Semega-Janneh	GPP	331
	Alasan Jaye	Independent	105
Kombo St. Mary AA (total)		PPP	11,319
		NCP	9,275
		GPP	1,497
		PDOIS	1,023
Bakau	Dembo Bojang	NCP	2,313
	Famara S. Bojang	PPP	1,464
	Alieu O. Drammeh	GPP	127[a,c]
Serrekunda East	Omar A. Jallow	PPP	5,861
	Idrissa O. I. Manneh	NCP	2,808
	Halifa Sallah	PDOIS	1,023
	Ebrima O. Ndure	GPP	753[a]
Serrekunda West	Gibou M. Jagne	NCP	4,154
	Abdoulie A. N'Jie	PPP	3,994
	William S. Mendy	GPP	617
Brikama AA (WD) (total)		PPP	21,986
		NCP	12,932
		GPP	5,129
		PDOIS	338
Northern Kombo	Nyimasata Sanneh-Bojang (Mrs.)	PPP	3,633
	Abdou K. Jatta	NCP	2,445
	Kemo Jarju	GPP	616
	Abbas Manneh	PDOIS	338

Table C.7. (*continued*)

Constituency	Candidate	Party	Vote
Southern Kombo	**Mbemba Jatta**	PPP	4,248
	Mamadou A. Scattred-Janneh	NCP	2,647
	Baba Jarju	GPP	322
Central Kombo	**Dembo A. S. Jatta**	PPP	5,160[d]
	Jereba Bojang	NCP	3,867[d]
	Ya Fatou Sonko (Mrs.)	GPP	1,396[d]
Eastern Kombo	**Lamin K. Jabang**	PPP	3,466
	Tapha T. Sanyang	NCP	1,523[a]
	Siaka Jarju	GPP	124
Eastern Foni	**Alkali James Gaye**	PPP	2,806
	Henry M. Jammeh	GPP	1,785
	Tombong Badjie	NCP	225
Western Foni	**B. L. Kuti Sanyang**	PPP	2,673[a]
	Ibrahim J. F. B. Sanyang	NCP	2,225
	Habibou Badjie	GPP	886
Mansakonko AA (LRD)		PPP	11,677
(total)		NCP	5,356
		GPP	1,368
		Independent	128
Eastern Jarra	**Saihou Barrow**	PPP	2,109
	Mbye Kanyi	NCP	1,074
	Saidi A. Kanyi	GPP	556[a,c]
	Dodou A. Ceesay	Independent	128[a]
Western Jarra	**Yaya Ceesay**	PPP	3,160
	Kemeseng S. M. Jammeh	NCP	1,475
	Bekai Baldeh	GPP	508
Eastern Kiang	**Jallow Sanneh**	PPP	2,755
	Wally S. M. Sanneh	NCP	1,929
	Kassim Fadera	GPP	183
Western Kiang	**Bakary B. Dabo**	PPP	3,653
	F. Omar S. Jarju	NCP	878
	Boto B. Camara	GPP	121
Kerewan AA (NBD)		PPP	21,859
(total)		NCP	14,352
		GPP	4,992
Sabach Sanjal	**Saihou S. Sabally**	PPP	4,391
	Momodou P. Gaye	NCP	2,151
	Baboucar Samba	GPP	289

Table C.7. (*continued*)

Constituency	Candidate	Party	Vote
Illiassa	**Fodayba Jammeh**	**NCP**	3,670
	Abdoulie E. Jammeh	PPP	3,315
Central Baddibu	**Lamin K. Saho**	**PPP**	2,844
	Sheriff M. Dibba	NCP	2,749
	Abdoulie Jaiteh	GPP	114
Lower Baddibu	**Foday A. K. Makalo**	**NCP**	2,747
	Kebba F. Singhateh	PPP	2,124
	Lang Kinteh	GPP	63
Jokadu	**Dodou A. S. Jome**	**PPP**	3,015
	Famara B. O. Seckan	NCP	1,069[a]
Lower Niumi	**Dodou N'Gum**	**PPP**	3,337
	Jain Coli Fye	GPP	3,286[a]
	Jerreba J. Jammeh	NCP	905
Upper Niumi	**Landing J. Sonko**	**PPP**	2,833
	Momodou L. Bah	GPP	1,240
	Kebba F. Jatta	NCP	1,061
Georgetown AA (MID) (total)		PPP	26,330
		NCP	7,059
		GPP	8,032
Sami	**Sarjo Touray**	**PPP**	3,199
	Kopi Mbake	NCP	1,216[a]
	Noperi K. Kandeh	GPP	405
Niani	**Talib O. Bensouda**	**PPP**	4,432[a]
	Alpha K. Sabally	NCP	743
	Bura A. Jawo	GPP	713
Saloum	**Amulai Janneh**	**PPP**	5,900
	Nganyie K. Touray	GPP	1,807[a]
	Kebba A. Bayo	NCP	494
Lower Fulladu West	**Mathew Y. Baldeh**	**PPP**	4,845
	Bakary D.T. Jallow	GPP	1,613
	Kekoi S. Fatty	NCP	1,118
Upper Fulladu West	**Kebba K. Jawara**	**PPP**	4,256
	Mawdo Suso	NCP	3,068
	Keita M.M. Baldeh	GPP	855
Niamina	**Lamin B. M'Boge**	**PPP**	3,698
	Malick B. Sabally	GPP	2,639[a]
	Baba M. Sawaneh	NCP	420[a]

Table C.7. (*continued*)

Constituency	Candidate	Party	Vote
Basse AA (URD)		PPP	21,859
(total)		NCP	6,277
		GPP	8,781
		PDOIS	222
Jimara	**Momodou C. Jallow**	PPP	4,745
	Yero B. A. K. Mballow	GPP	1,819[a]
	Hamadi Krubally	NCP	263
Kantora	**Pa Mandu Sanyang**	PPP	2,911
	Assan M. Camara	GPP	2,401[c]
	Baboucarr Sanyang	NCP	379
Tumana	**Momodou C. Cham**	PPP	3,270
	Mbemba M. Tambedou	GPP	2,451
	Kebba M. J. Sissoko	NCP	136
Basse	**Omar B. A. Sey**	PPP	4,216
	Ousainou Baldeh	NCP	1,466
	Sulaymen Sumbundu	GPP	1,283
Eastern Wuli	**Seni Singhateh**	PPP	1,862
	Mohammed S. Darbo	NCP	1,417
	Nyanamang Wally	GPP	235
	Sidia Jatta	PDOIS	222
Western Wuli	**Malang A. K. Sawo**	PPP	2,653
	Karamang L. Jawuneh	NCP	809
	Kissima A. K. Sillah	GPP	411
Sandu	**Musa Drammeh**	PPP	2,202
	A. K. Touray	NCP	1,807
	Binna B. Drammeh	GPP	181

Notes: [a]Results differ in Sagnia.
[b]Listed as NCP in Sagnia.
[c]Result differs in *The Nation*.
[d]Result not given in *GNB*. The results in Sagnia are very different: Jatta, 3,511; Bojang, 2,686; Sonko, 404.
Winning candidates are noted in bold.

Sources: Gambia News Bulletin, March 18, 1987; *The Nation*, March 14, 1987 (results by party only); Sagnia, *Gambian Legislature*, 77–80. Except in the case of Central Kombo, the results in *GNB* and *The Nation* are almost identical and have been followed in preference to those in Sagnia.

Table C.7. (*continued*)

SUMMARY OF RESULTS

Party	Number of votes	Percentage of votes
PPP	119,248	56.35
NCP/UP (total):	58,461	27.63
NCP	55,251	26.11
UP/NCP	3,210	1.52
GPP	31,604	14.93
PDOIS	2,069	0.98
Independents	233	0.11
Total votes cast	211,615	100.00

Table C.8. General Election Results: 1992

Constituency	Candidate	Party	Vote
Banjul AA (total)		PPP	4,759
		UP/NCP	2,892
		PDOIS	1,179
		Independent	309
Banjul North	**I. B. A. Kelepha-Samba**	**PPP**	1,780
	Housainou N'Jai	UP/NCP	974
	Baboucarr Sise	PDOIS	650
	Dodou Gaye	Independent	75
Banjul Central	**Ebrima A. B. ("Pesseh") N'Jie**	**PPP**	1,444
	N'Janko N'Jie	UP/NCP	966
	David Jones	PDOIS	293
	Anna F. Thomas (Mrs.)	Independent	63
Banjul South	**Momodou M. Taal**	**PPP**	1,535
	Babou S. N'Jie	UP/NCP	952
	Amie Sillah (Mrs.)	PDOIS	236
	Papa M. N'Diaye	Independent	171
Kombo St. Mary AA (total)		PPP	10,153
		NCP	7,229
		PDP	42
		PDOIS	1,158
Bakau	**Dembo Bojang**	**NCP**	2,198
	Sam Sillah	PPP	1,904
	Alpha O. Jallow	PDP	42
Serrekunda East	**Omar A. Jallow**	**PPP**	4,443
	Ousainou Jaiteh	NCP	2,236
	Halifa Sallah	PDOIS	833
Serrekunda West	**Abdoulie A. N'Jie**	**PPP**	3,806
	Gibou M. Jagne	NCP	2,795
	Adama Bah	PDOIS	325
Brikama AA (WD) (total)		PPP	21,051
		NCP	12,257
		GPP	571
		PDP	3,025
		PDOIS	654
Northern Kombo	**Ebrima K. Sarr**	**PPP**	4,646
	Yusupha F. A. Cham	NCP	3,322
	Abbas Manneh	PDOIS	328
Southern Kombo	**Mbemba Jatta**	**PPP**	5,667
	Bouba M. M. Touray	NCP	2,338
	Momodou N. Kassama	PDP	592
	Dodou M. L. Sarr Demba	GPP	201

Table C.8. (*continued*)

Constituency	Candidate	Party	Vote
Central Kombo	**Dembo A. S. Jatta**	**PPP**	3,315
	L. K. Dembo Bojang	NCP	2,263
	Lamin Bojang	PDP	432
	Edrissa Jarju	PDOIS	226
	Fatou Sanneh Colley (Mrs.)	GPP	142
Eastern Kombo	**Lamin K. Jabang**	**PPP**	3,073
	N'Fansu B. K. Conteh	PDP	1,139
	Saikou Kujabi	NCP	788
	Siaka Jarju	GPP	125
Eastern Foni	**Alkali James Gaye**	**PPP**	2,096
	Kausu L. Gibba	NCP	991
	Ibrahim B. Sanneh	PDP	616
	Modou L. S. Fatty	GPP	103
	Lebage Bojang	PDOIS	100
Western Foni	**Ibrahim J. F. B. Sanyang**	**NCP**	2,555
	B. L. Kuti Sanyang	PPP	2,254
	Momodou L. Bojang	PDP	246
Mansakonko AA (LRD)		PPP	9,621
(total)		NCP	3,714
		GPP	1,224
		PDP	539
		Independent	1,513
Eastern Jarra	**Momodou Saidywane**	**NCP**	1,627
	Fafanding Dabo	PPP	1,336
	Musa M. Sabally	GPP	477
	Yaya S. Dabo	PDP	133
Western Jarra	**Yaya Ceesay**	**PPP**	2,629
	Kemeseng S. M. Jammeh	NCP	1,437
	Bekai Baldeh	GPP	634
	Famara L. Jobe	PDP	178
Eastern Kiang	**Wally S. M. Sanneh**	**PPP**	2,145
	Buba Samura	Independent	1,191
	Demba B. Komma	Independent	322
	Bubakary S. Fadera	PDP	228
	Sidisi Dibba	NCP	132
	Fakebba Colly	GPP	113
Western Kiang	**Bakary B. Dabo**	**PPP**	3,511
	Momodou L. Drammeh	NCP	518

Table C.8. (*continued*)

Constituency	Candidate	Party	Vote
Kerewan AA (NBD) (total)		PPP	21,668
		NCP	15,113
		GPP	1,048
		PDP	535
		PDOIS	539
		Independent	5,277
Sabach Sanjal	**Saihou S. Sabally**	**PPP**	4,347
	Momodou B. Camara	Independent	2,114
	Yoro Bah	NCP	541
Illiassa	**Kebba T. Jammeh**	**PPP**	4,143
	Fodayba Jammeh	NCP	3,116
	Sulayman Kanyi	PDP	281
	Alhaji Dampha	GPP	155
Central Baddibu	**Sheriff M. Dibba**	**NCP**	3,233
	Lamin K. Saho	PPP	2,726
	Lamin Camara	GPP	62
Lower Baddibu	**Majanko Samusa**	**NCP**	2,531
	Kebba F. Singhateh	PPP	2,340
	Lamin Jeng	PDP	110
Jokadu	**Momodou S. K. Manneh**	**Independent**	2,327
	Amadou Lowe	PPP	1,033
	Yougo T. Kebbeh	Independent	836
	Famara B. O. Seckan	NCP	497
	Ansumana K. Fadera	PDP	144
Lower Niumi	**Jerreba J. Jammeh**	**NCP**	3,439
	Dodou N'Gum	PPP	2,733
	Musa M. Sonko	GPP	831
	A. Baboucarr Gaye	PDOIS	539
Upper Niumi	**Landing J. Sonko**	**PPP**	4,346
	Landing L. Sonko	NCP	1,756
Georgetown AA (MID) (total)		PPP	21,843
		NCP	4,668
		GPP	6,021
		PDP	1,527
		PDOIS	139
		Independent	6,493
Sami	**Sarjo Touray**	**PPP**	3,082
	Bakary K. Sidibeh	GPP	1,171
	Kanjura Kanyi	NCP	349
	Omar K. Touray	PDOIS	139

Table C.8. (*continued*)

Constituency	Candidate	Party	Vote
Niani	**Almamy A. Touray**	**Independent**	2,908
	Talib O. Bensouda	PPP	2,739
	Bura A. Jawo	GPP	454
	Alpha K. Sabally	NCP	163
Saloum	**Amulai Janneh**	**PPP**	5,629
	Jabel Sallah	PDP	1,527
	Kebba A. Bayo	NCP	459
Lower Fulladu West	**Mathew Y. Baldeh**	**PPP**	4,280
	Malang Fatty	NCP	2,080
	Samba Baldeh	GPP	565
Upper Fulladu West	**M. J. M. ("Babung") Phatty**	**GPP**	3,338
	Kebba K. Jawara	PPP	2,950
	Mawdo Suso	NCP	1,617
Niamina	**Lamin W. Juwara**	**Independent**	3,585
	Malanding Ceesay	PPP	3,163
	Sana Y. H. Jallow	GPP	493
Basse AA (URD) (total)		PPP	19,964
		NCP	2,972
		GPP	5,073
		PDP	3,623
		PDOIS	963
		Independent	1,739
Jimara	**Bubacarr M. Baldeh**	**PPP**	6,028
	Bakary B. Sonko	NCP	355
Kantora	**Pa Mandu Sanyang**	**PPP**	2,722
	Assan M. Camara	GPP	2,054
Tumana	**Mbemba M. Tambedou**	**GPP**	2,829
	Momodou C. Cham	PPP	2,179
	Faye Suso	PDOIS	88
Basse	**Omar B. A. Sey**	**PPP**	2,791
	Sidia K. L. Sanyang	Independent	1,739
	Ousainou Baldeh	NCP	747
	Peter Baldeh	GPP	190
	Aruna Jobe	PDOIS	186
Eastern Wuli	**Seni Singhateh**	**PPP**	1,527
	Salifu Darbo	PDP	804
	Mohammed S. Darbo	NCP	584
	Sidia Jatta	PDOIS	535

Table C.8. (*continued*)

Constituency	Candidate	Party	Vote
Western Wuli	**Malang A. K. Sawo**	**PPP**	1,540
	Karamang L. Jawuneh	NCP	1,222
	Foday M. Y. Kebbeh	PDP	1,118
	Swaebou Touray	PDOIS	154
Sandu	**Musa Drammeh**	**PPP**	3,177
	A. K. Touray	PDP	1,701
	Amadou K. Conteh	NCP	64

Note: Winning candidates are noted in bold.

Sources: Gambia Weekly, May 1, 1992 and May 8, 1992 (which contains various corrections); *The Gambia News and (Special) Report,* April 30, 1992.

SUMMARY OF RESULTS

Party	Number of votes	Percentage of votes
PPP	109,059	54.23
NCP/UP (total):	48,845	24.29
NCP	45,953	22.85
UP/NCP	2,892	1.44
GPP	13,937	6.93
PDP	9,291	4.62
PDOIS	4,632	2.30
Independents	15,331	7.62
Total votes cast	201,095	100.00

Table C.9. By-Election Results: 1961–93

Constituency	Reason for by-election	Date of by-election	Candidate	Party	Vote
Niani-Saloum[a]	Successful PPP appeal against UP winner (Alasan Touray)	Jan 1961	**Ebrima D. N'Jie** Omar J. Sise	UP PPP	2,499 1,794
Sabach Sanjal[b]	Successful UP appeal against PPP winner (Yusupha Samba)	Oct 1962	**Yusupha** **S. Samba** Mamadi Sabally	PPP UP	2,918 2,142
Basse[c]	Death of PPP MP (Michael Baldeh)	Oct 1965	**Kebba** **J. Krubally** Momodou C. Jallow	PPP UP	1,998 1,443
Western Kiang[d]	Death of PPP MP (Amang Kanyi)	Oct 1968	**Howsoon** **O. Semega-Janneh**	PPP	Unopposed
Lower Fulladu West[e]	Death of PPA MP (Paul Baldeh)	Feb 1969	**Abdul** **M'Ballow** Augustin A. Sabally	PPP UP	1,956 1,230
Wuli[f]	Jailing of PPP MP (Bangally Singhateh)	Mar 1969	**Della** **Singhateh** Momodou M. N'Jie	PPP UP	1,860 537
Eastern Kombo[g]	PPP MP (Sir Dawda Jawara) becomes president	July 1970	**Lamin K.** **Jabang**	PPP	Unopposed
Upper Fulladu West[h]	Jailing of UP MP (Numukunda Darbo)	Oct 1970	**Kebba** **K. Jawara** Sheikh S. Jobe	PPP UP	3,906 1,657
Saloum[i]	Death of UP MP (E. D. N'Jie)	Jan 1971	**Kebba A. Bayo** Kebba W. Foon	PPP UP	2,125 1,947
Jokadu[j]	Jailing of PPP MP (K. C. A. Kah)	Mar 1971	**Maja O. Sonko** Abdoulie M. Drammeh	IND PPP	1,795 1,437
Bathurst North[k]	UP MP (P. S. N'Jie) forfeits seat for nonattendance	Dec 1972	**Musa A. Jobe** I. B. A. Kelepha-Samba	UP PPP	1,365 1,308

Table C.9. (*continued*)

Constituency	Reason for by-election	Date of by-election	Candidate	Party	Vote
Sandu[l]	Independent MP (Batapa Drammeh) forfeits seat for nonattendance	Nov 1973	**Musa S. Dabo** Morro Drammeh	PPP IND	2,634 2,253
Eastern Foni[m]	Death of PPP MP (Momodou Sanyang)	Nov 1973	**Ismaila B. Jammeh**	PPP	Unopposed
Banjul Central[n]	Death of UP MP (J. R. Forster)	May 1977	**Horace R. Monday** Kebba W. Foon Pap C. Secka Lilian Johnson (Ms) Noble H. Allen	PPP UP NLP IND IND	1,414 1,294 123 30 18
Bakau[o]	Death of NCP MP (Bakary Camara)	June 1978	**Dembo Bojang** Famara S. Bojang	NCP PPP	2,211 1,573
Eastern Jarra[p]	Resignation of Independent MP (Saihou Barrow) to seek PPP nomination	April 1983	**Saihou Barrow** Samba Baldeh	PPP NCP	2,450 974
Eastern Kiang[q]	Resignation of Independent MP (Kebba Fadera) to seek PPP nomination	July 1983	**Jallow Sanneh** Wally S. M. Sanneh	PPP IND	2,275 1,381
Sami[r]	Resignation of PPP MP (Kebba Leigh) due to ill health	Nov 1984	**Sarjo Touray**	PPP	Unopposed
Basse[s]	Independent MP (Bubacarr Baldeh) forfeits seat for nonattendance	Dec 1985	**Omar B. A. Sey** Ousainou Baldeh	PPP NCP	N/a N/a

Table C.9. (*continued*)

Constituency	Reason for by-election	Date of by-election	Candidate	Party	Vote
Tumana[t]	Successful PPP appeal against GPP winner (Mbemba Tambedou)	June 1993	**Mbemba M. Tambedou**	**GPP**	**4,519**
			Momodou C. Cham	PPP	2,707
Jokadu[u]	Successful PPP appeal against Independent winner (M. S. K. Manneh)	June 1993	**Momodou S. K. Manneh**	**IND**	**2,330**
			Amadou Lowe	PPP	1,159
			Yougo T. Kebbeh	IND	672

Note: Winning candidates are noted in bold.

Sources: [a]*Gambia Echo,* January 16, 1961.
[b]*Gambia Echo,* October 8, 1962.
[c]*Gambia News Bulletin,* October 9, 1965.
[d]*Gambia Gazette,* October 18, 1968.
[e]*Gambia Gazette,* February 12, 1969. Abdul M'Ballow, formerly Andrew M'Ballow.
[f]*Gambia Gazette,* March 28, 1969.
[g]Sagnia, *Gambian Legislature,* 44.
[h]*Gambia Gazette,* October 22, 1970.
[i]*Gambia News Bulletin,* January 28, 1971.
[j]*Gambia Gazette,* March 5, 1971.
[k]*Gambia Gazette,* December 15, 1972.
[l]Sagnia, *Gambian Legislature,* 44–45; FCO 65/1452, Diplomatic Report no. 95/174, Report by J. R. W. Parker, January 9, 1974.
[m]*West Africa,* December 10, 1973, 1748; FCO 65/1452, Diplomatic Report no. 95/174, Report by J. R. W. Parker, January 9, 1974.
[n]*West Africa,* June 13, 1978, 1182.
[o]Ba Tarawally, "How Gambia's By-Election Was Fought," *West Africa,* June 26, 1978, 1216–17.
[p]"Barrow Wins," *West Africa,* April 11, 1983, 920.
[q]"PPP Wins By-Election," *West Africa,* July 4, 1983, 1581.
[r]Eddie Momoh, "No Easy Promises," *WA,* February 18, 1985, 297–98.
[s]Baboucar Gaye, "Basse Poll," *West Africa,* December 9, 1985, 2617; Fatou Sey, "Jawara's Toughest Test," *West Africa,* March 9, 1987, 452–53, who states that Omar Sey won by less than 60 votes.
[t]*Gambia Weekly,* June 4, 1993.
[u]*Gambia Weekly,* June 11, 1993.

APPENDIX D

PRESIDENTIAL ELECTION RESULTS, 1982—92

Table D.1. Presidential Election Results: 1982

Administrative area	Candidate	Party	Vote
Banjul	**Dawda K. Jawara**	**PPP**	7,338
	Sheriff M. Dibba	NCP	4,108
Kombo St. Mary	**Dawda K. Jawara**	**PPP**	10,135
	Sheriff M. Dibba	NCP	7,089
Brikama (WD)	**Dawda K. Jawara**	**PPP**	21,640
	Sheriff M. Dibba	NCP	13,132
Mansakonko (LRD)	**Dawda K. Jawara**	**PPP**	13,396
	Sheriff M. Dibba	NCP	4,990
Kerewan (NBD)	**Dawda K. Jawara**	**PPP**	25,600
	Sheriff M. Dibba	NCP	12,412
Georgetown (MID)	**Dawda K. Jawara**	**PPP**	32,840
	Sheriff M. Dibba	NCP	5,416
Basse (URD)	**Dawda K. Jawara**	**PPP**	26,071
	Sheriff M. Dibba	NCP	4,948
The Gambia	**Dawda K. Jawara**	**PPP**	137,020 (72.45%)
	Sheriff M. Dibba	NCP	52,095 (27.55%)
	Total votes cast		189,115

Note: Winning candidates are noted in bold.
Source: Gambia News Bulletin, May 12, 1982.

Table D.2. Presidential Election Results: 1987

Constituency	Candidate	Party	Vote
Banjul AA (total)	**Dawda K. Jawara**	**PPP**	4,463[a]
	Assan M. Camara	GPP	3,172
	Sheriff M. Dibba	NCP	2,171
Banjul North	**Dawda K. Jawara**	**PPP**	1,566
	Assan M. Camara	GPP	1,135
	Sheriff M. Dibba	NCP	734
Banjul Central	**Dawda K. Jawara**	**PPP**	1,238
	Assan M. Camara	GPP	1,020
	Sheriff M. Dibba	NCP	667
Banjul South	**Dawda K. Jawara**	**PPP**	1,659
	Assan M. Camara	GPP	1,017
	Sheriff M. Dibba	NCP	770
Kombo St. Mary AA (total)	**Dawda K. Jawara**	**PPP**	10,933
	Sheriff M. Dibba	NCP	9,547
	Assan M. Camara	GPP	2,619
Bakau	**Sheriff M. Dibba**	**NCP**	2,179
	Dawda K. Jawara	PPP	1,547
	Assan M. Camara	GPP	177
Serrekunda East	**Dawda K. Jawara**	**PPP**	5,174
	Sheriff M. Dibba	NCP	3,867
	Assan M. Camara	GPP	1,396[b]
Serrekunda West	**Dawda K. Jawara**	**PPP**	4,212
	Sheriff M. Dibba	NCP	3,501
	Assan M. Camara	GPP	1,046
Brikama AA (WD) (total)	**Dawda K. Jawara**	**PPP**	20,715
	Sheriff M. Dibba	NCP	12,470
	Assan M. Camara	GPP	3,485
Northern Kombo	**Dawda K. Jawara**	**PPP**	3,811
	Sheriff M. Dibba	NCP	2,730
	Assan M. Camara	GPP	492
Southern Kombo	**Dawda K. Jawara**	**PPP**	4,167
	Sheriff M. Dibba	NCP	2,778
	Assan M. Camara	GPP	296
Central Kombo	**Dawda K. Jawara**	**PPP**	3,584
	Sheriff M. Dibba	NCP	2,591
	Assan M. Camara	GPP	450
Eastern Kombo	**Dawda K. Jawara**	**PPP**	3,518
	Sheriff M. Dibba	NCP	1,437
	Assan M. Camara	GPP	163

Table D.2. (*continued*)

Constituency	Candidate	Party	Vote
Eastern Foni	**Dawda K. Jawara**	**PPP**	2,798
	Assan M. Camara	GPP	1,469
	Sheriff M. Dibba	NCP	583
Western Foni	**Dawda K. Jawara**	**PPP**	2,837
	Sheriff M. Dibba	NCP	2,351
	Assan M. Camara	GPP	615
Mansakonko AA (LRD) (total)	**Dawda K. Jawara**	**PPP**	12,102
	Sheriff M. Dibba	NCP	5,246
	Assan M. Camara	GPP	1,309
Eastern Jarra	**Dawda K. Jawara**	**PPP**	2,347
	Sheriff M. Dibba	NCP	1,049[b]
	Assan M. Camara	GPP	495
Western Jarra	**Dawda K. Jawara**	**PPP**	3,251
	Sheriff M. Dibba	NCP	1,502
	Assan M. Camara	GPP	426
Eastern Kiang	**Dawda K. Jawara**	**PPP**	3,070
	Sheriff M. Dibba	NCP	1,528
	Assan M. Camara	GPP	298
Western Kiang	**Dawda K. Jawara**	**PPP**	3,434
	Sheriff M. Dibba	NCP	1,167
	Assan M. Camara	GPP	90
Kerewan AA (NBD) (total)	**Dawda K. Jawara**	**PPP**	22,871
	Sheriff M. Dibba	NCP	14,877
	Assan M. Camara	GPP	3,534[a]
Sabach Sanjal	**Dawda K. Jawara**	**PPP**	4,746
	Sheriff M. Dibba	NCP	1,775
	Assan M. Camara	GPP	329
Illiassa	**Sheriff M. Dibba**	**NCP**	3,469
	Dawda K. Jawara	PPP	3,213
	Assan M. Camara	GPP	321
Central Baddibu	**Sheriff M. Dibba**	**NCP**	2,866
	Dawda K. Jawara	PPP	2,682[b]
	Assan M. Camara	GPP	169
Lower Baddibu	**Sheriff M. Dibba**	**NCP**	2,831
	Dawda K. Jawara	PPP	2,020
	Assan M. Camara	GPP	91
Jokadu	**Dawda K. Jawara**	**PPP**	2,879
	Sheriff M. Dibba	NCP	992
	Assan M. Camara	GPP	210

Table D.2. (*continued*)

Constituency	Candidate	Party	Vote
Lower Niumi	**Dawda K. Jawara**	**PPP**	4,423
	Sheriff M. Dibba	NCP	1,615
	Assan M. Camara	GPP	1,506
Upper Niumi	**Dawda K. Jawara**	**PPP**	2,908
	Sheriff M. Dibba	NCP	1,329
	Assan M. Camara	GPP	908
Georgetown AA (MID) (total)	**Dawda K. Jawara**	**PPP**	28,510
	Sheriff M. Dibba	NCP	6,591
	Assan M. Camara	GPP	6,543
Sami	**Dawda K. Jawara**	**PPP**	3,454
	Sheriff M. Dibba	NCP	1,058
	Assan M. Camara	GPP	358
Niani	**Dawda K. Jawara**	**PPP**	4,583
	Sheriff M. Dibba	NCP	686
	Assan M. Camara	GPP	638
Saloum	**Dawda K. Jawara**	**PPP**	5,906
	Assan M. Camara	GPP	1,634
	Sheriff M. Dibba	NCP	675
Lower Fulladu West	**Dawda K. Jawara**	**PPP**	5,419
	Assan M. Camara	GPP	1,157
	Sheriff M. Dibba	NCP	1,024
Upper Fulladu West	**Dawda K. Jawara**	**PPP**	4,920
	Sheriff M. Dibba	NCP	2,346
	Assan M. Camara	GPP	953
Niamina	**Dawda K. Jawara**	**PPP**	4,228
	Assan M. Camara	GPP	1,803
	Sheriff M. Dibba	NCP	802
Basse AA (URD) (total)	**Dawda K. Jawara**	**PPP**	23,791
	Assan M. Camara	GPP	7,089
	Sheriff M. Dibba	NCP	6,441
Jimara	**Dawda K. Jawara**	**PPP**	4,936
	Assan M. Camara	GPP	1,250
	Sheriff M. Dibba	NCP	646
Kantora	**Dawda K. Jawara**	**PPP**	2,923
	Assan M. Camara	GPP	2,334[b]
	Sheriff M. Dibba	NCP	458
Tumana	**Dawda K. Jawara**	**PPP**	4,034
	Assan M. Camara	GPP	1,317
	Sheriff M. Dibba	NCP	525

Table D.2. (*continued*)

Constituency	Candidate	Party	Vote
Basse	**Dawda K. Jawara**	**PPP**	4,341
	Assan M. Camara	GPP	1,337
	Sheriff M. Dibba	NCP	1,307
Eastern Wuli	**Dawda K. Jawara**	**PPP**	2,113[c]
	Sheriff M. Dibba	NCP	1,462[c]
	Assan M. Camara	GPP	250[c]
Western Wuli	**Dawda K. Jawara**	**PPP**	2,804
	Sheriff M. Dibba	NCP	758
	Assan M. Camara	GPP	318
Sandu	**Dawda K. Jawara**	**PPP**	2,640
	Sheriff M. Dibba	NCP	1,285
	Assan M. Camara	GPP	283
The Gambia[a]	**Dawda K. Jawara**	**PPP**	123,385 (59.18%)
	Sheriff M. Dibba	NCP	57,343 (27.51%)
	Assan M. Camara	GPP	27,751[a] (13.31%)
	Total votes cast		208,479[a]
	Registered electorate		262,593[d]

Notes: [a]Results differ in *Gambia News Bulletin,* but recalculated from votes in each constituency.
[b]Results differ in *The Nation.*
[c]Result given in *The Nation* was for Western Wuli.
[d]Total given in *Gambia News Bulletin* is 262,143, but recalculated from total for each Administrative Area.
Winning candidates are noted in bold.

Sources: The Nation, March 14, 1987; Gambia *News Bulletin,* March 18, 1987 (Administrative Areas only). Additional information given to Hughes by the Election Office, Banjul, provided a further means to check the published sources.

Table D.3. Presidential Election Results: 1992

Constituency	Candidate	Party	Vote
Banjul AA (total)	**Dawda K. Jawara**	**PPP**	5,565
	Sheriff M. Dibba	NCP	1,670
	Sidia Jatta	PDOIS	1,118
	Assan M. Camara	GPP	526
	Lamin Bojang	PDP	247
Banjul North	**Dawda K. Jawara**	**PPP**	2,069
	Sheriff M. Dibba	NCP	582
	Sidia Jatta	PDOIS	488
	Assan M. Camara	GPP	258
	Lamin Bojang	PDP	86
Banjul Central	**Dawda K. Jawara**	**PPP**	1,585
	Sheriff M. Dibba	NCP	622
	Sidia Jatta	PDOIS	313
	Assan M. Camara	GPP	155
	Lamin Bojang	PDP	88
Banjul South	**Dawda K. Jawara**	**PPP**	1,911
	Sheriff M. Dibba	NCP	466
	Sidia Jatta	PDOIS	317
	Assan M. Camara	GPP	113
	Lamin Bojang	PDP	73
Kombo St. Mary AA (total)	**Dawda K. Jawara**	**PPP**	9,513
	Sheriff M. Dibba	NCP	5,987
	Sidia Jatta	PDOIS	1,296
	Lamin Bojang	PDP	700
	Assan M. Camara	GPP	689
Bakau	**Sheriff M. Dibba**	**NCP**	2,017
	Dawda K. Jawara	PPP	1,836
	Sidia Jatta	PDOIS	132
	Assan M. Camara	GPP	105
	Lamin Bojang	PDP	37
Serrekunda East	**Dawda K. Jawara**	**PPP**	3,908
	Sheriff M. Dibba	NCP	2,014
	Sidia Jatta	PDOIS	616
	Lamin Bojang	PDP	304
	Assan M. Camara	GPP	287
Serrekunda West	**Dawda K. Jawara**	**PPP**	3,769
	Sheriff M. Dibba	NCP	1,956
	Sidia Jatta	PDOIS	548
	Lamin Bojang	PDP	359
	Assan M. Camara	GPP	297

Table D.3. (*continued*)

Constituency	Candidate	Party	Vote
Brikama AA (WD) (total)	**Dawda K. Jawara**	**PPP**	21,791
	Sheriff M. Dibba	NCP	10,447
	Lamin Bojang	PDP	2,552
	Sidia Jatta	PDOIS	1,568
	Assan M. Camara	GPP	1,331
Northern Kombo	**Dawda K. Jawara**	**PPP**	4,833
	Sheriff M. Dibba	NCP	2,546
	Sidia Jatta	PDOIS	386
	Assan M. Camara	GPP	287
	Lamin Bojang	PDP	272
Southern Kombo	**Dawda K. Jawara**	**PPP**	5,572
	Sheriff M. Dibba	NCP	2,273
	Lamin Bojang	PDP	402
	Assan M. Camara	GPP	305
	Sidia Jatta	PDOIS	266
Central Kombo	**Dawda K. Jawara**	**PPP**	3,624
	Sheriff M. Dibba	NCP	1,706
	Lamin Bojang	PDP	557
	Sidia Jatta	PDOIS	320
	Assan M. Camara	GPP	199
Eastern Kombo	**Dawda K. Jawara**	**PPP**	3,309
	Sheriff M. Dibba	NCP	989
	Lamin Bojang	PDP	540
	Assan M. Camara	GPP	166
	Sidia Jatta	PDOIS	146
Eastern Foni	**Dawda K. Jawara**	**PPP**	2,197
	Sheriff M. Dibba	NCP	872
	Lamin Bojang	PDP	534
	Sidia Jatta	PDOIS	193
	Assan M. Camara	GPP	128
Western Foni	**Dawda K. Jawara**	**PPP**	2,256
	Sheriff M. Dibba	NCP	2,061
	Sidia Jatta	PDOIS	257
	Lamin Bojang	PDP	247
	Assan M. Camara	GPP	246
Mansakonko AA (LRD) (total)	**Dawda K. Jawara**	**PPP**	10,985
	Sheriff M. Dibba	NCP	3,797
	Assan M. Camara	GPP	1,064
	Lamin Bojang	PDP	452
	Sidia Jatta	PDOIS	428

Table D.3. (*continued*)

Constituency	Candidate	Party	Vote
Eastern Jarra	**Dawda K. Jawara**	**PPP**	1,789
	Sheriff M. Dibba	NCP	1,194
	Assan M. Camara	GPP	377
	Lamin Bojang	PDP	134
	Sidia Jatta	PDOIS	109
Western Jarra	**Dawda K. Jawara**	**PPP**	2,894
	Sheriff M. Dibba	NCP	1,319
	Assan M. Camara	GPP	406
	Lamin Bojang	PDP	145
	Sidia Jatta	PDOIS	119
Eastern Kiang	**Dawda K. Jawara**	**PPP**	2,946
	Sheriff M. Dibba	NCP	735
	Assan M. Camara	GPP	212
	Sidia Jatta	PDOIS	138
	Lamin Bojang	PDP	127
Western Kiang	**Dawda K. Jawara**	**PPP**	3,356
	Sheriff M. Dibba	NCP	549
	Assan M. Camara	GPP	69
	Sidia Jatta	PDOIS	62
	Lamin Bojang	PDP	46
Kerewan AA (NBD)	**Dawda K. Jawara**	**PPP**	23,899
(total)	Sheriff M. Dibba	NCP	14,670
	Assan M. Camara	GPP	2,228
	Sidia Jatta	PDOIS	1,784
	Lamin Bojang	PDP	1,540
Sabach Sanjal	**Dawda K. Jawara**	**PPP**	4,669
	Sheriff M. Dibba	NCP	1,210
	Assan M. Camara	GPP	495
	Lamin Bojang	PDP	429
	Sidia Jatta	PDOIS	206
Illiassa	**Dawda K. Jawara**	**PPP**	4,079
	Sheriff M. Dibba	NCP	2,922
	Assan M. Camara	GPP	282
	Sidia Jatta	PDOIS	229
	Lamin Bojang	PDP	224
Central Baddibu	**Sheriff M. Dibba**	**NCP**	3,087
	Dawda K. Jawara	PPP	2,537
	Assan M. Camara	GPP	147
	Sidia Jatta	PDOIS	55
	Lamin Bojang	PDP	47

Table D.3. (*continued*)

Constituency	Candidate	Party	Vote
Jokadu	**Dawda K. Jawara**	**PPP**	2,788
	Sheriff M. Dibba	NCP	1,019
	Assan M. Camara	GPP	410
	Sidia Jatta	PDOIS	348
	Lamin Bojang	PDP	272
Lower Baddibu	**Sheriff M. Dibba**	**NCP**	2,483
	Dawda K. Jawara	PPP	2,181
	Sidia Jatta	PDOIS	133
	Assan M. Camara	GPP	100
	Lamin Bojang	PDP	94
Lower Niumi	**Dawda K. Jawara**	**PPP**	3,456
	Sheriff M. Dibba	NCP	2,759
	Sidia Jatta	PDOIS	539
	Assan M. Camara	GPP	502
	Lamin Bojang	PDP	307
Upper Niumi	**Dawda K. Jawara**	**PPP**	4,189
	Sheriff M. Dibba	NCP	1,190
	Assan M. Camara	GPP	292
	Sidia Jatta	PDOIS	274
	Lamin Bojang	PDP	167
Georgetown AA (MID) (total)	**Dawda K. Jawara**	**PPP**	25,409
	Assan M. Camara	GPP	5,779
	Sheriff M. Dibba	NCP	4,909
	Lamin Bojang	PDP	2,554
	Sidia Jatta	PDOIS	2,129
Sami[a]	**Dawda K. Jawara**	**PPP**	3,106
	Assan M. Camara	GPP	639
	Sheriff M. Dibba	NCP	531
	Sidia Jatta	PDOIS	423
	Lamin Bojang	PDP	61
Niani	**Dawda K. Jawara**	**PPP**	3,151
	Assan M. Camara	GPP	1,486
	Sheriff M. Dibba	NCP	880
	Sidia Jatta	PDOIS	487
	Lamin Bojang	PDP	258
Saloum	**Dawda K. Jawara**	**PPP**	5,621
	Lamin Bojang	PDP	869
	Sheriff M. Dibba	NCP	572
	Assan M. Camara	GPP	298
	Sidia Jatta	PDOIS	280

Table D.3. (*continued*)

Constituency	Candidate	Party	Vote
Lower Fulladu West	**Dawda K. Jawara**	**PPP**	4,451
	Sheriff M. Dibba	NCP	1,332
	Assan M. Camara	GPP	656
	Sidia Jatta	PDOIS	303
	Lamin Bojang	PDP	223
Upper Fulladu West	**Dawda K. Jawara**	**PPP**	4,129
	Assan M. Camara	GPP	1,865
	Sheriff M. Dibba	NCP	993
	Lamin Bojang	PDP	674
	Sidia Jatta	PDOIS	248
Niamina	**Dawda K. Jawara**	**PPP**	4,951
	Assan M. Camara	GPP	835
	Sheriff M. Dibba	NCP	601
	Lamin Bojang	PDP	469
	Sidia Jatta	PDOIS	388
Basse AA (URD) (total)	**Dawda K. Jawara**	**PPP**	20,387
	Assan M. Camara	GPP	4,670
	Lamin Bojang	PDP	3,954
	Sheriff M. Dibba	NCP	3,159
	Sidia Jatta	PDOIS	2,220
Jimara	**Dawda K. Jawara**	**PPP**	5,390
	Assan M. Camara	GPP	280
	Sheriff M. Dibba	NCP	267
	Lamin Bojang	PDP	229
	Sidia Jatta	PDOIS	217
Kantora	**Dawda K. Jawara**	**PPP**	2,395
	Assan M. Camara	GPP	1,740
	Lamin Bojang	PDP	254
	Sidia Jatta	PDOIS	223
	Sheriff M. Dibba	NCP	184
Tumana	**Dawda K. Jawara**	**PPP**	2,797
	Assan M. Camara	GPP	1,453
	Lamin Bojang	PDP	306
	Sheriff M. Dibba	NCP	294
	Sidia Jatta	PDOIS	268
Basse	**Dawda K. Jawara**	**PPP**	3,407
	Sheriff M. Dibba	NCP	898
	Assan M. Camara	GPP	608
	Sidia Jatta	PDOIS	391
	Lamin Bojang	PDP	332

Table D.3. (*continued*)

Constituency	Candidate	Party	Vote
Eastern Wuli	**Dawda K. Jawara**	**PPP**	1,535
	Lamin Bojang	PDP	664
	Sidia Jatta	PDOIS	622
	Sheriff M. Dibba	NCP	475
	Assan M. Camara	GPP	174
Western Wuli	**Dawda K. Jawara**	**PPP**	1,724
	Lamin Bojang	PDP	941
	Sheriff M. Dibba	NCP	922
	Sidia Jatta	PDOIS	293
	Assan M. Camara	GPP	162
Sandu	**Dawda K. Jawara**	**PPP**	3,139
	Lamin Bojang	PDP	1,228
	Assan M. Camara	GPP	253
	Sidia Jatta	PDOIS	206
	Sheriff M. Dibba	NCP	119
The Gambia[a]	**Dawda K. Jawara**	**PPP**	117,549 (58.48%)
	Sheriff M. Dibba	NCP	44,639 (22.21%)
	Assan M. Camara	GPP	16,287 (8.10%)
	Lamin Bojang	PDP	11,999 (5.97%)
	Sidia Jatta	PDOIS	10,543 (5.24%)
	Total votes cast		201,017[a]
	Registered electorate		338,739

Notes: [a]The Sami results, which were omitted in *GW*, have been calculated by subtracting the total number of votes for each candidate in all other constituencies from their total national vote. Winning candidates are noted in bold.

Source: Gambia Weekly, May 1, 1992.

APPENDIX E

REPUBLIC REFERENDUM RESULTS, 1970

Table E.1. Republic Referendum Results: 1970

Constituency	Yes	No
Bathurst AA (total)	3,288	5,303
Bathurst North	1,217	2,155
Bathurst Central	1,081	1,586
Bathurst South	990	1,562
Kombo St. Mary AA (total)	1,809	1,647
Bakau	1,240	510
Serrekunda	569	1,137
Brikama AA (total)	22,150	3,340
Northern Kombo	2,673	565
Southern Kombo	4,070	841
Eastern Kombo	6,436	794
Eastern Foni	4,726	520
Western Foni	4,245	620
Mansakonko AA (total)	14,679	1,309
Eastern Jarra	3,504	351
Western Jarra	3,739	675
Eastern Kiang	3,494	206
Western Kiang	3,942	77
Kerewan AA (total)	24,678	8,155
Sabach Sanjal	2,879	1,826
Illiassa	5,393	1,258[a]
Central Baddibu	4,266	291
Lower Baddibu	3,790	323
Jokadu	3,030	1,217
Niumi	5,320	3,240

Table E.1. (*continued*)

Constituency	Yes	No
Georgetown AA (total)	10,389	9,587
Sami	2,318	1,067
Niani	2,251	935
Saloum	1,651	2,860
Lower Fulladu West	1,841	1,220
Upper Fulladu West	929	1,606
Niamina	1,399	1,899
Basse AA (total)	7,975	6,297
Jimara	760	759
Kantora	1,326	1,060
Tumana	1,310	1,619
Basse	1,393	1,025
Wuli	1,252	1,132
Sandu	1,934	702[a]
Total	**84,968**	**35,638**
Registered electorate		133,813

Notes: [a]Results differ in Ramage to Stewart.

Sources: FCO 65/596, annex to Ramage to Stewart, April 24, 1970; Bakarr, *Gambia Yesterday*, 26. The results by Administrative Area in *West Africa*, May 9, 1970, 534, are inaccurate.

APPENDIX F

PRIMARY SOURCES

PUBLIC RECORD OFFICE DOCUMENTS:

COLONIAL OFFICE DOCUMENTS:

Specific documents cited:

CO 89/12, "Report on the Affiliated Elementary Schools for 1918."
CO 89/33, "Report of the Chief Superintendent of The Gambia Police Force for the Year 1954."
CO 89/39, "Police Report, 1958."
CO 89/39, "Police Report, 1960."
CO 554/1513, "Constitutional Advance 1958: Note for Mr Windley," April 1958.
CO 554/2279, "Gambia Constitutional Conference 1961."
CO 554/2279, "Gambia Constitutional Conference Briefs."
CO 554/2623, "Biographical Notes of Gambia Government Delegates," July 1964.

Files in CO series consulted and cited:

87/19	87/113	87/161	87/222
87/28	87/117	87/163	87/225/13
87/46	87/118	87/176	87/225/14
87/47	87/119	87/177	87/228/20
87/66	87/120	87/186	87/229/12
87/67	87/128	87/189	87/230/8
87/74	87/129	87/190	87/231/11
87/80	87/133	87/191	87/232/11
87/82	87/137	87/194	87/235/10
87/83	87/139	87/209	87/236/19
87/96	87/141	87/212	87/237/6
87/99	87/146	87/213	87/237/7
87/104	87/149	87/216	87/237/8
87/109	87/150	87/217	87/237/9
87/111	87/156	87/220	87/238/2

87/238/5	89/23	850/207/3
87/238/9	89/30	
87/239/6	89/33	854/173
87/239/15	89/39	
87/240/5		879/13
87/240/10	267/655/11	879/152
87/240/11		879/183
87/251/6	537/3651	879/189
87/253/4		
87/253/5	554/131/4	1032/131
87/256/1	554/250	
87/256/3	554/251	1037/46
87/256/4	554/422	
87/258/13	554/536	
87/259/1	554/801	
87/259/7	554/1217	
87/259/11	554/1218	
87/260/1	554/1513	
87/260/2	554/1517	
87/260/7	554/1518	
87/260/8	554/1872	
87/266/1	554/1967	
87/266/2	554/2051	
	554/2138	
89/1	554/2147	
89/3	554/2148	
89/4	554/2150	
89/5	554/2153	
89/6	554/2164	
89/7	554/2279	
89/8	554/2498	
89/9	554/2622	
89/10	554/2635	
89/11	554/2636	
89/12	554/2623	
89/14	554/2626	

DOMINION OFFICE DOCUMENTS:

Specific documents cited:

DO 195/382, "Biographical notes for visit of Secretary of State for the Colonies."

Files in DO series consulted and cited:

195/243	195/385	195/392	195/406
195/382	195/388	195/399	195/407
195/384	195/389	195/401	

FOREIGN OFFICE DOCUMENTS:

Files in FO series consulted and cited:

371/146484	371/161579	371/167336	371/181786
371/146485	371/161581	371/176512	371/181861
371/146486	371/161582	371/176586	371/181866
371/147289	371/167335	371/176778	

FOREIGN AND COMMONWEALTH OFFICE DOCUMENTS:

Specific documents cited:

FCO 65/597, Diplomatic Report no. 128/70, Report by J .G. W. Ramage, February 3, 1970.

FCO 65/599, Draft final report prepared by K .W. J. Lane as the UN's Regional Adviser. Enclosure to Collins to Barmby, November 26, 1970.

FCO 65/915, Diplomatic Report no. 145/71, Report by J. G. W. Ramage, February 11, 1971.

FCO 65/1091, Diplomatic Report no. 191/72, Report by M. B. Collins, January 26, 1972.

FCO 65/1285, Diplomatic Report no. 186/73, Report by J. R. W. Parker, January 8, 1973.

FCO 65/1452, Diplomatic Report no. 195/74, Report by J. R. W. Parker, January, 9, 1974.

FCO 65/1611, Diplomatic Report no. 90/75, Report by J. R. W. Parker, January, 10, 1975.

Files in FCO series consulted and cited:

26/1412	65/596	65/1287	65/1458
	65/597	65/1452	65/1611
38/136	65/599	65/916	65/1453
38/137	65/601	65/1454	65/1613
38/138	65/602	65/1455	65/1614
38/139	65/915	65/1456	
38/140	65/44	65/1457	
	65/918		
45/699	65/1090		
	65/1091		
65/32	65/1285		
65/40			
65/41			
65/42			
65/1612			

GAMBIA NATIONAL ARCHIVES DOCUMENTS

Specific documents cited:
GA C1210/1929, Aitken to Colonial Secretary, March 28, 1929 ("Aitken Judgment").

(Original references)	665/1932	S3008/1945
C309/1918	1187/1932	C2079B/1946
732/1919	C1553/1932	A3888/1951
C498/1920	707/1933	
C766/1920	C1685 I/1933	(Modern references etc)
C633/1921	S135/1933	2/2832
C1526/1921	S135 A/1933	4/368
C727/1922	635/1934	9/284
581/1923	683/1934	54/65
C936/1924	C1769/1934	54/231
160/1925	C1771/1934	81/1
C1206/1929	S140 I/1934	82/1
C1210/1929	301/1935	84/43
C1216/1929	C1898/1935	84/266
C1250/1929	C1951/1935	L1/1947
C1251/1929	C2077/1936	
C1268/1929	S179/1938	GA – despatches (1937)
818/1930	214/1939	
C1308/1930	12840/1940	
CF13/1930	S23840/1940	
S116 I/1930	56/1941	
S125/1930	237/1941	
C1466/1931	L56/1941	
C1476/1931	C2371A/1942	
C1477/1931	109/1943	
S131 I/1931	S2502A I/1943	
S140/1931	A350/1944	

OTHER ARCHIVES DOCUMENTS

Election Office (Banjul – "Gambia Elections Results" file)
Gambia Labour Department (Banjul – Gambia Workers' Union file 1b/1)
Gambia Workers' Union files (Banjul – various documents)
Labour Research Department (London – Bathurst Trade Union file)
Ministry of Local Government and Lands (Banjul – file LG/1301)
Senegal National Archives (Dakar – file SA 17G/58)

APPENDIX G

NEWSPAPERS AND MAGAZINES CONSULTED

It should be noted that there are few, if any, surviving complete holdings of Gambian newspapers. The incomplete runs listed here have been read in a variety of sources in The Gambia and England, principally the Gambia National Archives in Banjul and the British Newspaper Library and the Institute of Commonwealth Studies Library in London.

Gambian newspapers (& years consulted):
The Bathurst Observer and West African Gazette (1883–87)
The Bathurst Times (1871)*
The Daily Observer (1994–2006)
Foroyaa (1988–95)
The Gambia Daily (1995–99)
The Gambia Echo (1936–70)
The Gambia News and Special Report (1992)*
The Gambia News Bulletin (1947–87)
The Gambia Onward (1968–84)
The Gambia Outlook and Senegambian Reporter/The Gambia Outlook (1930–80)
The Gambia Times (1981–95)
The Gambia Weekly (1989–94)
The Gambia Weekly News (1951)*
The Hibarr (1954)*
The Independent (2002–4)*
Kent Street Vous (1969)*
The Nation (1972–87)*
New Citizen (1995)*
New Gambia (1966–70)*
The Point (1992–2006)*
The Progressive (1966–76)
The Senegambia Sun (1983–84)
The Vanguard (1958–60)
The Voice (1978–79)*
The Weekend Observer (1994–97)
The Worker (1975–84)

* Only a few issues within the period consulted.

London newspapers and magazines:
The African Times (1864–95)
Crown Colonist (1947)
New African (1981–84)
New Commonwealth (1961–63)
West Africa (1924–95)

Official publication:
The Gambia Gazette (1889–1982)

NOTE$

Chapter 1

1. R. J. Harrison Church, "The Gambia: Physical and Social Geography," in *Africa South of the Sahara 1992*, 21st ed. (London: Europa Publications Ltd, 1992), 488, gives a total area of 11,295 square kilometers, whereas [Gambia Government], *Statistical Abstract of The Gambia 1991* (Banjul: Central Statistics Department, Ministry of Finance and Economic Affairs, 1992), Table 1, gives a total area of 10,689 square kilometers. Small ocean-going vessels used to call regularly at Basse and, more rarely, Fatoto (464 km upstream), but no longer go beyond Kaur and Kuntaur.

2. Harry A. Gailey, *A History of the Gambia* (London: Routledge & Kegan Paul, 1964), 104–10. For a comprehensive description of The Gambia's borders with Senegal, see Ian Brownlie, *African Boundaries: A Legal and Diplomatic Encyclopedia* (London: C. Hurst, 1979), 213–29. Brownlie notes (213) that the border at Kantora and Wuli was slightly adjusted in 1976. As discussed in Chapter 2, the 1889 agreement was a comprehensive one and affected the boundaries of all the British settlements in West Africa.

3. These acquisitions are described by Gailey, *History*, 61–73; J. M. Gray, *A History of the Gambia*, 2nd ed. (London: Frank Cass, 1966), 297–410; Florence K. O. Mahoney, "Government and Opinion in the Gambia 1816–1901" (Ph.D. diss., University of London, 1963), 25–124; and R. R. Kuczynski, *Demographic Survey of the British Colonial Empire*, 2 vols. (London: Oxford University Press, 1948), vol. 1, 324–30. MacCarthy Island (or Lemain Island as it was known at the time) was actually first purchased in 1785, but this fact appeared not to be known by the Gambian government of the 1820s. See Gray, *History*, 277–79; 335. As noted by Francis Bisset Archer, *The Gambia Colony and Protectorate: An Official Handbook*, reprint of 1906 ed. (London: Frank Cass, 1967), 114, the name Kombo St. Mary was used instead of British Kombo by the early 1900s. Bathurst was renamed Banjul in April 1973.

4. Gray, *History*, 479–84; Gailey, *History*, 115–21; and Kuczynski, *Demographic Survey*, vol. 1, 330–31. See also Sir Phillip Bridges, "A Note on Law in The Gambia," in *The Gambia: Studies in Society and Politics*, ed. Arnold Hughes (Birmingham: Birmingham University African Studies Series no. 3, 1991), 55–63. The Gambia Protectorate Ordinance no. 7 of 1902, which transferred the former territories of the Colony to the Protectorate, is reprinted in Archer, *Colony and Protectorate*, 160–77; see also Colonial Office file, Public Record Office (PRO), Kew (hence CO), CO 89/30, Minutes of the Legislative Council (hence Leg. Co. Minutes), November 28, 1946, for the debate on the Protectorate Ordinance that transferred Kombo St. Mary back to the Colony.

5. Harrison Church, "The Gambia"; and Gailey, *History*, 2–3. R. N. C. Anyadike, "Patterns and Variations of Rainfall Over Banjul, Gambia," *Singapore Journal of Tropical Geography* 14, no. 1: (1993), 1–14, examines data on rainfall between 1886 and 1987 as measured at

Yundum (just outside the capital), whereas [Gambia Government], *Statistical Abstract 1991*, Table 4, provides more recent monthly rainfall data.

6. Gailey, *History*, 118. The first "travelling commissioners," J. H. Ozanne (North Bank) and C. F. Sitwell (South Bank) were appointed in 1893; their successors covered a more restricted area. See Arnold Hughes and Harry A. Gailey, *Historical Dictionary of The Gambia*, African Historical Dictionaries no. 79, 3rd ed. (Lanham, MD: Scarecrow Press, 1999), 137; 164; 174. In 1930, the number of Provinces was reduced to four, with the abolition of Kombo-Foni Province, which was incorporated into South Bank Province. See [Colonial Office], *The Gambia, Report for 1930*. Colonial Report no. 1543 (London: HMSO, 1931), 5.

7. [Gambia Government] *Report on the Census of Population of the Gambia Taken on 17th/18th April 1963 by H. A. Oliver* (Sessional Paper [SP] no. 13 of 1965) (Bathurst: Government Printer, 1965), 1; and K. C. Zachariah and Julien Condé, *Migration in West Africa: Demographic Aspects* (Oxford: Oxford University Press, 1981), 30. On local government reorganization in the early 1960s, see M. H. Orde, "Development of Local Government in Rural Areas in the Gambia," *Journal of Local Administration Overseas* 4, no. 1: (1965), 51–59. For later changes, see David P. Gamble, *The North Bank of The Gambia: Places, People and Population,* 3 vols. (Brisbane, CA: Gamble and Rahman, 1999), vol. C, 100; and [Gambia Government], *Population Databank 1995* (Banjul: National Population Commission Secretariat, 1996), Table 1.2. As noted in Hughes and Gailey, *Historical Dictionary*, 116, Janjangbureh was the original local name of what later became MacCarthy Island.

8. Kuczynski, *Demographic Survey*, vol. 1, 318–28. The troops who were stationed in Bathurst formed part of the Gambia Expedition against Fodi Kabba, on which see Gray, *History*, 468–72.

9. Kuczynski, *Demographic Survey*, vol. 1, 330–33, discusses the widely divergent estimates of the Protectorate's population in the early years of the twentieth century; the 1921 Protectorate overestimate was due to overcounting in North Bank Province. The number of "temporary" residents in Bathurst fell from 5,169 in 1944 to 3,046 in 1951 (temporary residents were defined as those who had been in Bathurst for less than five years). See [Gambia Government], *Report of the Census Commissioner for Bathurst, 1944* (SP no. 2 of 1945) (Bathurst: Government Printer, 1945); and [Gambia Government], *Report of the Census Commissioner for the Colony—1951* (SP no. 4 of 1952) (Bathurst: Government Printer, 1952).

10. World Bank, *World Development Indicators 1997* (Washington: World Bank, 1997), Table 1.1. Only six African countries (Burundi, The Comoros, Mauritius, Nigeria, Rwanda, and Seychelles) were considered by this source to have a higher population density in 1995. Table 2.1 of the same source gives an annual population growth rate for The Gambia of 3.7 percent per annum between 1980 and 1995, one of the highest listed.

11. [Gambia Government], *Population Databank*, Table 1.8. World Bank, *African Development Indicators 2003* (Washington: World Bank, 2003), 312 (Table 13.4), gives lower urbanization estimates of 24.9 percent in 1990 and 31.3 percent in 2001.

12. No full-length ethnographic account of the peoples of The Gambia has been published, although there are brief descriptions in Patience Sonko-Godwin, *Ethnic Groups of the Senegambia: A Brief History* (Banjul: Book Production and Material Resources Unit, 1985); Burama K. Sagnia, *A Concise Account of the History and Traditions of Origin of Major Ethnic Groups* (Banjul: Office of the Vice-President, 1984); Sulayman S. Nyang, "Colonialism and the Integration of the Gambian Ethnic Groups" in *State and Society in Africa: Perspectives on Continuity and Change,* ed. Feraidoon Shams (Lanham, MD: University Press of America, 1995), 88–115; and B. K. Sidibe (Bakary Sidibeh) and Winifred Galloway, *The Gambian Peoples* (Banjul: Oral History & Antiquities Division, Vice-President's Office, 1975). This section is therefore mainly based on the census reports of 1881–1993, particularly those of 1911 and 1963–93, on which see [Colonial Office], *Report and Summary of the Census of the Gambia 1911* (London: HMSO, 1911).

This can be found in CO 87/186, Denton to Secretary of State, June 27, 1911; [Gambia Government], *Census Report, 1963*; [Gambia Government], *Population and Housing Census 1983* (Banjul: Central Statistics Department, Ministry of Economic Planning and Industrial Development, 1987), vol. 1; and [Gambia Government], *Population Databank*. Additional comparative data for 1973–93 were supplied to the authors by the Central Statistics Department, Banjul. Useful secondary sources include Gailey, *History*, 9–16; Gray, *History*, 325–32; Henry F. Reeve, *The Gambia, Its History: Ancient, Medieval and Modern* (London: Smith, Elder and Co., 1912), 168–207; Charlotte A. Quinn, *Mandingo Kingdoms in the Senegambia: Traditionalism, Islam and European Expansion* (Evanston: Northwestern University Press, 1972); Peter M. Weil, "Mandinka Mansaya: The Role of the Mandinka in the Political System of The Gambia" (Ph.D. diss., University of Oregon, 1968); David P. Gamble, *the Wolof of Senegambia, Together With Notes on the Lebu and the Serer* (London: International African Institute, 1957); David P. Gamble, *Contributions to a Socio-Economic Survey of the Gambia* (London: Colonial Office Research Department, 1949), 25; and Michael Tomkinson, *The Gambia: A Holiday Guide* (London: Michael Tomkinson, 1983), 26–32. An early account by Administrator Gilbert T. Carter is also useful. See [Colonial Office], "Gambia: Report on the Blue Book for 1888," in *Papers Relating to Her Majesty's Colonial Possessions*, no. 61. (London: HMSO, 1889), 29–39.

13. The analysis is made more difficult by the fact that only limited data have been published in the census reports. It is not possible, for example, to show occupational structure or religious belief by ethnic group.

14. Quinn, *Mandingo Kingdoms*, 24, notes that by the mid-nineteenth century, the Wolof had long been intermarrying with the Serere, Mandinka, and Fula Torodo, whereas Gamble, *Socio-Economic Survey*, 28, writing in the late 1940s, commented on the close relationship between the Mandinka and the Serere. On the use of Wolof as a "lingua franca" in Senegal, see Donal Cruise O'Brien, "The Shadow-Politics of Wolofisation," *Journal of Modern African Studies* 36, no. 1: (1998), 25–46. Among the examples of Wolofized politicians were the Serahuli brothers, B. O. and H. O. Semega-Janneh. See also note 43.

15. Quinn, *Mandingo Kingdoms*, 24, notes that the Mandinka, Wolof, Serere, and Fula all had a similar caste system in the nineteenth century. Indeed, it would appear that only the Aku and the Jola of the major Gambian ethnic groups have no caste system.

16. The first simultaneous census was not conducted until 1963. Previously, the Protectorate census had been carried out by provincial/divisional commissioners over a four- or five-month period. Commissioners depended on estimates made by heads of the household and did not visit all villages in their Divisions personally. See [Gambia Government], *Census Report, 1963*, 8; Gamble, *Socio-Economic Survey*, 25.

17. Sidibe and Galloway, *The Gambian Peoples*, describe some of the other minor ethnic groups.

18. See J. D. Fage, *A History of West Africa: An Introductory Survey*, 4th ed. (Cambridge: Cambridge University Press, 1969), 21–22; Quinn, *Mandingo Kingdoms*, 10–11; 29; Gray, *History*, 325; and Sonko-Godwin, *Ethnic Groups*, 3–4.

19. The other three Provinces at this time were Kombo-Foni, Upper River, and MacCarthy Island; see Gailey, *History*, 118.

20. Gray, *History*, 319–20.

21. Quinn, *Mandingo Kingdoms*, 15–17; and Weil, "Mandinka Mansaya," 72–76.

22. Judith Carney and Michael Watts, "Disciplining Women? Rice, Mechanization, and the Evolution of Mandinka Gender Relations in Senegambia," *Signs* 16, 4: (1991), 651–81, examine the gender division of labor in Mandinka households. See also Arnold Hughes, "From Green Uprising to National Reconciliation: The People's Progressive Party in the Gambia 1959–1973," *Canadian Journal of African Studies* 9, no. 1: (1975), 67–70. Charles O. van der Plas, "Report of a Socio-Economic Survey of Bathurst and Kombo St. Mary in the

Gambia," 127, noted that the Mandinka were often employed as drivers and laborers (including seasonal laborers) in the urban areas. Van Der Plas' report (which was produced for the Gambian government in 1956) may be found in the Gambian National Archives, Banjul (hence GA), GA 54/65. On Mandinka occupations in the 1990s, see Rohey Wadda and Russell Craig, *Report on the 1992 Priority Survey* (Banjul: Ministry of Finance and Economic Affairs, 1993), 21 (Table 2.4).

23. Administrator Carter claimed in [Colonial Office], "1888 Blue Book Report," 30, that "as a rule," the Mandinka were Muslims. Similarly, Quinn, *Mandingo Kingdoms*, 192, argued that by the 1890s, "many Mandingo . . . had come to call themselves Muslim." Allister Macmillan, *The Red Book of West Africa*. New impression. (London: Frank Cass, 1968), 278 (writing in 1920), stated simply that "They are Mohammedans." The circumstances of Jawara's conversion to Christianity are outlined in Chapter 6.

24. Sources have disagreed over whether the Tukulor and the Fula should be regarded as the same or as different ethnic groups. For example, Administrator Carter argued that the two were practically the same race; fifty years later, the historian J. M. Gray suggested that the Tukulor were "one section" of the Fula people. See [Colonial Office], "1888 Blue Book Report," 38–39; and Gray, *History*, 326. Conversely, Reeve, *The Gambia*, 201, described the Tukulor as being of mixed Fula/Wolof/Mandinka blood. Although the Tukulor were separately classified in the 1963 census, the census controller, Henry Oliver, stated that they could equally have been recorded as Fula; see [Gambia Government], *Census Report, 1963*, 24. See also Sonko-Godwin, *Ethnic Groups*, 29.

25. Quinn, *Mandingo Kingdoms*, 18–19, suggests that the Fula may be subdivided into nine dialect groups. She did not include the Tukulor within this total.

26. On Musa Molloh (whom she terms "Molo"), see Quinn, *Mandingo Kingdoms*, 174–90.

27. On rural Fula, see Quinn, *Mandingo Kingdoms*, 21; Kenneth Swindell, *The Strange Farmers of The Gambia: A Study in the Redistribution of African Population*. Monograph 15. (Swansea: Centre for Development Studies, University College of Swansea, 1981), 41; Sonko-Godwin, *Ethnic Groups*, 27; and Sidibe and Galloway, *The Gambian Peoples*, 5–6. On urban Fula, see Van der Plas, "Socio-Economic Survey," 127.

28. Quinn, *Mandingo Kingdoms*, 21, argues that by the nineteenth century, four Fula sub-groups were thoroughly Islamized, two were in the process of conversion, and three remained firmly animist. Gray, *History*, 326, noted that the Tukulor were "for the most part Mohammedans," but added that Islam "had not made as great strides" among other Fula subgroups.

29. The 1830s mission is described by Gray, *History*, 362–63, and that of the 1940s in S. H. M. Jones, *The Diocese of Gambia and the Rio Pongas 1935–1951: Its Origins and Early History* (Banjul: Book Production and Material Resources Unit, 1986), 41–50. A notable convert was Andrew D. Camara. As noted in Chapter 9, Camara became a Muslim in the 1970s and changed his name to Assan Musa Camara.

30. Quinn, *Mandingo Kingdoms*, 23–25 (who notes that the population of Saloum was largely Serere rather than Wolof in the nineteenth century); and Gray, *History*, 325–27. In 1988, the Wolof population of Senegal was 2.9 million, 43 percent of the country's total population. See "Senegal," *The Europa World Year Book 1999*, 40th ed. 2 vols. (London: Europa Publications Ltd, 1999), vol. 2, 3085.

31. See Gray, *History*, 316–19; Quinn, *Mandingo Kingdoms*, 23–24; and Gamble, *Wolof of Senegambia*, 79.

32. See Gray, *History*, 325; Gamble, *Wolof of Senegambia*, 11; and Sulayman S. Nyang, "The Role of the Gambian Political Parties in National Integration" (Ph.D. diss., University of Virginia, 1979), 47–48.

33. These definitions were adopted in the 1992 Priority Survey, which was a nationally representative survey of 2,000 households. See Wadda and Craig, *Priority Survey*, 21 (Table 2.4). On rural Wolof, see also Gamble, *Wolof of Senegambia*, 30.

34. Van der Plas, "Socio-Economic Survey," 127, notes that urban Wolof were still mainly employed in manual occupations in the mid-1950s, although some were employed as clerks by the government or commercial firms. Gamble, *Wolof of Senegambia*, 79 (writing in the late 1950s), noted that a much higher proportion of Wolof had attended school in recent years and were gradually taking over posts in the civil service from the Aku. In addition, in 1948, the first Wolof (P. S. N'Jie) was called to the bar; see Chapter 5.

35. Quinn, *Mandingo Kingdoms*, 23, notes that the Wolof of Baddibu and Saloum dominated the Muslim revivalist movement of the mid-nineteenth century. Similarly, Carter described the Wolof as "fervent Mohammedans"; see [Colonial Office], "1888 Blue Book Report," 37. See also Reeve, *The Gambia*, 182.

36. See William Moister, *Memorials of Missionary Labours in Western Africa, the West Indies and at the Cape of Good Hope* (London: William Nichols, 1866), 136–41; Barbara Prickett, *Island Base—A History of the Methodist Church in The Gambia, 1921–1969* (Bathurst: Methodist Church, Gambia, 1971), 38–43; and Gray, *History*, 319. For further information on the background and later careers of the two men, see Prickett, passim; and Mahoney, "Government and Opinion," 149; 161.

37. James Africanus Horton, *West African Countries and Peoples*. Reprint of 1868 ed. (Edinburgh: Edinburgh University Press, 1969), 70, writing about the Wolof of Bathurst, stated that "the Roman Catholic religion is professed by them." Prickett, *Island Base*, 94, attributes the growth of Catholicism among the Wolof to the fact that Wolof-speaking priests were sent to Bathurst in the 1860s. Gamble, *Wolof of Senegambia*, 72, argued that Christian Wolof in the 1950s were mainly Catholic. One reason for the decline in the Protestant share of the Wolof population may have been because the children of Wolof Protestants (and of mixed Aku/Wolof parents) were apparently generally considered to be Aku; see Nyang, "Gambian Political Parties," 50.

38. There has been no major study of Gambian Jola, but on the Jola in Casamance, see Olga F. Linares, *Power, Prayer and Production: The Jola of Casamance, Senegal* (Cambridge: Cambridge University Press, 1992). Sonko-Godwin, *Ethnic Groups*, 35, argues that the Jola moved north to the area due south of the River Gambia following the arrival of the Mandinka in the thirteenth and fourteenth centuries.

39. According to Gray, *History*, 319, the Jola had formed a separate community in "Jola Town" since the early days of the settlement. See Sonko-Godwin, *Ethnic Groups*, 35–37, on the structure of Jola society.

40. Van der Plas, "Socio-Economic Survey," 127; and Nyang, "Gambian Political Parties," 49. On rural Jola, see Quinn, *Mandingo Kingdoms*, 25–27; and Sonko-Godwin, *Ethnic Groups*, 37.

41. Carter noted that Muslims had "utterly failed" to introduce Islam to the Jola, while the Portuguese had been equally unsuccessful in establishing Catholicism; see [Colonial Office], "1888 Blue Book Report," 36. Gray (writing in the late 1930s), noted that "there still exist strong pagan elements amongst the Jolas" (although he considered the majority were Muslims). Quinn believed in the 1970s that "some" were still animist, while Madge argued in the early 1990s that the Jola in The Gambia were largely Muslims. Rice noted in the 1960s that "a few" Jola were Catholic. See Gray, *History*, 328; Quinn, *Mandingo Kingdoms*, 27; Clare Madge, "Intra-Household Use of Income and Informal Credit Schemes in The Gambia," in *Studies in Society and Politics*, ed. Hughes, 29–41; and Berkeley Rice, *Enter Gambia: The Birth of an Improbable Nation* (London: Angus and Robertson, 1968), 228.

42. See Reeve, *The Gambia*, 202; and Sonko-Godwin, *Ethnic Groups*, 32–33, on the origins of the Serahuli. Kenneth Swindell, "Serawoollies, Tillibunkas and Strange Farmers: The Development of Migrant Groundnut Farming Along the Gambia River, 1848–95," *Journal of African History* 21, no. 1: (1980), 93–104; and Quinn, *Mandingo Kingdoms*, 27, discuss the Serahuli in the nineteenth century.

43. On rural Serahuli, see Gailey, *History*, 15; and Sidibe and Galloway, *The Gambian Peoples*, 7. On modern Serahuli businessmen, see Tomkinson, *The Gambia*, 28–29. Interestingly, the most successful Serahuli professional and political family, the Semega-Jannehs, originated from Mauritania and were thus not strictly speaking "Gambian" Serahuli. See also note 14.

44. Sonko-Godwin, *Ethnic Groups*, 33–34, notes that a Serahuli marabout, Momadou Lamin Drammeh, settled with his followers in Gambia in the 1880s. She argues that thereafter the Serahuli were strong adherents of Islam (and hostile to Christianity). Similarly, Quinn, *Mandingo Kingdoms*, 192, argues that the Serahuli were "devoutly Muslim" by the 1890s. The 1993 census found that the Serahuli had the highest proportion of the population with no formal Western education (76 percent); it was suggested that this was because Serahuli parents preferred to send their children to Muslim "Madrassahs". See [Gambia Government], *Population and Housing Census 1993* (Banjul: Central Statistics Department, Department of State for Finance and Economic Affairs, 1996), vol. 8 (Education Statistics), 6–7.

45. On the Serere, see Gamble, *Wolof of Senegambia*, 97–103. On their counterparts in Senegal, see [Europa Publications], "Senegal," *Europa World Year Book 1999*, vol. 2, 3085. Serer is the preferred spelling in Senegal and has often been used in The Gambia as well.

46. Archer, *Colony and Protectorate*, 67–68.

47. Both Horton, *West African Countries*, 72; and Carter in [Colonial Office], "1888 Blue Book Report," 31, noted that Serere men tended to be laborers. See Sidibe and Galloway, *The Gambian Peoples*, 4; and Tomkinson, *The Gambia*, 29, on modern rural Serere.

48. Carter described the Serere as "infidels," who resisted Islam; see [Colonial Office], "1888 Blue Book Report," 31. Reeve, *The Gambia*, 174, writing in 1912, noted that the Serere were generally still "Pagans." For Methodist efforts to convert the Serere to Christianity in the 1870s, see G. G. Findlay and W. W. Holdsworth, *The History of the Wesleyan Methodist Missionary Society*, 5 vols. (London: Epworth, 1922), vol. 4, 140. On the religious affiliation of Serere in Senegal, see Andrew F. Clark and Lucie Colvin Phillips, *Historical Dictionary of Senegal*, African Historical Dictionaries no. 65, 2nd ed. (Metuchen, NJ: Scarecrow Press, 1994), 245.

49. On the Manjago in Guinea-Bissau, see Rosemary E. Galli, *Guinea-Bissau* (Oxford: Clio Press, 1990); and Joshua B. Forrest, *Guinea-Bissau: Power, Conflict and Renewal in a West African Nation* (Boulder, CO: Westview Press, 1992). Forrest notes (118), that the Mandjack comprised 11 percent of the population of Guinea-Bissau in 1979. Peter B. Clarke, *West Africa and Christianity* (London: Edward Arnold, 1986), 79, suggests there were Manjago in Bathurst as early as the 1840s.

50. Rice, *Enter Gambia*, 176; and Sidibe and Galloway, *The Gambian Peoples*, 2. Mahoney, "Government and Opinion," 64–65, notes that many captains of vessels (as well as painters and skilled mechanics) in the nineteenth century were immigrants from the Cape Verde Islands and Portuguese Guinea, and Manjago sailors were also involved in a major strike in 1929; see David M. R. Perfect, "Organised Labour and Politics in The Gambia: 1920–1984" (Ph.D. diss., University of Birmingham, 1987), 72 (note 8). On the higher than average Manjago educational standards (and their predominant Christian religion), see [Gambia Government], *Census Report, 1993*, vol. 8, 7.

51. Gray, *History*, 335, reports a Bambara presence in Gambia in the 1830s. On the Bambara in Mali, see Pascal James Imperato, *Historical Dictionary of Mali*, African Historical Dictionaries no. 11, 2nd ed. (Metuchen, NJ: Scarecrow Press, 1986), 95.

52. For example, at least until the 1970s, the Sanitary Night Service workers in Bathurst tended to be Bambara; other Gambian ethnic groups would not take on the work. See, for example, *The Progressive*, September 10, 1973.

53. On the nineteenth-century Liberated Africans and their descendants, see especially Mahoney, "Government and Opinion"; Florence K. Mahoney, "African Leadership in Bathurst in the Nineteenth Century," *Tarikh* 2, no. 2: (1968), 25–38; Gray, *History*, 315–16; 357–65; and Patrick Webb, "Guests of the Crown: Convicts and Liberated Slaves on McCarthy [*sic*] Island, The Gambia," *Geographical Journal* 160, no. 2: (1994), 136–42. There has been no full-length study of the Aku in The Gambia. In contrast, their counterparts in Sierra Leone, the Creoles/Krio, have been studied in detail; see especially Akintola J. G. Wyse, *The Krio of Sierra Leone* (London: C. Hurst, 1989).

54. Kuczynski, *Demographic Survey*, vol. 1, 116, presents documentary evidence from the Liberated African Department in Freetown that a total of 1,599 Liberated Africans were sent to Gambia between 1818 and 1833 (of whom 1,073 were sent in 1832 and 1833); he also cites (126), the contemporary evidence of Lieutenant Governor H. V. Huntley to a Parliamentary Committee that 2,914 Liberated Africans had been transferred to Gambia by 1841. A modern estimate by Webb, "Guests of the Crown," 139, is that more than 4,000 Liberated Africans were transferred to The Gambia between 1832 and 1843.

55. Mahoney, "African Leadership," 30, citing the estimate of Commissioner Dr. R. R. Madden (see note 60).

56. Mahoney, "African Leadership," 28–29; 37. See also Horton, *West African Countries*, 71. See Christopher Fyfe, *A History of Sierra Leone* (London: Oxford University Press, 1962), 170, on the use of the term Aku in Freetown.

57. The 1911 census report in fact stated simply that the Aku were "the descendants of Liberated Africans." [Colonial Office], *Census Report, 1911*. Harry A. Gailey, *Historical Dictionary of The Gambia*, African Historical Dictionaries no. 4. (Metuchen, NJ: Scarecrow Press, 1975), 23, also notes how Aku came to be wrongly applied to the descendants of all Recaptives. See also note 37.

58. A total of 1,059 people living in Bathurst in 1931 were reported to have been born in Sierra Leone; perhaps many of these were classified as Aku in 1944. See Kuczynski, *Demographic Survey*, vol. 1, 342 (Table 5).

59. On the rise and fall of these communities, see Gray, *History*, 360–64; 481–84; Mahoney, "Government and Opinion," 75–77; Webb, "Guests of the Crown"; and Kuczynski, *Demographic Survey*, vol. 1, 324–28.

60. Mahoney, "African Leadership," 29–30; and [House of Commons (HC)], "Report of Her Majesty's Commissioner [Dr. R. R. Madden] on the State of the British Settlements on the Western Coast of Africa," in *British Parliamentary Papers Colonies Africa 2* (hence *PPCA 2*) (Shannon: Irish University Press, 1968), 186–88. At the time of Madden's visit to the colony in 1841, there were no Liberated Africans enrolled in the only school in Bathurst.

61. Horton, *West African Countries*, 71; and [Colonial Office], *Census Report, 1911*. For a detailed analysis of the rise of the Liberated Africans in the nineteenth century, see Mahoney, "Government and Opinion"; and Mahoney, "African Leadership."

62. Gamble, *Wolof of Senegambia*, 79, argued that in the mid-1930s, 80 percent of the clerks on the government staff list had Aku names; however, by the late 1950s, their dominance had been reduced as Wolof were gradually increasing their share of posts. Rice, *Enter Gambia*, 11, who visited Gambia on the eve of independence, reported that the Aku still held "many" senior posts in the civil service. Hughes, "Green Uprising," 70, found that twenty-seven out of thirty-one "Super Scale" posts in the civil service were held by Aku or Wolof in 1973.

63. [Gambia Government], *Census Report, 1993*, vol. 8, 6–7.

64. Horton, *West African Countries,* 71. Clarke, *West Africa Christianity,* 79–80, notes the failure of Catholic missionaries to convert many Aku in the nineteenth century, but also suggests (125) that most Catholics in The Gambia in the early 1970s were descended from Liberated Africans. See also Nyang, "Gambian Political Parties," 50.

65. An analysis of the minutes of the Annual Synod Meeting of The Gambia District of the Wesleyan Methodist Society indicates that between the late 1880s and World War I, virtually all the leading lay members of the Wesleyan Church were Aku. See "West Africa Synod Minutes: Gambia, 1842–1910; 1912–46," microfiche box numbers 1 and 10, Wesleyan Methodist Missionary Society (hence WMMS) Archives, School of Oriental and African Studies, University of London.

66. On strange farmers, see Gamble, *Socio-Economic Survey,* 71–78; Swindell, *Strange Farmers;* and A. F. Robertson, *The Dynamics of Productive Relationships: African Share Contracts in Comparative Perspective* (Cambridge: Cambridge University Press, 1987), Chapter 6.

67. The various estimates are by Gamble, *Socio-Economic Survey,* 78; Swindell, *Strange Farmers,* 39–40; and Malcolm F. McPherson, "Macroeconomic Reform and Agriculture," in *Economic Recovery in The Gambia: Insights for Adjustment in Sub-Saharan Africa,* ed. Malcolm F. McPherson and Steven C. Radelet (Cambridge, MA: Harvard Institute for International Development, 1995), 202–3 (note 3). McPherson cites other estimates that there were approximately 12,000–17,000 strange farmers in The Gambia in the mid-1970s.

68. Horton, *West African Countries,* 71, noted the presence of traders from Sierra Leone in the 1860s; see also Chapter 3 on the influx of Creoles in the 1870s.

69. Zachariah and Condé, *Migration in West Africa,* 35, reported that whereas 3,400 Gambians were living in Sierra Leone in the mid-1970s, only 400 Sierra Leoneans were then living in The Gambia.

70. In 1931, there were 2,989 Senegalese-born persons in Bathurst (21 percent of the total population); see Kuczynski, *Demographic Survey,* vol. 1, 342 (Table 6). Christopher Allen, "African Trade Unionism in Microcosm: The Gambia Labour Movement, 1939–67," in *African Perspectives: Papers in the History, Politics and Economics of Africa Presented to Thomas Hodgkin,* ed. Christopher Allen and R. W. Johnson (Cambridge: Cambridge University Press, 1970), 397, estimates that in the late 1930s there were 3,500 seasonal immigrant workers from French and Portuguese territories in Bathurst and its vicinity.

71. Zachariah and Condé, *Migration in West Africa,* 34–35. See also David Cooke and Arnold Hughes, "The Politics of Economic Recovery: The Gambia's Experience of Structural Adjustment, 1985–1994," *Journal of Commonwealth & Comparative Politics* 35, no. 1: (1997), 111–12.

72. Wadda and Craig, *Priority Survey,* 21 (Table 2.4).

73. Mahoney, "Government and Opinion," 31–32.

74. Kuczynski, *Demographic Survey,* vol. 1, 318–47, provides data on the European population until the 1940s; see also [Gambia Government], *Census Report, 1963,* Table 10. Macmillan, *Red Book,* 291, notes the establishment of Maurel Frères in Bathurst.

75. Prominent merchants like Thomas Brown and Thomas Quin frequently assumed official posts in the 1850s and 1860s. For example, in 1854, Quin held the posts of superintendent of police, justice of the peace, and clerk of the Legislative and Executive Councils; see Quinn, *Mandingo Kingdoms,* 92.

76. Kuczynski, *Demographic Survey,* vol. 1, 346 (Table 10), provides data on European government officials and other Europeans between 1910 and 1939.

77. The most detailed analysis of the Mulattos in Gambia is by Florence K. O. Mahoney, "Notes on Mulattoes of the Gambia Before the Mid-Nineteenth Century," *Transactions of the Historical Society of Ghana* 8 (1965), 120–29; see also Mahoney, "Government and Opinion," 407; and Gray, *History,* 316. On the Mulattos in Senegal, see G. Wesley Johnson, *The*

Emergence of Black Politics in Senegal: The Struggle for Power in the Four Communes, 1900–1920 (Stanford, CA: Stanford University Press, 1971).

78. For example, Archer, *Colony and Protectorate*, 68, noted that in the early 1860s, discharged men of the West Indian regiments settled in Kombo. Mahoney, "Government and Opinion," 167, gives one such example. There has been no detailed study of the West Indian community in Gambia, but on their counterparts in Sierra Leone, see Nemata Amelia Blyden, *West Indians in West Africa, 1808–1880: The African Diaspora in Reverse* (Rochester, NY: University of Rochester Press, 2000).

79. [Colonial Office], *Census of the British Empire 1901* (London: HMSO, 1906), Gambia, Table 6. The first significant migration of Lebanese to Senegal occurred after 1902 when Governor-General Roume made a specific appeal for settlers to move to the colony. See Saïd Boumedouha, "Adjustment to West African Realities: The Lebanese in Senegal," *Africa* 60, no. 4 (1990), 547 (note 1). Lebanon was not created as a separate country until 1920.

80. There has as yet been no specific study of the Lebanese in The Gambia. On Lebanese communities elsewhere in West Africa, see for example H. L. van der Laan, *The Lebanese Traders in Sierra Leone* (The Hague: Mouton, 1975); Rita Cruise O'Brien, "Lebanese Entrepreneurs in Senegal: Economic Integration and the Politics of Protection," *Cahiers d'Études Africaines* 15, no. 1 (1975), 95–115; Boumedouha, "Lebanese in Senegal"; Chris Bierwirth, "The Lebanese Communities of Côte d'Ivoire," *African Affairs* 98, no. 390 (1999), 79–99; and Toyin Falola, "Lebanese Traders in Southwestern Nigeria, 1900–1960," *African Affairs* 89, no. 357 (1990), 523–53. Tomkinson, *The Gambia*, 31, gives a brief description of the postindependence community in The Gambia.

81. [Gambia Government], *Population Databank*, Table 1.6.

82. Quinn, *Mandingo Kingdoms*, provides a comprehensive account of the rise of Islam in The Gambia. She argues (192), that until the jihad of the 1860s, Muslims were outnumbered by animists in the river states. On Maba Diakhou/Jaakhu, see also Boubacar Barry, *Senegambia and the Atlantic Slave Trade* (Cambridge: Cambridge University Press, 1998), especially 196–99.

83. According to the 1911 census, 85 percent of the population of the Protectorate was Muslim, 15 percent was "pagan," and 0.6 percent (or 792 people) was Christian. See [Colonial Office], *Census Report, 1911*. Similarly, in 1931, 86 percent of the Protectorate's population was Muslim, 13 percent was "pagan," and 0.4 percent was Christian. Of the 767 Christians in the Protectorate in 1931, 421 were Catholic, 216 were Methodist, and 130 were Anglican. See [Colonial Office], *Annual Report on the Social and Economic Progress of the People of the Gambia, 1931* (Colonial Reports no. 1572) (London: HMSO, 1932), Table 9. On the situation in the 1950s, see J. Spencer Trimingham, *A History of Islam in West Africa* (Oxford: Oxford University Press, 1962), 228 (who cites official estimates for 1947–50). However, these estimates should be viewed with caution, because the number of animists implausibly fell from 49,236 in 1949 to 19,382 in 1950.

84. Calculated from [Gambia Government], *Population Databank*, Table 1.6. The timing of the decline of the animist population cannot be stated with any precision, because religious affiliation was not recorded in either the 1963 or 1973 censuses. On the situation in Cameroon and Liberia, see Jeff Haynes, *Religion and Politics in Africa* (London: Zed Books, 1996), 73; 113.

85. The first missionary to arrive in Gambia was actually William Singleton of the Society of Friends (Quakers) in January 1821. But Singleton's role was to explore the possibility of missionary work in Gambia; the first Quaker missionaries, a group of four Europeans and two Gambians educated in England led by Hannah Kilham, did not arrive until December 1823. The mission collapsed in 1824 and the Society was not active in Gambia thereafter. See Gray, *History*, 311–13; and Hughes and Gailey, *Historical Dictionary*, 110.

86. John Morgan, William Moister, and William Fox, three of the Wesleyan missionaries to Gambia in the 1820s and 1830s, later wrote accounts of their time there. See John Morgan, *Reminiscences of the Founding of a Christian Mission on the Gambia* (London: Wesleyan Mission House, 1864); William Moister, *Memorials*; William Moister, *A History of Wesleyan Missions in all Parts of the World from Their Commencement to the Present Time* (London: Elliot Stock, 1870); and William Fox, *A Brief History of the Wesleyan Missions on the Western Coast of Africa* (London: Aylott and Jones, 1851). The main secondary source is Prickett, *Island Base*. See also Mahoney, "Government and Opinion," 143–86; Findlay and Holdsworth, *Methodist Missionary Society*, vol. 4, passim; Gray, *History*, 310–14; and Lamin Sanneh, *West African Christianity: The Religious Impact* (London: C. Hurst, 1983), 140–46. The brief account by Gailey, *History*, 68–69, is inaccurate.

87. The figures are from Moister, *Memorials*, 40; Gray, *History*, 314; Findlay and Holdsworth, *Methodist Missionary Society*, vol. 4, 87; and [HC], "Madden Report," *PPCA 2*, 187. It is probable that the figures refer only to adult members of the church. Church membership fluctuated from year to year; for example, following the first full Wesleyan District Meeting in March 1842, recorded membership fell to 554 (a slight majority lived on St. Mary's Island). See Prickett, *Island Base*, 63–64.

88. Gray, *History*, 315; 384–85.

89. See [Gambia Government], "Census Report, 1871." This unpublished report can be found in CO 87/99, Administrator Anton to Kennedy, May 16, 1871, which forms an enclosure to Kennedy to Kimberley, June 7, 1871. Clarke, *West Africa and Christianity*, 79–80, provides the estimate for the 1890s. Quinn, *Mandingo Kingdoms*, 94, suggests that one-third of the population of Bathurst may have been Catholic in the 1860s; this was probably an exaggeration. Rev. W. H. Findlay, who visited Gambia and Sierra Leone in 1900 on behalf of the Wesleyan Methodist Missionary Society (WMMS), reported that there were 705 full members of the Wesleyan Church in 1870 (601 in Bathurst and 104 on MacCarthy Island); 633 in 1880; 721 in 1890; and 730 in 1900. See Findlay, "Report of a Visit to the Sierra Leone and Gambia District" (privately printed for WMMS, 1900, WMMS Archives), 15.

90. Quinn, *Mandingo Kingdoms*, 97, notes that Governor D'Arcy estimated that 400 "Marabouts" lived in Bathurst in 1866.

91. In 1881, 80 percent of all Christians lived in Bathurst and 20 percent in other parts of the Colony; by 1901, 91 percent lived in Bathurst. Similarly, by 1898, all bar 51 of the 669 Wesleyan full church members lived in Bathurst. See [Gambia Government], *Detailed Account of the Census of the Population of the British Settlement on the River Gambia, taken on the 4th April 1881* (Bathurst: Government Printer, 1881), which is in CO 87/117, Gouldsbury to Rowe, September 9, 1881 and [Colonial Office], *Census, 1901, Report of the Superintendent* (London: HMSO, 1902), which is in CO 87/163, enclosure to Denton to Chamberlain, June 24, 1901. See also Findlay and Holdsworth, *Methodist Missionary Society*, vol. 4, 141–42.

92. The Christian population of Kombo St. Mary in 1951 was 1,130, 867 of whom were Catholic, 148 Methodist, and 115 Anglican. There were also 6,184 Muslims and 381 "pagans." For details, see [Gambia Government], *Census Report, 1951*, Table 18.

93. [Europa Publications], "The Gambia," *Europa World Year Book 1999*, vol. 1, 1498; and [Gambia Government], *Population Databank*, Table 1.6. There has been no official recent estimate by the Methodist Church. Clarke, *West Africa and Christianity*, 125–26, provides the estimated Christian population in 1970. Prickett, *Island Base*, 7, suggested that there were around 2,000 Methodists in The Gambia in 1969.

94. [HC], "Madden Report," *PPCA 2*, 186.

95. Macmillan, *Red Book*, 283, who (owing to a misprint in the *Annual Report of the Gambia*) gives the date as 1917; CO 89/12, "Report on the Affiliated Elementary Schools for 1918," Appendix II. Gray, *History*, 495, notes that an Anglican church school was opened in

1869, whereas Sanneh, *West African Christianity,* 144, states that the first Catholic school was opened in 1849.

96. Macmillan, *Red Book,* 283. In 1887, for example, 36 Muslims were enrolled in a mission school. They represented 3 percent of total enrolment. See [Colonial Office], *Blue Book,* 1887.

97. Mahoney, "Government and Opinion," 182–83; Macmillan, *Red Book,* 284; and Sanneh, *West African Christianity,* 143.

98. Gailey, *History,* 178–80; and [Gambia Government], *Report of a Commission Appointed to Make Recommendations on the Aims, Scope, Contents and Methods of Education in the Gambia, by T. H. Baldwin* (SP no. 7 of 1951) (Bathurst: Government Printer, 1951). See also CO 87/256/4, on the government's take over of the mission's elementary schools. Catholic opposition to the proposed establishment of a single nondenominational secondary school in the 1950s is outlined in Chapter 5.

99. Macmillan, *Red Book,* 283; Gailey, *History,* 177–78 (who incorrectly gives the foundation of Armitage as 1923); and Sanneh, *West African Christianity,* 144. See also [Colonial Office], *Annual Report of the Gambia* (London: HMSO), various issues, 1926–38. On Bo School, see Mark Walton, "Bo School: A Case Study of 'Adapted Education,' " in *Sierra Leone Studies at Birmingham 1985,* ed. Peter K. Mitchell and Adam Jones (Birmingham: University of Birmingham, 1987), 173–91. In 1962, Armitage School had 180 pupils; see CO 554/2138, Governor of Gambia to Secretary of State, July 19, 1962.

100. Gailey, *History,* 180; and Nyang, "Gambian Political Parties," 79–80.

101. Data are from the census returns of 1921 and 1951 for Bathurst; see [Gambia Government], *Report and Summary of the Census of the Gambia* (Bathurst: Government Printer, 1921); and [Gambia Government], *Census Report, 1951.* See also [Gambia Government], *Report of the Senior Commissioner on the Annual Census of the Protectorate of the Gambia, 1945* (SP no. 5 of 1946) (Bathurst: Government Printer, 1946); and Sanneh, *West African Christianity,* 144–45.

102. Douglas Rimmer, *The Economies of West Africa* (London: Weidenfeld and Nicolson, 1984), 82–83, cites UNESCO estimates on the numbers enrolled in schools as a percentage of six- to eleven-year-old children (or slightly differing age groups) in 1960 in fifteen West African states. Only 12 percent of children aged six to eleven were enrolled in Gambia, a lower figure than in all countries except Mali, Mauritania, Niger, and Upper Volta.

103. [Gambia Government], *Second Five Year Plan for Economic and Social Development 1981/82–1985/86* (Banjul: Ministry of Economic Planning and Industrial Development, 1983), 268; [Gambia Government], *Statistical Abstract 1991,* Tables 15–17; [Gambia Government], *Statistical Abstract of The Gambia 1995* (Banjul: Central Statistics Department, Department of State for Finance and Economic Affairs, 1996), Table 19; [Europa Publications], "The Gambia," *Europa World Year Book 1999,* vol. 1, 1499; United Nations Development Programme (UNDP), *Human Development Report 1995* (New York: Oxford University Press, 1995), Table 1; and World Bank, *World Development Indicators 1997,* Table 2.8. The enrolment data for 1964–65 appear to have been calculated on a slightly different basis from later data.

104. J. Erik De Vrijer, Robin Kibuka, Byung K. Jang, Ivailo V. Izvorski, and Christian H. Beddies, *The Gambia: Selected Issues.* IMF Staff Country Report no. 99/71. (Washington: IMF, 1999), 6; and World Bank, *World Development Indicators 1997,* Table 2.8. [Gambia Government], *Statistical Abstract 1995,* Table 7.9, reports literacy rates for those aged twenty and over in each Division in 1993; these ranged from 73 percent in Banjul to only 21 percent in the URD. In all Divisions, the male literacy rate was at least 20 percentage points above the female rate (in the LRD, the gender gap was as high as 61 percentage points). [Gambia Government], *1998 National Household Poverty Survey Report* (Banjul: Ministry of

Finance and Economic Affairs, 2000), found that net primary enrolment in regular schools was 57 percent in urban areas in 1998, but only 44 percent in rural areas; the difference in net secondary enrolment was wider (30 percent versus 8 percent).

105. For an overview of disease and mortality in the nineteenth and first half of the twentieth centuries, see Kuczynski, *Demographic Survey*, vol. 1, 363–88. There were yellow fever epidemics in 1837, 1859, 1872, 1912, and 1934 and a devastating cholera epidemic in 1869.

106. Roosevelt's statement is quoted in Wm. Roger Louis, *Imperialism at Bay 1941–1945* (Oxford: Clarendon Press, 1977), 356–57. Roosevelt briefly visited Bathurst in January 1943 en route to and from a wartime conference with the British prime minister, Winston Churchill, in Casablanca.

107. World Bank, *World Development Report 1997* (New York: Oxford University Press, 1997), 214 (Table 1).

108. [Gambia Government], *Second Five Year Plan*, 296; and [Gambia Government], *Statistical Abstract 1991*, Table 15. It should be noted that some of the improvement in health facilities in the rural areas was due to the activities of nongovernmental organizations; see Daniel Davis, David Hulme and Philip Woodhouse, "Decentralization by Default: Local Governance and the View from the Village in The Gambia," *Public Administration and Development* 14, no. 3: (1994), 260.

109. [Gambia Government], *Statistical Abstract 1995*, Table 1; and World Bank, *World Development Indicators 1998* (Washington: World Bank, 1998), Table 2.17. These estimates should be viewed with considerable caution.

110. Data are from World Bank, *World Development Report 1997*, Table 2.12 (for access to sanitation); De Vrijer et al., *The Gambia*, 6; and [Gambia Government], *Statistical Abstract 1995*, Table 1 (for access to safe water). The World Bank figure for access to safe water was much lower at 61 percent. It was estimated that in 1983, 97 percent of the urban population, compared with only 50 percent of the rural population, had access to safe water.

111. See [Gambia Government], *1992–93 Household Economic Survey Report: The Gambia* (Banjul: Central Statistics Department, Ministry of Finance and Economic Affairs, 1994), Chapters 4 and 5; [Gambia Government], *1998 National Household Poverty Survey Report*. See also Detlev Puetz and Xiao Ye, "The Gambia National Household Poverty Survey, 1998." World Bank Report no. 26664. In *Standardized Survey Bulletin*, no. 6: (2003, June), 1–8.

112. Brendan M. Walsh, "The Program for Sustained Development," in *Economic Recovery*, ed. McPherson and Radelet, 290; and UNDP, *Human Development Report 1995*, Table 2.1. The UNDP report (15–23) describes the HDI.

113. This is based on an analysis of the 1881 census.

114. Seasonal migration into Bathurst continued on a large scale until after World War II. Bathurst residents would also travel up river to trade during the "dry" season. See Kuczynski, *Demographic Survey*, vol. 1, 319–23.

115. This analysis is based on the census returns for Bathurst (1911–51) and for Kombo St. Mary (1951).

116. Allen, "African Trade Unionism," 397.

117. Data are from [Gambia Government], *Census Report, 1993*, vol. 9 (Gender Statistics). See also [Gambia Government], *Urban Labour Force Survey 1974–75* (Banjul: Central Statistics Division, 1975); [Gambia Government], *Survey of Employment, Earnings and Hours of Work (December 1986)* (Banjul: Central Statistics Department, Ministry of Economic Planning and Industrial Development, 1987); [Gambia Government], *Statistical Abstract 1991*, Table 9 (on the 1983 census). World Bank, *African Development Indicators 2003*, Table 11.5, gives very different estimates for the structure of the economically active population, suggesting that in 2000, as many as 74 percent of active men and 92 percent of active women were employed in agriculture.

118. The Labour Department Report of 1940 suggested that at the peak of the trade season, the European import/export firms might employ between 1,500 and 1,800 people, whereas the government employed fewer than 1,000 even at the busiest times. However, the government may have employed a greater number of workers in the off season. See Perfect, "Organised Labour," 7.

119. Malcolm F. McPherson and Steven C. Radelet, "The Economic Recovery Program: Background and Formulation," in *Economic Recovery*, ed. McPherson and Radelet, 22–23. See also Perfect "Organised Labour," 10 (Tables 1.6 and 1.7) for employment data between 1963 and 1983. Similarly, Tijan M. Sallah, "Economics and Politics in The Gambia," *Journal of Modern African Studies* 28, no. 4: (1990), 628, notes that over 4,500 posts were created in the civil service.

120. The number of civil servants who were laid off in 1986 is disputed. According to Paul E. McNamara, "Budget Reform," in *Economic Recovery*, ed. McPherson and Radelet, 114, 922 established staff and 1,935 temporary staff were laid off and 1,096 vacant civil service posts were eliminated in 1986. Michael T. Hadjimichael, Thomas Rumbaugh, and Eric Verreydt (with Philippe Beaugrand and Christopher Chirwa), *The Gambia: Economic Adjustment in a Small Open Economy*. IMF Occasional Paper no. 100. (Washington: IMF, 1992), 23, agree that 900 established staff were dismissed, but suggest that 2,600 temporary staff were removed in early 1986, and 300 additional temporary staff were taken on in August 1986. See also [Gambia Government], *Survey of Employment 1986*.

121. J. Kakoza, R. Basanti, T. Ehrbeck, and R. Prem, *The Gambia: Recent Economic Developments*. IMF Staff Country Report no. 95/123. (Washington: IMF, 1995), 6, 38; and Peter U. C. Dieke, "The Political Economy of Tourism in The Gambia," *Review of African Political Economy*, no. 62 (1994), 621.

122. See A. G. Hopkins, *An Economic History of West Africa* (Harlow: Longman, 1973), for a detailed examination of West African colonial economies.

123. For example, during World War I, customs revenue accounted for about 70 percent of total revenue; see Macmillan, *Red Book*, 282. The proportion derived from customs was often much higher in the nineteenth century; for details, see the Colonial Office's annual *Blue Books*. The political response to the introduction of income tax is noted in Chapter 4.

124. Data for 1965–66 (and for selected years thereafter) are in Clive S. Gray and Malcolm F. McPherson, "Tax Reform," in *Economic Recovery*, ed. McPherson and Radelet, 128. Data for the 1980s are in Hadjimichael et al., *Economic Adjustment*, 20–22; and Priya Basu and Norman Gemmell, *Fiscal Adjustment in The Gambia: A Case Study*. UNCTAD Discussion Papers no. 74 (Geneva: United Nations Conference on Trade and Development, 1993). The sources differ slightly.

125. Basu and Gemmell, *Fiscal Adjustment*, 11–13, who note that international trade accounts for 40 percent of revenue of sub-Saharan less developed countries on average. Later data (covering the period up to 1994–95), which are provided in Kakoza et al., *Economic Developments*, 48 (Table 22), are calculated in a different way from the sources cited in note 124. The sales tax on imports is regarded as a tax on international trade, but petroleum duty is not. On this basis, international trade accounted for 52 percent of total revenue in 1989–90 and 38 percent in 1994–95. If petroleum duty is also counted as a tax on international trade, the respective percentages increase to 65 percent in 1989–90 and 59 percent in 1994–95.

126. On the direction of trade up to 1920, see Macmillan, *Red Book*, 282. On the changes to the trade which resulted from the First World War, see P. H. S. Hatton, "The Gambia, the Colonial Office, and the Opening Months of the First World War," *Journal of African History* 7, no. 1: (1966), 123–31. The emergence of Gambian trade with Sierra Leone in the 1880s is discussed in Mahoney, "Government and Opinion," Chapter VI.

127. [Central Bank of The Gambia], *Quarterly Bulletin,* no. 1, April 1971, Tables 16 and 17, gives data on the direction of trade in 1965–66; International Monetary Fund (IMF), *Surveys of African Economies* (Washington: IMF, 1975), 78 (Table 23), provides data for 1966–67 to 1972–73.

128. Omar A. Touray, *The Gambia and the World: A History of the Foreign Policy of Africa's Smallest State, 1965–1995.* Hamburg African Studies no. 9. (Hamburg: Institute of African Affairs, 2000), 59.

129. Gailey, *History,* 142.

130. Gamble, *Socio-Economic Survey,* 58–62; and Hazel R. Barrett, *The Marketing of Foodstuffs in The Gambia, 1400–1980* (Aldershot: Avebury, 1988), 27–29. For further information on the volume and value of individual imports and exports, see [Colonial Office], *Blue Books.*

131. On the nineteenth century groundnut trade, see Barrett, *Marketing of Foodstuffs,* 36–43; George E. Brooks, "Peanuts and Colonialism: Consequences of the Commercialization of Peanuts in West Africa, 1830–70," *Journal of African History* 16, no. 1: (1975), 29–54; Gamble, *Socio-Economic Survey,* 58–65; Barry, *Senegambia,* 142–47; Alieu A. O. Jeng, "An Economic History of the Gambian Groundnut Industry, 1830–1924: The Evolution of an Export Economy" (Ph.D. diss., University of Birmingham, 1978); and Robertson, *African Share Contracts,* 208–11.

132. Gamble, *Socio-Economic Survey,* 64; and Jeng, "Gambian Groundnut Industry." On strange farmers in the nineteenth and twentieth centuries, see Swindell, "Serawoollies"; Gamble, *Socio-Economic Survey,* 71–78; and Robertson, *African Share Contracts,* 205–19.

133. Carney and Watts, "Disciplining Women," 656–59; and Gamble, *Socio-Economic Survey,* 63.

134. Mahoney, "Government and Opinion," 239–41; and Gamble, *Socio-Economic Survey,* 62–63.

135. Data are from [Colonial Office], *Blue Books.* On the groundnut trade up to the mid-1920s, see Jeng, "Gambian Groundnut Industry"; Barrett, *Marketing of Foodstuffs,* 40–43; and Gamble, *Socio-Economic Survey,* 65–69.

136. Data are from [Colonial Office], *Annual Report of the Gambia* (various issues). The various projects are examined by Gailey, *History,* 147–59.

137. [Central Bank of The Gambia], *Bulletins,* various issues. See also IMF, *Surveys of African Economies,* Table 21; and [Gambia Government], *Second Five Year Plan,* 30 (Table 7A). There are some differences between these sources.

138. Hadjimichael et al., *Economic Adjustment,* 18 (Table 6); and Kakoza et al., *Economic Developments,* 40 (Table 14), present data on a consistent basis. Data on groundnut output are from [Central Bank of The Gambia], *Bulletins.*

139. On the collapse of the groundnut trade, see Christine Jones and Steven C. Radelet, "The Groundnut Sector," in *Economic Recovery,* ed. McPherson and Radelet, 207–8. For recent data on production, see Kakoza et al., *Economic Developments,* 31 (Table 5); and [Food and Agriculture Organization] (FAO), *Production Yearbook 1997.* FAO Statistics Series no. 142, vol. 51. (Rome: FAO, 1997), Table 38. See also Cooke and Hughes, "Politics of Economic Recovery," 94–99.

140. Data for the 1970s and 1980s are from [Gambia Government], *Second Five Year Plan,* 32 (Table 8); and Hadjimichael et al., *Economic Adjustment,* 10 (Table 3). Claude E. Welch Jr., *Dream of Unity: Pan-Africanism and Political Unification in West Africa* (Ithaca, NY: Cornell University Press, 1966), 269, provides the 1960s estimate. See also Kakoza et al., *Economic Developments,* 7; and Peter Robson, *Economic Integration in Africa* (London: George Allen and Unwin, 1968), 277–78.

141. On the growth (and partial decline) of the re-export sector, see Hadjimichael et al., *Economic Adjustment*, 13; Kakoza et al., *Economic Developments*, 7–10; and Cooke and Hughes, "Politics of Economic Recovery," 99. Chapter 10 examines the changing relationship between The Gambia and Senegal since independence.

142. Hadjimichael et al., *Economic Adjustment*, 18 (Table 6).

143. The tourism statistics are from [Central Bank of The Gambia], *Quarterly Survey*, no. 2 (1975, April–June), Table 23; [Gambia Government], *Statistical Abstract 1991*, Table 29; World Tourism Organization, *Yearbook of Tourism Statistics*. 49th ed. (Madrid: World Tourism Organization, 1997), vol. 1, 33; and Dieke, "Political Economy of Tourism," 617. Kakoza et al., *Economic Developments*, 39 (Table 13), gives data on travel income. On the impact of the coup, see Kaye Whiteman, "Tourism at Risk," *West Africa (WA)*, 9–15 January 1995, 10–11; and Carlene J. Edie, "Democracy in The Gambia: Past, Present and Prospects for the Future," *Africa Development*, 25, no. 3–4 (2000), 183.

144. C. W. Newbury, *British Policy Towards West Africa: Select Documents 1875–1914* (Oxford: Clarendon Press, 1971), Statistical Appendix Table VII, contains the available data on revenue and expenditure between 1828 and 1914. Table V contains data on imports and exports between 1828 and 1914. However, the data are incomplete for this period.

145. Mahoney, "Government and Opinion," 90–97, examines the impact of French activities at Albreda, arguing that in 1824, French evasion of customs duties reduced government revenue from £4,000 to £2,000. Newbury, *Select Documents 1875–1914*, Table VII, shows government revenue for this period, but the data are incomplete.

146. Mahoney, "Government and Opinion," 120–21; 237–40; Gamble, *Socio-Economic Survey*, 59; and [HC], "Report of Colonel Ord into the Condition of the British Settlements on the West Coast of Africa, 1864," in *British Parliamentary Papers Colonies Africa 5* (hence *PPCA 5*) (Shannon: Irish University Press, 1968), 345. See also Newbury, *Select Documents 1875–1914*, Table VII.

147. In 1860, for example, two-thirds of the public expenditure was consumed by the civil establishment. See [HC], "Ord Report," *PPCA 5*, 368. See also Newbury, *Select Documents 1875–1914*, Table VII.

148. Gamble, *Socio-Economic Survey*, 60–61; and Newbury, *Select Documents 1875–1914*, Table VII.

149. For example in 1911, the total education budget (including salaries) was a mere £1,965. There were budget surpluses in all bar two years between 1901 and 1914. See Newbury, *Select Documents 1875–1914*, Table VII. Gamble, *Socio-Economic Survey*, 65–66, examines the groundnut trade in this period.

150. Gailey, *History*, Appendix IV, contains data on revenue and expenditure between 1914 and 1959 (see also 166). See also Macmillan, *Red Book*, 282; and Hatton, "The Gambia," on the impact on trade of the First World War. Perfect, "Organised Labour," 43 (note 9), states that it was estimated by an official Arbitration Board in November 1920 that the cost of living had increased by 200 percent since 1914.

151. Groundnut exports were worth £20 per ton between 1925 and 1929; see [Colonial Office], *Blue Books*, 1925–29.

152. On demonetization and its impact, see Gailey, *History*, 167–69; and Hughes and Gailey, *Historical Dictionary*, 66–67. The exchange rate for the five franc piece had been set at three shillings, ten and one-half pence by an Order in Council in the late nineteenth or early twentieth centuries. When its value fell, Gambia alone failed to adjust the official rate to the world rate and the coin could be exchanged in the colony at a rate approximately 1.75 times its real value. Consequently, five franc pieces flooded into the colony even when their importation was prohibited in April 1921. When the Gambian government demonetized, it bought back all the five franc pieces at the legal rate, which cost over £200,000.

153. Gross expenditure gradually declined from £290,000 in 1929 to £175,000 in 1934 (the lowest figure since 1920) and did not exceed the 1929 total again until 1942. This helped to produce budget surpluses each year between 1932 and 1937; see Gailey, *History*, Appendix IV. Employment and unemployment statistics were not collected systematically in the 1930s and the available data are summarized by Perfect, "Organised Labour," 7–8. See also G. St. J. Orde-Browne, *Labour Conditions in West Africa.* Cmnd 6277. (London: HMSO, 1941), 144.

154. The impact of World War II on the Gambian economy is discussed by Sir Kenneth Blackburne, *Lasting Legacy: A Story of British Colonialism* (London: Johnson, 1976), 58–61. The political implications of the introduction of income tax are discussed in Chapter 4.

155. A cost of living index (which was heavily criticized for being inaccurate and unrepresentative of the cost of living) was established in Bathurst in 1940 with a base of 1938 prices being equal to 100. The index reached 217 in the fourth quarter of 1942, before fluctuating between 170 and 190 for most of the rest of the war. See GA L56/1941.

156. Recorded employment by larger employers fell from a monthly average of 8,901 in 1943 to 4,669 in 1944. See Perfect, "Organised Labour," 8.

157. There were surpluses between 1952 and 1955, when capital assets were run down, and again in 1957 and 1962. Recurrent revenue and expenditure for each year between 1947 and 1964 is examined in the Foreign Office file, PRO (hence FO), FO 371/176512, which was prepared for the 1964 Constitutional Conference. Gailey, *History*, Appendix IV, has data up to 1959 (the 1959 data are different).

158. See Gailey, *History*, 162–63.

159. FO 371/176512. See also Perfect, "Organised Labour," 174–76, on its consequences for public sector employment.

160. This period is analyzed by McPherson and Radelet, "Economic Recovery Program," 20–23. See also McPherson, "Macroeconomic Reform," 192–93. Hadjimichael et al., *Economic Adjustment*, 1, reached similar conclusions over the economic performance in this period. The consumer price index for the low-income group in Banjul and Kombo St. Mary (1990 = 100) rose from 7.0 in 1966 to 7.8 in 1971, which represented an average annual inflation rate of only 2 percent. This rose to 8 percent between 1972 and 1974. See IMF, *International Financial Statistics Yearbook 1996* (Washington: IMF, 1996), 372–73. According to the British high commissioner, who noted the rising cost of living in early 1972, unemployment of school leavers also began to increase around this time; see Foreign and Commonwealth Office file, PRO (hence FCO), FCO 65/1285, Diplomatic Report no. 186/73, Report by J. R. W. Parker, January 8, 1973 (hence "Parker Report 1973").

161. The annual inflation rate rose from 8.8 percent in 1974 to 25.5 percent in 1975, before gradually falling to 6.1 percent in 1979; see [Gambia Government], *Consumer Price Index of The Gambia 1991* (Banjul: Central Statistics Department, Ministry of Finance and Economic Affairs, 1992), Table 1.

162. Twenty parastatals were established between 1971 and 1981. For a review of their performance (and that of the older established parastatals), see Richard M. Hook, Richard D. Mallon, and Malcolm F. McPherson, "Parastatal Reform, Performance Contracts, and Privatization," in *Economic Recovery*, ed. McPherson and Radelet, 235–49.

163. For brief details, see Paul McNamara and Parker Shipton, "Rural Credit and Savings," in *Economic Recovery*, ed. McPherson and Radelet, 103–4.

164. Steven C. Radelet, "Donor Support for the Economic Recovery Program," in *Economic Recovery*, ed. McPherson and Radelet, 49.

165. McPherson and Radelet, "Economic Recovery Program," 23–24; Radelet, "Donor Support," 49; and Cooke and Hughes, "Politics of Economic Recovery," 95–96. The annual inflation rates in 1984 and 1985 were 22.1 and 18.3 percent, respectively. Jawara's support

for the program, which was essential if it were to be adopted, is discussed in Steven C. Radelet and Malcolm F. McPherson, "The Politics of Economic Reform," in *Economic Recovery*, ed. McPherson and Radelet, 36–38.

166. Although the IMF responded favorably to the ERP in August 1985, a new agreement was not signed with it until August 1986; see Radelet, "Donor Support," 50–51.

167. The ERP objectives are summarized in McPherson and Radelet, "Economic Recovery Program," 25–27. See also [Gambia Government], *The Economic Recovery Programme* (Banjul: Government Printer, 1986).

168. The reforms are examined in *Economic Recovery*, ed. McPherson and Radelet. See also Hadjimichael et al., *Economic Adjustment*; Cooke and Hughes, "Politics of Economic Recovery"; Cathy Jabara, "Structural Adjustment in a Small, Open Economy: The Case of Gambia," in *Adjusting to Policy Failure in African Economies*, ed. David E. Sahn (Ithaca, NY: Cornell University Press, 1994), 302–31; and Tony Killick, *IMF Programmes in Developing Countries* (London: Routledge, 1995). The Gambia was one of eight case studies (five in Africa, plus Bangladesh, Costa Rica and Jamaica) analyzed by Killick.

169. The record of nine African countries (Central African Republic, The Gambia, Malawi, Mali, Niger, Somalia, Sudan, Togo, and Uganda) in implementing IMF structural adjustment programs in the 1980s is examined by Ikubolajeh B. Logan and Kidane Mengisteaib, "IMF–World Bank Adjustment and Structural Transformation in Sub-Saharan Africa," *Economic Geography* 69, no. 1 (1993), 1–24. They list (9, Table 1) seven measures that could be adopted under IMF programs; only The Gambia implemented them all. Similarly, a report by the World Bank of structural adjustment programs in twenty-six African countries, concluded that The Gambia was one of six countries that had made large improvements in macroeconomic policies. See World Bank, *Adjustment in Africa: Reforms, Results and the Road Ahead* (Oxford: Oxford University Press, 1994). See also Douglas Rimmer, "Adjustment Blues," *African Affairs*, 94, no. 374 (1995), 109–13, for a detailed review of this report.

170. For brief overall assessments of the ERP, see McPherson and Radelet, "Economic Recovery Program," 28–30; and Cooke and Hughes, "Politics of Economic Recovery," 97–99. See also [Gambia Government], *Consumer Price Index*, Table 1. Jones and Radelet, "The Groundnut Sector," 211, provide the estimate on the increase in rural areas. However, Cooke and Hughes, "Politics of Economic Recovery," 99, argue that living standards remained largely unchanged.

171. Jabara, "Structural Adjustment in a Small, Open Economy," 323.

172. For example, the HIID team concluded that "The ERP was successful in the sense that policy reforms were introduced, and within a relatively brief period, the Gambian economy recovered from a decade of stagnation and began to grow effectively. But a closer look at the ERP package shows that while several crucial reforms were implemented successfully, several were not." See Merilee S. Grindle and Michael Roemer, "Insights from the Economic Recovery Program for Sub-Saharan Africa," in *Economic Recovery*, ed. McPherson and Radelet, 303. Similarly, the overall appraisal by Killick, *IMF Programmes*, 100–101 (Table 3.6), was that in The Gambia, there was "Clear overall improvement but fragile and data unreliable." Cooke and Hughes, "Politics of Economic Recovery," also regarded the ERP as a success.

173. On the aims of the PSD, see Walsh, "Sustained Development," 281–92. See also Cooke and Hughes, "Politics of Economic Recovery," 107–8; and, for the official view, [Gambia Government], *Report of the Third Roundtable Conference for The Gambia* (Banjul: Government Printer, 1992).

174. On the impact of PSD, see Cooke and Hughes, "Politics of Economic Recovery," 107–12; and Kakoza et al., *Economic Developments*. The annual inflation rate fell to 0.3 percent in 1992, the lowest figure since 1970. See IMF, *International Financial Statistics Yearbook 1996*, 372–73.

Chapter 2

1. The background to the establishment of the Bathurst settlement is described by Gray, *History*, 297–302; Gailey, *History*, 61–62; and Mahoney, "Government and Opinion," 25–30.

2. For a detailed history of the James Island settlement, see Gray, *History*, 52–265; and Gailey, *History*, 22–33.

3. On the Company of Merchants, see Gray, *History*, 217–33; 276–77; and Gailey, *History*, 30–34.

4. Gailey, *History*, 62, estimates that this was worth about £25.

5. Gray, *History*, 322–23. On the reasons for the ending of Company rule, see G. E. Metcalfe, *Great Britain and Ghana: Documents of Ghana History 1807–1957* (London: Thomas Nelson, 1964), 49–68, which contains the debate in the House of Commons of February 1821.

6. Gray, *History*, 234–75, describes this period.

7. Gray, *History*, 323.

8. The Executive Council of Sierra Leone was retained, while Governor Freeman appears to have governed Lagos without an Executive Council. See Newbury, *Select Documents 1875–1914*, 524–32. These events are analyzed in detail in Chapter 3.

9. Governor D'Arcy led one expedition into Baddibu in 1861 and another to Albreda and Tubab Kolon in July 1866, but these operations were not repeated in the 1870s and 1880s. Subsidies were paid to two of the rulers of Baddibu, Mamur Nderi Ba and Saer Mati Ba, in the 1870s and 1880s, for example, while D'Arcy mediated between the Soninkes and the Marabouts in Baddibu in 1863. The leaders of both factions urged Governor D'Arcy to take Niumi under British protection in 1862; a similar appeal was made to the administrator by the rulers of Kataba and Nyanibintang in 1870 and by the ruler of Brikama in 1873. All these appeals were rejected. For details, see Quinn, *Mandingo Kingdoms*, 100–105, 133–42; Gray, *History*, 417–63; and Gailey, *History*, 46–57.

10. This decision was taken because the Colonial Office concluded that centralization had not proved effective during the recent Asante War. See David Kimble, *A Political History of Ghana: The Rise of Gold Coast Nationalism 1850–1928* (Oxford: Clarendon Press, 1963), 270–74; and Francis Agbodeka, *African Politics and British Policy in the Gold Coast 1868–1900: A Study in the Forms and Force of Protest* (London: Longman, 1971), 44–55.

11. On the separation of Lagos and the Gold Coast, see Patrick Cole, *Modern and Traditional Elites in the Politics of Lagos* (Cambridge: Cambridge University Press, 1975), 53–56; and Tekena N. Tamuno, *Nigeria and Elective Representation 1923–1947* (London: Heinemann, 1966), 8–11. The reasons for the separation of Gambia and Sierra Leone are discussed in Chapter 4. The first governor was Sir George Denton.

12. The fullest account of the negotiations in the 1870s is in John D. Hargreaves, *Prelude to the Partition of West Africa* (London: Macmillan, 1963), 125–95. The opposition to the proposal in Bathurst and London is analyzed in Chapter 3.

13. See John D. Hargreaves, *West Africa Partitioned: The Loaded Pause, 1885–1889* (London: Macmillan, 1974), 228–29; Gray, *History*, 463–64; and Gailey, *History*, 57–58. For a general account of the French conquest of West Africa during this period, see also Michael Crowder, *West Africa Under Colonial Rule* (London: Hutchinson, 1968), 69–115.

14. The background to the convention is discussed by Hargreaves, *West Africa Partitioned*, 230–46; and Gailey, *History*, 96–104. See also William G. Hynes, *The Economics of Empire: Britain, Africa and the New Imperialism,. 1870–95* (London: Longman, 1979), 96–122. The treaty is given in full in Brownlie, *African Boundaries*, 215–20.

15. On the process by which the boundary was drawn up, the details of the early Protectorate Ordinances and the successful expeditions against Fodi Sillah and Fodi Kabba, see Gailey, *History*, 96–122.

16. Akintola J. G. Wyse, "The Gambia in Anglo-French Relations, 1905–12," *Journal of Imperial and Commonwealth History* 4, no. 2: (1976), 164–75. As late as 1915, William Ponty, the governor general of French West Africa, hoped to achieve the eventual cession of Gambia; see Welch, *Dream of Unity*, 259–60.

17. John Kent, "Regionalism or Territorial Autonomy? The Case of British West African Development, 1939–49," *Journal of Imperial and Commonwealth History* 18, no. 1: (1990) (78, note 3). The proposal does not appear to have received serious consideration by the Colonial Office.

18. CO 1032/131, memorandum by Hammer, March 2, 1959. The response of Wyn-Harris is contained in CO 554/250, Wyn-Harris to Lloyd, March 7, 1952. Further information from Wyn-Harris (Hughes interview, Woodbridge, April 1974).

19. The events are analyzed in full in Dennis Austin, *Malta and the End of Empire* (London: Frank Cass, 1971). On the GMC's endorsement of the Malta option, see Welch, *Dream of Unity*, 271; and Austin, *Malta*, 84.

20. FO 371/146485, memorandum by MacLeod, December 6, 1960; see also CO 554/2154, note by Eastwood, November 3, 1960. On the alleged support for federation in Freetown, see FO 371/146484, Watson to Foreign Office, September 3, 1960 (citing the fears of President Senghor of Senegal).

21. For the views of the Colonial Office and Foreign Office, see the memoranda by MacLeod, December 6, 1960 (FO 371/146485) and Boothby, December 21, 1960 (FO 371/146486). On the opinions of Senghor and Windley, see Welch, *Dream of Unity*, 264–78; and FO 371/146484, Windley to Eastwood, May 4, 1960.

22. FO 371/146485, December 2, 1960, notes of meeting between Iain Macleod, the secretary of state for the colonies, and three Gambian ministers; and Welch, *Dream of Unity*, 283. British Somaliland had become independent at the end of June 1960 and five days later had joined an independent Somalia. See Anthony Low, "The End of the British Empire in Africa," in *Decolonization and African Independence: The Transfers of Power, 1960–1980*, ed. Prosser Gifford and Wm. Roger Louis (New Haven, CT: Yale University Press, 1988), 43.

23. Welch, *Dream of Unity*, 282–91. See also Hubertus J. van Mook, Max Graessli, Henri Monfrini, and Hendrik Weisfelt, *Report on the Alternatives for Association Between the Gambia and Senegal* (SP no. 13 of 1964) (Bathurst: Government Printer, 1964).

24. The adoption of the capital *T* was apparently to avoid confusion with Zambia. See also [Gambia Government], *The Gambia: Independence Conference 1964* (SP no. 21 of 1964) (Bathurst: Government Printer, 1964).

25. The constitutional position is summarized in "How to Create Senegambia?" *WA*, August 8, 1964, 873–74. The 1961 Sierra Leone constitution laid down that the monarchy could only be abolished if there was a two-thirds majority in Parliament in favor of a republic bill, an election was held and the new Parliament also approved the legislation. See John R. Cartwright, *Politics in Sierra Leone 1947–67* (Toronto: University of Toronto Press, 1970), 239–40. At a constitutional conference in London in 1964, the Gambian government originally proposed that the Sierra Leonean constitutional provisions be adopted, but the Colonial Office preferred the idea of a referendum. See CO 554/2622, UK Government, no. 25.

26. The referenda are discussed in Chapter 7.

27. The constitutional change of 1982 and the formal powers of the presidency are discussed in John A. Wiseman, "The Role of the House of Representatives in the Gambian Political System," in *Studies in Society and Politics*, ed. Hughes, 81–83. See Chapter 9 on the elections.

28. See Chapters 8 and 10.

29. See John A. Wiseman, "The Gambia: From Coup to Elections," *Journal of Democracy* 9, no. 2: (1998), 64–75; and Abdoulaye S. M. Saine, "The 1996/1997 Presidential and National Assembly Elections in The Gambia," *Electoral Studies* 16, no. 4: (1997), 554–59.

30. See Martin Wight, *The Development of the Legislative Council 1606–1945* (London: Faber and Faber, 1946), 74; 126–29.

31. Wight, *Development of the Legislative Council*, 149–50. The Letters Patent issued to Governor Seagram in 1843 may be found in C. W. Newbury, *British Policy Towards West Africa: Select Documents 1786–1874* (Oxford: Clarendon Press, 1964), 515–17.

32. Gray, *History*, 378; CO 89/1, Minutes of the Executive Council (hence Ex. Co. Minutes), October 25, 1843; February 21, 1853; and Mahoney, "Government and Opinion," 213. Merchants were represented on the Gold Coast Executive Council in the 1850s and 1860s; see Kimble, *History of Ghana*, 406–7. Brown's career is discussed in Chapter 3.

33. The unusual circumstances of Topp's appointment are discussed in Chapter 4. It was customary for unofficials to attend Executive Council meetings as "extraordinary" members only; see CO 87/149, Ripon to Llewelyn, March 28, 1895. See also CO 87/146, Llewelyn to Ripon, May 29, 1894, when the administrator termed Topp a "general obstructionist" and called for the constitution of the Executive Council to be modified so as to include officials only. The Colonial Office concurred.

34. See GA C1771/1934, Oke to Cunliffe-Lister, February 9, 1934, commenting on a petition from Small and others of October 31, 1933 in the same file. Governor Thompson called for the appointment of two unofficials to the Nigeria Executive Council in 1930, as noted in R. D. Pearce, *The Turning Point in Africa: British Colonial Policy 1938–1948* (London: Frank Cass, 1982), 76.

35. The Burns initiative is examined in Curtis R. Nordman, "The Decision to Admit Unofficials to the Executive Councils of British West Africa," *Journal of Imperial and Commonwealth History* 4, no. 2: (1976), 194–205. See also Pearce, *Turning Point*, 76–79. For the Gambian response, see GA 4/368, Southorn to Moyne, December 31, 1941; and CO 554/131/4, Blood to Cranborne, August 4, 1942.

36. CO 87/260/2, Wright to Creech Jones, April 16, 1947; Creech Jones to Wright, May 9, 1947. The political careers of Small and Faye are discussed in detail in Chapters 4 and 5. On Jammeh, who had been appointed Seyfu of Upper Baddibu in 1928 (having previously been the Deputy), see CO 87/260/2, Wright to Creech Jones, September 27, 1947; and Gamble, *North Bank*, vol. C, 123.

37. See CO 87/266/1 for details of the discussions between Wyn-Harris and the Colonial Office. The Colonial Office would have been prepared to allow parity between officials and unofficials (as in the 1951 Sierra Leone constitution), but this was rejected by Wyn-Harris. The circumstances of Faye's dismissal are discussed in Chapter 5.

38. The Consultative Committee's report was published in *The Gambia Gazette* (*GG*), July 31, 1953. Its membership is discussed in Chapter 5.

39. The constitution was published as [Colonial Office], *The Gambia (Constitution) Order in Council 1954* (London: HMSO, 1954). Its provisions are summarized by Gailey, *History*, 188–89. The political implications of the constitution are analyzed in Chapter 5.

40. The ministerial appointments and the circumstances of P. S. N'Jie's dismissal are examined in Chapter 5. The other unofficials appointed to the Executive Council were Henry Madi (who was elected to the Legislative Council for Kombo St. Mary); Seyfu Landing Sonko of Lower Niumi and Seyfu K. K. Sanneh of Kiang East; and a barrister, Jacob L. Mahoney. See CO 554/1513, "Constitutional Advance 1958: Note for Mr Windley," April 12, 1958 (which was written by Windley's predecessor, Wyn-Harris).

41. The Windley Constitution was published as [Gambia Government], *Constitutional Developments in Gambia: Exchange of Despatches* (SP no. 4 of 1959) (Bathurst: Government Printer, 1959). See Chapter 6 on the selection of the ministers.

42. See Chapter 6.

43. The conference proceedings were published as [Gambia Government], *Constitutional Developments in the Gambia: Exchange of Despatches* (SP no. 6 of 1961) (Bathurst: Government Printer, 1961); and [Gambia Government], *Report of the Gambia Constitutional Conference* (SP no. 8 of 1961) (Bathurst: Government Printer, 1961). They are analyzed in Jeggan C. Senghor, "Politics and the Functional Strategy to International Integration: Gambia in Senegambian Integration, 1958–1974" (Ph.D. diss., Yale University, 1979), 241–45; and Perfect, "Organised Labour," 166–68. The 1962 constitution, which was published in full in *GG*, Supplement A to April 26, 1962, is summarized in "Self-Government for the Gambia," *WA*, August 5, 1961, 851.

44. In Sierra Leone, for example, an all-African cabinet (apart from the governor) was created as early as 1958. See Cartwright, *Politics in Sierra Leone*, 99–100.

45. See Chapter 9 for a discussion of the new cabinet.

46. Newbury, *Select Documents 1786–1874*, 515.

47. Wight, *Development of the Legislative Council*, 152.

48. Gray, *History*, 378; Mahoney, "Government and Opinion," 202; CO 89/1, Leg. Co. Minutes, November 10, 1843; March 27, 1844; December 30, 1847; May 4, 1850; and [Colonial Office], *Blue Book*, 1861. Although Goddard attended meetings of the council in 1843, his appointment dated officially from May 1844. On Lloyd and Goddard, see Mahoney, "Government and Opinion," 42–45. On the situation in the Gold Coast and Sierra Leone, see Kimble, *History of Ghana*, 405; and Fyfe, *History of Sierra Leone*, 318–19.

49. James Bannerman was appointed to the Gold Coast Legislative Council and John Ezzidio to the Sierra Leone Legislative Council. The first African unofficial member of the Lagos Legislative Council was Captain James Pinson Labulo Davies, who was appointed in 1872. All three were merchants. See Kimble, *History of Ghana*, 405; Fyfe, *History of Sierra Leone*, 231–32; and Tamuno, *Nigeria and Elective Representation*, 7.

50. Hughes and Gailey, *Historical Dictionary*, 114, suggest that the council was abolished. Technically this appears to be correct, but in fact the council was merely reconstituted. See also [Colonial Office], *Blue Book*, 1866, which lists the members of the council at the time of its downgrading in February 1866. Kimble, *History of Ghana*, 408, notes developments in the Gold Coast.

51. A second European was selected in 1878, but for unknown reasons did not take his seat. See Chapter 3 on this incident and the appointment of Richards.

52. These appointments are discussed in Chapter 4. The Gambia Trading Company (which became the Bathurst Trading Company in 1880) was set up in 1860 by W. H. Goddard (probably H. C. Goddard's father). See Macmillan, *Red Book*, 289.

53. The vacancy was filled by A. L. Bennett. In February 1907, Goddard returned to the council when Bennett resigned, but in June he himself was replaced by the new manager of the Bathurst Trading Company, Ernest Baily. Baily was reappointed in 1912, but ceased to be a member of the council in 1914. See CO 87/177, Denton to Secretary of State, February 12, 1907; and CO 87/189, Galway to Harcourt, January 4, 1912. See also CO 87/186, enclosure to Denton to Harcourt, June 28, 1911.

54. These developments are discussed in Chapter 4. The first African professional to serve on a Legislative Council was Samuel Lewis, a barrister like Forster, who had been appointed to the Sierra Leone Legislative Council in 1883. See Fyfe, *History of Sierra Leone*, 457.

55. CO 87/189, Galway to Harcourt, January 4, 1912; and CO 89/11, Leg. Co. Minutes, December 18, 1912. See also CO 87/186, enclosure to Denton to Secretary of State, June 28, 1911. See Chapter 4 on Bishop.

56. There were Muslim members of the Nigerian Council established in 1914, but apparently not of the Legislative Council itself. See Tamuno, *Nigeria and Elective Representation*, 16. Jeng's appointment is analyzed in Chapter 4.

57. The Chamber of Commerce was founded in 1886; see CO 87/128, Hay to Governor-in-Chief, Sierra Leone, June 8, 1886; and *The Bathurst Observer and West African Gazette* (*BO*), December 20, 1887. The nine members of the Chamber of Commerce (four English and five French firms) may be found in [Colonial Office], *Gambia: Annual Report for 1922* (London: HMSO, 1923), Appendix 1.

58. These appointments are discussed in Chapter 4.

59. Bathurst was the last capital of a British West African colony to gain a municipal council. Freetown City Council was established in 1893 (but dissolved in 1926), Accra Town Council in 1898 and Lagos Town Council in 1917. See Akintola J. G. Wyse, *H.C. Bankole-Bright and Politics in Colonial Sierra Leone, 1919–1958* (Cambridge: Cambridge University Press, 1990), 76–80; Kimble, *History of Ghana*, 422–25; and Tamuno, *Nigeria and Elective Representation*, 19. On the BUDC and Carrol's appointment, see Chapter 4.

60. The BATC's establishment and electoral role is discussed in Chapter 4.

61. These appointments are analyzed in Chapter 5.

62. CO 87/253/5, Ward to Stanley, February 18, 1943.

63. The 1946 constitution is discussed in Chapter 5. In Nigeria, voters had to possess an annual income of £100 (reduced to £50 by the Richards Constitution of 1946); in Sierra Leone, they had to be literate in English or Arabic and either own or occupy a property of a ratable value of £10 p.a.; and in the Gold Coast, there was a property qualification of a ratable value of £80 p.a. See Tamuno, *Nigeria and Elective Representation*, 34–38; Martin Kilson, *Political Change in a West African State: A Study of the Modernization Process in Sierra Leone* (Cambridge: Harvard University Press, 1966), 125; and Kimble, *History of Ghana*, 441.

64. The Creole response to the 1947 constitution (which reached its climax when independence for the Colony was demanded in 1951) is discussed by Cartwright, *Politics in Sierra Leone*, 43–54. See CO 87/260/2, Wright to Creech Jones, September 27, 1947; Creech Jones to Wright, October 17, 1947, on the Gambian position.

65. CO 87/260/2, Wright to Creech Jones, September 27, 1947, discusses the process of selection of the Protectorate members. The 1946 Richards Constitution allowed the House of Chiefs and House of Assembly to nominate candidates; see Tamuno, *Nigeria and Elective Representation*, 94–95. Under the Burns Constitution of 1944, four chiefs were to be elected indirectly by Asante and nine by the Eastern and Western Provincial Councils; see Pearce, *Turning Point*, 80. The Stevenson Constitution permitted the Protectorate Assembly to elect ten members from among its own ranks. See Cartwright, *Politics in Sierra Leone*, 43–44.

66. The election is analyzed in Chapter 5. See also CO 87/260/2, Wright to Creech Jones, September 27, 1947, on the appointment of the other unofficial members. If a Muslim had won the election, Wright would have appointed Edward Lloyd-Evans, a Mulatto businessman, to ensure that both religious communities were represented.

67. The Gambia (Legislative Council) (Amendment) Order-in-Council 1951 was published in *GG*, July 12, 1951. See also CO 87/266/2 on the constitution. The 1951 election is discussed in Chapter 5.

68. The constitutional negotiations between Wyn-Harris and the Colonial Office may be found in CO 554/250 and CO 554/251. See especially CO 554/250, Report of Consultative Committee, May 1953. The 1954 election is analyzed in Chapter 5.

69. Gailey, *History*, 120. The two killed were C. F. Sitwell, the first commissioner of the South Bank, and his designated successor, F. E. Silva, both of whom were killed at Sankandi by Marabout forces in 1900.

70. For example, Jata Silang Jame, a member of the Soninke ruling family driven out by Maba Diakhou in the 1860s, became chief of British Baddibu; a Sonko was confirmed as Mansa Niumi; the Wali family retained power in Wuli; and the Sanyangs remained in control in Kantora. On the reappearance of the Soninkes, see Quinn, *Mandingo Kingdoms*,

184–86; on the situation in Niumi, see also Donald R. Wright, *The World and a Very Small Place in Africa* (Armonk, NY: ME Sharpe, 1997). This is an expansion of his earlier account of Niumi history—*The Early History of Niumi: Settlement and Foundation of a Mandinka State on the Gambia River*. Papers in International Studies Africa Series no. 32. (Athens: Ohio University Center for International Studies, 1977).

71. Quinn, *Mandingo Kingdoms*, 180–81.

72. Gailey, *History*, 114; Gray, *History*, 475–76; and Quinn, *Mandingo Kingdoms*, 180.

73. Gailey, *History*, 126–37, analyzes the Protectorate Ordinances and their consequences.

74. There has been little published research to date on local politics in the Protectorate during the colonial period. The exceptions include Wright, *The World and a Very Small Place* (on Niumi); Alice Bellagamba, "Portrait of a Chief Between Past and Present: Memory at Work in Colonial and Post-colonial Gambia," *Political and Legal Anthropology Review* 25, no. 2: (2002), 21–49 (on Fulladu West); Stephen H. Challis, *A History of Local Government in Kombo North District, Western Division, The Gambia: 1889–1944* (Banjul: Oral History and Administrative Division, Vice-President's Office, 1980); and B. K. Sidibe (Sidibeh), *The Balde Family of Fuladu* (Banjul: Oral History Division, Vice-President's Office, 1984). Among the long-serving seyfolu was Tamba Jammeh (note 36). A shorter, but informed review of the changing role of chieftaincy is provided by M. Baikoro Sillah, "The Demise of Kings," *WA*, June 6, 1983, 1351–53.

75. The emergence of a distinctive Protectorate political voice is examined in Chapter 6; see Gailey, *History*, 134–35, on the annual Chiefs' Conference.

76. Wiseman, "House of Representatives," 86–90.

77. [Gambia Government], *Constitutional Developments, 1959*. On average a constituency in Bathurst and Kombo St. Mary had approximately 4,000 voters and a Protectorate constituency, 20,000 voters (or 12,000 if the eight seats reserved for the chiefs were taken into account). See CO 554/1517, Windley to Lennox-Boyd, May 7, 1959.

78. Wiseman, "House of Representatives," 83–84, discusses the implications of abandoning English in the House.

79. See note 43.

80. See *GG*, February 4, 1965, Supplement A.

81. As noted in Chapter 1, table 1.3, the population was 1,038,145 in 1993. Official, as well as secondary, sources have used both Serekunda and Serrekunda. We have used the latter throughout except where citing a source that uses the former version in the title.

82. Wiseman, "House of Representatives," 83–84.

83. Wiseman, "House of Representatives," 84–85. The first woman nominated to the House was Lucretia St. Clair Joof in December 1968; see *GG*, October 3, 1969. The trade union leader appointed was Araba Bah, a former leader of the Gambia Workers' Union; see Arnold Hughes and David Perfect, "Trade Unionism in The Gambia," *African Affairs* 88, no. 353 (1989), 569.

84. Peter da Costa, "Jawara's New Government," *WA*, May 25–31, 1992, 876–77.

85. See Chapter 9.

86. See Wiseman "From Coup to Elections."

87. See Chapter 10.

Chapter 3

1. Quinn, *Mandingo Kingdoms*, 91, citing Daniel Robertson, the colonial secretary in the Gambian government.

2. Gray, *History*, 322. On Grant and MacCarthy, see Hughes and Gailey, *Historical Dictionary*, 86–87; 115–16. On the latter, see also A. P. Kup, "Sir Charles MacCarthy (1768–1824) Soldier and Administrator," *Bulletin of the John Rylands University Library of Manchester* 60, no. 1: (1977), 52–94.

3. On the lack of success of many of the early Gambia merchants, see the evidence of G. C. Redman to the 1842 Parliamentary Select Committee in [HC], *PPCA* 2, 175. On these merchants, see Gray, *History*, 309; Mahoney, "Government and Opinion," 45; 124–25; The Gambia Committee, *The Proposed Cession of the Gambia* (Westminster: The Gambia Committee, 1876), 25–29; Prickett, *Island Base*, 26; 60; and *The African Times* (*AT*), August 1873, 167.

4. Mahoney, "Government and Opinion," 39–42; and Edward Reynolds, *Trade and Economic Change on the Gold Coast 1807–1874* (Harlow: Longman, 1974), 55. However, according to William Fox, *History of the Wesleyan Missions in Western Africa* (London: Nichols, 1851), 448, the merchants frequently differed on policy issues. On the commercial activities of Forster and Smith in the Gold Coast, see Reynolds, *Trade and Economic Change*, passim.

5. Gray, *History*, 322–23; and Mahoney, "Government and Opinion," 53–54. See also [HC], "Sierra Leone: Report of the Commissioners of Inquiry [Major James Rowan] into the State of the Colony of Sierra Leone Second Part: I: Dependencies in the Gambia" (hence "Rowan Report"), which may be found in *British Parliamentary Papers Colonies Africa 52* (hence *PPCA 52*) (Shannon: Irish University Press, 1968), 211–25.

6. For contrasting views of how effectively this work was done, see [HC], *British Parliamentary Papers Colonies Africa 3* (hence *PPCA 3*) (Shannon: Irish University Press, 1968) 234–41, Forster et al. to Stanley, March 11, 1842; Ingram to Stanley, April 2, 1842. See also Gray, *History*, 321–22.

7. Parties and witnesses could also in theory go to Freetown for the hearing, but in practice no litigation was ever taken there. See Gray, *History*, 323–24; 375–76; Mahoney, "Government and Opinion," 55–56; [HC], "Rowan Report," *PPCA 52*, 223.

8. [HC], "Rowan Report," *PPCA 52*, 223; see also Mahoney, "Government and Opinion," 188–89; and Gray, *History*, 323–24. The secretary of state even ordered the abolition of two advisory Boards of Commerce established by Governor Campbell of Sierra Leone in 1826 and revived by the commandant, Major Findlay, in 1828. On developments in the Gold Coast, see Metcalfe, *Great Britain and Ghana*, 121.

9. These included the decision by the acting commandant, Captain Alexander Fraser, to declare forfeit a large number of plots in the town without any legal process being served, or the occupants being given time to make good their claims. See [HC], *PPCA 3*, 239, Forster et al. to Stanley, March 11, 1842.

10. Gray, *History*, 334–39; and Mahoney, "Government and Opinion," 47–52. Morgan, *Reminiscences*, 87–89, provides an eyewitness account of the annexation of MacCarthy Island. The "Ceded Mile" was a one-mile-deep strip of land from Jinnak creek in the west to Jokadu creek in the east.

11. Gray, *History*, 399–402; and Mahoney, "Government and Opinion," 90–97. See also Fox, *History of the Wesleyan Missions in Western Africa*, 263–64, who maintains that the French traders also covertly engaged in slave trading.

12. Gray, *History*, 339–42; and [HC], *PPCA 3*, 236–40. The Hutton treaty is an enclosure to Brown to Carnarvon, February 8, 1877, [HC], *British Parliamentary Papers Colonies Africa 56* (hence *PPCA 56*) (Shannon: Irish University Press, 1971), 366–67. Similar constraints were imposed on the government of Sierra Leone; for example, Governor Campbell was forced by the secretary of state to annul various territorial annexations carried out by his predecessor, Governor Turner. See Fyfe, *History of Sierra Leone*, 156–59.

13. Gray, *History*, 324; 344; and Mahoney, "Government and Opinion," 56. On Findlay, see [HC], *PPCA 2*, 150–51; Fyfe, *History of Sierra Leone*, 177–90; and Cyril P. Foray,

Historical Dictionary of Sierra Leone. African Historical Dictionaries no. 12. (Metuchen, NJ: Scarecrow Press, 1977), 70–71. On Rendall, see Hughes and Gailey, *Historical Dictionary*, 147–48.

14. Three other examples of Rendall's pro-mercantile policies were his encouragement of the Tendah Company, which was set up in 1831 to exploit the resources of the interior beyond the Barrakunda Falls; the attack on Dungassen in 1835; and the proposal to annex Sine Saloum in 1836. For details, see Mahoney, "Government and Opinion," 98–106; and Gray, *History*, 342–72, passim.

15. Gray, *History*, 374–77; and Mahoney, "Government and Opinion," 190–91. See also Sir Henry Huntley, *Seven Years' Service on the Slave Coast of Western Africa*. 2 vols. (London: Newby, 1850), vol. II, 133–35; and his evidence to the 1841 Madden Commission in [HC], *PPCA 3*, 211–12.

16. [HC], "Madden Report"; and evidence to the Select Committee in *PPCA 2.* For comments on both, see Gray, *History*, 378; Mahoney, "Government and Opinion," 200–202; Metcalfe, *Great Britain and Ghana*, 160–88; Newbury, *Select Documents 1786–1874*, 510–13; Fyfe, *History of Sierra Leone*, 223–24; and Kimble, *History of Ghana*, 194–95.

17. The two men's evidence may be found in [HC], *PPCA 2*, 489–519; 650–51; 699–744. On Forster, see also Michael Stenton, *Who's Who of British Members of Parliament*, 4 vols. (Hassocks, Sussex: Harvester Press, 1976), vol. I (1832–85), 146. On Hughes, see Mahoney, "Notes on Mulattoes," 125.

18. Fox, *History of the Wesleyan Missions in Western Africa*, 426–34, who provides a graphic eyewitness account, states that half of the Europeans in Bathurst, as well as many Mulattos and Africans, died. Prickett, *Island Base*, 54–55, also describes the epidemic (and states that 18 out of 40 Europeans died). However, according to one of Rendall's successors as lieutenant governor, Captain H. V. Huntley, Rendall "thought little beyond eating and drinking, in which occupation he fattened himself up to 20 stone and died"; the letter, dated July 19, 1840, is cited in *WA*, November 12, 1979, 2116.

19. No official could match the twenty years' service in Gambia of such merchants as William Forster, Edward Lloyd, Thomas Chown, and W. H. Goddard, on whom see Mahoney, "Government and Opinion," 38–45; and Gray, *History*, 309.

20. Evidence of Findlay to the 1842 Select Committee [HC], *PPCA 2*, 154–55. Findlay does not indicate who was originally offered the post, but it was probably A. Clogstown who, as noted in [HC], *PPCA 2*, 494, was acting lieutenant governor between September 1837 and September 1838. See also CO 87/19, Clogstown to Secretary of State, September 20, 1838, where Forster's criticisms of his administration are outlined.

21. [HC], *PPCA 3*, 238, Forster et al. to Stanley, March 11, 1842. See also [HC], *PPCA 2*, 466–68 (evidence of F. W. Finden, a Gambia merchant); and Huntley, *Seven Years' Service*, vol. II, 41–42; 135–38. Gray, *History*, 366, offers a more favorable opinion of Mackie.

22. Mahoney, "Government and Opinion," 199–200.

23. CO 87/46, MacDonnell to Grey, November 20, 1849; and [HC], *PPCA 2*, 494. See also Huntley, *Seven Years' Service*, vol. II, 228–29, whose oblique reference indicates that he believed Ingram to have acted correctly. Pine again served as queen's advocate in Gambia in the 1850s and later became governor of the Gold Coast. Kimble, *History of Ghana*, 199–205, describes his governorship.

24. [HC], *PPCA 3*, 238–40, Forster et al. to Stanley, March 11, 1842; Ingram to Stanley, April 2, 1842. Ingram argued that Government House was so dilapidated that repairs had been essential and claimed the Colonial Office approved of his interior policy. See also Archer, *Colony and Protectorate*, 42; Gray, *History*, 367–71; Huntley, *Seven Years' Service*, vol. II, passim; and Hughes and Gailey, *Historical Dictionary*, 92.

25. See Chapter 1, 31.

26. Gray, *History*, 371; Mahoney, "Government and Opinion," 191–202; and Huntley, *Seven Years' Service*, vol. II, 341–43. See also [HC], *PPCA 3*, 234–37, Ingram to Stanley, April 2, 1842.

27. CO 87/28, Ingram to Stanley, October 22, 1842, gives details of some of the petitioners. That clerks and traders were sometimes instructed to sign "mercantile" petitions is suggested by "A Gambian," letter to *AT*, August 1865, 22.

28. Mahoney, "Government and Opinion," 192, 203; see also CO 87/46, MacDonnell to Grey, September 8, 1849. Ironically, Mantell was to become a strong ally of the merchants in the 1860s.

29. For background details of the three men, see Mahoney, "Government and Opinion," 42–46; Hughes and Gailey, *Historical Dictionary*, 45; and Fox, *History of the Wesleyan Missions in Western Africa*, passim. See also [HC], *PPCA 3*, 229; and Reynolds, *Trade and Economic Change*, 55. It should also be noted that Brown supposedly had had an "unorthodox relationship" with Ingram's Mulatta wife; see Mahoney, "Government and Opinion," 68.

30. [HC], "Madden Report," *PPCA 3*, 182. W. H. Goddard and Richard Lloyd were the first two unofficial members; significantly, neither was amongst Ingram's opponents. See Mahoney, "Government and Opinion," 202.

31. The first governor, Commander Henry Seagram, died of fever after only six months in the colony; the second, Lieutenant E. Norcott, also survived for only a few months. See Gray, *History*, 385; and Archer, *Colony and Protectorate*, 44–45.

32. Archer, *Colony and Protectorate*, 46. According to *AT*, March 1864, 90, "native friends" in Bathurst claimed that only Rendall and Fitzgerald had ever done anything to promote their interests.

33. Quinn, *Mandingo Kingdoms*, 84. On MacDonnell (who was a qualified barrister, which pleased the merchants), see Hughes and Gailey, *Historical Dictionary*, 116–17; and for his later career [Oxford University Press (OUP)], *The Dictionary of National Biography* (London: OUP, 1921–22), vol. 12, 502–3.

34. CO 87/46, MacDonnell to Grey, September 18, 1849 and enclosures, including petition of the Black Inhabitants to Grey, August 24, 1849; MacDonnell to Grey, November 8, 1849; Committee of the Black Inhabitants to MacDonnell, September 19, 1849; and CO 87/47, Lome and others to Grey, September 4, 1849. On Prophet and Bocock, see [HC], *PPCA 3*, 241; [HC] *PPCA 56*, 156–57; and *AT*, June 1865, 154. A plaque in St Mary's Cathedral, Banjul, commemorates Doyery (noted by Perfect in May 1992). For a later claim that petitioners were generally ignorant of the contents of petitions, see CO 87/111, Gouldsbury to Rowe, April 20, 1878.

35. Mahoney, "African Leadership," 31. See also CO 87/19, Clogstown to Glenelg, May 1, 1838; and *AT*, December 1865, 58 (for the account of Joseph Reffles); May 1871, 123. Mahoney prefers the surname Reffell for both father and son, but the latter signed himself Reffles in his correspondence to the *African Times*. Moreover, a memorial plaque in Dobson Street Methodist Church in Banjul (noted by Perfect in May 1992) gave his name as Reffles (and his date of death as December 29, 1849 aged fifty-five). Fox was probably the only Wesleyan missionary in Bathurst in 1842. See also Hughes and Gailey, *Historical Dictionary*, 146; and [Colonial Office], *Blue Book*, 1842.

36. On the establishment of the Shipwrights' Society, see Perfect, "Organised Labour," 28. On friendly societies in Freetown, see Fyfe, *History of Sierra Leone*, 170–72.

37. Quinn, *Mandingo Kingdoms*, 84–95; Archer, *Colony and Protectorate*, 47–48; and Gray, *History*, 385–403 (who offers a less sanguine interpretation of the outcome of the blockade). See also CO 87/46, MacDonnell to Grey, September 18, 1849, in which the governor referred to having received two "very flattering" addresses from the merchants. MacDonnell rose to become governor of Hong Kong and to be knighted.

38. Archer, *Colony and Protectorate*, 48–49; and CO 87/46, MacDonnell to Grey, September 18, 1849; Lome and Doyery to Grey, August 24, 1849.

39. On O'Connor, see Quinn, *Mandingo Kingdoms*, 86; and Hughes and Gailey, *Historical Dictionary*, 133–34. Kennedy's appointment in 1852 is noted by Gailey, *History*, 83.

40. Brown had been appointed a justice of the peace in 1845 and a member of the Legislative Council in 1850. See CO 89/1, Leg. Co. Minutes, May 4, 1850; Ex. Co. Minutes, February 21, 1853; and [Colonial Office], *Blue Book*, 1866.

41. Quinn, *Mandingo Kingdoms*, 86–87, who points out the contradictions in the governor's strategy.

42. Quinn, *Mandingo Kingdoms*, 53–70.

43. Quinn, *Mandingo Kingdoms*, 85–91. See also Gray, *History*, 367–68; and Huntley, *Seven Years' Service*, vol. II, passim, on the acquisition of the Kombo. The attack on Sabajy is described in less flattering terms by J. F. Napier Hewett, *European Settlements on the West Coast of Africa*, reprint of 1862 ed. (New York: Negro Universities Press, 1969), 239–42.

44. Quinn, *Mandingo Kingdoms*, 88–93.

45. See [HC], *PPCA 56*, 21–42, on the Convention and related correspondence. The benefits of the treaty are emphasized by Gray, *History*, 409–10; and Gailey, *History*, 73. Its disadvantages for the British merchants are noted by Quinn, *Mandingo Kingdoms*, 95; and Mahoney, "Government and Opinion," 121–24. The first French business house established in Bathurst may have been Maurel Frères, which began operating in the town in 1860. See Macmillan, *Red Book*, 291.

46. CO 87/83, Memorial of Friendly Societies to Cardwell, October 20, 1865, which is also found in *AT*, November 1865, 46. T. S. Ashton, *The Industrial Revolution 1760–1830*. Reprint of 1948 ed. (London: Oxford University Press, 1975), 81, notes that the truck system was commonplace in Great Britain in the early nineteenth century.

47. The Grumetta Act was passed in Sierra Leone in 1825, but was not implemented in Gambia until the 1840s; the initiative for its repeal was taken by the Colonial Office, but was strongly supported by O'Connor. See Mahoney, "Government and Opinion," 207–9, for a discussion of the act and the merchants' resistance to its repeal. For further details, see CO 87/66, O'Connor to Secretary of State, August 3, 1858; and CO 87/67, O'Connor to Lytton, March 1, 1859.

48. Reffles' death was recorded in Dobson Street Methodist Church; see note 35. On Finden, see *AT*, May 1866, 118–19, letter from Joseph Reffles; Mahoney, "African Leadership," 31; Prickett, *Island Base*, 102, who describes him as a wine and spirit merchant; Hughes and Gailey, *Historical Dictionary*, 66; and CO 87/96, Kennedy to Granville, April 30, 1870. For details of his property and assets in the 1870s, see [HC], *PPCA 56*, 156–59; 313; 342. Hewett, who was writing about his visit to Bathurst in c. 1854, stated that the colonel of the militia was "the proprietor of a grog shop"; see *European Settlements*, 283. This was apparently an oblique reference to Harry Finden; in fact, the lieutenant colonel of the Gambian militia was John Finden, the colonial engineer. See [Colonial Office], *Blue Book*, 1854.

49. [HC], *PPCA 56*, 84, Patey to Kennedy, June 22, 1869. See also Quinn, *Mandingo Kingdoms*, 91 (citing the opinion of the colonial secretary, Daniel Robertson); and Mahoney, "Government and Opinion," 220. See also Hughes and Gailey, *Historical Dictionary*, 56–57, on D'Arcy.

50. The merchants were only too aware of their financial clout; for example, in a minute they submitted to the Legislative Council, their representatives pointed out that the colony "has nothing but its commerce to rely on for a revenue." See CO 89/3, Leg. Co. Minutes, February 6, 1863.

51. Hargreaves, *Prelude*, 154; Mahoney, "Government and Opinion," 211–13; and Prickett, *Island Base*, 93, who notes that six Europeans died of yellow fever in the space of

one week. See Chapter 1, 35, on the budgetary position in these years. On Quin, who had entered government service as early as 1839, see Mahoney, "Government and Opinion," 207; Quinn, *Mandingo Kingdoms*, 92; and [Colonial Office], *Blue Book*, 1842; 1866. During a meeting of the Executive Council in 1864, D'Arcy criticized its members for opposing his measures in the Legislative Council; see CO 89/3, Ex. Co. Minutes, May 3, 1864.

52. See Chapter 1, 23.

53. Mahoney, "Government and Opinion," 239–42; see also [HC], *British Parliamentary Papers Colonies Africa 5* (hence *PPCA 5*) (Shannon: Irish University Press, 1968), 345; and Hargreaves, *Prelude*, 154–55. That the 1865 tariff was deliberately designed to fall on Liberated African entrepreneurs and French firms is evident from CO 87/82, D'Arcy to Caldwell, May 17, 1865, cited by Mahoney.

54. Mahoney, "Government and Opinion," 136–37; 245–46. The 1862 petition, which received 375 signatures, may be found as an enclosure to CO 87/74, D'Arcy to Newcastle, September 27, 1862. On the Bankruptcy Bill, see CO 87/82, D'Arcy to Caldwell, May 18, 1865. See also CO 89/3, Leg. Co. Minutes, May 16, 1863; Ex. Co. Minutes, May 3, 1864; and various issues of *AT*, 1872–73.

55. Mahoney, "Government and Opinion," 216–17; see also CO 87/82, D'Arcy to Cardwell, June 21, 1865; CO 87/83, Primet to Cardwell, October 22, 1865 (which contains the Memorial of the Friendly Societies); and *AT*, May 1865, 136–37; October 1865, 65–66; April 1866, 104; 112. D'Arcy used Sherwood as an agent during negotiations with the Marabout party in 1864; Campbell was a signatory to a treaty between Soninkes and Marabouts in 1863. See [HC], *PPCA 5*, 415; 431.

56. Mahoney, "Government and Opinion," 213–15; and *AT*, May 1866, 118–19. See also *BO*, May 1, 1883, on Johnson. Mahoney also notes that the appointments of Johnson and Seymour Gay (a Gorée Wolof), were subsequently cancelled by D'Arcy after pressure from the merchants. On Gay's appointment, see also CO 87/74, D'Arcy to Newcastle, November 24, 1862.

57. CO 87/80, enclosure to D'Arcy to Secretary of State, August 25, 1864. The petitioners provided details of a number of specific benefits both to the colony, in general, and to the Liberated African community, in particular, that had resulted from D'Arcy's administration. In forwarding the petition to the Colonial Office, the governor claimed that it had been signed by all the native inhabitants who could write.

58. Mahoney, "Government and Opinion," 217–18; see also CO 89/3, Ex. Co. Minutes, December 18, 1865; Prickett, *Island Base*, 102; and *AT*, January 1866, 69–70; March 1866, 94–99; October 1869, 45; February 1870, 88–90. There was an unpleasant postscript to the whole incident when Finden was insulted and then physically attacked by two European army medical officers, Dr. Elliott and Dr. Oakes, in his shop in November 1866. The former was later arrested, tried, and fined a paltry sum, and the latter escaped by boarding a ship in the harbor. Finden believed that Governor D'Arcy deliberately intervened to prevent a more severe sentence being given against Dr. Elliott by passing an ordinance to allow the case to be tried by one magistrate, rather than by two. For details of the case, see *AT*, January 1867, 78–79; February 1867, 89; November 1867, 59–63. The editor of the *African Times*, Ferdinand Fitzgerald, believed that Finden was attacked and insulted solely because he was the agent in Bathurst for his newspaper.

59. Hargreaves, *Prelude*, 62–69.

60. See [HC], "Ord Report," *PPCA 5*, 343–66; the same volume also contains the Select Committee report. For further comment, see Hargreaves, *Prelude*, 64–91; Gray, *History*, 432–35; Kimble, *History of Ghana*, 205–15; Fyfe, *History of Sierra Leone*, 336–39; and Metcalfe, *Great Britain and Ghana*, 305–15. The Select Committee did recommend the abandonment of MacCarthy Island, but, although the garrison on the island was withdrawn, the settlement remained part of the colony.

61. *AT*, September 1865, 22; and Mahoney, "Government and Opinion," 219–20.

62. The only "Gambian" witness was Daniel Robertson, the colonial secretary, whose evidence is in [HC], *PPCA 5*, 267–74. Robertson did argue that centralization would not be in the interests of Gambia, but without great conviction. It is likely that the British merchants (or most of them) were in Bathurst at the time of the Select Committee's examination of the issue. This would explain why none gave evidence, although it is perhaps surprising that a retired merchant (such as Thomas Chown) did not do so.

63. According to Mahoney, "Government and Opinion," 222, Brown was retained on the recommendation of D'Arcy. On Patey, see Hughes and Gailey, *Historical Dictionary*, 138–39. The governor of the Gold Coast, Richard Pine, was also replaced; see Metcalfe, *Great Britain and Ghana*, 314–15.

64. [HC], *PPCA 56*, 84, Patey to Kennedy, June 22, 1869. It should be recognized that Patey had some success; the colony's expenditure fell in 1868 to its lowest level since 1862, but then rose to a record high in 1869.

65. *AT*, July 1867, 1–2; February 1870, 89; and Mahoney, "Government and Opinion," 244.

66. [HC], *PPCA 56*, 81–87, Patey to Kennedy, June 22, 1869; Goddard et al. to Granville, June 8, 1869. See also the report of a meeting between the Manchester Chamber of Commerce and Earl of Kimberley, *AT*, May 1873, 133–34, which notes the ending of the merchants' role as magistrates in 1869.

67. [HC], *PPCA 56*, 43–118, provides a full description of the epidemic. The account by Gray, *History*, 444–46, is misleading, because the political dimension to the issue is ignored. See also *AT*, June–October 1869; February 1870; and Prickett, *Island Base*, 105–6.

68. [HC], *PPCA 56*, Goddard et al. to Granville, June 8, 1869, 85–87 (which lists Finden as a petitioner). The alleged ill treatment of prisoners, which included the use of the shot drill and treadmill, is described in *AT*, May 1869, 125–26; June 1869, 145–52; July 1869, 19.

69. On the younger Reffles, see Mahoney, "African Leadership," 32–34; and Hughes and Gailey, *Historical Dictionary*, 145–46. See also CO 87/99, Kennedy to Kimberley, June 7, 1871 and its enclosure, Anton to Kennedy, May 5, 1871; and various issues of *AT* between 1865 and 1870. Mahoney suggests that Reffles was allowed to resign from his government post; however, in a letter to *AT*, May 1866, 120, Reffles stated that he had in fact been dismissed from the Ordnance Department "for no cause." Details of two cases in which Reffles acted as the attorney for two defendants in cases brought by Thomas Brown and W. H. Goddard can be found in *AT*, October 1867, 42.

70. *AT*, October 1869, 44; [HC], *PPCA 56*, 98, Granville to Patey, June 22, 1869; CO 87/99, Fowler to Anton, May 13, 1871; and CO 89/4, Leg. Co. Minutes, February 10, 1871.

71. *AT*, November 1869, 55, notes that Bravo's appointment caused alarm because of his conduct while police magistrate in Freetown. See issues of *AT*, September 1869–May 1870.

72. Hargreaves, *Prelude*, 125–95, passim. See also Mahoney, "Government and Opinion," 264–98; Gray, *History*, 431–43; and Gailey, *History*, 81–95. These accounts are based primarily on [HC], *PPCA 56*, 119–348. Cession was also covered extensively in *AT* in 1870–71 and again in 1875–76.

73. Hargreaves, *Prelude*, 129–53. Mahoney, "Government and Opinion," 269–71, points out that both Colonel Ord and the 1865 Select Committee concluded that capital would not be attracted to a disturbed neighborhood. Both authors note that the Colonial Office considered it preferable to hand over Gambia to France without seeking any territory in exchange, but it was thought that this would not be acceptable to public opinion.

74. Hargreaves, *Prelude*, 153.

75. Hargreaves, *Prelude*, 164–65. As Hargreaves points out (138), colonies had in the past been ceded without any prior consultation with Parliament. The decision in 1870 to secure

Parliamentary assent was therefore "a political, rather than a constitutional, judgment" (155).

76. [HC], *PPCA 56*, 129, Quin to Granville, January 12, 1870. To publicize the issue, this letter was reprinted by *AT*, February 1870. 85–86.

77. See [HC], *PPCA 56*, 179–91; and Manchester Chamber of Commerce (MCC) "Proceedings," July 1, 1870; July 20, 1870. Central Library, Manchester, England.

78. Gailey, *History*, 87, summarizes the merchants' calculations (based on their letters in [HC], *PPCA 56*, 171–201). But see also [HC], *PPCA 56*, 132–36, memorandum by Fowler (now acting collector of customs), March 12, 1870, for a differing view of the financial position of the firms.

79. Hargreaves, *Prelude*, 158–59; and Mahoney, "Government and Opinion," 274. The address to Brown from Finden and other Liberated Africans (published in *The Bathurst Times* of May 1871) may be found as an enclosure to CO 87/99, Kennedy to Kimberley, June 9, 1871.

80. For details of the petitions and the Liberated African petitioners, see [HC], *PPCA 56*, 149–63; and *AT*, June 1870, 134–35; July 1870, 2; January 1871, 74. Bravo's comment may be found in [HC], *PPCA 56*, 157–58, Bravo to Granville, May 13, 1870.

81. See [HC], *PPCA 56*, 158–59, Kennedy to Granville, June 2, 1870; see also CO 87/99, Kennedy to Kimberley, June 7, 1871; *AT*, November 1869, 50; CO 87/133, Carter to Knutsford, September 1888; and Fyfe, *History of Sierra Leone*, 330–74, passim. By the late 1880s, Walcott had become such a respectable figure that Administrator Carter considered him a suitable candidate for the Executive Council; see Chapter 4, note 7.

82. The leaders are listed in [HC], *PPCA 56*, 156, Finden to Kennedy, May 6, 1870. For more details of their background and property, see also *PPCA 56*, 156–63; 313–15; 333–48. See also *BO*, January 15, 1884; February 5, 1884 and *AT*, February 1876, 120, on Barber; Mahoney, "Government and Opinion," 129, on King; Prickett, *Island Base*, 77, on Goddard; note 34 on Prophet and Bocock; and note 48 on Finden. On Reffles' part in the opposition to cession, see also Mahoney, "African Leadership," 34–35. See also CO 87/80, King to D'Arcy, August 23, 1864.

83. The fullest account of Richards' early life is from his obituary in the *Sierra Leone Weekly News* (*SLWN*), November 16, 1917. Further details are in CO 87/120, Gouldsbury to Havelock, February 12, 1883; see also *AT*, October 1864, 49; May 1876, 122. Further information on him was provided by Sam Goddard (Perfect interview, Banjul, April 1992). On Forster, see Chapter 4.

84. Joof was listed as one of the two leaders of the Carpenters' Society in the Memorial of the Friendly Societies of 1865; see CO 87/83, Primet to Cardwell, October 22, 1865.

85. The dispute between "Sierra Leoneans" and "Gambians" is analyzed in Mahoney, "African Leadership," 34; and Mahoney, "Government and Opinion," 176–79. See also CO 87/99, Kennedy to Kimberley, June 7, 1871 and enclosures; and *AT*, January 1873, 78.

86. [HC], *PPCA 56*, 156–57. Mahoney, "Government and Opinion," 277–79, also emphasizes the emotional attachment of Liberated Africans to British rule, which is evident in the April petition.

87. Hargreaves, *Prelude*, 174–95 (the quote is on 178).

88. Hargreaves, *Prelude*, 175–77; and Mahoney, "Government and Opinion," 296.

89. See [HC], *PPCA 56*, 296–307; CO 87/148, Brown et al. to Carnarvon, February 29, 1876; J. F. Hutton, *The Proposed Cession of the British Colony of the Gambia to France* (Manchester: Privately Published, 1876) (this is reproduced in CO 87/109, Cooper to Under-Secretary of State for the Colonies, March 21, 1876); The Gambia Committee, *Cession*; and "MCC Proceedings," September 29, 1875; October 20, 1875. See also Hargreaves, *Prelude*, 184–93. The first reaction of Lintott and Spink was in fact to demand compensation. On Kortright,

see Hughes and Gailey, *Historical Dictionary*, 111–12. On Topp (who was a Mulatto), see CO 87/148, Llewelyn to Ripon, May 29, 1894.

90. As Hargreaves, *Prelude*, 187, points out, the Colonial Office was convinced that the opposition of the merchants was designed only to secure compensation. One merchant (J. F. Hutton) was later an advocate of exchange, which lends some credence to this theory. See Hargreaves, *Prelude*, 307–8; and Hargreaves, *West Africa Partitioned*, 236–42.

91. Richards' financial position, as assessed by Administrator Cooper, is contained in an enclosure to Rowe to Carnarvon, February 17, 1876 (see [HC], *PPCA, 56*, 342). Cooper noted that Richards resided at his mother's property and owned only one open boat of about five tons. However, in a letter to *AT* dated February 1876, "Opiner du Bonnet" claimed that Richards had property and land and had only moved to his mother's house for reasons of convenience and the healthiness of the locality; moreover, a ship, which would cost no less than £700, was being built for him. See *AT*, May 1876, 122.

92. On the petitions and the petitioners, see [HC], *PPCA 56*, 311–48, passim; and CO 87/109, Brown et al. to Carnarvon, February 29, 1876. The GNAssocn leaders are listed in *The Hour*, November 5, 1875. See also Mahoney, "Government and Opinion," 333, on Dodgin; and Prickett, *Island Base*, 137, on Shyngle.

93. Mahoney, "African Leadership," 35–37, while noting Reffles' absence from the documentary evidence after 1876, implies that he was a political leader in 1875–76. On his position in 1875, see [WMMS], "Gambia Correspondence, 1877–84," WMMS fiche box no. 4, box 296, no. 911, Adcock to Wesleyan Methodist Missionary Society, December 7, 1877. The dispute between Reffles and Adcock is summarized in Prickett, *Island Base*, 125–26, who notes that Reffles' old enemy, Thomas Brown, gave his services to Adcock for free. For a fuller discussion, see *AT*, February 1878, 14–20; April 1878, 39; June 1878, 69–70. See also the correspondence between the Bathurst missionaries and the London headquarters in 1877–78 in WMMS fiche box no. 4, box 296. Prickett, passim, also provides more background information on Adcock.

94. A point noted by Gray, *History*, 441.

95. Hargreaves, *Prelude*, 160–61; 183–84, discusses the response of the Wesleyan missionaries in 1870 and 1875–76. See also [WMMS], "Gambia Correspondence, 1843–76," WMMS fiche box no. 4, box 296, no. 903, Babcock et al. to General Secretary, Wesleyan Methodist Missionary Society, January 29, 1876. Curiously, Prickett, *Island Base*, 120–21, while discussing cession, does not mention the opposition to it of the European missionaries.

96. [HC], *PPCA 56*, 311, Richards et al. to Carnarvon, October 7, 1875. See also Gray, *History*, 440–41.

97. [HC], *PPCA 56*, 330–33, Richards et al. to Carnarvon, December 31, 1875.

98. Hargreaves, *Prelude*, 234–37; 307–14; and Hargreaves, *West Africa Partitioned*, 223–46.

99. For details, see Wyse, "Gambia in Anglo-French Relations."

100. Mahoney, "Government and Opinion," 274.

101. See CO 87/99, Brown to Kimberley, March 31, 1871; and CO 87/109, Brown to Cooper, May 2, 1876 (enclosure) for the views of the merchants. *AT*, January 1871, 74–75, outlines the views of the Liberated Africans. On Kennedy's dismissive attitude to the petitioners, see Hargreaves, *Prelude*, 161–62; and Mahoney, "Government and Opinion," 277–78. His attempt to revive exchange in 1871 is noted by Gailey, *History*, 89–90.

102. Hargreaves, *Prelude*, 164. For the reaction of the European merchants, see also *AT*, February 1871, 86–87; May 1871, 122–23; and CO 87/99, Kennedy to Kimberley, February 9, 1871; Kennedy to Kimberley, March 23, 1871; Kennedy to Kimberley, May 6, 1871.

103. Between the departure of Patey in 1869 and the arrival of Gouldsbury in March 1877, there were three substantive and six acting administrators. Three of these, Anton,

W. H. Simpson and H. T. M. Cooper, died in office; T. F. Callaghan resigned his post because of ill health; see *AT*, November 1872, 54; May 1873, 133–34; March 1877, 26.

104. CO 87/99, Brown to Anton, January 31, 1871; [HC], *PPCA 56*, 379–80, McArthur et al. to Carnarvon, April 16, 1877; and CO 89/4, Leg. Co. Minutes, June 20, 1873; June 24, 1873. These complaints echoed the criticisms of Lieutenant Governor Huntley in the early 1840s.

105. Mahoney, "Government and Opinion," 252–57; 286–88; and *AT*, September 1869, 26–27; October 1870, 45–46; January 1871, 74–75. The expense of the local establishment rose from £9,340 in 1869 to £12,680 in 1877; see [HC], *PPCA 56*, 380–81, McArthur to Carnarvon, April 28, 1877. The most detailed description of the consular system in Eastern Nigeria is by K. Onwuka Dike, *Trade and Politics in the Niger Delta 1830–1885*. 2nd ed. (Oxford: Clarendon, 1966), especially 128–52.

106. Hargreaves, *Prelude*, 153; 159. The business interests of Goddard and Quin were taken on by their Mulatto sons, William Goddard and T. F. J. Quin. On the latter, see Mahoney, "Government and Opinion," 291; and *AT*, July 1883, 73–74.

107. For examples of Brown being outvoted by the official members, see CO 89/4, Leg. Co. Minutes, February 10, 1871; August 30, 1871; April 21, 1873; June 20, 1873; June 24, 1873. See also CO 87/104, Cooper to Governor-in-Chief, March 24, 1873; Brown to Kimberley, March 18, 1873. In his petition to the secretary of state, Brown complained in painstaking detail about unnecessary increases to government expenditure; in refuting these, Cooper noted that Brown was absent from the colony between July 1872 and February 1873 and also commented that Brown tended to criticize the expenditure when he was not in receipt of government contracts.

108. The Anna Evans case is covered in detail in CO 87/104; see especially Chalmers to Harley, June 21, 1873. It is briefly referred to in Mahoney, "Government and Opinion," 296. Brown's resignation from the council and his brief reinstatement are noted in CO 89/4, Leg. Co. Minutes, May 30, 1874; January 27, 1879. See also CO 87/109, Cooper to Herbert, March 21, 1876, comment by an official in the Colonial Office on Hutton, *Proposed Cession*, 3. At the same time as seeking to refute the allegations against him, Fowler also accused the chief magistrate (and his fellow councilor), T. W. Jackson, of raping another woman, a charge that the latter strenuously denied; for details, see CO 87/107. [Colonial Office], *Blue Book*, 1874, notes Fowler's promotion, but without of course giving any of the reasons that lay behind the decision. A letter from Speer to *AT*, March 1882, 28–29, notes Brown's death the previous year.

109. Helm was appointed because no Englishman of sufficient standing could be found; see [HC], *PPCA 56*, 384–85, Colonial Office to Brown, March 29, 1876. See also CO 89/4, Leg. Co. Minutes, December 17, 1874, when Helm unsuccessfully opposed the extension of navigation rights on the river to all foreign ships. On Helm, see also CO 879/13, Gouldsbury to Rowe, July 8, 1878; and CO 87/111, Gouldsbury to Rowe, April 20, 1878.

110. Rowe was acting governor of Sierra Leone virtually from the moment he was appointed administrator of Gambia in 1875. See Fyfe, *History of Sierra Leone*, 402–10. On Gouldsbury, see Hughes and Gailey, *Historical Dictionary*, 85–86.

111. See Newbury, *Select Documents 1875–1914*, Table VII.

112. See CO 87/111, Gouldsbury to Rowe, March 9, 1878; April 20, 1878; and CO 89/4, Leg. Co. Minutes, January 23–March 7, 1878. Helm forfeited his seat because he was absent for many months during 1875 and it was thought unlikely that he would return; see CO 89/4, Leg. Co. Minutes, August 14, 1875; November 6, 1875; April 1, 1876.

113. *AT*, March 1883, 26, which contains the Memorial of the Bathurst (Gambia) Native Association to Rowe, 1879; see also CO 87/111, petition of Speer et al. to Hicks Beach, April 1878; Rowe to Hicks Beach, May 12, 1878 and enclosures; Gouldsbury to Hicks Beach, June 21, 1878.

114. This ordinance (and an earlier attempt to amend one of 1873, which allowed debtors to be imprisoned for fraud that was vetoed by the secretary of state) is discussed in CO 87/117, Havelock to Kimberley, October 13, 1881; and CO 87/118, Gouldsbury to Havelock, March 10, 1882; Havelock to Kimberley, June 9, 1882. See also CO 89/5, Leg. Co. Minutes for 1882 and various issues of *AT*, 1881–83.

115. The first Gambian newspaper, *The Bathurst Times*, was established in May 1871 (the first edition survives in CO 87/99) by Thomas Brown; however, it is doubtful whether this paper ran to more than a few issues. On this and the *Bathurst Observer*, see Nana Grey-Johnson, "The Story of the Newspaper in The Gambia," in *African Media Cultures: Transdisciplinary Perspectives,* ed. Rose Marie Beck and Frank Wittmann (Köln: Rüdiger Köpper Verlag, 2004), 20–21. Grey-Johnson does not, however, refer to the political divisions within the Liberated African community. On the ordinances and the response of merchants and traders, see various issues of *AT*, September 1881–April 1883; *BO*, March 6, 1883; and Mahoney, "Government and Opinion," 138.

116. The four were Richards, Harry Finden, J. H. Finden (a shopkeeper) and J. D. Jones. According to Gouldsbury, the inspiration for the petition was Frederick Speer, a European involved in trade as a dealer. See CO 87/111, Gouldsbury to Rowe, April 20, 1878. Speer was a regular correspondent to *AT* before his death in Bathurst in July 1882 and frequently criticized Bauer. On Speer, see also Hargreaves, *Prelude*, 232–33; and *AT*, December 1881, 134–37.

117. On Jones, see [HC], *PPCA 56*, 163; 313; 333; 343; and CO 87/118, petition of merchants, February 21, 1882, enclosure to Gouldsbury to Havelock, March 10, 1882 (which discusses Jones' trial for fraud in 1879 in detail). See also *AT*, March 1882, 26–28; April 1882, 38–39; May 1883, 50; and *BO*, March 6, 1883, which criticized the fact that Jones was the first name on petitions.

118. See CO 87/111, Gouldsbury to Rowe, April 20, 1878. See also Hargreaves, *Prelude*, 155 (note 1) on Cole.

119. Hutton, *Proposed Cession*, 3; and "MCC Proceedings," May 28, 1873. See also [HC], *PPCA 56*, 383–85, Colonial Office to Brown, March 29, 1876; Herbert to McArthur, May 8, 1877; and *AT*, May 1873, 126; 133–34. That the appointment of another European merchant to the Legislative Council would not have met with universal approval from the Liberated African community is demonstrated by a letter from "A Native of the Soil" to *AT*; see *AT*, August 1873, 166–67.

120. CO 879/13, McArthur to Hicks Beach, May 9, 1878; Gouldsbury to Rowe, July 8, 1878; Hicks Beach to Rowe, September 23, 1878. On McArthur, see also Hargreaves, *Prelude*, 188; and Stenton, *Members of Parliament*, vol. I, 248. On Bowman's naturalization, see CO 89/4, Leg. Co. Minutes, August 28, 1872; October 21, 1873; November 19, 1873.

121. CO 87/119, Havelock to Kimberley, November 27, 1882; Gouldsbury to Havelock, September 20, 1882; Gouldsbury to Havelock, November 21, 1882; and CO 87/133, Carter to Knutsford, September 10, 1888. For examples of Topp's criticisms of the government, see CO 89/4, Leg. Co. Minutes, June 7, 1877; January–March 1878; June 13, 1878; and CO 89/5, Leg. Co. Minutes, July 15, 1881; January 13, 1882; March 8, 1882. Gouldsbury's expedition is described in Gray, *History*, 458–59; and Barry, *Senegambia*, 274–75.

122. CO 87/119, Gouldsbury to Havelock, November 21, 1882; Kimberley to Havelock, December 26, 1882; and CO 87/120, Gouldsbury to Havelock, February 12, 1883. Richards' appointment was delayed until the secretary of state received confirmation that he was a British subject. A letter in *AT*, December 1884, 169, claimed that Richards had supported the merchants' petition, which called for tighter restrictions on fraudulent traders, but in fact it was signed by only two African merchants, S. J. Forster and G. N. Shyngle; see CO 87/118, enclosure to Gouldsbury to Havelock, March 10, 1882. In his dispatch of November

1882, Gouldsbury stated that Richards had recently sided with "native trading classes" against the merchants in their "conflicting interests and views," but did not go into further detail.

123. *AT*, May 1883, 50, citing a petition from Jones et al. to Gouldsbury, March 2, 1883, presents the GNAssocn standpoint. *BO*, March 20, 1883; April 3, 1883, outlines Walcott's perspective.

124. CO 87/133, Carter to Knutsford September 10, 1888; and CO 89/5, Leg. Co. Minutes, March 27, 1883; October 3, 1883; May 7, 1886.

125. CO 89/5, Leg. Co. Minutes, August 9, 1883; August 14, 1883; October 4, 1883; January 9, 1884; February 24, 1885; December 14, 1886. On Moloney, see Hughes and Gailey, *Historical Dictionary*, 123.

Chapter 4

1. For other studies of "clientelist" politics in this period, see Kimble, *History of Ghana*; Cole, *Elites in Lagos*; and Johnson, *Black Politics*.

2. Forster's origins were outlined by John R. Forster (his grandson) (Hughes interview, Bathurst, February 1972). See also CO 87/99, Anton to Kennedy, May 5, 1871, for his career in government service; and [HC], *PPCA 56*, 313; 342, which provides details of his birthplace and property. Although Forster's date of birth is not known, his daughter was born in 1863/4; see *AT*, August 1885, 118.

3. Mahoney, "Government and Opinion," 394, citing CO 87/128, Hay to Granville, August 5, 1886. On his earlier appointments, see *AT*, October 1884, 144; December 1884, 169; and *BO*, April 32, 1885. On Hay, see Hughes and Gailey, *Historical Dictionary*, 89–90.

4. Hargreaves, *West Africa Partitioned*, 226–30. For further details on the mail service controversy, see [HC], *PPCA 56*, 453–568. As early as 1879, the leading Gambian merchants and traders had petitioned the governor in chief, Samuel Rowe, either to take more direct control of the settlement or to encourage the restoration of its independence from Sierra Leone; see CO 87/113, Brown et al. to Rowe March 21, 1879, which forms an enclosure to Rowe to Hicks Beach, April 7, 1879. Although the bulk of the signatories of the petitions were Europeans, they did include both J. D. Richards and S. J. Forster. On the agitation in Lagos, see Cole, *Elites in Lagos*, 53–56; and Tamuno, *Nigeria and Elective Representation*, 10–11.

5. See [HC], *PPCA 56*, 522–51, passim; and CO 87/133, Carter to Knutsford, September 10, 1888. On Hutton, see also "The late Mr J. F. Hutton," *Manchester Faces and Places* 1, no. 7 (1890), 107–8; and Stenton and Lees, *Who's Who of British Members of Parliament*, 186. Hutton's impact on British policy on Africa is discussed in Hargreaves, *Prelude*, 184–93; Hargreaves, *West Africa Partitioned*, 227–40; and Ronald Robinson and John Gallagher (with Alice Denny), *Africa and the Victorians* (New York: St Martin's Press, 1967), 193–96 (on his East Africa interests).

6. CO 87/133, Carter to Knutsford, September 10, 1888; Hargreaves, *West Africa Partitioned*, 226–27; and [HC], *PPCA 56*, 507–9, Richards to Radcliffe, May 28, 1886; Richards to Radcliffe, June 15, 1886. When Carter served as postmaster in the colony in 1885, Jones accused him of being affected by "personal motives" in the discharge of his public duty. The incident was a trivial one; Carter was prepared to bend the strict rules for the payment of money orders for some people, but not for Jones. See *AT*, May 1885, 75, letters from Jones and Syrett. See also CO 87/129, Carter to Hay, August 25, 1886, when Carter rejected a petition from Richards, Jones and others who complained about the appointment of Thomas Spilsbury as colonial surgeon. On Carter, see Hughes and Gailey, *Historical*

Dictionary, 49. On Spilsbury, who was from Sierra Leone, see Fyfe, *History of Sierra Leone*, 348; and Adell Patton, *Physicians, Colonial Racism, and Diaspora in West Africa* (Gainesville: University Press of Florida, 1996), 87.

7. Both Forster and Topp argued that no subsidy should be paid for the mail service; see CO 89/6, Leg. Co. Minutes, February 1, 1887. It should be borne in mind that neither had close commercial ties with Freetown. See also *GG*, December 31, 1889; and CO 87/137, Carter to Knutsford, February 15, 1890. Carter had previously argued that either H. H. Lee or W. C. Walcott (the latter, one of the leading opponents of cession in the 1870s), could usefully be appointed to the Executive Council as an "unofficial member." Lee was now already a member of the council, but it is not known why Topp was preferred to Walcott. See CO 87/133, Carter to Knutsford, September 10, 1888.

8. Mahoney, "Government and Opinion," 362; 407; and CO 89/6, Leg. Co. Minutes, January 3, 1889. Goddard is commemorated by a plaque in St. Mary's Anglican Cathedral, Banjul. The Mulattos in Gambia had no independent political role, unlike their equivalents (the "métis") in Senegal, on whom see Johnson, *Black Politics*, especially 106–22.

9. CO 89/7, Ex. Co. Minutes, February 7, 1894; December 21, 1894; November 19, 1895. On Llewelyn, see Hughes and Gailey, *Historical Dictionary*, 115.

10. Letter from "Nettle," in *AT*, October 1884, 144. But another letter from "Truth" in the December 1884 issue (165) argued that there was no more suitable candidate in Bathurst than Forster.

11. J. D. Hargreaves, *A Life of Sir Samuel Lewis* (London: Oxford University Press, 1958), 33.

12. CO 89/8, Leg. Co. Minutes, April 6, 1894.

13. CO 89/8, Leg. Co. Minutes, March 27, 1894; May 12, 1896; June 30, 1898. See also CO 87/156, Griffith to Secretary of State, July 1, 1898; Forster to Griffith, June 14, 1898.

14. See Grey-Johnson, "The Newpaper in The Gambia," 21–22, who notes that the *Intelligencer* had been first published in July 1893 with the capital for its production being put up by four Gambian merchants: Forster, Sam Jones (Samuel Horton Jones), H. R. Carrol, and A. W. Carrol. The *Intelligencer* ceased publication in June 1896; see David P. Gamble and Louise Sperling, *A General Bibliography of The Gambia (up to 31 December 1977)* (Boston: G. K. Hall, 1977), 13. Unfortunately, we have not been able to read any copies of this newspaper, so have not been able to explore this issue more fully.

15. One reason for this is that no newspapers survive from this period. The *Bathurst Observer* ceased publication about 1888 and the *Intelligencer* folded in 1896; see Grey-Johnson, "The Newspaper in The Gambia," 23–24.

16. CO 87/149, Ripon circular despatch, March 28, 1895. On Lagos, see Tamuno, *Nigeria and Elective Representation*, 11–12. Fyfe, *History of Sierra Leone*, 538, reports that Samuel Lewis, the senior unofficial member of the Sierra Leone Legislative Council, objected to the proposal on the grounds that it would favor the subservient.

17. Newbury, *Select Documents 1875–1914*, 280–81, citing Cardew to Ripon, May 23, 1892.

18. The "election" is described in detail in CO 87/150, Llewelyn to Chamberlain, August 19, 1895. The circular, which was sent out on August 9, with a deadline of sunset on August 10, forms an enclosure to this despatch. See also CO 89/7, Ex. Co. Minutes, May 7, 1895; November 14, 1895; and CO 87/161, Griffith to Secretary of State, December 6, 1900. The account in Mahoney, "Government and Opinion," 396, is slightly misleading. On Thomas, see Macmillan, *Red Book*, 293. Richards did not vote on the grounds that insufficient time had been allowed for him to consider the matter fully; had he done so, and voted for himself, he would have won. His letter to Llewelyn of August 10 forms another enclosure to the administrator's despatch.

19. CO 87/150, Llewelyn to Chamberlain, August 19, 1895. See also Mahoney, "Government and Opinion," 397–98; and CO 87/141, Llewelyn to Secretary of State, April 13, 1892. Richards wished the board to have control over all money raised by the rates and for it to gain an elected chairman (who would presumably be himself). Probably because he was dissatisfied by its limited powers, Richards declined an invitation from Llewelyn in 1893 to remain on the Board of Health; see CO 89/7, Ex. Co. Minutes, January 3, 1893.

20. Llewelyn informed the members of the Executive Council that Goddard had headed the poll and that Richards, Forster, and Thomas were the only others to have received "any number of votes"; he was careful not to point out that Richards received more votes than Forster (or the same number as Goddard). See CO 89/7, Ex. Co. Minutes, November 14, 1895. See also CO 87/150, Llewelyn to Chamberlain, August 19, 1895; Secretary of State to Llewelyn, September 18, 1895. Llewelyn preferred Forster to Thomas because the latter had little influence over the local population.

21. On Topp's enforced retirement, see CO 87/146, Llewelyn to Ripon, May 29, 1894; and CO 87/150, Llewelyn to Chamberlain, September 26, 1895. See also CO 89/7, Ex. Co. Minutes, November 14, 1895; April 13, 1896; and CO 87/150, Llewelyn to Hemmurg, September 18, 1895. Although several European officials attended Executive Council meetings in the period up to World War I, we could find no record of Forster (before his death in 1906) or Goddard having done so. See CO 89/7; and CO 89/10.

22. Mahoney, "Government and Opinion," 396; and CO 87/161, Griffith to Chamberlain, December 6, 1900. On Gibson, who had been transferred when civil service posts were opened up to competitive examination by Governor Kennedy in 1868, see Archer, *Colony and Protectorate*, 313; and CO 87/99, Kennedy to Kimberley, June 7, 1871.

23. CO 87/161, Griffith to Chamberlain, December 6, 1900. On the situation in the Gold Coast and Griffith's background, see Kimble, *History of Ghana*, 97; 428–29; and [Adam and Charles Black], *Who Was Who*, 5th ed. (London: Adam and Charles Black, 1967), vol. I (1897–1915), 297–98. The fullest analysis of the Easmon case is in Patton, *Physicians*, 93–122. There is fragmentary evidence from the *Sierra Leone Weekly News* of Richards' family connections in Freetown; for example, in 1889, his daughter, Annie, married Alpheus Richards (who was presumably a relative) in St. George's Cathedral in Freetown. See *SLWN*, June 8, 1889.

24. For Forster and Richards' response to the 1871 petition, see CO 87/99, Kennedy to Kimberley, June 7, 1871, enclosures by Anton and Nicol.

25. CO 87/176, Griffith to Secretary of State, October 24, 1906. The minutes of the Legislative Council reveal that Forster often missed meetings because of ill health in 1905–06. On Jones, see Macmillan, *Red Book*, 292; and CO 89/9, Leg. Co. Minutes, June 23, 1906. On Richards' later life and political career, see *SLWN*, November 16, 1917; and CO 87/194, petition by Richards et al., which forms an enclosure to Galway to Secretary of State, July 14, 1913. Unlike Griffith, Denton did not serve in the Gold Coast. As noted by Hughes and Gailey, *Historical Dictionary*, 58, his previous post was acting governor of Lagos.

26. Forster's provisional appointment is noted in CO 89/9, Leg. Co. Minutes, November 19, 1906. Even such stalwarts as Nana Ofori Atta I (Gold Coast), H. C. Bankole-Bright and C. E. Wright (both Sierra Leone) could not match Forster's length of service.

27. On Forster's early career, see Macmillan, *Red Book*, 294; and his obituary notice in *The Gambia Echo* (hence *GE*), July 15, 1940. See also CO 87/163, Denton to Secretary of State, June 17, 1901. On Shyngle (who practiced at the Lagos Bar from 1892), see Tamuno, *Nigeria and Elective Representation*, 80. Wyse, *Krio of Sierra Leone*, 34, states that Krio parents who could afford to do so sent their children to England for education; Hargreaves, *Samuel Lewis*, 11, points out that West African lawyers usually practiced both as solicitors and barristers.

28. For example, CO 89/11, Leg. Co. Minutes, November 9, 1911, when he objected to an increase in salary for the new governor.

29. CO 87/189, Galway to Secretary of State, January 4, 1912. It should be pointed out that this was often used as an excuse when African unofficials were reappointed. See for example, John D. Hargreaves, "Assumptions, Expectations and Plans: Approaches to Decolonisation in Sierra Leone," in *Decolonisation and After: The British and French Experience*, ed. W. H. Morris-Jones and Georges Fischer (London: Frank Cass, 1980), 82, on the approach adopted by Governor Jardine of Sierra Leone with regard to the pro-government candidate, C. E. Wright, in 1939.

30. On the two bills, see CO 89/11, Leg. Co. Minutes, May 14, 1912; May 27, 1912; June 4, 1912; January 22, 1913; March 12, 1913; March 19, 1913. See also CO 87/190, Galway to Secretary of State, May 20, 1912; Galway to Secretary of State, June 13, 1912; and CO 87/191, Galway to Secretary of State, August 12, 1912; O'Brien to Secretary of State, October 14, 1912; Galway to Secretary of State, July 9, 1913.

31. Martin Kilson, "The National Congress of British West Africa, 1918–1935," in *Protest and Power in Black Africa*, ed. Robert I. Rotberg and Ali A. Mazrui (London: Oxford University Press, 1970), 581–84, distinguishes between an "upper-level" elite of lawyers, merchants, and clergymen and a "lower-level" elite of clerks, primary school teachers, and artisans. See also Kilson, *Political Change in a West African State*, 68–76. The foundation of the Reform Club is noted in *GE*, July 15, 1940. On the Committee of Gentlemen, see J. Ayodele Langley, *Pan-Africanism and Nationalism in West Africa, 1900–1945: A Study in Ideology and Social Classes* (Oxford: Clarendon Press, 1973), 136 (note 6).

32. CO 87/109, Galway to Secretary of State, January 4, 1912; and *GG*, July 31, 1916; December 15, 1916. See also Macmillan, *Red Book*, 292–94; and Fyfe, *History of Sierra Leone*, 493; 523, who states that Bishop was the nephew of the former Sierra Leonean councilor, T. C. Bishop.

33. CO 87/109, Harcourt to Galway, February 1, 1912. The reasons for Cameron's choice of Forster are not known; nor is it known whether the Colonial Office made any reaction to the fact that Forster was being offered a third term of office. On Cameron, see Hughes and Gailey, *Historical Dictionary*, 48.

34. Small was born either in January 1890 or January 1891. Most sources (e.g. Langley, *Pan-Africanism*, 137) give Small's date of birth as 1890 in line with GA C633/1921, Armitage to Secretary of State, May 7, 1921; moreover, *The Gambia Weekly* (*GW*), February 2, 1990, reported on events commemorating the centenary of his birth. However, a plaque in Banjul, which commemorates his career, and *The Gambia Outlook and Senegambian Reporter* (hence *GO*), January 4, 1958, both give a date of 1891. David Perfect, "The Political Career of Edward Francis Small," in Hughes, ed. *Studies in Society and Politics*, 64, suggested that the date of birth was 1891, but we now think that the 1890 date is more probable.

35. Small's father was listed as John W. Small in *GO*, January 4, 1958. J. W. Small first appears in official files in December 1875, when he signed the anti-cession petition; he then described himself as a tailor and a freeholder of house property. He had not signed the anti-cession petition of April 1870. However, this was signed by a W. R. Small, who was stated to be a tailor with house and land worth £50 and may have been John Small's father; see [HC], *PPCA 56*, 162; 341; 348. John Small's advertisement appears in *BO*, January 27, 1885. He was described as one of Bathurst "principal artisans" by the then colonial secretary, Francis Bisset Archer in *Colony and Protectorate*, 314. J. W. Small served on the Methodist Church District Extension Fund Committee for several years and was its Chairman in 1908. See [WMMS], "West Africa Synod Minutes: Gambia, 1842–1910," WMMS fiche box no. 1.

36. Small's mother (who died in December 1937) was listed as Annie Eliza Thomas in *GO*, January 1, 1938. She certainly married a Mr. Johnson (possibly W. E. Johnson, the

headmaster of the Methodist School in Bathurst) and probably also a Mr. Oldfield, because Small's half brothers included Victor E. Johnson and M. S. Oldfield. See GA C1308/1930, minute by Finn, December 3, 1930, who calls her Mrs. Johnson; *GE*, December 9, 1957; December 16, 1957; and GA C498/1920, note on signatories to Congress petition of May 6, 1924. Small's mother was described as a "basket woman" by Rev. J. C. Faye (Perfect interview, Banjul, September 1984). Small was also described as illegitimate by Governor Palmer; see GA S135/1933, Palmer to Cunliffe-Lister, January 10, 1933. It should be noted that it was commonplace in Aku families for illegitimate children to be named after their fathers rather than their mothers. *GO*, November 23, 1935, reports the death of John Small's wife, Ellen, at the age of 82, but does not indicate when they were married.

37. *GE*, December 16, 1957; and GA C633/1921, Armitage to Secretary of State, May 7, 1921, describe his education. Small's intelligence and his willingness to give up a position worth £95 p.a. with Maurel et Prom for one worth only £60 p.a. was noted in [WMMS], "Gambia Correspondence 1916–1922," fiche box no. 8, box 762, Toye to Goudie, January 14, 1916; Toye to Goudie, December 21, 1916. The date of John Small's death is not known, but his name disappears from the records of lay officials of the Methodist Church after 1908; see [WMMS], "West Africa Synod Minutes: Gambia, 1842–1910." Langley, *Pan-Africanism*, 137, summarizes Armitage's despatch, but incorrectly states that Small returned to Bathurst after his application for promotion in Freetown was denied.

38. [WMMS], "Gambia Correspondence 1916–22," Memorial of Native Gentlemen, January 11, 1916.

39. [WMMS], "Gambia Correspondence 1916–22," Toye to Goudie, December 21, 1916; Goudie to Toye, January 10, 1917. The Ballanghar station was established in 1908; see [WMMS], *Report of the Wesleyan Methodist Missionary Society 1909* (London: WMMS, 1909).

40. The incident is discussed in Perfect, "E. F. Small," 66; and Langley, *Pan-Africanism*, 137. For the reaction of local Methodists (including Forster), see [WMMS], "Gambia Correspondence 1916–22," Leonard to Gouldie, September 5, 1918. It is interesting to note that shortly afterward, McCallum was dismissed from government service for misconduct, having allegedly come under the influence of Fatu Khan, the niece of the Seyfu of Upper Saloum. For details, see J. H. Price, "Some Notes on the Influence of Women in Gambian Politics," in *Nigerian Institute of Social and Economic Research (NISER) Conference Proceedings, December 1958* (Ibadan: NISER, 1958), 151–58.

41. Langley, *Pan-Africanism*, 136, accepts the (later) view of the Gambian government that the GNDU was a society of government clerks that had "no known political aims." In fact, it was formed by clerks and agents of trading firms and had a strongly political focus. This interpretation is based both on the known membership of the GNDU and on an account in *GO*, January 11, 1958.

42. Perfect, "Organised Labour," 33–34. MacCarthy was a close confidant of Small in 1920 (and may have been related to him); he was hanged in 1922 for the murder of an elderly trader, Charles Goddard. See GA C633/1921, Small to MacCarthy, June 21, 1920; CO 87/217, Armitage to Secretary of State, November 4, 1922; minute by Ellis, c. December 5, 1922, and *GO*, February 4, 1950. On Jones (who, like Small, was twenty-eight in 1919), see also Langley, *Pan-Africanism*, 135; Macmillan, *Red Book*, 292; and GA C633/1921, Armitage to Secretary of State, May 7, 1921.

43. See James S. Coleman, *Nigeria: Background to Nationalism* (Berkeley: University of California Press, 1958), 197; Cole, *Elites in Lagos*, 76; and Kimble, *History of Ghana*, 95. Another prominent nationalist of the 1920s, Kobina Sekyi, was radicalized by his experiences of racism. See J. Ayodele Langley, Introduction to *The Blinkards* by Kobina Sekyi (London: Heinemann Educational, 1974), 1–17.

44. Langley, *Pan-Africanism*, 178–79; and Kimble, *History of Ghana*, 375.

45. Perfect, "Organised Labour," 34–35. Langley, *Pan-Africanism*, 135–36, offers a slightly different version of events. On Roberts, see also Macmillan, *Red Book*, 294.

46. On the conference, see Langley, *Pan-Africanism*, 125–31; and Kimble, *History of Ghana*, 381–85. For analyses of the Congress branches in the other colonies, see Langley, *Pan-Africanism*, 134–94; Kimble, *History of Ghana*, 375–403; Kilson, "National Congress"; Akintola J. G. Wyse, "The Sierra Leone Branch of the National Congress of British West Africa, 1918–1946," *International Journal of African Historical Studies* 18, no. 4 (1985), 675–98; G. O. Olusanya, "The Lagos Branch of the National Congress of British West Africa," *Journal of the Historical Society of Nigeria* 4, no. 2: (1968), 321–33; and Gabriel I. C. Eluwa, "The National Congress of British West Africa: A Pioneer Nationalist Movement," *Genève Afrique* 11, no. 1: (1972), 38–51.

47. A partial list of the Congress members in 1920 is in Langley, *Pan-Africanism*, 139; this is based on GA C766/1920, Small to Colonial Secretary, June 1, 1920. The occupations of some of these individuals are given in GA C498/1920. The Rev. F. S. Oldfield seems to have lost his position as acting colonial chaplain in 1923 because of his support for the Congress; see GA C766/1920, minute by Finn, October 4, 1923. See also GA C498/1920, minutes by Commissioner of Police, March 7, 1922; May 23, 1925.

48. CO 87/213, Armitage to Secretary of State, March 7, 1921 (reporting on a tour of the Protectorate in January); Kimble, *History of Ghana*, 375–99; and Langley, *Pan-Africanism*, 164–74. On the situation in Sierra Leone and Nigeria, see Wyse, "Sierra Leone Branch," 684–90; Langley, *Pan-Africanism*, 182; and Tamuno, *Nigeria and Elective Representation*, 29.

49. GA C766/1920, Small to Henniker Heaton, June 1, 1920, contains a list of the branch members at that time; an incomplete list is in Langley, *Pan-Africanism*, 139. The same letter describes the difference between the General Committee and the Working Committee. See also Perfect, "E. F. Small," 69; and, on Pratt, *GO*, February 5, 1938. Further information from Sam Goddard (Hughes interview, Banjul, April 1977).

50. The views of Forster and Bishop were outlined in CO 89/14, Leg. Co. Minutes, January 10, 1921; Pratt appears to have played no further part in the Congress. Another leading member of the Congress, James T. Roberts (a trader), told a meeting in May 1924 that, although an original member, he had later disassociated himself from the movement because of its domination by "Extremists"; see Langley, *Pan-Africanism*, 150. Langley does not mention that Forster turned against the Congress.

51. GA C766/1920, Acting Governor Henniker Heaton to Small, June 2, 1920. See Tamuno, *Nigeria and Elective Representation*, 44–45; Langley, *Pan-Africanism*, 163–84; Kimble, *History of Ghana*, 374–403; and Wyse, "Sierra Leone Branch," 679–80, for developments in the other three colonies.

52. *SLWN*, October 16, 1920. Jones may have been selected because he had commercial interests in London and may therefore have subsidized the delegation; see Langley, *Pan-Africanism*, 243. Delegates were also elected in Sierra Leone, according to Wyse, "Sierra Leone Branch," 682 (note 32). But in Lagos, the selection of Chief T. M. Oluwa and J. E. Shyngle (who were already in London) caused great controversy as Olusanya, "Lagos Branch," 327–30, points out.

53. The branch leaders included B. J. George and Cyril Richards of the GNDU. The acting secretary of the branch, Anthony H. Jones, was another who may have nursed a grievance. He had resigned from his position as a government clerk because he had not received the promotion he expected (GA C498/1920, minute by Finn, May 23, 1921). The president, Moses Richards (a trader), who was another son of J. D. Richards, was a more conservative figure. See GA C498/1920. On Small's view of Moses Richards, see GA C633/1921, Small to MacCarthy, June 21, 1920.

54. The Muslim Section apparently contributed £350 to the London delegation fund. See GA 581/1923, George to Bulstrode, August 30, 1923. See also CO 87/216, Armitage to Secretary of State, August 15, 1922, who claimed that Muslims were promised various unspecified benefits when the delegates returned from London.

55. GA C766/1920, Small to Colonial Secretary, June 1, 1920; Greig to Colonial Secretary, October 31, 1922. A photograph of Congress leaders, which was probably taken in 1920, includes Jallow (see GA C633/1921), on whom see also GA C766/1920, Jeng to Colonial Secretary, October 31, 1922. GA C498/1920, minute by Finn, June 26, 1924, notes that Sowe was associated with the Congress before he became Almami. Gormack N'Jie had been Almami between 1882 and 1890; see A. E. Cham-Joof, "The History of the Banjul Mosque," *Weekend Observer* (*WO*), May 5–7, 1995.

56. Langley, *Pan-Africanism*, 142; GA C633/1921, Armitage to Secretary of State, May 7, 1921; N'Jai to Finn, July 4, 1921; and CO 87/216, Armitage to Secretary of State, August 15, 1922, who also notes that N'Jai (or N'Jie) was Almani between 1902 and 1922. An Imam, H. Deen, was a founding member of the Sierra Leone Congress in 1918, but may have been the only Muslim and was never prominent in the organization. See Wyse, *Bankole-Bright*, 35.

57. On Jeng's background, see GA C1526/1921, Barbou Jallow et al. to Workman, November 22, 1921; Workman to Secretary of State, December 1, 1921. See also Burama K. Sagnia, *Historical Development of the Gambian Legislature* (Lawrenceville, VA: Brunswick, 1991), 13–14. For a brief description of the origins of the three Sufi brotherhoods in West Africa (Muridiyya, Tijaniyya, and Qadiriyya), see Trimingham, *Islam in West Africa*, 157–60; 227–28.

58. According to the commissioner of police, C. Greig. See GA C766/1920, Greig to Colonial Secretary, October 31, 1922.

59. CO 87/213, Armitage to Secretary of State, March 2, 1921. The furor over the Peace Celebrations is referred to in GA C1477/1931, minute by Workman, July 31, 1922. However, it should be noted that Forster organized a Grand Victory Ball in Bathurst in February 1919, which makes Cameron's response surprising; see *SLWN*, February 8, 1919. See also GA C1526/1921, minute by Finn, February 3, 1921. On Armitage, see Hughes and Gailey, *Historical Dictionary*, 32.

60. Kimble, *History of Ghana*, 81–83. Armitage himself informed a Congress deputation in 1926 that he had revived the powers of the chiefs in the Northern Territories; see GA 581/1923, minute by Workman, January 4, 1926. As stated in Chapter 1, 27–28, Armitage also founded the Armitage School in Georgetown specifically to cater for the sons and relatives of chiefs.

61. GA C1526/1921, minutes by Armitage, February 12, 1921; Finn, March 1, 1921.

62. GA C1526/1921, Barbou Jallow et al. to Workman, November 22, 1921; and CO 87/216, Yerim N'Dure to Armitage, August 10, 1922. *GO*, November 19, 1950, notes that Jeng married Omar Sowe's eldest daughter, Aminata, around 1906.

63. GA C1526/1921, Jallow et al. to Workman, November 22, 1921; Workman to Secretary of State, December 1, 1921. See also GA—despatches, 1937, Oke to Secretary of State, February 26, 1937; and GA C498/1920, Webley to Acting Colonial Secretary, October 30, 1923. Fye was certainly employed by the Bathurst Trading Company in the mid-1920s; see GA C936/1924, minute by Finn, October 28, 1924.

64. Fye's supporters are listed in GA C1526/1921. The members of the Advisory Committee are given in CO 87/216, Yerim N'Dure to Armitage, August 10, 1922. On N'Jie and Cham, see also GA 732/1919, Harley N'Jie et al. to Acting Colonial Engineer, June 13, 1919.

65. CO 89/9, Leg. Co. Minutes, July 4, 1905; and GA C1268/1929, enclosure to Jahumpa and Darameh to Colonial Secretary, September 28, 1929; memo by Judge Horne, March 1929.

66. GA C1526/1921, Jallow to Workman, November 22, 1921; see also minute by E. Hopkinson, Commissioner North Bank Province to Officer in Charge of Secretariat,

November 26, 1921. Hopkinson considered the reason given "an absolute bar" to Fye's appointment. For a discussion of "griots" in Wolof society, see Gamble, *Wolof of Senegambia*, 44–45.

67. GA C1526/1921, Armitage to Secretary of State, March 24, 1922. Forster's part in securing Jeng's selection was noted by his son, J. R. Forster (Hughes interview, Bathurst, February 1972).

68. GA C1526/1921, Armitage to Secretary of State, March 24, 1922, who stated that the Muslims refused to allow Small to address them about the Congress. Langley, *Pan-Africanism*, 143, notes that Jallow was opposed to the Congress in 1922. But by 1924, he was again a Congress supporter, as is evident from GA C498/1920, May 6, 1924. Ousman N'Jie's rejection of the Congress was noted in GA C633/1921, minute by Greig, October 31, 1922.

69. CO 89/14, Leg. Co. Minutes, January 10, 1921. Armitage also quoted, with approval, a famous speech by Governor Clifford to the Nigerian Council in December 1920, in which he denounced the Congress. Clifford's address is summarized by Coleman, *Nigeria: Background to Nationalism*, 192–94. See also Tamuno, *Nigeria and Elective Representation*, 26.

70. Jones was expelled from the Wesleyan Church body in Bathurst in 1921 for committing bigamy. He married a second woman while in London, even though his first wife was still alive in Freetown; see GA C633/1921, Armitage to Secretary of State, May 7, 1921. His fall from grace probably explains why Jones, although still a member of the Congress, was not a leader of the local branch after 1920. Even Colonial Office officials considered that Armitage's reaction to any criticism was excessive; see, for example, comment by Ellis on CO 87/217, Armitage to Secretary of State, November 4, 1922.

71. GA C1526/1921, Workman to Secretary of State, December 1, 1921, noted that Fye initially refused to join the Congress, which may explain why he appears originally to have been Armitage's preferred choice; see also GA C1526/1921, Jallow to Workman, November 22, 1921. See GA C766/1920, Omar Jallow to Jeng, October 18, 1922, on the attempt to win over Wakka Bah; see also CO 87/216, Yerim N'Dure to Armitage, August 10, 1922. Fye was listed as a branch member in October 1923; see GA C498/1920, Webley to Acting Colonial Secretary, October 30, 1923.

72. See for example, GA 581/1923, Workman to George, July 11, 1923; and GA C498/1920, Armitage to Secretary of State, January 2, 1925. See also Langley, *Pan-Africanism*, 145; and CO 267/655, minute by I. J. T. Turbett (a former Gambian police magistrate), September 16, 1936. The hostility toward "Sierra Leoneans" recalled the objections to J. D. Richards at the turn of the century.

73. *GW*, February 2, 1990, records that Small moved to Rufisque, but states that he did so in 1920, not 1922. Another explanation for Small's departure to Senegal was that he could obtain a printing press there, as noted in *GE*, November 2, 1957. Grey-Johnson, "The Newspaper in The Gambia," 23, claims that, during an earlier visit to France, Small met Blaise Diagne, who in 1914 became the first black African to be elected to the French Chamber of Deputies. But there is no confirmation of this in other sources. On the political rights of the inhabitants of Rufisque and Diagne's election, see Crowder, *West Africa Under Colonial Rule*, 414–19.

74. The last Gambian newspaper was *The Gambia Intelligencer*, which ceased to exist in 1896; see note 15.

75. See GA C309/1918, Small to Workman, August 11, 1922; Armitage to Secretary of State for the Colonies, November 4, 1922; Maugham to Workman, November 2, 1922; and CO 87/217, Small to British Consul-General, Dakar (R. C. Maugham), September 1, 1922, which forms an enclosure to Small to Secretary of State for Foreign Affairs, September 1, 1922. Unfortunately, Maugham did not specify exactly what problems Small caused.

76. See GA C727/1922, Maugham to Armitage, June 15, 1922; Armitage to Maugham, June 28, 1922. According to Armitage, Small's supporters made contact with Garvey's

emissaries in Senegal; see GA C309/1918, Armitage to Secretary of State, November 4, 1922. For a brief discussion of the UNIA branch in Senegal, see G. O. Olusanya, "Garvey and Nigeria," in *Garvey: Africa, Europe, the Americas,* 2nd ed., ed. Rupert Lewis and Maureen Warner-Lewis (Trenton, NJ: Africa World Press, 1994), 128. See also Robert A. Hill ed., *The Marcus Garvey Papers.* 8 vols. (Berkeley: University of California Press, 1995), vol. IX, 442–43; 501–12.

77. A Senegalese government Police Report of November 24, 1930, notes that during a brief stay in Dakar en route from Europe to Gambia, Small met "William Winstone," who was suspected of being a member of the UNIA in 1922; the latter was apparently now a police informer (it is likely that Winstone was in fact Wilson and the police records were inaccurate). But Small did not tell Winstone/Wilson a great deal about his activities. See Senegalese National Archives, Dakar (hence SA), SA 17G/58 "M. Small. Edouard Francis (Propagandiste a tendances communistes)" [1931]. It is significant that the French regarded Small as a "communist" rather than as a Garveyite subversive.

78. Olusanya, "Garvey and Nigeria," discusses the relationship between the UNIA and the NCBWA. But Arnold Hughes, "Africa and the Garvey Movement in the Interwar Years," in *Garvey*, ed. Lewis and Warner-Lewis, 104, while noting that no UNIA branch was ever established in The Gambia, does point out that one of the founders of the NCBWA, J. E. Casely-Hayford, appeared to be close to the UNIA. Yet, though honored by the UNIA, he never belonged to any of its branches in the Gold Coast.

79. GA C1308/1930, Fiddian to Commissioner of Police, December 13, 1926, contains a letter dated August 1925 from Mrs. F. R. Avis, a London landlady, who stated that Small stayed with her between July 29, 1923 and the end of December 1923.

80. CO 87/225/14, Armitage to Secretary of State, November 6, 1926 and other correspondence in this file. Small's former landlady, Mrs. Avis, claimed that Small owed her over £27 in unpaid rent; she had apparently searched for him across London, but without success. According to Armitage, at least one issue of the *Gambia Outlook* was published while Small was in London, but it has not survived.

81. GA C498/1920, Armitage to Secretary of State, December 11, 1924, which also briefly mentions Mahoney's background. For more details on Mahoney, see "The Gambia's 'Speaker,'" *WA*, July 4, 1953, 605; and GA C1308/1930, minute by Finn, December 3, 1930. See also CO 554/2051, Smith to Eastwood, July 8, 1959. On several occasions, J. E. Mahoney signed petitions presented to the Gambian government by European and African merchants. These included a petition against the reenactment of the Customs Ordinance in 1898 and one in 1911 which called for an increase in the number of customs staff; see CO 87/156, merchants to S. J. Forster, June 14, 1898, which forms an enclosure to Griffith to Secretary of State, July 1, 1898; and CO 87/186, merchants and traders to Denton, which forms an enclosure to Denton to Secretary of State, June 28, 1911. Mahoney's death was recorded in the Gambia District Synod Minutes for 1911; see [WMMS], "West Africa Synod Minutes: Gambia 1912–1946," WMMS, fiche box no. 10.

82. For differing accounts of the reasons for the concession of the franchise in Nigeria, see Tamuno, *Nigeria and Elective Representation,* 18–32; and Langley, *Pan-Africanism,* 265–85. On the concession of the franchise in Sierra Leone, see Wyse, *Bankole-Bright,* 47–56.

83. GA 581/1923, George to Armitage, July 4, 1923; Workman to George, July 11, 1923; George to Bulstrode, August 30, 1923; Mahoney to Colonial Secretary, March 26, 1924. The official replies (in the same file) are Workman to George, July 5, 1923; Workman to Secretary, Congress, February 27, 1924; Workman to Secretary, Congress, March 28, 1924. See also Langley, *Pan-Africanism,* 145–46.

84. GA 581/1923, Mahoney to Thomas, May 6, 1924; Thomas to Armitage, June 18, 1924. See also CO 87/220, Armitage to Thomas, May 9, 1924 and the comments on the petition

by Colonial Office officials in this file; and *WA*, August 23, 1924, 866. For the views of the other governors, see Langley, *Pan-Africanism*, 256–85; Wyse, *Bankole-Bright*, 47–48; and Kimble, *History of Ghana*, 438–41.

85. Langley, *Pan-Africanism*, 147. See also GA 160/1925, minute by Armitage, April 30, 1925.

86. "The Gambia Government and Municipal Politics," *WA*, November 8, 1924, 1252–53.

87. Under the Supreme Court Ordinance, the crown could elect to hold trials in capital cases before a judge and assessors. The Licensing Bill imposed a licensing fee on shop-keepers and petty traders. For details, see CO 87/220, Armitage to Secretary of State, April 8, 1924; and CO 87/222, Armitage to Secretary of State, January 16, 1925. See also GA C498/1920, Armitage to Secretary of State, January 16, 1925; and GA 160/1925, Sowe to Colonial Secretary, May 4, 1925. Sowe claimed that he had been tricked into signing the petition. Sowe's appointment is noted in Cham-Joof, "Banjul Mosque."

88. GA 160/1925, January 4, 1926, report by Workman on the meeting between Armitage and the Congress delegation.

89. CO 87/225/13, Armitage to Secretary of State, October 26, 1926. When drawing up lists of Congress leaders, the government often distinguished between "Sierra Leoneans" and "Gambians"; see, for example, its analysis of the signatories to a "franchise" petition of May 6, 1924 in GA C498/1920.

90. On the 1926 strike and its political repercussions, see Akintola J. G. Wyse, "The 1926 Railway Strike and Anglo-Krio Relations: An Interpretation," *International Journal of African Historical Studies* 14, no. 1: (1981), 93–123; Wyse, *Bankole-Bright*, 69–76; and David Fasholé Luke, *Labour and Parastatal Politics in Sierra Leone: A Study of African Working-Class Ambivalence* (Lanham, MD: University Press of America, 1984), 26–29. See also CO 87/225/13, minute by Strachey, November 23, 1926.

91. CO 87/225/13, minute by Ormsby-Gore, November 30, 1926. See also [Colonial Office], *Report by the Hon. W.G.A. Ormsby-Gore, M.P. on His Visit to West Africa During the Year 1926* (London: HMSO, 1926), 161–68; and "Mr Ormsby-Gore and the Affairs of The Gambia," *WA*, July 3, 1926, 807–8. On the foundation of the GRC, see two articles by J. A. N'Jai-Gomez in *GO*, November 22, 1930 and July 9, 1932. See also *GO*, November 1, 1930; June 25, 1932; *GE*, April 11, 1938; May 28, 1945; and (on N'Jai-Gomez) CO 87/212, Henniker Heaton to Secretary of State, November 10, 1920. Further information was provided by Rev. J. C. Faye (Perfect interview, Banjul, June 1984). Unfortunately, the names of the other GRC delegates are not known.

92. GA C1526/1921, Small to Secretary of State, September 12, 1929, notes the rejection of Armitage's "promise" of the franchise; see also *GO*, April 30, 1932, which interestingly reports that the local press argued at the time that if an election had been held, Forster and Jeng would have been returned. (No copies of the only contemporary newspaper, the *Gambia Outlook*, have survived from this period.) On Middleton, see Hughes and Gailey, *Historical Dictionary*, 122.

93. There was a meeting in March 1928; see GA C766/1920, report by Sawyerr, March 27, 1928. But this was probably convened by the Gambia Representative Committee. On his arrival in Bathurst, Governor Denham was greeted by a Congress deputation headed by its new secretary, J. F. Senegal; see GA 160/1925, Senegal to Colonial Secretary, December 7, 1928. As stated by Langley, *Pan-Africanism*, 135, Gambia was represented at the fourth Congress Session in 1930 by I. J. Roberts, but it is doubtful if the Bathurst branch was still then functioning.

94. GA C1268/1929, enclosure to Jahumpa and Darameh to Colonial Secretary, September 28, 1929. Jahumpa had been one of the three representatives sent by Almami Momadu N'Jai to attend the Congress meeting in June 1921; see GA C633/1921, Finn to

Almami, June 30, 1921. Jahumpa's father, Sereng, a Koranic teacher, had been one of Bathurst's earliest inhabitants, having moved to Gambia from Gorée; see "The Gambia's First Minister?" *WA*, December 12, 1953, 1157. Further information on his father was provided by I. M. Garba-Jahumpa (Perfect interview, Banjul, June 1984).

95. GA C1216/1929, Jahumpa et al. to Denham, June 4, 1929; report by Greig, Commissioner of Police, April 13, 1929. See also enclosure to GA C1210/1929, Aitken to Colonial Secretary, March 28, 1929 (hence "Aitken Judgment"). Judge Aitken accepted that the Juma Society (or the Mohammedan Carpenters' Society as it was also known) had indeed nominated all the Almamis.

96. GA C1216/1929, Jahumpa and Darameh to Secretary of State, September 2, 1929; minute by Greig, April 13, 1929. See also GA C1210/1929, "Aitken Judgment."

97. GA C1210/1929, "Aitken Judgment." A rumor that Fye was covertly supporting Jahumpa was reported by the director of agriculture in February 1929; see GA C1206/1929, Brooks to Acting Colonial Secretary, February 4, 1929. However, the latter considered (minute, February 13) that the report could not be substantiated. Indeed, on the only occasion when Fye intervened in the matter, he apparently acted as a mediator (see GA C1210/1929, report by Greig, April 8, 1929).

98. GA C1210/1929, Jahumpa and Darameh to Colonial Secretary, October 11, 1929. The two men also protested to the secretary of state, but to no avail; see Passfield to Denham, November 25, 1929, in the same file.

99. Control over the school was valued not only because of the prestige derived, but also because fees were charged for hiring out the school premises. Both Jahumpa and Jeng attempted to set up their own school Managing Committee in 1929, neither of which was recognized by the other. Governor Denham then intervened and both sides agreed in October 1929 that the (European) inspector of schools should control the keys to the school. For a summary of the dispute, see C1216/1929, memo by Judge Horne, March 1931. See also Densham Smith to Cadi, April 13, 1931, in the same file. On Palmer, see Hughes and Gailey, *Historical Dictionary*, 137–38.

100. See GA C936/1924, minute by Acting Colonial Secretary, Finn, August 6, 1924; and GA C1526/1921, Sowe to Governor Middleton, April 8, 1928; Workman to Sowe, April 24, 1928.

101. For the first known indication of Fye's political stance, see GA S135A/1933, Fye to Acting Governor Parish, November 10, 1933. It is, however, possible that Fye had made clear his opposition to Small before his appointment to the council.

102. Langley, *Pan-Africanism*, 139, states that Roberts was a member of the Gambia Section in 1920. His financial support for Small was noted by Sam Goddard in interviews in Banjul with Hughes (April 1977) and Perfect (April 1992).

103. There has been no full analysis of the GFCMA (which apparently did not include Fye). For brief secondary discussions, see Perfect, "Organised Labour," 40–81, passim; Wright, *The World and a Very Small Place*, 212–13; and [Gambia Government], *Annual Report of the Registrar of Co-operative Societies, 1964* (SP no. 4 of 1965) (Bathurst: Government Printer, 1965), 1–2. The aims of the syndicate are outlined in GA C1206/1929, Small to Prentis, January 16, 1929 (which names Fye as the co-promoter). The activities of the GFCMA are covered in a range of official files in Banjul and London: see especially GA C1206/1929; GA CF13/1930; GA 54/231; and CO 87/232/11. This was one of several unsuccessful ventures by Africans in British West Africa during the inter-war period to challenge the price-fixing cartels of European produce buyers. See Hopkins, *An Economic History of West Africa*, 254–56, for the general economic context and other examples.

104. Small had certainly intervened in the dispute by October 1929; see GA C1268/1929, Denham to Secretary of State, October 25, 1929, which refers to a petition by Small of

October 12. However, G. W. S. Ladepon-Thomas, who was a leading member of the RPA (and Small's solicitor), also acted as Jahumpa's solicitor from February (see GA C1210/1929, "Aitken Judgment"). The union's foundation is discussed in Perfect, "Organised Labour," 40–42.

105. See Perfect, "Organised Labour," 31–63, for a detailed account of the strike.

106. The sharpest contrast is with the 1926 Freetown railway strike. After six weeks, the strikers were forced to return on the government's terms and 37 pensionable and 200 daily paid workers were dismissed. See Wyse, "1926 Railway Strike," 111.

107. GA S135/1933, Governor Palmer to Secretary of State, January 10, 1933. See Perfect, "Organised Labour," 63, for the actions of the two councilors during the strike. On Denham, see Hughes and Gailey, *Historical Dictionary*, 58.

108. The Passfield Memorandum can be found in CO 854/173. It has drawn a mixed response from writers on colonial trade unionism. It is viewed positively by B. C. Roberts, *Labour in the Tropical Territories of the Commonwealth* (London: Bell for London School of Economics, 1964); and by Sahadeo Basdeo, *Labour Organisation and Labour Reform in Trinidad 1919–1939* (St. Augustine, Trinidad: Institute of Social and Economic Research, University of West Indies, 1983). However, Milcah Amolo, "Sierra Leone and British Colonial Labour Policy 1930–1945" (Ph.D. diss., Dalhousie University, 1978), 23, describes it as "a masterpiece of sly manipulation." This view is largely shared by Perfect, "Organised Labour," 66–70, who demonstrates that the Bathurst strike provided the impetus for the legislation.

109. Because Small was under close surveillance by the colonial authorities during 1930, it is possible to trace his movements into and out of Gambia through a careful analysis of surviving official files in Banjul and Dakar. Crucially, however, it is not known precisely where he went once he was in Europe. See GA C1251/1929, Consul-General to Acting Governor, Gambia, February 28, 1930; GA C1308/1930; and SA 17G/58.

110. GA C1553/1932, Bridgeman to Cunliffe-Lister, January 28, 1932, describes the Senegalese trip; see also SA 17G/58. GA C1206/1929, Small to Acting Colonial Secretary, May 14, 1931, notes that he had recently returned from Accra. Small went to the Gold Coast to open negotiations with Winfried Tete-Ansa's West African American Corporation, but these eventually broke down. See Langley, *Pan-Africanism*, 232–35; Perfect, "Organised Labour," 81; CO 87/232/11, Parish to Fiddian, September 9, 1931; and GA C1466/1931.

111. According to Small's later account, the BTU's problems had begun when Fye allegedly misappropriated union funds; see Perfect, "Organised Labour," 79–80. On Fye, see also S116 I/1930, minute by Webley, January 9, 1931.

112. The fullest account of the LAI and Bridgeman is in Joyce M. Bellamy and John Saville, *Dictionary of Labour Biography*. 10 vols. (London: Macmillan, 1984), vol. VII, 26–50 (44). See also Edward T. Wilson, *Russia and Black Africa Before World War II* (New York: Holmes and Meier, 1974), 176–85; 226–29; Perfect, "Organised Labour," 64–65; and Langley, *Pan-Africanism*, 309–10.

113. On Small's links with the LRDept and the PLP, see Hughes and Perfect, "Trade Unionism," 553–55. On the LRDept, see "80 Years Combating Inequality," *Labour Research*, July 1992, 15–16; and Margaret Cole, *The Life of G. D. H. Cole* (London: Macmillan, 1971), 124–28.

114. See Perfect, "Organised Labour," 55; and Hughes and Perfect, "Trade Unionism," 555.

115. See Wilson, *Russia and Black Africa*, 175–223; and James R. Hooker, *Black Revolutionary: George Padmore's Path from Communism to Pan-Africanism* (New York: Praeger, 1967).

116. Padmore was certainly in London in April 1930 and subsequently gave his address there as 2 Torrington Square, the house where Small was staying in May 1930; he also visited

Berlin (where he obtained his visa to visit West Africa) during an extensive European tour in 1930. According to both the Gambian government and the Colonial Office, Small traveled to Berlin, but this cannot be confirmed from other sources. See GA S131 I/1931, Workman to Kell, June 17, 1930; GA C1308/1930, Workman to Passfield, June 2, 1930; and CO 87/230/8, Flood to Foreign Office, June 11, 1930. Wilson, *Russia and Black Africa*, 243, considers that Workman's reference to the Berlin meeting may have been an erroneous reference to the Hamburg Conference, but this did not take place until July 7–9.

117. On Padmore's visit to West Africa, see GA S131 I/1931; and GA C1308/1930, Workman to Passfield, June 2, 1930. Secondary accounts are by Wilson, *Russia and Black Africa*, 191; and Arnold Hughes and Robin Cohen, "An Emerging Nigerian Working Class: The Lagos Experience 1897–1939," in *African Labor History*, ed. Peter C. W. Gutkind, Robin Cohen, and Jean Copans (Beverly Hills, CA: Sage, 1978), 47. GA S131 I/1931, Phillips to Workman, August 16, 1930, reported that Padmore collected six African delegates who traveled with him on the *S. S. Abinsi*. One of these was certainly the Nigerian, Frank Macaulay (the son of Herbert Macaulay), who was on board the ship when it docked at Bathurst on June 13. The other five are not known, but may have included Small if the *S. S. Abinsi* docked at Dakar en route to England.

118. Small's speech is reported in full in International Trade Union Committee of Negro Workers, *A Report of Proceedings and Decisions of the First Conference of Negro Workers* (Hamburg: ITUC-NW, 1930), 21–23 (which can be found in CO 87/237/8). He claimed that the "Gambia Labour Union" (as Small rather confusingly termed it) had 3,500 members, 2,500 of whom were "peasants." See also Wilson, *Russia and Black Africa*, 185; 242; and Perfect, "Organised Labour," 64–65. Wilson does not name the conference delegates who attended the RILU Congress and there is no firm evidence that Small did so. However, it is known that after returning to London following the Hamburg Conference, he was at least planning to go back to Germany (to Berlin). Assuming he did so, he may well have gone on to Moscow from there; see GA S125/1930, Small to Evans, July 27, 1930. Langley, *Pan-Africanism*, 138, states that Small did go to Moscow in 1930, but suggests that this was to attend a meeting of the Krestintern (the Red Peasant International, another affiliate of the Comintern).

119. Denham Diaries (Rhodes House, Oxford) [Sir Edward Denham, Governor of Gambia, 1928–30] vol. X 29/11/28–5/5/29. Entry, December 12, 1928. Small soon changed his mind about the government's attitude to his newspaper; by September 1929, he was complaining to the secretary of state for the colonies about official discourtesy toward the press. See GA C1250/1929, Small to Passfield, September 7, 1929. In his response in the same file (Denham to Passfield, October 3, 1929), the governor stated that "I fear however that Mr Small's activities are at times merely mischievous and that his object is not to supply accurate information."

120. In GA C1308/1930, Workman to Passfield, June 2, 1930, the acting governor admitted that he was not aware whether Small had definitely joined the Communist Party, but stated that his meeting in Berlin (see note 116) and his correspondence with the League Against Imperialism, "sufficiently indicate his attitude." The Senegalese government and the Colonial Office held similar views. See SA 17G/58; CO 87/229/12, minute by Flood, January 8, 1930; and CO 87/238/9, minute by Hazelrigg, September 20, 1933.

121. GA C1206/1929, minute by Workman, June 11, 1930, notes Small's denial of the charge. Small also claimed in this interview that the offending articles were published in the newspaper without his consent by his "agent," Eustace Richards (on whom see S116 I/1930, minute by Webley, January 9, 1931). According to the colonial authorities, Padmore landed in Bathurst on April 26 and departed for Sierra Leone three days later. The *Negro Worker* articles appeared in the *Gambia Outlook* between March 29 and May 10, and another article

written by Padmore himself was in the issue of April 26. It is certainly possible that Padmore brought copies of the *Negro Worker* with him, and the *GO* articles were wrongly dated, rather than that they were necessarily sent to Bathurst by Small from London.

122. On the instruction of the commissioner of police (H. L. Webley), Small's baggage was certainly searched on his return to Gambia and his passport temporarily detained, but there is no evidence from surviving Gambian government files that anything else was seized (and Small did not complain that it had been). See GA C1250/1929, Small to Colonial Secretary, November 25, 1930; Small to Acting Colonial Secretary, September 3, 1931; and GA C1308/1930, minute by Webley, June 12, 1930; minute by Receiver General, November 25, 1930. The view of the French consul in Bathurst (Orcel) was outlined in SA 17G/58, enclosure to Consul, Bathurst, to Governor-General, French West Africa, December 1, 1930.

123. See GA 1250/1929; and GA S116 I/1930, minute by Webley, March 12, 1931.

124. See C1553/1932, Bridgeman to Cunliffe-Lister, January 28, 1932, for Small's perspective.

125. The incident is discussed in CO 87/230/8; and GA C1308/1930.

126. Perfect, "Organised Labour," 66–67, citing GA C1206/1929, Macklin to Colonial Secretary July 20, 1930. For other examples of government hostility to the GFCMA, see GA S140/1931; and GA CF13/1930.

127. See GA S140 I/1934, Oke to Cunliffe-Lister, March 29, 1934, cited by Langley, *Pan-Africanism*, 138.

128. Wilson, *Russia and Black Africa*, 242–43; 277; and Langley, *Pan-Africanism*, 138.

129. See Perfect, "E. F. Small," 75–76; and Perfect, "Organised Labour," 65–66 (who cites specific examples of Small's appeals to the LRDept and LAI).

130. GA S135/1933, Rendall to Secretary, Parliamentary Conservative Party, December 22, 1932. On Rendall, see Perfect, "Organised Labour," 83–98; GA S2502A I/1943, minute by Wilkinson, January 5, 1943; and GA S135/1933, report by Webley, June 2, 1932. Further information on his background was from Rev. J. C. Faye (Perfect interview, Banjul, September 1984).

131. Forster's appointments meant that an unofficial member of the Legislative Council was in receipt of a position of profit. This caused the Colonial Office some disquiet, but was permitted because of Forster's conspicuous service to the government. For details, see CO 87/228/20. See also the acting governor's address to the Legislative Council in CO 89/23, Leg. Co. Minutes, July 9, 1940.

132. *GO*, October 18, 1930, contains a list of the GRC members who signed a "welcome address" to Governor Palmer. On the Carrols, see GA 237/1941; and Macmillan, *Red Book*, 293. Further information was provided by Sam Goddard (Perfect interview, Banjul, April 1992). Carrol's role in WASU is discussed by S. K. B. Asante, *Pan-African Protest: West Africa and the Italo-Ethiopian Crisis, 1934–1941* (London: Longman, 1977), 48. Other WASU pioneers included J. B. Danquah.

133. GA C1526/1921, minute by Palmer, September 22, 1930; and GA C1476/1931, minute by Palmer, January 18, 1932. See also CO 87/231/11, Palmer to Passfield, November 25, 1930; and CO 87/237/7, Palmer to Passfield, May 6, 1931. For the response of the Colonial Office, see CO 87/231/11, minute by Fiddian, December 18, 1930; Passfield to Palmer, January 20, 1931.

134. GA 818/1930, minute by Assistant Colonial Secretary, January 31, 1931; GA 81/1, Minutes of the Bathurst Urban District Council (hence BUDC Minutes), March 16, 1932; and GA 707/1933, N'Jai-Gomez to Colonial Secretary, January 9, 1935. A total of 551 votes were cast in the 1931 election. For opposing views of Senegal's politics, see *GO*, May 14, 1932; and GA S135/1933, Palmer to Cunliffe-Lister, January 10, 1933. See also Grey-Johnson, "Newspaper in The Gambia," 24–25. A plaque in Dobson Street Methodist

Church, Banjul (noted by Perfect in May 1992) commemorates Allen. Little is known about, the victor in Half Die in 1931, R. J. Hall.

135. Forster's reappointment is discussed in GA C1477/1931. In a letter to the colonial secretary dated February 1, 1932, he expressed a wish to retire. But he was persuaded to stay on by the members of the Gambia Representative Committee as Forster to Palmer, February 6, 1932, makes clear.

136. For a full discussion of the dispute, see Perfect, "Organised Labour," 79–87. See also C1685 I/1933, especially Small to Cunliffe-Lister, July 19, 1933 (and enclosures).

137. GA S135/1933, memo by Horne, June 16, 1932. The appointment of the committee, which consisted of the police magistrate, S. J. Forster, and M. J. R. Pratt, was announced in *GG* on May 16, 1932. On the debate over the codes, see GA S135/1933; CO 87/235/10; and issues of *GO*, May 21–July 2, 1932.

138. Wyse, *Krio of Sierra Leone*, 86. At a public meeting in Bathurst, Ladepon-Thomas (Small's solicitor) reminded his audience of this resistance. See GA S135/1933, report by Webley (Commissioner of Police), June 2, 1932; and note 104.

139. *GO*, May 21, 1932. The same arguments were constantly reiterated in the press and in petitions over the next few months.

140. The first public meetings, held on May 21 and May 23, allegedly attracted 500 and 2,000 people respectively; see GA S135/1933, Rendall to Colonial Secretary, June 9, 1932. Wyse, *Bankole-Bright*, 125, states that a Committee of Citizens was established in Freetown in 1938.

141. Having at first declined to attend the public meetings, the councilors later did so in order to criticize the campaign. See GA S135/1933, Rendall to Colonial Secretary, June 9, 1932; GA 665/1932, report by Sub-Inspector A. K. John, July 11, 1932; and GA 81/1, BUDC Minutes, June 15, 1932. For press and public criticisms of the Legislative and BUDC councilors, see *GO*, May 28–August 13, 1932. On the Gold Coast response, see Crowder, *West Africa Under Colonial Rule*, 458.

142. GA 665/1932, Rendall to Colonial Secretary, July 25, 1932; and GA S135/1933, Rendall to Colonial Secretary, June 9, 1932. See Kimble, *History of Ghana*, 451–55; and Kilson, "National Congress," 583, on the establishment of other ratepayers' associations for electoral purposes.

143. An estimate of the number of persons on the rating list can be taken from the number of eligible voters in 1934 (GA 635/1934). In the six constituencies, there were 1,663 voters, most of whom, it can be assumed, were ratepayers rather than government employees.

144. The first chairman of the RPA was S. E. J. Thomas (a tailor); Rendall was secretary. Other committee members included Eustace Richards (a former justice of the peace, who had been a founding member of the Congress in 1920); Bai Ceesay (a prominent member of the BTU); Matarr Mboge (a Muslim who supported the Jahumpa party in the intra-Muslim conflict); and Edward Lloyd-Evans (a Mulatto clerk). See GA 665/1932, report by Sub-Inspector John, August 3, 1932. Unflattering descriptions of some of these individuals are in GA S135/1933, report by Webley, June 2, 1932. See also GA S116 I/1930, minute by Webley, January 9, 1931. On Richards, see also note 121.

145. According to Edward Lloyd-Evans, the Committee of Citizens was founded in 1931 and organized the RPA; see *GE*, October 15, 1951. Rendall served as its secretary in 1932–33, a role later filled by Small. See GA S135A/1933, Rendall to Acting Colonial Secretary, November 10, 1933 (and enclosure); and GA C2077/1936, Small to Thomas, April 23, 1936.

146. GA S135/1933, Palmer to Cunliffe-Lister, January 10, 1933; minute by Parish, October 20, 1932.

147. These ordinances are discussed in CO 87/236/19; CO 87/237/7; CO 87/237/8; and CO 87/238/5; see also GA S135/1933. The most important sources are the despatches

from Governor Palmer: CO 87/237/8, Palmer to Cunliffe-Lister, January 10, 1933; Palmer to Cunliffe-Lister, March 3, 1933; and CO 87/237/7, Palmer to Cunliffe-Lister, February 28, 1933. On the Protectorate legislation, see also Gailey, *History*, 126–32 (126).

148. For details, see CO 87/236/19, minutes by Pedler, December 19, 1931; February 28, 1933; CO 87/237/7, Palmer to Cunliffe-Lister, February 28, 1933 and enclosures; minute by Pedler, April 10, 1933; and CO 87/237/8, Palmer to Cunliffe-Lister, January 10, 1933. See also CO 89/23, Leg. Co. Minutes, November 9, 1932; and *WA*, January 21, 1933, 37.

149. CO 87/230/8, Rendall to Cunliffe-Lister, February 25, 1933; Palmer to Cunliffe-Lister, March 3, 1933; minute by Pedler, April 1, 1933; minute by Hazelrigg, June 12, 1933. A complaint by the RPA that rate defaulters had been harshly treated was also ignored. See GA S135/1933, Rendall to Cunliffe-Lister, October 25, 1932; and CO 87/230/8, Palmer to Cunliffe-Lister, January 10, 1933; Cunliffe-Lister to Pickering, February 27, 1933.

150. For Small's reaction to the ordinance see his letter to the Secretary of the Labour Research Department, W. H. Williams, November 18, 1932; this can be found in the Bathurst Trade Union file, Labour Research Department archives, London. Not surprisingly, Small complained that the new tax was a political and fiscal measure, a view that some officials in the Colonial Office shared; see CO 87/236/19, minute by Pedler, December 19, 1931. See also *GO*, June 9, 1934; and GA C1308/1930, minute by Palmer, March 11, 1932, which described Small as "down and out."

151. Perfect, "Organised Labour," 69–70, discusses the differing response to the despatch of the four British West African Governments. No Trade Union Ordinance was enacted in Nigeria until 1938; in Sierra Leone until 1939; and in the Gold Coast until 1941.

152. Perfect, "Organised Labour," 84–88, provides a detailed analysis. See also C1685 I/1933, especially Small to Cunliffe-Lister, July 19, 1933.

153. The election results are in GA 1187/1932. N'Jai-Gomez's two opponents (J. J. Oldfield and J. F. Senegal) received a grand total of seven votes between them. Governor Palmer interpreted this result as a major setback for the RPA on the grounds that Senegal had "some connection with Small." See GA S135/1933, Palmer to Secretary of State, January 10, 1933. The quote is from Small to Registrar-General, June 10, 1933 (an enclosure to this document). But this seems unlikely (see note 134) and it appears that the RPA did not nominate any candidates until 1933.

154. The process is discussed in CO 87/237/6, Palmer to Cunliffe-Lister, March 22, 1933. See also GA 81/1, BUDC Minutes, March 17, 1933; GA 665/1932, petition of the Elected Members of the Bathurst Advisory Town Council (BATC), April 1938; and GA C1476/1931, minute by Palmer, January 18, 1932.

155. The results are in GA 707/1933. Two other Committee of Citizens candidates, Ousman Jeng and the Rev. H. Newman Hunter, withdrew from the contest, perhaps after the RPA decided to allow the other three incumbents one more year to mend their ways. See CO 87/237/9, petition from Small et al., December 14, 1933; and S135A/1933, report by Sub-Inspector John, December 6, 1933. See note 144 on Lloyd-Evans.

156. For details of the councilors' interventions and the RPA's protests, see GA S135/1933, Rendall to Parish, November 9, 1933; Rendall to Acting Colonial Secretary, November 21, 1933; Small et al. to the Privy Council, December 12, 1933 (and enclosures); CO 87/238/2, Parish to Fiddian, November 27, 1933; minute by Maclennan, February 6, 1934; and CO 87/237/9, Parish to Fiddian, December 20, 1933; Parish to Cunliffe-Lister, December 21, 1933. See also CO 89/23, Leg. Co. Minutes, December 5, 1933; December 12, 1933.

157. Grey-Johnson, "The Newspaper in The Gambia," 25–26, gives details of the establishment of the *Gambia Echo* and lists the members of the syndicate; he suggests, however, that the purpose of the newspaper was to investigate the local Church and the Gambian

government and to monitor the behavior of expatriate officials, rather than to counter the RPA.

158. The election results are in GA 635/1934. On Carrol's conduct, see *GO*, December 22, 1934; on the contest in New Town, see GA 635/1934, Cole to Commissioner of Police, December 18, 1934. See also *GO*, November 10–December 22, 1934, especially December 22, 1934.

159. See Asante, *Pan-African Protest*, 112–19; CO 87/239/6, minute by Roberts-Wray, December 6, 1934; CO 87/240/11, Cunliffe-Lister to Parkinson, February 28, 1935; GA 707/1933, N'Jai-Gomez to Colonial Secretary, January 9, 1935; and *GO*, November 10, 1934. Asante states that economic factors also played a part in the 1935 Gold Coast election.

160. On the yellow fever outbreak, see CO 87/239/15; CO 87/240/5; GA 683/1934; and GA C1898/1935. Prickett, *Island Base*, 201–3, contains an account of the epidemic by one of the European Methodist missionaries, J. J. Baker. Four Europeans (including the colonial secretary, G. C. B. Parish) died of yellow fever, but there was only one African fatality.

161. On the establishment of the BATC, see GA 301/1935; GA C1951/1935; CO 87/240/10; and CO 89/23, Leg. Co. Minutes, May 21, 1935.

162. See GA C1769/1934, Small to Oke, January 27, 1934; *GO*, May 25, 1935; June 1, 1935; GA 301/1935, Rendall to Richards, May 18, 1935; and GA S135A/1933, minute by Parish, January 10, 1934.

163. GA 82/1, BATC Minutes, June 30, 1936; *GO*, May 23–June 20, 1936; and *GE*, June 1, 1936; June 8, 1936.

164. See GA 214/1939, Acting Governor Oke, minute of May 17, 1939, who noted that there had been no contested elections since 1936. On the 1940–43 elections, see GA 12840/1940; and *GO*, June 7, 1941; May 30, 1942; May 22, 1943; May 29, 1943. The process of selection of candidates is described in *GO*, May 16, 1936; June 27, 1936; November 28, 1942.

165. *GO*, October 12, 1935; and GA C1268/1929, minute by Sub-Inspector John, September 30, 1935. On the reconciliation between the two men (and Small's role in achieving it), see *GO*, October 5–November 9, 1935.

166. GA C1268/1929, minutes by Webley and Clark, September 30, 1935. See also minute by Assheton, January 18, 1936, in which it is stated that Jeng had been elected supervising manager of the Mohammedan School by the Board of Management, defeating Fye by four votes to one. Cham-Joof, "Banjul Mosque" notes that Sowe ceased to be Almami in 1937.

167. On the unpopularity of Fye, see GA C1268/1929, minute by Webley, September 30, 1935. For criticisms of both reappointments, see *GO*, July 31, 1937.

168. GA 82/1, BATC Minutes, March 29, 1938; and GA 665/1932, Lloyd-Evans et al. to Colonial Secretary, April 7, 1938. See also CO 87/253/4, Southorn to Moyne, December 3, 1941. On Southorn, see Hughes and Gailey, *Historical Dictionary*, 169–70.

169. CO 87/251/6, Small to MacDonald, May 10, 1940; and CO 89/23, Leg. Co. Minutes, April 23–May 7, 1940. See also *GE*, April 1–May 20, 1940; *GO*, March 9–April 27, 1940; and CO 87/253/4, Southorn to Moyne, December 3, 1941. See also Tamuno, *Nigeria and Elective Representation*, 44; Martin Wight, *The Gold Coast Legislative Council* (London: Faber and Faber, 1947), 30; and on Sierra Leone, Hargreaves, "Approaches to Decolonisation," 88–89, who states that Jardine also had reservations about income tax.

170. CO 267/655/11, report by Turbett, September 18, 1936 (enclosure to Blood to Ormsby-Gore, September 20, 1936).

171. GA S23840/1940; GA 237/1941; and *GE*, July 15, 1940. There was some discussion that Forster might be replaced by his brother, Thomas, a groundnut dealer, but this came to nothing. See GA C1526/1921, minute by Plant, February 21, 1941.

Chapter 5

1. William Tordoff, *Government and Politics in Africa* (Basingstoke: Macmillan, 1984), 63–64. See also Thomas Hodgkin, *African Political Parties: An Introductory Survey* (Harmondsworth: Penguin Books, 1961), Chapters 3 and 4, on the evolution and typologies of political organizations.

2. See Hodgkin, *African Political Parties*, 68–75, for the distinction between "elite" ("patron") and "mass" parties; and Christopher Clapham, *Third World Politics: An Introduction* (London: Croom Helm, 1985), 54–59, for a concise discussion of "patron-clientage" in the politics of African and other Third World countries.

3. GA 581/1923, minute by Plant, January 8, 1941. Southorn received no criticism for this decision, even from Small, as *GO*, March 8, 1941, makes clear.

4. CO 87/253/4, Southorn to Moyne, December 3, 1941; and GA 82/1, BATC Minutes, November 13, 1941. Editorials in *GO*, January 4, 1941; April 26, 1941; May 31, 1941, demonstrate Small's attitude toward the war. On Riley, see also *GO*, June 27, 1936 (where he is described as the RPA Treasurer); GA 635/1934; and his obituary notice in *GO*, August 17, 1946.

5. CO 87/253/4, Southorn to Moyne, December 3, 1941. Mahoney is not mentioned as supporting the various RPA petitions of the 1930s, nor was he a member of the RPA Executive in 1936 (*GO*, June 27, 1936). However, his half-brother, L. S. Mahoney, was a RPA councilor in 1935–36, before being forced to retire through ill health. On the elder Mahoney, see *GO*, December 22, 1934; June 27, 1936; May 7, 1938.

6. CO 87/253/4, Southorn to Moyne, March 4, 1942. The only other Muslim worthy of consideration was a government official and thus ineligible, although Southorn did hope that suitable younger Muslims might be available in a few years' time.

7. CO 87/253/5, Ward to Stanley, February 18, 1943 (a despatch approved by Blood). See also CO 87/253/4, Southorn to Moyne, December 3, 1941; and CO 87/260/2, Blood to Hall, April 16, 1946. On the situation elsewhere in West Africa, see John D. Hargreaves, "Toward the Transfer of Power in British West Africa," in *The Transfer of Power in Africa*, ed. Prosser Gifford and Wm. Roger Louis (New Haven, CT: Yale University Press, 1982), 117–40; Pearce, *Turning Point*, 76–85; and Richard Crook, "Decolonization, the Colonial State and Chieftaincy in the Gold Coast," *African Affairs* 85, no. 338: (1986), 75–105. Blood is profiled in Hughes and Gailey, *Historical Dictionary*, 41–42.

8. [Gambia Government], *Report of the Committee on the Legislative Council Franchise* (SP no. 2 of 1944) (Bathurst: Government Printer, 1944); CO 87/256/1, Blood to Stanley, February 28, 1944; and CO 89/30, Leg. Co. Minutes, April 25, 1944. See also CO 87/253/5, Ward to Stanley, February 10, 1943, on Fye.

9. CO 87/256/1, Blood to Stanley, May 11, 1944; Blood to Gater, September 13, 1944; Stanley to Blood, December 11, 1944; minute by Williams, August 1, 1944. In a minute dated October 20, 1944, the Secretary of State, Lord Stanley, termed universal suffrage for Gambia "a rather foolish proposal." He accepted it because the Colonial Office was already in dispute with Blood over other matters and did not wish to add a fresh issue to the list.

10. CO 89/30, Leg. Co. Minutes, October 29, 1942; April 22, 1943; January 18, 1944; January 25, 1944; September 22, 1945; June 25, 1946; November 12, 1946. See also CO 87/258/13; CO 87/259/1; and GA 109/1943.

11. The Faal case is described in GA C2709B/1946; and CO 87/260/7.

12. *GE*, May 28, 1945, provides the first reference to the two organizations. The People's Party is also mentioned in Langley, *Pan-Africanism*, 351; and *GO*, October 20, 1945.

13. The founding date of the BYMS is given as August 1936 in *GO*, May 24, 1941; and Nyang, "Gambian Political Parties," 103. See also *GE*, July 5, 1937. Its revival as a political organization is noted in *GO*, May 11, 1946; June 8, 1946; June 29, 1946. See also GA S179/1938, minute by Superintendent of Police, June 18, 1946; and *West African Pilot*, May 29, 1946. The developments in Nigeria are noted by Tordoff, *Government and Politics*, 65–66.

14. Garba-Jahumpa's early career is outlined in *WA*, "The Gambia's First Minister?" December 12, 1953; and Sulayman S. Nyang, "Ibrahim Garba-Jahumpa, 1912–1994," *WA*, September 12–18, 1994, 1581. The appointments are noted in *GE*, June 12, 1941; June 8, 1942. See also Hughes and Gailey, *Historical Dictionary*, 82–84. Further information from Garba-Jahumpa (Perfect interview, Banjul, June 1984).

15. On the establishment of the GLU and the background to the conference, see Perfect, "Organised Labour," 88–108; Allen, "African Trade Unionism," 405–9; and Hughes and Perfect, "Trade Unionism," 557–58. It is an indication of how official attitudes toward Small had changed from the 1930s that the Gambian government was prepared to subsidize his visit to London; see GA A350/1944.

16. The dispute is discussed in Perfect "Organised Labour," 108–10; and Langley, *Pan-Africanism*, 349–50. See also GA S3008/1945. On the conference, see Langley, *Pan-Africanism*, 347–57: and George Padmore, ed., *History of the Pan-African Congress*. 2nd ed. (London: The Hammersmith Bookshop, 1963). On Downes-Thomas, see also Grey-Johnson, "The Newspaper in The Gambia," 26–27.

17. On the split between Nkrumah and Danquah, see Bankole Timothy, *Kwame Nkrumah—From Cradle to Grave* (Dorchester: Gavin Press, 1981), 40–53.

18. For details of Wallace-Johnson's visit to Bathurst, see Asante, *Pan-African Protest*, 195–96.

19. See Asante, *Pan-African Protest*, 111, on the WAYL appeal to Muslims. It was initially announced that the BYMS intended to form a "Moslem League," but this was later denied by Garba-Jahumpa; see *GO*, May 11, 1946; June 8, 1946; and GA S179/1938, minute by Commissioner of Police, June 18, 1946.

20. As stated in Chapter 4, 164, there had been no contests at all between 1937 and 1942. One seat was fought in 1943 and two in 1944 (*GO*, May 22, 1943; May 29, 1943; May 13, 1944; June 3, 1944), but the RPA's opponents were apparently Independents. No election took place in 1945.

21. On the BTC, see CO 87/259/7; see also CO 89/30, Leg. Co. Minutes, June 25, 1946; July 2, 1946. The estimate of the size of the electorate is in CO 87/259/7, Blood to Creech Jones, October 23, 1946.

22. CO 87/259/7, Blood to Creech Jones, October 23, 1946. Small also disliked the fact that civil servants were allowed to stand for election. See CO 89/30, Leg. Co. Minutes, April 25, 1944; July 2, 1946. Blood concluded that Small's stance proved that he was a "reactionary."

23. The background to the election and the results may be found in various issues of *GO*, July 20–October 26, 1946. See also "Bathurst at the Polls," *West African Review*, December 1946, 1367–68; and CO 87/259/7, Blood to Creech Jones, October 23, 1946. On Kuye and Gibbs, see also *GO*, November 28, 1942; December 5, 1942; July 20, 1946.

24. The BYMS' relatively unsuccessful performance was in contrast to the much stronger showing made by the various youth movements of British West Africa in the 1930s. The Nigerian Youth Movement won all three Lagos seats in the 1938 Legislative Council election and a by-election in Lagos in 1940. The West African Youth League's candidate won the 1935 Gold Coast Legislative Council election and the Sierra Leone Youth League swept the board in the Freetown municipal election in 1938. For details, see Tamuno, *Nigeria and Elective Representation*, 84–90; and Asante, *Pan-African Protest*, 112–14; 198.

25. Hughes and Perfect, "Trade Unionism," 558, citing Elliot J. Berg and Jeffrey Butler, "Trade Unions," in *Political Parties and National Integration in Tropical Africa*, ed. James S. Coleman and Carl G. Rosberg (Berkeley: University of California Press, 1964), 362. On the GATU, see Perfect, "Organised Labour," 111–14.

26. There were more than 4,000 enlisted Gambians in August 1945 when World War II ended; the majority of these were in the army. See GA 2/2832.

27. See Wright, *The World and a Very Small Place*, 211. The ordinance can be found in CO 87/259/11. In [Gambia Government], *Annual Report on the Labour Department 1946* (SP no. 3 of 1947) (Bathurst: Government Printer, 1947), 3, the Labour Officer noted that out of 4,000 demobilized servicemen, 1,500 had registered under the Ex-Servicemen Ordinance.

28. CO 87/256/1, Creasy to Blood, March 1, 1945; Stanley to Ward, March 18, 1945; and CO 87/260/2, Hall to Blood, April 4, 1946; minute by Williams, April 30, 1946. The Order-in-Council, dated November 29, 1946, may be found in CO 87/256/3.

29. Wright succeeded Sir Hilary Blood in January 1947 following the latter's promotion to be governor of Barbados. Wright, who had previously been colonial secretary of Trinidad, is profiled in Hughes and Gailey, *Historical Dictionary*, 182; see also CO 850/207/3. His proposals for the Executive Council are outlined in CO 87/260/2 and summarized in Chapter 2, 46.

30. *GO*, October 25, 1947, lists the candidates in 1947. Finden Dailey was sentenced to a seven-year jail sentence in 1919 for misappropriating the property of deceased persons when in government employment (he was the curator's agent of interstate estates). He was released in 1922 and made an appeal for a free pardon in 1936; but this was rejected, and so he remained a felon. In Nigeria, Herbert Macaulay was imprisoned and permanently barred from political office for a similar offence (the Mary Franklin Estate case). On Finden Dailey, see GA 84/43; see also Grey-Johnson, "The Newspaper in The Gambia," 26; and CO 87/209, Cameron to Secretary of State, March 25, 1919 (and enclosed report by J. L. Fenton, January 21, 1919). On the Mary Franklin case, see Tekena N. Tamuno, *Herbert Macaulay, Nigerian Patriot* (Ibadan: Heinemann, 1975), 17.

31. *GO*, October 19, 1946; October 18, 1947, provide the BTC election results. Finden Dailey had opposed the anti-codes campaign of the 1930s and supported the introduction of income tax in 1940. See his letter to *WA*, September 17, 1932, 978; and CO 87/251/6, Oke to Lloyd, August 20, 1940 (noting the stance of the *Gambia Weekly News*). There is no indication that the RPA functioned after 1946.

32. "New Constitution for the Gambia," *Crown Colonist*, October 1947, 558. The correspondent was probably a colonial official.

33. See Chapter 1, tables 1.5 and 1.9; see also [Gambia Government], *Census Report, 1951*, on religious affiliation in Kombo St. Mary.

34. *GO*, October 25, 1947; and *GE*, August 27, 1945. In addition, Fye had recently been awarded the OBE, *Crown Colonist*, August 1947, 444, which further increased his prestige (*Crown Colonist*, August 1947, 444). Bah served as Almami between 1937 and 1953; see Cham-Joof, "Banjul Mosque."

35. For example, Small was described as a recluse in the Gambian Political Report for April 1948; see CO 537/3651.

36. Perfect, "Organised Labour," 114; and Tamuno, *Nigeria and Elective Representation*, 86–88.

37. See CO 87/259/7, Blood to Creech Jones, October 23, 1946; and [Colonial Office], *Annual Report of the Gambia*, 1947, 3, on the number of registered voters in the two elections. Appendix table B.1 gives the full results. These may be found in *GO*, November 1, 1947. See Kilson, "National Congress," 583, on the 1924 Sierra Leone election. In the Lagos election of 1923, there were approximately 4,000 persons on the electoral list and 1,649 votes were cast; in Accra in 1927, 780 out of the 1,816 registered electors voted. See Tamuno, *Nigeria and Elective Representation*, Appendix B; and Kimble, *History of Ghana*, 452.

38. *GO*, October 25, 1947, lists Small's nominees. As noted in Chapter 2, 50, M'Bye was appointed to the Legislative Council after the election.

39. Perfect, "E. F. Small," 72.

40. That Small should be elected because he had gained the franchise was certainly argued before the 1951 election; see *GO*, October 6, 1951.

41. *Crown Colonist*, August 1947, 444. In 1942–43, Fye made a determined attempt to get the internal banishment of Alhaji Salim Jaite of Njaba Kunda, North Bank Province, reversed. See GA C2371A/1942.

42. Interviews by Perfect with Garba-Jahumpa (Banjul, June 1984) and Sam Goddard (Banjul, April 1992) and by Hughes with Goddard (Banjul, February 1977).

43. *Crown Colonist*, December 1947, 669, notes the nonregistration of farmers; see Perfect, "Organised Labour," 115, on Small's alleged support from the Kombo chiefs.

44. Perfect, "Organised Labour," 119; and GA L1/1947, Minutes of the Labour Advisory Board, August 1949. Further information from Garba-Jahumpa (Perfect interview, Banjul, June 1984).

45. CO 87/266/2, Wyn-Harris to Griffiths, May 18, 1950; Wyn-Harris to Cohen, August 18, 1950; Griffiths to Wyn-Harris, September 9, 1950.

46. CO 87/266/2, Cohen to Wyn-Harris, August 9, 1950; Wyn-Harris to Cohen, August 18, 1950; Cohen to Wyn-Harris, September 1, 1950.

47. CO 87/266/1, Wyn-Harris to Gorsuch, May 9, 1951; Griffiths to Officer Administering the Government, Gambia, August 4, 1951; and *The Gambia News Bulletin* (*GNB*), August 17, 1951.

48. On Faye's early career, see "The Gambia's Amiable Example," *WA*, May 30, 1952, 803; Jones, *Diocese of Gambia and the Rio Pongas*, 49–51; Nyang, "Gambian Political Parties," 97 (who notes Faye's mixed origin); and Perfect, "Organised Labour," 117–18. Further information from A. M. Camara (Hughes interview, Banjul, December 1997). His appointment to the Executive Council is discussed in CO 87/260/2, Wright to Creech Jones, September 27, 1947. On the establishment of Kristikunda, see also John Laughton, *Gambia: Country, People and Church in the Diocese of Gambia and the Rio Pongas*, 2nd ed. (London: SPG, 1949), 37–40.

49. See GA 12840/1940; and GA 56/1941. Most accounts (e.g., *WA*, "The Gambia's Amiable Example") wrongly assume that he represented both wards simultaneously. In an interview with Perfect (Banjul, June 1984), Faye stated that he was persuaded to stand for election in 1940 by Eustace Richards, one of Small's leading supporters in the early 1930s. On Richards, see Chapter 4, notes 121 and 144.

50. Nyang, "Gambian Political Parties," 91, gives the date of the foundation of the GDP as February 1951, but *GE*, September 10, 1951, makes it clear that the new party was not officially established until June (although it had been building up support since February). See Perfect, "Organised Labour," 117–20, on the MDMU, which at the height of its fortunes claimed to represent 662 drivers, of whom 338 were dues payers.

51. Nyang, "Gambian Political Parties," 96–101, analyzes the GDP's membership. See also CO 554/536, Ward to Rowland, November 17, 1951; additional information from Faye (Perfect interview, Banjul, June 1984). According to Nyang (91), Faye was persuaded to stand for election by Muslim dignitaries.

52. On Senegal's original election to the BUDC, see GA 818/1930; see *GO*, October 19, 1946; October 8, 1949, for his more recent successes. A former editor of the *Gambia Echo* (*GE*, October 8, 1945), he was described as an auctioneer in *GNB*, October 15, 1951.

53. On N'Jie's background, see Hughes and Gailey, *Historical Dictionary*, 132; see also "P. S. N'Jie," *WA*, May 3, 1958, 411. Details of his career up to 1943 can be found in CO 87/260/8, N'Jie to Creech Jones, May 13, 1949. N'Jie was described as being of part Jola descent in CO 554/2623, "Biographical Notes of Gambia Government Delegates," July 1964.

54. Full details of the case can be found in CO 87/260/8; see especially N'Jie to Creech Jones, May 13, 1949; N'Jie to Sorensen, August 24, 1949. Roberts apparently fathered a child by one of N'Jie's nieces and "set his eyes" on a Gambian woman whom N'Jie wished to marry.

55. CO 87/260/8, Creech Jones to Wyn-Harris, February 15, 1950.

56. Roberts was later transferred to Uganda. In 1949, he was serving a jail sentence for taking bribes, which gave further credence to N'Jie's allegations; see CO 87/260/8, N'Jie to Creech Jones, May 13, 1949; Governor's Deputy to Secretary of State, December 19, 1949. See also Chapter 4, note 40, which notes that Small's accuser, J. L. McCallum, was later dismissed from government service.

57. *GE*, September 10, 1951; October 22, 1951. A more cynical interpretation of the support Roman Catholics gave to N'Jie was that he made a handsome donation to their building fund; see *GE*, October 8, 1951. An indication of his good relations with Muslims was that although P. S. N'Jie converted to Catholicism around 1929, he nevertheless served as honorary secretary of the BYMS in 1937; see *WA*, "P. S. N'Jie," May 13, 1958; and *GE*, July 5, 1937.

58. On the links between Colley and the BTU, see Perfect, "Organised Labour," 118; see also the *Gambia Weekly News*, September 5, 1951; September 11, 1951 (both issues can be found in CO 554/536) on Finden Dailey's campaign. The 1951 BTC election results are in *GE*, October 22, 1951. Colley and Finden Dailey were apparently the only candidates to fight on a common platform, but because the former was a Muslim and the latter a Catholic, they were effectively seeking support from different sections of the population.

59. Perfect, "Organised Labour," 117–18. Further information from Garba-Jahumpa (Perfect interview, Banjul, June 1984).

60. Perfect, "E. F. Small," 74; and Perfect, "Organised Labour," 119. The Africa Conference is reported in full in CO 879/152; the protests against the transfer of Wright are in CO 87/260/1.

61. The comment about Madi is in CO 554/250, Wyn-Harris note for Lyttleton, June 7, 1952. Wyn-Harris (Hughes interview, Woodbridge, April 1974) considered that Madi was "the most powerful man in the Gambia." Paul Gore, the Financial Secretary and subsequently chief secretary to the government of Gambia in the early 1960s (Hughes interview, Woodbridge, February 1992), thought Madi might have become involved in politics through Garba-Jahumpa, but ended up financing all groups. Another former senior colonial official (colonial secretary), Kenneth Smith (Hughes interview, Sherborne, August 1985), also believed Madi backed all African political groups in his time. Madi's unexpected death in 1965 at the relatively early age of fifty-two, brought to an end the Madi family's direct involvement in Gambian politics, although his younger brothers, Joseph and Robert (Bobby), served successively as "nominated" MPs from the mid-1960s to the early 1970s. See Hughes and Gailey, *Historical Dictionary*, 117.

62. See CO 554/536, Ward to Rowland, November 17, 1951 (which lists the occupations of the candidates). A. M. Camara (Hughes interview, Banjul, December 1997) stated that the Semega-Jannehs were Mauritanian, not Gambian, Serahulis; certainly, they appear to have had few links with the indigenous Serahuli of the Upper River Division. B. M. Tarawale described Semega-Janneh as a Wolofized Serahuli (Hughes interview, Latrikunda, December 1999).

63. Full results are in Appendix table B.2. These may be found in *GNB*, October 26, 1951. See also *GO*, October 27, 1951; *GE*, November 5, 1951; and [Gambia Government], *Revision of Electoral Machinery Committee Report, 1953* (hence *Spurling Report*) (SP no. 4 of 1953) (Bathurst: Government Printer, 1953).

64. CO 554/536, Ward to Rowland, November 17, 1951; and Perfect, "Organised Labour," 117–21. Soon after the election, the MDMU fell into abeyance. In an interview

with Perfect (Banjul, September 1984), Faye claimed that the union was undermined by Garba-Jahumpa, who successfully persuaded pro-GMC drivers that it had only been established to promote Faye's political career. The union ceased to function until its revival by Kebba N'Jie in 1962. On the importance of griots in Gambian elections in the 1950s, see also Price, "Women in Gambian Politics," 154.

65. *GNB*, October 15, 1951, lists the GDP's candidates and their sponsors. On M. M. N'Jie, see "Momodou Musa N'Jie," *WA*, August 13–19, 1990, 2272; and Rice, *Enter Gambia*, 215–18.

66. *GE*, September 10, 1951; September 24, 1951, outline the GDP's policies.

67. See GA 84/266, "Election Campaigns 1951."

68. His adoption of a star and crescent reinforced his Islamic identity. In contrast, Faye chose a snake, Small a fish, and N'Jie a lion (his Wolof clan totem). Symbols were normally selected from an official list. See *GG*, October 15, 1951.

69. CO 554/536, BYMS manifesto of August 8, 1951; BYMS release of August 29, 1951; Ward to Rowland, November 17, 1951. See also *GNB*, October 15, 1951. On the GATU's winding up, see Perfect, "Organised Labour," 115–16.

70. *GNB*, October 15, 1951, on Jeng's endorsement of N'Jie; Jeng, of course, supported Small in 1947. Press reports indicate that N'Jie ignored the constitution in his pre-election speeches. As noted by Grey-Johnson, "The Newspaper in The Gambia," 27–28, N'Jie was a member of the syndicate that administered the *GE* and a friend of its editor, Lenrie Peters (not be confused with Lenrie Peters, the doctor and poet).

71. CO 554/536, Ward to Rowland, November 17, 1951; Clark to Williamson, September 24, 1951 (which encloses the GNL manifesto). On Small's campaign, see *GE*, October 8, 1951; October 15, 1951. See *GO*, January 27, 1951, for Small's endorsement of the constitution.

72. Perfect, "E. F. Small," 74–77. Interestingly, Wyn-Harris (Hughes interview, Woodbridge, April 1974) was completely unaware of the existence of government files on Small's radical past, remembering him as a very cooperative old man.

73. See Hughes, "Green Uprising" 67–70. The Aku maintained a political foothold in Central Bathurst/Banjul, until 1982. A comparison may be drawn between the Aku and the Creoles (or Krio, as Wyse prefers) of Sierra Leone under the Margais and Siaka Stevens. Wyse argues that the Krio remained influential under Sir Milton Margai, but lost ground under both Albert Margai and Stevens, so that, by the start of the 1980s, the civil service was no longer a bastion of Krio power. See Wyse, *Krio of Sierra Leone*, 115–20; and John R. Cartwright, *Political Leadership in Sierra Leone* (London: Croom Helm, 1978), 172–75. On the 1957 Sierra Leone election, see Cartwright, *Politics in Sierra Leone*, 96–97. Wyse, *Krio of Sierra Leone*, 107, examines the effect on the Krio of the NCSL's defeat.

74. CO 554/250, notes of meeting between Wyn-Harris and Colonial Office officials, October 9, 1952.

75. CO 554/250, Wyn-Harris to Lyttleton, May 22, 1953. An enclosure to this despatch contains the names of the committee's members; the two non-Africans were Henry Madi and C. L. Page, the former manager of the United Africa Company. Gailey, *History*, 188, states erroneously that all the members of the Consultative Committee were ex-members of the Executive and Legislative Councils; in fact, only half a dozen were. Four Protectorate chiefs attended the first two meetings as observers, but played no further role.

76. Report of the Consultative Committee, *GG*, July 31, 1953. Wyn-Harris regarded the single vote device as a way to ensure Christian representation on the council; see CO 554/250, Wyn-Harris to Lyttleton, May 22, 1953.

77. *GG*, July 31, 1953, includes the exchanges of despatches between Governor Wyn-Harris and the secretary of state. See also "New Constitution for the Gambia," *WA*, August 8, 1953, 724; and CO 554/251, Gorell Barnes to Wyn-Harris, November 14, 1953; Gorell Barnes to Wyn-Harris, December 17, 1953.

78. St. Clair Joof was elected in New Town East in the 1946 BTC election, but resigned in January 1948; see *GO*, October 19, 1946; January 31, 1948. He represented the hitherto obscure Gambia People's Party; the first known reference to this party is in *GNB*, March 20, 1954, when St. Clair Joof was stated to be its candidate.

79. On the GMC, see Nyang, "Gambian Political Parties," 101–9; and Sulayman S. Nyang, "Local and National Elites and Islam in The Gambia: An African Case Study," *International Journal of Islamic and Arabic Studies* 1, no. 2: (1984), 57–67. See also *The Hibarr* (the GMC's newspaper) (January 1954); *GE*, December 3, 1951; September 1, 1952; and *GNB*, August 17, 1954.

80. The conflicting accounts are in Gailey, *Historical Dictionary*, 125; and Andria J. Fletcher, "Party Politics in The Gambia," (Ph.D. diss., University of California at Los Angeles, 1979), 72. The Intelligence Report may be found in CO 554/250. The first known contemporary reference to the UP is in *GNB*, June 19, 1954.

81. On the UP's support, see Nyang, "Gambian Political Parties," 110–25; see also Senghor, "Senegambian Integration," 179 (note 121); and Price, "Women in Gambian Politics," 155. Yayi Kompins were the mothers ("yayi") or heads of neighborhood associations ("kompins"). They were used by the GDP as well as the UP, although not as successfully; the GDP even had a "Yayi Partibi" (mother of the party)—Ya Fatou Manneh. See Nyang, "Gambian Political Parties," 96 (and footnote 11); 113–17.

82. Full results are in Appendix table B.3. These may be found in *GNB*, October 20, 1954. On the registration system, see "The Gambia's General Election," *WA*, November 6, 1954, 1036; and [Gambia Government], *Spurling Report*. See also CO 89/33, "Report of the Chief Superintendent of the Gambia Police Force for the Year 1954."

83. Fletcher, "Party Politics," 72–73 (who also suggests that the overwhelming majority of first-time voters supported N'Jie, but without producing any evidence for the statement); Price, "Women in Gambian Politics," 155; and CO 554/1217, minute by Vile, December 6, 1954.

84. Wyn-Harris noted in 1958 that "Larger sums than [£5 per head] in bribes were reported at the last General Election"; see CO 554/1513, "Note for Windley." For the GDP view, see their memorandum on the constitution, which forms an enclosure to Smith to Lennox-Boyd, May 17, 1958, in the same file. See also CO 554/1217, minute by Vile, December 6, 1954, on N'Jie's land transactions.

85. Fletcher, "Party Politics," 71, stresses the importance of this factor. N'Jie is named as a member of the Consultative Committee in CO 554/250, Wyn-Harris to Lyttleton, May 22, 1953.

86. Faye's financial affairs are discussed in CO 554/422; see especially Waddell to Williamson, March 21, 1953; Wyn-Harris to Lyttleton, 31 October 1953.

87. The incident is analyzed in detail in CO 554/250; and CO 554/422. The governor's assessment of the deputation is in CO 554/422, Wyn-Harris to Gorell Barnes, July 10, 1952. See also "Rev. Faye Asked to Resign," *WA*, July 19, 1952, 659; and "The Governor, the Bishop and the Rev. John Faye," *WA*, August 2, 1952, 705. Further information was supplied to Perfect by Right Rev. R. N. Coote in November 1997.

88. CO 554/422, Wyn-Harris to Secretary of State, August 16, 1952. Further information from Right Rev. R. N. Coote, November 1997.

89. CO 554/422, Garba-Jahumpa to Wyn-Harris, July 1, 1952. Sam Goddard stated (Perfect interview, Banjul, April 1992) that Garba-Jahumpa was generally blamed for causing Faye's downfall.

90. "Mr Faye's Complaint," *WA*, October 17, 1953, 962; letter from Faye to *WA*, October 17, 1953, 971. See also CO 554/251, Wyn-Harris to Gorell Barnes, November 14, 1953; CO 554/422, Wyn-Harris to Lyttleton, October 31, 1953; Lyttleton to Wyn-Harris, November 23, 1953; and *GE*, December 7, 1953.

91. CO 554/422, Wyn-Harris to Gorell Barnes, July 5, 1952. Ken Smith (Hughes interview, Sherborne, August 1985), wryly observed that Garba-Jahumpa was always surrounded by young female "assistants."

92. On Garba-Jahumpa's support for the new constitution, see *WA*, "The Gambia's First Minister?," December 12, 1953. Senghor, "Senegambian Integration," 153, states that Garba-Jahumpa was known as Wyn-Harris' "man."

93. CO 554/801, Wyn-Harris to Secretary of State, November 10, 1954. Further information from S. Goddard (Perfect interview, Banjul, April 1992).

94. See Appendix table B.3; and *GNB*, October 20, 1954, for the results. *WA*, "The Gambia's General Election," November 6, 1954, gives the turnout. Further information on Oldfield from Rev. J. C. Faye (Perfect interview, Banjul, September 1984).

95. See CO 554/1513, "Note for Windley," for details of those elected in 1954. This secret memo prepared by Wyn-Harris on the eve of his departure from Gambia forms an enclosure to Wyn-Harris to Eastwood, April 13, 1958. On M'Baki, see Hughes and Gailey, *Historical Dictionary*, 121–22; CO 554/2279, "Gambia Constitutional Conference 1961"; and CO 554/2623, "Biographical Notes of Gambia Government Delegates." See also "Gambia's Progressive Chief," *WA*, April 8, 1961, 369; and Jay Saidy, "Omar Mbacke as Chief among Chiefs was the Kingmaker in 1962," *The Point*, September 15, 1994. (This alternative spelling of M'Baki has often been used.)

96. The successful candidates are listed in CO 554/1513, "Note for Windley." See also CO 554/2051, Smith to Eastwood, July 8, 1959. Details of the process by which the BTC and Kombo Rural Authority arrived at the list of candidates are in *GNB*, October 29, 1954; October 30, 1954.

97. The selection process is discussed in CO 554/801, Wyn-Harris to Secretary of State, November 4, 1954. His earlier opposition to the appointment of a third minister is in CO 554/250, Wyn-Harris to Secretary of State, May 20, 1952. The ministerial portfolios are given in full in *WA*, December 4, 1954, 1143.

98. See Hodgkin, *African Political Parties*, Chapter 4, for the characteristics of "mass" parties.

99. The best example of this process is provided by Nigeria where there were also three major parties. The shifting set of alliances between the parties are analyzed by Coleman, *Nigeria: Background to Nationalism*; and Kenneth W. J. Post and Michael Vickers, *Structure and Conflict in Nigeria, 1960–1966* (London: Heinemann Educational, 1973). There were similar developments in the Gold Coast after the emergence of the Convention People's Party; see Dennis Austin, *Politics in Ghana, 1946–1960* (London: Oxford University Press, 1964).

100. *GE*, October 10, 1955; October 17, 1955; November 14, 1955.

101. The affray and its aftermath is discussed in detail in [Gambia Government], *Report of a Commission Appointed to Inquire into the Conduct of the Gambia Police Force in Connection With an Affray Which Took Place in Bathurst on 16th October, 1955* (hence *Baker Report*) (SP no. 15 of 1955) (Bathurst: Government Printer, 1955). See especially the report by the attorney general of his meeting with N'Jie on October 18 and N'Jie's letter to the Superintendent of Police, October 20, 1955. See also CO 554/1218; and CO 1037/46.

102. [Gambia Government], *Baker Report*. See also Wyn-Harris's address to Leg. Co., December 22, 1955, which was reprinted in *West African Review*, February 1956, 169–70; and CO 1037/46.

103. Full details of the process are in CO 554/1218; and CO 1037/46. Hughes and Gailey, *Historical Dictionary*, 132; and Nyang, "Gambian Political Parties," 111, both state inaccurately that N'Jie resigned. Fletcher, "Party Politics," 73–75, maintains that the clash between N'Jie and Wyn-Harris came about because of the determination of the former to improve conditions in Bathurst, but provides no evidence for her contention.

104. CO 554/1513, "Note for Windley." The charge that Garba-Jahumpa engineered the whole affair was accepted by Fletcher, "Party Politics," 74, on the basis of interviews with P. S. N'Jie and a former GMC member, M. S. Ceesay.

105. The election results are in October 22, 1956; over 1,400 votes were cast in the constituency, compared with 1,259 in 1953. Wyn-Harris also believed that Garba-Jahumpa lost much popularity; see CO 554/801, minute by Godden, December 13, 1956, reporting on a meeting between Wyn-Harris and officials at the Colonial Office.

106. On developments in Ghana and Sierra Leone, see Austin, *Politics in Ghana;* and Cartwright, *Politics in Sierra Leone,* 103–22. The impact of West African events on Gambia was acknowledged by Wyn-Harris; see CO 554/1513, "Note for Windley."

107. CO 554/801, minute by Godden, December 13, 1956.

108. The two sets of proposals may be found in CO 554/1513 as enclosures to Smith to Lennox-Boyd, May 7, 1958. In his "Note for Windley," Wyn-Harris made clear their similarities, but added that the GDP's were the more carefully thought out.

109. See CO 554/1513, "Note for Windley."

110. This was the view of Henry Oliver, who was a senior member of the Protectorate administration at the time (Hughes interview, Bakau, September 1973). Perhaps it was fitting that Wyn-Harris left from up river for, according to Oliver, he was happiest there, unlike other governors who seldom ventured beyond Brikama, where he was far removed from Bathurst and its political turmoil. CO 89/39, "Police Report, 1958," describes the official ceremonies that did take place. See also CO 554/1967, "Annual Report of the Secretary of State to Parliament" (for 1957) on the earlier announcement of Wyn-Harris' retirement.

111. See Hughes and Gailey, *Historical Dictionary,* 181, on Windley's background.

112. CO 879/189, Windley to Eastwood, November 13, 1958, contains a report of the Brikama Conference and the "All Party Constitutional Proposals"; see also Michael Crowder, "Chiefs in Gambia Politics: I," *WA,* October 18, 1958, 987; and Michael Crowder, "Chiefs in Gambia Politics: II," October 25, 1958, 1017. On the Georgetown Conference, see CO 879/189, Windley to Eastwood, February 27, 1959, and on the Bathurst Conference, [Gambia Government], *Record of the Constitutional Conference Held from the 6th to 11th March, 1959 With His Excellency the Governor's Opening Address* (SP no. 3 of 1959) (Bathurst: Government Printer, 1959). The discussions were also widely covered in the local press. GA 9/284, contains useful additional information on the background and proceedings of the Brikama and Georgetown Conferences. *GE,* June 30, 1958, reports Windley's arrival in Gambia.

113. The resolution forms another enclosure to Smith to Lennox-Boyd, May 7, 1958. See also Senghor, "Senegambian Integration," 153–54.

114. On the GNP's origins and leaders, see *GE,* August 5, 1957; and Michael Crowder, *Pagans and Politicians* (London: Hutchinson, 1959), 37–38. See also Michael Crowder, "The Gambian Political Scene," *WA,* November 2, 1957, 1035; Fletcher, "Party Politics," 75–76 (who gives a date of January 1956 for the party's foundation); CO 554/1518, Windley to Eastwood, October 27, 1959; CO 554/1513, Gambian Intelligence Reports for March and October 1958; and CO 879/189, Windley to Eastwood, November 13, 1958. On Foon, see also Hughes and Gailey, *Historical Dictionary,* 70 (which incorrectly gives his date of birth as 1902, not 1923); and CO 554/2623, "Biographical Notes of Gambia Government Delegates." Further information from M. B. Jones (Hughes interview, Banjul, April 1975).

115. For example, at a public meeting in February 1958, Samba accused Windley of sowing enmity between the Colony and the Protectorate; Jones criticized the fact that expatriates were given loans to buy cars and also denounced the role played by Garba-Jahumpa as minister of agriculture. See CO 554/1513, Gambian Intelligence Report, March 1958. In July 1958, an expatriate dentist sued Bidwell-Bright for libel for comments in *The Vanguard,* but the case was dismissed (see issues of May 17, 1958; July 12, 1958; July 19, 1958); nevertheless,

Jones was dismissed as editor. One GNP leader, K. W. Foon, stood in the 1956 BTC election as an Independent, but no candidates were put forward in 1957 or 1958.

116. CO 554/1513, Wyn-Harris to Lennox-Boyd, March 17, 1958; Smith to Lennox-Boyd, May 17, 1958 (and enclosure). See also Gambian Intelligence Report for March 1958 (in the same file), which reports that N'Jie had accused Garba-Jahumpa in the previous month of breaking the agreement.

117. GA 9/284, Record of Meeting of Chiefs' Conference, Brikama, February 21, 1958; M'Baki to Senior Commissioner, May 20, 1958. The chiefs also petitioned Governor Wyn-Harris for an increase in Protectorate membership of the Legislative Council; the petition dated February 19, 1958 is in the same file. Subsequently, the draft agenda for the October 1958 Brikama Conference included an item, "to form the Gambia Protectorate Party," but this was later deleted, and was not discussed at the conference.

118. Crowder, "Chiefs in Gambia Politics: I," on his speech at Brikama; see *GE*, February 9, 1959 for his position at Georgetown.

119. CO 554/1513, Wyn-Harris to Lennox-Boyd, March 17, 1958, notes that it was known in the Protectorate that Garba-Jahumpa had been little involved with agricultural development since 1954.

120. Garba-Jahumpa supported the UP/GDP line that candidates should be able to stand anywhere, whereas the chiefs insisted that the Protectorate should be represented by its own men only. See [Gambia Government], *Constitutional Conference 1959*; and CO 879/189, Windley to Eastwood, March 24, 1959.

121. The results are in *GNB*, October 16, 1957; and *GE*, October 20, 1958; see also Crowder, "Gambian Political Scene," for a discussion of the 1957 election. It is unclear if A. B. N'Jie stood in 1958 for the GDP or as an Independent (as in 1955).

122. CO 554/1518, record of the meeting with Lennox-Boyd, June 5, 1959, which forms an enclosure to Windley to MacLeod, November 3, 1959.

123. On the demonstration, see Perfect, "Organised Labour," 160. Further details are in CO 554/1518; and CO 879/189, Windley to Eastwood, June 15, 1959. See *WA*, June 15, 1959, 569 on the demonstration in Freetown.

124. CO 554/1518, record of the meeting with Lennox-Boyd, June 5, 1959. See also Cartwright, *Politics in Sierra Leone*, 67–86; and Austin, *Politics in Ghana*, 250–315.

125. [Gambia Government], *Constitutional Conference 1959*.

126. [Gambia Government], *Constitutional Developments, 1959*. See also CO 879/189, Eastwood to Windley, May 4, 1959; Windley to Lennox-Boyd, May 7, 1959; minute by Carter, August 6, 1959.

127. CO 879/189, Windley to Lennox-Boyd, May 7, 1959. See also Windley to Eastwood, November 13, 1958; Windley to Eastwood, March 24, 1959, in the same file.

128. [Gambia Government], *Constitutional Conference 1959*; and [Gambia Government], *Constitutional Developments, 1959*. The decision over candidates in the Protectorate was something of a compromise; initially the chiefs wished only those of Protectorate birth to be able to stand for election outside the Colony. See CO 879/189, Windley to Eastwood, November 13, 1958; Windley to Eastwood March 24, 1959; Windley to Eastwood, May 7, 1959, for the debate over this issue.

129. CO 879/189, Windley to Eastwood, March 24, 1959; Windley to Eastwood, May 7, 1959. The Colonial Office shared Windley's opinion as CO 554/1513, Eastwood to Windley, April 13, 1959, makes clear.

130. CO 879/189, Windley to MacLeod, December 3, 1959.

131. The Committee members are given in *GE*, November 2, 1959. On the political position of the GWU at this time, see Perfect, "Organised Labour," 159–61.

132. The petitions form enclosures in CO 554/1518, Windley to Eastwood, October 27, 1959; Windley to MacLeod, November 3, 1959. See also MacLeod to Windley, November 20, 1959 in the same file.

133. Senghor, "Senegambian Integration," 165. See also CO 554/1518, Windley to Eastwood, October 27, 1959; Windley to Macleod, November 3, 1959; *The Vanguard*, September 26, 1959; October 24, 1959 (letter from J. D. Cole); and *GE*, July 11, 1960 (article by Samba). On the N'Jie case, see Senghor, "Senegambian Integration," 209; and CO 554/1872.

134. CO 879/189, Windley to Eastwood, June 15, 1959.

135. The election result is in *GNB*, October 16, 1959. For the governor's interpretation of the outcome, see CO 554/1518, Windley to Eastwood, October 27, 1959.

136. M. B. Jones, who was elected as an Independent in 1960, declared for the UP immediately afterward; and K. W. Foon was on the UP Executive Committee in the early 1960s and represented the UP at the 1964 Constitutional Conference in London. J. W. Bidwell-Bright probably joined the GDP. See CO 879/189, Windley to Eastwood, June 17, 1960; CO 554/2623; Nyang, "Gambian Political Parties," 123; and Perfect, "Organised Labour," 165.

137. See Cartwright, *Politics in Sierra Leone*, 55–63, on the origins of the SLPP.

Chapter 6

1. Samuel P. Huntington, *Political Order in Changing Societies* (New Haven, CT: Yale University Press, 1968), sets out the concept of "Green Uprising" (433–34) and the characteristics of a "ruralizing election" (459–60). See also Hughes, "Green Uprising."

2. At least three Armitage graduates (Sheriff Sisay, Sheriff Dibba, and Jerreh Daffeh) were elected for the PPP in 1960, and three others (Kalilou Singhateh, Lamin M'Boge, and Kuti Sanyang) were elected in 1962; all except Sanyang, who was a Jola, were Mandinka. See CO 554/2623, "Biographical Notes of Gambia Government Delegates"; and [Africa Books], *Africa Who's Who*, 3rd ed. (London: Africa Books, 1996), 208. Further information from B. M. Tarawale (Hughes interview, Bathurst, 1972).

3. Sir Dawda Jawara provides the best example of this process.

4. See PPP, *The Voice: The Story of the PPP 1959–1989* (Banjul: Baroueli, 1992), 9; and three articles by Sheriff Bojang, "Sanjally Bojang: An Encounter With a Living Legend," *WO*, March 31–April 2, 1995; "Sanjally Bojang Passes Away," *Daily Observer*, October 24, 1995; and "Sanjally Bojang: When the Darling of the Gods Die [*sic*] Old," *WO*, October 27–29, 1995. Further information from Sanjally Bojang and Sheriff Sisay (Hughes interviews, Kembuje, February 1972 and Banjul, September 1973). See also Perfect, "Organised Labour," 180, note 53. The Arabic spelling of Bojang's society varies in the sources.

5. See also Nyang, "Gambian Political Parties," 121, on N'Jie. That he remained loyal to the UP is indicated by his signature of the UP Memorial of June 24, 1960, which is in CO 554/2147.

6. G. H. Smith, "Study of Social and Economic Conditions in the Western Division," 1. [Gambia] Confidential Paper no. 1, August 22, 1955. This can be found in Rhodes House Library, Oxford, in the Gerald H. Smith MSS Afr. 1022 PA/203 collection.

7. Smith, "Social and Economic Conditions," 2.

8. On the origins of the PPS and its key figures, see PPP, *Voice*, vii; 10–11; further details are in GA 9/284. On Farimang Singhateh, see also Hughes and Gailey, *Historical Dictionary*, 162–63. Further details from B. K. Sidibeh and A. M. Camara (Hughes interviews, Banjul,

September 1973 and December 1997). On Sidibeh, Sagnia, M. F. Singhateh, and Fofana, see also *GG*, June 16, 1958; April 30, 1960; July 30, 1960; March 15, 1962.

9. On M'Boge, see [Gambia Government], *Members of the Government October 1984* (Banjul: Government Printer, 1984). On Sisay, see Hughes and Gailey, *Historical Dictionary*, 163–64; "The Gambia's Number Two," *WA*, October 31, 1964, 1219; and CO 554/2623, "Biographical Notes of Gambia Government Delegates." On Seyfu M'Boge and Koba Leigh, see also S. A. Bakarr, *The Gambia Yesterday: 1447–1979* (Banjul: Gambia Press Union, 1980), 22; *GG*, June 11, 1966; David P. Gamble, *The South Bank of The Gambia: Places, People and Population*, 3 vols. (Brisbane, CA: Gamble and Rahman, 1996), vol. A, 60b; vol. B, 20; and CO 554/1513, "Note for Windley." Further information on Leigh from Tarawale and Sidibeh; Hughes interviews (Bathurst/Banjul, 1972–73).

10. PPP, *Voice*, 10. For example, M'Boge was born in 1932 and Sisay in 1935. There were a number of exceptions to this: Sagnia (who retired on pension from the Medical and Health Department in May 1960) and Sanyang were apparently regarded as the "elders" of the group; Leigh was born around 1907 and Farimang Singhateh in 1912. See notes 8 and 9 for sources on M'Boge, Sagnia, Sisay, and Singhateh; and *WA*, September 4, 1978, 1768, on Leigh.

11. M. B. Sagnia, Sidibeh, M'Boge, Sisay, Leigh, and Farimang Singhateh were certainly all Mandinka (as were probably most of the other members). See Nyang, "Gambian Political Parties," 245; further information from B. M. Tarawale (Hughes interview, Latrikunda, December 1999). According to Sheriff Sisay (Hughes interview, Banjul, September 1973), the Mandinka were better educated than the other predominantly rural ethnic groups, which would help to explain their predominance within the PPS.

12. PPP, *Voice*, 11–18; see also an article by one of the GNP leaders, Henry Joof, in *The Vanguard*, November 8, 1958, which expresses strongly anti-Protectorate sentiments. As noted in Chapter 5, 120, a not dissimilar protest had been organized against the transfer of Wyn-Harris's predecessor, Andrew Wright, in 1949. As recently as early October, the PPS secretary, Sheriff Sisay, had informed the colonial authorities that Bojang should not represent the PPS at the Brikama Conference as he was not a member of it; see GA 9/284, Sisay to Oliver, October 3, 1958.

13. Because the PPS was a society and not a party, it was only granted observer status at the Brikama Conference in October 1958. It was allowed to send one delegate (Leigh) to the Georgetown Conference in January 1959, but the Bathurst parties complained to the colonial secretary about this decision. See GA 9/284, note of the meeting between the colonial secretary and the Bathurst political leaders, February 2, 1959. Sheriff Sisay also emphasized that the constitutional talks served as a catalyst for the establishment of the ProtPP (Hughes interview, Banjul, September 1973).

14. The PPS' representative at Basse, Leigh, was not, however, permitted to address the chiefs because he only had observer status at the conference. See PPP, *Voice*, 18–19; see also GA 9/284, Bojang to Oliver, February 6, 1959; Oliver to Bojang, February 9, 1959.

15. On the early support of the Protectorate chiefs, see PPP, *Voice*, 27; and Hughes, "Green Uprising," 65.

16. PPP, *Voice*, 18–25. Further information from Sanjally Bojang (Hughes interview, Kembuje, February 1972).

17. On Jawara's early life and career, see "Gambian Leader," *WA*, January 21, 1961, 61; Hughes and Gailey, *Historical Dictionary*, 98–100; Rice, *Enter Gambia*, 135–36; Sulayman S. Nyang, "Sir Dawda Kairaba Jawara," in *Political Leaders of Contemporary Africa South of the Sahara: A Biographical Dictionary*, ed. Harvey Glickman (Westport, CT: Greenwood Press, 1992), 95–96; and CO 554/2623, "Biographical Notes of Gambia Government Delegates." Further information from Jawara (Hughes interview, Haywards Heath, August 1998), who

claimed that only Aku boys received full scholarships. Jawara's original Mandinka name was Kairaba. Kwesi is a Ghanaian name, which dated from his period at Achimota; Dawda is the Arabic equivalent of David.

18. Apparently Mahoney and other members of his family objected to the proposed marriage on religious grounds; these objections were overcome by Jawara's timely conversion to Christianity. See FO 371/181861, Scragg to Duff, May 12, 1965, which forms an enclosure to Peck to Brown, May 19, 1965. The expediency of Jawara's conversion was also noted by Rev. R. N. Coote (information supplied to Perfect, December 1997). On Augusta Jawara, see also *WA*, "Gambian Leader," January 21, 1961. As he noted in his interview with Hughes (August 1998), Jawara changed his name to David Kwesi when he converted to Christianity.

19. The election of the party leader is discussed in PPP, *Voice*, 23–25; and Hughes, "Green Uprising," 68–69. See CO 554/2148, Paul to Maudling, June 7, 1962, on Sisay. Bojang, "Sanjally Bojang: An Encounter With a Living Legend," suggests that Marenah withdrew from the contest.

20. *GNB*, April 19, 1960.

21. PPP, *Voice*, 28–39, lists a number of the PPP candidates, but examines the selection process in detail in only one constituency (Basse). The recollections of the European commissioner of the URD, R. T. Addis, provide further insights into the process. See "Groundnut Stew—Gambia: Recollections of the First General Election 1960" (1963). ADDIS MSS Afr. s 2129, Rhodes House Library, Oxford.

22. Sidibeh also later claimed (Hughes interview, Banjul, September 1973) that the local chief (presumably Koba Leigh) feared that if Sidibeh were elected, he would seek to replace him with his own father (Sidibeh's grandfather was a chief).

23. On Dibba's background, see Hughes and Gailey, *Historical Dictionary*, 59–60; "Guardian of the Gambia's Finances," *WA*, December 6, 1969, 1477; Rice, *Enter Gambia*, 279; and Peter da Costa, "An Obsessive Disciplinarian," *WA*, April 16–22, 1990, 615.

24. On the political role of civil servants in the 1960 election, see CO 879/183, Colonial Office Brief No 2B for the July 1961 Constitutional Conference. Gambia had the same policy as Kenya with regard to civil servants standing for election. On Dabo and Daffeh, see CO 554/2148, Paul to Secretary of State, June 15, 1962. Further information from B. M. Tarawale (Hughes interview, Bathurst, 1972).

25. For the PPP view of Baldeh's chicanery, see PPP, *Voice*, 37–39; see also Bojang, "Sanjally Bojang: An Encounter with a Living Legend." An official view is in CO 554/2147, enclosure to Windley to Eastwood, June 1, 1960; and CO 554/2153, Officer Acting as Governor of Gambia to Secretary of State, July 4, 1960. CO 554/2147, UP Memorial to Secretary of State, June 27, 1960, reports the alleged view of Governor Windley that Baldeh was previously a member of the GDP.

26. Interviews by Hughes with Sanjally Bojang and B. M. Tarawale (Kembuje and Bathurst, 1972). See also Hassoum Ceesay, "Author of the PPP/UP Coalition Government 1965," *WO*, December 6–8, 1996; and Gamble, *North Bank*, vol. C, 100. On Yaya Ceesay, see [Gambia Government], *Members of the Government*; [Friedrich Ebert Stiftung], *African Biographies: Gambia* (Bonn: Verlag Neue Gesellschaft, c. 1974); and Ebrima Sillah, "Yaya Ceesay Before Public Assets Commission," *New Citizen*, February 17, 1995. Yaya Ceesay was born in 1937, so was twenty-two or twenty-three at the time of the election. According to Bojang, "Sanjally Bojang: An Encounter With a Living Legend," however, the choice of Daffeh (and Momodou Sanyang in Foni) was at first unacceptable to the chiefs.

27. [Gambia Government], *Census Report, 1963*, Table 12, gives the ethnic breakdown of the Gambian population of Soldier Town in 1963. Demba's previous employment (in the Department of Agriculture) was noted in *The Vanguard*, May 14, 1960. He was previously a

policeman, as noted in CO 89/39, "Police Report, 1960." As early as 1946, two Aku women, Hannah Forster and Cecilia Davies, were elected to the Bathurst Town Council in Soldier Town ward; see *GO*, October 19, 1946.

28. PPP, *Voice*, 39, states that there were only two PPP candidates in the Colony, but *The Vanguard*, May 14, 1960, lists Able-Thomas as a PPP candidate. That Able-Thomas was sympathetic to the PPP in this period is confirmed by PPP, *Voice*, 35. According to Sir Dawda Jawara (Hughes interview, Haywards Heath, August 1998), Able-Thomas stood as an Independent for tactical reasons.

29. Our assessment is largely based on Nyang, "Gambian Political Parties," 140; 225–27; and on information from A. M. Camara and B. M. Tarawale (Hughes interviews, Banjul, December 1997 and Latrikunda, December 1999). Dabo was regarded as a Serahuli by both Nyang and Governor John Paul (CO 554/2148, Paul to Maudling, June 7, 1962); however, Tarawale informed Hughes in 1972 that Dabo was the grandson of the famous Fula warrior, Musa Molloh, but possibly by a Mandinka or a Serahuli mother. Sanyang was described as a Mandinka by Tarawale and may be considered to have been a "Mandinkanized" Jola.

30. This was J. L. B. Daffeh, who had been jailed for misappropriating public funds when serving as a district treasurer; see CO 554/2148, Paul to Maudling, June 7, 1962. Further information from B. M. Tarawale (Hughes interview, Bathurst, 1972).

31. CO 554/2147, Smith to M. B. N'Jie, June 28, 1960, argued that the total vote of all the candidates who declared for the UP before the election was just over 6,000. The combined vote of its five candidates in the Colony (who were listed as UP supporters in *The Vanguard*, May 14, 1960), together with A. N. Touray (Niani-Saloum) was 6,320.

32. *GE*, October 9, 1959, gives the BTC election results; for further details on these candidates, see also *The Vanguard*, May 14, 1960; *GNB*, October 1, 1959; and Nyang, "Gambian Political Parties," 122. On E. D. N'Jie, see also Hughes and Gailey, *Historical Dictionary*, 131; *GE*, February 17, 1958; and CO 554/2623, "Biographical Notes of Gambia Government Delegates."

33. The Wolof made up 36 percent of the Gambian population of Niani-Saloum in 1963 (including 53 percent of the Gambian population of the Saloum part of the constituency). See *Census Report, 1963*, Table 12. That Touray was definitely a UP candidate is confirmed by the official results cited in CO 554/2147, Windley to Eastwood, June 1, 1960.

34. See letter from M. B. N'Jie to *GE*, July 11, 1960. Baldeh was described in the official results as a UP candidate; see CO 554/2147, Windley to Eastwood, June 1, 1960. On his links to the UP, see also PPP, *Voice*, 37–39, which argues that Baldeh was financially dependent on Alhaji Saihou N'Jie, a local trader associated with P. S. N'Jie. Darbo was listed as a UP supporter in a letter from E. D. N'Jie to *GE*, May 29, 1961, and described as a UP candidate by A. M. Camara (Hughes interview, Banjul, December 1997). See also Rice, *Enter Gambia*, 110–15; and Alice Bellagamba, "Entrustment and Its Changing Political Meanings in Fuladu, The Gambia (1880–1994)," *Africa* 74, no. 3 (2004), 399, for more information on Darbo.

35. Our assessment of the ethnic origins (and religious persuasion) of these candidates is based on Nyang, "Gambian Political Parties," 122, and information from Camara (Hughes interview, December 1997). In CO 554/2623, "Biographical Notes of Gambia Government Delegates," E. D. N'Jie was said to be a Jola, but we have followed Nyang's assessment. According to Sanjally Bojang (Hughes interview, Kembuje, February 1972), N'Jie's mother was a Jola.

36. See letter from M. B. N'Jie to *GE*, July 11, 1960; CO 554/2147, Smith to N'Jie, June 28, 1960; and (on Jones' links with the UP), CO 554/2147, Windley to Eastwood, June 1, 1960.

37. Camara stated that he received support, but not financial assistance, from the UP in 1960 (Hughes interviews, Banjul, November and December 1997). He was described as an

Independent (supporting UP) in the official results; see CO 554/2147, Windley to Eastwood, June 1, 1960. Ceesay was listed as a member of the UP in a letter from E. D. N'Jie to *GE*, May 29, 1961. According to Camara, Biyai and Juwara were UP candidates in 1960; the former was the UP candidate in Western Foni in 1962 and the latter the UP candidate in Wuli in 1966. Dabo contested Eastern Jarra for the UP in 1966 (see Appendix tables C.1–C.3). It is difficult to decide which candidate in Niumi-Jokadu, the UP supported. PPP, *Voice*, 42, states that the seat was won by the UP, which would make L. O. Sonko the UP candidate. Although we think this is incorrect—Sonko was described in the official results as an Independent—it perhaps indicates that he received some UP support in the campaign.

38. *GE*, April 25, 1960, lists the office holders in the new party.

39. *The Vanguard*, May 14, 1960, lists the DCA candidates in the Colony. *GE*, April 25, 1960, gives its office holders. On N'Jie, see also Hughes and Gailey, *Historical Dictionary*, 131; and CO 554/2623, "Biographical Notes of Gambia Government Delegates." On Sallah, see also Rice, *Enter Gambia*, 255–56. According to Governor Windley, there were DCA candidates in all seven Colony seats; see CO 554/2147, Windley to Eastwood, May 17, 1960. If his assessment was at least partially correct, then the DCA must have supported Oldfield.

40. Other sources suggest that the DCA did have candidates in some Protectorate constituencies. PPP, *Voice*, 39, states that the DCA contested "very few" seats there, and Gailey, *History*, 217 (Appendix VII), argues that the DCA won 11 percent of the Protectorate vote. Senghor, "Senegambian Integration," 201 (note 8), outlines Faye's intentions. Faye later claimed (Hughes interview, Banjul, April 1975) that the DCA won Kantora and Niumi-Jokadu through Andrew Camara and L. O. Sonko respectively, but this can be discounted.

41. This is based on Nyang, "Gambian Political Parties," 97, and additional information from A. M. Camara (Hughes interview, Banjul, December 1997).

42. CO 554/2147, Windley to Eastwood, May 17, 1960.

43. Both Burang-John and Gaye were listed as leading members of the GMC in the 1950s by Nyang, "Gambian Political Parties," 108. CO 554/2051, Smith to Eastwood, July 8, 1959, notes that Gaye was a founding member of the GMC and he was certainly still the GMC general secretary in 1959 (see the GMC manifesto in *GE*, September 14, 1959). Burang-John was elected to the BTC for the GMC; see *GNB*, October 7, 1957; October 16, 1957. See also *The Vanguard*, May 14, 1960, on their backgrounds.

44. On Camara's background, see Hughes and Gailey, *Historical Dictionary*, 47; [Africa Books], *Africa Who's Who*, 310–11; and [Friedrich Ebert Stiftung], *African Biographies: Gambia*. Further information from Camara (Hughes interviews, Banjul, November and December 1997).

45. B. M. Tarawale (Hughes interview, Banjul, May 1992), noted that the three sons of Jewru Krubally stood for election in 1960. See also CO 554/1513, "Note for Windley," on Muhammadou Krubally, the candidate in Basse. Jammeh was listed as "K. B. Janneh" in the results in *GNB*, May 24, 1960; see also Gailey, *History*, 211, on Sonko. That the chiefs put forward their own candidates is also suggested by *GE*, December 5, 1960; and "Role of the Chiefs in the Gambia," *New Commonwealth*, January 1961, 54.

46. See GA 9/284, Commissioner, MacCarthy Island Division to Senior Commissioner, September 26, 1959.

47. For example, according to Tordoff, *Government and Politics*, 65, the Union Progressiste Mauritanienne and the Union Démocratique Tchadienne received such strong official backing that they were known as "partis de l'Administration."

48. In the Gold Coast, for example, several prominent trade union leaders were elected to the Legislative Assembly on the Convention People's Party ticket; see Jon Kraus, "The Political Economy of Industrial Relations in Ghana," in *Industrial Relations in Africa*, ed. Ukandi G. Damachi, H. Dieter Seibel and Lester Trachtman (London: Macmillan, 1979), 130–31.

49. CO 554/2498, Windley to Eastwood, February 29, 1960, reporting conversations between Jallow and other GWU leaders, the colonial secretary, and Henry Madi. A full account of the rise of the GWU and the 1960 strike is in Perfect, "Organised Labour," 129–41.

50. Hughes and Perfect, "Trade Unionism," 559–60. Sources agree that most rank and file union members were either UP or GMC (DCA) supporters at this time (although they disagree which party had the most union support). Some GWU leaders were also known to be supporters of either the UP or GMC, although Jallow was himself on close terms with leading PPP members, particularly Lamin M'Boge. See Fletcher, "Party Politics," 76–77; Senghor, "Senegambian Integration," 184; and Perfect "Organised Labour," 161–64. The other main trade union, the Gambia Labour Union, whose leaders supported different parties, also remained neutral during the election; see Perfect, "Organised Labour," 165–66.

51. CO 554/2147, Windley to Eastwood, June 1, 1960. For a detailed account of the "drum and marble" method, see Marion Foon, "Operation Ping-Pong to Beat Votes Fiddlers," *Journal of African Administration* 13, no. 1 (1961), 35–37. The system was invented by the colonial secretary, Ken Smith, and the attorney general, Lionel Weston, and was jokingly known as the "Smith and Weston," a play on the American Smith and Wesson handgun (Smith interview with Hughes, Sherborne, August 1985).

52. See CO 89/39, "Police Report, 1960," 5; and *GNB*, Election Supplement, May 14, 1960. Further information from Sanjally Bojang (Hughes interview, Kembuje, February 1972). On the violence in the Gold Coast and Nigeria, respectively, see Austin, *Politics in Ghana*, 316–62; and Kenneth W. J. Post, *The Nigerian Federal Election of 1959: Politics and Administration in a Developing Political System* (London: Oxford University Press, 1963).

53. Full results are given in Appendix table C.1. These may be found in *GNB*, June 24, 1960. *The Vanguard*, June 4, 1960; and CO 554/2147, Windley to Eastwood, June 1, 1960, provide partial results. According to PPP, *Voice*, 29, the only likely opponent of Jawara, E. Ngorr Sarge, a trader from Bwiam and a former nominated member of the Legislative Council, failed to turn up. On Ngorr Sarge, see CO 554/1513, "Note for Windley."

54. The inadequacy of the registers was later admitted by the colonial secretary, Duncan Sandys. See *The Times*, May 29, 1963, 6. See also the background note on the electoral registers case, which was prepared for the 1964 Constitutional Conference in FO 371/176512. On the turnout in the Colony and Protectorate, see CO 554/2147, Windley to Eastwood, June 1, 1960; and Gailey, *History*, 217.

55. Gailey, *History*, 197–98, suggests that the PPP won eight seats, the UP six, the DCA three, and two were won by Independents. Fletcher, "Party Politics," 94, argues that the PPP won eight seats, the UP seven, the DCA one and Independents three. The least accurate assessment is "General Election in the Gambia," *New Commonwealth*, July 1960, 468, which gave the UP victory with eight seats to the PPP's five, with six Independent successes. An earlier assessment by Perfect, "Organised Labour," 14, was that the PPP won ten seats, the UP six, the DCA one, and Independents two. But one Independent candidate was incorrectly described as a PPP supporter and it is now our view that Jones should be regarded as an Independent candidate.

56. Senghor, "Senegambian Integration," 400, cites the initial report in the *GNB*, June 2, 1960, that 62,604 votes were cast and provides a breakdown by party. The final results were published in *GNB*, June 24, 1960. The PPP final share of the vote was lower than that recorded initially in *GNB*, because Michael Baldeh's 4,561 votes have been reallocated to the UP. Presumably in the initial account, some pro-UP Independents were counted as UP candidates, which would explain why its final vote was also lower.

57. See CO 554/2147, Windley to Eastwood, May 17, 1960. See also Addis, "Groundnut Stew," 13; *WA*, "Gambian Leader," January 21, 1961; and PPP, *Voice*, 30–31. In an interview

with Hughes (Haywards Heath, August 1998), Jawara emphasized the superior organization of the PPP as a key factor in his party's victory.

58. The tour is discussed in PPP, *Voice*, 31–34. See also *WA*, "Gambian Leader," January 21, 1961. Further details from Bojang (Hughes interview, Kembuje, February 1972).

59. Jawara noted the importance of the rinderpest campaign (Hughes interview, August 1998).

60. Hughes interview with Henry Oliver, a former senior commissioner (Bakau, September 1973).

61. The Gambian population for each of the constituencies used in the 1962 election is given in [Gambia Government], *Census Report, 1963*, Table 12. It is possible from this information to estimate the ethnic composition of the population of each constituency in 1960.

62. One Colonial Office official even argued that the PPP won the election because of its overall opposition to the chiefs. See CO 554/2147, "Background Note on the Gambia," December 29, 1960. A report by the senior commissioner in October 1959 noted that three important chiefs, Landing Sonko, Omar M'Baki, and Karamo K. Sanneh, had expressed their anxiety about the activities of PPP agents in their districts. However, the chiefs did not collectively show their hostility to the PPP until the end of July 1960. See GA 9/284, Senior Commissioner to Colonial Secretary, October 23, 1959; and CO 554/2147, petition by Chiefs to Officer Acting Governor of Gambia, July 25, 1960.

63. The Mandinka comprised 49 percent of the Gambian population of Bakau (which approximated to the Kombo East constituency in 1960) in 1963, the Aku only 1 percent; see [Gambia Government], *Census Report, 1963*, Table 12. This constituency should not be confused with the Eastern Kombo constituency, which was created for the 1962 election and was in the Protectorate.

64. See Chapter 5, note 81, on the Kompins. Three UP candidates, P. S. N'Jie, J. H. Joof, and Michael Baldeh, were Catholic.

65. It is not known exactly when N'Jie switched from the GDP to the UP; he was listed as a UP leader (1951/60) by Nyang, "Gambian Political Parties," 120. On his support for the UP in the 1960s, see also Rice, *Enter Gambia*, 215–18; and PPP, *Voice*, 122.

66. On N'Jie's descent from the ruling family of the Saloums and his appeal to Saloum Kheet [Het], see Nyang, "Gambian Political Parties," 114; Senghor, "Senegambian Integration," 179; and Rice, *Enter Gambia*, 277. N'Jie's claims to royal blood are also reported in CO 554/2150, Windley to Eastwood, April 5, 1961. However, according to Bakary Dabo (Hughes interview, Birmingham, July 1995), Saloum Het was a construction of P. S. N'Jie's, rather than a historical reality.

67. The charge was reported in *GE*, July 25, 1960. See also Rice, *Enter Gambia*, 275, citing an interview with Garba-Jahumpa, which probably refers to this election.

68. See CO 879/189, Windley to Eastwood, June 17, 1960; and a letter from E. D. N'Jie to *GE*, May 29, 1961 (which lists all three men as UP members).

69. The petitioners were listed in *GG*, June 30, 1960; July 4, 1960; see also *GE*, October 31, 1960; January 16, 1961, on the decision in Niani-Saloum.

70. *GG*, May 19, 1960, lists the successful candidates; see also CO 554/2147, Windley to Eastwood, May 17, 1960.

71. CO 879/189, Windley to Eastwood, June 17, 1960, describes the process of selecting the new ministers in detail and notes Camara's alleged links with the chiefs. However, Camara emphasized (Hughes interview, December 1997) that he was regarded as a radical by British officials because of his stance against the chiefs, whom he regarded as overbearing and undemocratic. See also Senghor, "Senegambian Integration," 208–9.

72. CO 879/189, Windley to Eastwood, June 17, 1960.

73. CO 879/189, Windley to Eastwood, June 17, 1960. See also Chapter 5, 133, on N'Jie's disbarment.

74. For the UP reaction to N'Jie's appointment, see CO 879/189, Windley to Eastwood, June 17, 1960; Senghor, "Senegambian Integration," 210–12; issues of the *Gambia Echo,* June 28–July 18, 1960; and "One Gambia Party Now Seeks Independence," *New Commonwealth,* September 1960, 606. The memorial and the correspondence between the UP and the Gambian government may also be found in CO 554/2147. For a cynical assessment of the UP's tactics, see the article by the former leader of the GNP, E. J. Samba, in *GE,* July 11, 1960.

75. PPP, *Voice,* 44–47. The manifesto is reprinted in PPP, *Voice,* 225–27; and CO 554/2150, enclosure to Windley to Eastwood, November 3, 1960. Jawara noted that the manifesto was secretly published in Lagos, but leaked ahead of his return to Gambia (Hughes interview, August 1998).

76. The course of events is outlined in Harry A. Gailey, "Gambia Moves Forward," *WA,* April 1, 1961, 339; and Senghor, "Senegambian Integration," 212–17. See also correspondence between Governor Windley and the Colonial Office in CO 554/2147; CO 554/2150; and *GNB,* March 16, 1961.

77. CO 554/2147, Smith to Eastwood, July 28, 1960; Chiefs to Officer Administering the Gambia Government, July 25, 1960. See also Gailey, "Gambia Moves Forward"; and Senghor, "Senegambian Integration," 215. CO 89/39, "Police Report, 1960," 5, reported on a number of incidents between "adherents of a political party" (presumably the PPP) and the district chiefs of Eastern Jarra and Gunjur between August and November 1960.

78. PPP, *Voice,* 54, states that some chiefs were alleged to have signed a document declaring their support for the UP, although in its view, the document was "bogus." On the UP's view of the political role of the chiefs, see its "memorial" of June 24, 1960 in CO 554/2147.

79. CO 554/2147, Windley to Secretary of State, March 14, 1961; and *GNB,* March 16, 1961.

80. CO 554/2147, Windley to Eastwood, March 3, 1961. Smith (Hughes interview, Sherborne, August 1985) claimed that Windley liked N'Jie more than Jawara.

81. The importance of this argument was emphasized by Gailey, "Gambia Moves Forward." Certainly it helped to shape the governor's thinking as CO 554/2147, Windley to Eastwood, March 3, 1961, makes clear. But as Perfect, "Organised Labour," 179 (note 38), points out, the UP won the seat in 1960 with a higher share of the vote. Moreover, as noted by PPP, *Voice,* 42, N'Jie was a much stronger candidate than Touray.

82. For a full account of the 1961 general strike, see Perfect "Organised Labour," Chapter 6. See also CO 554/2498, Windley to Eastwood, January 31, 1961; and CO 554/2147, Windley to Eastwood, March 3, 1961. In fact, P. S. N'Jie had an unfavorable attitude toward Jallow (at least in the mid-1960s); see Rice, *Enter Gambia,* 278, where N'Jie was quoted as describing Jallow as "a ruffian."

83. CO 554/2147, Windley to Secretary of State, March 14, 1961; Windley to Secretary of State, March 21, 1961; and *GNB,* March 16, 1961. For a different assessment of A. B. N'Jie's motives for resigning, see PPP, *Voice,* 54 (which claims that originally Camara had promised to resign as well). P. S. N'Jie apparently looked down on A. B. N'Jie; see CO 554/2150, Windley to Eastwood, April 5, 1961.

84. The proceedings of the conferences were published as [Gambia Government], *Constitutional Development 1961*; and [Gambia Government], *Constitutional Conference 1961.* They are discussed in Perfect, "Organised Labour," 167–68; Senghor, "Senegambian Integration," 242–45; and PPP, *Voice,* 56–58. See also CO 554/2148; and CO 554/2279, "Gambia Constitutional Conference Briefs."

85. See *WA,* "Self-Government for the Gambia," August 5, 1961.

86. The dates are given in *GG,* June 21, 1962.

87. Senghor, "Senegambian Integration," 244–50; and PPP, *Voice*, 56–58. On the BTC election, see also "Blow to Gambia's Ruling Party," *New Commonwealth*, December (1961), 807–8. The full results are in *GO*, October 14, 1961.

88. PPP, *Voice*, 50; 113. Edie, "Democracy in The Gambia," 164, incorrectly states that the pact was formed after the 1962 election.

89. A rumor reported by Governor Paul; see CO 554/2148, Paul to Maudling, June 7, 1962. Further information on Garba-Jahumpa's links with Nkrumah at this time was provided by Ibrahima Jallow, a former radical activist (Hughes interview, Birmingham, November 1997). Hughes, "Green Uprising," 69 (note 29), reports information given him confidentially by a former senior aide of Jawara that the PPP received money from President Senghor of Senegal to finance his election campaign. Senghor might well have feared that links would be established between a new PPP administration and rival, radical, West African governments. Addis, "Groundnut Stew," states that Jawara "flirted" with Nkrumah and Sékou Touré of Guinea while out of office, but subsequently came to consider Senghor to be the most realistic ally.

90. Omar J. Sise, the defeated PPP candidate in Niani-Saloum, both in the 1960 general election and the 1961 by-election, succeeded his father as Seyfu of Upper Saloum in 1961 and was thus not eligible to stand again. See Gamble, *North Bank*, vol. A, 54.

91. On F. W. Touray, see CO 554/2623, "Biographical Notes of Gambia Government Delegates"; and PPP, *Voice*, 18; 61. Touray was the grandson of the famous Marabout warrior ruler of Gunjur, Fodi Sillah. On B. M. Touray's role in the PPP Youth Wing, see *GE*, December 12, 1960.

92. At the time of the election, Touray was employed in the Marine Department, M'Boge in the Customs Department, and Singhateh in the Audit Department; Cham was a Health Inspector. See *GG*, February 16, 1961; April 30, 1962; [Gambia Government], *Members of the Government*; and [Friedrich Ebert Stiftung], *African Biographies: Gambia*. Further information from Tarawale (Hughes interview, Bathurst, 1972).

93. See CO 554/2148, Paul to Maudling, June 7, 1962; Dominion Office file, PRO (hence DO), DO 195/382, "Biographical Notes for Visit of Secretary of State for the Colonies," August 1965; Hughes and Gailey, *Historical Dictionary*, 37; and Bellagamba, "Entrustment and Its Changing Political Meanings in Fuladu," 399–400. Further information on Baldeh from Bakary Dabo (Hughes interview, July 1995); and from Alice Bellagamba on interviews on the history of late colonial and postcolonial Gambia carried out by Bakary Sidibeh and herself in 2000. Cherno Kady Baldeh's career is discussed in Alice Bellagamba, "Portrait of a Chief Between Past and Present," 21–49.

94. See *GE*, October 8, 1960; PPP, *Voice*, 48–49; 115–16; and FCO 65/1453, Parker to Date, October 3, 1974. Further information on the Gambia Progressive Union from Bojang and Jawara (Hughes interviews, February 1972 and August 1998).

95. On the GNU, see Senghor, "Senegambian Integration," 252–58; Gailey, *History*, 195–96; Perfect, "Organised Labour," 170–71; PPP, *Voice*, 116; Sulayman S. Nyang, "The Historical Development of Political Parties in the Gambia," *Africana Research Bulletin* 5, no. 4: (1975), 27; and "Campaigning in the Gambia," *WA*, May 19, 1962, 535. Further information from Bojang and Foon (Hughes interviews, Kembuje, 1972 and Banjul, September 1973). By 1963, Bojang had made his peace with the PPP.

96. PPP, *Voice*, 61; and CO 554/2148, Paul to Eastwood, May 23, 1962.

97. Hughes interview with Camara (December 1997).

98. Gaye (who was a Wolof) had represented the UP at the first 1961 Constitutional Conference in Bathurst and now represented the Joloff/Portuguese Town ward on the BTC; see *GE*, May 8, 1961; and DO 195/382, Gambian Intelligence Report, November 1964. On Kah (who was a Tukulor), see Hughes and Gailey, *Historical Dictionary*, 107; and DO 195/382, "Biographical notes for Secretary of State." His dismissal from the civil service was

reported in *GG*, April 14, 1962. Biyai was a Jola and Sonko and Jammeh were Mandinka. As noted by Wright, *The World and a Very Small Place*, 157–58; 219, Sonko was the great-grandson of Maranta Sonko, the Seyfu of Niumi between 1897 and 1911.

99. On the two men, see [Gambia Government], *Members of the Government*; [Africa Books], *Africa Who's Who*, 317; CO 554/2623, "Biographical Notes of Gambia Government Delegates" (where Cham is described as a Taranko); *GG*, June 4, 1962; and Rice, *Enter Gambia*, 192; 258–59.

100. The ethnic origin of all the candidates is given in Appendix table C.2. Our assessment is based on Nyang, "Gambian Political Parties," 122; 140; 225–29; 245; and on information from B. M. Tarawale (Hughes interview, December 1999). Where the sources differ, we have generally followed the latter.

101. For example, Harry Land, "The Gambia—Politics and Groundnuts," *New Commonwealth*, September 1962, 561. For other accounts, which did emphasize the differences between the parties, see "New Men in the Gambia," *WA*, June 9, 1962, 619; Raya Dunayevskaya, "The Gambia Takes the Hard, Long Road to Independence," *Contemporary Issues*, January 1963, 18–25; Weil, "Mandinka Mansaya," 35–36; PPP, *Voice*, 58–62; and Gailey, *History*, 199–200.

102. CO 554/2148, Paul to Eastwood, May 23, 1962; and Dunayevskaya, "Road to Independence," 18; 22.

103. Dunayevskaya, "Road to Independence," 23. See also CO 554/2148, Paul to Eastwood, May 23, 1962; and FO 371/161579, Windley to Colonial Office, February 8, 1962.

104. Dunayevskaya, "Road to Independence (citing Jawara)," 23; Fletcher, "Party Politics," 116; and Weil, "Mandinka Mansaya," 36. Weil disagrees with the assertion by Gailey, *History*, 199, that the PPP had modified its radical anti-chief stance since 1960. For a detailed discussion of the Area Councils, see Orde, "Development of Local Government."

105. Gailey, *History*, 199; Weil, "Mandinka Mansaya," 35; and Dunayevskaya, "Road to Independence," 23.

106. Dunayevskaya, "Road to Independence," 18.

107. PPP, *Voice*, 60, apparently quoting a speech by N'Jie on Radio Gambia. See also Dunayevskaya, "Road to Independence," 22.

108. See PPP, *Voice*, 60–61; and Senghor, "Senegambian Integration," 262–63.

109. See Appendix table C.2 for the full results. These may be found in *GNB*, June 1, 1962. They are also reported in DO 195/382, Crombie to Greenhill, May 2, 1966. CO 554/2148, Paul to Eastwood, June 7, 1962; and Senghor, "Senegambian Integration," 400, also discuss the results.

110. The four who polled less than 60 percent of the vote were Paul Baldeh (Lower Fulladu West) with 59 percent; Lamin M'Boge (Illiassa) with 58 percent; Yusupha Samba (Sabach Sanjal) with 52 percent; and Bangally Singhateh (Wuli) with 51 percent. Seven of the eight sitting MPs received at least three-quarters of the vote, the exception being Kebba Leigh (Sami) with 63 percent of the vote.

111. These were H. O. Semega-Janneh, who gained 66 percent of the vote in Serrekunda and E. D. N'Jie, who won 65 percent of the vote in Saloum.

112. See Weil, "Mandinka Mansaya," 36; and *WA*, "New Men in the Gambia," June 9, 1962. The latter article noted that the UP was badly organized in the up river constituencies until just before the election and was surprised that it had won as many as thirteen seats. A. M. Camara also emphasized the disorganization of the UP in 1962 (Hughes interview, December 1997).

113. Camara also pointed out (Hughes interview, December 1997) that P. S. N'Jie (his party leader at the time) did not campaign in the URD during the election campaign. He also claimed that N'Jie was indolent, eccentric, drunk, and arrogant.

114. The chiefs' election result is given in *GG*, June 5, 1962; see also DO 195/382, Crombie to Greenhill, May 20, 1966.

115. CO 554/2148, Paul to Maudling, June 7, 1962. The members of the 1962 cabinet (except Dabo) are given by Nyang, "Gambian Political Parties," 141. After his appointment, M'Baki resigned as Seyfu of Sami District in favor of his uncle, resuming the post after his resignation from the cabinet in September 1964; see Saidy, "Omar Mbacke."

116. Samba was described as a Mandinka in *WA*, "New Men in the Gambia," June 9, 1962; and CO 554/2148, Paul to Maudling, June 7, 1962. But Nyang, "Gambian Political Parties," 41, and Tarawale (Hughes interview, December 1999), agree that he was a rural Wolof.

117. CO 554/2148, Paul to Maudling, June 7, 1962. Sallah became one of Jawara's most loyal supporters in Parliament, according to Rice, *Enter Gambia*, 267.

118. On Jack, who was a Bathurst Wolof and a Muslim, see Hughes and Gailey, *Historical Dictionary*, 94; *WA*, "New Men in the Gambia," June 9, 1962; and FCO 65/1457, Parker to Date, May 24, 1974. Jack was assistant secretary general of the DCA in 1960, as *GE*, April 25, 1960, indicates. In the 1950s, he was a leading member of the GMC; see Nyang, "Gambian Political Parties," 108.

119. On the GCP, see Fletcher, "Party Politics," 162–68; and Rice, *Enter Gambia*, 273–75. PPP, *Voice*, 73–74, states that the GCP was founded in 1963, but see Perfect, "Organised Labour," 171. Among those who remained in the DCA were N'Jie, Faye, Cham-Joof, and Grey-Johnson as noted in *GNB*, October 27, 1964.

120. On the GCP's links with the GLU, see Perfect, "Organised Labour," 171. John also later rejoined the DCA, as *GNB*, October 27, 1964, notes.

121. *GE*, October 15, 1962, notes the 1962 electoral pact. DO 195/382, Gambian Intelligence Report, November 1964, reports on the strains in the relationship.

122. The Gambian government made frequent disapproving comments about Garba-Jahumpa's external connections. See, for example, DO 195/382, Paul to Secretary of State, January 8, 1965, on his links with Chinese Communists; the governor argued that this reinforced local opinion that Garba-Jahumpa was "utterly unscrupulous and self-seeking." See also Rice, *Enter Gambia*, 274–75.

123. "Mr Sandys Explains Decision to Validate Gambia Elections," *The Times*, May 29, 1963, 6; and PPP, *Voice*, 64–66. For a list of the election petitions, see *GG*, June 20, 1962; July 6, 1962. Nineteen petitions were initially brought forward because Kebba Leigh in Sami was challenged not only by the UP's Samba Jobe (who subsequently withdrew it), but also by Makam Sidibeh. Addis, "Groundnut Stew," accuses N'Jie of hypocrisy in that, as chief minister in 1961, he introduced the new registers.

124. See FO 371/176512, background note on electoral registers case; "Validating Gambia Election," *The Times*, May 21, 1963, 10; *The Times*, "Mr Sandys Explains Decision"; letters from P. S. N'Jie to *The Times*, May 23, 1963, 13; June 5, 1963, 13; and DO 195/382 (which contains *The Times*' report of the final legal judgment). See also Laurie [Lenrie] Peters, "Election Controversy in Gambia," *New Commonwealth*, October 1963, 679; and PPP, *Voice*, 64–66, which claims that the UP found it difficult to pay Macauley's fees.

125. A decade later, N'Jie was still complaining about the way he had been treated; see, for example, FCO 65/1453, N'Jie to Hart, February 28, 1974.

126. CO 554/2148, Paul to Maudling, June 7, 1962.

127. See PPP, *Voice*, 38; 66–70; Hughes, "Green Uprising," 68; Rice, *Enter Gambia*, 141–44 (who states that Mustapha Dibba was Sheriff Dibba's brother); Gamble, *South Bank*, vol. A, 143 (who asserts that the former was the latter's father); and Gamble, *North Bank*, vol. C, 117. Rice outlines Dibba's viewpoint and suggests that only two of the seven chiefs removed in 1965, one of whom was M'Baki, were pro-UP. Further information on the reasons for the sacking of the chiefs was provided by Henry Oliver (Hughes interview, Bakau, September 1973), who emphasized Dibba's personal role in the process. See also *GE*, October 22, 1965, for a list of the dismissed chiefs.

128. *GG*, October 11, 1963; September 3, 1964. DO 195/382, Paul to Secretary of State, October 12, 1964, noted that the stated reason (as given in *GNB*, September 8, 1964) for M'Baki's resignation from the cabinet was that he wished to replace his ageing uncle as chief, but added that it was generally thought that he resigned to avoid being dismissed.

129. DO 195/382, "Biographical Notes for Secretary of State."

130. In an interview with Hughes (Banjul, December 1997), Camara stated that he joined the PPP in 1963 and that Baldeh switched parties soon after him; Camara's switch in 1963 was also noted in *GE*, October 28, 1963. Although the timing of the defection of Sonko and Jobe is not known, both men voted with the PPP (and against the UP) in a key debate in the House of Representatives on January 10, 1964. They had certainly left the UP formally by July 1964, when the governor reported that only eight UP MPs remained; see FO 371/176512, Paul to Eastwood, July 1, 1964. P. S. N'Jie later claimed that Camara and Baldeh joined the PPP (in 1962) to avoid paying back money that he had given them to fight their election campaigns. See FCO 65/1453, N'Jie to Date, October 3, 1974.

131. These defections are noted in DO 195/382, Gambian Intelligence Reports for September and October 1964; see also *GNB*, October 27, 1964, on Jones.

132. See issues of the *GG*, which record P. S. N'Jie's absences from the House; and Senghor, "Senegambian Integration," 347. See also CO 554/2626, N'Jie to Sandys, July 30, 1964. In his interview with Hughes in December 1997, Camara stated that he joined the PPP because he had become disillusioned with P. S. N'Jie's leadership; he also disliked the fact that N'Jie had moved from favoring closer links with Senegal to attacking the PPP for adopting a pro-Senegal stance.

133. *GG*, November 8, 1963; January 2, 1964. Nyang, "Gambian Political Parties," 150, incorrectly states that H. O. Semega-Janneh was appointed to a ministerial position, but he did not gain preferment until 1969.

134. Four of the eight who defected—Sonko, Jobe, Michael Baldeh and Kah—won 55 percent of the total vote or less in their constituencies in 1962. Yet the UP MP with the smallest majority—J. H. Joof—stayed loyal to the party, whereas the MP with the largest—H. O. Semega-Janneh—defected to the PPP.

135. The Joint Statement between the PPP/DCA and the UP can be found in *GE*, December 28, 1964. An editorial in the same issue noted how the UP had been reduced from its original thirteen members to five by October 1964 and added that the UP had been engulfed in an uneven coalition of five to twenty-seven. See also DO 195/382, Gambian Intelligence Report, December 1964. Edie, "Democracy in The Gambia," 164, incorrectly states that the UP and PPP formed a coalition between 1963 and 1965.

136. Nyang, "Gambian Political Parties," 148–54; PPP, *Voice*, 110–12; Senghor, "Senegambian Integration," 347; 363–67; Perfect, "Organised Labour," 185–86; and DO 195/382, Paul to Secretary of State, January 8, 1965; Paul to Secretary of State, February 6, 1965; Crombie to Commonwealth Relations Office, March 6, 1965. Rice, *Enter Gambia*, 277, argues that P. S. N'Jie was hostile to the coalition.

137. PPP, *Voice*, 65–68; 112–15. See also DO 195/382, Gambia Government to Commonwealth Relations Office, August 17, 1965.

Chapter 7

1. On the 1965 referendum, see Perfect, "Organised Labour," 184–94; PPP, *Voice*, 79–85; Senghor, "Senegambian Integration," 363–74; Fletcher, "Party Politics," 172–73; and Weil, "Mandinka Mansaya," 40–41. Two PRO files, DO 195/406 and 195/407, which were

released in the 1990s, contain new information that is not discussed in any of these earlier sources.

2. DO 195/406, Paul to Harrison, April 22, 1965.

3. See Jawara's speech to the House of Representatives as reported in *GNB*, June 3, 1965; *GE*, June 14, 1965; "A Republic for The Gambia?" *WA*, June 5, 1965, 614; and DO 195/406, Britten to Duff, June 2, 1965. There are slight differences in the sources in the reasons given for the constitutional change. See also *GNB*, November 14, 1965, for their reiteration as outlined by the governor general, Sir John Paul. It was Sir John, "anxious to be on my way with precious little else to do" who drafted the republican constitution, and even "engaging myself in explaining its provisions on an extended tour up and down the River—needless to say on a strictly impartial basis!" (according to a written reply to a questionnaire sent him by David Gamble [date not given]); copy given to Hughes.

4. On the UP's opposition to the republic bill, see Perfect, "Organised Labour," 185–86; Senghor, "Senegambian Integration," 367–68; DO 195/406, Britten to Duff, June 2, 1965; and *WA*, "A Republic for The Gambia?" June 5, 1965 (which wrongly states that the vote on the first reading was unanimous). DO 195/406, Paul to Harrison, April 22, 1965, notes Jawara's original wish to introduce a republican constitution via an election.

5. Nyang, "Gambian Political Parties," 152. Paul was dismissive of the UP leader's suitability for the post: "any idea that P. S. N'Jie may have had about assuming the post of Governor General can only be described as a moonbeam from the larger lunacy" (written reply to Gamble questionnaire).

6. Perfect, "Organised Labour," 185–86, summarizes the GCP's arguments.

7. On the merger and the expulsion of Fadia, see PPP, *Voice*, 114–17; and DO 195/382, Gambia Government to Commonwealth Relations Office, August 17, 1965. It would seem that Fadia later rejoined the PPP and was again expelled in 1973 for attacking the Government for neglecting the Mandinka; see Hughes, "Green Uprising," 73. Nyang, "Gambian Political Parties," 140, lists Fadia as one of ten PPP leaders in 1960–61.

8. See *GNB*, June 10, 1965; and DO 195/406, Britten to Duff, June 9, 1965. Nyang, "Gambian Political Parties," 152–53 (citing an interview with N'Jie's sister, Yadicone), emphasizes his opposition to the coalition. See also *GE*, May 31, 1965; June 14, 1965.

9. For example, in the Adjournment debate of December 1964, all three bitterly criticized government policies. See DO 195/382, Paul to Secretary of State, January 8, 1965. According to B. M. Tarawale (Hughes interview, Bathurst, April 1972), M'Boge was regarded by elements of the party leadership as one of an incipient "left wing" grouping in the ruling party with the others being Sheriff Sisay, Paul Baldeh, Kuti Sanyang, and himself. Sir Dawda Jawara (Hughes interview, Haywards Heath, August 1998) confirmed this, describing M'Boge as being "too radical" and critical of the government's pro-Western foreign policy.

10. Interviews by Hughes with Jawara (1998) and Dibba (Banjul, March 1983); the latter stated that M'Boge was felt to be "Jallow's man in the Cabinet."

11. *GNB*, May 20, 1965, reports his expulsion from the PPP. PPP, *Voice*, 117, also notes M'Boge's expulsion, but dates this to around the time of the referendum. DO 195/243, Britten to Duff, June 3, 1966, notes that he was replaced as deputy speaker on June 1. See also DO 195/382, Crombie to Greenhill, May 2, 1966, which suggests that he was sacked as the deputy speaker because of drunkenness.

12. PPP, *Voice*, 114; Senghor, "Senegambian Integration," 369–71; and *GNB*, September 30, 1965.

13. Perfect, "Organised Labour," 186–90.

14. Perfect, "Organised Labour," 194; and PPP, *Voice*, 84.

15. As reported in *GNB*, November 13, 1965, the second reading was supported by twenty-eight votes to five and the third was passed unanimously.

16. The results are in PPP, *Voice*, 82. Fletcher, "Party Politics," 173, states that there were 154,626 eligible voters. See also DO 195/406, Paul to Chadwick, December 3, 1965; and DO 195/407, Crombie to Bottomley, December 9, 1965. Unfortunately, neither the vote nor the turnout in individual constituencies was recorded. P. S. N'Jie later claimed that 22,000 (or 27,000) "no" votes "disappeared" and were transferred to the "yes" vote, but there is no evidence to support this; see FCO 65/1453, P. S. N'Jie, "Notes" for FCO, May 1974 (received by FCO, May 20, 1974); N'Jie to Date, October 3, 1974.

17. DO 195/406, Paul to Chadwick, December 3, 1965. It may be argued that if Paul's theory about the Fula and Serahuli in URD were correct, they would have voted *against* the referendum in large numbers, not merely abstained.

18. Perfect, "Organised Labour," 192–94, discusses the extent of opposition campaigning, and PPP, *Voice*, 84, notes the role played by the ex-chiefs. Weil, "Mandinka Mansaya," 40, who carried out fieldwork in The Gambia in the mid-1960s, reported that "many Mandinka informants," who were usually PPP supporters, opposed the referendum.

19. See PPP, *Voice*, 85. But Paul probably did not share this view; in an earlier despatch (DO 195/406, Paul to Chadwick, June 4, 1965), he had argued that by the time of the referendum, farming should have been completed.

20. On the response of PPP ministers and Jawara's response, see DO 195/407, Crombie to Bottomley, December 9, 1965. PPP, *Voice*, 82–83, describes the reaction of the rank and file membership, but not that of the ministers.

21. On Singhateh, see Chapter 6, note 8; and Hughes and Gailey, *Historical Dictionary*, 162–63; and DO 195/382, Crombie to Greenhill, December 22, 1965. B. M. Tarawale (Hughes interview, Bathurst, April 1972) stated that Singhateh's appointment was pressed by Sheriff Sisay. The other symbolic and honorific position, that of speaker of the House of Representatives went initially to an Aku, and successive speakers would always be either Aku or urban Wolof; a choice that would rankle with some Mandinka.

22. The signing of the pact was recorded by Bakarr, *Gambia Yesterday*, 20. See also Perfect, "Organised Labour," 195; and Senghor, "Senegambian Integration," 374–79. Fletcher, "Party Politics," 173, wrongly states that the pact broke down even before the election. The UP may also have hoped to benefit from the external financial donations that Garba-Jahumpa periodically received.

23. There has been no detailed analysis of the 1966 election. The fullest secondary accounts are by Fletcher, "Party Politics," 174–81; and PPP, *Voice*, 85–86.

24. See [Gambia Government], *Report of the Constituency Boundaries Commission* (SP no. 2 of 1966) (Bathurst: Government Printer, 1966). The boundary changes are outlined in *GG*, April 12, 1966. While noting that these changes benefited the PPP, Weil, "Mandinka Mansaya," 41, argues that this was not the Commission's intention. See also DO 195/406, Paul to Chadwick December 3, 1965.

25. The number of registered voters was 175,733, an increase of more than 20,000 since the referendum, and of more than 40,000 since 1962. See Bakarr, *Gambia Yesterday*, 82; and DO 195/382, Crombie to Bottomley, June 2, 1966, Annex 1. Fletcher, "Party Politics," 174, also points out that steps were taken to improve voter registration before the 1966 election.

26. On Touray's earlier career as a trade union leader, see Perfect, "Organised Labour," 191–92. It is not known why Demba was not selected again. The nominated candidates for all parties are in *GNB*, May 10, 1966.

27. Jobe may have been living in Senegal at this time. Senghor, "Senegambian Integration," 380, reports that an "Ismaila Jobe" (quite possibly the former UP MP, Ishmael Jobe), a Gambian resident in Senegal, was instrumental in persuading the two parties to discuss the formation of a coalition in 1967.

28. See *GNB*, July 26, 1965; October 9, 1965. Krubally's victory was not surprising; the PPP had won nine out of twelve seats in the 1964 Area Council election in Basse, whereas in the previous local election, it won only three seats, compared with nine for the UP. In addition, Jawara personally visited the constituency before the by-election to shore up the PPP's support. See CO 554/2636, Paul to Eastwood, May 19, 1964; and DO 195/382, Gambia Fortnightly Summary, October 4, 1965.

29. This estimate is based on sources outlined in Chapter 6, note 100.

30. DO 195/382, Crombie to Greenhill, May 2, 1966. Crombie himself thought that the UP would be lucky to win more than twelve seats.

31. *GNB*, May 10, 1966, shows the party affiliation of the candidates. As noted in *GNB*, May 17, 1966, those candidates who wished to be publicly accepted as representing both opposition parties had to notify the acting information officer. It is unclear whether the eighteen candidates who represented the UP alone made a conscious decision not to be associated with the GCP, or simply failed to inform this official in time.

32. Perfect, "Organised Labour," 195; and Senghor, "Senegambian Integration," 379. On Burang-John, see also Nyang, "Gambian Political Parties," 122.

33. Jallow's background is described in Chapter 6. According to his own account, he was known as "Jallow Vertinary [*sic*]" as late as the 1990s; see *Foroyaa*, March 30, 1991.

34. These were K. W. Foon in Bakau and Malick Sabally in Sabach Sanjal. In addition, Karamo Kinteh, who contested Lower Baddibu in 1962 as an Independent, stood for the UP in the same seat. It is not clear why so few were reselected; some may have been dropped for their poor performance in 1962, and others may have joined the PPP. For example, Andrew M'Ballow, who stood for the UP in Lower Fulladu West in 1962, but did not stand in 1966, fought a by-election in the same seat on behalf of the PPP in February 1969 (by which time he had converted to Islam and changed his name to Abdul M'Ballow). It is not known when M'Ballow joined the PPP, but because he performed reasonably well in 1962, capturing 41 percent of the vote, it is reasonable to assume from his nonselection in 1966 that it occurred prior to the election. See Appendix tables C.3 and C.9.

35. On Forster, see Perfect, "Organised Labour," 165. Further information from Forster (Hughes interview, Bathurst, February 1972). Forster's early interest in local politics was fostered by E. F. Small, but he did not enter national politics until his retirement from public service (the Post Office) in 1959. As a UP candidate, he had already defeated his parliamentary rivals, Faye and Jones, in Bathurst Central in the municipal election of February 1966. Details in *GNB*, February 12, 1966. Forster also replaced Burang-John as editor of the pro-UP *Gambia Echo* until its demise in the early 1970s; see Grey-Johnson, "The Newspaper in The Gambia," 19.

36. Our assessment largely follows that of B. M. Tarawale (Hughes interview, Latrikunda, December 1999).

37. Fletcher, "Party Politics," 158–62.

38. Fletcher, "Party Politics," 158.

39. According to Rice, *Enter Gambia*, 273–74. One of the GCP defectors was certainly Alasan N'Dure (the GCP's national propaganda secretary), who accused Garba-Jahumpa of misusing party funds, and the other was probably Kisima Semega-Janneh (its general secretary). Both later became PPP councilors. See also *GNB*, February 24, 1966; Nyang, "Gambian Political Parties," 199; Bakarr, *Gambia Yesterday*, 19; 88; and DO 195/382, Gambian Intelligence Report, September 1964, which lists the four recently elected GCP councilors (the other two were Alieu Ceesay and Garba-Jahumpa himself).

40. Perfect, "Organised Labour," 195–98. Because Jallow withdrew only shortly before the deadline for nominations, the UP was unable to find another candidate to contest Western Kiang.

Notes to pages 166–169

41. *GNB*, May 10, 1966.

42. Transcripts are to be found in *GNB*, May 3, 1966 (Sisay); May 5, 1966 (P. S. N'Jie); May 7, 1966 (A. B. N'Jie); May 10, 1966 (Garba-Jahumpa); May 14, 1966 (Jawara). For a critical comment on Garba-Jahumpa's speech, see also DO 195/382, Seaward to Hunter, May 17, 1966.

43. See Chapter 10, 273.

44. Full results are in Appendix table C.3. These are based on three sources: *GNB*, May 28, 1966; Bakarr, *Gambia Yesterday*, 81–82; and Sagnia, *Gambian Legislature*, 61–64. Where these differ, we have followed *GNB*. DO 195/382, Crombie to Bottomley, June 2, 1966, Annex 1, gives the turnout.

45. M. B. Jones (Hughes interview, Banjul, April 1975), admitted that his shift to the PPP, brought about by disillusionment with the UP leader, P. S. N'Jie, was unpopular with Aku voters, but claimed that he lost because of constituency boundary changes, which transferred some "500 Jahumpa voters" from Bathurst South to Bathurst Central.

46. This estimate differs from that of Weil, "Mandinka Mansaya," 236, who states that after the election, the PPP had twelve Mandinka, three Wolof, three Tukulor, two Fula, two Jola, and two Serahuli members.

47. Nyang, "Gambian Political Parties," 154–55; and Allen "African Trade Unionism," 404. Both suggest that he owed his victory largely to UP support.

48. On Jallow's subsequent trade union career, see Perfect "Organised Labour," 194–289.

49. See PPP, *Voice*, 115; Bakarr, *Gambia Yesterday*, 88; *GO*, January 18, 1973; and *GNB*, December 11, 1985. See also *The Nation*, January 15, 1977, which lists Faye as part of a UP delegation that discussed a possible electoral alliance with the National Liberation Party.

50. According to Garba-Jahumpa, the PPP's use of government vehicles had played an important part in boosting the "yes" vote in the previous referendum; see *WA*, December 25, 1965, 1471. He made other accusations against the PPP government during the debate on the Speech from the Throne, June 27–30, 1966. Forster, for the UP, supported Garba-Jahumpa's claim of the partisan access to Radio Gambia. Predictably, the accusation, and one of intimidation of opposition supporters up river, were denied by Jawara. This accusation recurred in subsequent elections and not without some justification. See B. M. Tarawally [Tarawale], *In Parliament in The Gambia. Report of the Proceedings of the House of Representatives 27–30 June 1966* (Bathurst: Government Printer, 1966). Interestingly, the official record of these debates as reported in *GG*, December 15, 1967 (Supplement E), makes no mention of Garba-Jahumpa's criticisms.

51. DO 195/382, Crombie to Bottomley, June 2, 1966. The British high commissioner in fact attributed much of the credit for the PPP's success to Jawara personally.

52. Interviews by Hughes with N'Jie (Bathurst/Banjul, March 1972 and August 1973). John Wiseman also told Hughes that similar views were expressed to him.

53. DO 195/382, Crombie to Bottomley, June 2, 1966; and DO 195/407, Crombie to Greenhill, June 9, 1966.

54. FCO 65/1453, N'Jie to Hart, February 28, 1974; N'Jie, "Notes" for FCO, May 1974.

55. The talks are discussed, from a PPP perspective, in PPP, *Voice*, 119–21 and, from a UP perspective, in FCO 65/1453, N'Jie to Date, October 3, 1974; see also Senghor, "Senegambian Integration," 380–81. In N'Jie's account, the meeting with Jawara took place in 1967, not 1968. There was also opposition to a coalition from backbench PPP MPs, whose prospects for promotion might therefore be reduced, as FCO 38/137, Crombie to Miles, August 4, 1967, makes clear.

56. The relationship between Dawda and Augusta Jawara is discussed in FCO 38/136. On the reaction to the Marriage Bill, see *GE*, July 31, 1967; August 32, 1967; and Senghor, "Senegambian Integration," 388. Chilel is profiled in FCO 65/1455, Parker to Date, February 21, 1974, which also refers to Jawara's relationship with his first wife.

57. FCO 38/136, Seaward to Moberly, March 21, 1968, discusses the reasons for the marriage. See also PPP, *Voice*, 122; and Nyang, "Gambian Political Parties," 183–85.

58. On the relationship between Cham and M. M. N'Jie, see *WA*, "Momodou Musa N'Jie" August 13–19, 1990. The defection of Bah and Ndow is noted in Sulayman S. Nyang, "Politics of Defection in The Gambia," *WA*, April 16, 1979, 664–67. Bah was Almami between 1953 and 1983, as noted in Cham-Joof, "Banjul Mosque."

59. The reasons for Garba-Jahumpa's defection are discussed in PPP, *Voice*, 121; Senghor, "Senegambian Integration," 381–82; Fletcher, "Party Politics," 189–90 (who wrongly suggests that the merger occurred as a result of the formation of the PPA); and Nyang, "Gambian Political Parties," 154–56; 194–96. See also *GE*, March 18, 1968; and FCO 38/138, Seaward to Moberly, March 14, 1968. The press release issued by Garba-Jahumpa on March 7 to announce the merger may be found in FCO 38/138.

60. Bakarr, *Gambia Yesterday*, 88. The first three candidates in each ward were elected to the BCC.

61. See FCO 38/138, Seaward to Moberly, April 4, 1968; the appointment had been announced on the previous day.

62. Nyang, "Gambian Political Parties," 155; and FCO 38/138, Seaward to Moberly, March 14, 1968.

63. See *GNB*, August 26, 1969; October 23, 1969, on Cham and Kinteh. See PPP, *Voice*, 122; and [Gambia Government], *Members of the Government*, on Sanneh. Appendix table C.2 outlines their showing in the 1966 election. Sanneh subsequently joined the PPP's administrative bureau in Bathurst and was rewarded by being appointed as a "nominated" MP after the 1972 election; see Nyang, "Gambian Political Parties," 245; and Arnold Hughes, "Jawara Wins Again," *WA*, April 21, 1972, 453.

64. This approach shares similarities with the "consociational democracy" model of governing plural societies, first set out and advocated by the Dutch political scientist, Arend Lijphart in *Democracy in Plural Societies: A Comparative Exploration* (New Haven, CT: Yale University Press, 1977) and elsewhere. The Gambian parallels of rule through ethnic elite consensus and power sharing are discussed further in Arnold Hughes, "The Limits of 'Consociational Democracy' in The Gambia," *Civilisations* 22, no. 2 and 23, no. 1: (1982–83), 65–95.

65. These appointments are noted in Bakarr, *Gambia Yesterday*, 25–28. See also Nyang, "Gambian Political Parties," 170; and FCO 38/138, Ramage to Tebbit, September 10, 1968. On Saho, see Hughes and Gailey, *Historical Dictionary*, 153.

66. See Robert H. Jackson and Carl G. Rosberg, *Personal Rule in Black Africa* (Berkeley: University of California Press, 1982), 77–78; 83–89. Although it is the Senegalese president, Léopold Senghor, whose style of leadership is discussed in detail as epitomizing the "princely" subtype, the depiction fits Jawara equally well.

67. On the new party (which was also called the Gambia Convention Party), see *GE*, May 15, 1967, which announced its formation and named Sanyang as leader; and FCO 38/137, Crombie to Miles, August 4, 1967. The latter source (which calls Sanyang, Nuha Sagnia) gives the other leaders. Tarawale's break with the PPP is noted in *GE*, July 25, 1966. See also Senghor, "Senegambian Integration," 382.

68. Sanyang had gained 43 percent of the vote in the constituency in 1962, whereas Kandeh won 44 percent of the vote in 1966. See Appendix tables C.2 and C.3.

69. FCO 38/137, Crombie to Miles, August 4, 1967, reports on the resignations of M'Boge and Tarawale. Bakarr, *Gambia Yesterday*, 32, notes Sanyang's readmittance to the

PPP. See also Senghor, "Senegambian Integration," 385, on the links between the National Convention Party and the PPA.

70. For previous discussion of the creation and collapse of the PPA, see Nyang, "Gambian Political Parties," 156–59; Fletcher, "Party Politics," 188–94; and Senghor, "Senegambian Integration," 382–98.

71. See PPP, *Voice*, 117, which claims that Tarawale transformed the *New Gambia* from a pro-PPP newspaper into "a virulent machine for anti-party campaign and smear."

72. For an analysis of the cabinet changes in January 1968, see FCO 38/137, Seaward to Moberly, January 6, 1968; February 7, 1968. For earlier references to Sisay's relationship with Jawara in 1966–67, see especially Crombie to Norris, December 30, 1966, in the same file. See also Sulayman S. Nyang, "Politics in Post-Independence Gambia," *A Current Bibliography on African Affairs* 8, no. 2: (1975), 118; Senghor, "Senegambian Integration," 382–83; and *GE*, January 1, 1968; January 8, 1968.

73. *GE*, June 17, 1968.

74. These cabinet changes are reported in *GG*, April 4, 1968. See also *GE*, April 8, 1968; April 15, 1968; Nyang, "Politics in Post-Independence Gambia," 118; Senghor, "Senegambian Integration," 381–83; and FCO 38/138, Seaward to Moberly, April 4, 1968.

75. See FCO 38/138, Ramage to Tebbit, September 10, 1968, for a detailed analysis. See also Senghor, "Senegambian Integration," 383–84; and Fletcher, "Party Politics," 188 (who incorrectly states that the proposal to increase the number of "nominated" MPs was defeated).

76. Senghor, "Senegambian Integration," 387 (note 90), notes that M'Boge claimed he returned to the PPP "on the advice of my parents." According to Tarawale (Hughes interviews, Bathurst, March–April 1972), his application for readmission was assisted by a deputation of PPP supporters from Western Kiang, who were in Bathurst in September for the funeral of their MP, Amang Kanyi, and were anxious to reunite the party.

77. *The Progressive*, September 2, 1968; and FCO 38/138, Ramage to Tebbitt, September 10, 1968.

78. Senghor, "Senegambian Integration," 384.

79. Senghor, "Senegambian Integration," 385. On the support of the ex-GNP leaders (and other prominent Bathurst citizens), see PPP, *Voice*, 125. According to Tarawale, although the PPA sought to create country-wide branches, its support in the Provinces was uneven: strongest in Gunjur, Jarras (supported by a leading marabout [Muslim spiritual leader]), Niamina (Sisay's home area), Lower Fulladu West (Paul Baldeh's constituency), Illiassa and Sabach Sanjal and weakest in the Baddibus, the Fonis, the Kombos, and Basse. Serahuli backing gave it some support elsewhere in URD. Various interviews given by Tarawale to Hughes (Bathurst, March–April 1972). The authors have benefited greatly from Tarawale's insider account of the brief history of the PPA. Sisay, though interviewed by Hughes in Bathurst in 1972, understandably refused to be drawn on this subject.

80. See Nyang, "Gambian Political Parties," 157–58; and Nyang, "Politics in Post-Independence Gambia," 118–19. For the reaction of the PPP militants, see Nyang, "Local and National Elites," 64.

81. Bakarr, *Gambia Yesterday*, 29; and *The Progressive*, December 19, 1968. *GE*, December 23, 1968, gives his age as thirty-two, but according to Hughes and Gailey, *Historical Dictionary*, 37, he was born in 1937. Baldeh's serious drinking problem probably accounted for his early death.

82. Senghor, "Senegambian Integration," 386.

83. See *GE*, October 13, 1969; and Hughes and Gailey, *Historical Dictionary*, 107. Kah's appeal against his sentence was rejected by the Gambia Court of Appeal on November 26, 1970 and because he failed to contest this judgment within a forty-two-day period of grace,

he was unseated and a by-election held. See "Gambia Election Results" file, Election Office, Banjul.

84. A point noted by Senghor, "Senegambian Integration," 386.

85. For earlier accounts of the 1970 referendum, see Senghor, "Senegambian Integration," 387–94; PPP, *Voice*, 86–88; 124–25; Perfect, "Organised Labour," 218–22; and Fletcher, "Party Politics," 192–95. See also FCO 65/32; and FCO 65/596. These PRO files, which were released in the early 2000s, contain new information not discussed by the earlier secondary sources.

86. FCO 65/32, Ramage to Barder, September 9, 1969. The Wuli by-election was brought about by the unseating of Bangally Singhateh, who was sentenced to two years' imprisonment in 1968; see *GE*, March 18, 1968. The results are in Appendix table C.9.

87. FCO 65/32, Ramage to Barder, November 12, 1969.

88. See FCO 65/32, Thatcher to Thomas, June 3, 1969, enclosing a letter to her from N'Jie dated May 29. Mrs. Thatcher had met N'Jie when visiting The Gambia in 1967 as part of a parliamentary delegation.

89. On the PPA's reasons for opposing the bill, see Perfect, "Organised Labour," 192, citing a PPA document of June 1969; see also *GE*, January 5, 1970.

90. For a discussion of notions of Mandinka political culture informing PPP attitudes on consensus and the inclusiveness of the political community, see Peter M. Weil, "Political Structure and Process Among the Gambian Mandinka: The Village Parapolitical System," in *Papers on the Manding*, ed. Carleton T. Hodge (Bloomington, IN: Indiana University Press, 1971), 267. See also Weil, "Mandinka Mansaya," Chapter IX.

91. "Power in The Gambia," *WA*, May 2, 1970, 481, gives the electorate as 133,813. Fletcher, "Party Politics," 194, gives a slightly higher figure of 135,000. See also FCO 65/32, Sullis to Middleton, June 12, 1969, on the revisions to the registers.

92. Full results in each constituency are in Appendix table E.1. These can be found in an annex to FCO 65/596, Ramage to Stewart, April 24, 1970; and Bakarr, *Gambia Yesterday*, 26. Perhaps not surprisingly, N'Jie later claimed that he actually won the 1970 referendum, but that Jawara manipulated the results to bring victory to the PPP; see FCO 65/1453, N'Jie to Hart, February 28, 1974.

93. According to Tarawale (Hughes interviews, Bathurst, March–April 1972), Singhateh was already on leave before the referendum and was criticized in government circles for alleged pro-PPA and anti-republican sympathies. He was also felt to lack the necessary attributes for such an elevated position. A. S. Jack, the speaker of the House, deputed in his absence. Additional information from former Gambian vice president, B. B. Dabo (Hughes interview, Birmingham, July 1995).

94. Sagnia, *Gambian Legislature*, 62, notes Jabang's election. For his background, see [Gambia Government], *Members of the Government*.

95. Senghor, "Senegambian Integration," 397–98; and PPP, *Voice*, 125. FCO 65/1091, Diplomatic Report no. 191/72, Report by M. B. Collins, January 26, 1972 (hence "Collins Report"), states that the two men rejoined the PPP on December 18, 1971. Bakarr, *Gambia Yesterday*, 44, notes that the PPA was dissolved on February 12, 1972. See also Nyang, "Local and National Elites," 64, who claims that Sisay agreed publicly to repent of his actions in 1971. As noted by the British high commissioner, Jawara insisted on this as the price for reconciliation; see FCO 65/916, Collins to Bambury, December 3, 1971.

96. *Gambia Onward*, December 8, 1972. As noted in FCO 65/1090, Collins to Seaward, March 9, 1972, prior to this appointment, Sisay considered moving to London to take a law degree.

97. *GNB*, June 12, 1971.

98. See FCO 65/1091, "Collins Report"; and a letter from the Attorney General's Office to Tarawale, in March 1972, which was shown to Hughes. The action was legally disputable,

but Tarawale lacked the resources to contest it and publication of the newspaper was discontinued after the first issue.

99. Provincial Area Councils were established in 1961–62; see Orde, "Development of Local Government," 54–55. For full details of the 1972 election, see File LG/1301, Ministry of Local Government and Lands, Banjul.

100. On the 1972 election, see three articles by Arnold Hughes in *West Africa*: "Jawara Wins Again," (April 14, 1972); "After the Gambian Elections," *WA*, April 21, 1972, 475; and "After the Elections," *WA*, April 28, 1972, 511. Hughes undertook research in The Gambia in January–April 1972. See also PPP, *Voice*, 125–28; *GNB*, March 30, 1972; and Fletcher, "Party Politics," 203–12 (but note that there are numerous errors in her electoral statistics).

101. Sabally, who was the son of a prosperous trader, was born in 1947; see [Gambia Government], *Members of the Government*. In recent years, M'Boge had served as the PPP's senior administrative secretary; see Nyang, "Gambian Political Parties," 245.

102. On Sonko and Jallow, see [Gambia Government], *Members of the Government*. On Drammeh, who had stood as a PPP candidate in Bathurst South in 1966, see Nyang, "Gambian Political Parties," 193.

103. On Kelepha-Samba, see Hughes and Gailey, *Historical Dictionary*, 107–8; and his obituary notice in *Gambia Times*, July 19, 1995. On Monday, see Nyang, "Gambian Political Parties," 187–88; and FCO 65/44, note by West African Department, December 10, 1968. See also *GNB*, August 5, 1971, which notes that he had also served since 1971 as the chairman of the Management Committee of the BCC.

104. Sulayman S. Nyang, "Decline and Fall of a Party," *WA*, April 23, 1979, 711, suggests that the key appointment for Christian civil servants was that of Eric Christensen, a Roman Catholic of mixed Gambian–Danish parentage. Christensen became the first Gambian head (secretary general) of the civil service in 1967 and retained this post until his retirement in 1978. He was also secretary to the cabinet. Christensen is profiled in Hughes and Gailey, *Historical Dictionary*, 51; and FCO 65/1455, Parker to Date, February 21, 1974.

105. Kelepha-Samba's reputation was, however, dented by his arrest on corruption charges in June 1971 following the dissolution of the BCC; see *GNB*, June 6, 1971. He was subsequently acquitted. Bakarr, *Gambia Yesterday*, 25, notes that he was first elected mayor in May 1967.

106. Hughes interviews with Lamin M'Boge, then the PPP administrative secretary (Banjul, September 1973).

107. See *GNB*, April 21, 1970 (letter from Burang-John); April 23, 1970; August 27, 1970; PPP, *Voice*, 122–23; and Grey-Johnson, "The Newspaper in The Gambia," 28–29.

108. The dispute was covered (from a PPP perspective) in *GNB*, May 14, 1970; May 16, 1970; see also *GE*, May 18, 1970; and Fletcher, "Party Politics," 198–99; 214 (note 20). FCO 65/1090, Collins to Bambury, March 24, 1972, reports on P. S. N'Jie's conduct after 1970. On P. S. N'Jie's earlier drinking habits, see, for example, CO 554/2626, minute by Eastwood, October 23, 1964. *GNB*, July 1, 1970, notes E. D. N'Jie's appointment as official leader of the opposition.

109. E. D. N'Jie's death is noted in *GNB*, October 20, 1970 (which outlines his career); and "Opposition Leader Dies After Crash," *WA*, October 24, 1970, 1264. It is no coincidence that Cham joined the PPP within a day or so of N'Jie's death; see *GE*, November 2, 1970; and Bakarr, *Gambia Yesterday*, 38. PPP, *Voice*, 123, incorrectly states that N'Jie died during the 1970 referendum campaign. P. S. N'Jie later sourly claimed that Cham had defected after stealing his money and damaging his Landrover; see FCO 65/1453, N'Jie to Date, October 3, 1974.

110. The by-election results are in Appendix table C.9; Jawara won 46 percent and Bayo 39 percent of the vote in the same constituencies in 1966. Darbo's disqualification was

noted in *GG*, July 31, 1970. Arnold Hughes, "Jawara's New Team," *WA*, May 24, 1982, 1361, notes that Kebba Jawara was a relative of the president (nephew). On Jobe, who was a retired health inspector, see *GG*, April 9, 1966. Bellagamba, "Entrustment and Its Changing Political Meanings in Fuladu," 400, gives further information on the selection of Jawara as the PPP candidate.

111. FCO 65/916, Collins to Bambury, December 3, 1971; and FCO 65/1090, Parker to Date, September 22, 1972. M. B. Jones (Hughes interview, Banjul, March 1984) later claimed that both E. D. N'Jie and John Forster were contemplating defecting to the PPP at the time of the former's death. P. S. N'Jie also doubted Forster's loyalty to the UP; see FCO 65/1453, N'Jie to Date, October 3, 1974. Although N'Jie's suspicion of his fellow-UP MPs and parliamentary candidates may be partly justified given their high defection rate, this could only work against party morale and efficiency. Further information from N'Jie (Hughes interview, Banjul, September 1973).

112. Fletcher, "Party Politics," 200, incorrectly states that the UP had 16 candidates in 1972. The British high commissioner noted that a potential UP candidate in Wuli had withdrawn because of intimidation and suspected that this had occurred in other constituencies where the PPP was unopposed; see FCO 65/1090, Collins to Bambury, March 24, 1972.

113. Taal was financial secretary/treasurer of the GNYC in 1966–67, became its president in 1969, and held this position until at least 1971; see note on GNYC Congress, April 1967 (Gambia Workers' Union (GWU) files, Banjul); *GNB*, May 15, 1969; and *Gambia Onward*, February 24, 1971. See Bakarr, *Gambia Yesterday*, 88, on his election to the BCC in 1968.

114. On the Independents, see Hughes, "Jawara Wins Again"; PPP, *Voice*, 125–26; Nyang, "Gambian Political Parties," 172–73 (although this is inaccurate); and Fletcher, "Party Politics," 200–203. Their viewpoint was outlined in a series of pamphlets: [Independents], "Gambia Betrayed!! Down With UP. Down With PPP. Vote Independent"; [Independents], "The Type of Gambia We Want"; and [Independents], "Communique" [*sic*]. The first two pamphlets were issued before the election and the third after it. The pamphlets were read in the Institute of Commonwealth Studies Library (ICS), London; the final pamphlet is also summarized in *Foroyaa*, April 15, 1991. Further information was acquired by Hughes during visits to The Gambia in 1972–73.

115. John A. Wiseman, "The Social and Economic Bases of Party Political Support in Serekunda, The Gambia," *Journal of Commonwealth & Comparative Politics* 23, no. 1: (1985), 4–5. See Chapter 2, note 81, on the spelling of Serekunda/Serrekunda.

116. Bakarr, *Gambia Yesterday*, 40; and FCO 65/1091, "Collins Report," note Sonko's removal. See also *GNB*, March 4, 1971; March 9, 1971; and *GG*, March 5, 1971 (which gives the home addresses of the two by-election candidates). See also *The Nation*, April 8, 1972. The by-election result is in Appendix table C.9.

117. Sagnia, *Gambian Legislature*, 68, states the candidate in Kantora was Momodou Sanyang, but PPP, *Voice*, 126, notes that it was M. B. Sagnia (we think these are variants of the same name). It is not known if the Yaya Dabo who fought Jarra in 1962 and in Eastern Jarra in 1972 was the same person, but it is assumed that it was.

118. According to Lamin M'Boge (Hughes interview, Banjul, September 1973). Fletcher, "Party Politics," 201, suggests that all nineteen candidates had previously been identified with the PPA or UP, but gives no evidence for this improbable claim.

119. Dabo was later acquitted, but remained discredited; see *GNB*, January 8, 1970; June 18, 1970; and *GE*, June 29, 1970.

120. The main exceptions to this were M. E. Jallow (Bathurst North); L. O. Sonko and Jerreh Manneh (both Niumi); and M. B. Sagnia (Kantora). See PPP, *Voice*, 126, which states that otherwise the Independents consisted "mainly of inexperienced novices."

121. See Hughes, "Green Uprising," 73 (note 44).

122. FCO 65/1090, Collins to Bambury, March 24, 1972.

123. Hughes, field observations, 1972.

124. Hughes, "Green Uprising," 72.

125. The backgrounds of Manneh (born in 1947) and Saho (born in 1944) are described in [Gambia Government], *Members of the Government*, and S. B. Danso, "Development Takes Many Ways . . . Dr. Saho," *Daily Observer*, February 28, 1995. See also Sulayman S. Nyang, "Recent Trends in Gambian Politics," *L'Afrique et l'Asie Modernes*, no. 109 (1976), 41–42; PPP, *Voice*, 126–27; and Baboucar Gaye, "Rumbles in the PPP," *WA*, January 21, 1985, 103.

126. See, for example, [Independents], "Gambia Betrayed!"; and [Independents], "The Type of Gambia We Want." An independent observer, the British high commissioner, M. B. Collins, also considered that corruption was increasing; see FCO 65/1091, "Collins Report." FCO 65/1285, "Parker Report 1973," notes that unemployment and the cost of living were both rising at the time of the election, and there was economic uncertainty because of the imminent departure of one major expatriate commercial firm, the United Africa Company (which ceased to operate in The Gambia in September 1972) and doubts over the remainder. See also Chapter 1, 37.

127. This ambiguity has been observed elsewhere; see for example, Margaret Peil, *Nigerian Politics: The People's View* (London: Cassell, 1976), Chapter 3 (particularly 52–56).

128. Two of the leading Independent critics of the PPP's misrule, Dr. M. S. K. Manneh and Dr. L. K. Saho, would be dismissed as ministers from the PPP government for corruption. See Chapter 9, 233; 240.

129. See Chapter 5, 121.

130. Between them, the nineteen Independent candidates selected eight different symbols (two chose no symbol at all); see FCO 65/1090, Collins to Bambury, April 6, 1972 Annex A. The disunity of the Independents was also noted in [Independents], "Communique" [*sic*].

131. Hughes, field observations, 1972. Plans to summon a "constituent assembly" after the election, announced in [Independents], "Communique" [*sic*], similarly foundered.

132. PPP, *Voice*, 128, suggests the UP "opted to encourage" the Independents. P. S. N'Jie claimed to have provided some financial assistance and that Maja Sonko in Jokadu reneged on a promise to stand for the UP in 1972. Basically, N'Jie did not feel able to trust any of the Independent candidates, the most articulate of whom, M. E. Jallow, was again standing against him in Bathurst North. Additionally, he was financially overstretched trying to assist UP candidates. Interviews with Hughes (Bathurst/Banjul, March 1972 and September 1973).

133. See FCO 65/1090, Collins to Bambury, March 24, 1972, who notes that the decision provoked a hostile reaction from local inhabitants in Sandu; see also P. S. N'Jie, "Points From Election Speeches," *The Nation*, April 8, 1972. This was consistent with the PPP practice of bringing pressure to bear on chiefs, either to keep out of politics or actively to support ruling party candidates. Four chieftaincies were vacant at the time of the election, which favored the PPP, as aspirants would not wish to antagonize the government. Although chiefs were legally prohibited from such partisan activities, there was no refuting opposition claims to their involvement, on this and other occasions. While observing the election up river, Hughes several times saw chiefs among PPP campaign teams. Lamin M'Boge, Sheriff Dibba, and Assan Musa (Andrew) Camara, all subsequently admitted this took place (interviews with Hughes in Banjul, 1973, 1977, and 1990). N'Jie elaborated further on alleged PPP electoral malpractices in an interview with Hughes (Bathurst, March 1972), given two days after the election. He blamed these as the main reasons for the UP failure to put up candidates in six of the seven uncontested seats, although he conceded that in Bakau it was because of his own party's incompetence in sorting out the necessary documentation and deposit in time.

134. A point noted by PPP, *Voice*, 126; and [Independents], "Communique" [*sic*]. As a result, the latter called for the voting age to be reduced from 21 to 18.

135. Hughes, "Green Uprising," 72.

136. The British high commissioner argued that some ministers (including Sheriff Dibba) only won because Jawara made a personal appearance in their wavering constituencies; see FCO 65/1285, "Parker Report 1973"; and FCO 65/1612, Parker to Lewis, September 10, 1975.

137. On Sonko, who had previously sought to contest the seat for the PPP, but was turned down, see Omar Bah, "Ya Fatou Sonko: Nadd Executive Member," *Daily Observer*, February 12, 2005. After her election defeat, Sonko lost her job as a PPP election clerk, but nevertheless soon rejoined the party. Further information on the election campaign in Eastern Kombo was from Hughes field observations and interviews, 1972.

138. [Independents], "Communique" [*sic*], specifically criticized the role of chiefs and headmen in the election.

139. FCO 65/1090, Collins to Bambury, April 6, 1972; and *GG*, April 6, 1972. The total number of registered voters was 168,771, a much higher figure than for the 1970 referendum reflecting the increasing population, although lower than in 1966. The turnout was based on the electorate in the twenty-five constituencies where there were contested ballots (136,521).

140. Excluding the special case of Tumana (where the PPP candidate in 1972, M. C. Cham, had won for the UP in 1966), the PPP had won 75 percent of the vote in these seats in the 1966 election. Detailed results are in Appendix table C.4. These can be found in Bakarr, *Gambia Yesterday*, 84; Sagnia, *Gambian Legislature*, 65–68; and FCO 65/1090, annex to Collins to Bambury, April 6, 1972. Edie, "Democracy in The Gambia," 166, gives a slightly different summary of the results.

141. Over the years, N'Jie spent an estimated £80,000 of his family's money, necessitating the selling of several properties, to fund his failing party; Hughes interview with P. S. N'Jie (Bathurst, September 1973). Nyang, "Decline and Fall of a Party," 712, states that N'Jie was called "Samba Lingerr" (a Wolof title of honor) because of his extravagant expenditure during elections. It appears that the main source of the N'Jie family income was P. S.' lawyer brother, Sheriff; see FCO 65/1457, Parker to Date, June 14, 1974.

142. N'Jie, "Points from Election Speeches."

143. Coker was president of the UP and had served as an elected councilor on the BCC. Nyang, "Gambian Political Parties," 119–22, lists Coker as a leader of the UP in the 1950s, but not in the early 1960s. He had worked as a trader and produce inspector for the Gambia Produce Marketing Board; see *Gambia Onward*, March 17, 1981. According to the British high commissioner, a kindly description of Coker was that he was "a venerable gentleman of failing faculties" and that other views about him were more terse and less courteous; see FCO 65/1090, Collins to Bambury, March 24, 1972.

144. The cabinet reshuffle is discussed in Hughes, "After the Elections"; PPP, *Voice*, 129; and FCO 65/1090, Collins to Bambury, April 6, 1972 (who gives full details of the changes). It was rumored around this time that Jawara wanted to appoint Jack as vice president, but that this was deemed unacceptable to the Mandinka and some sections of the Wolof communities; see FCO 65/1457, enclosure to Parker to Date, May 24, 1974.

145. The expulsion of N'Jie is noted in Bakarr, *Gambia Yesterday*, 46; and FCO 65/1090, Parker to Date, September 22, 1972 (who suggests that N'Jie's refusal to take the required oath was another factor). N'Jie argued that he was unjustly removed from the House; see FCO 65/1453, N'Jie to Hart, February 28, 1974.

146. See FCO 65/1453, note by Date, June 7, 1974. Prior to his arrival in London that April, N'Jie appealed directly to Judith Hart, then minister of overseas development, to assist him in his quest; see N'Jie to Hart, February 28, 1974 in the same file.

147.. See Appendix table C.9 for the by-election result. N'Jie later claimed that Jawara spent more than £4,600 on the contest, apart from illegal gifts in kind, and around 800 PPP supporters had newly registered in the constituency, having transferred from other constituencies in Banjul and the provinces; see FCO 65/1453, N'Jie to Hart, February 28, 1974; N'Jie, "Notes" for FCO, May 1974. On Jobe (who had retired from the Attorney General's Department in 1966), see *GG*, July 2, 1966.

148. A circular letter found in the GWU files, which was issued by M. L. K. Cham, the president of the Independent group in Kombo North, and dated May 5, 1973, suggests that this followed a meeting between Landing O. Sonko and Jawara. It is, however, evident from Cham's letter that not all the Independent candidates and their supporters wished to rejoin the PPP. According to Nyang, "Recent Trends," 41, Dr. Lamin Saho, one of the leaders of the Independent movement, had sought to join the PPP in 1972, but his application was blocked by Sheriff Dibba, who regarded him as a dangerous political rival in the Baddibu area.

149. Drammeh was believed to have suffered some kind of mental breakdown after his victory and traveled to a spiritual guide (marabout) in Mauritania with his father after the election. Local rumors had it that he was placed under a spell by his PPP rival, Dabo. See *WA*, November 26, 1973, 1680; December 10, 1973, 1748; FCO 65/1452, Diplomatic Report no. 195/74, Report by J. R. W. Parker, January 9, 1974 (hence "Parker Report 1974"); Hughes, "Green Uprising," 72 (note 42); Sagnia, *Gambian Legislature*, 44–45 (who incorrectly states that the by-election was held in December); and Nyang, "Gambian Political Parties," 173.

150. These appointments are listed in Hughes and Gailey, *Historical Dictionary*, 59.

151. The most detailed account of the affair is in FCO 65/1090, Parker to Date, September 22, 1972. See also "Dibba and the Butut Affair," *WA*, October 2, 1972, 1321; da Costa, "An Obsessive Disciplinarian"; PPP, *Voice*, 130; *GNB*, September 16, 1972; and Hughes, "Green Uprising," 72–73. See also *Foroyaa*, December 30, 1988, which contains the exchange of correspondence between Dibba and Jawara in September 1972. Dibba admitted (Hughes interview, Banjul, March 1984) that his brother did take contraband radios to Senegal, but claimed that it was a Senegalese trader, traveling in the same vehicle, who was dealing in the coins. Dibba believed that the Senegalese Customs were tipped off, possibly by one of his political rivals.

152. FCO 65/1090, Macrae to Date, October 13, 1972, describes the reshuffle and notes that apart from Jawara himself, there were only two Mandinka in the cabinet, Yaya Ceesay and Kalilou Singhateh, and that both were regarded as lightweights by the Mandinka community. See also "Dibba for Brussels," *WA*, October 23, 1972, 1440.

153. The cabinet reshuffle is discussed in detail in FCO 65/1453, Ashbourne to Date, July 12, 1974.

154. For the PPP viewpoint, see PPP, *Voice*, 130–31. See also FCO 65/1612, Parker to Lewis, August 6, 1975, which is a strongly pro-Jawara account. Dibba's opinion is outlined in Fletcher, "Party Politics," 232–33; and da Costa, "An Obsessive Disciplinarian." See also Nyang, "Recent Trends," 36–37; and Lamin Sanneh, "Political Innovation in The Gambia," *WA*, May 7, 1979, 787–88. None of these sources identify Dibba's main opponents. For a discussion of the strike and Dibba's role in it, see Perfect, "Organised Labour," 225–32. Nyang also suggests that Dibba's political rivals had made several earlier abortive attempts to get him expelled from the government. Dibba identified his party rivals in an interview with Hughes (Banjul, April 1977).

155. FCO 65/1612, Parker to Lewis, September 10, 1975; and NCP, *Constitution of the National Convention Party* (Banjul: National Convention Party, 1975). The Busumbala rally is also described in *Foroyaa*, June 30, 1991; July 15, 1991. Fletcher, "Party Politics," 233, incorrecty states that Dibba was expelled on September 8 and that the NCP was formed on September 23.

156. See Nyang, "recent trends," 38–40, and FCO 65/1612, Parker to Lewis, September 10, 1975, for the economic factors behind the NCP support. Parker noted that it had been suggested to him that the NCP was receiving financial support from Mandinka petty traders in Banjul, who were facing competition from Mauritanians and other more successful groups. See also Chapter 1, 37, for a review of the economic situation at this time.

157. Another Head Chief, Kebba T. Jammeh, of Upper Baddibu (a former deputy speaker of the House of Representatives) also joined the NCP. On Dibba and Jammeh, see Bakarr, *Gambia Yesterday*, 36; 57–58; Gamble, *North Bank*, vol. C, 117; [Gambia Government], *Gambia Staff List 1967*, iv (Bathurst: Government Printer, 1967); and *GW*, June 22, 1990.

158. On the NCP's initial support, and Jawara's response, see Fletcher, "Party Politics," 234–36; PPP, *Voice*, 131–32; and FCO 65/1612, Parker to Lewis, September 10, 1975. It is not clear whether Gibou Jagne joined the NCP on its foundation or later.

159. Hughes, "Green Uprising," 73; see also FCO 65/1452, "Parker Report 1974." Sanneh, "Political innovation," 787, also claims that the opposition of Banjul politicians prevented Mandinka being used as the language of primary schools and that this caused further resentment within the community.

160. Dibba public speeches and interviews with Hughes (Banjul, 1977).

161. See NCP, *The Farafenni Declaration* (Banjul: National Convention Party, 1976). For a discussion of the NCP program, see Arnold Hughes, "Election Time in The Gambia," *WA*, April 4, 1977, 649–50. See also FCO 65/1612, Parker to Lewis, September 10, 1975, on the NCP's policies. The PPP motto is given in PPP, *Voice*, unnumbered preliminary page. See Chapter 6, 144, on its emblem.

162. For accounts of the election, see Arnold Hughes, "Election Time in The Gambia"; Hughes, "Gambia Election Report," *WA*, April 18, 1977, 743–45; Fletcher, "Party Politics," 241–54; and PPP, *Voice*, 132–35.

163. The official number of voters was recorded as 212,688 for thirty-four out of thirty-five constituencies (excluding Jokadu); see *GG*, April 3, 1977. Fletcher, "Party Politics," 251, gives a (total) figure of 211,300.

164. Bakarr, *Gambia Yesterday*, 57, notes that Saho was selected as the new PPP candidate in Central Baddibu as early as the end of October 1975. See also PPP, *Voice*, 125–26; and FCO 65/1612, Parker to Lewis, September 10, 1975; Rogers to Gore, November 18, 1975. On Singhateh, Janneh, and N'Jie, see [Gambia Government], *Members of the Government.* Manneh gained a doctorate from Rutgers University (U.S.) and Saho one from the Ruhr University, Bochum (Germany).

165. The PPP campaign is discussed in Hughes, "Election Time in The Gambia," and Fletcher, "Party Politics," 248–49.

166. In addition, it is probable that M. K. Sanneh, the Independent candidate in Western Kiang in 1972, contested the same constituency for the NCP in 1977, but was wrongly listed in the results as "M. L. Sanneh." See Sagnia, *Gambian Legislature*, 66–72. See also PPP, *Voice*, 132, on Sidibeh.

167. Sanyang's elder brother, Momodou L. Sanyang, stood as an Independent in Eastern Foni in 1972; see Hughes and Gailey, *Historical Dictionary*, 154. Kukoi Sanyang's background is discussed in Chapter 8, 210–11.

168. The only source for the reasons for Darbo's defection is Sheriff Dibba, who was interviewed by *Foroyaa*, July 30, 1991; see also Hughes, "Election Time in The Gambia"; and Nyang, "Gambian Political Parties," 186–87, on Darbo. M. S. Darbo was duly selected as the NCP candidate in Wuli. The Darbo brothers were also called Dabo or Darboe.

169. On the NCP campaign, see Hughes, "Election Time in The Gambia," and Fletcher, "Party Politics," 245–49.

170. All four candidates used the UP symbol of an umbrella; see *GG*, April 13, 1977. A meeting was held in January 1977 between some members of the UP leadership (but not P. S. N'Jie) and the NLP's Alasan N'Dure and Pap Secka to discuss electoral collaboration, but it is not clear whether a formal pact was agreed either then or subsequently; see *The Nation*, January 15, 1977 and *Foroyaa*, July 30, 1991. In practice, according to Fletcher, "Party Politics," 247, there was virtually no joint campaigning between the parties. In Banjul South, the UP and NLP formed a joint Strategy Committee to oppose Garba-Jahumpa. See UP/NLP Banjul South Strategy Committee, "The Next General Elections: An Open Letter Replying to the PPP Member (Candidate) for Banjul South (Half Die)" (ICS Library, London).

171. Fletcher, "Party Politics," 244.

172. *The Nation*, October 11, 1975. *Foroyaa*, July 30, 1991, describes the sequence of events. See also Sheriff Bojang, "Pap Cheyassin Secka: A Man for All Seasons," *WO*, May 24–26, 1996; this was an interview with Secka.

173. On Secka and the NLP, see Bojang, "Secka"; Hughes and Gailey, *Historical Dictionary*, 127; Nyang, "Recent Trends," 39–40; Fletcher, "Party Politics," 229–31; *WA*, December 22, 1975, 1590; FCO 65/1612, Parker to Lewis, September 10, 1975; S. A. Bakarr, *The Treason Trial of Trials: The Republican State of The Gambia Versus S. M. Dibba, Pap Cheyassin Secka and Five Others* (Banjul: The Author, 1982); and S. A. Bakarr, *The Law of Treason in the Republic of The Gambia Versus Alieu Sallah & 6 Revolutionists* (Banjul: the author, 1981), 3.

174. The death of N'Dure is noted in Bakarr, *Gambia Yesterday*, 60. See Fletcher, "Party Politics," 253, on the extent of NLP campaigning.

175. On Juwara, see S. B. Danso, "Detained Politician Named Man of the Year," *Daily Observer*, January 6, 1997; and Omar Bah, "Lamin Waa Juwara: Ndam Leader," *Daily Observer*, August 1, 2004 (an interview with him).

176. The various estimates are by John A. Wiseman, *Democracy in Black Africa: Survival and Revival* (New York: Paragon, 1990), 54 (82 percent); Sagnia, *Gambian Legislature*, 72 (83 percent); and Fletcher, "Party Politics," 4 (84 percent). The official return was given as 83.3 percent as stated in *GG*, April 3, 1977.

177. Detailed election results are in Appendix table C.5. These are from *GNB*, April 7, 1977; Bakarr, *Gambia Yesterday*, 87–88; and Sagnia, *Gambian Legislature*, 69–72. We follow *GNB* where the results differ. The Jokadu result (which was technically a by-election) is included in these results. It took the NCP 8,042 votes to return an MP, whereas the PPP required 5,024 votes only; figures for the thirty-one contested seats. Edie, "Democracy in The Gambia," 166, gives a slightly different summary.

178. A claim set out at some length after the election by the defeated NCP candidate, Antoine (Antouman) Jatta (Hughes interview, Banjul, April 1977).

179. Singhateh was also unpopular with working-class voters and trade unionists for his perceived role in bringing about the downfall of the GWU, which was deregistered in January 1977; see Perfect, "Organised Labour," Chapter 10, for a full discussion of the events leading up to deregistration.

180. Authors' calculations. This updates an earlier assessment by Hughes, "Gambia Election Report," that only five NCP candidates were not Mandinka.

181. Fletcher, "Party Politics," 245–46.

182. The uncharitable PPP view was that the NCP stretched its scarce resources too widely because of "vanity"; see PPP, *Voice*, 132. However, as indicated, Dibba was seeking to supplant the PPP, not to create yet another ineffectual party.

183. As in previous elections, opposition parties disputed a number of election results, but their claims of irregularities by the PPP were turned down by the courts. Less partisan observers would concede only a handful of constituency results to be "fixed," certainly too

few to alter the overall results. As noted, it was not vote fixing, so much as the unfair (and sometimes improper) advantages enjoyed by the ruling party, as well as the shortcomings of its opponents, which determined the outcome of this and other Gambian elections. Dibba's views are outlined in "Democracy at Work," *WA*, May 15, 1978, 917.

184. *Foroyaa*, August 30, 1991; and Bakarr, *Gambia Yesterday*, 61. Both sources state that he died on April 7.

185. Perfect, "Organised Labour," 257; and Hughes and Gailey, *Historical Dictionary*, 84. Garba-Jahumpa (Hughes interview, Banjul, April 1977) blamed Jack for his downfall. The criticisms of Garba-Jahumpa's record as a constituency MP were also effective; he was also attacked, for example, for allowing the boat building industry to decline and for failing to improve housing in the area. See UP/NLP, Banjul South Strategy Committee, "The Next General Election."

186. Hughes interviews with P. S. N'Jie and Kebba Foon (Banjul, March 1977). Fletcher, "Party Politics," 244, notes that the UP carried out very little campaigning even in Banjul, where it complacently assumed that it would retain both its seats.

187. See Appendix table C.9.

188. Bakarr, *Gambia Yesterday*, 66; and PPP, *Voice*, 138.

189. Hughes and Gailey, *Historical Dictionary*, 132.

190. The turnout in Sami was particularly high; see "Matchet's Diary," *WA*, April 18, 1977, 756–57.

191. The cabinet changes are discussed in Hughes, "Gambia Election Report." Although not discussed in this article, it should also be noted that political gossip in Banjul linked Jack's name to allegations of corruption involving the importation of British Leyland buses into The Gambia. However, these were never substantiated. Jack subsequently took on his old position of speaker of the House; see *WA*, May 23, 1977, 107.

192. Only Jabang of the three new ministers was under forty. Jallow was now fifty-seven, while Semega-Janneh (who had been active in politics since the early 1950s) may well have been in his sixties.

193. According to Ba Tarawally, "How Gambia's By-Election Was Fought," *WA*, June 26, 1978, 1216–17. See also "Dembo Bojang: The Gambia's Longest Serving MP," *The Gambia Daily* (*GD*), May 1999, which attributes his success to the emphasis he gave to local issues. *Foroyaa*, August 30, 1991, records Camara's death.

194. See John A. Wiseman, "Local Elections in The Gambia: Where the Marble Rings the Bell," *The Round Table*, no. 275 (1979, July), 237. The local election had been delayed since the previous summer because of the drought; see *WA*, June 26, 1978, 1216.

Chapter 8

1. The main source on the 1981 coup is Arnold Hughes, "The Attempted Gambian Coup d'Etat of 27 [30] July 1981," in *Studies in Society and Politics*, ed. Hughes, 92–106, which was published in 1991. Two useful sources published since 1991 are PPP, *Voice*, 90–107, which assesses the coup from the PPP perspective; and Codou Mbassy Diene-Njie, *Gambia: The Fall of the Old Order* (Dakar: les Editions Cheikh Anta Diop, 1996), 63–71. Earlier analyses by Hughes and Wiseman also remain useful. See Hughes, "The Gambia at the Crossroads," *Contemporary Review* 239, no. 1390: (1981), 225–30; "Why the Gambian Coup Failed," *WA*, October 26, 1981, 2498–2502; and "The Gambia After the Coup Attempt," *WA*, November 2, 1981, 2570–73. See John A. Wiseman, "Revolt in The Gambia: A Pointless Tragedy," *The Round Table*, no. 284 (1981, October), 373–80; and "Attempted Coup in The Gambia:

Marxist Revolution or Punk Rebellion?" *Communist Affairs* 1, no. 2 (1982), 434–43. See also Sallah, "Economics and Politics," 632–39. The published sources are supplemented through interviews by Hughes with former radicals and with senior political leaders (Dawda Jawara, Sheriff Dibba, and Assan Musa Camara) in The Gambia and England.

2. The term "verandah boys," is widely used in the literature on post-war Gold Coast nationalism; see, for example, David Apter, "Ghana," in *Political Parties and National Integration*, ed. Coleman and Rosberg, 279; 404. Similarly, Austin, *Politics in Ghana*, 13–18, discusses the important political role played by elementary school teachers (Standard VII boys) in the Gold Coast in the 1940s and 1950s.

3. Hughes, "Gambian Coup," 94. The phrase "neocolonial stooges or puppets," was used by one of Hughes's "radical" informants.

4. Nyang, "Garba-Jahumpa." According to Acting Governor Smith, around ninety Gambian boys were then in Accra in the Ghanaian Young Pioneers. Smith added that the course was originally intended to last for six months, but might be extended to a year; see FO 371/161579, Smith to Watson, March 15, 1962.

5. On Guinean aid to the GWU, see Perfect, "Organised Labour," 132. The British high commissioner noted in 1973 that Guinean propaganda was popular amongst the young urban unemployed and self-styled "intellectuals"; see FCO 65/1287, Parker to Date, February 23, 1973; and FCO 65/1452, "Parker Report 1974."

6. Several of Hughes' informants in Banjul spoke of these countries as helping to inform and influence radical thinking. The British high commissioner also noted with concern in 1973 that there was some evidence that the *Soviet News*, the *Peking Review*, and some North Korean magazines were gaining subscribers amongst younger student elements; see FCO 26/1412, Annex to Parker to Brinson, August 30, 1973.

7. FCO 65/915, Diplomatic Report no. 145/71, Report by J. G. W. Ramage, February 11, 1971 (hence "Ramage Report 1971"). *GE*, May 11, 1970, notes that Jones was the president of the society. He was also president of the (North) Korean–Gambian Friendship Association; see T. M. Sosseh to Choi Chol Sun, July 30, 1970 (GWU files). Jones told Hughes (interview, Banjul, April 1975), that he turned to the Russians after 1966, when he felt abandoned politically and economically by the PPP. He first visited North Korea in 1968.

8. The GLU first affiliated with the WFTU in 1945, but then affiliated with the rival, pro-American, International Confederation of Free Trade Unions in 1949. See Hughes and Perfect, "Trade Unionism," 568. On the GLU's admiration for Kim Il Sung, see issues of *The Worker*, especially that of November 19, 1976. It should be noted, though, that such "admiration" often owed as much to financial factors as to ideological sympathy. Both M. B. Jones and Rudolph Allen (the editor of the *Gambia Onward*) admitted that financial considerations determined their links to international Communism. Allen profitably published Kim Il Sung's turgid "Juche" ("self-reliance") philosophy in the *Onward*, but had no interest in its subject matter.

9. Hughes, "Gambian Coup," 94.

10. Wiseman, "Party Political Support," 17. See also Chapter 1, 8–9; 37, for a discussion of the population expansion of the 1960s and 1970s and the economic problems of the 1970s. An article published in the government's *Gambia News Bulletin* shortly before the coup also pointed out the economic and social problems faced by rural migrants to the urban areas; see Gumbo Touray, "Rural–Urban Migration: The Gambia Example," *GNB*, January 5, 1981.

11. Hughes, "Gambian Coup," 94. The two best examples of involvement in violent clashes were the 1955 clash between GMC and UP supporters, which resulted in P. S. N'Jie's removal from the Legislative Council, and the anti-chiefs campaign by PPP youths in 1960. See Chapter 5, 128; Chapter 6, 148.

12. On the 1961 general strike and the subsequent decline of the GWU after 1961, see Perfect, "Organised Labour," 142–91.

13. The formation of the GNYC and its ideology is noted in *GNB*, November 7, 1963. However, it should be noted that two of its seven listed officers, O. C. Bunhatab Jallow and William E. Hydara-Colley, represented the PPP Youth Movement. The other organizations represented on the GNYC were the GWU's Young Workers Movement; the Mansakonko Welfare Society; the Yundum College Students Association; and the Central Council of Youth Clubs. The last-named was established in the mid-1950s. Further information on the Central Council of Youth Clubs was provided by A. E. Cham-Joof (its founder) (Perfect interview, Banjul, May 1984).

14. Hughes, "Gambian Coup," 94–97.

15. Our main oral sources are two former radical activists, Ibrahima Jallow (Hughes interview, Birmingham, August 1997) and Femi Peters (Hughes interviews, Banjul, November and December 1997). Additional oral information from Halifa Sallah (Hughes interview, Bakotu, April 1992) and two one-hour tapes of a radical discussion group organized for Hughes by Jonkunda Daffeh in Banjul in 1991. Interviewing major participants in radical Gambian political organizations, or indeed, establishing the veracity of their accounts, has proved challenging. In addition to the ephemeral and obscure nature of these movements, and the conflicting accounts given by rival informants, obtaining interviews has never been easy. Possible sources of information were not always available; some were dead, others abroad, yet others no longer wished to be reminded of their youthful activities. There was also a lingering suspicion of "Western" academics.

16. See *Tonya Menta*, September 6, 1965, in GWU file, 1b/1, Gambia Labour Department, Banjul.

17. A strike was organized by the Gambia Teachers' Union over the sacking of three teachers at the Gambia High School in May 1966; Yundum College had a tradition for militancy. On the strike, see *GNB*, April 23, 1966; May 26, 1966; and Gambia Teachers' Union documents in the files of the GWU. See also [Gambia Government], *Report of an Enquiry Into the Complaints Made by Students of Yundum College in January 1964 by S. H. M. Jones* (SP no. 18 of 1964) (Bathurst: Government Printer, 1964).

18. Sallah and Bala-Gaye both eventually reached the highest civil service rank of permanent secretary. Sallah was serving as permanent secretary in the Office of the Vice Chairman in 1995. See [Gambia Government], *Gambia Staff List 1970* (Bathurst: Government Printer, 1970), 86; and *New Citizen*, April 21, 1995. Bala-Gaye (who joined the civil service in 1971) rose to become permanent secretary in the Ministry of Finance in 1982. After leaving the civil service for a business career, he was appointed secretary of state for finance and economic affairs by President Jammeh in September 2003. Details of his curriculum vitae were downloaded from the Gambian government cabinet Web site http://www.statehouse.gm/cabinet.html, in December 2004. Semega-Janneh was called to the bar in London in 1975 (*WA*, December 8, 1975, 1503) and sought the PPP nomination in Banjul South in 1992.

19. On Taal, see Chapter 7, note 133.

20. See *Kent Street Vous Journal* II, no. 6: (issued late 1969) (GWU files). This is the only issue of the *Journal* that we have seen.

21. For details of the protest and the KSV's role within it, see FCO 65/918. The names of the KSV leaders involved in organizing the demonstration are not given. *Gambia Onward*, February 24, 1971, reports the GNYC's condemnation of the Senegalese position. Because M. M. Taal was president of the GNYC, it is likely that it supported the demonstration led by his brother.

22. FCO 65/916, Ramage to Foreign and Commonwealth Office, March 31, 1971. Unfortunately, Ramage does not provide either the name of the individual or the organization to which he belonged.

23. Hughes interview with Ibrahima Jallow, who also suggested that Manjang was one of Sallah's pupils at Crab Island School. On Sallah, see Amnesty International International Secretariat, *Amnesty International Trial Observation Missions to the Republic of The Gambia (December 1980/January 1982)* (London: Amnesty International, 1983), 2; Hughes, "Gambian Coup," 96–97; and "Opposition View of The Gambia," *WA*, December 15, 1980, 2553. Tamsir Jallow rose to prominence after the 1994 coup; see Arnold Hughes, "'Democratisation' Under the Military in The Gambia: 1994–2000," *Commonwealth & Comparative Politics* 38, no. 3: (2000), 46–47. Nothing is known of the background of the other BBM leaders.

24. See *WA*, January 3, 1970, 24; and FCO 65/915, "Ramage Report 1971," on Carmichael's visit.

25. On Sanyang's alleged role, see Hughes and Gailey, *Historical Dictionary*, 154.

26. See Bakarr, *Gambia Yesterday*, 33; and *WA*, December 13, 1969, 1528; January 3, 1970, 24.

27. The main source on the events of the KNMF foundation is Peters (Hughes interviews, Banjul, 1997). Unfortunately, we have not been able to ascertain the date of the demonstration and symposium, but believe that it occurred fairly soon after Nkrumah's death. Zaya Yeebo, *State of Fear in Paradise: The Military Coup in The Gambia and Its Implications for Democracy* (London: Africa Research and Information Bureau, 1995), 117, also gives a foundation date for the KNMF of 1972. Peters briefly described his background in an interview with Perfect (Banjul, August 1984).

28. Yeebo, *State of Fear*, 117, lists Manjang, Sarr, Sallah, and Fatty as among the founders of the KNMF; Peters mentioned himself and Marenah (Hughes interviews, Banjul, 1997). On Sarr, who was employed as a mathematics and/or physics teacher at the Gambia High School in 1983, see Baboucar Gaye, "Arrests and Detention in Banjul," WA, November 14, 1983, 2652; and Baboucar Gaye, "Six Detainees Released," *WA*, May 28, 1984, 1142.

29. Jatta was only mentioned by Ibrahima Jallow, who was possibly not directly involved in the KNMF; in any case, because Jatta went to France in 1972, he can only have been an active member for a short time. His biographical details are from *GW*, April 17, 1992; and Sheriff Bojang, "PDOIS Leader, Sidia Jatta Speaks Out," *Daily Observer*, September 5, 1996.

30. *GD*, October 11, 1995, describes his later career.

31. Yeebo, *State of Fear*, 117. Further information from Femi Peters (Hughes interviews, Banjul, 1997).

32. Amnesty International, *Trial Observation*, 2. This is presumably based on Sallah's testimony. On his brother, see *WA*, December 17, 1974, 1785.

33. On Jatta, see *GW*, April 17, 1992. Details on Manjang were supplied by Ibrahima Jallow (Hughes interview, August 1997).

34. On Peters' political career, see *WO*, January 4–5, 1997. Information on his earlier trade union career was from his interview with Perfect (Banjul, August 1984).

35. On Marenah, see *GW*, March 12, 1993; and John A. Wiseman, "Military Rule in The Gambia: An Interim Assessment," *Third World Quarterly* 17, no. 5: (1996), 929.

36. See FCO 65/1091, "Collins Report."

37. See Nenneh Faye, "Taking Stock," *WA*, September 4–10, 1995, 1402–3, citing Ndey Jobarteh, on the KNMF's lack of interest in women's issues. See Chapter 2, 53, on the PPP's willingness to use nominations to Parliament to promote women in politics; for an opposite perspective, see Diene-Njie, *Fall of the Old Order*, 59.

38. The Nigerian trade union leader, Michael Imoudu, provides one such example; see Robin Cohen, *Labour and Politics in Nigeria, 1945–71* (London: Heinemann, 1974).

39. Perfect, "Organised Labour," 188. Jallow's political role is discussed in Chapter 7.

40. The GLU newspaper, *The Worker*, contains many references to such visits made by GLU leaders and members. For example, the issue of April 20, 1981, reported on the visit of M. M. Ceesay to attend the May Day celebrations in Cuba.

41. Gaye, "Six Detainees Released." Yeebo, *State of Fear*, 117, gives a later date of 1979 for its establishment.

42. The first issue of *The Voice* appeared some time between October 1978 and January 1979; the second number, which was entitled "In Search of Scapegoats," appeared in early January 1979. See "Glimpses of The Gambia," *WA*, March 12, 1979, 436–39. *New African*, January 1984, 35; and Gaye, "Six Detainees Released," list the names of those suspected of being involved in the group. On Sarho (who is called Sahor in *West Africa*), see Cherno Baba Jallow, "MOJA Activist Unburdens His Soul to *Daily Observer*," *Daily Observer*, March 23, 1995.

43. Among the epithets applied to various named ministers and ex-ministers included: "embezzler and bribe taker"; "big crook"; "thief"; "gangster"; and "mugger." Collectively they were described as "untrained, unschooled and parasitic bush pigs." See *The Voice*, "In Search of Scapegoats," 3–4.

44. Radelet and McPherson, "The Politics of Economic Reform," 34, make the connection between the growth of the public sector and an increased ability for politicians, bureaucrats, and special interest groups "for manipulating public resources for their own benefit."

45. Ben Asante, "Prescription for Conflict," *New African*, January 1981, 19–21 (interview with Secka).

46. Ceesay was first replaced as minister of agriculture and then, having served for a fortnight as a minister of state in the President's Office, was sacked from the cabinet altogether. See "Ceesay Dismissed," *WA*, October 9, 1978, 2020; *WA*, January 15, 1979, 109; *GNB*, September 14, 1978; and Sillah, "Yaya Ceesay." Ceesay, who was called "a thief" by *The Voice*, 3, revealed in his evidence to the Commission of Inquiry into Land Administration after the 1994 coup that he acquired fourteen plots of land; see *Daily Observer*, April 19, 1995. See also FCO 65/1453, Ashbourne to Date, July 12, 1974, who states that Ceesay notoriously used his (previous) position as minister of local government and lands "to further his land-owning interests."

47. For example, after resigning from the cabinet in September 1978 allegedly on the grounds of old age, Kebba Leigh, whom *The Voice*, 3, called a "big crook," was almost immediately appointed a director of the Seagull Cold Stores Ltd. Seagull was partially owned by the government. See also *WA*, September 4, 1978, 1768; October 9, 1978, 3020. On Seagull, see [Gambia Government], *Second Five Year Plan*, 365.

48. The RDP I report is summarized in "Round Holes: Square Pegs," *WA*, November 14, 1983, 2610–11, which notes that the secretary general of the Civil Service, Francis Mboge, who was strongly criticized by the commission, was allowed to retire on a full pension. See also McNamara and Shipton, "Rural Credit and Savings," 103–4. Asante, "Prescription for Conflict," reports Secka's complaint that the commission's report had not yet been published.

49. *The Voice*, "In Search of Scapegoats," 4; and Asante, "Prescription for Conflict."

50. See Chapter 11, 284.

51. *The Voice*, "In Search of Scapegoats."

52. For a detailed discussion of the general strike and the deregistration of the GWU, see Perfect, "Organised Labour," Chapter 10; see also, Wogu Ananaba, *The Trade Union Movement in Africa: Promise and Performance* (London: C. Hurst, 1979), 19–21. As Perfect points out, the restrictions imposed on trade unions by the 1976 act were comparatively

mild by African standards. By the mid-1970s, the right to strike was severely limited in most African states and curtailed altogether in many; even in another liberal democracy, Botswana, strikes had only been legal since 1969, but a long and detailed procedure had to be followed in advance. See Dave Cooper, "Unions in Botswana: Comparisons With Lesotho," *South African Labour Bulletin* 10, no. 8: (1985), 109.

53. Yeebo, *State of Fear*, 117; Diene-NJie, *Fall of the Old Order*, 64; and "The Gambia's MOJA," *WA*, November 3, 1980, 2172 (which suggests that MOJA was formed in late 1979). As noted in Amnesty International, *Trial Observation*, 6, MOJA held its first Congress on August 24, 1980.

54. Yeeb, *State of Fear*, 117, lists the three men as founders of MOJA-G. On Sarho's earlier political affiliations, see Jallow, "MOJA Activist." Amnesty International, *Trial Observation*, 2, notes that Sallah was unemployed at the time of his arrest. It is unclear if Manjang had returned to The Gambia from Scandinavia.

55. Christopher Clapham, "Liberia," in *Contemporary West African States*, ed. Donal B. Cruise O'Brien, John Dunn, and Richard Rathbone (Cambridge: Cambridge University Press, 1989), 101–3, describes MOJA's foundation and notes its lack of involvement in the coup. "Matchet's Diary," *WA*, February 2, 1981, 206, states that no contact between the two MOJA organizations had been established.

56. It is significant that Sarho, a MOJA member, was arrested for distributing *The Voice*.

57. *WA*, "The Gambia's MOJA," November 3, 1980. See also Nii K. Bentsi-Enchill, "Koro Sallah Interview—1," *WA*, March 22, 1982, 761–65; "Koro Sallah Interview—2," March 29, 1982, 851–58.

58. Juwara was a building assistant, and the others were all unemployed. Modu Jobe was a police officer; M'Boge and Tamba, clerks in the Public Works Department; and Bekai Jobe, an apprentice mechanic. See Amnesty International, *Trial Observation*, 2. See also Sallah, "Economics and Politics," 632.

59. Amnesty International, *Trial Observation*, 36.

60. The attorney general, Fafa M'Bai, rejected Amnesty International's claim. See *Trial Observation*, especially 6–8; 23–25. See also *WA*, "Matchet's Diary," February 2, 1981, 206.

61. PPP, *Voice*, 103. Secka had also been involved in a business venture as managing director of Boye Sajo's Enterprises Ltd; see Bakarr, *Trial of Trials*, 3.

62. Asante, "Prescription for Conflict"; and *WA*, "Opposition View of The Gambia," December 15, 1980. The latter was an interview with Secka (wrongly called Pap Seega in the article).

63. S. A. Bakarr, "The Gambia in Perspective," *WA*, January 26, 1981, 165.

64. See PPP, *Voice*, 96–97. *WA*, "Matchet's Diary," February 2, 1981, 206, notes that the incidents occurred "Some weeks ago," but does not give a precise date.

65. On George and Kah, see Hughes, "Gambian Coup," 96; PPP, *Voice*, 103; and *The Sun*, July 29, 1980, which terms the original party, the GSRP and its successor, the Gambia Underground Socialist Revolutionary Party. See also *GG*, October 30, 1980.

66. On the origins of the Field Force, see Hughes and Gailey, *Historical Dictionary*, 79.

67. The estimate by N'Dow N'Jie is in "118 Field Force Rebels Cashiered," *WA*, September 14, 1981, 2154. Colonel Ngom, the commander of the Senegalese troops, gave the same figure in an interview; see Nii K. Bentsi-Enchill, "Senegalese Presence in The Gambia," *WA*, January 11, 1982, 78–79. The higher estimate by Hughes, "Gambian Coup," 97, was based on the evidence of Commander E. S. Nicol, the acting commander of the Depot at the time of the coup. Nicol stated in his trial evidence that there were "over 400 but less than 500 men at the Depot"; see [Gambia Court of Appeal], *Criminal Appeal no. 5–11/81* (Banjul: Gambia Court of Appeal, 1982), 43. In addition, there were several dozen Field Force men at the Pioneer Unit at Farafenni and others on duty at State

House in Central Banjul, Cape Point State House, and elsewhere. Two earlier estimates by Richard Booth and the British High Commission gave the Field Force strength as 150 (1970) and 250 (1974). See Booth, *The Armed Forces of African States, 1970.* Adelphi Paper no. 67. (London: Institute for Strategic Studies, 1970) 10; and FCO 65/1454, White to Lewis, May 3, 1974. On N'Dow N'Jie, see Kaye Whiteman, "Top Brass in Banjul," *WA*, February 19–25, 1990, 278–79.

68. For brief details, see FCO 38/137, Crombie to Norris, June 16, 1967.

69. Hughes, "Gambian Coup," 97; and PPP, *Voice*, 98. See also "Senegal's Tensions With The Gambia," *WA*, November 17, 1980, 2278–79.

70. Hughes, "Gambian Coup," 97–98; and PPP, *Voice*, 100 (which incorrectly calls the assistant commander, Bakary Bojang). In an interview with Hughes (Haywards Heath, August 1998), Jawara also confirmed Bojang's envy and disaffection; he also regarded him as "more Jola than Mandinka."

71. Hughes, "Gambian Coup," 97; Diene-Njie, *Fall of the Old Order*, 64–65; PPP, *Voice*, 98; "The Gambia Breaks Off Relations With Libya," *WA*, November 10, 1980, 2216–17; and *GNB*, January 5, 1981 (which reports Jawara's New Year message). See also *WA*, "Opposition View of The Gambia," December 15, 1980, 2553, in which Secka alleged that diplomatic relations were severed with Libya at Senghor's request.

72. This reconstruction of events largely follows Hughes, "Gambian Coup," 98–101. Additional information is from PPP, *Voice*, 99–106; and Diene-Njie, *Fall of the Old Order*, 67–70. Differences between these sources are noted. Much valuable information, though requiring cautious interpretation, is to be obtained from the two trial records of those accused of plotting the insurrection. See [Gambia Court of Appeal], *Criminal Appeal no. 5–11/81*; and *Criminal Appeal no. 29/82* (Banjul: Gambia Court of Appeal, 1982). See also Bakarr, *Trial of Trials*.

73. On Sanyang's background, see "Samba Sanyang: From the Monastery to Become a Coup Maker," *Africa Now*, September 1981, 36–37; and Hughes and Gailey, *Historical Dictionary*, 154–55. The latter provides additional information to that presented in Hughes, "Gambian Coup," 96–97, and corrects several statements. Additional information is to be found in S. A. Bakarr, *The Gambia Mourns Her Image: Thursday 30th July to Thursday 6th August* (Serrekunda: The Author, 1981), 6–7.

74. *Africa Now*, "Samba Sanyang," notes his membership of the Gambia Socialist Party. See note 25 on his clandestine membership of the Black Scorpions.

75. He did not contest the by election which was held in December 1973 after the death of M. N. Sanyang, which allowed Ismaila Jammeh to be elected unopposed. See Appendix table C.9; and *GG*, November 14, 1975 (citing the minutes of the House of Representatives in December 1973).

76. *Africa Now*, "Samba Sanyang," states that he went to Guinea. PPP, *Voice*, 106, suggests that Sanyang had attempted and failed to become a teacher, but does not give further details.

77. *Africa Now*, "Samba Sanyang"; see also "Matchet's Diary," *WA*, August 17, 1981, 1865–69, which states that "Kukoi" (or "Kekoi", as the article calls him) means "sweep clean" in Mandinka.

78. *Africa Now*, "Samba Sanyang," states that he left The Gambia in 1978 and traveled to Senegal, Sierra Leone, North Africa, and Sweden over the next two years. A former teacher of Sanyang's, James Gomez, claimed in an interview that he visited Libya; see Nick Fadugba, "The Gambia: Battle for Banjul," *Africa*, September 1981, 18–19. Hughes and Perfect, "Trade Unionism," 567, report the unsubstantiated claim made by a GWU leader that Sanyang received a scholarship from the GLU. See Appendix table C.5 on the election result.

79. *Africa Now,* "Samba Sanyang."

80. Hughes and Gailey, *Historical Dictionary,* 155; Bakarr, *The Gambia Mourns Her Image,* 6–7; Bojang, "Secka"; and the trial evidence of Secka which is in [Gambia Court of Appeal], *Criminal Appeal, no. 29/82,* 121–24, Exhibit FF, Statement to Police by Secka, September 15, 1982. Another coup leader, Appai Sonko, claimed in his evidence that some of the plotters had met from January 1, 1981 onward. See [Gambia Court of Appeal], *Criminal Appeal no. 5–11/81,* 30.

81. Hughes, "Gambian Coup," 103, citing the statement of Simon Sanneh. See also [Gambia Court of Appeal], *Criminal Appeal no. 5–11/81,* Exhibit "C," 100–115; 226–29.

82. Bentsi-Enchill, "Sallah Interview—2" 855; Sallah claimed that the six MOJA activists who were arrested in October 1980 were placed on the list to implicate the organization. See also Yeebo, *State of Fear,* 117. It should be noted that, on the basis of other articles written by Bentsi-Enchill in *West Africa,* he can be regarded as strongly supportive of the Gambian radicals with whom he shared a similar pan-Africanist outlook.

83. Bojang, "Secka." According to Appai Sonko, the date of the coup was to be determined by a marabout; see [Gambia Court of Appeal], *Criminal Appeal no. 5–11/81,* 23–24.

84. Hughes, "Gambian Coup," 98, names eleven of the principal conspirators. Sallah, "Economics and Politics," 633, citing a MOJA-G source, gives a similar list with one addition (Momodou Sanyang), although with different spellings. Several other people attended at least one of the meetings in Serrekunda; see [Gambia Court of Appeal], *Criminal Appeal no. 5–11/81,* 29–30; 177–83; 226–29; 271–75. On Secka's position, see Bojang, "Secka."

85. Hughes, "Gambian Coup," 98–99. Further information from the trial evidence of Taffa Camara and M'Bemba Camara; see [Gambia Court of Appeal], *Criminal Appeal no. 5–11/81,* 177–83. Perfect, "Organised Labour," 294 (note 65), states that Kebba N'Jie, the leader of the Gambia General Transport Union (a small trade union of taxi drivers) announced his support for the coup in a radio broadcast. He later claimed that he was forced to do so and escaped punishment after the coup.

86. See Chapter 10, 261.

87. See Hughes, "Gambian Coup," 100, on the ethnic origin of George, Secka and Bojang; and Chapter 7, 192, on Secka's education.

88. Hughes, "Gambian Coup," 103; and Bojang, "Secka." Tapes of Kukoi's radio broadcasts were made available to Hughes in October 1981. Transcripts of several of these; a number of speeches made involuntarily over Radio Gambia by hostages; and broadcasts and interviews by President Jawara, are to be found in Bakarr, *The Gambia Mourns Her Image,* 10–20; 30; 38–59.

89. Trial evidence of M'Bemba Camara in [Gambia Court of Appeal], *Criminal Appeal no. 5–11/81,* 218.

90. Ibid. It was a widely held belief that the rebels avoided damaging the houses of the political elite because they intended taking them over themselves. Hughes observations.

91. Evidence of M'Bemba Camara [Gambia Court of Appeal], *Criminal Appeal no. 5–11/81,* 224. This was a widely held view in Banjul in the aftermath of the coup; Hughes observations.

92. PPP, *Voice,* 99, also notes that the coup coincided with the Muslim end-of-fast festivities and suggests that this helped to lull the vigilance of the security forces. In Jawara's view (Hughes interview, Haywards Heath, August 1998), the inspector general of police, A. S. M'Boob, and the Field Force commander, John Clews (a Briton), ignored growing evidence of unrest in the Field Force and he only learned of this from his aide de camp, N'Dow N'Jie, who would replace M'Boob after the insurrection.

93. Hughes, "Gambian Coup," 99; and PPP, *Voice,* 100. Baldeh was amongst those posthumously decorated by Jawara; see *GG,* February 18, 1982 (which wrongly spells his name as Bandeh).

94. According to N'Dow N'Jie (wrongly termed Ndaw Njie in the article), of the 358 members of the Field Force at the time of the coup, 179 were still in service in September 1981; six loyalists had been killed. Of the remainder, 118 were detained, ten insurgents were killed, twelve were cashiered, eleven were at large and were being sought, and the remaining twenty-two were unaccounted for. Although this might suggest that almost half the Field Force joined the coup, it should be noted that not all were eventually charged, suggesting some coercion. See *WA*, "118 Field Force Rebels Cashiered," September 14, 1981. Moreover, as stated in note 67, the Field Force strength may well have been higher at the time of the coup.

95. Hughes, "Gambian Coup," 99; and *GNB*, May 29, 1981.

96. Hughes, "Gambian Coup," 100. These figures were supplied to Hughes by Gambian police officials in October 1981. A slightly lower estimate of 2,500 Senegalese troops being involved is reported in Alex Rondos, "Socialist Look at Africa," *WA*, August 31, 1981, citing the Senegalese newspaper, *Le Soleil* (although Rondos has reservations about these figures). Radelet and McPherson, "The Politics of Economic Reform," 35, suggest, however, that only 1,500 Senegalese troops were involved.

97. Diene-Njie, *Fall of the Old Order*, 68, suggests that Jawara returned in Diouf's plane; this was confirmed by Jawara (Hughes interview, August 1998). Further information from A. M. Camara (Hughes interview, Banjul, December 1997).

98. The descriptions of the Senegalese campaign in Diene-Njie, *Fall of the Old Order*, 67; and PPP, *Voice*, 103, differ slightly from this account.

99. According to Diene-Njie, *Fall of the Old Order*, 68, M'Boob had collected Camara on the first day of the coup; further information from Camara (Hughes interview, December 1997). *GNB*, November 11, 1981, reports his new appointment. However, the decision to "promote" M'Boob was partly determined by Jawara's wish to replace him as operational head of the security forces.

100. The conflicting figures were given in Parliament by M. C. Jallow, the minister of labor, and the NCP MP, Foday Makalo; see *GNB*, November 16, 1981. Perfect, "Organised Labour" 294 (note 66), reports a claim by a pro-PPP union leader that the dockers were in fact dismissed because they were NCP supporters.

101. For a brief discussion, see Hughes and Perfect, "Trade Unionism," 568–69.

102. Dibba's version of events is presented in "My Conscience is Clear," *Africa*, no. 121, 1981, September 18–19 (interview with Dibba). See also his evidence at his trial, which is reported in "The Sheriff Dibba Case," *WA*, July 19, 1982, 1870; and [Gambia Court of Appeal], *Criminal Appeal, no. 29/82*, "Cautionary Statement Sheriff Dibba," 62–63; "Exhibits J–J3, Voluntary Statements Sheriff Dibba," 74–77. Further information from Dibba (Hughes interview, Banjul, March 1984). The PPP's hostile interpretation of his actions and those of the NCP is in PPP, *Voice*, 106–7.

103. On the arrests of Jagne and Sidibeh, see "Matchet's Diary," *WA*, August 24, 1981, 1914; and Amnesty International, *Trial Observation*, 14 (which notes that Sidibeh was apparently only arrested because he was confused with someone of the same name). In the same source (28), see the letter from Fafa M'Bai, the attorney general, which reveals that neither Bojang nor Makalo were detained. It is clear from the *West Africa* article that the fifth NCP MP, Fodayba Jammeh (Illiassa) was not arrested either.

104. *WA*, "The Sheriff Dibba Case," July 19, 1982, 1868–71; see Chapter 9, 223, on Jagne and Sidibeh's release.

105. Evidence of Commander M. B. Khan, [Gambia Court of Appeal], *Criminal Appeal no. 5–11/81*, 57; and "The Gambia: Sir Dawda Fights Back," *Africa Now*, September 1981, 35–36. Further information from Khan (Hughes interview, Banjul, October 1981). Diene-Njie, *Fall of the Old Order*, 69, gives a slightly different list of those detained. "Senegalere

Troops Free 135 Hostages," *The Times*, August 6, 1981, 5, citing the U.S. ambassador to The Gambia, states that about 135 hostages were released.

106. *WA*, "The Sheriff Dibba Case," July 19, 1982, 1868, reports Bojang's dismissal, and Jatta and Touray's resignations are noted in *GNB*, August 24, 1981. For a sympathetic account of Bojang's actions during the coup, which emphasizes the ill treatment handed out to one of his wives, see Bojang, "Sanjally Bojang Passes Away."

107. According to Ibrahima Jallow (Hughes interview, Birmingham, August 1997), his brother, Captain Sallah, lost his job as managing director of the Gambia Ports Authority as a result. Sallah claimed that "the people" smuggled him out of hospital; see Bentsi-Enchill, "Sallah Interview—1," 761.

108. Information on the SAS actions was provided by M. B. Khan, one of those who was rescued by them, and by A. M. Camara (Hughes interviews, Banjul, October 1981 and December 1997). For published accounts, see PPP, *Voice*, 105–6; and James Adams, *Secret Armies* (London: Hutchinson, 1987), 172–76. But see also Eddie Momoh, "Jawara and the SAS," *WA*, February 29, 1988, 352–53, for a skeptical review of the latter source.

109. Camara informed Hughes in his 1997 interview that the government genuinely tried to compile casualty figures, which were as accurate as possible under the circumstances. It relied on returns from the Royal Victoria Hospital, Banjul, and from health clinics and village chiefs in the districts around the capital. Similarly, in October 1981, some months after the coup, Hughes tried to calculate the number of deaths by interviewing hospital and cemetery employees, as well as security force contacts. Other estimates are higher. Radelet and McPherson, "The Politics of Economic Reform," 35, suggested that an estimated 1,000 Gambians died, whereas Koro Sallah—who probably exaggerated the number for political reasons—claimed that 2,000 died; see Bentsi-Enchill, "Sallah Interview—1," 763.

110. See Bentsi-Enchill, "Sallah Interview—1," 763, where Sallah claimed that hundreds of Senegalese soldiers were killed; again, this is an exaggeration. After the coup, Hughes tried to check the causes of the Senegalese military deaths. There were only two relatively serious verifiable fatal incidents; in one, a helicopter carrying a dozen or so soldiers crashed into the sea near Banjul, and in another, a lorry overturned near Kanifing. These incidents resulted in fewer than twenty deaths between them and neither could be attributed to enemy action.

111. For example, in Banjul, the Maurel et Prom supermarket and Sunar Stores were burned down, the government-owned NTC store was looted on July 31, and other expatriate-owned business premises were damaged; see *GNB*, September 2, 1981. The Banjul Chamber of Commerce later estimated that the cost to the private sector from looting and damage to equipment was D42 million; see *GNB*, January 6, 1982. Hughes, "Why the Gambian Coup Failed," reported the cost to commercial property to be £10 million.

112. PPP, *Voice*, 100, argues that the rebels received no support from police or other security units outside the main urban areas near Banjul, with the possible exception of Mansakonko. According to a British officer in charge of the Farafenni Pioneer Unit at the time of the coup, some men tried to mutiny, but were arrested, allowing him to travel to Banjul with a number of loyalists to help those besieged in the capital; Hughes interview (Banjul, October 1981).

113. Baboucar Gaye, "Coup: 24 Sentenced to Death," *WA*, April 30, 1984, 944. *GNB*, August 14, 1981, refers to the declaration of the State of Emergency. Sallah claimed that the *Gazette* list was incomplete and that more than 1,500 people were detained; see Bentsi-Enchill, "Sallah Interview—2," 855.

114. The precise number of death sentences that were imposed is not known. "The Shadow of 1981," *WA*, May 6, 1985, 870, notes that twenty-seven death sentences were

commuted in 1983 and a further sixteen in 1985, but these presumably did not include those who had escaped from The Gambia like Sanyang. Secka's release and later political activities are noted in Hughes, "Gambian Coup," 103; and Bojang, "Secka." See also *Foroyaa*, August 23–25, 2004. *WA*, October 12, 1981, 2423, reports Danso's execution.

115. See "Senegalese and Libyan 'Connections' Alleged in Treason Trial," *WA*, May 2, 1988, 815; and *WA*, July 4, 1988, 1232.

116. "Invasion Fear," *WA*, April 6–12, 1992, 600, reports on an alleged plot to invade The Gambia by a group of Gambians based in Ouagadougou who were led by Sanyang; Hughes, "'Democratisation' Under the Military," 47, notes that Sanyang's supporters launched an armed raid on the Farafenni Barracks of the Gambian National Army in November 1995.

117. "MOJA Members Held?" *WA*, May 21, 1984, 1096. The three were Batch Samba, an employee of the Gambia Ports Authority; Sarjo Bah, who worked for Action Aid; and Jennebah Bah, a cooperative secretary. Political refugee status did not stop MOJA activists from continuing to denounce the PPP government. In late 1983, a Swedish film maker, Lars Westman, clearly accepting MOJA's interpretation of events, released a highly controversial and partisan film about The Gambia post-1981, entitled "Balamba" or "The Resistance." For reactions to the film, see *The Senegambia Sun*, October 3, 1983; and *GNB*, October 5, 1983.

118. Sallah denied this charge in a letter to *WA*, May 23, 1988, 936.

119. *GW*, November 27, 1992, reports Jawara's speech to the House of Representatives that lifted the ban; the president argued that MOJA was now more mature and responsible in its political strategies.

120. According to his account, he spent fourteen months in prison; see Jallow, "MOJA Activist."

121. Gaye, "Arrests and Detention in Banjul"; Wiseman, *Democracy in Black Africa*, 59; and Chapter 9, 232.

122. Hughes, "Gambian Coup," 100–101, summarizes the external reaction; see also "Foreign Hands Are Blamed," *WA*, September 21, 1981, 2224, on the Saudi contribution. The foreign aid received was to cause the government some embarrassment as well as assistance, when it was discovered that the commissioner for administering the foreign aid fund, E. M. Taal (permanent secretary in the Ministry of External Affairs), with others, had defrauded the government. A commission of inquiry had to be set up and Taal was given a prison sentence. See [Gambia Government], *Report of the Commission to Inquire Into the Conduct and Management of the External Aid Fund* (Banjul: Government Printer, 1983).

123. Hughes, "Gambian Coup," 100–101; and "Vieira Mends Gambian Fences," *WA*, January 3, 1983, 51. In an interview with Hughes (Banjul, December 1997), Camara stated that that he was dispatched to Bissau to try and get Kukoi Sanyang extradited, but no treaty of extradition existed between the two countries. Vieira instead gave Sanyang the choice of deportation either to Cuba or to Morocco; not surprisingly, he chose the former. Camara immediately flew on to Guinea (Conakry) and Sierra Leone, whose governments promised to repatriate Sanyang if he turned up on their territory. Sékou Touré even offered to send troops to The Gambia, but this was tactfully turned down, so as not to complicate relations with Senegal.

124. "Restabilising The Gambia," *WA*, August 10, 1981, 1806, reports Libya's denials of any involvement and also notes that initially Jawara declined to accuse it specifically. This changed in later years; see especially Ad'Obe Obe, "A President's Story," *WA*, February 19–25, 1990, 265 (an interview with Jawara). In an interview with Hughes (Haywards Heath, August 1998), Jawara conceded that long-held suspicions of Libyan activities in the subregion colored his and Diouf's views. No proper investigation of the coup was held and nothing published, apparently to conceal the incompetence of senior security officials.

125. Diene-Njie, *Fall of the Old Order*, 65–66; and *GW*, November 25, 1994.

126. PPP, *Voice*, 198. Touray, *Gambia and the World*, 168, notes that North Korea condemned the coup.

127. Diene-Njie, *Fall of the Old Order*, 83–84; Arnold Hughes, "The Collapse of the Senegambian Confederation," *Journal of Commonwealth & Comparative Politics* 30, no. 2: (1992), 209; "Combined Forces," *WA*, February 7, 1983, 366; Baboucar Gaye, "National Army Created," *WA*, November 19, 1984, 2311; and *WA*, February 24–March 1992, 344.

Chapter 9

1. The State of Emergency was not lifted until February 1985; see Arnold Hughes, "The Gambia: Recent History," in *Africa South of the Sahara 1992*, 21st ed. (London: Europa Publications, 1992), 489.

2. There is no detailed study of the 1982 elections, but for shorter accounts and the results, see *GNB*, May 12, 1982; Arnold Hughes, "The Gambian General Elections," *WA*, May 10, 1982, 1241–42; Hughes, "The Gambia's Democratic Image Restored," *WA*, May 17, 1982, 1305–7; *Africa Contemporary Record* (*ACR*) 15: (1982–83), B441–43; and Elizabeth Vidler, "Regime Survival in The Gambia and Sierra Leone. A Comparative Study of the People's Progressive Party (1965–1994) and the All People's Congress (1968–1992)" (Ph.D. diss., University of Newcastle-upon-Tyne, 1998), Chapter 3, "The Role of Elections," 234–312, in which Vidler surveys the three elections between 1982 and 1992. For a partisan view see PPP, *Voice*, 140–50.

3. Arnold Hughes, "From Colonialism to Confederation: The Gambian Experience of Independence, 1965–1982," in *African Islands and Enclaves*, ed. Robin Cohen (Beverly Hills, CA: Sage, 1983), 74.

4. Wiseman, "House of Representatives" (2nd ref), 82; and *WA*, March 22, 1982, 826.

5. Hughes, "Gambian General Elections," 1241, notes that there were fourteen applicants in Northern Kombo alone. The full list of candidates was published in *GG*, May 8, 1982.

6. See Hughes, "Gambian General Elections," 1241; PPP, *Voice*, 140; and *ACR* 16: (1983–84), B422.

7. *GNB*, March 15, 1982; March 17, 1982; March 22, 1982, record the retirements of N'Jie and Sonko and that Monday and Cham withdrew their applications.

8. For a discussion of the reasons for N'Jie's resignation as vice president, see Ba Tarawally, "Not Just His Age . . .," *WA*, September 18, 1978, 1832–33. His death is noted in Hughes and Gailey, *Historical Dictionary*, 131.

9. PPP, *Voice*, 145–46, notes that Semega-Janneh was dropped by the party's central Selection Committee, but claims that Cham, M'Ballow, and Touray agreed to step down.

10. Jammeh was elected in a by-election in December 1973 following the death of Momodou Sanyang. Semega-Janneh lost his seat in 1966, but regained it in 1968, and M'Ballow was elected in 1969. See Appendix table C.9 for details.

11. One of these, I. M. Garba-Jahumpa, had retired and his successor, M. M. Taal, had defected from the UP to join the PPP. Another, A. K. N'Jie, had been replaced as the PPP candidate in Bakau in the by-election caused by the death of Bakary Camara in 1978. The others were Baba Touray (Illiassa) and Kalilou Singhateh (Lower Baddibu).

12. For the background of all four candidates, see [Gambia Government], *Members of the Government*. On Sanneh-Bojang, see also "The Gambia's Leading Lady," *WA*, July 5, 1982, 1760; and "New Health Minister Sworn In," *GD*, November 8, 1995. Further information

was supplied by Lianne Parrett, who interviewed Mrs. Nyimasata Sanneh-Bojang in April 1998.

13. Hughes, "Gambian General Elections," 1241; and PPP, *Voice*, 146. Presumably Saho stood for election because he had already been informed that he would be replaced as attorney general after the election and thus lose his seat in the House of Representatives. One former minister even informed Hughes that he was encouraged to stand by the president in the expectation that he would be defeated!

14. For details of Dabo's background and early career, see [Gambia Government], *Members of the Government*; Hughes and Gailey, *Historical Dictionary*, 55; and *The International Who's Who 1998–99*, 62nd ed. (London: Europa Publications, 1998), 355. See also *GNB*, October 5, 1981. Additional information provided by Dabo (Hughes interviews, Birmingham, May–June 1996).

15. On the Teeri Kafoo and Dabo's role in it, see Diene-Njie, *Fall of the Old Order*, 44–45; 58–59; 106–7. See also "'Tribalistic Government,'" *WA*, June 21, 1982, 1676, which reports an allegation made by the former attorney general, M. L. Saho, in *The Nation* newspaper (May 22, 1982), that Dabo had admitted that he joined the PPP in September 1981.

16. The deselection of Semega-Janneh is discussed (from a PPP viewpoint) in PPP, *Voice*, 145–46. See also "Janneh: First Victim," *WA*, August 16, 1982, 2140; and the letter from Semega-Janneh to *WA*, September 20, 1982, 2444–45, on his arrest and subsequent acquittal. *GNB*, November 17, 1982, lists the BanCC candidates.

17. Hughes, "Gambian General Elections," 1241.

18. The estimate of the number of NCP officials and supporters who were detained was by Dibba; see Baboucar Gaye, "'Jawara Must Resign'—Dibba," *WA*, September 16, 1985, 1940. The freeing of Jagne, Dibba, and Sidibeh was noted in *GG*, May 6, 1982; July 5, 1982. For a profile of Jammeh (who was released in May 1982), see http://www.udpgambia.org/ K_Jammeh.htm (downloaded March 2006).

19. On Juwara's defection, see *WA*, "The Gambia's MOJA," November 3, 1980, 2171, which reported that the NCP claimed he had been expelled for anti-party activities and for trying to usurp power. On Sanneh's defection and declining NCP support in the Baddibus see "Party Politics in Senegambia," *WA*, February 15, 1982, 427, which described Sanneh as easily the most popular NCP candidate in the Kombos. On falling support in Serrekunda West, see Bakarr, "The Gambia in Perspective," (although it should be remembered that Bakarr was a strong PPP supporter). Wiseman, "Party Political Support," 9, points out that the NCP won 51 percent of the vote in the two Serrekunda constituencies in the 1977 general election, but only 37 percent of the vote in the same constituencies in the 1979 local election. Dibba (Hughes interview, Banjul, March 1984) conceded that lack of adequate finances damaged his party's prospects. There was no money to set up a newspaper (although both the *Nation* and the *Gambia Outlook* offered some support) and the central office in Banjul was run on a shoestring. It had no paid staff and possessed only one typewriter. Its rented premises had to be given up later because it could not pay the rent.

20. The electoral pact between the NCP and the UP is noted in PPP, *Voice*, 141. Sagnia, *Gambian Legislature*, 73, lists the UP candidates. The pact between the NCP and the UP was facilitated by P. S. N'Jie's withdrawal from political life. In an interview with Hughes (Banjul, April 1982), N'Jie stated that he regarded the elections as a waste of time; the UP Central Committee was defunct and he had no knowledge of what "self-styled" UP candidates were up to.

21. This was Mohamed Jahanke in Lower Fulladu West; see *GNB*, April 19, 1982. See also *GG*, May 4, 1982 (where he is called Momadu Jamanka), which records his nomination.

22. "Expulsions Before Elections," *WA*, May 10, 1982, 1281; and *GNB*, April 16, 1982, which lists eleven of the Independents who were former members of the PPP. Only Sanna ("Ticks") Manneh (Banjul North), a journalist and former UP local councilor who claimed

to be standing as the candidate for "unemployed youth," Nganyie Touray (Saloum) and Momodou Lamin Drammeh (Jimara), were not former PPP members. On Manneh, see Hughes, "Democratic Image," 1305; and *The Hibarr* 1, no. 1 (1982). See also *Foroyaa*, February 20, 1989, which reported that he was elected to the BanCC in 1979 for the UP.

23. On Baldeh and his campaign, see Hughes, "Gambian General Elections," 1241; PPP, *Voice*, 143–44; and Hughes, field observations, 1982. Baldeh first came to public prominence at the PPP party congress in May 1979; see "Changing The Gambia," *WA*, July 30, 1979, 1361–62. The symbols of each candidate are listed in *GG*, May 4, 1982.

24. See Baboucar Gaye, "Jawara's New Opposition," *WA*, April 14, 1986, 771 (interview with Camara). Further information from Camara (Hughes interview, Banjul, January 1997).

25. Full results are in Appendix table C.6 and may be found in *GNB*, May 12, 1982; Bakarr, *Gambia Yesterday*, 87–88; and Sagnia, *Gambian Legislature*, 73–76.

26. *GNB*, May 10, 1982 gives the turnout. Sagnia, *Gambian Legislature*, 76; Hughes, "Democratic Image," 1306; and *GG*, May 8, 1982, all suggest a lower figure (58 percent), but this is misleading because it was based on the total electorate in all thirty-five constituencies, rather than on the thirty-one constituencies that were contested.

27. Ousman Manjang, "Gambian Liberation," *WA*, July 26, 1982, 1931.

28. Dibba later claimed that the "elections were, to all intents and purposes, rigged"; see Gaye, "Jawara Must Resign." Similarly, in his interview with Hughes (Banjul, March 1984), Dibba reiterated the now-familiar accusations of PPP malpractices of the kind made by all opposition parties, namely, doctoring of voters' lists, bribery and coercion, improper use of state resources, and excluding opposition agents from the counting. See also Badara K. Sidibeh, "A Code of Conduct for a Free and Fair Parliamentary and Presidential Elections in 1987." The document, which was issued on behalf of the NCP Executive Committee in February 1987, may be found in the ICS Library, London.

29. Wiseman, "Party Political Support," 21, suggests that the PPP victory in Serrekunda West occurred because a prominent former NCP supporter had rejoined the PPP after being out of the party for some years. This may have been Dembo Sanneh. See also Danso, "Saho." Sidibeh, "Code of Conduct," explicitly criticized Saho's campaign in 1982.

30. The four constituencies were Lower Fulladu West, Niani, Kantora, and Sabach Sanjal; in the first three of these, the PPP gained at least 80 percent of the vote in the preceding election. PPP, *Voice*, 141, states that the PPP was also unopposed in Sami, but this is incorrect. See also Wiseman, "Party Political Support," 25 (note 23).

31. Wiseman, "Party Political Support," 12.

32. Hughes, "Democratic Image," 1306. Prior to entering politics, Gaye was a teacher in a number of rural schools; see *GD*, October 25, 1995.

33. Results for each Administrative Area are in Appendix table D.1; these are from *GNB*, May 12, 1982. *GW*, May 1, 1992, gives a slightly higher total for Dibba of 52,136. Additional unpublished information on the outcome in certain constituencies was given to Hughes by the Election Office, Banjul, but the full results were apparently never officially published.

34. The cabinet changes are discussed in *GNB*, May 14, 1982; and Hughes, "Jawara's New Team."

35. Camara's ministerial appointments are outlined in Hughes and Gailey, *Historical Dictionary*, 47 (although they state that Camara regained the vice presidency in 1981, not 1978); see also "Mr A. M. Camara New Vice President," *WA*, September 4, 1978, 1768, on his reappointment to the post.

36. Hughes and Gailey, *Historical Dictionary*, 47, state that he remained in the cabinet as minister of education, youth and sport, but in fact this post went to A. A. N'Jie.

37. On Sabally's background and early career, see [Africa Books], *Africa Who's Who*, 1279; and [Gambia Government], *Members of the Government*. An official in the British High

Commission noted that three backbench MPs were appointed parliamentary secretaries as a way of silencing their persistent criticisms of government policies; this group would have included Sabally. See FCO 65/1453, Ashbourne to Date, July 12, 1974. Cham's sacking was noted in *Gambia Times*, January 22, 1981.

38. See Chapter 1, 37–38, page on the economic situation in the early 1980s.

39. On Sisay's career since 1972, see *GNB*, May 14, 1982.

40. On M'Bai's background, see [Africa Books], *Africa Who's Who*, 874–75.

41. On the aims and establishment of the commission, see "Rulers and Rebels," *WA*, April 19, 1982, 1042; and "Illegal Assets," *WA*, March 28, 1983, 812. For a detailed consideration of the scandal (including discussion of Nzeribe's role), see issues of *Gambia Onward*, Summer 1984. See also Baboucar Gaye, "Attorney-General Resigns," *WA*, July 2, 1984, 1348–49; Baboucar Gaye, "Fafa Mbai at Probe," *WA*, August 6, 1984, 1609; Eddie Momoh, "A Trial of Political Muscle," *WA*, October 22, 1984, 2114–15; and "M'bai's Revelations," *WA*, August 12, 1985, 1642.

42. On Jallow's case, see Baboucar Gaye, "Can the Assets Commission Survive?" *WA*, September 2, 1985, 1833.

43. On Saho's resignation, see PPP, *Voice*, 146–47; *WA*, " 'Tribalistic Government,' " June 21, 1982; and "The Gambia: Jawara Holds the Aces as Dibba Is Freed," *New African*, September 1982, 23.

44. See *GNB*, May 14, 1982, for the ages of the ministers; the article states that M'Bai was forty, but [Africa Books], *Africa Who's Who*, 874–75, states that he was only thirty-nine. Jabang and Sonko had been ministers since 1977 and 1978, respectively, and both O. A. Jallow and Manneh were promoted to the cabinet in the September 1981 reshuffle; see [Gambia Government], *Members of the Government*.

45. *GNB*, May 14, 1982; and [Gambia Government], *Members of the Government*. M'Boob, who had been appointed as minister of the interior in November 1981, held office for only a few months longer; he resigned in August 1982 after rumors (which he denied) that he was warned of a possible coup several months before it took actually took place. See *GNB*, November 11, 1981; and Baboucar Gaye, "Mboob—More Questions Than Answers," *WA*, August 23, 1982, 2190–91.

46. Hughes, "Jawara's New Team," gives the ethnic composition of the new cabinet. *New African*, "Jawara Holds the Aces," gives a slightly different view, suggesting there were eight Mandinka, five Wolof, and one Fula in the cabinet after the election.

47. According to the PDOIS Congress Report, August 26, 1986 (cited in *Foroyaa*, September 15, 1987), "DOI" meant "sufficient or adequate in one of the local languages."

48. See *GNB*, November 1, 1982; November 3, 1982. The second seminar organized by the foundation in January 1983 helped lead to the provisional re-registration of the Gambia Workers' Union later that year. See Perfect, "Organised Labour," 280–81, for a discussion. The PPP party reformers also initially supported this outcome.

49. The reforms are discussed in *ACR* 16: (1983–84), B422. To make the party newspaper a more effective voice for internal party reform, its editor, S. A. Bakarr, was replaced by a collective editorial board, chaired by the vice president, with Jay Saidy, the State House press officer, as editor-in-chief. Other members of the editorial board included Sheriff Sisay, Fafa M'Bai, and Louise N'Jie (all reform-minded ministers) and B. M. Tarawale, who was now reconciled with the party. President Jawara's wish for it to be published weekly suggested the highest support for the reformers at this time. An analysis of the editorial content of the *Gambia Times* throughout 1983 reveals a strong commitment to internal party reform aimed at mobilizing the rank and file and combating corruption and cronyism.

50. Jack's resignation is discussed in "Sir Alieu Resigns," *WA*, July 4, 1983, 1580.

51. Wiseman, "House of Representatives," 82–84, notes that the NCP did not, however, officially designate Makalo as its parliamentary leader.

52. "Resign and Be Re-Admitted," *WA*, January 10, 1983, 117.

53. On the by-election see "Barrow Wins," *WA*, April 11, 1983, 920; "PPP Wins By-Election," July 4, 1983, 1581; M. Baikoro Sillah, "Rumours and Hopes," *WA*, October 17, 1983, 2395; and *ACR* 16: (1983–84), B422. The results are in Appendix table C.9. See [Gambia Government], *Members of the Government*, on Jallow Sanneh.

54. Wiseman, "House of Representatives," 82; and PPP, *Voice*, 143–44. Views expressed to Hughes at the time.

55. *ACR* 19: (1986–87), B26; Baboucar Gaye, "Basse Poll," *WA*, December 9, 1985, 2617; and Fatou Sey, "Jawara's Toughest Test," *WA*, March 9, 1987, 452–53. Sidibeh, "Code of Conduct," claims that the PPP used government vehicles to help win the Basse by-election, which was also marred by electoral interference, intimidation, and harassment of its opponents.

56. See *GNB*, November 17, 1982, for a list of candidates in the December 1982 BanCC election; *ACR* 16: (1983–84), B422; and "PPP Wins All?" *WA*, May 16, 1983, 1212. The PPP won all bar one seat, Sandu, which was taken by an Independent.

57. "539 NCP Supporters Defect," *WA*, May 21, 1984, 1096. See also Eddie Momoh, "The Gulf Between," *WA*, December 22–29, 1986, 2648.

58. See Wiseman, *Democracy in Black Africa*, 58. In an interview with Hughes (Banjul, January 1997), Camara defended his loyalty to Jawara and the PPP; he blamed his political exclusion on Jawara's suspicious nature, fuelled by Vice President Dabo, whom Camara regarded as a Mandinka tribalist and opportunist.

59. PPP, *Voice*, 147–48; Baboucar Gaye, "Dissidents in the PPP?" *WA*, February 17, 1986, 378; Baboucar Gaye, "Fire Destroys Albert Market," *WA*, January 27, 1986, 217–18; and "Plans for New Party," *WA*, February 24, 1986, 436.

60. Wiseman, "House of Representatives," 89. On the Banjul Mafia, see also Diene-Njie, *Fall of the Old Order*, 44; Wiseman, "Military Rule" 930–31; and Ousman Manjang, "Marriage of Confusion–2," *WA*, November 10, 1986, 2360.

61. Baboucar Gaye, "GPP Leader Elected," *WA*, April 7, 1986, 749. See Gambia People's Party, *Manifesto of the Gambia People's Party: La Haula Wala Huata Ila Bilah* (Banjul: GPP, 1987) for the final version of the manifesto.

62. *WA*, "Plans for New Party," February 24, 1986; Baboucar Gaye, "New Party Announced," *WA*, March 3, 1986, 487; and Eddie Momoh, "Elections Update," *WA*, February 16, 1987, 305. Further information from Camara (Hughes interviews, Banjul, March 1987 and December 1999).

63. Baboucar Gaye, "On the Campaign Trail," *WA*, July 21, 1986, 1515–16; Gaye, "Jawara's New Opposition"; Momoh, "Elections Update"; and GPP, *Manifesto*.

64. Camara's conversion (which was sponsored by King Hassan of Morocco) was noted in *WA*, January 6, 1975, 23; and FCO 65/1611, Diplomatic Report no. 90/75, Report by J. R. W. Parker, January 10, 1975 (hence "Parker Report 1975"). According to Parker, Camara claimed to have converted to Islam because of pressure from his family and his ethnic group, not for political reasons. However, it may be no coincidence that he did so not long after he had been replaced as minister of external affairs by A. B. N'Jie in July 1974. It was suggested that this occurred because N'Jie was more acceptable to Arab opinion, which was increasingly the focus of Gambian foreign policy initiatives. See FCO 65/1453, Ashbourne to Date, July 12, 1974. Following this, Camara may have concluded that his future career prospects would be greatly enhanced if he became a Muslim.

65. The two cabinet ministers of Fula origin were M. C. Jallow and O. A. Jallow (although the latter was essentially a detribalized urbanite).

66. In fact the colors represented the sun (red) and agriculture (green).

67. On Jammeh and Fatty, see "Jammeh Joins GPP," *WA*, June 23, 1986, 1341; and Eddie Momoh, "On Your Marks . . .," *WA*, October 27, 1986, 2252–53. Momoh suggests that Fatty did not join the GPP until September 1986, but this must be incorrect if he signed the agreement with Nzeribe in May.

68. Baboucar Gaye, "Accusations and Counter-Accusations," *WA*, October 13, 1986, 2156–57, outlines the allegations and Camara's response to them. Fatty did not deny that he signed the agreement in Lagos, but claimed that he did so only under coercion. See "Fatty Defects From GPP to Join PPP," *WA*, October 20, 1986, 2237, where Fatty is described as the GPP's fourth-ranking member; and Momoh, "On Your Marks. . . ." Camara (videotape interview with Hughes, Banjul, March 1987), while admitting he visited Lagos to meet Nzeribe to discuss the terms of financial support, claimed that speculation of a 3 million dalasi payment was wildly inaccurate. Nothing came of the talks because the concessions demanded were unacceptable to Camara. He defended his quest for external funding on the grounds that most local businessmen helped to fund the PPP and that Jawara also had access to external sources of finance.

69. Fatou Sey, "The Elections Hot Up," *WA*, February 19, 1987, 109–10; see also Momoh, "The Gulf Between," 2648.

70. See Chapter 8, 206–7, on *The Voice*. On Jatta, see Bojang, "Sidia Jatta"; and *The Point*, April 13, 1982. The reasons for Jatta's resignation are given in a cyclostyled letter of resignation, "RE: Resignation of Senior Curriculum Development Officer to Serve my Nation" (Banjul, September 28, 1986). Jatta's frustration and anger at official failure to publish vernacular educational material for which he was responsible formed part of a wider denunciation of the government.

71. "Third Opposition Party Formed," *WA*, August 25, 1986, 1803. According to Jatta, the main priority issue for PDOIS was the Senegambia Confederation; see Bojang, "Sidia Jatta." The party's emblem was an "eight pointed red sun"; its flag was a rectangle with a green triangle (representing agriculture), a brown background (representing industry) and the sun (representing energy). See PDOIS, *The Constitution of the People's Democratic Organisation for Independence and Socialism* (Serrekunda: PDOIS, 1986), 19–20.

72. PDOIS' principal objectives were: "build[ing] an economically and politically independent Gambia free from all foreign domination and allegiances . . . [and] . . . to promote People's democracy in the Gambia." [underlining in original]; see PDOIS, *Constitution*, 2. Further information on PDOIS' political program and approach to the elections was obtained from Halifa Sallah (Hughes interview, Bakotu, April 1992) and from party publications. See also Vidler, "Regime Survival," 262.

73. Cooke and Hughes, "Politics of Economic Recovery," 102.

74. The reasons for the lack of political unrest are discussed in Cooke and Hughes, "Politics of Economic Recovery," 102–4; and Radelet and McPherson, "The Politics of Economic Reform," 40–41.

75. Deborah Brautigam, "The 'Mauritus Miracle': Democracy, Institutions, and Economic Policy," in *State, Conflict and Democracy in Africa*, ed. Richard Joseph (Boulder, CO: Lynne Rienner, 1999), 143, notes that the June 1982 election in Mauritius took place a few months after the country had successfully completed an International Monetary Fund stabilization program. All sixty seats in the election were won by the opposition coalition. Joan M. Nelson, ed., *Economic Crisis and Policy Choice—The Politics of Adjustment in the Third World* (Princeton, NJ: Princeton University Press, 1990), outlines the conventional wisdom that political leaders cannot introduce austerity measures just before an election.

76. The main secondary sources for this election are Arnold Hughes, "Les elections gambiennes de mars 1987," *Politique Africaine*, no. 26 (1987), 121–27; and John A. Wiseman,

"The Gambian Presidential and Parliamentary Elections of 1987," *Electoral Studies* 6, no. 3: (1987), 286–88. The full results are in *GNB*, March 18, 1987; *The Nation*, March 14, 1987; and Sagnia, *Gambian Legislature*, 77–80. Where these differ, we have followed the results in *GNB* and *The Nation* which are identical (except that only the latter has the Central Kombo result).

77. Sagnia, *Gambian Legislature*, 77, states that the candidate in Banjul South represented PDOIS and was called Alasan Gaye. But the alternative source, *GNB*, March 18, 1987, is supported by Hughes, "Les elections gambiennes," 122.

78. The registered electorate is given in *GNB*, March 14, 1987. There is a slight discrepancy between the total national electorate given of 262,143 and the sum of the electorate in the seven local government areas (262,593). The number of registered voters is also listed for thirty-three out of the thirty-six constituencies. Chapter 1, table 1.7, gives the population at the 1983 and 1993 censuses.

79. Baboucar Gaye, "The Parties Name Their Candidates," *WA*, February 2, 1987, 234; and Sey, "Jawara's Toughest Test." On Manneh's dismissal, see Gaye, "Rumbles in the PPP," and on Jome, see "Dodou A. Jome a Nationalist, Commercial Pundit," *The Independent*, April 23, 2004 (an interview). The four PPP MPs elected in by-elections were Saihou Barrow, Jallow Sanneh, Omar Sey, and Sarjo Touray. Following the resignation of Kebba Leigh due to ill health, Touray defeated sixteen other candidates for the PPP nomination in Sami, but then won the election unopposed. See Ba Tarawale, "Sarjo Touray for Sami Constituency," *Gambia Times*, November 30, 1984; and Eddie Momoh, "No Easy Promises," *WA*, February 18, 1985, 298.

80. See Sey, "The Elections Hot Up," 110; and Gaye, "Parties Name their Candidates," on these candidates. See also "Pesseh Has Not Run Off With UDP Funds," *Daily Observer*, September 17, 1996. Dabo informed Hughes (interview, Birmingham, July 1995) that the selection process was much better handled in 1987 than in the past, hence the paucity of Independent candidates.

81. Hughes, "Les elections gambiennes," 121.

82. Eddie Momoh, " 'The Elections Were Rigged,' " *WA*, March 30, 1987, 602 (an interview with Dibba). Further information from Dibba (Hughes videotape interview, Banjul, March 1987). Reminded that, in an interview with Hughes in 1983, he had stated that the NCP did not expect to win in 1987, but only in 1992, he claimed that the mood of the electorate had changed since 1983. Again, he blamed the NCP failure on PPP electoral irregularities, rather than on his own party's shortcomings.

83. Momoh, "The Gulf Between," 2647.

84. See PPP, *Voice*, 149; Hughes, "Les elections gambiennes," 124; Sey, "The Elections Hot Up," 110; Gaye, "Parties Name Their Candidates"; and Gaye, "Accusations."

85. It intended to stand in all seats, but its candidate in Illiassa was disqualified for having an invalid voter's card and its candidate in Jokadu withdrew at the last moment. See "113 Candidates File for the Elections," *WA*, March 2, 1987, 439; and Momoh, "Elections Update," 305.

86. Hughes, "Les elections gambiennes," 125. PPP, *Voice*, 150, disparagingly commented that this meant the GPP put up "nonentities just for a show."

87. PPP, *Voice*, 149, on the failure to recruit Bubacarr Baldeh. Tambedou, who is profiled in *Daily Observer*, July 28, 1994, was then working as the local manager of Rothmans International. On Fye, who later became an Alliance for Patriotic Re-orientation and Construction MP, see Omar Bah, "Jane Coli Faye [Jain Coli Fye]: NAM, Lower Niumi Constituency," *Daily Observer*, December 12, 2004 (an interview with him); Jeggan Grey-Johnson, "The MP of the Week," *GD*, May 1999. In an interview with the *Daily Observer*, Ya Fatou Sonko stated that she stood for the GPP in 1987 because she felt that she "had no place in the PPP," but refused to elaborate on the reasons for this; see Bah, "Ya Fatou Sonko."

88. Hughes, field observations, March 1987.

89. Hughes and Gailey, *Historical Dictionary*, 97.

90. Hughes interview with Halifa Sallah (Bakotu, April 1992). See also PDOIS, *Introduction: Manifesto of the Peoples Democratic Organization for Independence and Socialism* (Bundunga Kunda: PDOIS, 1986).

91. The turnout is based on the results in *GNB*, March 18, 1987. As noted in J. Denis Derbyshire and Ian Derbyshire, *Spotlight on World Political Systems: An Introduction to Comparative Government* (Edinburgh: W & R Chambers Ltd, 1991), 121, when compared with many other poorer liberal democracies, the turnout in The Gambia has generally been unusually high.

92. Full results are in Appendix table C.7. These are from *GNB*, March 18, 1987; *The Nation*, March 14, 1987; and Sagnia, *Gambian Legislature*, 77–80. Edie, "Democracy in The Gambia," 166, gives a slightly different summary of the results.

93. Hughes, "Les elections gambiennes," 126.

94. Hughes, "Les elections gambiennes," 123; and Sey, "The Elections Hot Up."

95. Gaye, "On the Campaign Trail," 1516.

96. Hughes, "Senegambian Confederation," 212.

97. Hughes, "Les elections gambiennes," 123; Wiseman, "1987 Elections," 287; and Edie, "Democracy in The Gambia," 171–72.

98. Ibid. See also Eddie Momoh, " 'We'll Continue the Struggle,' " *WA*, March 30, 1987, 601 (interview with Camara); Eddie Momoh, "Storm in a Tea Cup," *WA*, April 13, 1987, 705; and Eddie Momoh, " 'The Elections Were Rigged.' " PDOIS did not criticize the conduct of the elections at the time, but subsequently issued a press release attacking the registration process; see PDOIS, "Corrupt Registration Practice," Banjul, October 11, 1988. In 1991, PDOIS went to court to challenge the voter registration system in several constituencies, but its challenge was dismissed on a legal technicality; see Edie, "Democracy in The Gambia," 170–71.

99. "19 Petitions Thrown Out," *WA*, July 20, 1987, 1419.

100. According to *GNB*, March 18, 1987, the turnout in Illiassa was as high as 98.8 percent.

101. Radelet and McPherson, "The Politics of Economic Reform," 40. As noted in Chapter 1, 39, the groundnut subsidy alone accounted for an estimated increase of 7 percent in real rural wages. An econometric assessment of the likely impact of structural adjustment found that, under the "base" scenario adopted, the household income of both the "rural rich" and the "rural poor" increased; see Karl M. Rich, Alex Winter-Nelson, and Gerald C. Nelson, "Political Feasibility of Structural Adjustment in Africa: An Application of SAM Mixed Multipliers," *World Development* 25, no. 12: (1997), 2112.

102. Cooke and Hughes, "Politics of Economic Recovery," 104–5.

103. Rich et al., "Political Feasibility," 2112, suggest that, under the "base" scenario, the household income of both the "urban rich" and the "urban poor" declined as a result of the ERP.

104. The turnout in Banjul South was certainly the lowest of the thirty-three constituencies for which the electorate was given in *GNB*, March 18, 1987. Moreover, the turnout was almost certainly higher in the three remaining seats (Central Kombo, Eastern Wuli, and Western Wuli). Wiseman, "1987 Elections," 288, similarly suggests that the ERP had a negative effect for the PPP in the urban areas. Jagne's subsequent appointment is noted in *Foroyaa*, December 15, 1987.

105. Wiseman, "1987 Elections," 288; and Momoh, "Storm in a Tea Cup."

106. Hughes, "Les elections gambiennes," 125.

107. Momoh, " 'We'll Continue the Struggle.' "

108. Sagnia, *Gambian Legislature*, 78, suggests the margin was seventy-one votes.

109. The PPP claimed that the first installment of £100,000 was paid to the GPP, but Camara (Hughes interview, Banjul, March 1987) denied receiving a single butut. See also Gaye, "Accusations," 2156.

110. Hughes, "Les elections gambiennes," 124–25.

111. Camara claimed (Hughes interview, Banjul, January 1997) that key supporters in Kantora were offered inducements to change sides and that he himself turned down an offer of 1 million dalasi from the wealthy businessman and leading PPP financial patron, M. M. N'Jie, to return to the ruling party.

112. Hughes, "Les elections gambiennes," 125.

113. Hughes, "Les elections gambiennes," 126.

114. Results for each constituency and Administrative Area are given in Appendix table D.2. These are based on figures published in *The Nation*, March 14, 1987; and *GNB*, March 18, 1987. The results for each constituency were also supplied to Hughes by the Election Office, Banjul. It should be noted that there are some differences between these figures. The overall figures are also given in *GW*, May 1, 1992.

115. Wiseman, "House of Representatives," 90.

116. The student protests are discussed in Baba Sillah, "Neglected Youth," *WA*, April 20, 1987, 759.

117. The cabinet changes are listed in *ACR* 19: (1986–87), B25–26.

118. Hughes and Gailey, *Historical Dictionary*, 164.

119. See Peter da Costa, "Fêted but Fated," *WA*, June 25–July 1, 1990, 1067; see *GW*, April 14, 1989; and Aisha Davies, "Jawara Received £1 Million in Bribes, Manneh Claims," *GD*, October 25, 1995, where Manneh repeated the allegations against Saho. The first trial was covered extensively in issues of *Foroyaa* in 1988–89.

120. See *GW*, March 30, 1990 to June 8, 1990; December 6, 1991. This pro-PPP newspaper stated (May 4, 1990), that reliable sources claimed that Saho's replacement by James Gaye was unconnected with the ongoing libel case. However, it seems very likely that Jawara wanted to avoid the potential embarrassment of a court ruling against a minister whom he could afford to sack. See also *Foroyaa*, May 15, 1990; and da Costa, "Fêted but Fated." Saho later blamed his permanent secretary, Baba Jagne, for his downfall; see Cherno Baba Jallow, "My Sacking Was a Result of a Problem I Had With My P.S.," *Daily Observer*, April 6, 1995. Saho subsequently became executive director of the Atlantic Airlines Company.

121. Diene-Njie, *Fall of the Old Order*, 109. See also Paul E. McNamara and Malcolm F. McPherson, "Customs Reform"; and Steven C. Radelet and Malcolm F. McPherson, "Epilogue: The July 1994 Coup d'Etat," both in *Economic Recovery*, ed. McPherson and Radelet, 253–59; 313. See also Chapter 11, 283–84.

122. Baboucar Gaye, "In the Run up to the Coup . . .," *WA*, August 1–7, 1994, 1347, suggests that Jabang was a serious contender, but he is not listed by other sources. His demotion after the 1987 elections put paid to any prospects.

123. Jackson and Rosberg, *Personal Rule*, 70–73, discusses the role of the "dauphin."

124. Information from Dabo (Hughes interview, July 1995).

125. The fullest account of the events at the Mansakonko Congress and the subsequent developments is in Diene–Njie, *Fall of the Old Order*, 105–8. See also Peter da Costa, "Jawara Bows Out?" *WA*, December 16–22, 1991, 2106–7; and *GW*, December 6, 1991.

126. This is the view of Diene-Njie, *Fall of the Old Order*, 105–6, for example, although she also reports a rumor that a plot to assassinate Jawara was uncovered.

127. Diene-Njie, *Fall of the Old Order*, 107–8. See also *GW*, December 6, 1991.

128. *GW*, December 20, 1991; and Peter da Costa, "Christmas Cheer," *WA*, January 13–19, 1992, 68. Dabo stated (Hughes interview, July 1995) that he was effectively side tracked on the occasion, not realizing that what was meant to be a local rally by the Banjul

women's section of the PPP, turned out to be a national rally, where all senior figures were expected to be present. Much was subsequently made of his absence. O. A. Jallow later claimed that he was the only minister who openly disagreed with Jawara's decision to reverse his decision to retire; see Omar Bah, "Omar Jallow (OJ): Interim Leader, People's Progressive Party," *Daily Observer*, August 28, 2004 (an interview with him).

129. Information from Dabo (Hughes interview, July 1995).

130. No full account of the 1992 election exists; for shorter discussions, see *ACR* 24: (1992–94), B39–40; and Vidler, "Regime Survival," 262–67. A full list of the candidates can be found in *GW*, May 1, 1992.

131. The number of registered voters is from *ACR* 24: (1992–94), B39, citing *GW*, May 1, 1992; the estimated eligible population is taken from the Gambian entry on the International IDEA Web site www.idea.int/vt (downloaded March 2006). The Web site follows Peter da Costa, "Dawning of a New Era?" *WA*, April 27–May 5, 1992, 710–11, in giving the number of registered voters as 400,000, but the lower figure is preferred.

132. See *The Independent*, "Dodou A. Jome," which notes that Jome was a member of the editorial board of the *Gambia Times* between 1987 and 1992; and *GW*, March 13, 1992; March 20, 1992. Additional information on Sanneh-Bojang from Lianne Parrett (personal communication) and from Dabo (Hughes interview, July 1995).

133. There is a profile of Sillah—which does not mention his past links to the discredited NLP—in "Ex-Soldier Makes a Bid," *WA*, April 27–May 3, 1992, 711. He was appointed UDP national president in March 2000, but died the following December; see *Africa Research Bulletin, Political Series* 37, no. 4: (2000), 13941. On Jammeh, see *GW*, June 22, 1990. Gamble, *North Bank*, vol. C, 123, notes that he was Seyfu of Upper Baddibu between 1963 and 1983.

134. From Dabo's account (Hughes interview, July 1995) of the intrigue surrounding the selection of the Banjul candidates, his attempts to reform and democratize the selection system singularly failed here: instead, political connections and money determined the outcome. It was evident that in a number of other constituencies, unpopular previous candidates were reselected despite local opposition. For opposition to Cham and Sey, see da Costa, "Dawning of a New Era?" 711; and *The Point*, March 2, 1992; March 9, 1992, for a wider review of constituency selection disputes. "Pesseh" N'Jie joined the UDP in 1996 and was subsequently accused of absconding with party funds, a charge denied by its campaign manager, Femi Peters; see *Daily Observer*, "Pesseh Has Not Run Off With UDP Funds." On Sallah, who was the managing director of the Assets Management and Recovery Commission set up by Bakary Dabo, see also Yeebo, *State of Fear*, 27.

135. PPP, *Building Upon 27 Years of Continued Peace, Progress and Prosperity. Manifesto of the People's Progressive Party 1992* (Banjul: Government Printer, 1992).

136. See *GW*, October 26, 1990, on Gaye's defection; it is not known when Wally Sanneh joined the PPP. It should be noted that as a pro-PPP newspaper, the *Gambia Weekly* did not record any movement of PPP members into opposition parties. Sidibeh, "Code of Conduct," claims that Momodou Gaye and his pregnant wife were assaulted by supporters of Sabally in December 1986. He adds that, in a radio broadcast, Jawara subsequently blamed Gaye. It thus seems curious that he later joined the PPP.

137. See *GW*, November 16, 1990; May 31, 1991. Because Makalo was imprisoned in England (rather than in The Gambia), the attorney general ruled in June 1991 that he should not automatically forfeit his seat; see *Foroyaa*, June 30, 1991. But he was not eligible for selection in 1992. Makalo resurfaced politically after the 1994 coup to offer his support to Jammeh, when the latter decided to run for president. Dibba (Hughes interview, Banjul, May 1992), confirmed that Touray left the NCP following Solo Darbo's break with the party.

138. The dispute between Dibba and Darbo is discussed in *Foroyaa*, July 15, 1991; July 30, 1991. Further information from Dibba (Hughes interview, Banjul, May 1992).

139. The talks and the PPP's response are discussed in *GW*, August 31, 1990; October 26, 1990; April 24, 1992; and *Foroyaa*, August 30, 1990.

140. Da Costa, "Dawning of a New Era?"

141. For the NCP manifesto and statements by Dibba, see NCP, *The 1992 General Election Manifesto of the National Convention Party* (Banjul: NCP, 1992); and *The Point*, April 13, 1992. This issue also has photographs of all the NCP candidates.

142. Information from Dibba (Hughes interview, Banjul, May 1992).

143. For details, see *GW*, September 22, 1989; October 26, 1990; and *Foroyaa*, October 11, 1988.

144. Fye was working in New York as the designated representative for the Pan African Islamic Society for Agricultural Development at the United Nations; see Bah, "Jane Coli Faye." Why Jammeh did not stand in 1992 is not known.

145. On Tambedou and Phatty (who should not be confused with Suntu Fatty), see *GW*, May 24, 1991; October 2, 1992; [Gambia Government], *Staff List 1970*, 82; and *Foroyaa*, August 15, 1991. Phatty was a teacher in Georgetown before becoming a district commissioner, so had connections in the area. Further information from interviews on the history of late colonial and post-colonial Gambia carried out by Alice Bellagamba and Bakary Sidibeh in 2000.

146. Gambia People's Party, *Manifesto of the Gambia People's Party: La Haula Wala Huata Ila Bilah.* Revised version (Banjul: GPP, 1992), 1.

147. Hughes, personal observation of polling stations in Banjul and Serrekunda.

148. Da Costa, "Dawning of a New Era?" 710. PDOIS had issued a much longer manifesto (130 pages) in January 1992; see PDOIS, *The Way Forward* (Banjul: PDOIS, 1992). It also issued a revised 109 page constitution in March; see PDOIS, *Constitution of the People's Democratic Organisation for Independence and Socialism* (Banjul: PDOIS, 1992).

149. Jawara dismissed PDOIS as "immature adventurers who are trying to sell an autocratic ideology which had been tried, found useless and abandoned." Similarly, Bojang, the PDP leader, somewhat contradictorily, told his followers to shun these godless "communists" who believed only in "revolution which breeds anarchy and civil disorder"; see *GW*, April 24, 1992.

150. On the PDP and Bojang, see Peter da Costa, "New Party Launched," *WA*, September 30–October 6, 1991, 1656; Hughes and Gailey, *Historical Dictionary*, 140–41; Vidler, "Regime Survival," 265; *GW*, April 17, 1992; and *The Point*, April 13, 1992. Further information from Bojang (Hughes interview, Kembuje, April 1992).

151. See interview with Sallah in *The Point*, March 30, 1992. Edie, "Democracy in The Gambia," 165, suggests that the PDP was a PPP, not NCP, offshoot.

152. People's Democratic Party, *People's Democratic Party (PDP) Manifesto* (Banjul: PDP, 1992). Bojang made the claim in an interview in *The Point*, April 13, 1992. The PDP's motto was "In God We Trust."

153. *Foroyaa*, May 30, 1990, discusses the reasons for his sacking; see also Danso, "Detained Politician"; and Bah, "Lamin Waa Juwara."

154. See Appendix table C.8.

155. Hughes, "'Democratisation' Under the Military," 35. *GW*, January 3, 1992, reports the threat of a boycott. Both Dibba and Camara, in post-election interviews with Hughes, conceded that the 1992 elections were much fairer than previous ones.

156. In an interview with Hughes (Banjul, May 1992), Braimah Sanyang, acting director of information, pointed out that access to radio cover was much improved for opposition parties. All party leaders had thirty-minute interviews; all parties had twenty-minute party broadcasts by their leaders; all parties were given six ten-minute slots in their choice of languages; and there was broad coverage of rallies without particular parties being favored. Additionally, the *Gambia Weekly* published details of all candidates.

157. Da Costa, "Dawning of a New Era?" 710; and *ACR* 23: (1990–92), B39.

158. *GW*, August 7, 1992, lists the seven petitioners. See also *Foroyaa*, June 15, 1992; July 6, 1992; July 20, 1992. PDOIS refused to petition, accepting that the majority of voters succumbed to PPP inducements.

159. Full results are shown in Appendix C.9. These may be found in *GW*, May 1, 1992; May 8, 1992; and *The Gambia News and (Special) Report*, April 30, 1992. The turnout is in *ACR* 24: (1992–94), B39. The NCP's percentage share of the vote differs between the sources; we follow the detailed analysis in *GW*. The summary in Edie, "Democracy in The Gambia," 166, incorrectly omits the two GPP victories.

160. Ibrahim Sanyang lost to Kuti Sanyang in 1987 by fewer than 450 votes; see *GNB*, March 18, 1987.

161. *GW*, October 2, 1992, reports that Saidywane had been a PPP member.

162. The result is in Appendix table C.9. See also *GW*, October 2, 1992; March 19, 1993; June 4, 1993; and *The Point*, June 14, 1993.

163. See Appendix table C.9; and *GW*, April 30, 1993; June 11, 1993.

164. The overall results are in Hughes and Gailey, *Historical Dictionary*, 192. Results for each constituency are in Appendix table D.3; these are from *GW*, May 1, 1992.

165. *Da Costa,* "Jawara's New Government," 877, outlines the cabinet changes; see also Diene-Njie, *Fall of the Old Order*, 109. Ceesay was sacked as minister of agriculture in September 1978; see "Sanyang Removed," *WA*, January 15, 1979, 109.

166. Diene-Njie, *Fall of the Old Order*, 109–13; Gaye, "In the Run up to the Coup . . . "; and Yeebo, *State of Fear*, 26–29.

167. Da Costa, "Christmas Cheer," 68.

Chapter 10

1. The best studies of post-independence Gambian foreign policy are Touray, *Gambia and the World*; and Fatma Denton, "Foreign Policy Formulation in The Gambia, 1965–1994: Small Weak Developing States and their Foreign Policy Decisions and Choices" (Ph.D. diss., University of Birmingham, 1998). Earlier studies are by Solomon Gomez, "The External Relations of The Gambia: A Study of Internal and External Actors That Influenced Foreign Policy Positions, 1965–1975" (Ph.D. diss., The Johns Hopkins University, Baltimore, 1978); and Wendy C. Momen, "The Foreign Policy and Relations of The Gambia" (Ph.D. diss., London School of Economics, University of London, 1987). Touray (9) states that foreign policy objectives were to strengthen security, promote economic development and boost national prestige; Denton (58–67) lists them as security, peaceful coexistence, territorial integrity, nonalignment, and support for African liberation and human rights; and Gomez (287) states that they were to safeguard independence and sovereignty, and enhance economic viability.

2. For an analysis of decision-making agencies and processes, see Gomez, "External Relations," 221–84; Touray, *Gambia and the World*, 23–29; and Denton, "Foreign Policy Formulation," 115–64.

3. See FO 371/147289, Watson to Smith, November 30, 1960. Senghor did not himself come to Bathurst until 1964, his first visit since 1927! See note of cabinet meeting, March 14, 1964 in CO 554/2635.

4. During his regular visits to London, Jawara often held discussions with British officials; see, for example, the account of his 1969 visit in FCO 65/41 and 65/42. In addition, informal advice was offered to Jawara by successive British high commissioners (sometimes during games of golf). For example, G. E. Crombie advised the prime minister in March 1967

that he could safely accept most of the terms of the Treaty of Association drafted by the Senegalese government; see FCO 38/139, Crombie to Miles, March 29, 1967.

5. For an example of Lane's advice to Jawara, see his memorandum on Senegalo-Gambian relations of March 1967, which forms an enclosure to FCO 38/139, Crombie to Miles, March 17, 1967. Lane also drafted some of the agreements between the two countries; see FCO 65/599, Collins to Barder, February 11, 1970. Gomez, "External Relations," 228, claims that John Taylor, permanent secretary at the Ministry of Finance, was also influential at this time.

6. All three sources concur on the growing dominance of Jawara in determining foreign policy and in the conduct of "face-to-face" diplomacy with other national leaders. See Gomez, "External Relations," 221–84; Touray, *Gambia and the World*, 24–25; and Denton, "Foreign Policy Formulation," 10; 73; 126–30. Denton aptly sums up the situation when she states (18), that Jawara's "role [was] instrumental in the foreign policy formulation of The Gambia from its genesis in 1965 until 1994." Touray (24), observes that Jawara "remained a constant factor behind The Gambia's foreign policy." Such a role readily fits Skurnik's model of "idiosyncratic" decision making, which he observed of Senegal's first head of state, Léopold Senghor, and other African leaders, in which decision making is largely the private domain of the ruler. See W. E. A. Skurnik, *The Foreign Policy of Senegal* (Evanston, IL: Northwestern University Press, 1972), 257–58.

7. Touray, *Gambia and the World*, 25, lists the various ministers (but states that N'Jie did not become minister of external affairs until 1968). Denton, "Foreign Policy Formulation," 142–43, notes, however, that the personal links between ministers and external contacts (national leaders or ministers) allowed them some influence on specific topics. For example, Camara had close relations with Sékou Touré and Jabang with his Senegalese counterpart.

8. See Hughes and Gailey, *Historical Dictionary*, 52. Christensen spent many years working for the French and Senegalese consulates before joining the MEA in 1965. This explains his crucial role in defining relations with Senegal in the immediate post-independence period. See Gomez, "External Relations," 244–46; and Chapter 7, note 104.

9. Wiseman, "House of Representatives," 87–89, provides a brief discussion of the issues raised by PPP and NCP MPs in the 1970s and 1980s. An analysis of Gambian reports of parliamentary proceedings for the entire post-independence period shows clearly that the overwhelming preponderance of domestic issues in debates.

10. The main exception occurred in 1964 when the three "radical" MPs, Lamin M'Boge, Paul Baldeh, and Kalilou Singhateh, launched an attack on Gambian foreign policy in the House; see Chapter 7, 162. Copies of parliamentary debates are to be found at the Gambian National Archives and the National Assembly in Banjul.

11. According to the British high commissioner, prior to joining the PPP, Garba-Jahumpa publicly took an "extreme line" on the Vietnam War and the Arab-Israeli conflict as well as consistently being "a champion of the communist cause"; see FCO 38/138, Seaward to Moberly, March 14, 1968.

12. The weaknesses and limited impact of organizations within "civil society" and public opinion more generally are discussed in Gomez, "External Relations," 263–75; and Denton, "Foreign Policy Formulation," 74–114. It was only in the mid-1980s, with the arrival of PDOIS and its newspaper, *Foroyaa*, that an opposition party and a newspaper engaged in lengthy criticism of government foreign policy—in this instance, from a radical leftist perspective.

13. Touray, *Gambia and the World*, 9–10; Denton, "Foreign Policy Formulation," 58–67; and Gomez, "External Relations," 287.

14. Peter Calvert, *The Foreign Policy of New States* (Brighton: Wheatsheaf Books Ltd, 1986), viii; 169.

15. See, for example, "The Challenges Ahead," *WA*, July 5–11, 1993, 1146–47. This formed part of an address by Jawara to the World Conference on Human Rights in Vienna.

16. Denton, "Foreign Policy Formulation," 5–6.

17. The first high commissioner in London was Louis Valantine, who had previously served as commissioner; see DO 195/399.

18. The main secondary accounts on Gambian/Senegalese relations in this period are Welch, *Dream of Unity*; and Senghor, "Senegambian Integration," Chapters 4 to 6. See also Arnold Hughes, "Senegambia Revisited or Changing Gambian Perceptions of Integration With Senegal," in *Senegambia. Proceedings of a Colloquium at the University of Aberdeen*, ed. Roy C. Bridges (Aberdeen: African Studies Group, University of Aberdeen, 1974), 145–49; Touray, *Gambia and the World*, 31–36; and Denton, "Foreign Policy Formulation," 209–59. Additional information from Colonial Office and Foreign Office files.

19. For the views of the Colonial Office and Foreign Office, see the memoranda by MacLeod, December 6, 1960 (FO 371/146485) and Boothby, December 21, 1960 (FO 371/146486). Windley's views are discussed in Welch, *Dream of Unity*, 274–76. A number of despatches from the governor demonstrate the extent of his enthusiasm for union with Senegal; see, for example, FO 371/146484, Windley to Eastwood, May 4, 1960; and FO 371/161579, Windley to Eastwood, February 8, 1962.

20. Welch, *Dream of Unity*, 283 (note 60), cites Sandys' statement.

21. See DO 195/384, Paul to Kisch, January 7, 1964, in which the governor commented that he was sure that the British government would not entertain the postponement of independence on account of the failure to reach a satisfactory settlement with Senegal. See also the notes of a meeting with Lord Lansdowne (the colonial secretary), April 15, 1964, in the same file; at this meeting, the Colonial Office and Foreign Office officials accepted Paul's view that it would be "counterproductive" for the British government to insist that independence was dependent on an agreement with Senegal.

22. On the Senegalese perspective in 1964, see FO 371/176778, Peck to Foreign Office, January 6, 1964; Peck (the British ambassador in Dakar) was reporting the views of the Senegalese foreign minister, Dodou Thiam. On Senghor's views in 1960, see FO 371/147289, Watson to Smith, November 30, 1960.

23. On the Mali Federation and its demise, see William J. Foltz, *From French West Africa to the Mali Federation*. Yale Studies in Political Science no. 12. (New Haven, CT: Yale University Press, 1965), 97–196. Welch, *Dream of Unity*, 264–66, discusses the effect of its demise on Senghor's attitude toward political unification with Gambia. See also the Memorandum on Senegalo-Gambian Relations prepared by K. W. J. Lane for Jawara, March 1967, which is in FCO 38/139; Lane differentiated between Senghor and the Senegalese foreign minister, Dodou Thiam, who wanted to adopt a stronger line. Senghor himself stated in 1971 that he could have taken over The Gambia by 1965, but had chosen not to do so; see FCO 65/918, Ramage to Bambury, April 30, 1971.

24. For a brief discussion of smuggling before World War II, see F. A. Renner, "Ethnic Affinity, Partition and Political Integration in Senegambia," in *Partitioned Africans: Ethnic Relations Across Africa's International Boundaries 1884–1984*, ed. A. I. Asiwaju (London: C. Hurst, 1985), 79.

25. Robson, *Economic Integration in Africa*, 277–78; and Welch, *Dream of Unity*, 267–69.

26. Robson, *Economic Integration*, 278. Welch, *Dream of Unity*, 269, gives a similar estimate.

27. Welch, *Dream of Unity*, 268.

28. Robson, *Economic Integration*, 280; and Hughes, "From Colonialism to Confederation," 77.

29. FO 371/161581, Palliser to Foreign Office, October 23, 1962; Paul to Eastwood, January 19, 1963. Welch, *Dream of Unity*, 278–79, also suggests that the economic benefits to Senegal of association were not clear cut.

30. Hughes, "Senegambian Confederation," 203; Touray, *Gambia and the World*, 35–36; and CO 554/2635, Peck to Foreign Office, January 16, 1964. On the poor relations between Senegal and Mali and Guinea, see Sheldon Gellar, *Senegal: An African Nation Between Islam and the West* (Boulder, CO: Westview Press, 1982), 71–72. See also FO 371/181786, Peck to Stewart, February 18, 1965; Peck to Le Quesne, February 25, 1965, in which it was argued that the Senegalese were also concerned about possible future Egyptian, Algerian, Tanzanian, Russian, and Chinese influence in The Gambia.

31. For a brief discussion of the conflict in 1962 between Senghor and Dia, see Christian Coulon, "Senegal: The Development and Fragility of Semidemocracy," in *Democracy in Developing Countries: Africa*, ed. Larry Diamond, Juan J. Linz, and Seymour Martin Lipset (Boulder, CO: Lynne Rienner, 1988), 147–48.

32. Hughes, "From Colonialism to Confederation," 76; and Welch, *Dream of Unity*, 279. See also FO 371/167336, Peck to Millard, April 6, 1963. Although there was no fighting in the Casamance at this time, Peck's despatch shows that the Senegalese government was nevertheless concerned about the potential dangers. After independence (and probably before it), the Senegalese also believed that the Gambians operated the ferry inefficiently; see, for example, FCO 65/42, Tahourdin to Foreign and Commonwealth Office, June 28, 1969. See also Touray, *Gambia and the World*, 80, which perhaps substantiates the Senegalese argument.

33. The report is discussed in Robson, *Economic Integration*, 281. See also Hughes, "Senegambian Confederation," 207. It appears to have been the first study to examine the economic potential of the river basin in detail.

34. Welch, *Dream of Unity*, 269; and Robson, *Economic Integration*, 281–88, provide the estimates of the value of the trade. However, Jawara tended publicly to downplay the importance of smuggling, describing it as a negligible portion of the legitimate two-way trade; see FCO 65/41, memorandum by West African Department, Foreign and Commonwealth Office, May 8, 1969.

35. Although there do not appear to have been any estimates of the value of the trade for local businessmen at this time, it was suggested that in the late 1970s/early 1980s, Gambian traders could expect an 11 percent markup on re-exported goods; see Peter Robson, *Integration, Development and Equity* (London: Allen and Unwin, 1983), 132. See also *WA*, "Momodou Musa N'Jie," August 13–19, 1990, in which N'Jie is described as having been the doyen of the re-export trade. However, as a UP supporter at this time, M. M. N'Jie's political influence was limited (except perhaps when P. S. N'Jie was chief minister in 1961–62).

36. FO 371/161579, Smith to Watson, March 15, 1962.

37. All participants at the 1964 Independence Conference were in favor of Gambia joining the Commonwealth at independence; see DO 195/392, The Gambia Independence Briefs: Brief No. 8. If political union had occurred, the Foreign Office in Britain would certainly have opposed Senegambia joining the Commonwealth as FO 371/161581, Kisch to Chadwick, October 24, 1962, makes clear. Governor Paul also believed that Gambia could not join the Commonwealth under these circumstances; see FO 371/161582, Paul to Eastwood, December 7, 1962.

38. On N'Jie's initiatives and the Committee, see Welch, *Dream of Unity*, 276–82; and Senghor, "Senegambian Integration," 235–39. See also the report by Lane in FCO 65/599, Collins to Bambury, November 26, 1970. Welch makes the point that N'Jie assumed that the discussions with Senegal would improve his domestic political prospects.

39. Welch, *Dream of Unity*, 283–84, outlines the UP's reversal of its previous position after the 1962 election; see also CO 554/2636, Paul to Secretary of State, April 10, 1964, on the UP's reaction to Senghor's visit.

40. Welch, *Dream of Unity*, 280, points out, for example, that Jawara strongly criticized N'Jie for establishing the Inter-Ministerial Committee without seeking the approval of the

House of Representatives. Governor Windley certainly believed that the Senegalese favored N'Jie prior to the 1962 election; see FO 371/161579, Windley to Eastwood, February 8, 1962.

41. The new governor, J. W. (later Sir John) Paul, noted during the summer of 1962 that Jawara was becoming less antagonistic to the idea of political union with Senegal; see FO 371/161579, Paul to Eastwood, May 29, 1962; June 29, 1962. According to the colonial secretary, Ken Smith, the very noticeable increase in the transport available to the PPP before the 1962 election was due to financial help from Senegal; see FO 371/161579, Smith to Watson, March 15, 1962.

42. Welch, *Dream of Unity*, 281–85. See also CO 554/2635; and Nii K. Bentsi-Enchill, "Sir Dawda Explains the Confederation," *WA*, January 18, 1982, 138 (an interview with Jawara), in which Jawara emphasized that the invitation to the UN was on his initiative. The delay was primarily caused by disagreements over the composition of the UN team as FO 371/167335, makes clear.

43. See van Mook, et al., *Report on the Alternatives for Association Between the Gambia and Senegal*, 22–35. For secondary analyses of the report, see Welch, *Dream of Unity*, 285–88; Hughes, "Senegambia Revisited," 146–48; Robson, *Economic Integration*, 278–85; and Touray, *Gambia and the World*, 32–33. See also CO 554/2636, draft Gambia Cabinet Paper, April 22, 1964.

44. The process of negotiation is discussed in CO 554/2636; and summarized in Touray, *Gambia and the World*, 33. See also the draft final report prepared by K. W. J. Lane as the UN's Regional Adviser (hence "Lane Report") which is in FCO 65/599, Collins to Bambury, November 26, 1970. On the conflict within the PPP, see CO 554/2636, Paul to Secretary of State, April 10, 1964; and FO 371/176586, note of meeting between Jawara and Le Quesne, December 10, 1964.

45. The defense and security agreement, which was signed in June 1964, may be found in DO 195/401. The same file discusses the terms of the foreign policy agreement; see also CO 554/2636, Eastwood to Chadwick, June 4, 1964; Paul to Eastwood, June 2, 1964. For secondary accounts, see Welch, *Dream of Unity*, 288–90; Robson, *Economic Integration*, 285–86; Diene-Njie, *Fall of the Old Order*, 37–38; and Touray, *Gambia and the World*, 33–36. There was some opposition from Australia to Gambia joining the Commonwealth (on the grounds of its size), but its objections were withdrawn; see DO 195/392, Pettit to Duff, November 11, 1964. As noted in FCO 65/599, Langridge to Bambury, July 3, 1970, Senegal then still represented The Gambia in these nine countries (France, West Germany, Spain, Belgium, Italy, Switzerland, the United Arab Republic, Lebanon, and the USSR).

46. DO 195/384, N'Jie to Sandys, July 30, 1964; and DO 195/385, Sandys to Paul, September 30, 1964.

47. Robson, *Economic Integration*, 285, describes Senghor's reaction; see CO 554/2636, Paul to Eastwood, June 2, 1964, for Jawara's response (which was shared by the governor).

48. Senghor's visit and the Treaty of Association are discussed in FCO 38/139. See also Touray, *Gambia and the World*, 36, who states that the treaty was ratified in January 1968; and Denton, "Foreign Policy Formulation," 222–27.

49. The delay in establishing the Permanent Secretariat was due to differences between the two governments over the number of its staff and the size of its budget; the Gambian aim for a more modest body was eventually achieved. See FCO 38/140, Seaward to Moberly, February 15, 1968; Ramage to Tebbit, August 19, 1968; see also Touray, *Gambia and the World*, 37–38.

50. See Diene-Njie, *Fall of the Old Order*, 39–40; Robson, *Integration, Development and Equity*, 126–27; Touray, *Gambia and the World*, 43; and Denton, "Foreign Policy Formulation," 222–31. The Senegambia Permanent Secretariat (as it was renamed) was rendered largely superfluous by the establishment of the confederation in 1982 and was eventually dissolved in 1987; see "Permanent Secretariat Dissolved," *WA*, November 23, 1987, 2362.

51. Touray, *Gambia and the World*, 38–39; Hughes, "Senegambia Revisited," 151–52; Denton, "Foreign Policy Formulation," 227–31; and FCO 65/597, Diplomatic Report no. 128/70, Report by J. G. W. Ramage, February 3, 1970 (hence "Ramage Report 1970"). Ramage admitted that there had been a remarkable upsurge in unrecorded re-exports, although Jawara continued to insist that smuggling represented only a negligible percentage of the traditional two-way legitimate trade; see note by the West African Department of the Foreign and Commonwealth Office, May 8, 1969 in FCO 65/41. On Collin, see Kaye Whiteman, "From Javel to Joal," *WA*, November 8–14, 1993, 2020–21; Whiteman describes Collin as among the hardliners in Senegal's dealings with The Gambia.

52. Robson, *Integration, Development and Equity*, 133, argues that smuggling was predominantly a Senegalese, not a Gambian, activity and also suggests that traders from other West African countries were involved. Hughes, "Senegambian Confederation," 221 (note 20); and Peter da Costa and Baboucar [M.] Gaye, "A Thorn in the Side," *WA*, December 18–24 1989, 2098, both suggest that Mouride traders largely controlled the trade.

53. Renner, "Ethnic Affinity," 80; and "The Smuggling Problem," *WA*, April 19, 1969, 435. See also FCO 65/918, Ramage to Bambury, April 30, 1971, on Senghor's reaction. Curiously, the Senegalese government (at least publicly) maintained that the demonstration was aimed at Jawara, not Senghor, but this was certainly not the Gambian view; see FCO 65/1454, White to Lewis, May 3, 1974.

54. See FCO 65/41; FCO 65/42; and FCO 65/599, "Lane Report." On Senegalese border restrictions, see also Touray, *Gambia and the World*, 40.

55. For a detailed account of the incidents and the Gambian reaction, see FCO 65/918. See also Diene-Njie, *Fall of the Old Order*, 51–52; and Touray, *Gambia and the World*, 42 (which differ in minor respects from the account in the FCO files).

56. The incidents and Jawara's reaction are described in Bankole Timothy, "Senegambia: Myths and Realities," *Africa Special Report*, no. 38 (1974), 38–39; and FCO 65/1454, Gore to Jarrold, August 2, 1974. The two accounts differ slightly over the number of Gambians involved.

57. Touray, *Gambia and the World*, 103; and Augustine Oyowe, "A Future for Senegambia?" *WA*, March 8, 1976, 299. See also "Border Treaty With Senegal," *WA*, June 21, 1976, 896; and "Good News for River Gambia Bridge," *WA*, March 19, 1979, 516. See also Chapter 1, note 2.

58. On the OMVG, see especially Touray, *Gambia and the World*, 80–90. See also Robson, *Integration, Development and Equity*, 135–36; Hughes, "From Colonialism to Confederation," 77–78; Hughes, "Senegambian Confederation," 207; and M. B. Sillah, "Rice: Political Diet of The Gambia," *WA*, November 1, 1982, 2830.

59. FO 371/181786, Mellon to Renwick, August 12, 1965, reported that Jawara was asked by Sékou Touré and Modibo Keita to protest about the situation in Algeria, but refused to do so without consulting Senghor first. FO 371/181861, Crombie to Commonwealth Relations Office, April 3, 1965, states that two Parti Africain de l'Indépendance members had been arrested by the Gambian police and handed over to the Senegalese.

60. See FO 371/181786, Mellon to Renwick, August 12, 1965; and FCO 38/137, Crombie to Norris, June 16, 1967; Crombie to Norris, July 28, 1967. Crombie suggested that the Gambian government had taken the initiative in 1967 because of rumors that some of the lower ranks of the Field Force might be considering a coup; see also Chapter 8, 209.

61. See Chapter 8.

62. On Niasse, see *WA*, "Senegal's Tensions With The Gambia," November 17, 1980, 2278–79; and Touray, *Gambia and the World*, 67. On the rise of Muslim fundamentalism in Senegal, see Christian Coulon and Donal B. Cruise O'Brien, "Senegal," in *Contemporary West African States*, ed. Cruise O'Brien, Dunn, and Rathbone, 156–58.

63. The conflict is briefly discussed in Coulon and O'Brien, "Senegal," 158–60; and Richard Vengroff and Lucy Creevey, "Senegal: The Evolution of a Quasi Democracy," in *Political Reform in Francophone Africa*, ed. John F. Clark and David E. Gardinier (Boulder, CO: Westview Press, 1997), 210–11.

64. On the Confederation, see especially Hughes, "Senegambian Confederation"; Touray, *Gambia and the World*, 107–18; and Denton, "Foreign Policy Formulation," 234–57.

65. "50 Presidential Guards," *WA*, August 31, 1981, 2022, notes that Diouf placed fifty presidential guards and Senegalese security agents at Jawara's disposal.

66. Bentsi-Enchill, "Sir Dawda," 139; and Touray, *Gambia and the World*, 107–8. Eddie Momoh, "Signs of Strain in the Confederation," *WA*, October 29, 1984, 2158–59, outlines the apparent Senegalese viewpoint at the time and suggests that Bakary Dabo, then the Gambian ambassador to Senegal, was instrumental in persuading Jawara not to accept a more restrictive federation. Jawara stated (Hughes interview, Haywards Heath, August 1998), that he himself did not favor a close union; confederation was as far as he wanted to go. Security was the immediate concern, but economic integration was a longer term objective, preferably within a subregional, rather than a bilateral, framework. Denton, "Foreign Policy Formulation," 241 (note 97), cites correspondence with the former permanent secretary at the MEA, Ebou Taal (23 August 1997), who drew up draft alternatives for a treaty in November 1981, all of which were to stress the retention of the independence and sovereignty of the two states. Denton (240–42) also records that the Gambian government hired Berthan Macauley, a leading Sierra Leonean barrister, to scrutinize the draft treaty to ensure that Gambian interests were protected. Macauley's report, "Memorandum-Relations with Senegal," is reproduced in Denton's thesis.

67. See Diene-Njie, *Fall of the Old Order*, 73–78; Hughes, "Senegambian Confederation," 200–201; Touray, *Gambia and the World*, 108–10; and Nii K. Bentsi-Enchill, "Signing on the Dotted Line," *WA*, February 8, 1982, 353–54.

68. Touray, *Gambia and the World*, 110–11, lists the other Gambian ministers. These were Dr. M. S. K. Manneh, Lamin Jabang, and Alieu Badjie. The division of posts between Senegalese and Gambians remained unaltered until at least 1987; see "Senegambian Confederation," *WA*, June 1, 1987, 1080. Diene-Njie, *Fall of the Old Order*, 73, argues that the Gambians would have preferred a rotating presidency, an issue that would contribute to the demise of the confederation in 1989.

69. Diene-Njie, *Fall of the Old Order*, 82–83; and Hughes, "Senegambian Confederation," 210–11. The estimated population of the two countries in 1986 was 720,000 and 6.52 million respectively. See Alan Rake, ed., *New African Yearbook 1987–88*, 7th ed. (London: IC Magazines Ltd, 1987–88), 125; 282.

70. Diene-Njie, *Fall of the Old Order*, 76–77. See also Hughes, "Senegambian Confederation," 202–3; Touray, *Gambia and the World*, 110–11; and "Gendarmerie Formed," *WA*, April 7, 1986, 749. The official records of the Treaty, Protocols, and Acts of the Confederation (in French and English) are found in the *Official Gazette* of the Senegambia Confederation (Banjul and Dakar).

71. Diene-Njie, *Fall of the Old Order*, 83–84; Hughes, "Senegambian Confederation," 209; and *WA*, "Combined forces," February 7, 1983. See also Baboucar Gaye, "Strains Remain?" *WA*, November 18, 1985, 2445.

72. See, for example, Bentsi-Enchill, "Sir Dawda," in which the president strenuously denied that The Gambia had lost its sovereignty. See also Hughes, "Senegambian Confederation," 206.

73. Bentsi-Enchill, "Signing on the Dotted Line," 353–54; and Touray, *Gambia and the World*, 109.

74. See *WA*, "Party Politics in Senegambia," February 15, 1982.

75. Touray, *Gambia and the World*, 109; and "Senegambia's Arrival," *WA*, January 4, 1982, 10, stated that the vote in the National Assembly was unanimous. For a contrary view, see Nii K. Bentsi-Enchill, "Starting off on the Wrong Foot," and "No Valid Foundation" (interviews with Mamadou Dia and Fara N'Diaye, the leader of the Mouvement Democratique et Populaire and the deputy leader of the PDS respectively), *WA*, January 11, 1982, 79–81. According to Manjang, "Marriage of Confusion," 2360, most of the Senegalese opposition parties later jointly signed a declaration that called for the withdrawal of Senegalese troops from The Gambia and condemned the confederal accord. See also "Fifteen Opposition Members Arrested," *WA*, September 28, 1981, 2277, on the size of opposition representation in the National Assembly at this time.

76. Touray, *Gambia and the World*, 109; Bentsi-Enchill, "Signing on the Dotted Line," 353–54; and Nii K. Bentsi-Enchill, "Senegal Treads Softly," *WA*, 4 January 1982, 11–12. As stated in Chapter 9, 223, the other two NCP MPs, Sheriff Dibba and Gibou Jagne, remained in prison.

77. Hughes, "Senegambian Confederation," 211–12.

78. "Start of a New Era?" *WA*, January 24, 1983, 229, describes the first meeting; see also Hughes, "Senegambian Confederation," 210.

79. Touray, *Gambia and the World*, 113.

80. Ibid, 112–17; Diene-Njie, *Fall of the Old Order*, 89–91; Hughes, "Senegambian Confederation," 212–14; and Kending S. Hakilimah, "Integration in Limbo," *WA*, January 18, 1988, 76. See also Obe, "A President's Story," 267 (interview with Jawara).

81. Amadou Mactar Gueye, "Herculean Tasks," *WA*, 18–24 September 1989, 1551.

82. Denton, "Foreign Policy Formulation," Appendix 7, lists thirty-five agreements, protocols, and conventions signed between the two countries between 1965 and 1991; ten of these were during the confederation. Hughes, "Senegambian Confederation," 5 (citing an official source), stated that some thirty collaborative agreements were signed between 1965 and 1992. See also Radelet and McPherson, "The Politics of Economic Reform," 39; and "Unity That Was," *WA*, October 2–8, 1989, 1634.

83. Eddie Momoh, "Dams Against Drought," *WA*, February 11, 1985, 252–53.

84. See Peter da Costa, "Casamance Under Siege," *WA*, January 28–February 3, 1991, 101; and "Arms Shipment?" *WA*, January 7–13, 1991, 3163 [*sic*]. Both claims were strenuously denied by the Gambian government.

85. Momoh, "Signs of Strain"; and Hakilimah, "Integration in Limbo."

86. Radelet and McPherson, "The Politics of Economic Reform," 39, argue that a key reason why Jawara accepted the need for an ERP was that otherwise the government would have had to beg assistance from Senegal. It is therefore possible that the success of the ERP made Jawara more willing to risk Senegalese disapproval of his policies.

87. See, for example, Baboucar Gaye, "The Rumbles Within," *WA*, April 1, 1985, 608; "Monetary Union Pressed," *WA*, March 19, 1984, 635 (reporting on Senegalese press comment); and "Economic Union or Burst," *WA*, February 15, 1988, 290.

88. According to Bakary Dabo (Hughes interview, Birmingham, July 1995), the minister of external affairs, Omar Sey, most strongly voiced official Gambian dissatisfaction with what was felt to be the one-sided nature of the relationship with Senegal. Bade Omole, "De la coopération a la confédération: la Sénégambie: Contribution a l'analyse du thème de l'intégration politique régionale en Afrique" (doctorat de 3e cycle, université de Bordeaux, 1986), 245–50, in an admittedly small sample, found that 89 percent of Gambians wished confederation to "continue slowly." In a study carried out ten years earlier, Kebba M. Bayo, "Mass Orientation and Regional Integration: Environmental Variations in Gambian Orientations Towards Senegambia" (Ph.D. diss., Northwestern University, 1977), Table V, 1 (162), found in a larger survey that only some 13 percent of Gambians wanted political

integration with Senegal. In both instances, urban Gambians were the most hostile to political union.

89. Diene-Njie, *Fall of the Old Order*, 89–91. Jawara informed Hughes (interview, Haywards Heath, August 1998) that both he and Sey found this unacceptable, but when he wrote to Diouf to press for the rotation of the confederal presidency, he failed to get a reply. According to Dabo (Hughes interview, Birmingham, July 1995), Vice President Camara raised objections to the confederal presidency arrangements during negotiations in 1981, but his views were arrogantly dismissed by M. Lamin Saho (the minister of justice). The latter was known to enjoy close relations with the Senegalese ambassador and the head of the Senegalese military force in The Gambia.

90. Hughes, "Senegambian Confederation," 209–10; Gaye, "The Rumbles Within"; and Susan Macdonald, "Jawara Interview Angers Dakar," *WA*, April 29, 1985, 854.

91. On MOJA's opposition, see Bentsi-Enchill, "Sallah interview—2," 851; "MOJA's 1983 Message," *WA*, March 7, 1983, 636; Manjang, "Marriage of Confusion," 2359–60; and Hakilimah, "Integration in Limbo," 76. For a PDOIS critique of Senegambian relations, see Halifa Sallah, *The Senegambian Confederation: Facts, Myths, Doubts and the Truth* (Banjul: The Nation Publishers, 1985). The attitudes of PDOIS and MOJA-G are summarized in Amadou S. Janneh, "Dilemmas of Senegambian Integration," (Ph.D. diss, University of Tennessee, 1990), 103–17.

92. On the dispute between Senegal and Mauritania, see Diene-Njie, *Fall of the Old Order*, 95–96; Mark Doyle and Chris Simpson, "Another Week of Terror," *WA*, May 8–14, 1989, 725; and Mark Doyle, "Troubled Waters," *WA*, June 19–25, 1989, 1007–9. See also, "Targets Met Despite the Odds," *WA*, January 22–28, 1990, 105, which cites a report by the Central Bank of The Gambia that large numbers of Mauritanians who were resident in The Gambia left the country during the border dispute with Senegal.

93. In interviews with Fatma Denton and Hughes (Haywards Heath, March 1996 and August 1998), Jawara expressed astonishment about the sudden and unannounced departure of the Senegalese forces, including his State House guard. When contacted by telephone later in the day, Diouf merely said that he thought the Gambians could now look after themselves. The Gambians accurately saw this as a form of punishment for prevarication and a failure to rally to Senegal over the dispute with Mauritania. In an interview with Denton (Dakar, August 1996), the former Senegalese ambassador to The Gambia, Mbai (or M'Bye) M'Bengue, admitted the unilateral withdrawal was meant to frighten the Gambian president.

94. The events of August 1989 are discussed in Hughes, "Senegambian Confederation," 215–18; and Diene-Njie, *Fall of the Old Order*, 96–98. See also "Senegal and Its Neighbours," *WA*, August 28–September 3, 1989, 1407; and Gueye, "Herculean Tasks."

95. Hughes, "Senegambian Confederation," 200; and da Costa and Gaye, "A Thorn in the Side," 2097. Touray, *Gambia and the World*, 115, suggests that it was wound up in October 1989. Denton, "Foreign Policy Formulation," Appendix 7, stated the Agreement of the Dissolution of the Senegambia Confederation was signed on September 21, 1989.

96. Diene-Njie, *Fall of the Old Order*, 97–105, describes the measures; see also Hughes, "Senegambian Confederation," 218; "Gambians Protest Harassment," *WA*, November 27–December 3, 1989, 1971–72; and Justice Fofana, "Senegambia Feud," *WA*, January 8–14, 1990, 34.

97. Hughes, "Senegambian Confederation," 219, notes that the treaty was approved in May 1991. See also Peter da Costa, "Senegal-Gambia treaty," *WA*, January 14–20, 1991, 28; "Bilateral Treaty," *WA*, June 10–16, 1991, 964; and Touray, *Gambia and the World*, 116.

98. See Peter da Costa, "A Border Conflict," *WA*, December 13–19, 1993, 2250–52 (interview with Omar Sey, the Gambian minister of external affairs). The estimate of the impact

on the re-export trade is from De Vrijer et al., *The Gambia: Selected Issues*, Table 45. See also Chapter 1, 34.

99. The International Monetary Fund report states that the re-export trade did not begin to pick up until 1998, but its estimated value of SDR 82 million was still well below the 1992–93 level of 97 million. See De Vrijer et al., *The Gambia*, Table 41.

100. That Gambians continued to attend university in Sierra Leone well after independence is noted in "Jawara Assures Koso Thomas," *WA*, July 22, 1985, 1513–14. Earlier, in 1969–70, Hughes, "Senegambia Revisited," 154 (note 1), stated that there were twenty-one Gambian students at Fourah Bay University in Sierra Leone, compared with only one at Dakar University.

101. See FCO 65/602, Collins to Bambury, May 26, 1970.

102. As stated in Chapter 6, note 89, Senghor helped finance the PPP's 1962 election campaign.

103. For somewhat conflicting accounts of Jawara's opinion of Nkrumah, see "The Gambia and the OAU," *WA*, June 5, 1965, 618; and FO 371/161579, Watson to Smith, March 9, 1962. During a visit to Achimota College in Ghana in May 1965, Jawara apparently expressed some criticisms of the Nkrumah government; see DO 195/243, Walker to Bottomley, May 29, 1965.

104. Jawara's response to the coup was to state that he considered it was in line with the wishes of the Ghanaian people; see DO 195/243, Crombie to Greenhill, April 28, 1966.

105. For example, in his annual message to Parliament in 1980, Jawara noted The Gambia's good relations with Ghana; see "The Gambia's Need for Food Relief," *WA*, September 8, 1980, 1706. In addition, President Limann paid a state visit to The Gambia in February 1981; see "Limann Awards Decorations," *WA*, March 16, 1981, 596. See also Denton, "Foreign Policy Formulation," 179–82.

106. For a brief discussion of Nigerian foreign policy under Gowon, see Ray Ofoegbu, "Foreign Policy and Military Rule," in *Nigerian Government and Politics Under Military Rule, 1966–79*, ed. Oyeleye Oyediran (London: Macmillan, 1979), 125–33.

107. Gowon's visit is reported in Christian Coulon, "Les partis politiques Gambiens," *Revue francaise d'études politiques africaines* no. 89 (1973, May), 47 (note 19); see also FCO 65/918. See FCO 65/1452, "Parker Report 1974," on the establishment of the embassy. Ofoegbu, "Foreign Policy," 131, states that Gowon visited a number of West and Central African states to thank their governments for supporting the federal government during the civil war, but does not mention his visit to The Gambia. On Jawara's refusal to recognize Biafra, see FCO 38/138, Seaward to Moberley, July 11, 1967.

108. On ECOWAS, see Robson, *Integration, Development and Equity*, 86–123, who reports the initial Senegalese opposition to the idea. In an interview, Gowon also noted Senegalese opposition; see "The Long Road to the Treaty of Lagos," *WA*, May 24, 1982, 1367. Jawara's reaction to its formation is discussed in Touray, *Gambia and the World*, 95–96.

109. Denton, "Foreign Policy Formulation," 251 (note 130), citing a Senegalese journalist, said nongovernmental newspapers were outspoken in their condemnation of The Gambia, and helped fan official mistrust of the Jawara government. See, for example, *Wal Tadjiri*, avril 12, 1985 (which criticized the enforced withdrawal of the Senegalese ambassador). See also *Liberté*, no. 1, mars 1985; and *Le Politicien*, mars 1, 1985, both of which were critical of the military training agreement with Britain, which ended Senegalese training of the Gambian National Army. They also attacked The Gambia's attempts to draw closer to Nigeria and Libya. The Senegalese press was also suspicious of the Gambian government's attitude toward Casamance separatists in The Gambia, but claims that separatists were shipping arms via Gambian territory were strongly refuted by the PPP newspaper, the *Gambia Times*; see Hughes, "Senegambian Confederation," 221 (note 35). One dismissive

Senegalese reporter wrote: "Underneath their boubas the Gambians still wear English shorts"; this is cited in Arnold Hughes and Janet Lewis, "Beyond Francophonie? The Senegambia Confederation in Retrospect," in *State and Society in Francophone Africa Since Independence*, ed. Anthony Kirk-Greene and Daniel Bach (Basingstoke: Macmillan, 1995), 236.

110. Ofoegbu, "Foreign Policy," 141–42, discusses the strains in Nigerian/Senegalese relations in 1975–76 over the World Black and African Festival of Arts and Culture. See also Denton, "Foreign Policy Formulation," 174–75; and Oscar O. B. Ede, "Nigeria and Francophone Africa," in *Nigeria's External Relations: The First Twenty-Five Years*, ed. G. O. Olusanya and R. A. Akindele (Ibadan: University of Ibadan Press, 1986), 186–90. Nigeria's main criticism of Senegal was its continuing ties to France, which included French military bases. Apart from the Festival of Arts and Culture dispute, other issues dividing the two countries were Senegal's reluctance to join the Nigerian-sponsored ECOWAS; its sympathy toward Biafra during the Nigerian civil war (1967–70); and its opposition to the MPLA faction in Angola (which Nigeria backed). Senegal, in turn, feared the regional and wider impact of a reunited and oil-rich Nigeria.

111. Denton, "Foreign Policy Formulation," 176–78. On the accord and Buhari's visit, see "Lagos-Banjul Accord," *WA*, July 30, 1984, 1553; and "Buhari in Banjul," *WA*, February 25, 1985, 397. On Babangida's visits, see Peter da Costa, "Carnival in Banjul," *WA*, March 5–11, 1990, 361. As Denton indicates (251), the Senegalese opposition press was critical of the Gambian invitation to Buhari.

112. See Chapter 11.

113. On Touré, see Jackson and Rosberg, *Personal Rule*, 208–19. His relations with Senghor are briefly discussed in Gellar, *Senegal*, 72. On The Gambia's relations with Guinea, see Hughes, "Senegambia Revisited," 154–55; and Denton, "Foreign Policy Formulation," 185–87. A key intermediary between the two heads of state was the Gambian minister of external affairs, Andrew (Assan Musa) Camara. Camara informed Hughes (interview, Banjul, December 1997) that, unlike Jawara, he enjoyed a close friendship with Touré and was charged with the delicate issue of the deportees.

114. On the invasion plot, see Claude Rivière, *Guinea: Mobilisation of a People*, trans. Virginia Thompson and Richard Adloff (Ithaca, NY: Cornell University Press, 1977), 135–36; and Lansiné Kaba, "Guinean Politics: A Critical Historical Review," *Journal of Modern African Studies* 15, no. 1 (1977), 33. For a discussion of the Gambian reaction, see "Guineans Sentenced," *WA*, October 24, 1970, 1264; "Matchet's Diary," *WA*, December 19, 1970, 1471; "Sir Dauda [*sic*] on Guinea's Stability," *WA*, February 12, 1973, 213; FCO 65/915, "Ramage Report 1971"; and Touray, *Gambia and the World*, 41.

115. When Jawara made an official state visit to Guinea in January 1973, Touré produced a healthy group of men who were supposedly among those deported in December 1970; see FCO 65/1287, Parker to Date, February 23, 1973. However, as Denton, "Foreign Policy Formulation," 186–87 points out, Jawara (whom she interviewed in 1987) admitted that they had been executed. The arrival of the first Guinean ambassador in June 1971 was noted in FCO 65/1091, "Collins Report."

116. On the reaction of the Senegalese government, see Gellar, *Senegal*, 72, who notes that diplomatic relations between the two countries were broken off altogether in 1973. In contrast, as noted, Jawara visited Conakry in January 1973, albeit reluctantly. The Senegalese government subsequently asked The Gambia to represent its interests in Conakry; see FCO 65/1452, "Parker Report 1974."

117. Ebou Dibba, "Jawara's Mission and Convictions," *WA*, February 17–23, 1992, 285, describes Jawara's attempts to reconcile the two men; see also Touray, *Gambia and the World*, 83–84; and FCO 65/1614, Rogers to Heath, December 10, 1975. However, Lansiné Kaba,

"From Colonialism to Autocracy: Guinea Under Sékou Touré, 1957–1984," in *Decolonization and African Independence*, ed. Gifford and Louis, 242, attributes the key role in the eventual rapprochement to President William Tolbert of Liberia. In contrast, Guinea did not seek to rejoin the OMVS (which it had left in 1970) until 1987; see "Conté Seeks Return to OMVS," *WA*, November 9, 1987, 2233.

118. See DO 195/382, Paul to Secretary of State, October 5, 1964, who noted that most Mandinka Qadiriyya were followers of Sheikh Sidya of Mauritania; see also "Visit From Mauritania," *WA*, November 29, 1976, 1830, for an example of anti-Mauritanian sentiment in Banjul. Gambian resentment arose not only from business rivalry, but also from the reputation of the Mauritanians for tax evasion and repatriation of profits to Mauritania.

119. See FCO 65/597, "Ramage Report 1970"; *WA*, "Visit From Mauritania," 29 November 1976; and "Jawara Talks With Haidalla," *WA*, September 1, 1980, 1682, on the visits. See "The Gambia Asks for Senegal Troops," *WA*, January 12, 1981, 66, on the 1980 agreement.

120. According to Diene-Njie, *Fall of the Old Order*, 97, the Mauritanian government offered to provide the Gambian government with various forms of support, but the latter turned down the offer. See also "The Dream of Unity," *WA*, November 27–December 3, 1989, 1959.

121. FCO 65/1452, "Parker Report 1974."

122. An indication of the good relations between Guinea-Bissau, Senegal, and The Gambia was that the three countries signed an agreement for mutual administrative assistance in customs matters in 1978; see "Customs Experts Meet," *WA*, August 5, 1985, 1619.

123. Touray, *Gambia and the World*, 85; and Denton, "Foreign Policy Formulation," 187–90. See also Chapter 8, 219.

124. PPP, *Voice*, 214; Denton, "Foreign Policy Formulation," 193–96; and Nana Humasi, "A Year in Review," *WA*, December 26, 1988–January 8, 1989, 2422.

125. Touray, *Gambia and the World*, 156–61, provides the fullest discussion.

126. See Chapter 11, 281–83.

127. Touray, *Gambia and the World*, 90–95, discusses CILSS and Jawara's role within it. See also Denton, "Foreign Policy Formulation," 198–203; and "FAO Honours Sir Dawda," *WA*, May 12, 1980, 858, which reported that the FAO issued a special medal to the Gambian president for his efforts on behalf of CILSS.

128. Touray, *Gambia and the World*, 94–95, notes the aid received by The Gambia. However, "Fight Against Drought," *WA*, December 3, 1979, 2233–34, also states that there was some Gambian criticism of the amount of time that Jawara spent on CILSS activities. See also FCO 65/1452, "Parker Report 1974."

129. PPP, *Voice*, 225–27 (Appendix II), reproduces "The 'Independence' Manifesto of the Peoples Progressive Party." The document, which was signed by Jawara and dated October 1, 1960, noted that Gambia's drive for independence was part of a common struggle in colonial Africa for "freedom and self-determination."

130. See, for example, Jawara's speeches during a visit to The Gambia by the secretary of state for the colonies, as reported in DO 195/406, Britten to Bottomley, August 9, 1965; and at the Commonwealth Prime Ministers' Conference in 1969, as reported in FCO 65/40, Foreign and Commonwealth Office to British High Commission, Bathurst, January 14, 1969. Jawara was particularly critical of the announcement in 1970 by the newly elected Conservative government that it would reopen negotiations with Smith; see FCO 45/699, especially the press release issued by the Gambian government, July 25, 1970. See also Touray, *Gambia and the World*, 47–48.

131. Touray, *Gambia and the World*, 47–48; Denton, "Foreign Policy Formulation," 272; and FCO 38/138, Seaward to Moberley, July 11, 1967. Naomi Chazan, Peter Lewis, Robert A. Mortimer, Donald Rothchild, and Stephen John Stedman, *Politics and Society in*

Contemporary Africa, 3rd ed. (Boulder, CO: Lynne Rienner, 1999), 418 (note 37), list the nine countries (including Ghana, Guinea, and Mali) that implemented the OAU's resolution.

132. For example, in 1986, Jawara stated that The Gambia would not boycott the UK or quit the Commonwealth over the question of sanctions; see "'We Will Not Quit Commonwealth,'" *WA*, October 6, 1986, 2134. Some of Jawara's criticisms of British policy toward South Africa were, however, very strong; see, for example, FCO 45/699, Gambia government press release, July 25, 1970.

133. See Touray, *Gambia and the World*, 147–49; and Denton, "Foreign Policy Formulation," 204–5. See also FCO 65/1613, Gore to Date, December 19, 1975, on the pressure exerted by other governments on Jawara and the minister of external affairs, A. B. N'Jie, to recognize the MPLA.

134. Touray, *Gambia and the World*, 150–56. For wider discussions of the conflict and the OAU's response, see Chazan et al., *Contemporary Africa*, 378–83; and John Damis, "The OAU and Western Sahara," in *The OAU After Twenty Years*, ed. Yassin El-Ayouty and I. William Zartman (New York: Praeger, 1984), 273–96.

135. It joined the OAU at a meeting in Nairobi in February/March 1965; see Touray, *Gambia and the World*, 45; and Denton, "Foreign Policy Formulation," 196–97.

136. Dibba, "Jawara's Mission," 285.

137. "Jawara Attacks Idi Amin Dada," *WA*, April 9, 1979, 649.

138. Touray, *Gambia and the World*, 161–64. See also the letter from Richard Akinjide (one of the member of the committee which established the Charter), *WA*, October 24–30, 1988, 2011; and three articles in *WA*, 19–25 April 1993: K. Gyan-Apenteng, "Defining the Terrain in Banjul," 634–35; "Africa Centre for Democracy and Human Rights Centre," 635; "The African Commission on Human and People's Rights," 636–37. For a more critical view of the Banjul Charter, see the comments of Surahata Semega-Janneh, the president of the Gambia Bar Association, as reported in D. A. Jawo, "Banjul Charter: A Compromise Document," *Daily Observer*, July 10, 1995. In an interview with Denton (Haywards Heath, March 1996), Jawara remarked that the Gambian government was surprised that, under the circumstances, it succeeded in getting the OAU to accept the African Human Rights Charter.

139. The fullest discussion of Gambian–UK relations is in Denton, "Foreign Policy Formulation," 262–74.

140. On grant-in-aid, see Touray, *Gambia and the World*, 50; DO 195/385, Sandys to Paul, August 27, 1964; and FCO 65/44, note of meeting with H. R. Monday (Gambian high commissioner to London), December 10, 1968. FCO 38/137, Crombie to Norris, December 30, 1966, shows that the British high commissioner was opposed to the British government seeking the return of the surplus.

141. Touray, *Gambia and the World*, 50–51, states, for example, that external sources accounted for 84.5 percent of the finance for the first (1964–67) development programme.

142. Ibid, 59. Gomez, "External Relations," 524–25, asserts that British aid in the early years of independence allowed The Gambia to fend off union with Senegal.

143. Radelet, "Donor Support" 52–53; and "Petroleum Grant," *WA*, December 24, 1990–6 January 1991, 3116. See also Touray, *Gambia and the World*, 123–24; 135–36.

144. See DO 195/401, especially Chadwick to Kisch, July 22, 1964.

145. See FCO 65/41, Foley to Foreign and Commonwealth Office, May 28, 1969; and FCO 65/601, report of meeting between Jawara and Harold Wilson (UK prime minister), July 21, 1969. By 1970, the United Kingdom only had defense agreements with two independent countries in Africa, Kenya and Mauritius; see FCO 65/601, Smedley to Counsel, December 21, 1970.

146. Information given Hughes by the British High Commission, Bathurst, Spring 1972.

147. "British RAF Using Banjul," *WA*, May 17, 1982, 1347; and Gaye, "National Army Created." The Gambia also called on Argentina to withdraw from the Falklands; see "Argentina Call," *WA*, April 19, 1982, 1105.

148. On external diplomatic representation in The Gambia in 1965–66, see DO 195/388. The Americans were persuaded by the British not to establish an embassy in Bathurst; otherwise, other countries might feel the need to do so; see DO 195/399, note by Eastwood, November 3, 1964; and FO 371/181866, Crombie to Harrison, February 24, 1965. See also PPP, *Voice*, 212; and DO 195/389. Touray, *Gambia and the World*, 51, states that the PPP government had hoped the United States would establish an embassy in Bathurst at independence.

149. Radelet, "Donor Support," 48.

150. Touray, *Gambia and the World*, 60–61. As noted by Rimmer, *Economies of West Africa*, 144, the Treaty of Rome of 1956 laid down that the African dependencies of EEC members could automatically become associate EEC members if they chose to do so.

151. Touray, *Gambia and the World*, 122; 137, notes that The Gambia was allocated ECU 80 million under Lomé I—III. EEC/EU aid is also discussed in Denton, "Foreign Policy Formulation," 274–80.

152. For example, Radelet, "Donor Support," 53, notes that EEC provided SDR 13 million in STABEX grants between 1986 and 1988.

153. Touray, *Gambia and the World*, 63–64; and Denton, "Foreign Policy Formulation," 279.

154. Touray, *Gambia and the World*, 137; and Denton, "Foreign Policy Formulation," 278–79. Similarly, Radelet, "Donor Support," 53–54, states that America provided U.S. $6 million as a grant and supplied 24,000 tons of rice (worth U.S. $4 million) to support the ERP.

155. Despite the initiation of a "Roots Festival" in 1996, relatively few African-Africans visit The Gambia, when compared with the number of European tourists.

156. Touray, *Gambia and the World*, 124–26; 136; 141; and Denton, "Foreign Policy Formulation," 281–82. On the first festival, see *Daily Observer*, August 27, 1996.

157. Touray, *Gambia and the World*, 125–26.

158. Ibid, 20; 138. See also Chapter 11, 287–88.

159. See Chapter 1, 38–39; see also Radelet, "Donor Support," 52–53. As noted in IMF, *Surveys of African Economies*, 10. The Gambia joined both the IMF and the IDA in September 1967.

160. On relations with Israel, see FCO 65/597, "Ramage Report 1970"; ACR 6: (1973–74), B641; and Touray, *Gambia and the World*, 68, note the final breaking off of diplomatic ties. According to the British high commissioner, this occurred after a visit to Banjul by the Mauritanian foreign minister; see FCO 65/1452, "Parker Report 1974." See also "Resumption of Relations With Israel," *WA*, September 28–October 4, 1992, 1633.

161. Touray, *Gambia and the World*, 66–68; 129; and FCO 65/1611, "Parker Report, 1975." See also Hughes, "'Democratisation' Under the Military," 51 (note 17), who reports the restoration of diplomatic ties.

162. Touray, *Gambia and the World*, 150–56. Earlier, as stated in Chapter 9, note 64, King Hassan had sponsored the return to the Muslim fold of Vice President Camara in 1974.

163. Touray, *Gambia and the World*, 68–69; FCO 65/1611, "Parker Report, 1975"; and *WA*, November 25, 1974, 1494.

164. Touray, *Gambia and the World*, 127.

165. Ibid, 69. The Gambia's membership of the OIC dated from 1974 when Jawara attended a conference in Lahore; see FCO 65/1611, "Parker Report, 1975"; and *WA*, March 18, 1974, 318.

166. Touray, *Gambia and the World*, 126–28; 139. Gambian ties with Iraq were established in 1979 when Jawara paid an official visit to Baghdad; see "President in Iraq . . .," *WA*, July 16, 1979, 1290.

167. Touray, *Gambia and the World*, 128; 138–40, states that these banks provided the greater part of the multilateral loans between 1980 and 1985.

168. Ibid, 127–28; Dibba, "Jawara's Mission," 285; and [Gambia Government], *Members of the Government.*

169. See DO 195/388, Crombie to Duff, 8 November 1965; Seaward to Browne, September 13, 1966; FCO 65/1285, "Parker Report 1973"; and FCO 65/1452, "Parker Report 1974."

170. Touray, *Gambia and the World*, 72–73. Cultural relations were restored in 1984; see "Soviet Ties Re-Established," *WA*, November 26, 1984, 2422.

171. For example, diplomatic relations were established with Hungary and Rumania in 1971, the German Democratic Republic in 1973 and Cuba in 1979; see FCO 65/918, Collins to Bambury, June 17, 1971; FCO 65/1091, "Collins Report"; Touray, *Gambia and the World*, 71; and *WA*, May 28, 1979, 962.

172. See *WA*, November 30, 1968, 1422; Touray, *Gambia and the World*, 69–70; and FCO 65/1285, "Parker Report 1973." For example, on several occasions, the Gambian government stated that it had no objection to China entering the United Nations, but was opposed to the ejection of Taiwan; see *WA*, April 15, 1967, 510; February 3, 1968, 140; and FCO 65/1091, "Collins Report." FCO 65/1611, "Parker Report, 1975," argues that the decision to sever ties with Taiwan was "taken under considerable pressure."

173. See Bankole Timothy, "The Chinese in The Gambia," *WA*, February 4, 1974, 123; IMF, *Surveys of African Economies*, 18; and D. A. Brautigam, "Foreign Assistance and the Export of Ideas: Chinese Development Aid in The Gambia and Sierra Leone," *Journal of Commonwealth & Comparative Politics* 32, no. 3 (1994), 324–48.

174. Touray, *Gambia and the World*, 70–71; 129; 140.

175. South Korea sought diplomatic recognition with The Gambia soon after independence, although it is not clear when this actually occurred; see DO 195/388.

176. Touray, *Gambia and the World*, 71–72; 130 (for later Korean aid); and Gomez, "External Relations," 401–5. Chapter 8, 220, notes the closure of the North Korean embassy.

Chapter 11

1. John A. Wiseman and Elizabeth Vidler, "The July 1994 Coup d'Etat in The Gambia: The End of an Era," *The Round Table* no. 333 (1995, January), 53; and Abdoulaye Saine, "The Coup d'Etat in The Gambia, 1994: The End of the First Republic," *Armed Forces & Society* 23, no. 1: (1996), 97.

2. On the coup, see especially Wiseman and Vidler, "1994 Coup"; Wiseman, "Military rule," 917–21; Saine, "Coup d'Etat"; Yeebo, *State of Fear*; Diene-Njie, *Fall of the Old Order*, 115–64; Radelet and McPherson, "1994 Coup"; and Jimmy D. Kandeh, "What Does the 'Militariat' Do When it Rules? Military Regimes: The Gambia, Sierra Leone and Liberia," *Review of African Political Economy*, no. 69: (1996), 387–404. Shorter accounts are to be found in Touray, *Gambia and the World*, 173–77; Peter da Costa, "Out With the Old," *Africa Report* 40, no. 1 (1995), 48–51; Edie, "Democracy in The Gambia," 180–82; Baboucar Gaye, "Ousted Jawara flees," *WA*, August 1–7, 1994, 1346; Rodney D. Sieh and Momodou Musa Secka, "Who is Lt Yaya Jammeh?," *WA*, August 1–7, 1994, 1347–48 (a reproduction of an article by the same authors in *Daily Observer*, July 25, 1994); D. R. Oat Jr., [pseudonym],

"Anatomy of a Coup," *WA*, August 29–September 4, 1994, 1502–3; Ebenezer Obadare, "The Military and Democracy in The Gambia," in *Governance and Democratisation in West Africa*, ed. Dele Olowu, Adebayo Williams, and Kayode Soremekun (Dakar: CODESRIA, 1999), 347–49; and "Army Coup in Gambia," *Daily Observer*, July 25, 1994.

3. A ten-part series of articles were posted on the Internet between April and July 2001. Entitled "Coup in Gambia," they were written under the pseudonym "Ebou Colly" (the articles can no longer be downloaded). Colly is now believed to be Lieutenant Colonel (Retired) Sheriff Samsudeen Sarr. Sarr was a captain at the time of the coup and was closely involved with the personalities and the events that took place. Although highly partisan and often uncorroborated, his account rings true in many respects.

4. See Wiseman and Vidler, "1994 Coup," 55–59; and Saine, "Coup d'Etat," 102.

5. The size of the Gambian contingent is from Touray, *Gambia and the World*, 158. Yeebo, *State of Fear*, 49–50, suggests that around 150 Gambian soldiers served in ECOMOG in total. It is not known what proportion of these remained in the GNA in 1994. Wiseman and Vidler, "1994 Coup," 55; Yeebo, *State of Fear*, 7; and Touray, *Gambia and the World*, 166 (for 1990), all provide similar estimates of the size of the GNA.

6. Colly, "Coup in Gambia, Part 2," notes that the government failed to maintain the numerical strength of the TSG and also points out that the GNA had machine guns, mortars and self propelled grenades, whereas the TSG was only armed with lighter weaponry.

7. Wiseman and Vidler, "1994 Coup," 55. Yeebo, *State of Fear*, 50–51, suggests that another motive for Jawara was to introduce some professionalism into the army.

8. Wiseman and Vidler, "1994 Coup," 55–60. Similarly, Colly, "Coup in Gambia, Part 1," claimed that there were about eighty Nigerians in the GNA at the time of the coup. Yeebo, *State of Fear*, 51, gives an improbably high figure for the Nigerian contingent of 179.

9. Colly, "Coup in Gambia, Part 5," names the forty-four Gambian officers who were serving at the time of the coup; he added two more, who were serving abroad, in Part 6. There were five majors. It is not possible to verify the accuracy of this list.

10. Profiles of all four are in Hughes and Gailey, *Historical Dictionary*, 92–93; 96; 152–53; 163; these were based on information supplied to Hughes by the Gambian Ministry of Information. A fuller account of Jammeh's background is in Sheriff Bojang, "Yahya A. J. J. Jammeh," *WO*, July 21–23, 1995. Sabally is profiled in Mathew K. Jallow, "Sana Sabally: From Kassakunda to No. 2 Man," *The Point*, November 14, 1994; and Singhateh in *The Point*, February 2, 1995. Jammeh and Singhateh (called Singhatey by this source) are also profiled on the Gambian government cabinet Web site http://www.statehouse.gm (downloaded March 2006). Additional information from Colly, "Coup in Gambia, Part 1," (who paints a very different picture of Sabally and Singhateh); and Wiseman and Vidler, "1994 Coup," 60. There is no direct evidence to support the claim by Diene-Njie, *Fall of the Old Order*, 84, that some members of this group joined the GNA with the deliberate intention of seeking later on to overthrow the PPP government. However, a senior Gambian official in the Ministry of External Affairs informed Hughes some years before the 1994 coup that some educated young men were joining the GNA for that very purpose.

11. Kandeh, "Military Regimes," 391. In contrast, Saine, "Coup d'Etat," 102, states that some junior officers had attended university, but does not give any details. See Hughes and Gailey, *Historical Dictionary*, 96; 163, for details of Jammeh's and Singhateh's education. Sabally was educated at Armitage School; see Jallow, "Sana Sabally." On the economic problems of the mid-1980s, see Chapter 1, 38.

12. Those trained in America included Jammeh, Singhateh, and Sabally. See Hughes and Gailey, *Historical Dictionary*, 96; 163; and Jallow, "Sana Sabally." Two other prominent officers, Baboucarr Jatta and Yankuba Touray, were also trained in America; see http://www.statehouse.gm (downloaded March 2006) and notes 54 and 64.

13. John A. Wiseman, "Letting Yahya Jammeh Off Lightly?" *Review of African Political Economy*, no. 72 (1997), 269. See also Wiseman and Vidler, "1994 Coup," 60. Colly, "Coup in Gambia, Part 6," does discuss allegations of Wolof favoritism under N'Dow N'Jie, but dismisses them.

14. Colly, "Coup in Gambia, Parts 1 and 5." See also Wiseman and Vidler, "1994 Coup," 59–60; and Saine, "Coup d'Etat," 102. No doubt the discontent of the officers was accentuated by the fact that the first two commanders of the GNA, Colonel N'Dow N'Jie (1984–91) and Major Maba Jobe (1991–92), were Gambians. According to Yeebo, *State of Fear*, 51, the latter retired from the army after his replacement as acting commander in July 1992.

15. Wiseman, "Military Rule," 920. Jammeh later claimed that he was excluded from the Presidential Guard because his opponents alleged (incorrectly) that he was related to Kukoi Sanyang, the leader of the 1981 coup; see *The Point*, September 19, 1994.

16. These incidents are discussed by Wiseman and Vidler, "1994 Coup," 55–56; Yeebo, *State of Fear*, 50; Colly, "Coup in Gambia, Part 2"; and Oat, "Anatomy of a Coup." Oat suggests that Jobe successfully defused the situation in 1991; while Colly credits the TSG with thwarting the 1992 attempt.

17. The reforms are described in Wiseman and Vidler, "1994 Coup," 59–60.

18. For a detailed example of this issue, see Thomas S. Cox, *Civil-Military Relations in Sierra Leone: A Case Study of African Soldiers in Politics* (Cambridge, MA: Harvard University Press, 1976).

19. This cannot be quantified, given the absence of opinion polls on political matters in The Gambia, but it may be significant that the PPP lost both by-elections conducted in June 1993; see Chapter 9, 248.

20. Obadare, "Military and Democracy," 347–48; and Kandeh, "Military Regimes," 390–91.

21. Radelet and McPherson, "1994 Coup," 313, explicitly link the decline in support of the PPP to the appointment of Sabally.

22. On corruption in the early 1990s, see Yeebo, *State of Fear*, 22–30; Wiseman and Vidler, "1994 Coup," 57–58; Wiseman, "Military Rule," 930–32; Saine, "Coup d'Etat," 100–101; Diene-Njie, *Fall of the Old Order*, 108–13; da Costa, "Out With the Old," 49–50; and Radelet and McPherson, "1994 Coup," 313–16. Radelet and McPherson contrast Jawara's willingness to act quickly and forcefully to check corruption in customs administration in the late 1980s with his inaction in the early 1990s.

23. Wiseman and Vidler, "1994 Coup," 58.

24. Saine, "Coup d'Etat," 100–101; Radelet and McPherson, "1994 Coup," 312–13; and S. B. Danso, "Dibba, Others to Pay D23m," *Daily Observer*, November 28, 1994. Dibba and two other GCU senior managers were sacked at the end of September; see Godwin Okon, "100 Days of Military Rule," *The Point*, October 31, 1994. Jammeh shared the perception that Jawara was to blame for the lack of action against the GCU officials; see "PPP Regime Mismanaged Most Foreign Aid," *Daily Observer*, September 12, 1994. See also Chapter 9, 240.

25. Yeebo, *State of Fear*, 26–29; Saine, "Coup d'Etat," 100; Edie, "Democracy in The Gambia," 176; and Radelet and McPherson, "1994 Coup," 313.

26. For example, Yeebo, *State of Fear*, 24–25, notes that allegations of corruption were made against the director of the African Centre for Democracy and Human Rights Studies, Raymond Sock. See also *Daily Observer*, May 29, 1995.

27. Diene-Njie, *Fall of the Old Order*, 133; and Yeebo, *State of Fear*, 24–25. See also the interview by Elizabeth Ohene of the BBC Africa Service with Jawara, as reported in *Daily Observer*, September 26, 1994.

28. Wiseman, "Military Rule," 930–32.

29. Wiseman and Vidler, "1994 Coup," 57.

30. "Broadcast from the AFPRC," *Daily Observer*, July 25, 1994; and Sieh and Secka, "Jammeh."

31. On August 1, twelve former PPP ministers were placed under house arrest; they were not released until mid-September. Six were arrested and detained for a week in September and eleven in November; later in November, it was announced that the assets of nineteen former cabinet ministers would be investigated by the Public Assets and Properties Recovery Commission. Most were subsequently heavily fined and stripped of their assets. Two former PPP ministers, M. C. Cham and O. A. Jallow, were arrested once again in October 1995 and remained in detention in September 1996; another, Dr. Lamin K. Saho, was released from detention after five months in December 1996. A number of heads of parastatal organizations were also arrested on August 1, 1994. For details, see Ebrima Ceesay and Rodney D. Sieh, "NIB, GPA Bosses Held," *Daily Observer*, August 2, 1994; Lamin Ceesay, "12 PPP Ministers Free at Last," *The Point*, September 15, 1994; *Daily Observer*, September 26, 1994; November 20, 1994; September 19, 1996; December 23, 1996; and *WO*, November 11–13, 1994.

32. Diene-Njie, *Fall of the Old Order*, 133. See also Wiseman, "Military Rule," 919.

33. See, for example, *Daily Observer*, November 6, 1994 (interview with Jammeh); and da Costa, "Out With the Old," 50. Jawara was later found guilty by the oil contracts commission; see Alieu Badara N'Jie, "Oil Commission Finds Jawara and Nine Others Liable," *Daily Observer*, May 30, 1995; *Daily Observer*, January 4, 1996; and *GD*, January 5, 1996. By then, Jawara had rejected the junta's overtures and was seeking external assistance to restore himself to power.

34. See *Daily Observer*, September 29, 1994; October 27, 1994; December 14, 1995; and *GD*, December 13, 1995, for details. The State Counsel at the Public Assets Recovery Commission, Bright Akwetey, recommended that Jawara be required to refund D4 million for unspent allowances for himself and his security guards between 1989 and 1994.

35. This is emphasized by Wiseman, "Military Rule," 920; and Yeebo, *State of Fear*, 52, for example.

36. Corruption under the AFPRC is discussed in Yeebo, *State of Fear*, 66–79; Wiseman, "Yahya Jammeh"; Hughes, "'Democratisation' Under the Military," 44; and Kandeh, "Military Regimes," 394–95. All except Kandeh strongly criticize the extent of corruption under Jammeh. Colly, "Gambia Coup, Parts 1–10," also strongly condemned the coup, as much for the brutality of its perpetrators as their venal motivations.

37. See "Broadcast From the AFPRC," *Daily Observer*, July 25, 1994. The lack of an independent electoral commission is discussed by Obadare, "Military and Democracy," 346. See also Wiseman and Vidler, "1994 Coup," 58–59, for a general discussion of this motive.

38. Radelet and McPherson, "1994 Coup," 312–16, argue that there was little direct relationship between the coup and the economic policy reforms, although they suggest that the initial public support for the coup at least partly reflected economic concerns, including the absence of sustained development and the increase in corruption.

39. Perhaps not surprisingly, all four coup leaders were promoted in November 1994; see *The Point*, November 21, 1994. Yeebo, *State of Fear*, 43, states that they promoted themselves; although this is technically incorrect, because they were promoted by Lieutenant Colonel Jatta, the commander of the GNA, it is not an unreasonable assessment.

40. Saine, "Coup d'Etat," 104, gives the suggestion some credence. Wiseman and Vidler, "1994 Coup," 60, note that it is certainly possible that the Sierra Leonean example encouraged the Gambian soldiers to believe their coup would succeed, but state that it is far from clear that the Strasser coup more directly influenced events in The Gambia. Colly, "Coup in Gambia, Part 4," claims that Singhateh's attitude toward the junta's perceived enemies hardened after a visit to Strasser in Freetown as part of an AFPRC explanatory mission in the

wake of the coup. On the Strasser and Abacha coups, see for example, Alfred B. Zack-Williams, "Sierra Leone: The Political Economy of Civil War, 1991–98," *Third World Quarterly* 20, no. 1: (1999), 149–50; and Peter M. Lewis, "Endgame in Nigeria? The Politics of a Failed Democratic Transition," *African Affairs* 93, no. 372: (1994), 323–40.

41. As stated by Saine, "Coup d'Etat," 103, Rawlings was guest of honor at the July 22 anniversary celebration in 1995 marking the AFPRC's first year in office. Saine elaborates on the parallels and distinctions between Jammeh and Rawlings in Abdoulaye S. Saine, "The Soldier-Turned-Presidential Candidate: A Comparison of Flawed 'Democratic' Transitions in Ghana and Gambia," *Journal of Political and Military Sociology* 28, no. 2: (2000), 191–209.

42. This factor is particularly emphasized by Yeebo, *State of Fear*, 49–52. Jammeh apparently later claimed that he served with ECOMOG in Liberia; this is dismissed by Colly, "Coup in Gambia, Part 1."

43. It should be noted that Yeebo does not accuse the U.S. government of definitely organizing the coup, although he does suggest that "it is still doubtful if the U.S. Embassy were innocent bystanders in the whole affair"; see Yeebo, *State of Fear*, 31–42 (34); 62–64. The accusation was strongly denied by the U.S. ambassador in The Gambia, Andrew Winter; see *Daily Observer*, 28 July 1994. Similarly, Colly, "Coup in Gambia, Part 7," emphasizes that Winter was strongly against the coup. In an interview with Hughes (Banjul, August 1994), Winter denied U.S. involvement and added that his immediate concern was to get Jawara and his party to safety on board the U.S. warship. It is likely that it was the speed and lack of bloodshed in the execution of the coup, as well as the measure of public support for the coup (and lack of any rallying to Jawara) that led to the de facto acceptance of the coup. Jawara's relatively good democratic record, although tarnished by the corruption issue, was not enough to lead the U.S. government to engage in such a controversial act on his behalf, particularly given the U.S.'s tragic debacle during its intervention in Somalia in October 1993. There might well have been an unstated feeling that Jawara had been in power long enough and that the coup organizers did reflect a wider mood for change.

44. Diene-Njie, *Fall of the Old Order*, 119. Yeebo, *State of Fear*, 52, claims that the army was divided into pro-Dabo and pro-Sabally factions, but does not suggest that the coup was organized by the former.

45. Touray, *Gambia and the World*, 173–74.

46. See Colly, "Coup in Gambia, Part 2."

47. Sieh and Secka, "Jammeh." See also Wiseman and Vidler, "1994 Coup," 56.

48. Colly, "Coup in Gambia, Part 1," states that this version of events was outlined by Singhateh himself in the presence of the other coup leaders. He also suggests that initially the plotters intended to execute all government officials and all GNA officers of the rank of captain or above. Wiseman, "Military Rule," 921–22, also suggests that Barrow was a conspirator (although not the main one). Yeebo, *State of Fear*, 43–44, argues that Barrow was the real leader of the coup, but then declined to join the AFPRC, rather than withdrawing before it began, but this seems incorrect.

49. On the November coup, see Yeebo, *State of Fear*, 83–88; Wiseman, "Military Rule," 921–22; Diene-Njie, *Fall of the Old Order*, 151–52; Saine, "Coup d'Etat," 105–6; *GW*, November 18, 1994; and Colly, "Coup in Gambia, Parts 3 and 4." See also *The Point*, November 17, 1994; November 28, 1994; and *Daily Observer*, December 7, 1994. The number of casualties in the November coup remains unclear. Saine, for example, suggests that around forty soldiers were killed and many more may have been summarily executed. Wiseman's estimate is lower; apart from the three alleged coup leaders, he suggests that around twenty soldiers were killed. Barrow's post-coup appointment is noted in *GW*, November 18, 1994, which describes it as a promotion (although his rank did not change).

50. The course of events on July 22 is summarized in Gaye, "Ousted Jawara Flees"; Wiseman and Vidler, "1994 Coup," 56–57; and Colly, "Coup in Gambia," (various parts). Jammeh's own account is in Sieh and Secka, "Jammeh." Jawara (Hughes interview, Haywards Heath, August 1998) stated that he was let down by his intelligence service, which had failed to follow up information provided by PPP sources. Colly, "Coup in Gambia, Part 2," states that the joint exercise between U.S. units and the GNA in 1994 was the third biennial event of its kind, with the other two having taken place in 1990 and 1992.

51. Gaye, "Ousted Jawara Flees." See also Jawara's interviews with Elizabeth Ohene of the BBC and Richard Kotey of Voice of America, as reported in *Daily Observer*, September 26, 1994; September 28, 1994.

52. Colly, "Coup in Gambia, Part 4," claims that he (Sarr) personally persuaded the TSG unit led by Major Chongan not to fight. In his interview with Gambian journalists after the coup, Jammeh claimed that there was fierce resistance to the coup, but this was clearly not the case; see Sieh and Secka, "Jammeh."

53. Some of those who were detained after the coup remained in prison in 1996 without any charge having been brought against them, as Wiseman, "Military Rule," 921, points out. Ceesay was detained until December 1996, but later became head of Jammeh's National Intelligence Agency; see *Daily Observer*, December 23, 1996; and Colly, "Coup in Gambia, Part 2." Okon, "100 Days of Military Rule," also notes that the inspector general of police and other senior officers were retired by the AFPRC government after the coup.

54. Colly, "Coup in Gambia, Part 10." On the Nigerian inaction, see also Wiseman and Vidler, "1994 Coup," 60. Jatta is profiled on http://www.statehouse.gm (downloaded March 2006).

55. See "Arrests in Banjul," *WA*, 8–14 August 1994, 1395; and "After the Coup," *WA*, 8–August 14, 1994, 1388.

56. Wiseman and Vidler, "1994 Coup," 62. On the response to the coup of Dibba and Camara, see also two articles by Abdullah Savage, "Over 18 Months Is Not Acceptable," *Daily Observer*, October 27, 1994; and "The Press Has Been Good for the Country," *Daily Observer*, October 28–30, 1994.

57. "Politics Suspended," *WA*, August 15–21, 1994, 1435–36; and Hughes, "'Democratisation' Under the Military," 37–38. All individuals who had held presidential, vice presidential, or ministerial office since 1965 also remained banned. Some former PPP ministers were arrested in November 1994, in part for violating Decree No. 4; see *WO*, November 11–13, 1994.

58. The nominated candidates for the 1997 National Assembly election are listed in *Daily Observer*, December 9, 1996; the constituencies listed are those for 1997. See Appendix tables C.6 and C.7 for the candidates in 1987 and 1992.

59. For the differing views, see Kandeh, "Military Regimes," 387; Radelet and McPherson, "1994 Coup," 311; Saine, "Coup d'Etat," 105; da Costa, "Out With the Old," 51; Wiseman, "Military Rule," 926–27; and Wiseman, "Yahya Jammeh," 265–66. It should be noted that the GBA and GMDA did not publicly condemn the coup until November 1994. On the GWC's initial reaction to the coup, see Pa Modou Faal, "Timetable Is Too Long," *Daily Observer*, October 27, 1994.

60. In an interview with *The Independent* in London, Jawara stated that he was informed by the captain of *La Moure County* that the marines were not granted permission by Washington to prevent the coup; he added that he did not think that the United States was behind the coup. The interview is summarized in *WO*, September 30–October 2, 1994. However, privately Jawara felt betrayed by the lack of U.S. intervention as he later indicated to Hughes (interview, August 1998).

61. Diene-Njie, *Fall of the Old Order*, 117–26, discusses Jawara's unsuccessful attempts to persuade Diouf to intervene.

62. See Colly, "Coup in Gambia, Part 7." On Senegal's recognition of the AFPRC government, see S. B. Danso, "Senegal and Gambia Enjoy Excellent Relations," *Daily Observer*, November 28, 1994, reporting a speech by Jammeh. See also *WA*, August 15–21, 1994, 1436; and da Costa, "Out With the Old," 50–51. The granting of political asylum to Jawara and Sabally is noted in *Daily Observer*, July 25, 1994; July 28, 1994.

63. The initial AFPRC broadcasts are reproduced in *Daily Observer*, "Broadcast From the AFPRC." Decree No. 30 of April 1995 (backdated to July 1994) formally dissolved the 1970 constitution and proscribed all political parties; see *WO*, April 7–9, 1995.

64. Colly, "Coup in Gambia, Part 1," states that Sabally and Singhateh voted for Jammeh to head the AFPRC on July 24 and suggests that they regarded him as a malleable puppet. On Touray (who was born in 1966), see Hughes and Gailey, *Historical Dictionary*, 173–74; Wiseman, "Military Rule," 921; and his profile on http://www.statehouse.gm (downloaded March 2006). He was promoted to captain in November 1994; see *The Point*, November 21, 1994.

65. On Kanteh's rise and fall, see Yeebo, *State of Fear*, 43; Okon, "100 Days of Military Rule"; Saine, "Coup d'Etat," 109 (note 11); and *GW*, November 11, 1994. Diene-Njie, *Fall of the Old Order*, 123, incorrectly states that Kanteh was originally appointed to the AFPRC before being replaced by Touray. Alpha Kinteh, the other original coup leader who withdrew from the plot at the last moment, was probably arrested at the same time as Kanteh and released in early November. Although not named in the *Gambia Weekly* article as one of the eight men who were released at this time, he was included in a list outlined by Sadibou Hydara in an interview with *The Point*, November 10, 1994. Colly, "Coup in Gambia, Part 1," describes both Kanteh and Alpha Kinteh as captains, not lieutenants, so presumably they were both promoted after November 1994.

66. The original fifteen members were listed in *WA*, August 1–7, 1994, 1347. The civilian members of the cabinet are profiled in *Daily Observer*, July 28, 1994; August 2, 1994.

67. On the downfall of Cham and Sarr, see Colly, "Coup in Gambia, Parts 8–10"; Diene-Njie, *Fall of the Old Order*, 124–25; Wiseman and Vidler, "1994 Coup," 62; and *WA*, "Arrests in Banjul," August 8–14, 1994. Colly suggests (Part 6), that he (Sarr) and Cham were added to the government at the suggestion of Basiru Barrow because of their experience and that he was arrested because he publicly challenged Jammeh; he adds (Part 8) that Jammeh later informed a press conference that he had been dismissed and arrested for conspiring with a superpower (i.e., the United States) to sabotage the coup. Diene-Njie also suggests that military rank may have been an additional cause, because the two captains were reluctant to take orders from lieutenants and Wiseman and Vidler report that Cham and Sarr were accused of passing information to the PPP. Both men were released in May 1995; see *Daily Observer*, May 11, 1995.

68. The selection of Sonko (a son of the former Seyfu of Upper Niumi, Landing Omar Sonko) is discussed by Diene-Njie, *Fall of the Old Order*, 124, who states that he was known to be "very close" to Bakary Dabo. Sonko and Mbenga are profiled in *Daily Observer*, July 28, 1994; and the latter also in Hughes and Gailey, *Historical Dictionary*, 122. Sonko was to be sacked in March 1995; see *GD*, March 22, 1995. Three former permanent secretaries were forcibly retired in August 1994, and another was sacked and six others forcibly retired in October 1994; see *The Point*, September 12, 1994; and *Daily Observer*, October 6, 1994. Two more were retired in March 1995; see *Daily Observer*, March 23, 1995.

69. Dabo himself claimed that Jawara was "very understanding" and encouraged him to return in an interview with the Senegalese newspaper, *Le Soleil*, cited in *The Point*, September 22, 1994. But according to *Foroyaa*, February 3, 1995, many PPP supporters considered that he had betrayed Jawara. Further information from Jawara (Hughes interview, 1998).

70. Dabo's appointment and downfall are discussed by Diene-Njie, *Fall of the Old Order,* 122–35; 151; and Wiseman, "Military Rule," 919–20. See also *GW,* November 18, 1994. Jammeh outlined the "official" reasons for Dabo's appointment in *The Point,* September 19, 1994. Dabo was among the eleven ex-ministers who were briefly arrested before the Barrow coup; see *WO,* November 11–13, 1994. Dabo subsequently attacked AFPRC rule in an article in *WA;* see Bakary Dabo, "Living in Crisis," *WA,* February 13–19, 1995, 217–18.

71. Tambedou was officially sacked for failing to carry out road and bridge construction in the countryside; see "Minister Dismissed," *WA,* September 25–October 8, 1995, 1507.

72. Colly, "Coup in Gambia, Part 8," states that the appointment of M'Bai was suggested by Capt. Cham before his dismissal from the government. On M'Bai's role under the AFPRC, see Wiseman, "Military Rule," 919–20; and da Costa, "Out With the Old," 51. His dismissal and the subsequent charge against him were noted in *GD,* March 22, 1995; March 24, 1995; and *Daily Observer,* March 23, 1995. See also *Daily Observer,* May 8, 1995.

73. Diene-Njie, *Fall of the Old Order,* 124–25; and Colly, "Coup in Gambia, Part 9." All three are profiled in *Daily Observer,* August 2, 1994. Waffa-Ogoo is also profiled in Hughes and Gailey, *Historical Dictionary,* 178–79; in <http://www.statehouse.gm> (downloaded March 2006). Tambajang was the best known of the three, having previously served as chairperson of the National Women's Council. Bojang was sacked from the cabinet in March 1995, but was then appointed high commissioner to France; see *GD,* March 22, 1995; March 24, 1995; and *Daily Observer,* May 11, 1995.

74. This curious incident is discussed by Wiseman, "Military Rule," 921–22; Yeebo, *State of Fear,* 108–12; and Diene-Njie, *Fall of the Old Order,* 154–57. The official explanation was that he died of natural causes, but no independent autopsy was allowed.

75. Chazan et al., *Contemporary Africa,* 225–26.

76. Muctarr Jalloh, "Jawara Lobbies Hard," *WA,* March 6–12, 1995, 349; and Ebrima Ceesay, "Sir Dawda Visits USA," *Daily Observer,* February 14, 1995. On Gambian/American relations after the coup, see Touray, *Gambia and the World,* 176–77.

77. See *The Independent* (Banjul), September 23, 2002; September 27, 2002. Jawara was also granted D8,404,000 in seized assets and lost earnings.

78. Jawara emphasized this point in his interview with Hughes (August, 1998).

79. See Chapter 7, 163. According to an insider informant, Jawara also rejected demands within the PPP leadership to use the election landslide in 1972 to introduce a single-party state.

80. Wiseman, "Military Rule," 923–26, contrasts the approach to the independent press of the two governments; see also Yeebo, *State of Fear,* 92–100. Obadare, "Military and Democracy," 344, who is generally critical of Jawara, also states that the press was "relatively free" under him.

81. See Chapter 8, 207, on the deregistration of the GWU. The GWC established in 1985 was also permitted to operate freely.

82. The best known example of this was the Sanna Manneh case discussed in Chapter 9, 240. In contrast, Edie, "Democracy in The Gambia," 172–73, argues that under Jawara, the judiciary was perceived as a tool of the PPP and thus could not guarantee the protection of individual rights.

83. See Chapter 7, 188–89.

84. For example, Andrew Camara served as vice president in the early 1970s before he converted to Islam.

85. See Chapter 10, 265–66. Jawara continued to blame Senegal for the breakdown of the confederation; see his interview with Richard Kotey in the *Daily Observer,* September 29, 1994.

86. This was reimposed by the Jammeh government in August 1995; see Wiseman, "Military Rule," 928.

87. See Chapter 10, 271.

88. For an overall assessment of the record up to 2000, see Hughes, "'Democratisation' Under the Military." For earlier accounts, see Yeebo, *State of Fear*, 66–114; Wiseman, "Military Rule"; and Kandeh, "Military Regimes."

89. See Chapter 1, 38–39.

90. See Chapter 9, 240–41. Jawara, however, continued to deny that he had made a mistake by standing in 1992; see his interview with Kotey, *Daily Observer*, September 29, 1994. The examples of states where there was a peaceful handover to a chosen successor included Senegal (1981), Cameroon (1982), Sierra Leone (1985), and Tanzania (1985).

91. Obadare, "Military and Democracy," 344–45, provides a particularly critical assessment of the Jawara record on social and economic development. Chapter 1, 28–30, provides the data to allow a more balanced assessment.

92. Dibba was appointed speaker of the National Assembly in February 1992, but was dismissed in April 2006, following allegations of involvement in a failed coup of the previous month. See *African Research Bulletin, Political Series* 39, no. 2: (2002), 14746; and *The Point*, April 21, 2006.

93. See Wiseman, "Military Rule," for an earlier account. Hughes, "'Democratisation' Under the Military"; Edie, "Democracy in The Gambia," 182–94; and Abdoulaye Saine, "Post-Coup Politics in The Gambia," *Journal of Democracy* 13, no. 4: (2002), 167–72, offer more recent assessments.

BIBLIOGRAPHY

Adams, James. *Secret Armies*. London: Hutchinson, 1987.

Addis, R. T. "Groundnut Stew—Gambia: Recollections of the First General Election 1960." (1963). ADDIS MSS Afr. s 2129, Rhodes House Library, Oxford.

[Africa]. "My Conscience is Clear," *Africa*, no. 121 (1981, September) 18–19.

[Africa Books]. *Africa Who's Who*. 3rd ed. London: Africa Books, 1996.

[Africa Contemporary Record]. Vols. 6–24 (1973–74 to 1992–94) [Gambian entries by Arnold Hughes].

[Africa Now]. "The Gambia: Sir Dawda Fights Back," *Africa Now*, September 1981, 35–36.

———. "Samba Sanyang: From the Monastery to Become a Coup Maker," *Africa Now*, September 1981, 36–37.

Agbodeka, Francis. *African Politics and British Policy in the Gold Coast 1868–1900: A Study in the Forms and Force of Protest*. London: Longman, 1971.

Allen, Christopher. "African Trade Unionism in Microcosm: The Gambia Labour Movement, 1939–67." In *African Perspectives: Papers in the History, Politics and Economics of Africa Presented to Thomas Hodgkin*, edited by Christopher Allen and R. W. Johnson, 393–426. Cambridge: Cambridge University Press, 1970.

Amnesty International International Secretariat. *Amnesty International Trial Observation Missions to the Republic of The Gambia (December 1980/January 1982)*. London: Amnesty International, 1983.

Amolo, Milcah. "Sierra Leone and British Colonial Labour Policy 1930–1945." Ph.D. diss., Dalhousie University, 1978.

Ananaba, Wogu. *The Trade Union Movement in Africa: Promise and Performance*. London: C. Hurst, 1979.

Anyadike, R. N. C. "Patterns and Variations of Rainfall over Banjul, Gambia." *Singapore Journal of Tropical Geography* 14, no. 1 (1993): 1–14.

Apter, David. "Ghana." In *Political Parties and National Integration in Tropical Africa*, edited by James S. Coleman and Carl G. Rosberg, 259–315. Berkeley: University of California Press, 1964.

Archer, Francis Bisset. *The Gambia Colony and Protectorate: An Official Handbook*. London: Frank Cass, 1967. Reprint of 1906 ed. Originally published—London: St. Bride's Press, 1906.

Asante, Ben. "Prescription for Conflict," *New African*, January 1981, 19–21.

Asante, S. K. B. *Pan-African Protest: West Africa and the Italo-Ethiopian Crisis, 1934–1941*. London: Longman, 1977.

Ashton, T. S. *The Industrial Revolution 1760–1830.* Reprint of 1948 ed. London: Oxford University Press, 1975.

Austin, Dennis. *Malta and the End of Empire.* London: Frank Cass, 1971.

———. *Politics in Ghana, 1946–1960.* London: Oxford University Press, 1964.

Bah, Omar. "Lamin Waa Juwara: Ndam Leader," *Daily Observer,* August 1, 2004.

———. "Omar Jallow (OJ): Interim Leader, People's Progressive Party," *Daily Observer,* August 28, 2004.

———. "Jane Coli Faye [Jain Coli Fye]: NAM, Lower Niumi Constituency," *Daily Observer,* December 12, 2004.

———. "Ya Fatou Sonko: Nadd Executive Member," *Daily Observer,* February 12, 2005.

Bakarr, S. A. *The Gambia Yesterday: 1447–1979.* Banjul: Gambia Press Union, 1980.

———. "The Gambia in Perspective," *West Africa,* January 26, 1981, 165.

———. *The Law of Treason in the Republic of The Gambia Versus Alieu Sallah & 6 Revolutionists.* Banjul: The Author, 1981.

———. *The Gambia Mourns Her Image: Thursday 30th July to August 6th 1981.* Serrekunda: The Author, 1981.

———. *The Treason Trial of Trials. The Republican State of the Gambia Versus S. M. Dibba, Pap Cheyassin Secka and Five Others.* Banjul: The Author, 1982.

Barrett, Hazel R. *The Marketing of Foodstuffs in The Gambia, 1400–1980.* Aldershot: Avebury, 1988.

Barry, Boubacar. *Senegambia and the Atlantic Slave Trade.* Cambridge: Cambridge University Press, 1998.

Basdeo, Sahadeo. *Labour Organisation and Labour Reform in Trinidad 1919–1939.* St. Augustine, Trinidad: Institute of Social and Economic Research, University of West Indies, 1983.

Basu, Priya, and Norman Gemmell. *Fiscal Adjustment in The Gambia: A Case Study.* UNCTAD Discussion Papers no. 74. Geneva: United Nations Conference on Trade and Development, 1993.

Bayo, Kebba M. "Mass Orientation and Regional Integration: Environmental Variations in Gambian Orientations Towards Senegambia." Ph.D. diss., Northwestern University, 1977.

Bellagamba, Alice. "Portrait of a Chief Between Past and Present: Memory at Work in Colonial and Post-colonial Gambia." *Political and Legal Anthropology Review* 25, no. 2 (2002): 21–49.

———. "Entrustment and Its Changing Political Meanings in Fuladu, The Gambia (1880–1994)." *Africa* 74, no. 3 (2004): 383–410.

Bellamy, Joyce M., and John Saville. *Dictionary of Labour Biography.* Vol. VII. London: Macmillan, 1984.

Bentsi-Enchill, Nii K. "Senegal Treads Softly," *West Africa,* January 4, 1982, 11–12.

———. "Senegalese Presence in The Gambia," *West Africa,* January 11, 1982, 78–79.

———. "Starting Off on the Wrong Foot," *West Africa,* January 11, 1982, 79–81.

———. "No Valid Foundation," *West Africa,* January 11, 1982, 81.

———. "Sir Dawda Explains the Confederation," *West Africa,* January 18, 1982, 137–41.

———. "Signing on the Dotted Line," *West Africa,* February 8, 1982, 353–55.

———. "Koro Sallah Interview—1," *West Africa,* March 22, 1982, 761–65.

———. "Koro Sallah Interview—2," *West Africa,* March 29, 1982, 851–58.

Berg, Elliot J., and Jeffrey Butler. "Trade Unions." In *Political Parties and National Integration in Tropical Africa,* edited by James S. Coleman and Carl G. Rosberg, 340–81. Berkeley: University of California Press, 1964.

Bierwirth, Chris. "The Lebanese Communities of Côte d'Ivoire." *African Affairs* 98, no. 390 (1999): 79–99.

Black, Adam, [and Charles]. *Who Was Who.* 5th ed. Vol. I: 1897–1915. London: Adam and Charles Black, 1967.

Blackburne, Sir Kenneth. *Lasting Legacy: A Story of British Colonialism.* London: Johnson, 1976.

Blyden, Nemata Amelia. *West Indians in West Africa, 1808–1880: The African Diaspora in Reverse.* Rochester, NY: University of Rochester Press, 2000.

Bojang, Sheriff. "Sanjally Bojang: An Encounter with a Living Legend," *Weekend Observer,* March 31–April 2, 1995.

———. "Yahya A. J. J. Jammeh," *Weekend Observer,* July 21–23, 1995.

———. "Sanjally Bojang Passes Away," *Daily Observer,* October 24, 1995.

———. "Sanjally Bojang: When the Darling of the Gods Die [*sic*] Old," *Weekend Observer,* October 27–29, 1995.

———. "Pap Cheyassin Secka: A Man for All Seasons," *Weekend Observer,* May 24–26, 1996.

———. "PDOIS Leader, Sidia Jatta Speaks Out," *Daily Observer,* September 5, 1996.

Booth, Richard. *The Armed Forces of African States, 1970.* Adelphi Paper no. 67. London: Institute for Strategic Studies, 1970.

Boumedouha, Saïd. "Adjustment to West African Realities: The Lebanese in Senegal." *Africa* 60, no. 4 (1990): 538–49.

Brautigam, Deborah A. "Foreign Assistance and the Export of Ideas: Chinese Development Aid in The Gambia and Sierra Leone." *Journal of Commonwealth & Comparative Politics* 32, no. 3 (1994): 324–48.

———. "The 'Mauritius Miracle': Democracy, Institutions and Economic Policy." In *State, Conflict and Democracy in Africa,* edited by Richard Joseph, 137–62. Boulder, CO: Lynne Rienner, 1999.

Bridges, Sir Phillip. "A Note on Law in The Gambia." In *The Gambia: Studies in Society and Politics,* edited by Arnold Hughes, 55–63. Birmingham University African Studies Series no. 3. Birmingham: University of Birmingham, 1991.

Brooks, George E. "Peanuts and Colonialism: Consequences of the Commercialization of Peanuts in West Africa, 1830–70." *Journal of African History* 16, no. 1 (1975): 29–54.

Brownlie, Ian. *African Boundaries: A Legal and Diplomatic Encyclopedia.* London: C. Hurst, 1979.

Calvert, Peter. *The Foreign Policy of New States.* Brighton: Wheatsheaf Books Ltd, 1986.

Carney, Judith, and Michael Watts. "Disciplining Women? Rice, Mechanization, and the Evolution of Mandinka Gender Relations in Senegambia." *Signs* 16, no. 4 (1991): 651–81.

Cartwright, John R. *Politics in Sierra Leone 1947–67.* Toronto: University of Toronto Press, 1970.

———. *Political Leadership in Sierra Leone.* London: Croom Helm, 1978.

Ceesay, Ebrima. "Sir Dawda Visits USA," *Daily Observer,* February 14, 1995.

[Central Bank of The Gambia]. *Quarterly Bulletin* and *Bulletin,* 1971 to 1989–90.

———. *Quarterly Survey,* no. 2 (1975, April–June).

Ceesay, Ebrima, and Rodney D. Sieh. "NIB, GPA Bosses Held," *Daily Observer,* August 2, 1994.

Ceesay, Hassoum. "Author of the PPP/UP Coalition Government 1965," *Weekend Observer,* December 6–8, 1996.

Ceesay, Lamin. "12 PPP Ministers Free at Last," *The Point,* September 15, 1994.

Challis, Stephen H. *A History of Local Government in Kombo North District, Western Division, The Gambia: 1889–1944.* Banjul: Oral History and Administrative Division, Vice-President's Office, 1980.

Cham-Joof, A. E. "The History of the Banjul Mosque," *Weekend Observer,* May 5–7, 1995.

Chazan, Naomi, Peter Lewis, Robert A. Mortimer, Donald Rothchild, and Stephen John Stedman. *Politics and Society in Contemporary Africa.* 3rd ed. Boulder, CO: Lynne Rienner, 1999.

Clapham, Christopher. *Third World Politics An Introduction.* London: Croom Helm, 1985.

———. "Liberia." In *Contemporary West African States,* edited by Donal B. Cruise O'Brien, John Dunn, and Richard Rathbone, 99–111. Cambridge: Cambridge University Press, 1989.

Clark, Andrew F., and Lucie Colvin Phillips. *Historical Dictionary of Senegal.* African Historical Dictionaries no. 65. 2nd ed. Metuchen, NJ: Scarecrow Press, 1994.

Clarke, Peter B. *West Africa and Christianity.* London: Edward Arnold, 1986.

Cohen, Robin. *Labour and Politics in Nigeria, 1945–71.* London: Heinemann, 1974.

Cole, Margaret. *The Life of G. D. H. Cole.* London: Macmillan, 1971.

Cole, Patrick. *Modern and Traditional Elites in the Politics of Lagos.* Cambridge: Cambridge University Press, 1975.

Coleman, James S. *Nigeria: Background to Nationalism.* Berkeley: University of California Press, 1958.

Colly, Ebou [pseudonym]. "Coup in Gambia" (April–June 2001). Articles previously available on the Internet.

[Colonial Office]. *Blue Book of Statistics,* 1842–1938. Earlier editions unpublished; later editions published by HMSO.

———. "Gambia: Report on the Blue Book for 1888." In *Papers Relating to HM Colonial Possessions,* no. 61. London: HMSO, 1889.

———. *Colony of the Gambia, Census 1901, Report of the Superintendent.* (London: HMSO, 1902). This can also be found in CO 87/163, Denton to Chamberlain, June 24, 1901.

———. *Census of the British Empire 1901.* London: HMSO, 1906.

———. *Report and Summary of the Census of the Gambia 1911.* London: HMSO, 1911. This can also be found in CO 87/186, Denton to Secretary of State, June 27, 1911.

———. *Annual Report of the Gambia.* London: HMSO, 1922–47 (titles vary slightly).

———. *Report by the Hon. W. G. A. Ormsby-Gore, M.P. on His Visit to West Africa During the Year 1926.* London: HMSO, 1926.

———. *Annual Report on the Social and Economic Progress of the People of the Gambia, 1931.* Colonial Reports no. 1572. London: HMSO, 1932.

———. *The Gambia (Constitution) Order in Council 1954.* London: HMSO, 1954.

Cooke, David, and Arnold Hughes. "The Politics of Economic Recovery: The Gambia's Experience of Structural Adjustment, 1985–1994." *Journal of Commonwealth & Comparative Politics* 35, no. 1 (1997): 93–117.

Cooper, Dave. "Unions in Botswana: Comparisons with Lesotho." *South African Labour Bulletin* 10, no. 8 (1985): 103–14.

Coulon, Christian. "Les partis politiques Gambiens." *Revue francaise d'études politiques africaines*, no. 89 (1973, May): 31–49.

———. "Senegal: The Development and Fragility of Semidemocracy." In *Democracy in Developing Countries: Africa*, edited by Larry Diamond, Juan J. Linz, and Seymour Martin Lipset, 141–78. Boulder, CO: Lynne Rienner, 1988.

Coulon, Christian, and Donal B. Cruise O'Brien. "Senegal." In *Contemporary West African States*, edited by Donal B. Cruise O'Brien, John Dunn, and Richard Rathbone, 145–64. Cambridge: Cambridge University Press, 1989.

Cox, Thomas S. *Civil-Military Relations in Sierra Leone: A Case Study of African Soldiers in Politics*. Cambridge, MA: Harvard University Press, 1976.

Crook, Richard. "Decolonization, the Colonial State and Chieftaincy in the Gold Coast." *African Affairs* 85, no. 338 (1986): 75–105.

Crowder, Michael. "The Gambian Political Scene," *West Africa*, November 2, 1957, 1035.

———. "Chiefs in Gambia Politics: I," *West Africa*, October 18, 1958, 987.

———. "Chiefs in Gambia Politics: II," *West Africa*, October 25, 1958, 1017.

———. *Pagans and Politicians*. London: Hutchinson, 1959.

———. *West Africa Under Colonial Rule*. London: Hutchinson, 1968.

[Crown Colonist]. "New Constitution for the Gambia," *Crown Colonist*, October 1947, 558.

Cruise O'Brien, Donal. "The Shadow-Politics of Wolofisation." *Journal of Modern African Studies* 36, no. 1 (1998): 25–46.

Cruise O'Brien, Rita. "Lebanese Entrepreneurs in Senegal: Economic Integration and the Politics of Protection." *Cahiers d'Etudes Africaines* 15, no. 1 (1975): 95–115.

Dabo, Bakary. "Living in Crisis," *West Africa*, February 13–19, 1995, 217–18.

da Costa, Peter. "Carnival in Banjul," *West Africa*, March 5–11, 1990, 361.

———. "An Obsessive Disciplinarian," *West Africa*, April 16–22, 1990, 615.

———. "Fêted but Fated," *West Africa*, June 25–July 1, 1990, 1067.

———. "Senegal-Gambia Treaty," *West Africa*, January 14–20, 1991, 28.

———. "Casamance Under Siege," *West Africa*, January 28–February 3, 1991, 100–102.

———. "New Party Launched," *West Africa*, September 30–October 6, 1991, 656.

———. "Jawara Bows Out?" *West Africa*, December 16–22, 1991, 2106–7.

———. "Christmas Cheer," *West Africa*, January 13–19, 1992, 68–69.

———. "Dawning of a New Era?" *West Africa*, April 27–May 5, 1992, 710–11.

———. "Jawara's New Government," *West Africa*, May 25–31, 1992, 876–77.

———. "A Border Conflict," *West Africa*, December 13–19, 1993, 2250–52.

———. "Out With the Old." *Africa Report* 40, no. 1 (1995): 48–51.

da Costa, Peter, and Baboucar M. Gaye. "A Thorn in the Side," *West Africa*, December 18–24, 1989, 2097–98.

[Daily Observer]. "Army Coup in Gambia," *Daily Observer*, July 25, 1994.

———. "Broadcast from the AFPRC," *Daily Observer*, July 25, 1994.

———. "PPP Regime Mismanaged Most Foreign Aid," *Daily Observer*, September 12, 1994.

———. "The Press Has Been Good for the Country," *Daily Observer*, October 28–30, 1994.

———. "Pesseh Has Not Run Off With UDP Funds," *Daily Observer*, September 17, 1996.

Damis, John. "The OAU and Western Sahara." In *The OAU After Twenty Years*, edited by Yassin El-Ayouty and I. William Zartman, 273–96. New York: Praeger, 1984.

Danso, S. B. "Dibba, Others to Pay D23m," *Daily Observer*, November 28, 1994.

———. "Senegal and Gambia Enjoy Excellent Relations," *Daily Observer*, November 28, 1994.

———. "Development Takes Many Ways . . . Dr. Saho," *Daily Observer*, February 28, 1995.

———. "Detained Politician Named Man of the Year," *Daily Observer*, January 6, 1997.

Davies, Aisha. "Jawara Received £1 Million in Bribes, Manneh Claims," *Gambia Daily*, October 25, 1995.

Davis, Daniel, David Hulme, and Philip Woodhouse. "Decentralization by Default: Local Governance and the View from the Village in The Gambia." *Public Administration and Development* 14, no. 3 (1994): 253–69.

Denham Diaries (Rhodes House Oxford) [Sir Edward Denham, Governor of Gambia, 1928–30]. Vol. X 29/11/28–5/5/29.

Denton, Fatma. "Foreign Policy Formulation in The Gambia, 1965–1994: Small Weak Developing States and their Foreign Policy Decisions and Choices." Ph.D. diss., University of Birmingham, 1998.

Derbyshire, J. Denis, and Ian Derbyshire. *Spotlight on World Political Systems: An Introduction to Comparative Government*. Edinburgh: W & R Chambers Ltd, 1991.

De Vrijer, J. Erik, Robin Kibuka, Byung K. Jang, Ivailo V. Izvorski, and Christian H. Beddies. *The Gambia: Selected Issues*. IMF Staff Country report no. 99/71. Washington: IMF, 1999.

Dibba, Ebou. "Jawara's Mission and Convictions," *West Africa*, February 17–23, 1992, 284–85.

Dieke, Peter U. C. "The Political Economy of Tourism in The Gambia." *Review of African Political Economy*, no. 62 (1994): 611–27.

Diene-Njie, Codou Mbassy. *Gambia: The Fall of the Old Order*. Dakar: les Editions Cheikh Anta Diop, 1996.

Dike, K. Onwuka. *Trade and Politics in the Niger Delta 1830–1885*. 2nd ed. Oxford: Clarendon Press, 1966.

Doyle, Mark. "Troubled Waters," *West Africa*, June 19–25, 1989, 1007–9.

Doyle, Mark, and Chris Simpson. "Another Week of Terror," *West Africa*, May 8–14, 1989, 725.

Dunayevskaya, Raya. "The Gambia Takes the Hard, Long Road to Independence." *Contemporary Issues*, January 1963, 18–25.

Ede, Oscar O. B. "Nigeria and Francophone Africa." In *Nigeria's External Relations: The First Twenty-Five Years*, edited by G. O. Olusanya and R. A. Akindele, 176–95. Ibadan: University of Ibadan Press, 1986.

Edie, Carlene J. "Democracy in The Gambia: Past, Present and Prospects for the Future." *Africa Development* 25, no. 3–4 (2000): 161–99.

Eluwa, Gabriel I. C. "The National Congress of British West Africa: A Pioneer Nationalist Movement." *Genève Afrique* 11, no. 1 (1972): 38–51.

[Europa Publications]. *The International Who's Who 1998–99*. 62nd ed. London: Europa Publications, 1998.

———. *The Europa World Year Book 1999*. 40th ed. Vols. 1 and 2. London: Europa Publications Ltd, 1999.

Faal, Pa Modou. "Timetable Is Too Long," *Daily Observer*, October 27, 1994.

Fadugba, Nick. "The Gambia: Battle for Banjul," *Africa*, September 1981, 14–19.

Fage, J. D. *A History of West Africa: An Introductory Survey.* 4th ed. Cambridge: Cambridge University Press, 1969.

Falola, Toyin. "Lebanese Traders in Southwestern Nigeria, 1900–1960." *African Affairs* 89, no. 357 (1990): 523–53.

Fashole Luke, David. *Labour and Parastatal Politics in Sierra Leone: A Study of African Working-Class Ambivalence.* Lanham, MD: University Press of America, 1984.

Faye, Nenneh. "Taking Stock," *West Africa*, September 4–10, 1995, 1402–3.

Findlay, G. G., and W. W. Holdsworth. *The History of the Wesleyan Methodist Missionary Society.* Vol. 4. London: Epworth, 1922.

Findlay, Rev. W. H. "Report of a Visit to the Sierra Leone and Gambia District." Privately printed for Wesleyan Methodist Missionary Society, 1900. Wesleyan Methodist Missionary Society Archives, School of Oriental and African Studies, University of London.

Fletcher, Andria J. "Party Politics in The Gambia." Ph.D. diss., University of California at Los Angeles, 1979.

Fofana, Justice. "Senegambia Feud," *West Africa*, January 8–14, 1990, 34.

Foltz, William J. *From French West Africa to the Mali Federation.* Yale Studies in Political Science no. 12. New Haven, CT: Yale University Press, 1965.

[Food and Agriculture Organization]. *Production Yearbook 1997.* FAO Statistics Series no. 142. Vol. 51. Rome: FAO, 1997.

Foon, Marion. "Operation Ping-Pong to Beat Votes Fiddlers." *Journal of African Administration* 13, no. 1 (1961): 35–37.

Foray, Cyril P. *Historical Dictionary of Sierra Leone.* African Historical Dictionaries no. 12. Metuchen, NJ: Scarecrow Press, 1977.

Forrest, Joshua B. *Guinea-Bissau: Power, Conflict and Renewal in a West African Nation.* Boulder, CO: Westview Press, 1992.

Fox, William. *A Brief History of the Wesleyan Missions on the Western Coast of Africa.* London: Aylott and Jones, 1851.

———. *History of the Wesleyan Missions in Western Africa.* London: Nichols, 1851.

[Friedrich Ebert Stiftung]. *African Biographies: Gambia.* Bonn: Verlag Neue Gesellschaft, c. 1974.

Fyfe, Christopher. *A History of Sierra Leone.* London: Oxford University Press, 1962.

Gailey, Harry A. "Gambia Moves Forward," *West Africa*, April 1, 1961, 339.

———. *A History of the Gambia.* London: Routledge & Kegan Paul, 1964.

———. *Historical Dictionary of the Gambia.* African Historical Dictionaries no. 4. Metuchen, NJ: Scarecrow Press, 1975.

Galli, Rosemary E. *Guinea-Bissau.* Oxford: Clio Press, 1990.

The Gambia Committee. *The Proposed Cession of the Gambia.* Westminster: The Gambia Committee, 1876.

[Gambia Court of Appeal]. *Criminal Appeal no. 5–11/81.* Banjul: Gambia Court of Appeal, 1982.

[Gambia Court of Appeal]. *Criminal Appeal no. 29/82.* Banjul: Gambia Court of Appeal, 1982.

[Gambia Daily]. "New Health Minister Sworn In," *Gambia Daily*, November 8, 1995.

———. "Dembo Bojang: The Gambia's Longest Serving MP," *Gambia Daily*, May 1999.

[Gambia Government]. "Census Report, 1871." This unpublished report can be found in CO 87/99, enclosure to Kennedy to Kimberley, June 7, 1871.

————. *Detailed Account of the Census of the Population of the British Settlement on the River Gambia, taken on the 4th April 1881*. Bathurst: Government Printer, 1881. This can be found in CO 87/117, Gouldsbury to Rowe, September 9, 1881.

————. *A Report of 1891 Census by WC Cates Acting Registrar.* This can be found in CO 87/139, Llewelyn to Secretary of State, July 21, 1891.

————. *Report and Summary of the Census of the Gambia.* Bathurst: Government Printer, 1921.

————. *Report and Summary of the Census of the Gambia.* Bathurst: Government Printer, 1932.

————. *Report of the Committee on the Legislative Council Franchise.* Sessional Paper no. 2 of 1944. Bathurst: Government Printer, 1944.

————. *Report of the Census Commissioner for Bathurst, 1944.* Sessional Paper no. 2 of 1945. Bathurst: Government Printer, 1945.

————. *Report of the Senior Commissioner on the Annual Census of the Protectorate of the Gambia, 1945.* Sessional Paper no. 5 of 1946. Bathurst: Government Printer, 1946.

————. *Annual Report on the Labour Department 1946.* Sessional Paper no. 3 of 1947. Bathurst: Government Printer, 1947.

————. *Report of a Commission Appointed to Make Recommendations on the Aims, Scope, Contents and Methods of Education in the Gambia by T. H. Baldwin.* Sessional Paper no. 7 of 1951. Bathurst: Government Printer, 1951.

————. *Report of the Census Commissioner for the Colony—1951.* Sessional Paper no. 4 of 1952. Bathurst: Government Printer, 1952.

————. *Revision of Electoral Machinery Committee Report, 1953 [Spurling Report].* Sessional Paper no. 4 of 1953. Bathurst: Government Printer, 1953.

————. *Report of a Commission [F. H. Baker] Appointed to Inquire into the Conduct of the Gambia Police Force in Connection With an Affray Which Took Place in Bathurst on 16th October, 1955.* Sessional Paper no. 15 of 1955. Bathurst: Government Printer, 1955.

————. *Record of the Constitutional Conference Held from the 6th to 11th March, 1959 With His Excellency the Governor's Opening Address.* Sessional Paper no. 3 of 1959. Bathurst, Government Printer, 1959.

————. *Constitutional Developments in Gambia: Exchange of Despatches.* Sessional Paper no. 4 of 1959. Bathurst: Government Printer, 1959.

————. *Constitutional Development in the Gambia: Exchange of Despatches.* Sessional Paper no. 6 of 1961. Bathurst: Government Printer, 1961.

————. *Report of the Gambia Constitutional Conference.* Sessional Paper no. 8 of 1961. Bathurst: Government Printer, 1961.

————. *Report of an Enquiry Into the Complaints Made by Students of Yundum College in January 1964 by S. H. M. Jones.* Sessional Paper no. 18 of 1964. Bathurst: Government Printer, 1964.

————. *The Gambia: Independence Conference 1964.* Sessional Paper no. 21 of 1964. Bathurst: Government Printer, 1964.

————. *Annual Report of the Registrar of Co-operative Societies, 1964.* Sessional Paper no. 4 of 1965. Bathurst: Government Printer, 1965.

————. *Report on the Census of Population of the Gambia Taken on 17th/18th April 1963 by H. A. Oliver.* Sessional Paper no. 13 of 1965. Bathurst: Government Printer, 1965.

[Gambia Government]. *Report of the Constituency Boundaries Commission.* Sessional Paper no. 2 of 1966. Bathurst: Government Printer, 1966.

———. *Gambia Staff List 1967.* Bathurst: Government Printer, 1967.

———. *Gambia Staff List 1970.* Bathurst: Government Printer, 1970.

———. *Urban Labour Force Survey 1974–75.* Banjul: Central Statistics Division, 1975.

———. *Report of the Commission to Inquire Into the Conduct and Management of the External Aid Fund.* Banjul: Government Printer, 1983.

———. *Second Five Year Plan for Economic and Social Development 1981/82–1985/86.* Banjul: Ministry of Economic Planning and Industrial Development, 1983.

———. *Members of the Government October 1984.* Banjul: Government Printer, 1984.

———. *The Economic Recovery Programme.* Banjul: Government Printer, 1986.

———. *Population and Housing Census 1983.* Vol. 1. Banjul: Central Statistics Department, Ministry of Economic Planning and Industrial Development, 1987.

———. *Survey of Employment, Earnings and Hours of Work (December 1986).* Banjul: Central Statistics Department, Ministry of Economic Planning and Industrial Development, 1987.

———. *Consumer Price Index of The Gambia 1991.* Banjul: Central Statistics Department, Ministry of Finance and Economic Affairs, 1992.

———. *Report of the Third Roundtable Conference for The Gambia.* Banjul: Government Printer, 1992.

———. *Statistical Abstract of The Gambia 1991.* Banjul: Central Statistics Department, Ministry of Finance and Economic Affairs, 1992.

———. *1992–93 Household Economic Survey Report: The Gambia.* Banjul: Central Statistics Department, Ministry of Finance and Economic Affairs, 1994.

———. *Population and Housing Census 1993.* Vols. 8 & 9. Banjul: Central Statistics Department, Department of State for Finance and Economic Affairs, 1996.

———. *Population Databank 1995.* Banjul: National Population Commission Secretariat, 1996.

———. *Statistical Abstract of The Gambia 1995.* Banjul: Central Statistics Department, Department of State for Finance and Economic Affairs, 1996.

———. *1998 National Household Poverty Survey Report.* Banjul: Ministry of Finance and Economic Affairs, 2000.

Gambia People's Party. *Manifesto of the Gambia People's Party: La Haula Wala Huata Ila Bilah.* Banjul: GPP, 1987.

———. *Manifesto of the Gambia People's Party: La Haula Wala Huata Ila Bilah.* Revised version. Banjul: GPP, 1992.

Gamble, David P. *Contributions to a Socio-Economic Survey of the Gambia.* London: Colonial Office Research Department, 1949.

———. *The Wolof of Senegambia, Together with Notes on the Lebu and the Serer.* London: International African Institute, 1957.

———. *The South Bank of The Gambia: Places, People and Population.* Vols. A and B. Gambian Studies nos. 30 & 31. Brisbane, CA: Gamble and Rahman, 1996.

Gamble, David P. *The North Bank of The Gambia: Places, People and Population.* Vols. A and C. Gambian Studies nos. 37 & 38. Brisbane, CA: Gamble and Rahman, 1999.

Gamble, David P., and Louise Sterling. *A General Bibliography of The Gambia (up to 31 December 1977).* Boston: G. K. Hall, 1977.

Gaye, Baboucar. "Mboob—More Questions Than Answers," *West Africa*, August 23, 1982, 2190–91.

———. "Arrests and Detention in Banjul," *West Africa*, November 14, 1983, 2652.

———. "Coup: 24 Sentenced to Death," *West Africa*, April 30, 1984, 944.

———. "Six Detainees Released," *West Africa*, May 28, 1984, 1142.

———. "Attorney-General Resigns," *West Africa*, July 2, 1984, 1348–49.

———. "Fafa Mbai at Probe," *West Africa*, August 6, 1984, 1609.

———. "National Army Created," *West Africa*, November 19, 1984, 2311.

———. "Rumbles in the PPP," *West Africa*, January 21, 1985, 102–3.

———. "The Rumbles Within," *West Africa*, April 1, 1985, 608.

———. "Can the Assets Commission Survive?" *West Africa*, September 2, 1985, 1833.

———. " 'Jawara Must Resign'—Dibba," *West Africa*, September 16, 1985, 1940.

———. "Strains Remain?" *West Africa*, November 18, 1985, 2445.

———. "Basse Poll," *West Africa*, December 9, 1985, 2617.

———. "Fire Destroys Albert Market," *West Africa*, January 27, 1986, 217–18.

———. "Dissidents in the PPP?" *West Africa*, February 17, 1986, 378.

———. "New Party Announced," *West Africa*, March 3, 1986, 487.

———. "GPP Leader Elected," *West Africa*, April 7, 1986, 749.

———. "Jawara's New Opposition," *West Africa*, April 14, 1986, 770–71.

———. "On the Campaign Trail," *West Africa*, July 21, 1986, 1515–16.

———. "Accusations and Counter-Accusations," *West Africa*, October 13, 1986, 2156–57.

———. "The Parties Name Their Candidates," *West Africa*, February 2, 1987, 234.

———. "Ousted Jawara Flees," *West Africa*, August 1–7, 1994, 1346.

———. "In the Run up to the Coup . . .," *West Africa*, August 1–7, 1994, 1347.

Gellar, Sheldon. *Senegal: An African Nation Between Islam and the West.* Boulder, CO: Westview Press, 1982.

Gomez, Solomon. "The External Relations of The Gambia: A Study of Internal and External Actors That Influenced Foreign Policy Positions, 1965–1975." Ph.D. diss., The Johns Hopkins University, Baltimore, 1978.

Gray, Clive S., and Malcolm F. McPherson. "Tax Reform." In *Economic Recovery in The Gambia: Insights for Adjustment in Sub-Saharan Africa*, edited by Malcolm F. McPherson and Steven C. Radelet, 125–44. Cambridge, MA: Harvard Institute for International Development, 1995.

Gray, J. M. *A History of the Gambia.* 2nd ed. London: Frank Cass, 1966. Originally published—Cambridge: Cambridge University Press, 1940.

Grey-Johnson, Jeggan. "The MP of the Week," *Gambia Daily*, May 1999.

Grey-Johnson, Nana. "The Story of the Newspaper in The Gambia." In *African Media Cultures: Transdisciplinary Perspectives*, edited by Rose Marie Beck and Frank Wittmann, 17–41. Köln: Rüdiger Köpper Verlag, 2004.

Grindle, Merilee S., and Michael Roemer. "Insights from the Economic Recovery Program for Sub-Saharan Africa." In *Economic Recovery in The Gambia: Insights for Adjustment in Sub-Saharan Africa*, edited by Malcolm F. McPherson and Steven C. Radelet, 293–310. Cambridge, MA: Harvard Institute for International Development, 1995.

Gueye, Amadou Mactar. "Herculean Tasks," *West Africa*, September 18–24, 1989, 1551–52.

Gyan-Apenteng, K. "Defining the Terrain in Banjul," *West Africa*, April 19–25, 1993, 634–35.

Hadjimichael, Michael T., Thomas Rumbaugh, and Eric Verreydt (with Philippe Beaugrand, and Christopher Chirwa). *The Gambia: Economic Adjustment in a Small Open Economy*. IMF Occasional Paper no. 100. Washington: IMF, 1992.

Hakilimah, Kending S. "Integration in Limbo," *West Africa*, January 18, 1988, 75–76.

Hargreaves, John D. *A Life of Sir Samuel Lewis*. London: Oxford University Press, 1958.

———. *Prelude to the Partition of West Africa*. London: Macmillan, 1963.

———. *West Africa Partitioned: The Loaded Pause, 1885–1889*. London: Macmillan, 1974.

———. "Assumptions, Expectations and Plans: Approaches to Decolonisation in Sierra Leone." In *Decolonisation and After: The British and French Experience*, edited by W. H. Morris-Jones and Georges Fischer, 73–103. London: Frank Cass, 1980.

———. "Toward the Transfer of Power in British West Africa." In *The Transfer of Power in Africa*, edited by Prosser Gifford and Wm. Roger Louis, 117–40. New Haven, CT: Yale University Press, 1982.

Harrison Church, R. J. "The Gambia: Physical and Social Geography." In *Africa South of the Sahara 1992*. 21st ed., 488. London: Europa Publications, 1992.

Hatton, P. H. S. "The Gambia, the Colonial Office, and the Opening Months of the First World War." *Journal of African History* 7, no. 1 (1966): 123–31.

Haynes, Jeff. *Religion and Politics in Africa*. London: Zed Books, 1996.

Hewett, J. F. Napier, *European Settlements on the West Coast of Africa*. New York: Negro Universities Press, 1969. Reprint of 1862 ed. Originally published—London: Chapman and Hall, 1862.

Hill, Robert A., ed. *The Marcus Garvey Papers*. Vol. IX. Berkeley: University of California Press, 1995.

Hodgkin, Thomas. *African Political Parties: An Introductory Survey*. Harmondsworth: Penguin Books, 1961.

Hook, Richard M., Richard D. Mallon, and Malcolm F. McPherson. "Parastatal Reform, Performance Contracts, and Privatization." In *Economic Recovery in The Gambia: Insights for Adjustment in Sub-Saharan Africa*, edited by Malcolm F. McPherson and Steven C. Radelet, 235–49. Cambridge, MA: Harvard Institute for International Development, 1995.

Hooker, James R. *Black Revolutionary: George Padmore's Path from Communism to Pan-Africanism*. New York: Praeger, 1967.

Hopkins, A. G. *An Economic History of West Africa*. Harlow: Longman, 1973.

Horton, James Africanus. *West African Countries and Peoples*. Reprint of 1868 ed. Edinburgh: Edinburgh University Press, 1969. Originally published— London: W. J. Johnson, 1868.

[House of Commons]. *British Parliamentary Papers Colonies Africa* 2. Shannon: Irish University Press, 1968.

———. *British Parliamentary Papers Colonies Africa* 3. Shannon: Irish University Press, 1968.

———. *British Parliamentary Papers Colonies Africa* 5. Shannon: Irish University Press, 1968.

[House of Commons]. *British Parliamentary Papers Colonies Africa* 52. Shannon: Irish University Press, 1968.

———. *British Parliamentary Papers Colonies Africa* 56. Shannon: Irish University Press, 1971.

———. "Sierra Leone: Report of the Commissioners of Inquiry [James Rowan] into the State of the Colony of Sierra Leone Second Part: I: Dependencies in the Gambia." In *British Parliamentary Papers Colonies Africa 52*, 211–25. Shannon: Irish University Press, 1968.

———. "Report of Her Majesty's Commissioner [Dr. R. R. Madden] on the State of the British Settlements on the Western Coast of Africa." In *British Parliamentary Papers Colonies Africa* 2, 177–242. Shannon: Irish University Press, 1968.

———. "Report of Colonel Ord into the Condition of the British Settlements on the West Coast of Africa, 1864." In *British Parliamentary Papers Colonies Africa 5*, 343–66. Shannon: Irish University Press, 1968.

Hughes, Arnold. "Jawara Wins Again," *West Africa*, April 14, 1972, 453.

———. "After the Gambian Elections," *West Africa*, April 21, 1972, 475.

———. "After the Elections," *West Africa*, April 28, 1972, 511.

———. "From Green Uprising to National Reconciliation: The People's Progressive Party in the Gambia 1959–1973." *Canadian Journal of African Studies* 9, no. 1 (1975): 61–74.

———. "Senegambia Revisited or Changing Gambian Perceptions of Integration With Senegal." In *Senegambia. Proceedings of a Colloquium at the University of Aberdeen,* edited by Roy C. Bridges, 139–70. Aberdeen: African Studies Group, University of Aberdeen, 1974.

———. "Election Time in The Gambia," *West Africa*, April 4, 1977, 649–50.

———. "Gambia Election Report," *West Africa*, April 18, 1977, 743–45.

———. "Why the Gambian Coup Failed," *West Africa*, October 26, 1981, 2498–2502.

———. "The Gambia After the Coup Attempt," *West Africa*, November 2, 1981, 2570–73.

———. "The Gambia at the Crossroads." *Contemporary Review* 239, no. 1390 (1981): 225–30.

———. "The Gambian General Elections," *West Africa*, May 10, 1982, 1241–42.

———. "The Gambia's Democratic Image Restored," *West Africa*, May 17, 1982, 1305–7.

———. "Jawara's New Team," *West Africa*, May 24, 1982, 1361.

———. "The Limits of 'Consociational Democracy' in the Gambia." *Civilisations* 22, no. 2 and 23, no. 1 (1982–83): 65–95.

———. "From Colonialism to Confederation: The Gambian Experience of Independence, 1965–1982." In *African Islands and Enclaves,* edited by Robin Cohen, 57–80. Beverly Hills, CA: Sage, 1983.

———. "Les elections gambiennes de mars 1987." *Politique Africaine,* no. 26 (1987): 121–27.

———. ed. *The Gambia: Studies in Society and Politics.* Birmingham University African Studies Series no. 3. Birmingham: University of Birmingham, 1991.

———. "The Attempted Gambian Coup d'Etat of 27 [30] July 1981." In *The Gambia: Studies in Society and Politics,* edited by Arnold Hughes, 92–106. Birmingham University African Studies Series no. 3. Birmingham: University of Birmingham, 1991.

Hughes, Arnold. "The Gambia: Recent History." In *Africa South of the Sahara 1992*. 21st ed., 488–92. London: Europa Publications, 1992.

———. "The Collapse of the Senegambian Confederation." *Journal of Commonwealth & Comparative Politics* 30, no. 2 (1992): 200–222.

———. "Africa and the Garvey Movement in the Interwar Years." In *Garvey: Africa, Europe, The Americas*, edited by Rupert Lewis and Maureen Warner-Lewis, 99–120. 2nd ed. Trenton, NJ: Africa World Press, 1994.

———. "'Democratisation' Under the Military in The Gambia: 1994–2000." *Commonwealth & Comparative Politics* 38, no. 3 (2000): 35–52.

Hughes, Arnold, and Robin Cohen. "An Emerging Nigerian Working Class: The Lagos Experience 1897–1939." In *African Labor History*, edited by Peter C. W. Gutkind, Robin Cohen, and Jean Copans, 31–55. Beverly Hills, CA: Sage, 1978.

Hughes, Arnold, and Harry A. Gailey. *Historical Dictionary of The Gambia*. African Historical Dictionaries no. 79. 3rd ed. Lanham, MD: Scarecrow Press, 1999.

Hughes, Arnold, and Janet Lewis. "Beyond Francophonie? The Senegambia Confederation in Retrospect." In *State and Society in Francophone Africa Since Independence*, edited by Anthony Kirk-Greene and Daniel Bach, 228–43. Basingstoke: Macmillan, 1995.

Hughes, Arnold, and David Perfect. "Trade Unionism in The Gambia." *African Affairs* 88, no. 353 (1989): 549–72.

Humasi, Nana. "A Year in Review," *West Africa*, December 26, 1988–January 8, 1989, 2422.

Huntington, Samuel P. *Political Order in Changing Societies*. New Haven, CT: Yale University Press, 1968.

Huntley, Sir Henry. *Seven Years' Service on the Slave Coast of Western Africa*. Vol. II. London: Newby, 1850.

Hutton, J. F. *The Proposed Cession of the British Colony of the Gambia to France*. Manchester: Privately Published, 1876. This can be found in CO 87/109, Cooper to Under-Secretary of State for the Colonies, March 21, 1876.

Hynes, William G. *The Economics of Empire: Britain, Africa and the New Imperialism 1870–95*. London: Longman, 1979.

Imperato, Pascal James. *Historical Dictionary of Mali*. African Historical Dictionaries no. 11. 2nd ed. Metuchen, NJ: Scarecrow Press, 1986.

[The Independent]. "Dodou A. Jome a Nationalist, Commercial Pundit," *The Independent*, April 23, 2004.

Independents. "Gambia Betrayed!! Down with UP. Down with PPP. Vote Independent." (1972, cyclostyled). Institute of Commonwealth Studies Library, London.

———. "The Type of Gambia We Want." (1972, cyclostyled). Institute of Commonwealth Studies Library, London.

———. "Communique." [*sic*] (1972, cyclostyled). Institute of Commonwealth Studies Library, London.

International Monetary Fund. *Surveys of African Economies*. Washington: IMF, 1975.

———. *International Financial Statistics Yearbook 1996*. Washington: IMF, 1996.

International Trade Union Committee of Negro Workers. *A Report of Proceedings and Decisions of the First Conference of Negro Workers*. Hamburg: ITUC-NW, 1930.

Jabara, Cathy. "Structural Adjustment in a Small, Open Economy: The Case of Gambia." In *Adjusting to Policy Failure in African Economies*, edited by David E. Sahn, 302–31. Ithaca, NY: Cornell University Press, 1994.

Jackson, Robert H., and Carl G. Rosberg. *Personal Rule in Black Africa.* Berkeley: University of California Press, 1982.

Jalloh, Muctarr. "Jawara Lobbies Hard," *West Africa,* March 6–12, 1995, 349.

Jallow, Cherno Baba. "MOJA Activist Unburdens His Soul to *Daily Observer,*" *Daily Observer,* March 23, 1995.

———. "My Sacking Was a Result of a Problem I Had With My P.S.," *Daily Observer,* April 6, 1995.

Jallow, Mathew K. "Sana Sabally: From Kassakunda to No. 2 Man," *The Point,* November 14, 1994.

Janneh, Amadou S. "Dilemmas of Senegambian Integration." Ph.D. diss., University of Tennessee, 1990.

Jatta, Sidia. "RE: Resignation of Senior Curriculum Development Officer to Serve my Nation." Banjul, September 28, 1986. Cyclostyled letter.

Jawo, D. A. "Banjul Charter: A Compromise Document," *Daily Observer,* July 10, 1995.

Jeng, Alieu A. O. "An Economic History of the Gambian Groundnut Industry, 1830–1924: The Evolution of an Export Economy." Ph.D. diss., University of Birmingham, 1978.

Johnson, G. Wesley. *The Emergence of Black Politics in Senegal: The Struggle for Power in the Four Communes, 1900–1920.* Stanford, CA: Stanford University Press, 1971.

Jones, Christine, and Radelet, Steven C. "The Groundnut Sector." In *Economic Recovery in The Gambia: Insights for Adjustment in Sub-Saharan Africa,* edited by Malcolm F. McPherson and Steven C. Radelet, 205–17. Cambridge, MA: Harvard Institute for International Development, 1995.

Jones, S. H. M. *The Diocese of Gambia and the Rio Pongas 1935–1951: Its Origins and Early History.* Banjul: Book Production and Material Resources Unit, 1986.

Kaba, Lansiné. "Guinean Politics: A Critical Historical Review." *Journal of Modern African Studies* 15, no. 1 (1977): 25–45.

———. "From Colonialism to Autocracy: Guinea Under Sékou Touré, 1957–1984." In *Decolonization and African Independence: The Transfers of Power, 1960–1980,* edited by Prosser Gifford and Wm. Roger Louis, 225–44. New Haven, CT: Yale University Press, 1988.

Kakoza, J., R. Basanti, T. Ehrbeck, and R. Prem. *The Gambia: Recent Economic Developments.* IMF Staff Country Report no. 95/123. Washington: IMF, 1995.

Kandeh, Jimmy D. "What Does the 'Militariat' Do When it Rules? Military Regimes: The Gambia, Sierra Leone and Liberia." *Review of African Political Economy,* no. 69 (1996): 387–404.

Kent, John. "Regionalism or Territorial Autonomy? The Case of British West African Development, 1939–49." *Journal of Imperial and Commonwealth History* 18, no. 1 (1990): 61–80.

Killick, Tony. *IMF Programmes in Developing Countries.* London: Routledge, 1995.

Kilson, Martin. *Political Change in a West African State: A Study of the Modernization Process in Sierra Leone.* Cambridge: Harvard University Press, 1966.

———. "The National Congress of British West Africa, 1918–1935." In *Protest and Power in Black Africa,* edited by Robert I. Rotberg and Ali A. Mazrui, 571–88. London: Oxford University Press, 1970.

Kimble, David. *A Political History of Ghana: The Rise of Gold Coast Nationalism 1850–1928.* Oxford: Clarendon Press, 1963.

Kraus, Jon. "The Political Economy of Industrial Relations in Ghana." In *Industrial Relations in Africa*, edited by Ukandi G. Damachi, H. Dieter Seibel and Lester Trachtman, 106–68. London: Macmillan, 1979.

Kuczynski, R. R. *Demographic Survey of the British Colonial Empire*. Vol. 1. London: Oxford University Press, 1948.

Kup, A. P. "Sir Charles MacCarthy (1768–1824) Soldier and Administrator," *Bulletin of the John Rylands University Library of Manchester* 60, no. 1 (1977): 52–94.

[Labour Research]. "80 Years Combating Inequality." *Labour Research*, July 1992, 15–16.

Land, Harry. "The Gambia—Politics and Groundnuts." *New Commonwealth*, September 1962, 561–64.

Langley, J. Ayodele. *Pan-Africanism and Nationalism in West Africa, 1900–1945: A Study in Ideology and Social Classes*. Oxford: Clarendon Press, 1973.

———. Introduction to *The Blinkards*, by Kobina Sekyi. London: Heinemann Educational, 1974.

Laughton, John. *Gambia: Country, People and Church in the Diocese of Gambia and the Rio Pongas*. 2nd ed. London: SPG, 1949.

Lewis, Peter M. "Endgame in Nigeria? The Politics of a Failed Democratic Transition." *African Affairs* 93, no. 372 (1994): 323–40.

Lijphart, Arend. *Democracy in Plural Societies: A Comparative Exploration*. New Haven, CT: Yale University Press, 1977.

Linares, Olga F. *Power, Prayer and Production: The Jola of Casamance, Senegal*. Cambridge: Cambridge University Press, 1992.

Logan, Ikubolajeh B., and Kidane Mengisteaib. "IMF–World Bank Adjustment and Structural Transformation in Sub-Saharan Africa." *Economic Geography* 69, no. 1 (1993): 1–24.

Louis, Wm. Roger. *Imperialism at Bay 1941–1945*. Oxford: Clarendon Press, 1977.

Low, Anthony. "The End of the British Empire in Africa." In *Decolonization and African Independence: The Transfers of Power, 1960–1980*, edited by Prosser Gifford and Wm. Roger Louis, 33–72. New Haven, CT: Yale University Press, 1988.

Macdonald, Susan. "Jawara Interview Angers Dakar," *West Africa*, April 29, 1985, 854.

Macmillan, Allister. *The Red Book of West Africa*. New impression. London: Frank Cass, 1968. Originally published—London: Collingridge, 1920.

Madge, Clare. "Intra-Household Use of Income and Informal Credit Schemes in The Gambia." In *The Gambia: Studies in Society and Politics*, edited by Arnold Hughes, 29–41. Birmingham University African Studies Series no. 3. Birmingham: University of Birmingham, 1991.

Mahoney, Florence K. O. "Government and Opinion in The Gambia 1816–1901." Ph.D. diss., University of London, 1963.

———. "Notes on Mulattoes of the Gambia Before the Mid-Nineteenth Century." *Transactions of the Historical Society of Ghana* 8 (1965): 120–29.

———. "African Leadership in Bathurst in the Nineteenth Century." *Tarikh* 2, no. 2 (1968): 25–38.

[Manchester Chamber of Commerce]. "Proceedings: 1867–73." Local Studies Unit, Central Library, Manchester, England.

———. "Proceedings: 1873–79." Local Studies Unit, Central Library, Manchester, England.

[Manchester Faces and Places]. "The Late Mr J. F. Hutton," *Manchester Faces and Places* 1, no. 7 (1890): 107–8.

Manjang, Ousman. "Gambian Liberation," *West Africa*, July 26, 1982, 1929–31.

———. "Marriage of Confusion–2," *West Africa*, November 10, 1986, 2358–60.

McNamara, Paul E. "Budget Reform." In *Economic Recovery in The Gambia: Insights for Adjustment in Sub-Saharan Africa*, edited by Malcolm F. McPherson and Steven C. Radelet, 111–23. Cambridge, MA: Harvard Institute for International Development, 1995.

McNamara, Paul E., and Malcolm F. McPherson. "Customs Reform." In *Economic Recovery in The Gambia: Insights for Adjustment in Sub-Saharan Africa*, edited by Malcolm F. McPherson and Steven C. Radelet, 251–63. Cambridge, MA: Harvard Institute for International Development, 1995.

McNamara, Paul E., and Parker Shipton. "Rural Credit and Savings." In *Economic Recovery in The Gambia: Insights for Adjustment in Sub-Saharan Africa*, edited by Malcolm F. McPherson and Steven C. Radelet, 95–110. Cambridge, MA: Harvard Institute for International Development, 1995.

McPherson, Malcolm F. "Macroeconomic Reform and Agriculture." In *Economic Recovery in The Gambia: Insights for Adjustment in Sub–Saharan Africa*, edited by Malcolm F. McPherson and Steven C. Radelet, 191–203. Cambridge, MA: Harvard Institute for International Development, 1995.

McPherson, Malcolm F., and Steven C. Radelet, eds. *Economic Recovery in The Gambia: Insights for Adjustment in Sub-Saharan Africa*. Cambridge, MA: Harvard Institute for International Development, 1995.

———. "The Economic Recovery Program: Background and Formulation." In *Economic Recovery in The Gambia: Insights for Adjustment in Sub-Saharan Africa*, edited by Malcolm F. McPherson and Steven C. Radelet, 19–32. Cambridge, MA: Harvard Institute for International Development, 1995.

Metcalfe, G. E. *Great Britain and Ghana: Documents of Ghana History 1807–1957*. London: Thomas Nelson, 1964.

Moister, William. *Memorials of Missionary Labours in Western Africa, the West Indies and at the Cape of Good Hope*. London: William Nichols, 1866.

———. *A History of Wesleyan Missions in all Parts of the World From Their Commencement to the Present Time*. London: Elliot Stock, 1870.

Momen, Wendy C. "The Foreign Policy and Relations of The Gambia." Ph.D. diss., London School of Economics, University of London, 1987.

Momoh, Eddie. "A Trial of Political Muscle," *West Africa*, October 22, 1984, 2114–15.

———. "Signs of Strain in the Confederation," *West Africa*, October 29, 1984, 2158–59.

———. "Dams Against Drought," *West Africa*, February 11, 1985, 252–53.

———. "No Easy Promises," *West Africa*, February 18, 1985, 297–98.

———. "On Your Marks . . . ," *West Africa*, October 27, 1986, 2252–53.

———. "The Gulf Between," *West Africa*, December 22–29, 1986, 2647–48.

———. "Elections Update," *West Africa*, February 16, 1987, 304–5.

———. "'We'll Continue the Struggle,'" *West Africa*, March 30, 1987, 601.

———. "'The Elections Were Rigged,'" *West Africa*, March 30, 1987, 601–2.

———. "Storm in a Tea Cup," *West Africa*, April 13, 1987, 705.

———. "Jawara and the SAS," *West Africa*, February 29, 1988, 352–53.

Morgan, John. *Reminiscences of the Founding of a Christian Mission on the Gambia.* London: Wesleyan Mission House, 1864.

National Convention Party. *Constitution of the National Convention Party.* Banjul: National Convention Party, 1975.

———. *The Farafenni Declaration.* Banjul: National Convention Party, 1976.

———. *The 1992 General Election Manifesto of the National Convention Party.* Banjul: National Convention Party, 1992.

Nelson, Joan M., ed. *Economic Crisis and Policy Choice: The Politics of Adjustment in The Third World.* Princeton, NJ: Princeton University Press, 1990.

[New African]. "The Gambia: Jawara Holds the Aces as Dibba is Freed." *New African,* September 1982, 23.

Newbury, C. W. *British Policy Towards West Africa: Select Documents 1786–1874.* Oxford: Clarendon Press, 1964.

———. *British Policy Towards West Africa: Select Documents 1875–1914.* Oxford: Clarendon Press, 1971.

[New Commonwealth]. "General Election in the Gambia." *New Commonwealth,* July 1960, 468.

———. "One Gambia Party Now Seeks Independence." *New Commonwealth,* September 1960, 606.

———. "Role of the Chiefs in the Gambia." *New Commonwealth,* January 1961, 54.

———. "Blow to Gambia's Ruling Party." *New Commonwealth,* December 1961, 807–8.

N'Jie, Alieu Badara. "Oil Commission Finds Jawara and Nine Others Liable," *Daily Observer,* May 30, 1995.

N'Jie, P. S. "Points from Election Speeches," *The Nation,* April 8, 1972.

Nordman, Curtis R. "The Decision to Admit Unofficials to the Executive Councils of British West Africa." *Journal of Imperial and Commonwealth History* 4, no. 2 (1976): 194–205.

Nyang, Sulayman S. "Politics in Post-Independence Gambia." *A Current Bibliography on African Affairs* 8, no. 2 (1975): 113–26.

———. "The Historical Development of Political Parties in the Gambia." *Africana Research Bulletin* 5, no. 4 (1975): 3–38.

———. "Recent Trends in Gambian Politics." *L'Afrique et l'Asie Modernes,* no. 109 (1976): 34–44.

———. "The Role of the Gambian Political Parties in National Integration." Ph.D. diss., University of Virginia, 1979.

———. "Politics of Defection in The Gambia," *West Africa,* April 16, 1979, 664–67.

———. "Decline and Fall of a Party," *West Africa,* April 23, 1979, 711–14.

———. "Local and National Elites and Islam in The Gambia: An African Case Study." *International Journal of Islamic and Arabic Studies* 1, no. 2 (1984): 57–67.

———. "Sir Dawda Kairba Jawara." In *Political Leaders of Contemporary Africa South of the Sahara. A Biographical Dictionary,* edited by Harvey Glickman, 95–100. Westport, CT: Greenwood Press, 1992.

———. "Ibrahim Garba-Jahumpa, 1912–1994," *West Africa,* September 12–18, 1994, 1581.

———. "Colonialism and the Integration of the Gambian Ethnic Groups." In *State and Society in Africa: Perspectives on Continuity and Change* edited by Feraidoon Shams, 88–115, Lanham, MD: University Press of America, 1995.

Oat Jr., D. R. [pseudonym]. "Anatomy of a Coup," *West Africa*, August 29–September 4, 1994, 1502–3.

Obadare, Ebenezer. "The Military and Democracy in The Gambia." In *Governance and Democratisation in West Africa*, edited by Dele Olowu, Adebayo Williams, and Kayode Soremekun, 341–57. Dakar: CODESRIA, 1999.

Obe, Ad'Obe. "A President's Story," *West Africa*, February 19–25, 1990, 264–68.

Ofoegbu, Ray. "Foreign Policy and Military Rule." In *Nigerian Government and Politics Under Military Rule, 1966–79*, edited by Oyelele Oyediran, 124–49. London: Macmillan, 1979.

Okon, Godwin. "100 Days of Military Rule," *The Point*, October 31, 1994.

Olusanya, G. O. "The Lagos Branch of the National Congress of British West Africa." *Journal of the Historical Society of Nigeria* 4, no. 2 (1968): 321–33.

———. "Garvey and Nigeria." In *Garvey: Africa, Europe, The Americas*, edited by Rupert Lewis and Maureen Warner-Lewis, 121–34. 2nd ed. Trenton, NJ: Africa World Press, 1994.

Omole, Bade. "De la co-opération a la confédération: la Sénégambie: Contribution a l'analyse du thème de l'intégration politique régionale en Afrique." Doctorat de 3e cycle, université de Bordeaux, 1986.

Orde, M. H. "Development of Local Government in Rural Areas in the Gambia." *Journal of Local Administration Overseas* 4, no. 1 (1965): 51–59.

Orde-Browne, G. St. J. *Labour Conditions in West Africa*. Cmnd 6277. London: HMSO, 1941.

[Oxford University Press]. *The Dictionary of National Biography*. Revised edition, vol. 12. London: Oxford University Press, 1921–22.

Oyowe, Augustine. "A Future for Senegambia?," *West Africa*, March 8, 1976, 299.

Padmore, George, ed. *History of the Pan-African Congress*. 2nd ed. London: The Hammersmith Bookshop, 1963.

Patton, Adell. *Physicians, Colonial Racism and Diaspora in West Africa*. Gainesville: University Press of Florida, 1996.

Pearce, R. D. *The Turning Point in Africa: British Colonial Policy 1938–1948*. London: Frank Cass, 1982.

Peil, Margaret. *Nigerian Politics: The People's View*. London: Cassell, 1976.

People's Democratic Organisation for Independence and Socialism. *The Constitution of the People's Democratic Organisation for Independence and Socialism*. Serrekunda: PDOIS, 1986.

———. *Corrupt Registration Practice*. Banjul: PDOIS, October 11, 1988.

———. *The Way Forward*. Banjul: PDOIS, 1992.

———. *Constitution of the People's Democratic Organisation for Independence and Socialism*. Revised version. Banjul: PDOIS, 1992.

People's Democratic Party. *People's Democratic Party (P.D.P.) Manifesto*. Banjul: PDP, 1992.

People's Progressive Party. *The Voice: The Story of the PPP 1959–1989*. Banjul: Baroueli, 1992.

———. *Building Upon 27 Years of Continued Peace, Progress and Prosperity. Manifesto of the People's Progressive Party 1992*. Banjul: Government Printer, 1992.

Perfect, David M. R. "Organised Labour and Politics in The Gambia: 1920–1984." Ph.D. diss., University of Birmingham, 1987.

Perfect, David M. R. "The Political Career of Edward Francis Small." In *The Gambia: Studies in Society and Politics,* edited by Arnold Hughes, 64–79. Birmingham University African Studies Series no. 3. Birmingham: University of Birmingham, 1991.

Peters, Laurie [Lenrie]. "Election Controversy in Gambia." *New Commonwealth,* October 1963, 679.

Post, Kenneth W. J. *The Nigerian Federal Election of 1959: Politics and Administration in a Developing Political System.* London: Oxford University Press, 1963.

Post, Kenneth W. J., and Michael Vickers. *Structure and Conflict in Nigeria, 1960–1966.* London: Heinemann Educational, 1973.

Price, J. H. "Some Notes on the Influence of Women in Gambian Politics." In *Proceedings of the Nigerian Institute of Social and Economic Research,* 151–58. Ibadan: NISER, 1958.

Prickett, Barbara. *Island Base—A History of the Methodist Church in the Gambia, 1921–1969.* Bathurst: Methodist Church, Gambia, 1971.

Puetz, Detlev, and Xiao Ye. "The Gambia National Household Poverty Survey, 1998." World Bank Report no. 26664. In *Standardized Survey Bulletin,* no. 6 (2003, June): 1–8.

Quinn, Charlotte A. *Mandingo Kingdoms in the Senegambia: Traditionalism, Islam and European Expansion.* Evanston: Northwestern University Press, 1972.

Radelet, Steven C. "Donor Support for the Economic Recovery Program." In *Economic Recovery in The Gambia: Insights for Adjustment in Sub-Saharan Africa,* edited by Malcolm F. McPherson and Steven C. Radelet, 47–57. Cambridge, MA: Harvard Institute for International Development, 1995.

Radelet, Steven C., and Malcolm F. McPherson. "The Politics of Economic Reform." In *Economic Recovery in The Gambia: Insights for Adjustment in Sub-Saharan Africa,* edited by Malcolm F. McPherson and Steven C. Radelet, 33–45. Cambridge, MA: Harvard Institute for International Development, 1995.

———. "Epilogue: The July 1994 Coup d'Etat." In *Economic Recovery in The Gambia: Insights for Adjustment in Sub-Saharan Africa,* edited by Malcolm F. McPherson and Steven C. Radelet, 311–17. Cambridge, MA: Harvard Institute for International Development, 1995.

Rake, Alan, ed. *New African Yearbook 1987–88.* 7th ed. London: IC Magazines Ltd, 1987–88.

Reeve, Henry F. *The Gambia, Its History: Ancient, Medieval and Modern.* London: Smith, Elder and Co., 1912.

Renner, F. A. "Ethnic Affinity, Partition and Political Integration in Senegambia." In *Partitioned Africans: Ethnic Relations Across Africa's International Boundaries 1884–1984,* edited by A. I. Asiwaju, 71–85. London: C. Hurst, 1985.

Reynolds, Edward. *Trade and Economic Change on the Gold Coast, 1807–1874.* Harlow: Longman, 1974.

Rice, Berkeley. *Enter Gambia: The Birth of an Improbable Nation.* London: Angus and Robertson, 1968.

Rich, Karl M., Alex Winter-Nelson, and Gerald C. Nelson. "Political Feasibility of Structural Adjustment in Africa: An Application of SAM Mixed Multipliers." *World Development* 25, no. 12 (1997): 2105–14.

Rimmer, Douglas. *The Economies of West Africa.* London: Weidenfeld and Nicolson, 1984.

———. "Adjustment Blues." *African Affairs* 94, no. 374 (1995): 109–13.

Rivière, Claude. *Guinea: The Mobilization of a People*, translated by Virginia Thompson and Richard Adloff. Ithaca, NY: Cornell University Press, 1977.

Roberts, B. C. *Labour in the Tropical Territories of the Commonwealth.* London: Bell for London School of Economics, 1964.

Robertson, A. F. *The Dynamics of Productive Relationships: African Share Contracts in Comparative Perspective.* Cambridge: Cambridge University Press, 1987.

Robinson, Ronald, and John Gallagher (with Alice Denny). *Africa and the Victorians: The Official Mind of Imperialism.* Originally published in 1961. New York: St Martin's Press, 1967.

Robson, Peter. *Economic Integration in Africa.* London: George Allen and Unwin, 1968.

———. *Integration, Development and Equity.* London: Allen and Unwin, 1983.

Rondos, Alex. "Socialist Look at Africa," *West Africa*, August 31, 1981, 1980–81.

Sagnia, Burama K. *A Concise Account of the History and Traditions of Origin of Major Ethnic Groups.* Banjul: Office of the Vice-President, 1984.

———. *Historical Development of the Gambian Legislature.* Lawrenceville, VA: Brunswick, 1991.

Saidy, Jay. "Omar Mbacke as Chief Among Chiefs Was the Kingmaker in 1962," *The Point*, September 15, 1994.

Saine, Abdoulaye S. M. "The Coup d'Etat in The Gambia, 1994: The End of the First Republic." *Armed Forces & Society* 23, no. 1 (1996): 97–111.

———. "The 1996/1997 Presidential and National Assembly Elections in The Gambia." *Electoral Studies* 16, no. 4 (1997): 554–59.

———. "The Soldier-Turned-Presidential Candidate: A Comparison of Flawed 'Democratic' Transitions in Ghana and Gambia," *Journal of Political and Military Sociology* 28 no. 2: (2000): 191–209.

———. "Post-Coup Politics in The Gambia." *Journal of Democracy* 13, no. 4 (2002): 167–72.

Sallah, Halifa. *The Senegambian Confederation: Facts, Myths, Doubts and the Truth.* Banjul: The Nation Publishers, 1985.

Sallah, Tijan M. "Economics and Politics in The Gambia." *Journal of Modern African Studies* 28, no. 4 (1990): 621–48.

Sanneh, Lamin. "Political Innovation in The Gambia," *West Africa*, May 7, 1979, 787–88.

———. *West African Christianity: The Religious Impact.* London: C. Hurst, 1983.

Savage, Abdullah. "Over 18 Months Is Not Acceptable," *Daily Observer*, October 27, 1994.

Senghor, Jeggan C. "Politics and the Functional Strategy to International Integration: Gambia in Senegambian Integration, 1958–1974." Ph.D. diss., Yale University, 1979.

Sey, Fatou. "The Elections Hot Up," *West Africa*, February 19, 1987, 109–10.

———. "Jawara's Toughest Test," *West Africa*, March 9, 1987, 452–53.

Sidibe (Sidibeh), B(akary) K. *The Balde Family of Fuladu.* Banjul: Oral History Division, Vice-President's Office, 1984.

Sidibe (Sidibeh), B(akary) K., and Winifred Galloway. *The Gambian Peoples.* Banjul: Oral History & Antiquities Division, Vice-President's Office, 1975.

Sidibeh, B(adara) K. "A Code of Conduct for a Free and Fair Parliamentary and Presidential Elections in 1987." (February 1987). Institute of Commonwealth Studies Library, London.

Sieh, Rodney D., and Momodou Musa Secka. "Who Is Lt Yaya Jammeh?," *West Africa*, August 1–7, 1994, 1347–48.

Sillah, Baba. "Neglected Youth," *West Africa*, April 20, 1987, 757–60.

Sillah, Ebrima. "Yaya Ceesay Before Public Assets Commission," *New Citizen*, February 17, 1995

Sillah, M. Baikoro. "Rice: Political Diet of the Gambia," *West Africa*, November 1, 1982, 2829–30.

———. "The Demise of Kings," *West Africa*, June 6, 1983, 1351–53.

———. "Rumours and Hopes," *West Africa*, October 17, 1983, 2394–95.

Skurnik, W. E. A. *The Foreign Policy of Senegal*. Evanston, IL: Northwestern University Press, 1972.

Smith, Gerald H. "Study of Social and Economic Conditions in the Western Division," [Gambia] Confidential Paper no. 1, August 22, 1955. (Gerald H. Smith MSS Afr. 1022 PA/203), Rhodes House Library, Oxford.

Sonko-Godwin, Patience. *Ethnic Groups of the Senegambia: A Brief History*. Banjul: Book Production and Material Resources Unit, 1985.

Stenton, Michael, and Stephen Lees. *Who's Who of British Members of Parliament*. Vols. I and II. Hassocks, Sussex: Harvester Press, 1976–78.

Swindell, Kenneth. "Serawoollies, Tillibunkas and Strange Farmers: The Development of Migrant Groundnut Farming Along the Gambia River, 1848–95." *Journal of African History* 21, no. 1 (1980): 93–104.

———. *The Strange Farmers of The Gambia: A Study in the Redistribution of African Population*. Monograph 15. Swansea: Centre for Development Studies, University College of Swansea, 1981.

Tamuno, Tekena N. *Nigeria and Elective Representation 1923–1947*. London: Heinemann, 1966.

———. *Herbert Macaulay, Nigerian Patriot*. Ibadan: Heinemann, 1975.

Tarawale (Tarawally), Ba M. *In Parliament in The Gambia. Report of the Proceedings of the House of Representatives 27–30 June 1966*. Bathurst: Government Printer, 1966.

———. "How Gambia's By-Election Was Fought," *West Africa*, June 26, 1978, 1216–17.

———. "Not Just His Age . . .," *West Africa*, September 18, 1978, 1832–33.

———. "Sarjo Touray for Sami Constituency," *Gambia Times*, November 30, 1984.

[The Times]. "Validating Gambia Election," *The Times*, May 21, 1963, 10.

———. "Mr Sandys Explains Decision to Validate Gambia Elections," *The Times*, May 29, 1963, 6.

———. "Senegalese Troops Free 135 Hostages," *The Times*, August 6, 1981, 5.

Timothy, Bankole. "The Chinese in The Gambia," *West Africa*, February 4, 1974, 123.

———. "Senegambia: Myths and Realities." *Africa Special Report*, no. 38 (1974): 38–39.

———. *Kwame Nkrumah—From Cradle to Grave*. Dorchester: Gavin Press, 1981.

Tomkinson, Michael. *The Gambia: A Holiday Guide*. London: Michael Tomkinson, 1983.

Tordoff, William. *Government and Politics in Africa*. Basingstoke: Macmillan, 1984.

Touray, Gumbo. "Rural-Urban Migration: The Gambia Example," *Gambia News Bulletin*, January 5, 1981.

Touray, Omar A. *The Gambia and the World: A History of the Foreign Policy of Africa's Smallest State, 1965–1995*. Hamburg African Studies, no. 9. Hamburg: Institute of African Affairs, 2000.

Trimingham, J. Spencer. *A History of Islam in West Africa.* Oxford: Oxford University Press, 1962.

UNESCO. *Statistical Yearbook 1995.* Paris: UNESCO, 1995.

United Nations Development Programme. *Human Development Report 1995.* New York: Oxford University Press, 1995.

United Party/National Liberation Party Banjul South Strategy Committee, "The Next General Elections: An Open Letter Replying to the P.P.P. Member (Candidate) for Banjul South (Half Die)." Institute of Commonwealth Studies Library, London.

van der Laan, H. L. *The Lebanese Traders in Sierra Leone.* The Hague: Mouton, 1975.

van der Plas, Charles O. "Report of a Socio-Economic Survey of Bathurst and Kombo St. Mary in the Gambia." (GA 54/65). Unpublished report. Later published as *Report of Socio-Economic Survey of Bathurst and Kombo St. Mary in the Gambia (1954).* New York: United Nations Technical Assistance Administration, TAA/GAM/1, 1956.

van Mook, Hubertus J., Max Graessli, Henri Monfrini, and Hendrik Weisfelt. *Report on the Alternatives for Association Between the Gambia and Senegal.* Sessional Paper no. 13 of 1964. Bathurst: Government Printer, 1964.

Vengroff, Richard, and Lucy Creevey. "Senegal: The Evolution of a Quasi Democracy." In *Political Reform in Francophone Africa,* edited by John F. Clark and David E. Gardinier, 204–22. Boulder, CO: Westview Press, 1997.

Vidler, Elizabeth. "Regime Survival in The Gambia and Sierra Leone. A Comparative Study of the People's Progressive Party (1965–1994) and the All People's Congress (1968–1992)." Ph.D. diss., University of Newcastle-upon-Tyne, 1998.

[The Voice]. "In Search of Scapegoats," *The Voice* (January 1979).

Wadda, Rohey, and Russell Craig. *Report on the 1992 Priority Survey.* Banjul: Ministry of Finance and Economic Affairs, 1993.

Walsh, Brendan M. "The Program for Sustained Development." In *Economic Recovery in The Gambia: Insights for Adjustment in Sub-Saharan Africa,* edited by Malcolm F. McPherson and Steven C. Radelet, 281–92. Cambridge, MA: Harvard Institute for International Development, 1995.

Walton, Mark. "Bo School: A Case Study of 'Adapted Education.'" In *Sierra Leone Studies at Birmingham 1985,* edited by Peter K. Mitchell and Adam Jones, 173–91. Birmingham: University of Birmingham, 1987.

Webb, Patrick. "Guests of the Crown: Convicts and Liberated Slaves on McCarthy Island, The Gambia." *Geographical Journal* 160, no. 2 (1994): 136–42.

Weil, Peter M. "Mandinka Mansaya: The Role of the Mandinka in the Political System of The Gambia." Ph.D. diss., University of Oregon, 1968.

———. "Political Structure and Process Among the Gambian Mandinka: The Village Parapolitical System." In *Papers on the Manding,* edited by Carleton T. Hodge, 249–72. Bloomington, IN: Indiana University Press, 1971.

Welch, Jr., Claude E. *Dream of Unity: Pan-Africanism and Political Unification in West Africa.* Ithaca, NY: Cornell University Press, 1966.

Wesleyan Methodist Missionary Society. *Report of the Wesleyan Methodist Missionary Society 1909.* London: WMMS, 1909.

———. "Gambia Correspondence 1843–76," WMMS fiche box no. 4, box 296. Wesleyan Methodist Missionary Society Archives, School of Oriental and African Studies, University of London.

Wesleyan Methodist Missionary Society. "Gambia Correspondence 1877–84," WMMS fiche box no. 4, box 296. Wesleyan Methodist Missionary Society Archives, School of Oriental and African Studies, University of London.

———. "Gambia Correspondence 1916–1922," WMMS fiche box no. 8, box 762. Wesleyan Methodist Missionary Society Archives, School of Oriental and African Studies, University of London.

———. "West Africa Synod Minutes: Gambia, 1842–1910," WMMS fiche box no. 1. Wesleyan Methodist Missionary Society Archives, School of Oriental and African Studies, University of London.

———. "West Africa Synod Minutes: Gambia 1912–1946," WMMS fiche box no. 10. Wesleyan Methodist Missionary Society Archives, School of Oriental and African Studies, University of London.

[West Africa]. "The Gambia Government and Municipal Politics," *WA*, November 8, 1924, 1252–53.

———. "Mr Ormsby-Gore and the Affairs of the Gambia," *WA*, July 3, 1926, 807–8.

———. "The Gambia's Amiable Example," *WA*, May 30, 1952, 803.

———. "Rev. Faye Asked to Resign," *WA*, July 19, 1952, 659.

———. "The Governor, the Bishop and the Rev. John Faye," *WA*, August 2, 1952, 705.

———. "The Gambia's 'Speaker,'" *WA*, July 4, 1953, 605.

———. "New Constitution for the Gambia," *WA*, August 8, 1953, 724.

———. "Mr Faye's Complaint," *WA*, October 17, 1953, 962.

———. "The Gambia's First Minister?," *WA*, December 12, 1953, 1157.

———. "The Gambia's General Election," *WA*, November 6, 1954, 1036.

———. "P. S. N'Jie," *WA*, May 3, 1958, 411.

———. "Gambian Leader," *WA*, January 21, 1961, 61.

———. "Gambia's Progressive Chief," *WA*, April 8, 1961, 369.

———. "Self-Government for The Gambia," *WA*, August 5, 1961, 851.

———. "Campaigning in The Gambia," *WA*, May 19, 1962, 535.

———. "New Men in The Gambia," *WA*, June 9, 1962, 619.

———. "How to Create Senegambia?" *WA*, August 8, 1964, 873–74.

———. "The Gambia's Number Two," *WA*, October 31, 1964, 1219.

———. "A Republic for The Gambia?" *WA*, June 5, 1965, 614.

———. "The Gambia and the OAU," *WA*, June 5, 1965, 618.

———. "The Smuggling Problem," *WA*, April 19, 1969, 435.

———. "Guardian of the Gambia's Finances," *WA*, December 6, 1969, 1477.

———. "Power in The Gambia," *WA*, May 2, 1970, 481–82.

———. "Guineans Sentenced," *WA*, October 24, 1970, 1264.

———. "Opposition Leader Dies After Crash," *WA*, October 24, 1970, 1264.

———. "Matchet's Diary," *WA*, December 19, 1970, 1471.

———. "Dibba and the Butut Affair," *WA*, October 2, 1972, 1321.

———. "Dibba for Brussels," *WA*, October 23, 1972, 1440.

———. "Sir Dauda [*sic*] on Guinea's Stability," *WA*, February 12, 1973, 213.

———. "Border Treaty With Senegal," *WA*, June 21, 1976, 896.

———. "Visit From Mauritania," *WA*, November 29, 1976, 1830.

———. "Matchet's Diary," *WA*, April 18, 1977, 756–57.

———. "Democracy at Work," *WA*, May 15, 1978, 917.

———. "Mr A. M. Camara New Vice-President," *WA*, September 4, 1978, 1768.

[West Africa]. "Ceesay Dismissed," *WA*, October 9, 1978, 2020.

———. "Sanyang Removed," *WA*, January 15, 1979, 109.

———. "Glimpses of The Gambia," *WA*, March 12, 1979, 436–39.

———. "Good News for River Gambia Bridge," *WA*, March 19, 1979, 516.

———. "Jawara Attacks Idi Amin Dada," *WA*, April 9, 1979, 649.

———. "President in Iraq . . . ," *WA*, July 16, 1979, 1290.

———. "Changing The Gambia," *WA*, July 30, 1979, 1361–62.

———. "Fight Against Drought," *WA*, December 3, 1979, 2233–34.

———. "FAO Honours Sir Dawda," *WA*, May 12, 1980, 858.

———. "Jawara Talks With Haidalla," *WA*, September 1, 1980, 1682.

———. "The Gambia's Need for Food Relief," *WA*, September 8, 1980, 1705–7.

———. "The Gambia's MOJA," *WA*, November 3, 1980, 2171–72.

———. "The Gambia Breaks Off Relations With Libya," *WA*, November 10, 1980, 2216–17.

———. "Senegal's Tensions With The Gambia," *WA*, November 17, 1980, 2278–80.

———. "Opposition View of The Gambia," *WA*, December 15, 1980, 2553–54.

———. "The Gambia Asks for Senegal Troops," *WA*, January 12, 1981, 65–67.

———. "Matchet's Diary," *WA*, February 2, 1981, 206–7.

———. "Limann Awards Decorations," *WA*, March 16, 1981, 596.

———. "Restabilising The Gambia," *WA*, August 10, 1981, 1805–6.

———. "Matchet's Diary," *WA*, August 17, 1981, 1865–69.

———. "Matchet's Diary," *WA*, August 24, 1981, 1914–16.

———. "50 Presidential Guards," *WA*, August 31, 1981, 2022.

———. "118 Field Force Rebels Cashiered," *WA*, September 14, 1981, 2154.

———. "Foreign Hands Are Blamed," *WA*, September 21, 1981, 2224.

———. "Fifteen Opposition Members Arrested," *WA*, September 28, 1981, 2277.

———. "Senegambia's Arrival," *WA*, January 4, 1982, 10–11.

———. "Party Politics in Senegambia," *WA*, February 15, 1982, 427–28.

———. "Rulers and Rebels," *WA*, April 19, 1982, 1042.

———. "Argentina Call," *WA*, April 19, 1982, 1105.

———. "Expulsions Before Elections," *WA*, May 10, 1982, 1281.

———. "British RAF Using Banjul," *WA*, May 17, 1982, 1347.

———. "The Long Road to the Treaty of Lagos," *WA*, May 24, 1982, 1364–67.

———. " 'Tribalistic Government,' " *WA*, June 21, 1982, 1676.

———. "The Gambia's Leading Lady," *WA*, July 5, 1982, 1760.

———. "The Sheriff Dibba Case," *WA*, July 19, 1982, 1868–71.

———. "Janneh: First Victim," *WA*, August 16, 1982, 2140.

———. "Vieira Mends Gambian Fences," *WA*, January 3, 1983, 51.

———. "Resign and Be Re-Admitted," *WA*, January 10, 1983, 117.

———. "Start of a New Era?" *WA*, January 24, 1983, 229.

———. "Combined Forces," *WA*, February 7, 1983, 366.

———. "MOJA's 1983 Message," *WA*, March 7, 1983, 636.

———. "Illegal Assets," *WA*, March 28, 1983, 812.

———. "Barrow Wins," *WA*, April 11, 1983, 920.

———. "PPP Wins All?" *WA*, May 16, 1983, 1212.

———. "Sir Alieu Resigns," *WA*, July 4, 1983, 1580.

———. "PPP Wins By-Election," July 4, 1983, 1581.

[West Africa]. "Round Holes: Square Pegs," *WA*, November 14, 1983, 2610–11.

———. "Monetary Union Pressed," *WA*, March 19, 1984, 635.

———. "MOJA Members Held?" *WA*, May 21, 1984, 1096.

———. "539 NCP Supporters Defect," *WA*, May 21, 1984, 1096.

———. "Lagos-Banjul Accord," *WA*, July 30, 1984, 1553.

———. "Soviet Ties Re-Established," *WA*, November 26, 1984, 2422.

———. "Buhari in Banjul," *WA*, February 25, 1985, 397.

———. "The Shadow of 1981," *WA*, May 6, 1985, 870.

———. "Jawara Assures Koso Thomas," *WA*, July 22, 1985, 1513–14.

———. "Customs Experts Meet," *WA*, August 5, 1985, 1619.

———. "M'bai's Revelations," *WA*, August 12, 1985, 1642.

———. "Plans for New Party," *WA*, February 24, 1986 436.

———. "Gendarmerie Formed," *WA*, April 7, 1986, 749.

———. "Jammeh Joins GPP," *WA*, June 23, 1986, 1341.

———. "Third Opposition Party Formed," *WA*, August 25, 1986, 1803.

———. " 'We Will Not Quit Commonwealth,' " *WA*, October 6, 1986, 2134.

———. "Fatty Defects From GPP to Join PPP," *WA*, October 20, 1986, 2237.

———. "113 Candidates File for the Elections," *WA*, March 2, 1987, 439.

———. "Senegambian Confederation," *WA*, June 1, 1987, 1080.

———. "19 Petitions Thrown Out," *WA*, July 20, 1987, 1419.

———. "Conté Seeks Return to OMVS," *WA*, November 9, 1987, 2233.

———. "Permanent Secretariat Dissolved," *WA*, November 23, 1987, 2362.

———. "Economic Union or Burst," *WA*, February 15, 1988, 290.

———. "Senegalese and Libyan 'Connections' Alleged in Treason Trial," *WA*, May 2, 1988, 815.

———. "Senegal and Its Neighbours," *WA*, August 28–September 3, 1989, 1407.

———. "Unity That Was," *WA*, October 2–8, 1989, 1634–35.

———. "The Dream of Unity," *WA*, November 27–December 3, 1989, 1959.

———. "Gambians Protest Harassment," *WA*, November 27–December 3, 1989, 1971–72.

———. "Targets Met Despite the Odds," *WA*, January 22–28, 1990, 105.

———. "Momodou Musa N'Jie," *WA*, August 13–19, 1990, 2272.

———. "Petroleum Grant," *WA*, December 24, 1990–January 6, 1991, 3116.

———. "Arms Shipment?" *WA*, January 7–13, 1991, 3163 [*sic*].

———. "Bilateral Treaty," *WA*, June 10–16, 1991, 964.

———. "Invasion Fear," *WA*, April 6–12, 1992, 600.

———. "Ex-Soldier Makes a Bid," *WA*, April 27–May 31, 1992, 711.

———. "Resumption of Relations With Israel," *WA*, September 28–October 4, 1992, 1633.

———. "Africa Centre for Democracy and Human Rights Centre," *WA*, April 19–25, 1993, 635.

———. "The African Commission on Human and People's Rights," *WA*, April 19–25, 1993, 636–37.

———. "The Challenges Ahead," *WA*, July 5–11, 1993, 1146–47.

———. "After the Coup," *WA*, August 8–14, 1994, 1388.

———. "Arrests in Banjul," *WA*, August 8–14, 1994, 1395.

———. "Politics Suspended," *WA*, August 15–21, 1994, 1435–36.

———. "Minister Dismissed," *WA*, September 25–October 8, 1995, 1507.

[West African Review]. "Bathurst at the Polls." *West African Review*, December 1946, 1367–68.

Whiteman, Kaye. "Top Brass in Banjul," *West Africa*, February 19–25, 1990, 278–79.

———. "From Javel to Joal," *West Africa*, November 8–14, 1993, 2020–21.

———. "Tourism at Risk," *West Africa*, January 9–15, 1995, 10–11.

Wight, Martin. *The Development of the Legislative Council 1606–1945*. London: Faber and Faber, 1946.

———. *The Gold Coast Legislative Council*. London: Faber and Faber, 1947.

Wilson, Edward T. *Russia and Black Africa Before World War II*. New York: Holmes and Meier, 1974.

Wiseman, John A. "Local Elections in The Gambia: Where the Marble Rings the Bell." *The Round Table*, no. 275 (1979, July): 232–37.

———. "Revolt in The Gambia: A Pointless Tragedy." *The Round Table*, no. 284 (1981, October): 373–80.

———. "Attempted Coup in The Gambia: Marxist Revolution or Punk Rebellion?" *Communist Affairs* 1, no. 2 (1982): 434–43.

———. "The Social and Economic Bases of Party Political Support in Serekunda, The Gambia." *Journal of Commonwealth & Comparative Politics* 23, no. 1 (1985): 3–29.

———. "The Gambian Presidential and Parliamentary Elections of 1987." *Electoral Studies* 6, no. 3 (1987): 286–88.

———. *Democracy in Black Africa: Survival and Revival*. New York: Paragon, 1990.

———. "The Role of the House of Representatives in the Gambian Political System." In *The Gambia: Studies in Society and Politics*, edited by Arnold Hughes, 80–91. Birmingham University African Studies Series no. 3. Birmingham: University of Birmingham, 1991.

———. "Military Rule in The Gambia: An Interim Assessment." *Third World Quarterly* 17, no. 5 (1996): 917–40.

———. "Letting Yahya Jammeh Off Lightly?" *Review of African Political Economy*, no. 72 (1997): 265–76.

———. "The Gambia: From Coup to Elections." *Journal of Democracy* 9, no. 2 (1998): 64–75.

Wiseman, John A., and Elizabeth Vidler. "The July 1994 Coup d'Etat in The Gambia: The End of an Era." *The Round Table*, no. 333 (1995, January): 53–65.

World Bank. *Adjustment in Africa: Reforms, Results and the Road Ahead*. Oxford: Oxford University Press, 1994.

———. *World Development Indicators 1997*. Washington: World Bank, 1997.

———. *World Development Report 1997*. New York: Oxford University Press, 1997.

———. *World Development Indicators 1998*. Washington: World Bank, 1998.

———. *African Development Indicators 2003*. Washington: World Bank, 2003.

World Tourism Organization. *Yearbook of Tourism Statistics*. Vol. 1. 49th ed. Madrid: WTO, 1997.

Wright, Donald R. *The Early History of Niumi: Settlement and Foundation of a Mandinka State on the Gambia River*. Papers in International Studies Africa Series no. 32. Athens: Ohio University Center for International Studies, 1977.

———. *The World and a Very Small Place in Africa*. Armonk, NY: ME Sharpe, 1997.

Wyse, Akintola J. G. "The Gambia in Anglo-French Relations, 1905–12." *Journal of Imperial and Commonwealth History* 4, no. 2 (1976): 164–75.

Wyse, Akintola J. G. "The 1926 Railway Strike and Anglo–Krio Relations: An Interpretation." *International Journal of African Historical Studies* 14, no. 1 (1981): 93–123.

———. "The Sierra Leone Branch of the National Congress of British West Africa, 1918–1946." *International Journal of African Historical Studies* 18, no. 4 (1985): 675–98.

———. *The Krio of Sierra Leone.* London: C. Hurst, 1989.

———. *H.C. Bankole-Bright and Politics in Colonial Sierra Leone, 1919–1958.* Cambridge: Cambridge University Press, 1990.

Yeebo, Zaya. *State of Fear in Paradise: The Military Coup in The Gambia and Its Implications for Democarcy.* London: Africa Research and Information Bureau, 1995.

Zachariah, K. C., and Julien Condé. *Migration in West Africa: Demographic Aspects.* Oxford: Oxford University Press, 1981.

Zack-Williams, Alfred B. "Sierra Leone: The Political Economy of Civil War, 1991–98." *Third World Quarterly* 20, no. 1 (1999): 143–62.

INDEX

Able-Thomas, A. S. C., 139, 141, 150–51, 154, 416n28

Aborigines' Rights Protection Society (Gold Coast) (ARPS), 87–88

Accra Conference (1920), 86–87. *See also* National Congress of British West Africa

Adcock, Rev. George, 72, 383n93

Adderley, Sir Charles B., 65–66

African Charter on Human and People's Rights, 271, 292

Aitken, Judge, 95, 101, 396n95

Ajasa, Sir Kitoyi, 88

Akadjie, Colonel, Nigerian military mission, 286

Aku, characteristics of, 10–14, 20–22, 61, 114, 139, 355n15, 357n34, 357n37, 359n57–58, 359n62, 360n65, 390n36, 408n73, 414–15n17, 419n63; and politics, 69, 78, 83–84, 86–87, 93, 100, 109, 114–15, 118, 122, 129, 139–41, 145, 152, 154, 164–66, 169, 178, 195, 210, 212, 416n27, 426n21, 428n45

Albreda, (French trading post) 7, 23, 35, 57, 61, 63, 367n145

Allen, Noble J., 100, 103–4, 399–400n134

Alliance for Patriotic Re-Orientation and Construction (APRC), 45, 287–88, 456n87

Almami of Bathurst, Advisory Committee to, 88–90, 94–95, 392n64, 395n94

Anglicans, characteristics of, 16, 22, 25–27, 362n92, 362–63n95; and politics, 50, 61, 69, 83, 114, 117–18, 125, 142. *See also* Christians; Protestants

Anglo-French Convention (1857), 63, (1889), 6–7, 43

animists/"pagans," characteristics of, 15–16, 18–19, 24–26, 357n41, 361n83, 362n92

Anton, Lieutenant Colonel Henry, 25, 383–84n103

Area Councils: establishment, 153, 432n99; elections, 177–79, 196, 427n28

Armed Forces Provisional Ruling Council (AFPRC), 45, 280–81, 284–85, 288–90, 478n36, 478–79n40, 479n41, 479n48, 480n53, 481n62–65, 482n70, 482n72

Armitage, Sir Cecil H., 89–95, 392n54, 392n60, 393n68–71, 393–94n76

Armitage School, 27–28, 135, 138, 141, 363n99, 392n60, 413n2, 476n11

Assets Evaluation Commission, 227

Assets Management and Recovery Commission (AMRC), 249, 284

Atta I, Nana Ofori, 87, 388n26

Ayoola, Chief Justice F. Olayinka, 236

Baddibu War (1861), 65, 370n9

Bah, Adama, 206, 232

Bah, Almami Mama Tumani, 114, 121, 123, 405n34

Bah, Almami Momadou Lamin, 123, 126, 170, 429n58

Bah, Almami Wakka, 91, 93, 393n71

Baker, F. H., (Report, 1955), 128, 410n101–2

Bala-Gaye, Mousa G., 202, 441n18

Baldeh, Bubacarr M., 224–25, 229, 234, 242, 249, 452n23, 456n87

Baldeh, Seyfu Cherno Kady, 151, 222

Baldeh, Kikala, Assistant Commander, 212–14, 446n93

Baldeh, Mathew Yaya, 222

Baldeh, Michael, 138–40, 144, 146, 149, 158, 164, 169, 224, 415n25, 416n34, 418n56, 419n64, 424n130, 424n134

Baldeh, Paul L., 151, 155, 158, 162, 169, 172–75, 422n110, 425n9, 430n79, 430n81, 462n10

ROCHESTER STUDIES in
AFRICAN HISTORY and the DIASPORA

Toyin Falola, Senior Editor
The Frances Higginbotham Nalle Centennial Professor in History
University of Texas at Austin

A Political History of The Gambia: 1816–1994 is the first complete account of the political history of the former British West African dependency to be written. It makes use of much hitherto unconsulted or unavailable British and Gambian official and private documentary sources, as well as interviews with many Gambian politicians and former British colonial officials.

The first part of the book charts the origins and characteristics of modern politics in colonial Bathurst (Banjul) and its expansion into the Gambian interior (Protectorate) in the two decades after World War II. By independence in 1965, older urban-based parties in the capital had been defeated by a new, rural-based political organization, the People's Progressive Party (PPP).

The second part of the book analyzes the means by which the PPP, under President Sir Dawda Jawara, succeeded in defeating both existing and new rival political parties and an attempted coup in 1981. The book closes with an explanation of the demise of the PPP at the hands of an army coup in 1994.

The book not only establishes those distinctive aspects of Gambian political history, but also relates these to the wider regional and African context, during the colonial and independence periods.

Emeritus Professor Arnold Hughes was educated at the University of Wales, Aberystwyth and Ibadan University, Nigeria. Between 1966 and 2001 he taught at the Centre of West African Studies, University of Birmingham, becoming its director and professor of African politics. He has researched and published widely on various aspects of African politics and political history and, since 1972, developed a special interest in the political history of The Gambia. He has paid some twenty-five research visits to The Gambia and published two books, *The Gambia: Studies in Society and Politics* (1991) and *Historical Dictionary of The Gambia* [with H. A.Gailey] (1999); and over thirty articles and book chapters on Gambian politics. He also edited *Commonwealth and Comparative Politics* for ten years; and served as a consultant to the UN and the British Government on Gambian affairs.

Dr. David Perfect studied history at Cambridge University before completing his PhD at the Centre of West African Studies, University of Birmingham, in 1987. His thesis, *Organised Labour and Politics in The Gambia: 1920–1984*, was based on extensive primary research in The Gambia and England. Since 1988, he has worked for the Equal Opportunities Commission, the statutory body which deals with gender equality in Britain, where he is a research manager. During this period he has continued to undertake research on the political history of The Gambia, primarily through archival research at the National Archive in Kew, London, and elsewhere. He is the author of three articles on Gambian political and labor history.